ECONOMIC DEVELOPMENT
FOR LATIN AMERICA

ECONOMIC DEVELOPMENT
FOR
LATIN AMERICA

Proceedings of a Conference
held by the International Economic Association

EDITED BY
HOWARD S. ELLIS

ASSISTED BY
HENRY C. WALLICH

LONDON
MACMILLAN & CO LTD
NEW YORK · ST MARTIN'S PRESS
1961

MACMILLAN AND COMPANY LIMITED
London Bombay Calcutta Madras Melbourne

THE MACMILLAN COMPANY OF CANADA LIMITED
Toronto

ST MARTIN'S PRESS INC
New York

PRINTED IN GREAT BRITAIN

CONTENTS

v

LIST OF PARTICIPANTS

John H. Adler, Economic Development Institute, Washington, D.C., U.S.A.

Gerald H. Alter, International Bank for Reconstruction and Development, Washington, D.C., U.S.A.

Jacques Boudeville, University of Lyons, France

P. R. Brahmananda, University of Bombay, India

Otavio G. de Bulhões, Instituto Brasileiro de Economia, Rio de Janeiro, Brazil

Maurice Byé, University of Paris, France

Roberto de Oliveira Campos, Banco Nacional do Desenvimento Econômico, Rio de Janeiro, Brazil

L. M. Dominguez, Organization of American States, Pan-American Union, Washington, D.C., U.S.A.

Howard S. Ellis, University of California, Berkeley, California, U.S.A.

Celso Furtado, Economic Commission for Latin America, Mexico

Eugenio Gudin, Instituto Brasileiro de Economia, Rio de Janeiro, Brazil

Gottfried Haberler, Harvard University, Cambridge, Massachusetts, U.S.A.

Albert O. Hirschman, Yale University, New Haven, Connecticut, U.S.A.

H. D. Huggins, Institute of Social and Economic Research, University College of the West Indies, Jamaica

Alexandre Kafka, Instituto Brasileiro de Economia, Rio de Janeiro, Brazil

Flavian Levine, Compañía de Acero del Pacífico, Santiago, Chile

Javier Márquez, Centro de Estudios Monetarios Latinoamericanos, Mexico

Jorge Marshall, International Monetary Fund, Washington, D.C., U.S.A.

José Antonio Mayobre, Economic Commission for Latin America, Santiago, Chile

Ragnar Nurkse, Columbia University, New York, U.S.A.

Felipe Pazos, Banco Continental Cubano, Havana, Cuba

vii

Helio Schlittler-Silva, Banco Nacional do Desenvolvimento Econômico, Rio de Janeiro, Brazil

Theodore W. Schultz, University of Chicago, Illinois, U.S.A.

Jorge Sol, International Monetary Fund, Washington, D.C., U.S.A.

Dorival Teixeira Vieira, University of São Paulo, Brazil

Henry C. Wallich (Rapporteur), Yale University, New Haven, Connecticut, U.S.A.

H. M. Phillips (Observer), UNESCO, Paris, France

H. Berger Lieser, Secretary, International Economic Association

PROGRAMME COMMITTEE

Howard Ellis (Chairman)
Eugenio Gudin
Javier Márquez
Henry Wallich

INTRODUCTION

By HOWARD S. ELLIS

THE present volume embraces papers, critical comments prepared
in advance, and the informal discussions of a roundtable of the
International Economic Association held at Rio de Janeiro, August
19-28, 1957. The title which has been given to these proceedings
may require some explanation. In the first place, the emphasis is
not placed upon the operational problems of economic policy and
administration, but upon the theory of economic development and
its general application. In the second place, while participants in
the conference had in mind particularly the Latin-American scene,
the very fact that the orientation throughout was towards theory and
general questions of policy signifies that the analysis is not narrowly
restricted in a geographic sense. Finally, the Table of Contents
reveals that the conference did not attempt to cover all possible issues
in economic development but rather those chiefly involved with the
supply of capital, and with international economic relations.

Preliminary plans for the Rio de Janeiro roundtable were laid in
November 1954 in Mexico City in conferences involving Javier
Márquez, Felipe Pazos, Raul Prebisch, and myself. Subsequently
the International Economic Association constituted the following
programme committee : Eugenio Gudin, Javier Márquez, Henry C.
Wallich, and Howard S. Ellis (chairman).

On the score of regrets — fortunately much the shorter side of
the ledger — I must record the disappointment of the programme
committee that several members of the staff or officers of the
Economic Commission for Latin America originally scheduled to
present papers had, in the final event, to withdraw because of the
pressure of official duties. Several others who wrote papers incorporated into the present volume were unable to attend because of
political or personal factors.

On the asset side of the balance-sheet the most notable entry
was the generosity of the Brazilian hosts, the Fundação Getulio
Vargas, under the direction of Professor Eugenio Gudin. To staff
members of the Fundação's Institute and to academic and other
economists in Rio de Janeiro, the conference owes a debt of gratitude
for extensive preparations, untiring expenditures of time, and lavish
hospitality during the meetings. In addition, the Fundação supplied

generous financial subvention. The roundtable was also aided financially by a grant from UNESCO and by the participation of representatives of the Economic Commission for Latin America, the International Bank for Reconstruction and Development, the International Monetary Fund, the Panamerican Union.

According to the belief of several participants, this roundtable was the first occasion of a meeting of economists from Latin America (and elsewhere) under purely scholarly auspices, *i.e.* not under arrangements of national or international governmental agencies. The discussions were marked by a freedom of expression and by a scientific spirit which has characterized the meetings of the International Economic Association.

I wish, as editor of these proceedings, to express the thanks of conference members to Professor Henry C. Wallich, who undertook the difficult tasks of acting as reporter and writing the summary of informal discussions. Thanks are due also to Mrs. Dorothy Adler for editorial work on the final printer's manuscript.

Chapter 1

THE THEORETICAL INTERPRETATION OF LATIN AMERICAN ECONOMIC DEVELOPMENT

BY

ALEXANDRE KAFKA

United Nations [1]

I. INTRODUCTION

IDEALLY, a paper such as this one should be a body of generalizations based on the kind of study Svennilson has made of the European economy.[2] This was out of the question. I have, therefore, had to take the liberty of reducing the scope of the assignment. After a brief review of recent Latin American growth (Section II), and some general remarks on the basic factors which have determined the ability of the Latin American countries to undergo the structural economic change made necessary by growth (Section III), there are presented a few ideas (Sections IV-V) on three somewhat unique aspects of Latin American growth which appear to be of some historical interest and to have received far less attention than they merit. These three aspects are : first, the way in which growth appears to have been stimulated by shocks ; second, the rôle which regional and social inequalities appear to have played in the Latin American growth process ; and third, the entirely unorthodox way in which inflation has been connected with growth in Latin America. The first and third of these factors appear to have operated in part through a common mechanism. Where they have promoted growth, they have done so by promoting structural disequilibrium. On a non-technical definition of imbalance which would include the second case as well, imbalance seems to be an interesting part of the explanation of the successful economic development of important Latin American countries in a short period from quite low levels of

[1] The views expressed in this paper do not necessarily reflect those of the United Nations, with which the author is at present associated.
[2] Ingvar Svennilson, *Growth and Stagnation in the European Economy* (Geneva, 1954).

I

average income. Implicitly, at least, this paper takes issue with that school of thought which believes that satisfactory growth in the earliest stages of development can come about under all circumstances *only* if adequate balance is assured between the various parts of the growing economy.

It may be well to repeat that this paper is concerned only with specific aspects of the Latin American growth process. No claim is made that the factors discussed here are the only, or even the main causes of Latin America's growth experience. It seems obvious that there have been, and still are, a bewildering variety of economic mechanisms at work in Latin America. Any attempt to generalize, and to explain all Latin American growth or lack of it by one main mechanism, would seem unjustifiable. Furthermore, it may be well to stress that the ideas thrown out here are based on extremely slender evidence. They are suggestions for further investigation rather than an analysis complete in itself. Even had I not lacked time for preparation of the first draft of this paper for presentation to the Rio meeting,[1] the available data are rather incomplete. This is not to be taken as any disparagement of the efforts made during the last ten years by national and international organizations which have wrought a nearly miraculous improvement in the quality and quantity of information available about the Continent.

II. A BRIEF REVIEW OF RECENT LATIN AMERICAN ECONOMIC GROWTH

In what follows, I use average real income as a measure of growth for want of a better one, and only to indicate rough orders of magnitude. Wide differences in consumption and production patterns between various Latin American countries and between Latin American countries and other areas preclude any other meaning, not only in terms of welfare, but also in terms of comparative productive capacities.[2]

Average income in Latin America at present amounts to something between $200 and $300 of current purchasing power. A few

---

[1] Considerable changes have been made in the paper since it was first presented, but these changes bear mostly on the arrangement of the subject matter and on the drafting. Before presenting the paper I profited from discussions, particularly with Professors Nurkse, Hirschman, and Boudeville; since then from discussions with Professors Laursen, Haberler, Gudin, and Bulhões as well as with my colleagues Messrs. Chacel and Kerstenetsky at the Brazilian Institute of Economics.

[2] See G. Warren Nutter, 'On Measuring Economic Growth', *Journal of Political Economy*, February 1957, p. 51 *et seq.*

countries in the temperate zone, but also Venezuela and Cuba, exceed this upper limit, and some countries fall considerably below it. Average income is about half that of Western Europe, and more than double that of South-east Asia. The absolute range of incomes as between different countries in Latin America is also half that found in Western Europe and not quite double that of Asia.[1]

Since the beginning of the Great Depression, average real income in Latin America as a whole appears to have grown in only somewhat smaller proportion than in the industrial countries.[2] But the Latin American nations as a whole have done better during this period than almost any of the other so-called under-developed countries, except the petroleum countries of the Middle East.

Growth rates, however, have differed widely among the Latin American countries. Argentina, as well as some of the smaller countries, are outstanding cases for the period of near stagnation of average real income. Chile and some other countries are cases of slow growth. Brazil appears to have matched the growth rate of *per capita* real income of North America. Mexico, Colombia, and possibly Venezuela, have, in terms of average real income, grown at rates exceeding the contemporaneous ones of the industrialized countries.[3] The much discussed gap between the average real income of many Latin American countries and that of many developed countries has either shrunk or at least not widened in relative terms. Moreover, the Latin American countries where this has been the case comprise the greater part of Latin America's population, and were at the beginning of the period among the poorer of the continent's nations.

The rise of average real income in the fastest growing Latin American countries has been attained in the face of population growth rates which have exceeded substantially the contemporaneous ones of the industrialized countries. In other words, the rate of growth of total real income in some Latin American countries has far exceeded the current rate of growth of total real income in any

[1] See, for example, *Economic Bulletin for Latin America*, Vol. II, No. 1, February 1957, Table 26, and United Nations, *Per Capita National Product of Fifty-five Countries: 1953–1954*.

[2] For real income indications, see United Nations, *Economic Survey of Latin America*, 1954, Table 9 ; for population data, see United Nations, *Demographic Yearbook*, 1956, p. 152 *et seq.* ; see, also, United Nations, *Statistical Yearbook*, 1955, p. 433 *et seq.* and p. 453 *et seq.*

[3] Country data estimated on the basis of : United Nations, *Economic Survey of Latin America*, 1949, pp. 207-287, 404 ; *ibid.* 1954, Table 11 ; United Nations, *Statistical Yearbook*, 1957, Tables 160-162 ; United Nations, *Demographic Yearbook*, 1956 ; United Nations, Document E/CN 12/365, Tables 1-23 ; *Revista Brasileira de Economia*, December 1955 ; United Nations, Document E/CN 12/429/Add. 4, Table 1.

industrialized country. And there is reason to believe that the rate of growth of average as well as of total real income in some of these countries has approached the highest growth rates of average real income *ever* reached in the industrialized countries.[1]

For the period before the Great Depression, our information on Latin America is even more scanty than for more recent decades. In general, the twenties were more or less favourable to Latin American countries, though there were notable exceptions, such as Cuba. During the first two decades of the twentieth century, there is also evidence of rapid growth, for example, in Argentina and probably in Brazil, Chile, and also in Cuba.

What of still earlier periods ? We have seen that the average real income of some Latin American countries is even today extraordinarily low — around $100 of present purchasing power or less. In many countries that have grown most rapidly in recent years, similar levels prevailed around the turn of the century. We can, nevertheless, not be sure that any of these countries, still less those countries which even then had somewhat higher incomes, were previously stagnating or growing slowly. After all, the meaning of $100 in terms of the many things that are relevant to growth is ambiguous, and the figure cannot be accepted as excluding earlier rapid growth.

III. GROWTH AND STRUCTURAL CHANGE

As a first approximation, and practically as a tautology, it can be said that the differing growth experience of the Latin American countries is a matter of their varying ability to undergo structural economic change. This section will discuss some basic factors which have influenced that ability in Latin America.

1. *Types of Structural Change Required*

The need for structural economic change has presented itself most dramatically in the form of the need to shift the centre of growth from the export to the non-export sector. Over the last half century or so, most Latin American countries have shown growing total real exports. At the same time most of them, with the clear exception only of Venezuela, either reached a peak in their real exports *per capita* relatively early in the period or at least have seen

[1] See, for example, L. H. Dupriez, ed., *Economic Progress*, (Louvain, 1955), p. 44.

4

the rate of growth of real exports slow down drastically. To quote only a few figures which happen to be handy,[1] Brazil, Uruguay, and Costa Rica reached a peak (or near peak) in real exports *per capita* before the turn of the century ; Argentina, Chile, and Bolivia before the beginning of the First World War ; Cuba before the twenties ; and Mexico (at least if one excepts the export of tourist services) and Peru during the twenties. This has by no means implied the end of the positive contribution made by exports to the development of these countries. Nor should we take it for granted that exports, whether or not of primary products, will never again become the fastest growing sector of these economies. In fact, such a development is by no means unlikely for those Latin American countries which are not of continental size. The need for raw materials may make non-continental industrial countries much heavier traders at certain stages of growth than less developed continental countries of similar size. It will be well, moreover, to stress that there is no implication here of a failure of export demand. There can, in fact, be very little doubt that factors acting on the supply side have sometimes been as important as factors acting on the demand side in making it necessary for Latin American countries to change their economic structure with respect to the relative importance of the export sector. The case of Bolivia is an obvious example of the importance of the supply side. In Bolivia, the real cost of procuring import goods by exporting the basic export has risen more than in proportion to the deterioration of the terms of trade. By contrast, in Brazil it is only an improvement in the terms of trade which has so far prevented a rise in the real cost of procuring imports by exporting that country's basic export.

It is almost trivial to note that even in the absence of a need to shift the growth centre to the non-export sector, Latin American countries could not have avoided structural change. Thus, a structural change might have been required within the export sector itself. In the face of a falling demand for or supply of the traditional export product, development of new export products may be easier than, or as easy as, a shift from the export to the non-export sector. This was the case in Ecuador where the traditional basic exports have been replaced by bananas, and in Mexico where cotton, coffee, and tourism have replaced minerals.

On the other hand, even if no structural change is required within the export sector, or as between the export sector and the rest of the economy, the mere growth of an economy will require structural change within the non-export sector. In Argentina it was, apparently,

[1] See Pan American Union, Doc. S-16, December 29, 1953, Tables I and II.

5

largely difficulties of carrying out a needed change in the structure of the non-export sector — a shift from the production of consumer goods to the production of raw materials and equipment — which explain her relative stagnation.[1]

2. *Failures of Structural Change — Open and Disguised Stagnation*

Difficulties relating to structural change mean stagnation of real income. No rise in real income can take place which involves demand for a product-mix which the economy cannot supply either directly or by purchases from abroad paid for by exports. Total real output, measured in base period prices, may be rising, but real income will not rise at all if there is no demand for the additional outputs, and their prices, in terms of other goods, are falling (in the extreme case, to zero) ; while it is impossible to procure those outputs which would be in demand if real income were rising in correspondence to the rise in real output at base period prices. The difficulty here is a divergence between income elasticities of demand and output elasticities of supply — that is to say, a structural difficulty. The structural difficulty may, however, be reflected in a confusing way in various employment and monetary phenomena. The stagnation of real income may take the form of either no physical growth and rising (open) unemployment, with stable money wages and monetary stability ; or, of physical growth and falling money wages, with full employment and monetary stability ; or, of physical growth and full employment without falling money wages but with inflation. In both the latter cases, of course, part of the employment is disguised unemployment, and adds nothing useful to the national dividend. The first two cases will look like failures of money demand, and the last like an excess of money demand, although in all three cases money demand merely reflects the action of structural factors.

Genuine failures of overall money demand do not seem to have been too important in Latin America, except for rather short periods. The outstanding exception may be Cuba's stagnation in the twenties. Even there other factors were partly responsible.[2] There is, of course, no particular reason why any failure of overall demand should take place or, if it does, why it should not be easily rectified. One can hardly rely, for this purpose, on price flexibility, but the

[1] See Dr. Raul Prebisch's address to the meeting of the Economic Commission for Latin America, La Paz, 1957.
[2] See Henry C. Wallich, *Monetary Problems of an Export Economy* (Cambridge, Massachusetts, 1950).

majority of Latin American countries have long possessed a sufficient degree of monetary autonomy.

3. *The Capacity for Structural Change*

With a given demand structure (as a function of the growth of real income, its changing distribution and changing tastes), a country's potential growth rate depends in the first instance on the potential simultaneous rate of growth of the current supply of the services of each of the requisite human or material resources (given the growth of the others), and on the degree of substitutability between them, which is largely a question of technology. The fundamental supply factors just mentioned are, of course, those which economists have always listed in discussing the economic prospects of a country.[1] In so far as it is possible to influence the demand structure by influencing preferences and income distribution, the growth rate can be increased, but the welfare significance of such an increase is not clear. It is sometimes suggested that in the absence of such interference, resource endowments in under-developed countries may pose very restrictive conditions on growth potentialities, because when incomes are low, the price elasticity of demand is universally low. The contrary has also been suggested, for example, by Harrod in *The Trade Cycle*, but this question cannot be determined on logical grounds alone. Even if it could be shown on logical grounds that substitution effects are smaller at lower than at higher incomes, it is clear that the income effects must be larger, so that the net effect remains in doubt.

One can go extremely far in explaining differences in growth in Latin America in terms of the supply factors mentioned earlier and one can certainly never ignore them. But one must remember that the process of development itself changes not only the quality and number of the population but also leads to the discovery of additional natural resources and generally leads to a more rapid capital accumulation than is assumed in the Keynesian consumption function. Within the limitations of this paper only an extremely superficial discussion of the relation of the supply factors to growth differences could be attempted and this would not be worth while.

Institutions and attitudes are of equal importance. Three general points require mention in this connection. The first is the pro-

[1] On this point see, for example, Jacob Viner, 'Stability and Progress : The Poorer Countries' Problem', in Douglas Hague, ed., *Stability and Progress in the World Economy* (London, 1958).

nounced entrepreneurial propensity which the Latin American population has shown. There is a general sensitivity to, and preparedness to act on, economic incentives, which is evident not only in the more advanced urban centres but also in the hinterland.[1] The second point is the relatively high savings ratio of many Latin American countries.[2] They appear to save, relatively to their incomes, as much as some far more advanced countries in Europe. A related remarkable fact about Latin America's saving is that it appears to some degree to be personally, but not sectorally, tied. We find, for example, in Brazil and Colombia, agricultural savings going into industry controlled by the landlords, as well as a reverse flow, like the recent coffee investments financed partly from industrial profits. The third point refers to the crippling tradition of the notarial state, the complicated bureaucratic machinery based on distrust of citizen and civil servant alike, where every absurdity is possible provided the required documents can be produced, and where the most reasonable thing is impossible without them. This tradition limits not only private enterprise, but equally reduces the efficiency of public action.

We have been concerned, so far, with the basic — natural and institutional — factors which have affected Latin America's ability to undergo structural change. The following sections discuss some particular factors which have been of importance in determining that ability.

IV. Adverse Shocks, Imbalance, and Growth

It is one of the most interesting aspects of recent Latin American growth that relatively rapid progress not only of structural change, particularly of industrialization, but also of overall growth have sometimes been associated with violent adverse shocks to the economic system. Let me add at once that I do not affirm that these economies have grown faster than they would have done in the absence of adverse shocks. All I affirm is that they have done so well in the presence of adverse shocks that their success merits surprise and explanation.

Though to some extent the events of the two world wars were adverse in terms of immediately available goods and services, such

---

[1] Numerous examples could be quoted. An interesting aspect is discussed in Sol Tax, *Penny Capitalism: A Guatemalan Indian Economy* (Washington, 1953).
[2] See United Nations, *Statistics of National Income and Expenditure*, January 1957; see also J. H. Adler, 'World Economic Growth — Retrospect and Prospects', *Review of Economics and Statistics*, August 1956.

adverse shocks occurred most obviously during the Great Depression. One might almost say that the ability to get through the years of the Great Depression with a rise in average real product marks the dividing line between those countries which in this generation have grown rapidly (Brazil, Colombia, and Mexico) and those which have stagnated or grown slowly (Argentina and Chile). Exceptions to this rule either have obvious explanations, like Venezuela, or, like Cuba, represent a long delayed recovery.

In the Great Depression, there appears, moreover, to have been a curious association between the degree of violence of these adverse shocks and growth. In Argentina a relatively mild adverse shock preceded slow growth of the average product. Brazil, Colombia, and Mexico grew rapidly after adverse shocks which were very strong in the first two countries and fairly strong in the third. In Chile a particularly violent adverse shock initiated a period of relatively slow growth.[1] We shall return later to this curious association. But before we do so we must attempt to explain how adverse shocks can ever produce any growth at all.

1. *Depression and Growth*

(a) *Changes in Preferences.* If future income were an inferior good, saving and investment would increase upon an adverse shock even in the absence of any change in the preference system. This premise, however, is hardly likely to be true. But a sudden loss of wealth and income can obviously produce a change in the preference system of a community which will lead to greater efforts at work and saving.[2] The change in preferences may occur either on the individual plane or, more likely, on the governmental plane, stimulating it to promote savings.

(b) *Changes in the Structure of Distribution and Production.* The adverse shock first reduces immediate real income, either by a reduction in current, physical productive capacity (for example, by an earthquake), or by producing an unfavourable change in the current terms of trade. The equilibrium growth path, in addition to being initially lowered by the adverse shock, will also be different from what it would have been if the shock had not occurred. Thus, the new equilibrium growth path will be characterized by a change in the relative importance of the various sectors of the economy. In

---

[1] See footnote 2, p. 3 ; see also United Nations, *Economic Survey of Latin America*, 1949, pp. 98, 211, 271-272, 408-409 ; and United Nations, Document E/CN 12/365, especially Tables I and II.

[2] A Toynbeean challenge-and-response effect, as Professor Gudin has put it. I do not think that Toynbee's thesis implies a tautology.

other words, the adverse shock will have a structural or substitution effect in addition to the income effect. Thus, the Great Depression changed the relative importance of agriculture and mining on the one hand, and industry on the other hand, in equilibrium. This change can, and in the case of the Great Depression did, in certain cases, promote growth. The explanation may be based on a change in income distribution and/or on external economies brought about by the change in terms of trade.

With respect to a change in income distribution, if the entre-preneurs in the lines of activity which are made particularly profitable by the change in data have a higher than average propensity to save, this alone may increase investment and growth. This is precisely what is likely to have happened in some cases where the Great Depression made industry profitable relatively to agriculture. How-ever, industrial entrepreneurs in under-developed countries are only partly a different group from agricultural entrepreneurs, and the effect of changes in sectoral income distribution should therefore not be overrated. With respect to external economies, if economies of scale can be reaped in the sectors made to expand by the deterioration in the terms of trade, there will be an offset to that deterioration. The economies must be external and probably, but not necessarily, technological, in order to make sure that the affected industries could not have expanded before the deterioration. For some time after the Great Depression there seems to have been an unparalleled opportunity in Latin America to reap technological external economies — Marshall's first kind which depend on the size of local enterprise and are mostly irreversible because they depend on the cumulation of output over time [1] — by industrialization. Nobody who has lived in Latin America during the recent period of industrialization could fail to be impressed by the appearance and spread of technical skills in the industrial centres. Pecuniary external economies due to the appearance of ancillary service industries were of equal importance. External economies were also reaped, however, in new sectors of agriculture, for example, in growing cotton in São Paulo. It is hardly necessary to add that not all structural effects are such as to make external economies possible. In the case of Latin America, however, the change in the terms of trade during the Great Depres-sion did stress the relative and absolute growth of the sector where this was possible, that is to say, the manufacturing sector. The possibility of realizing external economies in manufacturing after a change in terms of trade seems to imply : first, that the previous

[1] See H. S. Ellis and W. Fellner, 'External Economies and Diseconomies', *American Economic Review*, September 1943.

equilibrium growth path was not a social, only a private, one ; and second, that the new private equilibrium growth path is nearer the social one than the earlier one was.

(c) *Disequilibrium.* The change in data, being a shock, will also have been unforeseen and will, therefore, create disequilibrium for a time. In particular, due to the unexpected adverse shock, it is now revealed that there was a disequilibrium in the past structure of investment. Had the adverse shock been correctly foreseen, there would have been less investment in primary products, and more in manufacturing industry. It is entirely possible that as a result of this structural disequilibrium in past investment, the rate of investment and saving and of growth will now accelerate and that gross national product will after a time be higher than if — other things, including the Great Depression, being equal — equilibrium had been preserved throughout. I stress that this is just an hypothesis. It does not mean that an entirely different conjunction would not have prompted growth even more.

Available information does not permit a certain judgment as to whether disequilibrium itself contributed to accelerated growth in Latin America after the Great Depression, or whether the disequilibrium merely accompanied accelerated growth due to other factors. In some cases, for example, in the case of Brazil, it is quite likely that the disequilibrium as such, brought about by the fact that the Great Depression was unforeseen, did lead to an acceleration of growth and to an eventually higher gross national product than if equilibrium had been preserved. Consider, first, the total volume of saving and investment in the twenties. Correct foresight of the effects on Brazil of the Great Depression might have led to more saving. But this increase in saving, as well as part of the fixed investment that actually was made in coffee, might well have been diverted to private hoards rather than used to increase investment in other fields of production than coffee. In this case, that is to say, taking the structure of fixed investment in the twenties as given, gross national product in the thirties would have been smaller than it actually was. The effect of this smaller gross national product on growth would have depended in part on the use made of hoards. I shall discuss this briefly below.

On the other hand, with correct foresight, the structure of investment in the twenties might also have been different. If investment had stressed industry relatively to agriculture more than it did, then, for any given volume of investment in the twenties, gross national product immediately after the depression would have been larger than it actually was. (We shall see presently that industrial investment was, indeed, larger than might have been expected.) This would have inhibited growth.

The fact of agricultural over-investment in the twenties and of the subsequent over-production helped to increase the profitability of industrial development in the early thirties. It did so relatively not only to agricultural investment but — and this is the crucial point — relatively also to the expansion of production and consumption of products of current consumption. It was particularly the cost of import goods, which, at that time, could be acquired only by expanding exports, which became almost prohibitive under the circumstances. This would not have happened to the same extent if private hoards had been available. It is entirely conceivable that, in this way, saving and investment in the thirties and growth were raised above the levels and rate that would have prevailed if equilibrium had been preserved throughout.

The Great Depression is apparently an example of growth-promoting disequilibrium. Much disequilibrium, in Latin America at least, has been brought about by misguided intervention by the state. One would hardly claim that these disequilibria have generally contributed to growth. But one need not deny either that in some cases these disequilibria may have led to a degree of effort which may have resulted in the end in more rapid growth than would have taken place in its absence. It may be well, however, to stress a general observation at this point. In theory at least, there are always other ways to obtain the same growth that can be obtained through disequilibrium. Certainly, no excuse can be found here for *prima facie* faulty economic policies which may, by great good chance, contribute to growth in the end.

2. *Degree of Depression and Growth*

The association between the degree of adverse shock and growth noted earlier implies that there is an optimum degree of adverse shock. (It does not, of course, imply that an adverse shock is better than a favourable one.) The explanation must be found in the fact that the growth-promoting effects of the adverse shock, via changes in preferences, changes in income distribution, or the appearance of external economies or disequilibria, outweigh the negative income effects of the shock. It is not difficult to see how such an association can come about. A very mild depression will not have much effect either way, and in a catastrophic one the direct income effects will necessarily outweigh any other effects. What is a mild depression must, of course, be determined in the context of each economy and each particular stage of development.

3. *Prosperity, Growth, and the Alleged Double Curse of Under-development*

We have so far talked of the growth-promoting effects of adverse shocks. Favourable shocks, such as an improvement in the terms of trade, can have doubly favourable effects. The problem here, if any, is not the income, but the structural effect of the favourable shock. Will not such an improvement in the terms of trade of a primary producing country stress the traditional exports ? Will it not stress those lines of production where the propensity to save is apt to be low and where external economies have been exhausted long ago ? Will it not, therefore, inhibit, or even contract, the growth of manufactures, the sector where the two factors just mentioned can be expected to be more favourable ?

This is not necessarily true. First, an improvement in the terms of trade can affect new rather than traditional exports of primary products. Here the two factors just mentioned may be just as favourable as they would be in the case of a new industry. Another consideration is also important. If economies of scale are important in certain lines of manufacturing, the widening of the market through the income effect of the favourable change may on balance stimulate new industries which are subject to external economies in spite of the fact that the improvement in the terms of trade will stimulate imports. Moreover, the propensity to save of the entrepreneurs engaged in new industries may be higher than that of the entrepreneurs in traditional lines of manufacturing. The consequent rise of the average propensity to save and the reaping of economies of scale may contribute to further growth in addition to the contribution made by the improvement in the terms of trade. In these conditions, we might expect to find that an improvement in the terms of trade would be associated not only with an expansion of primary production for export, and an expansion of *new* manufacturing industries, but also with a contraction of old industries where economies of scale are already exhausted and cannot neutralize (or overcome) the substitution effects of improved terms of trade.

Precisely this constellation of events seems to have taken place in Brazil during the twenties when the terms of trade were extremely favourable to that country's exports. At the same time that the old textile industry was finding it increasingly difficult to emerge from its post-war crisis, a host of new industries were being set up ; the mechanism described here was, however, helped in some cases by tariffs and subsidies. Similar processes may have been at work in other Latin American countries. It is impressive that in the late twenties, when the terms of trade were favourable to their exports, so large a part of the investment not only of Brazil but also of Colombia, should have been directed into manufacturing.[1] The above considerations on the effect of improving terms of trade on growth, together with the considerations set forth in earlier paragraphs about the effects on growth of adverse shocks due to deteriorating terms of trade, explain why by no means all under-developed countries suffer from what has often been represented to be a double curse. When the terms of trade are favourable they have the possibility, but not the incentive, to strengthen their economies by developing industrial production for the home market, and when their terms of trade are unfavourable they have the incentive, but not the possibility.[2]

4. *Growth and War*

The explanation of the favourable effects on Latin American growth of both world wars can be analysed on lines similar to those of the preceding paragraphs. Wars in which one is not involved can be optimal shocks because both their income and their structural effects are almost bound to go in the right direction. At least for raw material producing countries, wars elsewhere will mean better terms of trade. To the favourable income effect there is now sure to be added a favourable structural effect, which could ordinarily not be relied upon. At the beginning of a war, the relative cheapening of imports which would ordinarily inhibit certain industries will actually lead to the expansion of these industries in anticipation of later shortages. (In addition to imports of equipment for the new industries, there will, of course, be some stockpiling.) At the end of the war, the terms of trade may again become unfavourable. This will produce the right structural effects, but the usual unfavourable income effects will now be neutralized by the use of monetary reserves accumulated during the war.

V. GEOGRAPHY, INCOME DISTRIBUTION, AND GROWTH

One of the most important factors responsible for differences in growth rates between the Latin American countries is the degree to which they have been able, at more or less early stages of their growth process, to take advantage of economies of scale, both internal

---

[1] See United Nations, *Economic Survey of Latin America*, 1949, p. 206 ; see also United Nations Document E/CN 12/365, Tables 1-14, 1-28.

[2] Regarding the period of unfavourable terms of trade, it is necessary to assume not only that saving is stimulated, but that it can be adequately transformed into foreign exchange.

and external. This factor is, of course, only one among many which explain such differences in growth rates. But it does appear to have been an important cause in enabling certain countries, such as Brazil or Mexico, to sustain a relatively rapid process of development from rather low levels of average real income at the same time that other countries were unable to perform an equal feat.[1]

It is almost a commonplace of development theory that economies of scale lead poor countries to *relatively* larger geographical concentrations of production and to relatively larger geographical and social concentrations of income than are found in wealthier countries. But it also seems that this proposition can be turned around, and we can say that the ability to produce concentrations of production — and income — is important in accelerating the development process and making it possible to take advantage of economies of scale. It may be well to stress that two aspects are involved, social as well as geographical concentration. The reason is that in the absence of zero transport cost, geographical concentration aids the scale effects of income concentration.

It is clear that from the point of view of the demand for any product or group of products, where economies of scale, internal or external, can be realized, there is an optimum income distribution, both classwise and geographical, for any given absolute size of income. Any greater equality of income distribution than the optimum will restrict the market. Any greater inequality will also restrict it. From other points of view than that of demand, other patterns of income distribution may be more conducive to growth. One particular distribution will maximize growth for each constellation of circumstances. The other cases have been discussed often enough. But the relationship between the demand for industrial products at any given level of average income and income distribution is sufficient to ensure that an intermediate type of income distribution will always promote more rapid growth than either extreme equality or inequality.

Our data on Latin American countries' patterns of income distribution are extraordinarily scanty.[2] But there is very little doubt that they are not all of one pattern. In many of them we find sufficient income concentration in certain centres to produce a market for manufactured goods which will make economies of scale possible while in others at the same level of average income there is no such market because of either excessive or insufficient social and geographical income concentration. A country's experience in this

[1] See Simon Kuznets, 'Population, Income and Capital', in L. H. Dupriez, ed., *Economic Progress* (Louvain, 1955).
[2] See Jorge Kingston, 'A Disigualdade na Distribuição das Rendas', *Revista Brasileira de Economia*, March 1952.

respect depends not only on its size, but also on its endowment with natural resources, and the state of world demand for these resources.

The relationship between income concentration and the type of natural resources is, perhaps, less obvious. Thus, certain sectors of production involve factor proportions which in turn involve extreme inequality of income distribution. This seems to be the case with certain types of mining. The reason for the particular factor proportions found in these cases may not lie so much in the fact that a minimal amount of capital per worker is required for production, as in the lack of supervisory labour which makes it more profitable to operate with more rather than less capital per unit of common labour. If the necessary labour is available at a subsistence wage, income distribution will be more uneven than with a less capital intensive technique. The market-size effect of capital intensity must be considered an offset, in certain cases, to its savings promoting effect.[1] On the other hand, agricultural operations may or may not be connected with extreme income inequality. Thus, Brazil's rather mixed scale of agricultural operations, particularly since the Great Depression, and Colombia's smaller-scale agriculture have undoubtedly been reflected in income distributions which have powerfully extended the market for certain types of consumer goods. In these cases income distribution may seem to be a purely institutional question. In fact, however, it is no more so than in the preceding case. Just as there, education — investment in human capital — is an important factor. Along with tradition, it determines the scale of economic production, just as there it determined the factor proportions. The subject, of course, could be discussed in much greater detail. Here, only a few ideas are mentioned.

VI. Inflation and Growth in Latin America

We shall be concerned in this section with the unusual relationship between inflation and growth or stagnation in certain Latin American countries. At least until very recently, relatively more countries in Latin America have suffered from inflation than in the rest of the under-developed world. In Latin America as elsewhere, inflation or its absence has been associated with the most diverse

[1] The savings promoting effect of capital intensity has recently been suggested as a reason for not using the appropriate accounting (*i.e.* full employment equilibrium) prices in determining factor proportions in under-developed countries. See W. Galenson and H. Leibenstein, 'Investment Criteria, Productivity and Economic Development', *Quarterly Journal of Economics*, August 1955 ; A. O. Hirschmann, 'Investment Policies and "Dualism" in Underdeveloped Countries', *American Economic Review*, September 1957.

types of growth. Some countries, such as Brazil, Colombia, Mexico, and Peru, have had more or less rapid inflation associated with rapid growth. Some, like Chile and Argentina, have had rapid inflation with slow growth or stagnation. Some, like Venezuela and, at times, Ecuador, have had very rapid growth associated with the absence of substantial inflation. Moreover, in a large number of countries monetary stability has been associated with stagnation.[1] From this quick survey it is tempting to conclude that inflation has not borne any relationship either of cause or of effect to economic growth. But such a conclusion would be erroneous. There have been important relationships, but they have not been of a straightforward nature.[2]

1. *Origin and Mechanism of Inflation in Latin America*

When analysing the causes of inflation, modern theory often proceeds to portray central banks — particularly in under-developed countries — like the character in Oscar Wilde's play who could resist anything but temptation. In other words, the existence of inflationary pressure is taken as sufficient explanation of inflation. This is hardly convincing, and the following analysis of the non-monetary causes of inflation is not intended to exculpate monetary authorities.

The origin of inflation is to be found most commonly in dissatisfaction with the equilibrium relationship between prices in general and wages. This gives rise to investment or budgetary deficit inflation or to wage inflation. The latter has become increasingly important in Latin America as elsewhere. Less commonly, inflations originate in dissatisfaction with the equilibrium relationship between prices in general, including wages, and prices in particular sectors, especially prices in the foreign trade sector. It goes without saying that in inflation, as otherwise, motives are generally mixed.

It is not difficult to see how growth can lead to inflationary action by economic agents. Thus, the stimulation of the propensity to invest, resulting from previous growth, has led to investment or

---

[1] United Nations, *World Economic Survey*, 1956, chap. iii.

[2] The chief sources on which the following considerations are based are : United Nations, *World Economic Survey*, 1956, Tables 43, 33, 49, 51, and Charts 14, 15, 17 ; *Producto e ingreso de la República Argentina*, Tables 6, 7, 9, 14, 21, 29, 30, 31 ; *Revista Brasileira de Economia*, December 1955, Tables on pp. 65-77 ; International Bank for Reconstruction and Development, *The Economic Development of Mexico* : Report of the Combined Mexican Working Party, Tables 126, 127, 113-121, 145, 12, 13, 26 (Baltimore, 1953) ; United Nations, Analyses and Projections of Economic Development, Vol. II, *The Economic Development of Brazil*, Tables 11, 16, 24, 25 ; United Nations, Document E/CN, 12/365, pp. 132-134, Tables I-1, I-2, I-3, I-4, I-5, I-10, I-18, I-30 ; A. Sturmthal, 'Economic Development, Income Distribution, and Capital Formation in Mexico', *Journal of Political Economy*, June 1955 ; United Nations, *Economic Survey of Latin America*, 1954, pp. 23-39 ; various papers of the International Monetary Fund.

budgetary deficit inflation in many Latin American countries. In-dustrialization and urbanization have created the conditions under which wage inflation can develop. An inter-sectoral price relationship which is often changed by growth in a manner causing — in low income economies — acute dissatisfaction and leading to inflationary reactions, is the one between food prices and prices in general, where agriculture lags behind the general rate of growth. Inflation due to dissatisfaction with this price relationship may appear as a form of wage inflation because it will be wage earners who will set the inflationary process in motion. Nevertheless, the cause will not be dissatisfaction with the relationship between wages and prices in general but dissatisfaction with the relationship between wages on one hand, and food prices on the other hand. The process of inflation will be set in motion by the wage earners because it is in the latter's budget that food prices weigh most heavily.

Where an apparent wage inflation is really due to imbalance between sectoral growth rates in agriculture and elsewhere, we may find such a wage inflation taking place while real wages are rising rapidly in terms of manufactures. We may then also find depression in manufacturing industry and falling prices for manufactures at the same time that money demand in general is rising. It is interesting to note that in some countries such sectoral imbalance was itself clearly the result of previous inflation combined with successful price control policies. Other countries — Brazil, for example — which suffered from similar degrees of inflation escaped this sectoral imbalance because of the ineffectiveness of their price controls. In some cases, however, it is conceivable that more deep-seated factors may have been responsible for the sectoral imbalance. In correcting such factors, the opening up of new lands to cultivation, where possible, seems to have been quite as successful as any measures of land reform which may have been adopted.

Sectoral imbalances affecting exports, and originating in over-valued exchange rates may, after longer periods, result in explosive depreciation of exchange rates leading to inflationary pressures con-nected with the relationship between export-import prices and prices in general including wages. A worsening of the terms of trade will lead to an equilibrium price relationship which may induce importers to press for inflationary credit expansion and may lead exporters to demand an inflationary exchange rate adjustment. An improvement in the terms of trade will induce pressure from consumers of exports but not from exporters or consumers of imported commodities. But there may be a general desire to participate in the bonanza coming to exporters, and inflationary pressures may be resorted to in order to disturb the equilibrium income distribution between non-exporters and exporters consequent upon an improvement in the terms of trade. We shall later see that such a disturbance has been frequently a result of inflation in Latin America, more frequent there than elsewhere.[1] But it is not possible to say how far the desire to disturb this equilibrium price relationship was also the origin of inflation in these cases.

2. *Incidence and Effects of Inflation in Latin America*

The unusual association of inflation with growth in certain Latin American countries at certain periods is the result of the unusual incidence of inflation. This has unusually often affected inter-sectoral price relationships rather than, as is more common, the social income distribution, that is to say, the relationship between wages and prices in general. Specifically, inflation in Latin American countries has unusually often affected the relationship between the prices of exports-imports and the prices of goods and services in general. This appears to have been particularly the case in countries such as Brazil, Chile, and Colombia. By contrast, in countries such as Mexico and Peru, inflation has, except during a few post-war

---

[1] It would be wrong to ascribe this fact to a greater importance in Latin America than elsewhere of the foreign trade sector relatively to the rest of the economy. For the post-war period an explanation can perhaps be found in the fact that the terms of trade improved greatly over the depression period and that this appeared to threaten the strong position which industry had acquired in the meantime. For earlier periods there is no such obvious explanation of the greater frequency of inflation sparked off by a dissatisfaction with the equilibrium price relationship between exports-imports and other prices. For Brazil, an explanation may be found for the period preceding the First World War in the very high propensity to import of the export sector, by which practically the entire burden of the deterioration in the terms of trade was thrown upon the non-export sector (including the government), leading to an inflationary reaction on the part of the latter. It is probably not true that inflation was started deliberately in order to modify the relationship between export-import prices and prices in general. But it is not very different from that when inflations are continued, or resumed after an interruption, without change of exchange rates ; particularly when this is done rather obviously because an improvement in the terms of trade has taken place and reduced the balance of payments pressures due to the preceding inflation by, as it were, ratifying that preceding inflation relatively to the existing level of exchange rates. There are considerable indications that something like this may have happened in the case of Brazil, Chile, and Colombia after the Second World War. It may be claimed that we are here deducing a motivation from a sort of natural stickiness of the exchange rate. But it is hard to believe that there is anything natural about the one price which is everywhere subject to government decision. Often, of course, action resulting in inflation cannot be interpreted to be unambiguously motivated by dissatisfaction with one particular price relationship. Thus, the desire on the part of industrialists to increase investment in excess of desired savings may imply indifferently a desire to change the relationship between the prices of their products and prices in general including wages, or between the prices of their products and export-import prices only, as long as their industries are to a sufficient extent direct or indirect consumers of imports.

years, been predominantly of the more usual wage-price incidence. In Argentina, both types of incidence have been important. In all cases, the primary incidence has not excluded other types of incidence. Thus, even where the wage-price incidence has predominated, there have also been distortions affecting the exchange rate and other controlled prices, in particular, utility rates. The distortions affecting the exchange rate and other controlled prices have also generally accompanied inflation whose primary incidence was on other inter-sectoral price relationships. There is no question, however, that the wage-price incidence is coming to predominate.

The incidence and origin of inflation are so closely connected that it is not necessary to enumerate here those factors which have been responsible for the increasing importance, in Latin America and elsewhere, of wage inflation.[1] Nor need we discuss those factors which account for the fact that incidence on the relationship between the exchange rate and prices in general has been more common in Latin America than elsewhere. In some cases, however, the latter incidence has been almost accidental, the exchange rate being the only price over which control, attempted on a wide front, could be effectively exercised.

The effects in general and on growth in particular, of those Latin American inflations whose incidence has been predominantly on the relationship between wages and prices in general have been analysed often enough. More complicated and interesting, and much less frequently analysed, has been the effect of inflation whose incidence is predominantly on the relationship between the prices of exports-imports and those prices of goods and services in general.

---

[1] Inflation of this kind is found to be one way to resolve, very temporarily and very partially, the problem of the low standard of living, by benefiting one part of the working class at the expense of the rest of the community. Moreover, the Latin American experience seems to indicate that very pronounced inflations, whatever their original incidence, usually fall upon wages/prices in the end. There are psychological as well as purely technical reasons for this. Among the latter two should be mentioned. First, wage adjustments do not take place at the same time everywhere. Hence it is difficult to determine the equilibrium wage for any group on the basis of existing price relationships. (See Economic Commission for Latin America, *Estudio Economico de America Latina*, 1954, p. 22 *et seq.*) This would not matter if wage determination were left to a perfect market, but, of course, it is not. Second, wage adjustments come in large proportions and the short-term elasticities of supply of wage-goods in the face of such large changes are lower than the corresponding long-term elasticities. Hence, when an attempt is made at establishment of the equilibrium wage corresponding to a given price level (an equilibrium wage which takes into account the fact that in equilibrium, the price of wage-goods may — almost certainly — be somewhat higher relatively to other prices than before the wage increase) the prices of wage goods rise at once in excess of their long-term equilibrium levels. If the interval before the next wage adjustment is shorter than the one necessary to reach the long-term equilibrium level of wage-goods, no equilibrium is possible. See E. Bernstein and I. G. Patel, 'Inflation and Economic Development', *International Monetary Fund Staff Papers*, November 1952.

The primary effect has been to alter income distribution to the prejudice of the exposed sub-sectors of the export sector and of the import-competing sector. These qualifications are necessary because, in almost all cases, multiple rate practices have been employed to limit the incidence of this kind of inflation to traditional exports. Moreover, many import-competing home products have been protected from the effect of this type of inflation by protective multiple rate practices and/or by quantitative import restrictions.

The prejudice to affected sectors has sometimes been only relative. In those countries where the external terms of trade improved considerably, it has been by no means incompatible with an increase in the export sector's actual share in the national income. Still less, of course, has it been incompatible with an increase in the share of that sector, agriculture or mining, from which exports are mainly derived. Moreover, there is no reason why this type of inflation should have any effect at all on the distribution of income between wages and profits generally. If real wages in the export sector are at subsistence level the inflation may merely reduce the share in national income of the export sector's profits. This implies that wages in that sector were below equilibrium level, but it does not imply monopsony or conspiracies. Landlords may work their own land and employ no other labour so that a reduction in excess profits only means that a reduction in the landlord-labourers' total income will not make them move out of farming. Under these conditions, inflation will increase the share in income of the remaining sectors and it may easily not only maintain but increase the share in national income of wages in those sectors. There is certainly no reason why the share in national income of wages in general should be reduced.

These effects refer to changes in income distribution as compared with what would have happened in the absence of inflation, not as compared with past income distribution. This distinction is important because at the same time as this type of inflation is going on, other factors in the economy will be acting to change the relationship between wages and profits. In fact we find, in the case of Brazil, no reduction in the share of urban wages and salaries properly defined [1] even before the recent period of wage inflation. In Chile the share of wages plus salaries in national income barely changed but that of profits fell perceptibly to the benefit of direct or indirect taxes which are partly reflected in subsidies to lower income groups.

[1] We have no data on the distribution of agricultural income by distributive shares. Executive salaries should be excluded from labour income and included with profits since the income tax prevents salaries of owners from being recorded as salaries at their actual level but insists that the excess over a steadily falling real value be recorded as profits.

Here, however, there is evidence of earlier wage-push inflation than in Brazil. We have no comparable data for Colombia. In Argentina, there is no question that the share of wages and salaries increased, but there wage inflation set in earlier.

In view of its effects on income distribution, the other effects of inflation whose main incidence is on export-import prices relatively to prices in general are also different from those of the more usual type of inflation. Since there is, in the former case, no shift to profits, we would not expect overall domestic saving or investment to change relatively to income. Thus, there is, *prima facie*, no reason to expect an acceleration of growth from this type of inflation. One could, on the contrary, expect that the sectoral disequilibrium or imbalance brought about by inflation would reduce current real income and stifle growth.

Undoubtedly, this is precisely what has happened in many cases. In some cases, it did not happen immediately, because, despite the constancy of the savings ratio, investment could be increased temporarily because of the over-valuation of the exchange rate applicable to capital goods imports. Statistically, this means that where data on a current as well as on a constant price basis are available, investment at constant prices as a percentage of income at constant prices regularly exceeds investment at current prices, as a percentage of income at current prices, because the currency is more overvalued if used to import equipment than otherwise. In this way, the inflation does lead to an increase in real saving.[1,2] The behaviour of savings in these cases is, however, more clearly correlated with other factors than with the rate of inflation measured by price increases (the

[1] One can also infer from this fact that a stimulus has been given to the importation and use of equipment embodying a higher ratio of initial to operating cost than would otherwise have been the case. But it is doubtful what effects this has had, since the imports of capital goods under these conditions have been rationed by import control. Undoubtedly, it has had the effect of creating a very uneven degree of mechanization among firms belonging to the same sector or stage of production, a fact which causes an eternal headache to the authorities and leads to constant inflationary pressures by the firms equipped with more obsolete machinery. It must be doubted, on the other hand, that it has gone to the point of creating disguised unemployment because there has undoubtedly been enough flexibility in combining such modern machinery with antiquated machinery and common labour either at the same stage of production or in ancillary processes, so that despite other detrimental effects the average ratio between initial and operating cost for the economy as a whole probably does not diverge too much from what it should have been on the basis of relative factor endowments and demand. We have too few data on the structure of private investment to make it useful to speculate what effects inflation may have on it. Where reasonably reliable data are available, there seems to have been a correlation between structure and the difficulty with which capital goods could be imported, *i.e.* construction in general has been an alternative investment outlet if no other outlet was available.

[2] Or because inflation and overvalued exchange rates make importers willing to pay high interest rates for import credits and because balance of payments deficits are the indispensable condition of much, if not most, foreign aid.

appropriate measure in this case). In particular, it is correlated with the balance of payments situation and the corresponding import policy. These factors determine the extent to which the over-valuation of the currency becomes effective with respect to capital goods imports.

Apart from the two effects on investment mentioned above, it follows from the nature of this type of inflation that its influence on growth derives mainly from its effect in altering the relative importance of the various sectors of the economy, as compared to the structure corresponding to equilibrium. Several mechanisms of such structural disequilibria due to inflation can be distinguished. Most obviously, by expanding, relatively to equilibrium, the non-export sector, this type of inflation may lead to the realization of external economies, which are less likely to have been exhausted there than in older sectors of the economy. Again, the propensity to save in the non-export sector may be higher than elsewhere in the economy, so that the modification of the inter-sectoral income distribution by inflation may after all raise savings. Less obviously, the structural imbalance created may itself promote growth by raising the saving-investment ratio through raising the profitability of investment relatively to the profitability of current production. The case is similar to the one where similar effects explain the growth-promoting results of certain types of adverse shocks. There is also little question that in some other cases the imbalances created have reduced real income only from a short-term point of view, that is, where they have run counter to a merely temporary change in terms of trade.

But these are exceptions. In general, there can be no doubt at all that this kind of inflation has simply inhibited growth by stifling certain sectors, such as utilities, transport of certain types, those sectors competing with favoured imports, and especially exports, without a sufficient offset in the forms explained above. The extent to which a given degree of inflation, combined with a given effective depreciation of the exchange rate, has affected actual growth as compared with potential growth in this way, has been influenced particularly, in addition to resource endowments, by the terms of trade. Of course, the degree of inflation, relatively to exchange rates, has itself often been influenced by the terms of trade.

Thus, Argentina appears in the post-war period to have stifled her own growth particularly effectively by an inflation which, relatively to the depreciation of the effective exchange rate, was more pronounced, by comparison with Argentina's improvement in terms of trade, than was the case in most other Latin American countries. The same may have been true of Chile, whose resource endowments

— in which should be included the ability to attract foreign capital — appear to have been particularly concentrated on the export sector. By contrast, those countries such as Mexico or Peru which, although experiencing no improvement in their terms of trade, have prevented inflation from stifling exports, have done well. Those countries such as Brazil or Colombia which have stifled the growth of their export sectors through inflation, but which have also had a substantial improvement in their terms of trade, have also done rather well, but they have obviously gambled on the terms of trade. On the other hand, those countries, like Venezuela, which have had an improvement in the terms of trade and have not stifled their export sectors, have also done extremely well.

The imbalances created by inflation with main incidence on inter-sectoral price relations have, as already mentioned, set up inflationary spirals which are in no way different from the inflationary spirals created by the familiar tug-of-war between wages and profits. These spirals have sometimes expressed themselves directly in successive readjustments of the exchange rate, which in turn have led to increased demand for credit on the part of the non-export sector. Sometimes these demands have been expressed indirectly via an increased call for government subsidies for certain favoured imports or for certain basic sectors like public utilities, which in turn have led to reactions in the form of credit demands on the part of government.

Finally, one may ask why the inflations in Latin America have not exploded yet. They have never, of course, been allowed to approach the rate at which hyperinflation sets in. From time to time, governments have acted decisively. Other reasons seem to be of two kinds, one relating to the acceleration of the inflationary spiral and the other to the increase in the velocity of circulation due to the loss of confidence in money as a store of value. The acceleration of spirals has been prevented because the incidence of inflation has been largely on a price relationship where the injured party has been politically weak or where the injury, due to improving terms of trade, has been relative, not absolute. The velocity of circulation has been prevented from rising as much as it might have done otherwise, by a series of factors. First, alternatives to the holding of cash have been less easily available than, say, in Europe at the time of the post War I inflations. Second, attempts at flight into foreign currencies have been prevented, not so much directly because exchange control has limited the *supply* of exchange for financial transactions, as indirectly by reducing *demand*. The narrowness of the financial market under exchange control has vastly increased fluctuations, and has made it

24

extremely risky to convert anything but savings of a permanent or long-term nature into foreign currencies. Third, attempts at flight into commodities have been prevented by a similar mechanism, because import-export control has created similar risks in respect to commodities. Fourth, the spread in poor countries between actual and minimum safe cash holdings at any time is immensely smaller than in rich ones. Finally, the erratic way in which the banking system gives its clients access to its lending facilities undoubtedly contributes to keeping minimum safe cash holdings relatively high. In fact, there are indications that the working of banking systems in Latin America may have become more erratic under inflation, providing an offset against other factors making for an increase in the velocity of circulation.

DISCUSSION OF DR. KAFKA'S PAPER

DR. KAFKA'S paper attracted much comment and gave rise to a wide-ranging discussion. The concept of optimum imbalance, or shock effect, received most of the attention. Other points discussed were the rôle of concentration, inflation, the recent growth of the Latin American economies, and the function of the entrepreneur.

I. SHOCK EFFECT

Professor Haberler expressed interest in the concept but thought it might be dangerous as a basis for policy. Presumably we did not want to generate wars and depressions for the purpose of promoting economic development. The reaction to shocks depended on many circumstances and remained always uncertain.

Professor Levine felt that the essence of the shock mechanism lay in the response rather than the challenge. The capacity of a social group to react to adverse events would make a useful subject of analysis.

Dr. Mayobre argued that the shock effect explained only isolated cases. It did not explain the bulk of cases that represented fairly steady growth under stable conditions. Even where shocks did occur, the concept was unsatisfactory because it did not elucidate the real causes behind the response. There were negative responses to shock as well as positive. In no case, however, would he consider the element of the unforeseen, which admittedly was inherent in the shock process, as an argument against the need for global programming. Rather it was an argument in favour of forecasting and programming.

On the significance of the frequent occurrence of shocks for programming, various other views were expressed. *Professor Byé* argued that two kinds of response had to be distinguished : the market response and the policy response of the government. The market response in under-developed countries usually was limited by the lack of integration of the various sectors of an economy. Hence government action was required — either to respond to shocks, or to avoid them. *Dr. Campos* believed, on the contrary, that governmental responses to shocks were usually of the wrong kind. Governments tended to try to soften the effects of shocks, for instance, by supporting agricultural prices against market declines, instead of allowing the imbalance to work itself out constructively. He suggested that governments should keep their protective action to whatever minimum might be practicable and allow the market to resume its corrective function.

Dr. Kafka agreed that the more centres of decision there were to respond to a shock, the better. He added that he thought he had made it quite clear that he was trying to *explain* the positive growth effects of adverse shocks, not to *recommend* such shocks. He had not, moreover, suggested that the growth effects of adverse shocks depended only on their size, as Professor Levine seemed to think, but rather on the general conditions of the economy.

II. Concentration

A second dictum of Dr. Kafka's, relating to the virtues of concentration, encountered much interest. *Dr. Kafka* had suggested reversing the familiar proposition that scale effects led to regional concentrations. Countries which had favourable conditions for regional concentration, like Brazil and Mexico, had been able to take advantage of economies of scale, thereby attaining accelerated growth. He was not associating himself, however, with the theory of the big push.

Professor Haberler questioned whether the effects of concentration really were unambiguously favourable. While he did not share the views of those who regarded concentration of industry in large cities as a tremendous evil, he did not consider it an outstandingly favourable factor either. It undoubtedly had dangerous political and social consequences which, in turn were apt to react unfavourably on economic stability by creating social and political unrest. *Professor Byé* likewise questioned the supposed benefits of concentration. High concentration, whether of income or in a geographic sense, led to external diseconomies. Geographic concentration particularly meant severe regional differences that prevented full integration of the economy. He preferred a balanced geographical growth pattern.

Dr. Kafka said in reply that he might have been overimpressed by examples of the benefits of concentration that he had observed. It was true that regional concentration of the sort represented by the cities of Rio de Janeiro, São Paulo, and Buenos Aires might now be approaching an excessive stage. On the other hand, he thought that the positive evidence of centres like Monterey should not be overlooked; neither should the importance of income concentration for the development of savings and of markets for advanced consumer goods.

III. INFLATION

Dr. Kafka had said that while inflationary pressures today were stronger than in the nineteenth century, this was no excuse for the often observable tendency to yield to them. *Professor Haberler* concurred and declared himself unimpressed by the frequent plea that the presence of inflationary pressures constituted a valid reason for letting inflation occur. Inflationary pressures had existed at many times in many countries. More important was the question why in Latin America they often were not resisted. Presumably this was a matter of attitudes and institutions. Because modern inflations often were repressed, he added, especially in the utility, housing, and exchange rate sectors, the evils of inflation had become compounded by distortion of the economy. Such good effects as inflation sometimes might have had were lost thereby. This repression might also be the reason why Latin American inflations so far had never really exploded. It might be better if such explosions were allowed to occur, because that might force a revision of policy, at least for some time.

Dr. Campos added that inflations in Latin America usually began to be combated after they had reached a rate of 50 per cent. per annum. Prior to that point, they were apt not to be taken seriously.

Dr. Kafka's statement that Latin America as a whole had not fallen sensibly behind the United States in its growth of average income between 1929 and 1954 seemed to surprise several members of the group. *Professor Haberler* thought that the Latin American statistics of overall output might be subject to a comparative upward bias for the same reason that Russian figures were biased — namely, because in early stages of industrialization basic industries dominated the scene. In more highly developed countries quality changes, diversification and the rise of service industries, which were insufficiently reflected in output statistics, tended to produce a comparative downward bias.

IV. RÔLE OF THE ENTREPRENEUR

Professor Haberler, agreeing with Dr. Kafka, expressed himself out of sympathy with the view that attributed the lag in Latin American development to a lack of entrepreneurs. Capacity for enterprise, he said, was an almost universal trait and certainly existed in Latin America. In the United States one found many entrepreneurs from countries that had been said to lack entrepreneurial talents, such as France or Middle Eastern countries. If entrepreneurial activity did not come to the fore the fault lay with the institutions that inhibited it. *Dr. Kafka* said that entrepreneurs were playing a very important rôle in Latin American growth.

Economic Development for Latin America

He did not agree with Professor Wallich's view that in Latin American development the rôle of innovation and of the entrepreneur was less central than it had been in the industrial countries. In particular, he saw no great difference between an innovation such as occurred in the industrial countries and the transplanting of a known process to a totally new environment. He thought Professor Wallich's distinction between production-oriented and consumption-oriented economies interesting, although he would prefer to distinguish saving-oriented and consumption-oriented ones.

Chapter 2

GLOBAL PROGRAMMING AS AN INSTRU-MENT OF ECONOMIC DEVELOPMENT POLICY

BY

JOSÉ ANTONIO MAYOBRE

Economic Commission for Latin America

I. Introduction

THE purpose of the present study is twofold. It seeks, first, to explain why some Latin American economists are convinced of the advantages of a development policy linked to a programme that covers the whole of the economy and aims at maximum compatibility of the ends pursued ; and, second, to discuss and analyse the methodology which the Economic Commission for Latin America has been working out and applying in some countries for the formulation of projections on which development programmes can be based.

II. Need for an Energetic Development Policy

The inadequate economic growth of most of the so-called under-developed countries may be attributed to more or less powerful concrete causes, which persist through time, and which can be remedied only if the community takes positive steps to do so — especially in the form of state action, with clearly defined objectives and instruments. Such state action does not necessarily mean the direct intervention of government organizations in the economic process. It may equally well imply the creation of conditions in which private interests can function with greater freedom and efficiency. The point is that the removal of obstacles to more intensive economic development calls for a planned policy with this end in view.

Among the most familiar stumbling-blocks can be cited the lack of specific resources or the failure to make good use of those resources that do exist ; a low propensity to save and to invest productively,

29

or — what comes to the same thing — an exaggerated propensity towards consumption or hoarding, deriving in most cases from an unsatisfactory distribution of income ; an insufficiency of basic capital to facilitate the utilization of natural and human resources and the geographic and economic integration of the region ; the undue instability imparted to the economy by its pronounced vulnerability to fluctuations in the world-market situation of one or a few products ; and the politico-social conditions hindering optimum utilization of human capacity or physical resources, such as closed social groups, lack of general and technical education, poor sanitary conditions, and obsolescent land tenure systems.

A national economic development policy must be based on fairly accurate knowledge of the influence exerted in practice by each of these or other factors. It must, at the same time, be provided with effective weapons wherewith to combat these influences, since their reasonably rapid elimination cannot be expected to result from the spontaneous interplay of economic forces, except in very special circumstances arising from the emergence of new and powerful stimuli, such as an unusually large inflow of foreign capital attracted by the discovery of great natural sources. Even in such exceptional cases, these new stimuli can hardly produce their full effect without a complementary economic policy. Thus, if substantial amounts of foreign capital are invested in an export activity, unbalanced development will ensue, unless advantage is taken of foreign investment to raise productivity in the agricultural and other sectors, or unless part of the increment in income is used to spread education and technical progress throughout the population.

These assertions are so obvious as to appear superfluous. Nevertheless, in many of the under-developed countries even the most elementary form of economic development policy is lacking. Sometimes the small groups holding the reins of government are not interested in or conscious of the need to raise the income and standard of living of the rest of the population. Sometimes the scientific and technical levels reached are not yet high enough for a clear conception of the requirements and instruments of such a policy to be formed. Most frequently, in the case of Latin America, the entire attention of the economic authorities is taken up by the problems of the moment. Whatever the reason, in many countries public action reflects a general economic, fiscal, and monetary policy characterized by conflicting measures or systems of which the ultimate aims are not clearly distinguished and which in the final issue prove ineffective or prejudicial to the balanced development of the economy. Still more often does it happen that in some countries where there exists a desire and determination to promote economic development, the possible effects of measures adopted to this end are weakened or nullified by the counteracting influence of others. For instance, alongside isolated programmes for the provision of basic facilities and a policy for the protection of industry, existing fiscal and exchange regimes or inflationary situations continue to foster an income distribution which discourages saving and productive investment and stimulates the flight of capital or the diversion of capital to purely speculative activities.

All these circumstances indicate the urgency of the need to supplement theoretical studies of economic growth with a set of guiding principles to orient development policy. Unco-ordinated action and improvisation must be replaced by a line of conduct rationally mapped out with the greatest possible unity and consistency. Such a purpose may be achieved in various ways, of which an analysis will now be attempted.

III. Development Policy Based on the Creation of Favourable Overall Conditions

A development policy may aim at overcoming the most serious obstacles hampering the growth of the economy through the application of specific measures at given basic points, while leaving the attainment of higher income levels and standards of living to the free interplay of private forces. Thus, for example, encouragement would be given to private investment and conditions attractive to foreign capital would be created. Fiscal measures to promote saving would be introduced. Public health and educational services would be improved. Out-of-date land tenure systems would be reformed, and the provision of basic facilities would be undertaken in the fields of transport, irrigation, electricity, and perhaps in some branches of industry where private capital was unwilling to operate.

From the point of view of programming, the distinguishing feature of such a policy is that it does not set up quantified objectives to be attained within a given period by the economy as a whole or by its various sectors. The basic premise is that the optimum growth of income will be secured through the spontaneous action of private interests in taking advantage of the favourable overall conditions newly brought into being. Consequently, the establishment of numerical economic objectives whose pursuit would determine the course of economic policy (a specific rate of growth, such-and-such a volume of investment and saving, given increments in production in the different sectors, and so on) will be impossible, because of the infinite number of unpredictable individual decisions involved. Furthermore, it will be pointless. If overall conditions favourable to development are created, an increasingly rational utilization of the economy's resources will be naturally and spontaneously induced without need for the prior establishment of specific targets. Programmes are thus confined to the separate plans of enterprises and to state investment, and their co-ordination is not assumed to be an essential part of development policy.

The weakness of this type of economic policy lies in its failure to visualize the future of the economy as a whole and to recognize how closely the various sectors are interrelated. This may mean that utilization of the factors likely to promote development falls short of the real possibilities. For example, ignorance of the long-term trends of demand and of its probable composition may result in too much investment in some sectors and too little in others. Lack of co-ordination among the different investment programmes may involve over-production in some cases and bottlenecks in others. Foreign currency resources, which are usually very limited in under-developed economies, may not be turned to the best account unless the most rational allocation is thought out beforehand. Internal growth may also give rise to disequilibrium in the external accounts if co-ordination between domestic requirements and the capacity to import is not ensured in advance. In general, the policy will run the risk of leading to an unsatisfactory use of human and capital resources, a structure of production ill-adapted to the composition of demand, the formation of bottlenecks at specific points in the process of production and distribution, and disequilibria which have unfavourable repercussions on development itself. All these defects can be gradually remedied as they arise, but the final balance will invariably show a more or less serious waste of resources and effort.

Despite these drawbacks, it cannot be denied that the mere creation of overall conditions favourable to economic development, particularly if the steps taken are based on a conscientious study of the country's situation, implies progress in the field of economic policy. The adoption of such a course, as distinct from the absence of programming referred to in the foregoing section, alone represents an improvement which would have inestimably far-reaching consequences for many under-developed countries. Moreover, in certain cases various factors, such as the need for immediate action, technical difficulties, or the prevailing politico-social conditions, may leave no other alternative open.

IV. DEVELOPMENT POLICY BASED ON OVERALL PROGRAMMING

A development policy based on an overall programme would set up more specific targets to be attained by the community within a given period, and would attempt to see that, as far as possible, these objectives were compatible or consonant with one another, and that the chosen instruments of economic policy were satisfactorily adapted to the ends pursued. The aim would be to ensure that under prevailing conditions optimum use was made of natural, human, and capital resources ; that production, in so far as the technique of economic analysis permits, was commensurate with probable future demand, both external and internal ; that the maximum advantage was derived from investments both in expanding the social product and in contributing to the subsequent growth of the economy ; that waste and bottlenecks were eliminated or reduced as much as possible ; and that the capacity to import was utilized more fully in accordance with the country's development requirements.

To serve these ends, a programme must contain certain essential elements. The first element is a prior evaluation of the goods and services required by the community within reasonable hypotheses of growth. The second is an assessment of the resources of every kind available or potentially available for the satisfaction of these needs. A comparison between requirements and resources will then permit the appraisal of the economy's development prospects, as well as of the differing degrees of effort which may be expected or demanded of the community in order to attain more or less intensive rates of growth. The third element is the setting-up of targets to be aimed at by the economy as a whole and by its various sectors so that given levels of production and income may be reached. The fourth element is the establishment of priorities for the use of available resources, with a view to the achievement and co-ordination of the ends envisaged. And the last is the determination of the means to be employed for the utilization of resources and the pursuit of objectives — in other words, the selection of the instruments of economic policy to be adopted.

This last point requires some clarification. Programming does not imply state control of the economy. The establishment of specific targets does not involve any preconceived notion as to whose will be the responsibility or the task of attaining these objectives. A programme may be confined to showing private interests the paths they may best follow in order to avoid failures or setbacks and to reach a higher level of production. Or, as is more likely, a programme may help the authorities to plan public investment in the basic facilities in the best interests of development, and to impart unity and consistency to their economic policy, especially in the fiscal and monetary fields, thereby encouraging private effort to reach the goals proposed for the different sectors of production. Furthermore, it is possible that the public sector may decide to assume responsibility for activities hitherto belonging to the sphere of private enterprise. The extent of state participation or intervention in economic life will essentially depend upon the prevailing political philosophy, but the adoption of a development programme is feasible under any of the contemporary political ideologies.

There are several technical alternatives for the preparation of such development programmes. Much has been written during the last few years about a series of models and schemes designed for practical purposes. Among the plans drawn up for free enterprise economies, the programmes of Norway, the Netherlands, India, Pakistan, and other Asiatic countries, and those carried out in all parts of the world by the missions of the International Bank for Reconstruction and Development should be mentioned. The present study offers a brief outline of the methodology which has been worked out by the United Nations Economic Commission for Latin America for the guidance of economic programming in the under-developed countries of this region. This methodology is still in its experimental phase and the procedures employed are subject to modification.

V. The Technique of Projections of the Economic Commission for Latin America [1]

The method of programming used in the studies of the Economic Commission for Latin America comprises three stages. The first is the calculation of aggregate projections for the economy as a whole. The second is the preparation of projections for the different sectors, and the third is the comparison of the overall projections with the findings of the sectoral studies, so that the necessary corrections and adjustments may be made.

The working out of the projections must be closely linked to as complete an analysis as possible of the country's past economic

---

[1] This methodology is expounded in detail in United Nations, *Analyses and Projections of Economic Development, An Introduction to the Technique of Programming*. For its application to specific cases see 'Analyses and Projections of Economic Development', Vol. II, *The Economic Development of Brazil*, and Vol. III, *The Economic Development of Colombia*.

development and of its present situation. Such an analysis calls for a thorough study of the evolution and special features of this growth ; of the rates of increase of product and income ; of the breakdown of income between consumption and saving, as well as of income distribution ; of the composition of the population and the labour force, and lastly, of the extent and quality of the available natural and human resources. Only on the basis of such knowledge will it be possible to evaluate the behaviour of the different sectors of the domestic economy and of foreign trade in the course of development, and to determine the strategic points conditioning this process. Such an analysis, which is usually called the diagnosis of the economy, really constitutes the first step towards embarking on the work of programming proper.

A fundamental aspect of this methodology is the establishment, as a preliminary approximation, of alternative targets or objectives for the economy as a whole. Each of these alternatives depends upon the fulfilment of certain conditions in external economic relationships, on specific degrees of effort on the part of the community, and especially upon the readiness of the latter to devote a greater or smaller proportion of its future income to capital formation. These aggregate projections must take into consideration the probable or possible situations that may arise within a given period and the results that may be expected from a programme under these differing conditions, in order that the programme may be given enough flexibility to adapt its targets to any changes that may take place in the determining factors. The aggregate projections, then, attempt to forecast in quantitative terms the levels to be attained by the economy, within a prudential period, on the basis of the elements of analysis available and of reasonable hypotheses as to the behaviour of its dynamic factors. These latter are in essence exports, the rate of saving, the productivity of capital, the inflow of foreign capital, and the capacity to import.

The estimate of external demand for the country's goods and services is based on probable trends in the markets for the country's regular export products and on the possibilities of developing new exports. Such trends depend upon future income in the markets in question, on the income elasticity of the demand for exports, on the behaviour of prices, and on the competitive position, whether in relation to similar goods and services or in relation to potential substitutes. An analysis of this kind must be made for every important commodity, as market conditions tend to vary for the different items. Consideration will also have to be given to the influence which may be exerted on foreign markets by the exporter country's trade and price policy, and to the incidence of the corresponding measures on the domestic economy. Given these data it is possible to establish, for a specific number of years, one or more hypotheses of demand for the country's exports and of their contribution to the gross product.

The rate of saving is closely bound up with two other variables, income levels and the proportion of income absorbed by consumption. Past and present income statistics and rates of saving and consumption are ascertained when the diagnosis of the economy is made. But in projecting the future development of the economy it is assumed that these figures will be modified in relation to the rate of growth postulated in the programme. Present data, therefore, only provide auxiliary material for the evaluation of future possibilities. The possibilities themselves will have to be provisionally assessed, with due regard not only to experience but also to the need or desire for a specific expansion to be achieved within a given period, as well as to the probable behaviour of other factors. Thus, if a considerable increase in the demand for exports is forecast, there is a likelihood of a rise in income and in the rate of saving, compatible with substantially higher absolute levels of consumption. To take a further example, it may happen that the aim is an acceleration of development calling for a high rate of saving and severe restriction of increments in consumption. Subjective decisions of programmers or of the economic authorities, which are controlled, up to a point, by the data on past and present real phenomena, and by forecasts of the behaviour of the other strategic factors thus introduce discretionary elements. To limit such arbitrary elements, the methodology under discussion advocates the preparation of several alternatives or hypotheses of growth, based as far as possible on data representing the real state of affairs.

Once one or more growth hypotheses are established, the next step is to estimate the investment needed to attain the proposed product levels. Here the concept of the productivity of capital, the product-capital ratio, comes into play. This is the relationship existing in a given period between the net national product or national income and the capital which participated in production. Detailed consideration of the factors influencing the productivity of capital is outside the scope of the present study, as is also discussion of the validity or the usefulness of taking an overall product-capital ratio as against sectorial productivity ratios.[1] However, in the methodology at present under review, the overall product-capital

[1] For a fuller treatment of the problem, see *Introduction to the Technique of Programming*, p. 21 *et seq.*

ratio is used provisionally in predetermining the order of magnitude of investment required if specific income levels are to be attained. The data thus obtained will be revised at a later stage of the analysis, when more exact figures on investment in the different sectors are available.

If the estimates of the investment needed for given income levels are compared with estimates of future saving, foreign capital requirements can be deduced. It is, in fact, very likely that in some underdeveloped economies, characterized by low *per capita* income, deficient consumption and a very modest rate of saving, this last cannot be increased sufficiently to meet investment needs. In such an event, supplementary foreign capital becomes essential, at least until saving has caught up with investment requirements.

The next stage in the preparation of the overall projections is to calculate the capacity to import and the total volume of imports which will have to be replaced with domestic production if this capacity is to be utilized in the best interests of economic development. The capacity to import will depend, first, on the future volume of exports and the probable terms of trade, and second, on the net movement of capital. These factors can be estimated, and hypotheses can be formulated to serve as a basis for alternative projections.[1] The next step will be to compare the capacity to import with the country's probable import requirements at the income levels previously assumed. In cases where development is not accompanied by any major growth of exports or by an inflow of foreign capital, the capacity to import may prove insufficient to meet import needs. In fact, economic growth normally brings in its train an expansion of demand for manufactured goods and raw materials. Furthermore, the import coefficient is higher in the capital than in the consumer goods category, and development presupposes that a larger proportion of income will be used for the purchase of capital goods. Where this is the case, the difference between the probable demand for imports and the capacity to import will indicate how far imports will have to be replaced by domestic production if the programme is to be successfully executed.

Up to this point overall statistics have been used. By this means it has been possible to establish one or more hypotheses as to the probable growth of the economy, to determine an order of magnitude for the investment needed in each of these hypothetical situations, to calculate the degree of community effort required to increase capital formation, to estimate the supplementary need for foreign

[1] For further details, see *ibid.*, pp. 23-24 and 25-26.

capital, to quantify the capacity to import and — should the case arise — to assess import substitution requirements. The second stage consists in estimating how these overall statistics will be reflected in the various component sectors of the economy, that is, in the preparation of the sectoral projections.

The basic element in the calculation of sectoral projections is the estimate of the community's future demand for various goods and services. In a society where consumer freedom is assumed to exist, the structure of demand will depend upon an unlimited number of individual decisions as to the distribution of expenditure. Methods of formulating reasonable hypotheses as to the future composition of demand must therefore be discovered.

For programming purposes, the technique of the Economic Commission for Latin America bases the analysis of demand on four large categories : final consumer goods ; intermediate products ; services ; and capital goods.

In the case of the first category, historic income-elasticity co-efficients are used as a preliminary approximation if the statistical standards reached do not allow of more accurate methods. Wherever possible this method is supplemented by consultation of family budgets in order to project the composition of future demand on the basis of demographic structure and probable future income levels. Inter-country comparisons can also be of aid. As regards demand for intermediate goods, input-output matrices are utilized. In the projection of demand for services, separate consideration is given to those rendered to the final consumer (housing, professional services, and domestic services), intermediate services (energy and transport), and government services, and to each of these the method of analysis that seems most suitable is applied. Demand for capital goods is projected with the help of the input-output matrices, supplemented, at a later stage, by the findings of the research into the structure of the various sectors referred to below.[1]

Knowledge of the demand likely to arise during the implementation of the programme leads directly to the study of how this demand is to be satisfied, that is, to the calculation of supply, whether of imported or of domestically produced goods. The capacity to import having been computed when the aggregate projections were prepared, the next requisite is to project the distribution of the estimated foreign exchange resources among those goods which are

---

[1] It is impossible to sum up each of these procedures in a few paragraphs. Those interested will find both the procedures in question and the problems arising in each case briefly outlined in *Introduction to the Technique of Programming*, pp. 28-32, and 39-41.

not produced in the country. Should the resources in question be insufficient, a programme of import substitution by sectors will have to be laid down. To this end, marginal social productivity is proposed as the criterion for determining the adoption of substitution alternatives, although certain other considerations (for example, the desirability of developing specific sectors and industries of basic importance for future growth) must also be taken into account.[1]

Deduction of that part of internal demand which will presumably be satisfied by imports from total demand (domestic demand plus demand for exports) in each of the four categories will determine the volume of production to be attained in each branch of the economy. Next, the prerequisites for attainment of these levels of production will have to be defined ; that is, the sectoral programmes must be drawn up. This calls for a detailed technico-economic study of each activity. The existing situation in each sector must be examined from the most widely divergent standpoints, so that in each case as accurate a conclusion as possible may be reached as to the investment required, its composition, the necessary inputs and those economic, administrative, and technical measures whose application will facilitate or ensure the execution of the programme.

The third and last stage of the methodology described consists of cross-checking and adjustment. The findings of the sectoral projections are compared with the assumptions on which they were based, that is, with the aggregate projections. Considerable discrepancies and inconsistencies between the two sets of postulates are to be expected. The only way to reconcile them is to revise the previous hypotheses in the light of the more concrete data resulting from the detailed study of each sector. This involves making successive approximations on which can be based hypotheses or alternatives consistent both as a whole and as regards the relationships between their various components.

Projections are not a programme. They are the foundations on which a programme can be built. They present a general picture of the situations likely to arise, postulated on assumptions of the behaviour of the factors strategically important for development. A programme also includes the preparation of concrete projects in fields where this is feasible, an economic policy designed to serve the programme's ends, and a satisfactory administrative organization. These topics have not been dealt with in the present study.

[1] *Ibid*. pp. 37-39 and 42-43. Other alternative criteria which might be applied are at present being studied.

VI. Preliminary Evaluation of the Proposed Technique
of Overall Programming

The method of overall programming possesses weaknesses deriving from the present state of economic technique, from imperfections of data and analysis in the under-developed countries and from factors inherent in free enterprise economies which set limits to the value of forecasts. A few examples will illustrate these difficulties.

The calculation of possible future levels of demand, as regards both exportable products and domestic consumer goods and services, is a basic element in the preparation of projections. Considerable progress has been made in the techniques of demand analysis, and it may safely be asserted that, on the basis of such analysis and projection of family budgets at different income levels — as compared with the income-elasticity coefficients obtained by the other methods mentioned — the future composition of demand can be approximately forecast. But current technique does not allow for changes in taste or technological innovations, both of which may radically alter the demand for final, intermediate, and capital goods. Another no less difficult problem is that of estimating how far variations in relative prices may influence future demand.

Equally serious difficulties arise when the demand for exports is projected. In this case consideration must be given not only to the possible volume of demand for the good or goods under study, but also to the situation of other producer countries and their competitive position, to the emergence of substitute commodities, and to the price fluctuations that may be registered on buyer markets. The difficulties are perhaps even greater when the future price of imports has to be predicted in order to calculate the possible terms of trade.

Another example which may be cited is the calculation of the rate or rates of development which the economy will attain, a point of fundamental importance for the building-up of the programme. The historical analysis will permit the assessment of the rate of growth achieved during a given period, which is an essential element in forecasting immediate prospects. The course which may possibly be followed by exports is also of great significance in estimating possible rates of development. But other basic variables will still remain to be ascertained, such as the proportion of income which the community is prepared to save, and the productivity of new investment, as well as changes in productivity which may occur during the execution of the programme as a result of development itself and of technological and social progress. Here there is still much to be done before techniques can be considered satisfactory, and the economists responsible for the preparation of programmes have for the moment no other way open to them but the presentation of alternative possibilities and, in the last issue, subjective appraisal, which deprives the conclusions reached of some of their scientific validity.

Nor is the situation any more promising when one comes to the problems relating the different sectors and their interrelationships. The inputs of every kind required in the productive process serve in effect as a basis for the establishment of production or import targets in the different sectors and branches of activity. Current technique enables the present structure of such inputs to be ascertained, though not without burdensome effort in the case of under-developed countries. But the validity of these data, so far as their future application is concerned, is a controversial point, in view of technical variations and changes in relative prices.

Mention must be made of other risks attendant upon overall programming, which, although more of a political or psychological nature, are far from negligible. How far may the detailed projection of demand give rise to prejudices in favour of autarky, or of something approaching autarky, to the disparagement of the advantages deriving from specialization ? Similarly, may or may not the obviously greater degree of accuracy in the calculation of internal than of external demand lead the country to attach more importance to import substitution than to the expansion of its export trade, even when the latter might be the more beneficial ? May not the fact that a programme is a form of governmental action, even when its compatibility with economic freedom and private initiative is acknowledged, give rise to excessive state intervention because of the authorities' interest in urging on the implementation of the programme ? May not this have still more dangerous consequences in under-developed countries where public administration is as a rule defective ?

The comments made on the shortcomings in technique and sources of information may first be analysed. The weaknesses noted, and others which a more thorough examination would bring to light, are undeniable. This indicates two facts.

First, a programme cannot be taken as something perfect and final, but rather as a body of conditional but feasible possibilities. If the external circumstances taken as a basis for programming were to become reality, the programme would show how best they could be turned to account in the acceleration of development. As this is not certain to happen, the more alternative situations the programme takes into consideration, the more useful it will be. In other words, a programme should be sufficiently flexible for its objectives to be modified when changes take place in the basic assumptions, but it should indicate how, in each of the possible situations envisaged, available resources may be utilized to the best advantage. This is, at all events, better than groping blindly. Even an approximate assessment of the principal economic magnitudes, and of the effort that would be needed for the attainment of specific targets within the development policy, represents a valuable guide for economic policy and for the programmes of private entrepreneurs.

The second conclusion is that the possibilities of improving the sources of information and the techniques of analyses applicable to programming must on no account be disregarded. It is not that formulae or models of unquestionable accuracy are thought to be attainable. There will always be unforeseen circumstances or elements of human error causing disequilibria and modifications at certain points in the system and necessitating the revision and correction of data and of the targets proposed. But economic science can and must remedy many of the present weaknesses in analytical technique, and in the sources of statistical data and of general and technical information.

As for the political or psychological reservations made, their very mention indicates awareness of the dangers which they pose. Programming does not in itself presuppose an economic policy with a bias towards autarky, nor a preference for import substitution, nor a particular type of state intervention. Neither does it disregard the benefits of specialization, the rise in income resulting from foreign trade, and the advantages of private enterprise. If in a given country and under specific conditions a programme were to imply a modification of these principles, the cause would probably not lie in prejudices bred of programming, but in other factors, such as conditions prevailing in the economy in question or preconceived ideas which cannot be fully justified.

The problem of overall programming may therefore be presented in two parts. First, is it legitimate to hope that programming — if its technical shortcomings are for the moment set aside — may prove to be an advance over other systems of economic policy, in the sense that it secures more satisfactory and better co-ordinated utilization of the resources available for development ? The whole of the preceding series of arguments indicates an affirmative reply to this question. Although it is impossible to foresee all the contingencies of economic life, many disequilibria and conflicts may be avoided. If the conditions in which the economy could develop are worked out beforehand together with a policy aiming at the efficient utilization of available resources within the framework of such conditions, there is every prospect of achieving balanced development at an optimum rate.

Second, how far do the weaknesses of the existing technique of overall programming render it inappropriate for purposes of practical economic policy and, what is more, make it a dangerous instrument because of the illusions it may create as to the accuracy of data grounded only on inaccurate methods ? On this point a variety of attitudes might be adopted. One, an extreme position, would be to consider that until the technique of overall programming acquires a more strictly scientific character, it should not be employed for practical ends. Another would permit the use of the technique of programming, even with its present shortcomings, in attempts to solve problems which cannot be tackled with precision by empirical methods, so long as the weaknesses of the technique are not lost sight of and the programmes are endowed with sufficient flexibility for their constituent elements to be modified when the basic data alters.

A few examples will give a clearer idea of this last criterion. In the case of exports, at the present level of technique, it is recognized that projections covering many years cannot be precisely calculated. But it is feasible to estimate with approximate accuracy, and for a reasonable period, the prospects of demand for a country's staple products and, in some instances, the probable behaviour of prices. When this can be done, the programming of export activities on the basis of such data represents an advance over a policy that merely feels its way. In the field of domestic demand, the elements which modern techniques of analysis can provide may be of great assistance in establishing probable levels of consumption for the main groups of products and services. The changes which may take place as a result of altered preferences, technological progress, or relative price fluctuations can be dealt with in the course of application of the programmes, provided that these programmes have the necessary flexibility. Calculations as to the probable levels of income, saving, and the productivity of capital are inaccurate, and more intensive and thorough research will be required before a satisfactory degree of precision can be achieved. But the data supplied by statistics of a standard not difficult to attain in certain Latin American countries allow such relationships to be used as bases for fairly realistic hypotheses, which would permit, to begin with, the appraisal of important factors such as, for example, investment requirements and the need for foreign capital. These hypotheses would then be compared with the findings of the sectoral studies, and could be modified if necessary.

To acknowledge the advantages offered by overall programming as an instrument of economic development policy is not to deny the advantages of other types of policy, especially that which has been called 'creation of favourable conditions'. As has already been pointed out, everything that means co-ordinated and clearly defined action implies a great stride forward. Moreover, to confine these remarks to the case of Latin America, overall programming calls for a certain minimum of data which are not at present available in some countries. It also demands certain technical and administrative standards and some degree of confidence and collaboration on the part of the public, both in the preparation and in the execution of the programme. Where these conditions are lacking, it would be idle to hope that economic policy could be based on an overall programme such as has been described, just as resignation to the absence of any policy whatsoever would be barren. But in all these cases there should be a conscious effort to overcome these difficulties, so as to proceed to the utilization of more highly perfected instruments of development policy.

COMMENTS ON DR. MAYOBRE'S PAPER

BY

EUGENIO GUDIN
University of Brazil

I. INTRODUCTION

ECONOMIC development is, basically, the result of a number of elements, several of which are not or are hardly controllable, such as : climate, natural resources, size, population, rate of population growth, population origin and structure, religion, capacity of private initiative ; and other elements which depend on long-term and persistent efforts, the most important of which is education, especially political education.

In spite of this, economic development is a subject that lends itself rather easily to wishful thinking under the stimulus of a patriotic desire to promote the country's progress. There is hardly anything more tempting to an economist of an under-developed country than to get together forecasts of the national product, of income *per capita* and of capital formation, to show his fellow countrymen the possibilities of building up a great country in a short time. Recipes for a big push or a take-off or a five-year plan, even in non-totalitarian countries, are often of great

44

appeal to governing classes, anxious for prestige and glory. Nitti once expressed his admiration for government planners' solicitude for the happiness of their victims.

II. Programming and Government Intervention

Macro-economic programming is naturally a governmental task, as it does not make sense without government sponsorship. This explains its invariable bias towards government intervention and direct action in the economic field. The author of the paper under discussion is therefore quite wise in expressing the fear that programming may be seriously tainted with socialization.

I dare not express an opinion on Latin America in general. Among under-developed countries, most of which I once proposed to call reflex economies, the diversity of types is large. In some countries the *animus progrediendi* may be lacking. In some there is and in others there is no disguised unemployment. Some have, others have not, excess of population, and so forth. As for Brazil, however, I can definitely state that the spirit of enterprise and private initiative has never been lacking. The slow rate of progress never had its origin in a lack of initiative but in the low productivity resulting from the tremendous shortage of competent people in all sectors of the economy.

Nevertheless, the Brazilian Government has, during the last twenty-five years, absorbed a number of economic activities which in other countries, with much more capable governments, remain in the hands of private initiative. All the railways of any importance, except one, nearly all worth-while shipping lines, oil extraction and prospecting, the largest steel mill, and the alkali industry, have been taken over. The electric power industry is now also being absorbed. The liquidation, in the Stalinian sense, of private enterprise has been effected with the aid of two very simple weapons: first, enforced wage rises of a magnitude which the companies could not stand ; and second, in the case of public utilities, refusal of increases in rates necessary to compensate for the higher production costs due to inflation.

The next result is worth registering, for the example as well as for posterity. The government autarchies which replaced the previously existing private companies produce today an operational deficit (twelve billions of cruzeiros) equivalent to nearly 20 per cent. of the total budget receipts of the Federal Government. Furthermore, the inefficiency of railways and shipping, together with the shortage of electric power, has been for the last ten years the worst bottleneck in the Brazilian economy.

III. Difficulties of Forecasting for Latin American Countries

In the paper under discussion we read that the fundamental element in the elaboration of the projections is the forecasting of the possible

levels of demand during the next few years, starting from the analysis of the projections of family budgets of different income levels. From this one can easily form an idea of the Herculean task that global programming involves as well as of the high degree of uncertainty.

This might perhaps not be so in the case of countries and economies of small dimensions, great stability, ample administrative capacity and first-class statistical organization, like the Netherlands or Switzerland. But in countries in the process of full development, where economic disorder is frequent either through exogenous factors or through the incapacity of governments, countries unusually vulnerable to impact from outside, countries largely dependent on export prices and on the size of harvests, countries subject to chronic inflationary pressure, it seems to me that the forecasting of demand during the next few years by far exceeds the possibilities of the courageous economists who attempt it.

The problem is probably more concisely put in a recent report of the Economic Commission for Latin America, where it is stated that the first problem refers to the objectives to be attained, for which there must be a programme, and to the rate at which a country must grow in order to reach a certain level of production and consumption within a certain number of years. By combining the volume of savings with a certain ratio of capital to output, the desired rate of investment and income growth can be determined.

This is an application of the Harrod-Domar formula. This formula is undoubtedly very interesting and elegant, like most dynamic models, but as Professor Boulding comments in his article in the *Quarterly Journal of Economics* of November, 1955, such models should not be taken too seriously as,' Relationships and parameters which we must assume, for purposes of the model, to be constant turn out to be highly variable in practice'. Similarly, Mr. Nicholas Kaldor, in one of his recent lectures in Rio de Janeiro, said that Harrod's independent variables are interdependent ; for instance, it is saving that regulates investment, but at the same time it is investment which, by increasing income, determines saving.

The uncertainty of projections in these countries is aggravated by the circumstance that, for these countries, the value of exports is larger and exports therefore have greater weight than investment, a fact which makes the stability of their economic systems more vulnerable. How can one foretell the price of coffee next year or whether Colombia's coffee harvest is going to be as abundant as in 1954 or as scarce as in 1956 ?

Turning to the domestic economy, how can one estimate the capital-output ratio which is going to prevail without knowing the probable degree of inflation ? Will it be near 10 to 1 as when the building industry is booming, sustained by bank credit and stimulated by the flight from the currency or will it be a mere 3 to 1 or 4 to 1 as when the transformation industries prevail and there is no inflation ? How can one foresee the unpredictable production of oil, the changes in the exchange system or whether the government is going to enforce a new and disastrous rise in minimum wages or in the salaries of government officials ? Considering all these factors of uncertainty, it seems pointless to pretend to frame quantitative estimates of demand, supply, saving, and investment.

It is true that the author of the paper warns us that programming must have flexibility so that the objectives may be altered when the basic data vary. It seems that the programme has got to be constantly adapted to facts over which it has no control. In other words, the programme has to run after the facts instead of governing them.

IV. What Governments can do to aid Economic Development in Latin America

What the governments of these countries can do for the economic development is not programming. It is simply to refrain from impeding development by indulging in such evils as political warfare, demagogy, inflation, hostility, disguised or otherwise, to foreign capital, or unbalanced or excessive protection to industry and/or agriculture. If these evils can be avoided, then economic development, subject to the elements mentioned in the first paragraph of this paper, is almost automatic. If they cannot, then economic development is doomed. The great task of combating and avoiding these evils absorbs more of the energies and efforts of the country, including the economists, than it is capable of expending.

I am not recommending a *laissez-faire* attitude, which is the other extreme, although I believe in market prices to a large extent as a precious instrument of economic guidance. I also believe in the adoption of policies directed towards the creation of a climate favourable to economic development, such as, a wise political policy, a suitable monetary and fiscal policy, a well-directed foreign trade and exchange policy, an intelligent foreign capital policy, a rational wage policy exempt from demagogy, and a policy of co-operation and support of private enterprise, especially by stimulating investments of a high social marginal productivity and by never neglecting the external economies indispensable to expansion. For the rest, international peace, absence of depression in the leading economies and favourable weather for the harvests do not depend upon government action or upon entrepreneurs. They are exogenous factors for our purposes.

I do not wish my remarks to be interpreted as deprecating the worth and utility of economic statistics, especially those on national income and capital formation. I am connected with the institution which has made the largest contribution to the development of these economic statistics and to their analysis in this country. It is this analysis that provides guidance for economic policies, both short and long term.

V. Conclusion

If, instead of concentrating its efforts and energies on the drawing up of estimates, forecasts and programmes for every element of the economic system and of the rate at which the country is going to develop, the Economic Commission for Latin America were to devote its efforts : first, to the analysis of the economic situation and of the policies followed by each country ; second, to the improvement of economic statistics ; and third, to contributing to the solution of Latin America's two greatest economic problems — productivity and education, I contend that it would be of much greater assistance to Latin America.

What most Latin American countries sorely need for economic development is education. Imports of education into Latin America have been ridiculously small, notwithstanding the fact that the penetration of Western civilization into the hinterlands is perhaps the most important problem of these countries' political and economic development.

Finally, little attention has been given to the progress and productivity of agriculture, generally considered as a sort of inferior type of economic activity. This lack of assistance to agriculture is the more regrettable because agricultural techniques in tropical or semi-tropical countries must be developed *in loco* and cannot be copied from temperate or cold climates of the Northern Hemisphere, as can industrial techniques of transformation industries.

FURTHER COMMENTS ON DR. MAYOBRE'S PAPER

BY

H. D. HUGGINS
University College of the West Indies

I. Introduction

There are two types of reaction to global planning. There are those who, viewing the history of the under-developed territories of the world, feel some impatience with private initiative and its record. There are the others who, distrustful of central authority, feel apprehension at the degree to which planning of the order indicated by global programming will, or must, involve intervention by the State. Advocates on either side can usually provide case studies and historical references to justify their points of view, but there is a growing recognition that such partisan lines of argument throw little light on the actual process of development. In those countries with the most relevant experience, rapid economic development has taken place when there has been positive collaboration between private initiative and governments. England, America, and Japan illustrate this.

48

So far as England is concerned, the experience is both contemporary and historical. Cunningham describes how active the intervention of the Elizabethan government was in the economic development of the country in the sixteenth century. Some of the policies fathered by Cecil, Elizabeth's chief economic adviser, are appearing in the reports of planning organizations in the twentieth century accompanied by all the pride of presentation which one expects in connection with a first-born. In the United States, intervention by government at the federal, state, and municipal level has been, and continues to be, vigorous. In Japan[1] the strands of government and private initiative were even more demonstrably interwoven. It is in such a context, presumably, that Mayobre implies that global planning does not necessarily mean so much the direct intervention of government organizations in the economic process as the creation of conditions in which private interests can function with greater freedom and efficiency.

II. DIFFICULTIES OF GLOBAL PLANNING

One of the difficulties affecting plans for economic development is that some measures may be nullified by the counteracting influence of others. The force exerted by, and on, saving is a case in point. Saving helps to make possible investment in development programmes. But it is not easy in under-developed economies to maintain the level of investment from the income generated. Development programmes, if they are to be successful, must have differential rewards for varying levels of skills, but there is in contemporary life a good deal of pressure against inequality of incomes. With widespread poverty in the under-developed areas, handsome profits, especially to foreigners, do not meet with popular favour and can be supported in few of the countries which we are here considering. Yet high profits are necessary if one of the ingredients of development is to be achieved, namely, the raising of saving from 5–6 to 12–14 per cent. of the national income. It is the entrepreneurial class attracted by high profits who will primarily increase saving. If skills and saving were the only consideration, the normally large pool of unskilled workers would have their incomes lowered rather than raised relative to other income groups.

In spite — or, perhaps, because — of interactions of this type the Mayobre paper advocates global planning as a second, and advanced, step. The earlier step in most new programmes is usually the initiation of a policy based on the creation of favourable overall conditions. The

[1] E. H. Norman writes : 'The merchant princes were reluctant to become pioneers . . . so the Government with the aid at first of loans from these same magnates . . . had itself to develop industry. Thus early Japanese capitalism may be described as a hot-house variety growing under the shelter of state protection and subsidy' ; Norman also refers to 'this peculiarity in early Japanese industrialization — the predominance of state control over industrial enterprise', *Japan's Emergence as a Modern State* (New York, 1940, pp. 111, 127).

Global Programme, based on the technique of the Economic Commission for Latin America, calls for the calculations of aggregate projections for the economy as a whole, projections for the different sectors and the reconciliation of the overall projections with the findings of the sectoral estimates.[1] The aggregate projections attempt to forecast in quantitative terms the levels to be attained in such dynamic factors as exports, the rate of saving, the productivity of capital, the influx of foreign capital and the capacity to import. Those who work in this field are aware that the processes themselves, especially as revealed in under-developed countries, need more study if the aggregates are to throw light on what can happen in a dynamic and changing economy. More studies are needed in this uncharted area and reference can here be made to work carried out on a limited, but nonetheless interesting aspect of one of these processes — saving-depreciation-investment relationships.[2]

A main characteristic of Dr. Mayobre's paper is that the whole problem of economic development is analysed as an economic problem and that the criteria used are economic criteria and not technical, social or political ones. Such a treatment necessarily has many weaknesses, but it does permit the writer to present in a few pages a set of principles that are being increasingly accepted as a basis for techniques in the implementation of policies of promoting faster economic growth in both developed and under-developed economies.

III. GLOBAL PLANNING OR KEY POINT CONTROL

The paper seems to have fallen into an error in the definition of different types of development plans. Dr. Mayobre speaks of the type of policy which operates through the application of specific measures at given basic points leaving the rest to the free interplay of private forces, and identifies this with programmes which do not have quantitative global estimates. In fact, the distinction between policies which attempt control at specific points and those which attempt control of all activities is quite separate from the distinction between programmes (not policies) which attempt detailed overall forecasts and those which do not. It is doubtful if any government, whatever its outlook, in this part of the world would have the

---

[1] One of the ways in which a university can participate is by preparing pilot estimates and thus establishing a pattern for use by government agencies. Thus the Institute of Social and Economic Research of the University College of the West Indies functions in an area which has no body corresponding to ECLA. The Institute has embarked on a programme covering all the territories of the new Federation of the West Indies as well as British Honduras, and has three specified aims : first, to prepare estimates for a recent year ; second, to prepare estimates for previous years and for the Caribbean as a whole ; and third, to undertake analysis, with efforts to separate price and volume movements. A first study in the series has been published as a monograph ; see A. P. Thorne, *Size, Structure and Growth of the Economy of Jamaica.*

[2] H. D. Huggins, 'Some Investment, Depreciation, Size and Capital Productivity Relationships in Economic Growth', *Social and Economic Studies*, Vol. 4, No. 1.

power or the wish to do more than control key points. Such a policy can be consistent with global planning, but this gets back very close to development based on the creation of favourable conditions.

Many will not agree that the 'weakness of this type of economic policy (application of specific measures at given basic points) lies in its failure to visualize the future of the economy as a whole and to recognize how closely the various sectors are interrelated'. It is true that unbalanced development could take place through misjudgments in administration. For example, roads might be built in the wrong part of the country or might not be built at all, or there might be a lack of recognition of the part which public utilities have to play in an expanding investment programme. The administrators of such schemes will endeavour to arm themselves with data which will help them to predict the needs of the private sector, at basic points, and so to induce balanced growth.

One conclusion to be drawn from this paper is that, despite the safeguards made by the author, global planning must, in order to succeed, come pretty near to planning by direction. Undoubtedly there has to be some direction in the use of resources, because a fully operating price mechanism does not always give results which are in the best interests of the community. This direction should, however, be kept to a minimum and should interfere with the market mechanism only at the basic points. Planning which has become too centralized can have dangers. For example, since no one single group can foresee the interplay of forces even in a simple economy, too rigid plans cannot prepare adequately for the various results that will occur. The more comprehensive plans are, the more extensive the work that has gone into them and, therefore, understandably, the greater the tendency for them to become inflexible. Central planners ensure standardization, since it is more economic to plan for one line of activity than for two, and while this can have its advantages it can also have unfavourable consequences. Central comprehensive planning tends to be costly in terms of scarce resources — trained personnel.[1]

Another interpretation of this paper and one on which there is likely to be more general agreement is that global planning is the same as the creation of favourable overall conditions with the proviso that on five

[1] W. A. Lewis discusses the subject in *The Principles of Economic Planning* (London, 1949), pp. 7-29, and has this to say in *The Theory of Economic Growth* (London, 1955), p. 384 : 'The case for a comprehensive production programme therefore stands or falls by the case for planning the economy in detail from a central office. It would take us too far to discuss this case in all its detail here. Broadly speaking, the case against detailed central planning is that it is undemocratic, bureaucratic, inflexible, and subject to great error and confusion. It is also unnecessary. There is a much better case for piecemeal planning ; that is to say, for concentrating on a few matters which it is particularly desired to influence, such as the level of exports, or of capital formation, or of industrial production, or of food production ; and for leaving all the rest of the economy to adjust itself to demand and supply. Some planning is necessary, since the results of demand and supply are not socially acceptable in their entirety ; but planning can be confined to those spheres where it is considered most important to modify the results that market forces acting alone would yield.'

constituents those in charge of planning endeavour to secure much more information than is usual : first, goods and services required by the community within reasonable hypotheses of growth ; second, the resources available, or potentially available, for the satisfaction of these needs (comparison of the two providing the economy's development prospects) ; third, targets ; fourth, priorities for the use of available resources ; and fifth, the instruments of economic policy to be adopted. There is everything to be said for such a course and for the provision of information of the type indicated in order to permit the planners to apply specific measures at given basic points.

IV. OTHER RESERVATIONS ABOUT GLOBAL PLANNING

The paper has rightly emphasized the obstacles of insufficient statistical data, and the difficulties of projecting present data, particularly input-output data, into the future. The formulation of any such programme presupposes the availability of statistical and other information which is unlikely to be available in many under-developed countries. A fruitful line of enquiry for a country considering such a programme would be to study the items ideally required for overall programming. This would reveal gaps of information. Consideration could then be given as to which agencies could supply the missing data in future and whether it would in fact be likely to be worth while to allocate scarce resources and qualified economists to obtaining information of the particular type and in the volume envisaged.[1] Conceivably these shortcomings of statistical data could be so severe that an overall technique was unlikely to succeed except in a very largely controlled economy. Perhaps therefore it might be necessary to give more attention than the paper does to problems of adjustment between the controlled and uncontrollable sections of the economy. If, however, one accepts, as Dr. Mayobre agrees, that overall programming does not necessarily imply state control, then many projections will have to be based on how private firms are *likely* to behave, not on how they *ought* to behave, and business decisions are notoriously unpredictable.

Another reservation which must be ever present in considering the implications of global planning concerns the problem of the liaison between the planning administrators and the research group. This reservation must increase the greater the authority of the global planners becomes. There will be temptation for the planners to accept statistical data without sufficient consciousness of its weaknesses. Very little statistical data coming from under-developed countries can be relied on for this type of planning. Most national income studies, for instance, are just about

---

[1] For example, is it worth while to put an economist on the job of measuring the rate of saving exactly when he might be working at the Government Savings Bank, advising how existing saving can best be made available for local investment ? Or of obtaining employment figures when he might be advising the local development corporation how to increase employment through diversification of the economy by the establishment of new industries?

accurate enough to give a sketch of the economy during the period to which they apply. Such figures would be particularly dangerous in the hands of visiting experts, who are usually unable to measure the extent of the psychological and political resistance to carrying out a blue print programme. A favourable overall conditions programme is less dependent on mere factors and may be carried out by local administrators with perhaps technical advice on specific rather than on overall features of the plan.

There is a good deal of emphasis in the paper on market rather than institutional forces in regard to export markets. Dr. Mayobre is conscious of the importance of the terms of trade to the economies of under-developed countries. Most commodities are now covered by world price agreements and the future of world prices will depend on whether or not these are, to some extent, thrown aside. Thus, projections of world demand for commodities, and these are notoriously dubious, may supply only half the answer.

Mention is made in the paper of the dangers of encouraging prejudices in favour of autarky and the possible consequences of defective administration. The author suggests, as one of the methods of safeguarding against these risks, the improvement of sources of information and analytical techniques. One needs to go further. One suspects that what is needed in most under-developed countries really goes much beyond the formulation of a programme on the lines set out here. It is just as important to develop an informed and critical public opinion capable of discussing the policies, achievements and shortcomings of government in a rational and objective fashion. There are many institutions needed to play their part in this — the universities and the press are among the most prominent. Criticism must be free and government and politicians must get used to being criticized. This is probably the only safeguard against the undue influence of private interests and the risk that they will succeed in shaping policy to their own ends. Governments anxious to encourage development under the umbrella of global planning will always be subjected to strong temptation. An educated public opinion is the only influence likely to be able to keep such tendencies under proper control.

DISCUSSION OF DR. MAYOBRE'S PAPER

THE discussion of Dr. Mayobre's paper revolved around four principal topics : first, the precise meaning of global programming ; second, its feasibility and methods of procedure ; third, its merits ; and fourth, the relative merits of other approaches to programming.

THE MEANING OF GLOBAL PROGRAMMING

In response to questions, *Dr. Mayobre* gave as the salient characteristic of global programming the setting of precise targets. These targets, he said, would comprise not only specific project goals such as the achievement of a certain steel capacity or the completion of a certain road by a given time. They would also consist of national income targets, such as a given rate of increase in *per capita* income. Other forms of planning, such as key point programming, could not set such global targets. They could only try to make such improvements as were possible and let the economy work out the results.

An analysis of Dr. Mayobre's paper made it clear, as *Dr. Huggins* pointed out, that the distinction between key point planning and global programming was not necessarily great. Key point planning was actively practised by the governments of England (and even the England of Elizabeth I), the United States, and Japan. Without really centralized authority, pure global planning did not seem feasible.

FEASIBILITY AND METHODS OF PROCEDURE

Professor Levine raised various doubts about the feasibility of global programming, especially when carried to the extreme of detailed sectoral projections. Development meant structural change, hence programming could not proceed by simply expanding the scale of the existing economic structure. To keep the projections realistic, it would be advisable to draw heavily upon the concrete investment plans of business enterprises. These might be incorporated into the global plan in so far as they led to appropriate results. Planning and execution should not be separated. Rather, those responsible for the execution of the programme should also have a hand in its formulation. A programme that helped to analyse existing trends and conditions would, on the other hand, aid the administrators in their tasks. He suggested that attention be given to a more explicit statement of the responsibilities of a planning agency, since such analysis might shed light on the methodological problems of programming. He mentioned some of those responsibilities.

Professor Brahmananda shared these concerns and added others. Mayobre's paper seemed to assume certain fixed parameters, such as a constant savings ratio and capital-output ratio. This might be appropriate for advanced countries, but did not fit under-developed countries. The global capital-output ratio in particular was a dubious composite of different sectoral ratios. Development was not movement along some pre-existing track — there was no track for an under-developed country.

The Indian programming experience, he said, bore out these qualms. The first year of India's second Five Year Plan had proceeded along lines similar to ECLA's global planning. But the quantitative assumptions on which it was based had not been verified. Now there was increasing scepticism regarding the feasibility and usefulness of this sort of programming.

Dr. Campos thought that, although global programming was logically more satisfactory than key point programming, the latter was often the more practicable approach. The difficulties of global programming were of various sorts : (a) *technical* ; (b) *political* ; (c) those resulting from past distortions produced, for instance, by exchange and price controls.

MERITS

Professor Gudin delivered a vigorous attack upon global programming. The uncertainties of economic life, richly illustrated by Brazilian experience, were far too great to permit effective programming. In practice, moreover, governmental action often reflected political motives rather than the advice of the planner. Under such conditions, the best that could be expected of the government was that it should not interfere with the natural process of growth.

Professor Hirschman commented on the aprioristic nature of the discussion and suggested some concrete tests of the successes of global planning. Were there, he asked, instances where global programming had shown a project to be worth while that would not have been spotted by other methods ? Or conversely, had projects been rejected on the basis of global programming that seemed commendable on an *ad hoc* basis ? His Colombian experience did not suggest to him any such cases. In the case of countries where development was actively under way, the desirable projects were fairly obvious. In the case of stagnating countries, growth had to be started at a few key points and programming did not appear to yield a technique of identifying such points. However, global programming might have the virtue of producing a confrontation of views and attitudes that might lead to bargaining and feasible compromises.

Dr. Campos took a more positive view of global programming, although pointing out that its usefulness was much greater for the under-developed countries that did not possess a dynamic entrepreneurial group. In countries where such an entrepreneurial group existed, global programming was no better than the more modest key project approach. The global plan would need to be extremely flexible, but this would undermine its consistency. Except for the social overhead area, there was no reason to believe the judgment of the planner to be superior to the judgment of the entrepreneur.

In the Brazilian experience, he added, the development agencies, while continuing their efforts to improve data and techniques underlying global programming, in practice had fallen back on key sector programming. In certain areas the problem was to rate *growing points*, which were fairly obvious. Global programmes would then be useful primarily as devices to study the economy with a view to the foundation of general monetary and fiscal policies.

Dr. Mayobre made a spirited defence of the merits of global programming. Other approaches, especially fiscal and monetary policy, as applied currently in most Latin American countries, dealt with problems on an *ad hoc* basis. They failed to give proper co-ordination to the consequences

E

of these measures for long-term growth. The analytical work underlying global programming contributed itself to a better knowledge of the economy, even though the newness of the approach had not permitted implementation on an important scale. Some practical results, however, had already been achieved. The projections that ECLA had made for Brazil, for instance, had been of material help to the Brazilian National Development Bank in its loan operations.

ALTERNATIVE APPROACHES

Alternative methods of planning were discussed under the general titles of bottleneck planning, key point planning, growing point planning, and the like. *Dr. Campos* saw some advantages in bottleneck planning because it practically excluded the possibility of errors. It also appeared more feasible because it required less statistical information. This partial kind of planning could also be applied to 'growing points' from which further spontaneous growth was most likely to develop. Key point planning might also become necessary if the investment signals given by the market were weak. But it was logically unsatisfactory procedure, and it carried with it the danger of over-investment and consequent inflation.

Professor Boudeville suggested that planning should be carried on at the micro-level of the firm as well as at the macro-level of the region or economy. Because development, in his view, originated from specific local points, this combination of micro- and macro-analysis should be practicable. There might be cases where an investment that was not profitable from the view-point of the firm should yet be undertaken in the light of benefits discovered by macro-analysis. There might be others where the planning authorities might wish to accelerate the growth of particularly significant nodal points.

Most of the other speakers who had questioned global programming, especially Messrs. Huggins, Hirschman, Levine, and Brahmananda, expressed themselves in favour of key point planning. Only *Professor Gudin* went somewhat further in his rejection of government action, but he, too, rejected a *laissez-faire* attitude.

56

Chapter 3

NOTES ON THE THEORY OF THE 'BIG PUSH'

BY

P. N. ROSENSTEIN-RODAN
Massachusetts Institute of Technology

I. METHODOLOGY

'THERE is a minimum level of resources that must be devoted to
. . . a development program if it is to have any chance of success.
Launching a country into self-sustaining growth is a little like getting
an airplane off the ground. There is a critical ground speed which
must be passed before the craft can become airborne. . . .'[1] Pro-
ceeding 'bit by bit' will not add up in its effects to the sum total of
the single bits. A minimum quantum of investment is a necessary,
though not sufficient, condition of success. This, in a nutshell, is
the contention of the theory of the big push.

This theory seems to contradict the conclusions of the traditional
static equilibrium theory and to reverse its famous motto, *natura non
facit saltum*. It does so for three reasons. First, it is based on a
set of more realistic assumptions of certain indivisibilities and 'non-
appropriabilities' in the production functions even on the level of
static equilibrium theory. These indivisibilities give rise to increasing returns and to technological external economies. Second, in
dealing with problems of growth this theory examines the path
towards equilibrium, not the conditions at a point of equilibrium
only. At a point of static equilibrium net investment is zero. The
theory of growth is very largely a theory of investment. Moreover,
the allocation of investment — unlike the allocation of given stocks
of consumer goods (equilibrium of consumption), or of producers'
goods (equilibrium of production) — necessarily occurs in an imperfect market, that is, a market on which prices do not signal all

[1] Massachusetts Institute of Technology, Center for International Studies,
The Objectives of United States Economic Assistance Programs (Washington, 1957),
p. 70.

the information required for an optimum solution.[1] Given an imperfect investment market, pecuniary external economies have the same effect in the theory of growth as technological external economies. They are a cause of a possible divergence between the private and the social marginal net product.[2] Since pecuniary, unlike technological, external economies are all-pervading and frequent, the price mechanism does not necessarily put the economy on an optimum path. Therefore, additional signalling devices apart from market prices are required.[3] Many economists, including the author, believe that these additional signals can be provided by programming. Third, in addition to the risk phenomena and imperfections characterizing the investment equilibrium, markets in under-developed countries are even more imperfect than in developed countries. The price mechanism in such imperfect markets does not provide the signals which guide a perfectly competitive economy towards an optimum position.

II. Terminology

Indivisibilities and external economies are portmanteau expressions which are loosely used. Fortunately, recent publications have

[1] See P. N. Rosenstein-Rodan, 'Programming in Theory and in Italian Practice', in Massachusetts Institute of Technology, Center for International Studies, *Investment Criteria and Economic Growth* (Cambridge, Massachusetts, 1955).

[2] T. Scitovsky, 'Two Concepts of External Economies', *Journal of Political Economy*, April 1954.

[3] Futures markets and futures prices could perhaps provide such signalling devices. It is a moot point whether perfect futures markets for all goods can exist. The author's suspicion (without proof) is that they cannot exist for the same reasons for which perfect foresight is impossible. In reality they certainly do not exist.

'In an economy in which economic decisions are decentralized, a system of communications is needed to enable each person who makes economic decisions to learn about the economic decisions of others and co-ordinate his decisions with theirs. In the market economy, prices are the signalling device that informs each person of other people's economic decisions ; and the merit of perfect competition is that it would cause prices to transmit information reliably and people to respond to this information properly. Market prices, however, reflect the economic situation as it is and not as it will be. For this reason, they are more useful for co-ordinating current production decisions, which are immediately effective and guided by short-run considerations, than they are for co-ordinating investment decisions which have a delayed effect and — looking ahead to a long future period — should be governed not by what the present economic situation is but by what the future economic situation is expected to be. The proper co-ordination of investment decisions, therefore, would require a signalling device to transmit information about present plans and future conditions as they are determined by present plans ; and the pricing system fails to provide this'. T. Scitovsky, *op. cit.* p. 150.

clairfied the concepts.[1] Not all indivisibilities give rise to external economies and not all external economies are due to indivisibilities. Some external economies are due to the impossibility of appropriating a factor — even if divisible. Pecuniary external economies are an almost superfluous concept in static equilibrium theory. They refer to those inter-industry relations which are due to the fact that production functions of different industries are not linear[2] and homogeneous. Their true function in the theory of static equilibrium is to mark a place for a concept which will become important in the theory of growth. Technological external economies are rare in a static competitive economy with one important exception, the training of labour[3] and education. In the theory of growth, however, external economies abound. Given the inherent imperfection of the investment market, as well as imperfect knowledge and risks, pecuniary and technological external economies have a similarly disturbing effect on the path towards equilibrium. While the distinction between pecuniary and technological external economies becomes practically irrelevant in the theory of growth, three different kinds of indivisibilities and external economies may be distinguished.

First, there is indivisibility in the production function, especially indivisibility in the supply of social overhead capital (lumpiness of capital) which is discussed in Section III. Second, there is indivisibility of demand (complementarity of demand), discussed in Section IV. Third, there is indivisibility (kink) in the supply of saving, discussed in Section VI.

In one way the first indivisibility is fundamental. If it did not

[1] See H. W. Arndt, 'External Economies in Economic Growth', *Economic Record*, November 1955 ; T. Scitovsky, *op. cit.* ; F. M. Bator, *Capital, Growth and Welfare: Essays on the Theory of Allocation*, a doctoral dissertation submitted at Massachusetts Institute of Technology, 1956, Part III ; L. Lefeber, *External Economies and Transportation in the General Equilibrium System*, a doctoral dissertation submitted at Massachusetts Institute of Technology, 1957, Part I ; M. Fleming, 'External Economies and the Doctrine of Balanced Growth', *Economic Journal*, June 1955, confines his analysis largely to conditions of a static equilibrium.

[2] This is almost but not quite the same as saying that there are indivisibilities in the production functions. There can be continuous though non-linear production functions where, for instance, inputs and outputs are non-linearly linked. The decisive criterion is non-convexity of production possibility curves. In most cases that is due to indivisibilities.

[3] In a slave economy, investment in training slave workers may pay. In a non-slave economy in which mortgages on workers do not exist, a trained worker may contract at a higher wage rate with another firm which did not invest in his training. The supply of training facilities in a competitive economy will therefore be normally below optimum. The best way of training workers is probably on the job. Industrial workers in towns with many establishments and industries acquire skill by working, by talking to each other, exchanging experiences and changing jobs, much more quickly than isolated peasants. This fact alone, apart from better division of labour, is a source of increasing returns to the industrial system as a whole and a differential advantage of industrialization.

exist, the others would not arise. Linear homogeneous production functions are basic in this sense, but they are completely unrealistic. They imply no economies of scale or of agglomeration, no entrepreneurship, no phenomenon of minimum quantum or threshold, so that they threaten to obscure the nature of the economic process and the risks involved rather than throwing light on it. In reality there are indivisibilities in the production function. They create not only non-constant returns but also risks of investment and imperfect markets which give rise to the indivisibility (complementarity) of demand.

III. INDIVISIBILITY IN THE PRODUCTION FUNCTION
(LUMPINESS OF CAPITAL)

Indivisibilities of inputs, processes, or outputs give rise to increasing returns, that is, economies of scale, and may require a high optimum size of a firm. This is not a very important obstacle to development since with some exceptions (for instance in Central America) there is usually sufficient demand, even in small, poor countries, for at least one optimum scale firm in many industries. There may be room, however, only for one or a few firms with the obvious danger of monopolistic markets.

As Allyn Young pointed out, increasing returns accrue to a firm not only with the growth of its size but also with the growth of the industry and with the growth of the industrial system as a whole. Greater specialization and better use of resources become possible when growth helps to overcome indivisibilities generating pecuniary external economies. The range of increasing returns seems to be very wide indeed.[1]

Social overhead capital is the most important instance of indivisibility and hence of external economies on the supply side. Its services are indirectly productive and become available only after long gestation periods. Its most important products are investment opportunities created in other industries. Social overhead capital comprises all those basic industries like power, transport, or communications which must precede the more quickly yielding, directly

---

[1] The capital-output ratio in the United States has fallen over the last eighty years from around 4 : 1 to around 3 : 1, while income per head, wage-rates, and the relative importance of heavy industry were rising. This is due to technical progress (change in production functions), increasing returns on balance (increasing returns prevailing over decreasing returns), and to the rising demand for labour-intensive services characteristic of high-income economies. It is my conviction that increasing returns played a considerable part in it.

productive investments and which constitute the framework or infra-structure and the overhead costs of the economy as a whole. Its installations are characterized by a sizeable initial lump and low variable costs. Since the minimum size in these basic industries is large, excess capacity will be unavoidable over the initial period in under-developed countries.[1] In addition, there is also an irreducible minimum industry mix of different public utilities, so that an under-developed country will have to invest between 30–40 per cent. of its total investment in these channels. Since overall vision is required as well as a correct appraisal of future development, programming is undoubtedly required in this lumpy field. Normal market mechanisms will not provide an optimum supply.

Social overhead capital is characterized by four indivisibilities. First, it is indivisible (irreversible) in time. It must precede other directly productive investments. Second, its equipment has high minimum durability. Lesser durability is either technically impossible or much less efficient. For this and other reasons it is very lumpy. Third, it has long gestation periods. Fourth, an irreducible minimum social overhead capital industry mix is a condition for getting off the dead-end.

Because of these indivisibilities and because services of social overhead capital cannot be imported, a high initial investment in social overhead capital must either precede or be known to be certainly available in order to pave the way for additional more quickly yielding directly productive investments. This indivisibility of social overhead capital constitutes one of the main obstacles to development of under-developed countries.

IV. Indivisibility of Demand (Complementarity of Demand)

Relatively few investments are made in the small market of an under-developed country. If all investment projects were independent (which they are not) and if their number grew, the risk of each investment project would decline by simple actuarial rules. The lower marginal risk of each investment dose (or project) would lead to either higher or cheaper credit facilities and these would thus constitute internal economies. In reality, however, various

[1] We may distinguish in fact between the developmental social overhead capital which provides for a hoped for but uncertain future demand and the rehabilitation social overhead capital which caters to an unsatisfied demand of the past. The first with its excess capacity will necessarily have a big sectoral capital-output ratio (10–15 : 1) ; the second, through breaking bottlenecks, has a certain high indirect productivity and a much lower capital-output ratio.

investment decisions are not independent. Investment projects have high risks because of uncertainty as to whether their products will find a market.

Let us restate our old example,[1] at first for a closed economy.[2] If a hundred workers who were previously in disguised unemployment [3] (so that the marginal productivity of their labour was equal to zero) in an under-developed country are put into a shoe factory, their wages will constitute additional income. If the newly employed workers spend all of their additional income on the shoes they produce, the shoe factory will find a market and will succeed. In fact, however, they will not spend all of their additional income on shoes. There is no easy solution of creating an additional market in this way.[4] The risk of not finding a market reduces the incentive to invest, and the shoe factory investment project will probably be abandoned. Let us vary the example. Instead of putting a hundred previously unemployed workers in one shoe factory, let us put ten thousand workers in one hundred factories and farms which between them will produce the bulk of the wage-goods on which the newly employed workers will spend their wages. What was not true in the case of one single shoe factory will become true for the complementary system of one hundred factories and farms. The new producers will be each other's customers and will verify Say's Law by creating an additional market. The complementarity of demand will reduce the risk of not finding a market. Reducing such interdependent risks naturally increases the incentive to invest.

If one unit of any wage-good could be produced as efficiently as many units, that is to say, if there were no indivisibilities in the production functions of wage-goods, a relatively small investment might suffice to produce a product mix which would satisfy, and create, the additional market. Indivisibilities make the minimum investment much larger.

The risk of any single investment in any one industry is increased by the fact that various goods are highly imperfect substitutes for each other in low income under-developed countries. The south-west corner of the indifference map shows very high degrees of

[1] See P. N. Rosenstein-Rodan, 'Problems of Industrialisation of Eastern and South-Eastern Europe', *Economic Journal*, June-September 1943 ; R. Nurkse, *Problems of Capital Formation in Underdeveloped Countries* (Oxford, 1953).

[2] The assumption of a closed economy will be dropped in Section V.

[3] On the concept and measurement of disguised unemployment see P. N. Rosenstein-Rodan, *Notes on Disguised Unemployment*, Massachusetts Institute of Technology, Center for International Studies (Cambridge, Massachusetts, 1956), Part I.

[4] In an open economy the output of the shoe factory may replace former shoe imports, or may find export markets, although this too is uncertain. See Section V below.

convexity. Demand for most goods will therefore be highly inelastic. Low elasticities of demand make it much more difficult to fit supplies to demands. The difficulty of fitting demand to supply on a small scale constitutes a risk which is higher in a small than in a large and growing market. Complementarity of demand will reduce the marginal risk of growing and diversified investments but will be below a *minimum sensibile* for small doses of investment. There is therefore a minimum threshold at which the complementarity of demand manifests itself. The discontinuity in the complementarity of demand may therefore be called indivisibility of demand.

A minimum quantum of investment is required to produce the bulk of additional wage-goods on which additionally employed workers will spend their additional income. Unless it is probable that other investments will take place, many single investment projects may be too risky to be undertaken. The mobilization of sufficient investment to provide this minimum quantum is the first hurdle which under-developed countries must overcome, but it is not the only one. Even if saving and investment sufficient to provide a minimum quantum of wage-goods were forthcoming, the previous creation of a minimum quantum of social overhead capital constitutes a second hurdle which must be overcome. While the first minimum quantum of investment in wage-goods may amount to say $20 million, the minimum quantum of investment in social overhead capital may amount to $60 to $80 million. The effective minimum of total investment may thus amount to, and require a big push of, from $80 to $100 million.

V. International Trade Reduces the Size of the Minimum Push

Complementarity of demand was examined in Section IV above under the assumption of a closed economy. In an open economy a shoe factory may replace former imports or may be efficient enough to find export markets. The world market can be a substitute for the additional domestic market required in a closed economy. Can the world market provide enough continuity to obviate the need for a minimum quantum of investment? It is submitted that the mobility of products is in reality an imperfect substitute for the mobility of factors. International trade undoubtedly reduces the size of the minimum push required, so that not *all* the wage-goods need be produced in the developing country, but it does not eliminate it.

The great expansion of international trade in the nineteenth century led neither to an equalization nor even to a reduction in the inequality of factor rewards. Theoretically this fact may be due to three reasons : [1] first, transport costs as impediments to the mobility of factors ; second, complete rather than partial specialization of production ; and third, different production functions in different countries.

The fact that transport costs have been sharply reduced during the last 150 years should have led to a growing equalization of factor rewards. The increasing importance of partial, as opposed to complete, specialization of production should also have worked in this direction. The English Industrial Revolution may, indeed, have increased the share of complete specialization of production. In England during that period, export-gaining industries expanded more than import-saving industries. Nevertheless, subsequent industrial revolutions, for example, the industrial revolution in Germany, showed a greater expansion of import-saving than of export-gaining production, although exact statistical information does not seem to exist.[2]

Therefore, the main explanation of why this tendency to a growing equalization of factor rewards did not materialize — why, in fact, labour rewards tended to become more unequal [3] — must rest on the assumption that production functions are different in various parts of the world. 'The laws of nature may be the same everywhere, but the laws of nature and the economically relevant production function relating maximum output obtainable from specified concrete inputs are two quite different things. Effective knowledge ("know-how") is probably as important a variable in understanding economic history and geography as is specific factor endowment. . . . The "effective" organization is different.' [4] There is no doubt that differences in effectiveness of organization do exist in different countries and that effective knowledge cannot be acquired by reading a book or by editorial exhortation. It can be acquired, however, on the job ! This possibility is a major source of increasing returns to the industrial system as a whole. Perhaps the most important yield of development is a cumulative increase in effective knowledge!

[1] See P. A. Samuelson, 'International Trade and the Equalisation of Factor Prices', *Economic Journal*, June 1948, and 'International Factor-Price Equalisation Once Again', *ibid.* June 1949.
[2] Much depends, of course, on the definition of the *same* or *similar* products in various countries.
[3] This was not due to a differentially higher increase in population in the under-developed countries. On the contrary, their increase in population was smaller than that of developed countries.
[4] P. A. Samuelson, *op. cit.* (1948), p. 181.

The growth of international trade during the last 150 years has not reduced the inequality in this field.

We may conclude that international trade would not eliminate — although it would reduce — the indivisibility of demand, even if markets, other than the investment market, were more or less perfect. In reality, of course, markets are imperfect ; and those in under-developed countries are probably more imperfect than those in the developed countries. International trade does much to reduce the danger of monopolies. It also effectively reduces the size of the minimum quantum of investment. But it does not dispense with the need for a big push.

VI. INDIVISIBILITY IN THE SUPPLY OF SAVINGS

A high minimum quantum of investment requires a high volume of savings, which is difficult to achieve in low income, under-developed countries. There is a way out of this vicious circle. In the first stage when income is increased due to an increase in invest-ment which mobilizes additional latent resources, mechanisms must be provided which assure that in the second stage the marginal rate of saving is very much higher than the average rate of saving. Adam Smith's dictum that frugality is a virtue and prodigality a vice has to be adapted to a situation of growing income. Economic history does not show that the English Industrial Revolution was preceded by a period of falling consumption. It only shows that the proportion saved from the increase in income was higher than the previous average rate of saving.

A zero (or very low) price elasticity of the supply of saving and a high income elasticity of saving thus constitute the third indivisibility.

These three indivisibilities and the external economies to which they give rise, plus the external economies of training labour, form the characteristic pattern of models of growth of under-developed countries.

VII. PSYCHOLOGICAL INDIVISIBILITY OF THE DEVELOPMENT DRIVE

The economic factors discussed so far give only the necessary, but not the sufficient, conditions of growth. A big push seems to be required to jump over the economic obstacles [1] to development.

---

[1] The extent and relative importance of the three indivisibilities and external economies is greater in under-developed than in developed countries. The same applies to the degree of imperfect knowledge and of imperfect competition.

There may be finally a phenomenon of indivisibility in the vigour and drive required for a successful development policy. Isolated and small efforts may not add up to a sufficient impact on growth. An atmosphere of development may only arise with a minimum speed or size of investment. Our knowledge of psychology is far too deficient to theorize about this phenomenon. This does not make it a less important factor. It may well constitute the difference between necessary and sufficient conditions for success.

VIII. A GLANCE AT THE ECONOMIC HISTORY OF THE NINETEENTH CENTURY

Let us glance at the economic history of the last 150 years and see how the absence of a big push in those countries, which are today under-developed, prevented them from achieving a rate of growth comparable to that of the advanced Western world. The classical economists have taught us that, given a long period of peace, order and security and a reasonable economic policy of free trade and not too much government interference, the wealth of nations will increase ; and that, moreover, the difference in income *per capita* between different parts of the world will tend to diminish. This would be the effect of international trade even without major capital movements, since the mobility of products is a good, if not perfect, substitute for the mobility of factors. Between the Congress of Vienna in 1815 and the outbreak of the First World War in 1914, a period long enough even for classical economists, we had a century of peace, order, and security. It was, moreover, a century of maximum international trade, of technological progress, and of very large movements both of capital and of labour. According to the orthodox economic principles, abundant manpower should result in low wages which should attract capital and thereby increase employment, wages, and income. Yet international income differences increased over the nineteenth century instead of decreasing. Slightly over a quarter of the world population increased its income *per capita* considerably, while the rest had to run very fast in order to stand still. Lower wages in under-developed countries did not attract enough capital to reduce the inequality in factor rewards nor did international trade fully achieve this effect.

The classical economists' forecast proved wrong because they neglected external economies. The deficiency of social overhead capital caused diseconomies on capital account which more than outweighed any economies on wage account. Western industrialists were not induced to invest much in the industries of under-developed countries. Consider the Lancashire textile industrialists in the middle of the nineteenth century. India was firmly under British rule. There was neither insecurity nor balance of payments or transfer risks, and wages in India were very much lower than in Lancashire. Yet any project for a textile mill in India would have encountered an obstacle in the deficiency of social overhead capital which, for this single project alone, was insurmountable. Thus, the Lancashire textile industrialists could not avail themselves of the advantage of lower wages. The lumpiness of social overhead capital would have made one hundred single project investments pay if there had been a sufficiently integrated force to organize them. An investment trust or a chartered monopoly like the East India Company might have accomplished this, but the single project approach of the City of London made this integration impossible. Had there been an integrating, synchronizing big push, the course of economic history might have been different.

COMMENTS ON
PROFESSOR ROSENSTEIN-RODAN'S PAPER

BY

CELSO FURTADO
Economic Commission for Latin America

I. INTRODUCTION

THE central idea of Professor Rosenstein-Rodan's theory, if I understand it correctly, is that a stationary under-developed economy is not converted bit by bit into a dynamic system capable of self-generating expansion. To use a Hegelian expression, between a situation of stationary under-development and the process of growth there exists a difference of quality, and the more complex process cannot be explained solely on the basis of knowledge of the less complex situation.

The practical importance of this theory lies in its warning against the illusion that it is feasible to pass from stagnation to development by means of a steady though slight effort. It would seem at first sight that it is not difficult to pass from a negligible net rate of investment to a rate of 1 per cent. of the product, then to 2 per cent, then to 3 per cent., until a rate comparable to that registered in economies whose development tends to be self-generating is attained. Such a gradual rise in the rate of invest-ment, starting from nil, is virtually impossible, Professor Rosenstein-Rodan asserts, for a series of reasons ultimately based on the nature of the production functions. The lack of homogeneity and of continuity characteristic of these functions prevents the gradual growth of productive capacity. In other words, it is not possible to allocate a given quantity of additional resources — independently of their magnitude — in a way consonant with the composition of demand. If this quantity of resources does not attain a certain relative importance, supply cannot be expanded as required by the structure of demand, which, moreover, tends to become diversified as income increases.

To approach the problem from the opposite angle, the way in which demand grows as the level of income rises calls for changes in the composition of supply which cannot be brought about if the increment in investment does not exceed a given minimum. This minimum acquires a great relative importance when the transition from stagnation to development is in question. Even were the production functions linear, the mere fact that they are not homogeneous, that is, that they do not pass through the point of origin, is enough to account for the abruptness of the leap from stagnation to development. This being so, if an under-developed stationary economy is to begin to grow, a strong initial impulse — a big push — is required, and the initial volume of investment required is such that it can hardly be expected to materialize spontaneously and on a basis of domestic saving. Nor is this all. Even if the resources required for such investment were mobilized, by what criteria would entrepreneurs determine their investment ? If the allocation of investment is very imperfect in a developed and expanding economy, what is to be said of an economy that is barely emerging from stagnation, and in which the forecasts of entrepreneurs are supported by no empirical experience ? Consequently, the big push is incompatible with *laissez-faire*.

It would be hard to find anyone more fully in agreement with Professor Rosenstein-Rodan's ideas on this subject than myself. The remarks which follow reflect only my desire to obtain a better grasp of certain aspects of the problem he has stated.

II. Economic Under-development and the Utilization of the Surplus

In the first place, I fear we may incur the risk of over-generalization if we do not define at the outset what we understand by economic under-development. I think this concept has an historical dimension that must not be lost sight of. Economies are not under-developed *per se*, but in comparison with others existing in the same epoch. England in the eighteenth, or Italy in the sixteenth, century cannot be considered under-developed economies.

The second point to which attention may be drawn is the fact that economic development during the last 150 years, which is commonly described as industrialization, is a phenomenon qualitatively different from the development process undergone by the typically commercial economies. The growth of an industrial economy is fundamentally a vertical process, inseparable from the advance of technique, while commercial economies grew mainly by agglutination, that is, by horizontal expansion.

For the theory of the big push to be considered as a theory of economic development, at least three points would have to be elucidated. First, what conditions and factors accounted for the advent of the first industrial economies? It must not be forgotten that the formation of an industrial economy in Europe at the end of the eighteenth century provoked the breakup of the contemporary world economy. Second, the world economy being divided into industrial and stationary non-industrial systems, what are the requisites for the advancement of a system from the second group to the first? This is apparently the question which the theory of the big push claims to answer. Third, under what conditions can economies whose development is retarded bridge the gap separating them from those economies whose industrial development began between the end of the eighteenth and the first half of the nineteenth century? It is on this third question that the theory of retarded development bears, and, of the three, it is the one to which most practical interest attaches in the world of today.

Of these three questions, only the second, strictly speaking, falls within the field of analysis of the theory of the big push. It should, therefore, be given careful consideration. What is it that basically differentiates a stationary under-developed economy from an economy in process of growth? I do not think it is the form taken by income distribution. Indeed, in typical stationary economies, as can readily be observed in certain parts of Brazil, income is distributed quite as inequitably as in expanding economies, or more so. Nor do I believe it is the average level of productivity. There are no empirical grounds for the assertion that whenever an economy attains a given average level of productivity, it inevitably becomes a dynamic system, and that below such a level, every economic system is necessarily stationary.

It is a matter of common observation that even in communities where the level of productivity is lowest, production exceeds the subsistence requirements of the population. The way in which this surplus production is utilized is the feature that distinguishes stationary economies from those in process of development. Such a surplus may be absorbed by the consumption of a privileged class or it may be utilized to finance wars, to build ramparts and pyramids or even to provide employment for a sector of the population which represents a cause of social unrest. According to Plutarch, it was this last reason that induced Pericles to spend the treasure of Athens on those wonderful works that have been handed down to our times in the marble of Mount Pentelicus.

An economy which makes only unproductive investments will in the long run have to use up the whole of its surplus in the mere replacement of the stock of unproductive works. Indeed, as this stock grows, replacement requirements increase. Unless the share of the surplus in the product also rises, the trend of net investment will be in the direction of zero.

To sum up, in a typical stationary economy, consumption and unproductive investments absorb the whole of the product, regardless of the way in which income is distributed. Adam Smith's feudal baron was surrounded by an entourage big enough to consume all of the product that reached his hands. But, it must be stressed that, although consumption and the maintenance of unproductive undertakings absorb the entire product in a stationary economy, it cannot be said that no surplus exists.

Moreover, the problem of the utilization of the surplus cannot be kept separate from that of its appropriation. The rôle of the dominant groups in a society is therefore of basic importance from the point of view of the theory of development. Indeed, in a society where the prestige and power of these leading groups is based on the ownership of a limited asset such as land, it is not to be expected that the surplus will be utilized in the same way as in another where the power of the dominant group derives from the accumulation of transferable wealth, as in the commercial cities.

In order that a stationary economy may be converted into a system in process of expansion, what is needed is not so much an increment in the surplus, which would require a reduction of consumption or an increase in productivity, as a change in the method of utilizing this surplus. Such a change presupposes alterations in the way the surplus is appropriated, such as historically have been produced only by the action of exogenous factors.

III. DEVELOPMENT AND THE STRUCTURE OF DEMAND

The theory of the big push would seem to suggest that whenever a large scale influence is exerted on the process of capital formation, a stationary economy probably begins to develop. But the experience of history does not confirm this corollary. To take the example of Bolivia, the important nucleus of a modern economy, concentrated in one part of the country, was created, originally mainly with resources from abroad. Large investments were effected in social overhead capital. Even today Bolivia has more kilometres of railway *per capita* than Latin America on the average or than Brazil. Exports substantially increased, and even nowadays Bolivia's *per capita* exports exceed the Latin American average or those of Brazil. In fact, the only country in Latin America with a higher export coefficient is Venezuela. Nevertheless, the Bolivian economy has remained stationary, and its *per capita* income at the present time is below $100, or less than half the average for Latin America or for Brazil.

As investment in Bolivia is concentrated in the mining sector, it has made scarcely any contribution to modifying the system of appropriation and utilization of the country's surplus. Such a modification would only have been achieved if mining had substantially altered the structure of internal demand. But as mining employs only an infinitesimal fraction of the country's labour force, and the profits it generates have been transferred abroad almost in their entirety, the impact on the composition of internal demand has been slight and was able to be absorbed by the increment in imports.

Assuming that an initial investment on a scale comparable to that reported in Bolivia is effected in coffee or cacao plantations, the amount of labour absorbed will necessarily attain great relative importance. If the supply of manpower is elastic, the average wage in the area will not rise to any considerable extent, but there will inevitably be a substantial increment in the total volume of wages paid. This large increase in the volume of monetary wages will inevitably cause significant changes in the structure of demand. Urban production, whether artisan or industrial, will have to expand to meet the greater demand for consumer goods, and production of foodstuffs will also grow to satisfy higher urban demand.

If the impetus provided by external factors is sustained — if external demand absorbs increasing quantities of coffee or cacao over a prolonged period — a very substantial change may take place in the structure of demand. In so far as internal supply keeps pace with these changes, possession of the surplus will inevitably be transferred from the traditional landowner class to the commercial and industrial entrepreneurial class. As first generation entrepreneurial classes have a high propensity to save, the concentration of part of the surplus in their hands will be conducive to a considerable increase in reproductive investment. It is thus perfectly possible that the resources required for the big push may be accumulated within a relatively short period. In the São Paulo district, for instance, the great expansion of the railways was begun with resources of domestic origin. Foreign capital for the public services came only at a later stage, when a vigorous process of development was already under way.

What it is important to emphasize is that a formerly stationary economy can in a few years reach a net investment rate of up to 10 per cent. with its own resources, provided that the way in which the surplus is utilized is fundamentally altered. It is true that these changes do not come about gradually but relatively abruptly, as the accumulation of resources in the hands of the new entrepreneurial class increases much more rapidly than consumer expenditure. It is also true that the underlying process of social change takes place under the stimulus of exogenous factors, namely, the creation of a flow of exports or an inflow of resources from abroad.

IV. Development and the Level of Technique

The theory of the big push, by suggesting that investment must be effected on a given scale if it is to be economic, places too much emphasis on the problem of the indivisibility of processes, both on the supply and the demand sides. It therefore overlooks the broader aspects of social reform that are necessary if a stationary economy is to begin to develop on the basis of its own resources and incentives. The recognition and

F

identification of these necessary reforms is of fundamental practical importance, both for countries which are anxious to emerge from stagnation and for those desirous of intensifying their development.

This remark leads on to certain considerations with respect to the third problem raised. What has the theory of the big push to say with respect to an under-developed economy in process of growth, such as Brazil ? According to this theory, *ceteris paribus*, the same rate of growth calls for a greater investment effort in an under-developed than in a developed economy. It is for this very reason that the trend towards geographic concentration of income is a natural consequence of spontaneous development. Nevertheless, it does not seem to me correct to state this problem strictly in terms of indivisibilities, since technology too has an historical dimension.

The development of the more advanced industrial economies over the last three-quarters of a century very particularly reflects the progress of technique. Capital formation, although it has been the main vehicle of the assimilation of new techniques, is in itself responsible for only a relatively small fraction of the increase in the productivity of labour. Although in a country like Brazil the net investment rate today is similar to that registered in the United States some three-quarters of a century ago, and although such investments are accompanied by a much more advanced technique than that of seventy-five years back, Brazil has not attained a rate of growth higher than that of the United States in the last quarter of the past century. Apparently, the progress of technique has made necessary a greater concentration of resources. The replacement of horses by tractors is useful when land taken up for the maintenance of the horses can be utilized with greater economic efficiency. The mechanization of the textile industry is advantageous when there is a growing demand for manpower. But if there is no alternative means of employing the factors released by the progress of technique, the assimilation of new technical processes may have little or no effect on the average productivity of the labour force. In other words, the marginal physical productivity of specific sectors, such as manufacturing, may substantially increase without any improvement in the average productivity of the system as a whole. This phenomenon was very well described by Kindleberger as 'structural disequilibrium at the factor level'.

This is not a phenomenon that can be presented out of its historical context. Its essence may be summed up in the following proposition : in the historical context of today the effect of the assimilation of a technical innovation on the rate of growth is a function of the degree of development. The more highly developed an economy is, the greater is the positive effect of the assimilation of a technical innovation. In other words, development depends increasingly upon technique and less on direct capital formation in the productive processes.

This does not mean that the under-developed economies would expand to a greater extent, at a given rate of investment, if they assimilated outmoded techniques instead of the most advanced. But it does imply that sectoral inequalities in marginal physical productivities would be reduced. As these inequalities hamper the integration of the under-developed economies, they consequently hold up the entire process of social and political development. This is why the current growth of the under-developed economies tends to create internal tensions which are partly responsible for the increasing state intervention in the economic sphere.

V. Conclusion

The aim of the foregoing comments has been to call attention to what might be called the problematic elements of under-development at the present stage. It is essential to recognize that the mere coexistence of economies with widely different degrees of development, although all of them are in process of growth, constitutes in itself a vitally important topic for study. It is not enough to acknowledge that international trade alone does not help to reduce inequalities in the remuneration of the factors. It must be determined in what conditions the expansion of a stationary economy's foreign trade can initiate a process of economic growth capable of generating its own momentum.

The assimilation of more advanced techniques is an indispensable prerequisite of growth whatever the degree of development attained. Since these techniques bring about economies in the use of manpower which is now the most plentiful factor in under-developed countries, the process of growth at the present time is very different from that which occurred in the nineteenth century. The disparities between the marginal productivity of the enterprise and of society tend to become increasingly great in the under-developed countries. It is therefore not enough to recognize that the effects of indivisibility in the production functions hinder the transition from stagnation to growth. We must go further, and acknowledge that the big push solves only a small problem. The main question is not to launch the boat, but to diminish, or avoid widening, the distance that separates it from those that long ago put out to sea. The elucidation of this second problem calls for a theory of relationships between the effects of foreign trade, capital formation, the assimilation of techniques, the constellation of factors and resources and the rate of growth. The point is not, therefore, to show that there are indivisibilities in the production functions. The main interest lies in demonstrating how processes can be modified so as to elude the effects of these indivisibilities.

Economic Development for Latin America

FURTHER COMMENTS ON
PROFESSOR ROSENSTEIN-RODAN'S PAPER

BY

RAGNAR NURKSE
Columbia University

I. QUESTIONS OF TERMINOLOGY

BECAUSE I have little or no substantive criticism to offer, my comments on Professor Rosenstein-Rodan's stimulating paper will for the most part reduce themselves to a few terminological quibbles. To make room for these quibbles, however, let me begin by rejecting the view that matters of terminology have all been satisfactorily settled by previous writers.

Take first this interesting new term, the 'Big Push'. What does it mean ? It seems to mean that economic development is a big job and that a tremendous effort, in many directions at once, is needed to tackle it effectively. In the circumstances of our time, the poorer countries are not prepared to accept the inevitability of gradualness. The theory of the big push seems to embrace nothing less than the whole economics of development, but is it necessary to present it under this peculiar label ? Is there a competing theory of the little push ? We are nearly all agreed on the importance of public overhead investments, on the complement- arity of consumers' wants, on the need for large savings and the vital rôle of enterprise, private and public, in the drive for development. I am prepared also to recognize the largely cumulative nature of the develop- ment process, where nothing succeeds like success and nothing fails like failure. These are among the principal substantive points in the big push theory, and I for one have no quarrel with them.

Still on the terminological plane, I am not sure that anything is gained by stretching the concept of indivisibilities so as to apply it to all the various characteristics listed in Sections II and III and scattered elsewhere throughout the paper. The term is an elastic one and can no doubt be stretched even further. I suggest, however, that the notion of indivisi- bilities is more useful when confined to the specific sense of technical indivisibilities, in which it is applicable to the public utility field in particular.

I must confess that the economics of external economies still has some dark corners for me. Here again it seems better not to try to cover every- thing with the same label but rather to sort out and investigate the specific cases, such as the external economies that flow from the installation and increasingly full utilization of overhead capital facilities ; the improve- ments in industrial organization that become possible as output increases ; the enlargement of the aggregate market that results from consumable output expansion in accordance with income elasticities of demand.

The statement that 'prices reflect the economic situation as it is and not as it will be', quoted from Scitovsky, overlooks the fact that prices can and usually do reflect expectations as well as existing conditions. Yet I share some of the author's scepticism regarding the adequacy of market prices as signalling devices in the context of growth economics. In our economic analysis the price system is usually made to work with given stocks of goods and factors, within a given framework. Economic development consists essentially in an extension of that framework. To rely solely on the price system for the structural changes that constitute development may not be enough. But mere programming (whatever this now so fashionable term may mean) is probably not enough either. In the last resort we must rely on the acts of faith that spring from enterprise private or public, or both.

II. Public Overhead Investment and Programming

To illustrate, let me consider the public overhead investments to which this paper rightly attaches great importance. For this purpose we may leave aside that part of social overhead capital which includes facilities for education, sanitation, law enforcement, and so forth. Let us concentrate on the *hard* public utilities such as transport, communications, power and water supply. These are significant chiefly as producers' services.

To me, the most important substantive point, stressed in the paper before us, is that public overhead investment creates investment opportunities in directly productive activities. To simplify the terminology we may speak of overhead investment and direct investment respectively. These two categories of capital formation are complementary, and the relationship between them is a vertical relationship in the sense of the traditional theory of capital. They should not be treated as being on a par. Overhead investment lays down the essential framework for miscellaneous economic activity. It represents a non-specific, initiatory, pioneering type of investment. The demand for the basic services it provides may be totally inadequate to start with. Overhead capital may have to be built ahead of demand. Since it provides inducements for directly productive investments, it tends eventually to create its own demand. A structure of public overheads causes economic activity to grow up around it and creates in this way an increasingly full and profitable demand for the services which it provides.

On this view, overhead investment tends to generate direct investment. Is it not possible, however, to reverse the causal sequence? An increase in direct investment may lead to an increased demand for overhead facilities. In many parts of Latin America the vigorous activity of directly productive investment is pressing hard on the capacity of public utilities, which are indeed becoming a bottleneck. Overhead investment is needed, not to anticipate future demand, but to make up for arrears accumulated in this field in the past. This is a possible alternative sequence, but it represents in my opinion a relatively advanced phase of development. In earlier stages the lack of public overhead facilities is more likely to kill the will to invest in miscellaneous productive activities. If, therefore, such direct investment simply does not take place, there may be no basis for the price system to induce an extension of overhead structures. The lack of local investment incentives sometimes leads to an export of funds to countries with more attractive incentives based on mass markets and an ample supply of basic services.

The public overheads are a prerequisite for the take-off phase in economic development. I cannot see that physical durability is a major difficulty, nor would I attach much importance to the long gestation period, if this means the period of construction. The technical indivisibilities are important here, but perhaps even they are not necessarily a dominant factor. Even in the absence of such indivisibilities there may be a case for building ahead of demand in the expectation of growth in directly productive activities or indeed as a means of promoting such growth.

The crucial difficulty is that overhead investment is apt to be highly capital intensive and is subject to long-delayed returns because it takes time for it to attract the direct investments which will ultimately make it pay its way, in the sense of covering the fixed interest charge as well as operating costs. There is typically a period of infancy during which an overhead investment project cannot earn its keep. This is not a mere problem of rate-fixing. In an under-developed area the traffic needed to make an overhead capital installation pay for itself does not yet exist. How is this gap to be bridged ? Either new loans must be raised to pay for the deficit during the barren period or else the project must be subsidized from government tax revenue. The former method leads to an increase in the interest charge for which the project becomes liable. Both methods may retard the growth of direct investment on which the ultimate success of the project depends. Neither method is to be lightly recommended. The gap implies an additional need for investible funds, yet their use for this purpose may be perfectly justified financially as well as socially.

The case for investment in the overhead sector is that it creates the conditions necessary for the growth of direct investment, for foreign business firms as well as for domestic enterprise. The essential basis of development is a wide diffusion of individual effort and activity. Building the overheads ahead of demand lays the groundwork for the growth of such activity. Is there really any scope for programming here, with a view to promoting direct investment and so absorbing the temporary excess capacity in the overhead sector ? It seems to me impracticable, unless all the miscellaneous direct investment is to be subjected to government planning along with the strategic overhead sector. The overall planning of development in a backward economy is bound to be a very difficult undertaking.

What is more, overall programming is quite likely to inhibit the big push in the overhead sector. There will be a tendency to say, 'Don't start hydro-electric projects until they are really necessary. Where is the market for the power?' The answer is that projects of this sort are not built to meet an existing need but to create one. Their rôle is that of trail blazers. Whether they do it under public or private auspices is, in the present context, immaterial. They lay the basis for generalized individual activity in miscellaneous direct investment, in agriculture as well as manufacturing. I cannot see what other function programming can have in that vast field of heterogeneous small-scale activity, unless it concerns itself, as it should, with the removal of other obstacles to such activity, such as the lack of know-how, education, and law enforcement.

III. International Trade and Under-developed Countries

Finally let me touch upon three points in the trade field. The statement that 'international trade reduces the size of the minimum push' is suggestive, like everything else in Professor Rosenstein-Rodan's paper. Its concrete meaning lies chiefly, I think, in the fact that steel and engineering industries are not a necessary part of the big push, since steel and machinery can be imported. The basic services such as power and transport cannot be imported. In the overhead sector, therefore, international trade cannot reduce the size of the minimum push. This is one reason for the strategic importance of overhead investment.

Another suggestive remark on trade is this : 'The world market can be a substitute for the additional domestic market required in a closed economy'. This sounds entirely plausible, but it does not even begin to deal with the problem that may arise when a country has an outstanding comparative advantage in primary products and when these products face a price-inelastic demand abroad. It is not just a world market but a *growing* world market that is needed by countries in this situation. What if world demand for crude materials should fail to expand, or should fail to expand at anything like the rate of growth in the advanced countries' production and incomes ? It is in such circumstances that the complementarity of consumers' wants, which Rosenstein-Rodan has stressed so much, becomes significant as a basis for the balanced growth argument for home market expansion. International specialization is an excellent thing for the under-developed countries. But beyond a point it can offer no assurance of continued growth through trade unless world demand for primary products is expanding.

This leads me to my last question. The classical theory of international specialization, as I understand it, is a static doctrine showing how, under given conditions, output and welfare can be maximized. The fact that, in spite of international trade, differences in *per capita* incomes in different parts of the world have tended to widen rather than diminish should not surprise us when we reflect that conditions have not remained the same.

Nor does it conflict with international trade theory as the classics formulated it. Samuelson's factor-price equalization theory is built on a rather special set of carefully selected assumptions, and it would be misleading to represent it as *the* classical trade theory in its general form. I should be grateful for instruction on this point, but my impression is that international income differences are a modern obsession. At any rate by nineteenth-century classics (of whom Samuelson is not one) trade was supposed to *raise* income levels in all countries. Was anything said about its tending to *equalize* incomes as well ?

DISCUSSION OF
PROFESSOR ROSENSTEIN-RODAN'S PAPER

PROFESSOR ROSENSTEIN-RODAN's paper, which was summarized by Dr. Kafka, generated discussion on three principal topics : first, the meaning of big push and of balanced growth ; second, the importance of indivisibilities ; and, third, the rôle of economic overhead.

I. THE BIG PUSH AND BALANCED GROWTH

Professor Schultz raised various questions regarding the meaning of the big push. Did it mean big in relation to the economy, or to the size of the particular project, or to the resources available ? The United States government was now making a big push with a 60 billion dollar highway programme which, however, fitted quite well into the American economy. A young farmer buying a farm in Iowa had to make a big push relative to his own modest resources, but this meant little to the economy as a whole. The big push, he thought, was a phenomenon that was observable in the real world in various guises, but he did not think it was a useful analytical concept for economists.

Dr. Huggins thought that one of the major questions raised by the big push related to inflation. In a society where there were idle resources, but little idle capacity — and this was typical of an under-developed territory — did the big push threaten to cause chaos before supply could be reconciled with demand ? Could much of the argument be stated in terms of indivisibilities and therefore more moderately ? In terms of the social and economic environment, and therefore more analytically ?

Professor Nurkse expressed agreement with many of Professor Rosenstein-Rodan's ideas. He felt, however, that the theory of the big push had become a little too broad. It seemed to encompass most of the economics of the development. The principle of balanced growth, for which he himself had argued on many occasions, did not seem to him to be a necessary component of the big push theory. Balanced growth meant little more, after all, than Say's Law.

Professor Hirschman observed that balanced growth, as part of the big push, really went beyond Say's Law. It seemed to imply the creation of a new independently integrated economy on top of a pre-existing economy, instead of integration of the newly arising activities into the traditional sector.

Professor Brahmananda added that there were several possible interpretations of Say's Law. It might mean simply that each supply created its own demand, which Professor Nurske's principle of balanced growth certainly did not imply. Or it could mean that the various sectors of economy were in proper balance. *Professor Nurkse* replied that balanced growth of agriculture and industry was a typical example of what he had in mind. He agreed that this kind of balance had been a preoccupation of economists long before Say. But in contrast to the desirability of horizontal balance, he did not feel the same way about vertical balance, that is, the balance between the consumer goods industries, on one side, and the capital goods industries and economic overhead investment on the other. Rather it seemed to him that in the sector of economic overhead a big push was necessary to enable stagnant economies to 'take-off' in a development.

Professor Wallich doubted that a 'take-off' point was a useful concept or that it could be found in any concrete case. The assumption of a completely stagnant economy, he said, was not convincing. An economy in which population growth absorbed all increases in income he would not consider altogether stagnant. This economy had welfare gains from lower infant mortality and greater life expectancy. And an economy stagnant in the sense of experiencing no advance, whatever, either quantitatively or qualitatively through new consumer goods, probably did not exist in the world today.

II. INDIVISIBILITIES

Professor Haberler agreed that Rosenstein-Rodan's paper greatly exaggerated the importance of indivisibilities. Even where they existed, the lumpy factor could often be stretched to accommodate a varying amount of the co-operating factors. The big push was no substitute for normal piecemeal progress.

Dr. Kafka added that in this piecemeal progress, entrepreneurs should invest on a larger scale than that warranted by the existing size of the market, if they could reasonably count on continuous expansion of the market.

Professor Brahmananda observed that the concept of indivisibilities was a short-run phenomenon which diminished over time. Regarding the case of India, he added, the contention that the lack of development in India during the nineteenth century was attributable to low investment in railways and similar overheads was not borne out by the facts. Actually, there was considerable excess capacity in these sectors in India during that period.

Professor Ellis noted that even where indivisibilities existed they did not necessarily constitute a justification for a big push. On the contrary, they just meant that the investment would be more risky and a big push for that reason perhaps less advisable.

Professor Gudin said that he did not believe in the existence of indivisibilities on the scale argued by Rosenstein-Rodan. In practice, even very lumpy investments had a good deal of divisibility. Railroads could be built with a narrow gauge or preferably preceded by roads and only later expanded to double tracks or wide gauge. Electric power stations could be started with one unit and expanded as demand dictated. Technology in the sense of know-how was far more important as a factor of economic development than indivisibility as a deterrent of it. He believed that overhead capital could be incremented *pari passu* with development. He added that in his notes on Professor Nurkse's paper he had given other reasons why he was not a believer in the big push scheme.

III. Economic Overhead

While the discussion had gone predominantly against the big push as a general developmental device, *Professor Nurkse* suggested that in the field of economic overhead there might be a place for it. Public utilities, railroads, and similar overhead facilities were inevitably lumpy. Their absence inhibited growth. To build them ahead of demand meant to create excess capacity, but their availability was a strong incentive to subsequent balanced growth. He criticized the tendency of planners not to build overhead facilities until bottlenecks had arisen, because the prospect of bottlenecks discouraged growth even before they were actually reached. The cost of building ahead and creating excess capacity should, if necessary, be covered with a public subsidy. The case seemed to him analogous to the familiar infant industry argument in connection with tariffs.

He did not, however, regard the need to provide advance overhead as an argument for global programming. One could not predict just what types of demand would arise, even though the facilities would undoubtedly create their own demand in some form. He referred to the example of Turkey, which was keeping its public works organization together, building considerably into the future, rather than disbanding it because of balance of payments difficulties. He thought that the Turkish authorities were right in refusing to produce an overall investment programme of the kind sometimes suggested to them.

Professor Hirschman doubted that as a general rule overhead facilities would create a demand for their services. This depended on the kind of entrepreneurship available. Certainly there was no fixed short-run relation between investment in overhead and other investment, since overhead could be stretched. *Dr. Kafka* shared these doubts and added that in some cases overhead could be imported, as in the case of foreign shipping. *Dr. Alter* objected to the creation of overhead facilities 'on faith'. This seemed just as inadvisable as the contrary procedure of global planning. One had to make such estimates and projections as were possible.

Dr. Sol suggested that in so far as there was a case for advance overhead, its provision should be undertaken by the government, in order to take care of initial losses. Various speakers pointed to the experience of American railroad building during the nineteenth century as an example of advance overhead. It was agreed, however, that in many cases the motivation might have been profit from construction and financing rather than from operation.

Chapter 4

INFLATION AND BALANCED GROWTH

BY

ROBERTO DE OLIVEIRA CAMPOS

National Bank for Economic Development,
Rio de Janeiro

I. Vulnerability of Under-developed Countries to Inflation

It has often been observed that, while nineteenth-century economic development was, by and large, achieved without inflation, or at least without chronic and acute inflation, present-day development, in the vast majority of countries, seems to have as its natural accompaniment a continuous inflationary pressure translated, more often than not, into open and protracted inflation. The question that suggests itself is whether this is due to mere monetary mismanagement, or whether the trouble lies deeper. Are there institutional, social, or structural factors that render today's development process peculiarly vulnerable to inflation?

One possible reason for the strong inflationary bias in most of the under-developed countries derives from the fact that their growth process often finds its motivation on the demand rather than on the supply side. Theirs is not a Schumpeterian development arising from the entrepreneurs' spontaneous production drive. Rather it is the aspiration of the masses to improve their standard of consumption that prompts governments to assume entrepreneurial functions and to prod private entrepreneurs into embarking on development schemes that offer a promise of future increases in consumption. This type of 'derived development' (to borrow an expression used by Wallich and Singer) does tend to have a congenital inflationary bias.

A related but not identical factor is the asymmetrical impact of the demonstration effect. In the last century, in the absence of mass communication media, the habits and patterns of consumption of wealthier countries were much less easily transmitted to, and less readily imitated by, the under-developed countries. The latter had thus a greater propensity to save out of a given income level than is the case today for the average under-developed country. It is true

82

that there is also a demonstration effect for production techniques. Unfortunately, however, the impacts of the consumption demonstration effect and of the production demonstration effect are asymmetrical. Consumption habits are much more easily transmitted than production techniques. Thus, by operating more on the demand side than on the supply side, the demonstration effect tends to aggravate the congenital inflationary bias of the derived development type of economy.

But the degree of vulnerability to inflation is also considerably affected by differences in the structure of the primary production which normally represents the bulk of economic activity in under-developed countries. It would appear that the younger countries that were able, most successfully, to combine accelerated development with a lesser degree of price instability — such as the United States, Canada, Australia, New Zealand, and Argentina (before the Peron experiment) — were also countries which were surplus producers of basic food products, such as cereals and meat, developed on the basis of a technology imported ready-made from the temperate zones of Europe.[1]

From the view-point of resistance to inflation, it would appear that this production structure is more favourable than that of countries specializing in the production of tropical or mineral products for export. The reason is twofold. First, those countries producing basic foodstuffs were able to import advanced agricultural techniques from temperate zones and thus to achieve a high level of agricultural productivity and to expand their output while those countries with a tropical agriculture were handicapped by a technology which has only recently been developed and is still, in some cases, rather primitive. Countries specializing in mineral production are also vulnerable to inflation, but for a different reason to which I shall come later.

Second, in the case of an under-developed country which produces an exportable surplus of basic foodstuffs, the rise in income resulting from an increase in domestic or foreign investment need not, in the first instance, appreciably affect food prices and the food component of industrial production costs. The immediate effect may be a reduction of the surplus available for export, followed by a more or less rapid supply adjustment, depending on the supply elasticity of the food-producing sector. To the extent that a reduction

---

[1] Better systems of land tenure and tenancy than exist even today in many under-developed countries also played an important rôle in bringing about a more elastic food supply. This factor, however, has been more emphasized than the structural composition of their agricultural production and the easy transplantation of the food technology developed in temperate climates.

of the surplus available for export forces a corresponding reduction in imports, an inflationary pressure will result. But this is a lagged effect and in the past has been often neutralized by short-term capital movements that have permitted the maintenance of normal imports.

Thus, for under-developed countries whose export surplus consists of basic foodstuffs, the first impact of inflationary pressure will fall on the balance of payments. But in the case of countries whose export surplus consists of minerals or of agricultural raw materials, increases in income, particularly if these countries are still in the lowest stages of development so that the income elasticity for food is still fairly high, are immediately translated into an increased demand for food. The food-producing sector of such countries is usually characterized by a rather primitive technology. The first impact is, therefore, on domestic prices and the cost of living. Export availabilities are not necessarily affected.

It is true that inflationary pressure can be lessened by an increase in imports of food and other consumption goods. But this can only occur after a lag, during which the inflationary process may increase, ultimately affecting even the production costs of exports, and thus the balance of payments. Moreover, some countries may feel reluctant to permit increases in the importation of consumers' goods because of their wish to conserve exchange proceeds for the importation of capital goods needed for the development process, or as a protection against cyclical falls in export revenue.

There is still a third factor, of a social and institutional nature, which explains, in part at least, the ability of certain of the younger countries to achieve a higher rate of development with less inflation. This is immigration, a factor which played a very important rôle in the rapid development of the United States, Canada, Australia, and Argentina, but which is not significant for Asia, where the problem is one of over-population, and has now ceased to be important even in Latin America. The economic effect of immigration is to enable recipient countries to save an enormous amount of investment in the feeding, housing, and training of part of its manpower until the productive age. This advantage is greater the higher the technological background of the immigrant. Less domestic investment is thus needed to achieve the same degree of development.

The foregoing list of factors affecting the vulnerability of under-developed countries to inflation is not meant to be exhaustive. For example, such a crucial factor as the variation in the inflow of foreign capital is not mentioned. The only purpose of this list is to stress some factors which have not infrequently been under-estimated.

The fact that, from the narrow view-point of the degree of vulnerability to inflation, those younger countries which, at an early stage of their growth specialized in food production in temperate climates, were better situated than those whose export surplus consisted only of minerals or agricultural raw materials, does not imply that the production of basic foods is *per se* more conducive to economic development than the production of minerals or agricultural raw materials.

Differences in the degree of development have to be explained by a host of other factors such as the overall composition of natural resources, governmental policies, the inflow of foreign capital, the availability of entrepreneurial talents, the technological background of immigrants, and so forth. Nor should the basic importance of monetary management be ignored. Strict monetary management can always curb any inflationary pressure which may exist, for if the monetary authorities refuse to expand the money supply, inflation must sooner or later come to an end.

When, however, a country starts from a low income level and the agricultural food sector is relatively inelastic, it is very difficult to combat the pressure of demand resulting from rising income during development with the traditional weapon of monetary policy, and great vigour and competence in the adoption of monetary and fiscal measures is required. The tragedy is that those countries which are structurally more vulnerable to inflation are also those countries less equipped, through lack of managerial and administrative experience, to achieve technically adequate standards of monetary policy.

II. The Problem of Balanced Growth

The subject which I have been assigned, 'Inflation and Balanced Growth', suggests three questions. The first is whether inflation can ever be regarded as a stimulant to growth. The second is whether growth can ever be balanced. The third is the definition of balanced growth.

As to the first question, it may be noted that the economists of under-developed countries tend to adopt, or at least used to adopt, a much more optimistic attitude regarding the stimulating effect of inflation on growth than do economists of more developed countries. Moreover, it must be recognized from the outset that some amount of inflationary pressure is bound to be generated during the development process, for a number of reasons.

First, development involves structural changes with a shift of factors from primary into secondary and tertiary production. Given the imperfection of factor markets and the obstacles to factor mobility, the rapid diversification and growth of demand contrasts with a relatively inelastic supply schedule for the equipment, intermediate products, and technical skills needed both for industrialization and for the modernization of agricultural practices. Particularly during phases of rapid growth, the mobility of demand is likely to be greater than the mobility of supply.

Second, during certain crucial stages of growth, a large part of investment has to be concentrated on the creation of overhead capital, which has a long maturation period and a high capital-output ratio. It is true, of course, that the sluggishness of the domestic factor supply can be offset by resorting to imports. But this presupposes the existence, throughout the development period, of an adequate capacity to import, made possible by means of an inflow of foreign capital and/or an improvement in the terms of trade, variables which can be regarded as autonomous and largely beyond the control of the under-developed countries, or by an expansion of exports, which again depends on the elasticity of foreign markets.

But inflationary pressure does not translate itself into inflation — barring changes in the velocity of circulation or a decline in the supply of goods — unless the monetary authorities expand the money supply. That the monetary authorities of most under-developed countries have only too often been willing to do so is a matter confirmed by sad statistics. In many cases, such a policy does not reflect laxity in monetary management, but stems rather from the implicit or explicit faith, often held by economists in under-developed countries, in the legitimate use of the instrument of inflation to promote development. There has been ample discussion of this subject, and we may confine ourselves to a passing mention of the controversy.

Those economists of under-developed countries who believe in inflation as a stimulating factor argue : first, inflation transfers income from consumers or conservative savers to the more dynamic entrepreneurial minority, upon which the development process depends ; second, inflation leads to fuller utilization of resources, particularly if there is a surplus of agricultural labour with low productivity that can be shifted to more productive occupation without appreciable reduction of the supply of consumers' goods ; even when bottlenecks or short-run inelasticities of supply in certain sectors entail price-rises, there may still be slack in other sectors, which can be brought into utilization through the inflationary pressure of demand ; [1] and, third, inflation is politically easier than taxation.

The battery of counter-arguments is nevertheless impressive, and practical experience has rendered our economists increasingly more sceptical of the compatibility of inflation with development. The counter-arguments can be summarized as follows : first, the wage lag needed to ensure the transfer of resources to the entrepreneurial group becomes increasingly shorter and tends to disappear as wage and salary groups mobilize themselves for defence of their real income ; second, such transfer to the entrepreneurial group as may be realized is largely wasted through increases in luxury consumption, unproductive investments in real estate, leakage into foreign exchange or metal hoards, and so forth ; third, the overhead capital sector — public utilities, transportation — is price-controlled and investments in this sector tend to be discouraged by the practical impossibility of continuously adjusting tariffs to rising costs ; fourth, balance of payments' difficulties usually emerge, reducing the capacity to import ; and fifth, lack of interest in increased productivity and efficiency may occur. [2]

Recent theoretical discussion plus a better evaluation of recent experience in under-developed countries has led most of the economists in under-developed countries and probably many economists in developed countries to the conclusion that inflation, particularly if moderate and interrupted by periods of stable or falling prices, can at times promote a temporary spurt of growth, but cannot be relied upon to promote steady and continuous growth. [3] When inflation is used for this purpose, the social cost is usually great and its effectiveness smaller than that of alternative methods.

The second question is whether growth can ever be balanced.

[1] It must be noted, however, that the 'inflation barrier' is usually reached in under-developed countries well below the point of full employment. The shortage of complementary factors — capital or technology — makes it possible to employ productively only a part of the labour supply, the remainder having a low or even zero marginal productivity. Thus, the full capacity level of output determined by the ratio between labour and capital plus technology lies below the point of full employment. See H. Pilvin, 'Inflation and Economic Development', a paper presented to the Fourth Meeting of Central Bank Technicians of the American Continent, held at Washington and New York, April-May 1954.

[2] For a discussion of inflation in relation to growth, see the report of Nicholas Kaldor's fourth lecture at the Fundação Getulio Vargas in *Revista Brasileira de Economia*, March 1957.

[3] The difficulty is that if mild inflation is not occasional but results from a deliberate policy, it may, when detected by the public, generate expectations of further monetary depreciation and result in a reduction of cash balances leading eventually, as observed by Ellis, to progressive inflation. See H. S. Ellis, 'Monetary Policy as an Instrument of Progress', in L. H. Dupriez, ed., *Economic Progress* (Louvain, 1955).

The prevalence of the expression balanced growth in modern literature leads one to conclude that this is both a feasible objective and one which is unquestionably commendable. There is, however, little historical justification for such complacency. The Schumpeterian interpretation of capitalistic development certainly does not support the notion of balanced growth.[1] Growth has proceeded by surges and relapses, and the process of creative destruction has made frequent appearances. There have been over-investment booms as well as under-consumption crises. There has been unevenness both in the rate of expansion of the capacity to produce and in the degree of utilization of the productive capacity.

A look at history is hardly encouraging to under-developed countries pursuing the idea of balanced growth. But just as improvement in the understanding of the economic strategic variables determining the level of income and employment has enabled governments to achieve some success in maintaining stability at full employment, it has generated increasing hopes that stability in development can also be achieved.

But here the problem is more complex, for it seems that disproportionalities are an essential dynamic element in the development process. These disproportionalities may take the form of a rapid advance in agricultural productivity which releases manpower and creates favourable conditions for a simultaneous or subsequent industrial upsurge. Within the industrial sector, the growth of heavy industry has a greater dynamic effect than the development of light industry. Hence, a disproportionality in favour of the former may be natural in certain stages of growth. The division of effort between the production of exports and the production of import substitutes seems also to result almost inevitably in a pendulum movement. Some countries concentrate on the production of exports only to find that foreign markets will not absorb these exports except at falling prices. Hence they shift to import substitutes and often carry this shift to a point at which the capacity to export is unduly reduced, thus forcing a new swing of the pendulum. The lumpiness of investment, particularly in railways, electric power, and heavy industry itself, is likely to result in temporary

---

[1] 'It is the economy in which businessmen are reckless and speculative, where expectations are highly volatile, but with an underlying bias towards optimism, where high and growing profits are projected into the future and lead to the hasty adoption of "unsound" projects involving over-expansion, which is likely to show a higher rate of progress over longer periods ; while it is an economy of sound and cautious businessmen, who are slow at reacting to current events, which is likely to grow at a slow rate.' See Nicholas Kaldor, 'The Relation of Economic Growth and Cyclical Fluctuations', *Economic Journal*, March 1954.

imbalances and disproportionalities, which are technically un-avoidable.[1]

It would thus appear that the notion of balanced growth must be interpreted with appropriate qualifications. Strictly speaking, only an economy which has an infinitely elastic supply schedule for every commodity and which is perfectly adjustable to changes in the demand pattern can aspire to balanced growth. As this is obviously out of the question, the practical objective for under-developed countries is not to avoid temporary excess demand or excess supply, but rather to prevent disproportionalities from becoming cumulative and resulting in bottlenecks that impede the continuation of the process of growth.

As is usually the case in economics, it is all a question of degree. It is clear that unbalanced growth cannot long be sustained due to the emergence of bottlenecks. If, for instance, the agricultural sector lags seriously behind the industrial sector, development may be interrupted through inflationary pressure or balance of payments disequilibria. Agriculture, on the other hand, unless it is totally export-oriented, cannot grow disproportionately if the industrial sector is not able to develop sufficiently to create a steady increase in the demand for agricultural products. The heavy industry sector cannot grow irrespective of the wage-goods' sector, for this may result in a general deficiency of demand.

Perhaps the valid distinction that should be made is between *self-correcting disproportionalities*,[2] which provoke subsequent adjustments, and *induced disequilibria*, which result in bottlenecks leading to a stoppage of development. The latter, more often than not, are caused by government intervention aimed at promoting development but in practice inimical to it.

One example of induced disequilibrium is that deriving from a governmental policy of exchange overvaluation that chokes exports, discourages the inflow of foreign capital, and, finally, decreases the capacity to import. Rigidity of tariff rates for basic services, such as transportation and power, during periods of inflation, is yet another

---

[1] 'Indivisibilities and inelasticities in commodity supplies — due either to inelastic (or discontinuous) supply curves of factors or to the character of the technical processes — may lead to unavoidable demand-supply discrepancies in some markets. In consequence of these limitations on the supply side, perfect smoothness in growth cannot be expected even if entrepreneurial expectations regarding changing consumer demand are realized. It will rarely be possible to avoid the occurrence of some substantial demand-supply discrepancies in the various markets', Loreto N. Dominguez and Harold Pilvin, 'The Process of Balanced Economic Growth', *Social Research*, Winter 1954.

[2] A similar concept underlies the idea of leading growth sectors, advanced by W. W. Rostow. The leading sector creates a temporary disproportionality which is later corrected by the emergence of supplementary and derived growth sectors.

example, for it results in under-investment in those sectors leading to serious developmental bottlenecks. But I shall say more about this later.

A final comment should be made on the very definition of balanced growth. According to the narrower definition propounded in the discussions on the big push, balanced growth means simply a simultaneous advance, on a broad front, of inter-related industries capable of providing each other with markets that none can create in isolation. It is basically a concept related to the absence of horizontal maladjustments. This is the sense in which this term has been used by Rosenstein-Rodan and Nurkse. For the purposes of this paper, however, the term balanced growth will be used in a broader sense, to denote the absence of bottleneck-creating disequilibria of two main types, internal sectoral imbalance and external payments imbalance.

III. INFLATION AND SECTORAL IMBALANCES

In this section a few comments will be made on some of the imbalances and distortions in sectoral growth that are apt to result from inflation. The first subsection will deal with the effects of inflation on the development of agriculture ; the second with its effects on the growth of the economic overhead sector ; and, in the third, some comments will be made on the imbalances in industrial growth which arise during the inflationary process.

1. *Inflation and the Agricultural Sector*

There appears to be no *prima facie* reason why inflation should have unfavourable effects on the growth of agriculture. Since demand for food is generally inelastic, price inflation might be expected to result in a transfer of income to the food-producing sector. It is, in fact, a widely held view that the main beneficiaries of the inflationary process are the entrepreneurial group and the peasant classes, while the burden falls largely on the fixed salary and rentier groups.[1]

In practice, however, complicating factors are likely to arise in the course of the inflationary process that may tend to retard agricultural growth. Some of these complicating factors affect agriculture in general ; others bear directly on export agriculture. It is a matter of common observation that, as inflation grows in acuteness

[1] W. Arthur Lewis, *The Theory of Economic Growth* (London, 1955), p. 222.

and begins to generate social unrest, there seems to be an almost irresistible temptation for governments to impose price controls on basic food products. This is often only an attempt to cure the symptoms of inflation. Price controls are resorted to as a substitute for more difficult and less dramatic measures to curb overall excess monetary demand. In the long run the result is negative, since agricultural expansion and food production are discouraged. Such price control only acts as a subsidy to consumption, and as an impediment to enlarged supply. Even though the temporary restraint of food prices may increase the bargaining power of public and private employers in resisting wage claims, the growth in monetary demand, without an offsetting stimulus to agricultural production, makes it impossible to avoid inflationary break-through. The situation is much better if the control of food prices is a complement to, rather than a substitute for, measures intended to curb overall monetary demand. Even then the effort may prove self-defeating, if the relative price rigidity in the agricultural sector causes a reduction in its profitability and there is some amount of factor mobility from the agricultural to the industrial or service sector.

The almost universal experience in Latin America has been that in those countries where price controls on agricultural products have been effectively implemented, agriculture has stagnated, with a resulting aggravation of inflationary pressure. Such has been the experience in Chile and Argentina. In Brazil, agricultural production for home consumption has, in recent years, increased continuously even though at an unsatisfactory rate, but this has been due largely to the ineffectiveness of the food price controls.

Inflation may also indirectly discourage the expansion of agricultural production for export. This happens if overvalued exchange rates, either single or multiple, are maintained. In many cases in Latin America, the overvaluation of exchange rates, in the face of internal inflation, has acted as a tax on agricultural exports, the proceeds of which have been utilized to subsidize industry through favourable exchange rates for imports of equipment and raw materials, while protection against competing import goods has been secured through quantitative restrictions. In some instances, the overvalued multiple rates act as subsidies for imports of foodstuffs, a policy which has a clear disincentive effect on internal agriculture.

The taxing of agricultural exports through the exchange mechanism for the subsidization of industry was particularly evident during the post-war period in Brazil and Argentina, both of which suffered a heavy decline in the quantum of agricultural exports, including, in the case of Argentina, meat exports.

It may thus be concluded that while, in principle, inflation need not cause a sectoral imbalance to the detriment of agriculture, in practice, sectoral imbalance of this type has resulted in many under-developed countries. The effect of inflation on agricultural production for internal consumption will depend on whether a country adopts measures to control agricultural prices, which, though intended to have a cost-restraining effect, prove self-defeating through a long-run supply disincentive effect. The effect of inflation on agricultural production for export will depend on whether over-valued exchange rates result in a similar disincentive effect. Recent experience in Latin America indicates that those countries that have avoided reliance on price and exchange controls have achieved a more satisfactory rate of agricultural expansion.[1]

2. *Inflation and the Basic Services*

Perhaps the main imbalance created by inflation is the dis-incentive to investment in overhead capital facilities, such as transport, communications, and electric power. This sector is universally subject to price regulation, and, since prices in this sector are contractual in nature, they are not flexible enough to keep up with the inflationary trend.

Four factors are at the root of the difficulty. First, historical cost is frequently used as a basis for valuing capital investment. In times of inflation, rates fixed with reference to such valuations result in a reduction of the real profitability of investment. Second, profits are often limited by statute because of the monopoly character of many public services. Third, administrative difficulties and bureaucratic inertia inhibit prompt utility rate readjustments in response to continuing cost inflation. Fourthly, there is frequently political opposition to rate readjustments, on the ground that they operate as autonomous cost-increasing factors.

The field of public utilities typifies the main weakness of inflation in promoting development. Development requires massive investment in the creation of those external economies, but, unless the inflation is very moderate in degree, it soon becomes impossible to avoid the emergence of a wide gap between the relative profitability of investment in industry and agriculture, and investment in power and transportation. The natural result is the formation of bottle-necks, with resultant losses in productivity and misallocation of resources.

[1] For data, see Jorge Marshall, 'Exchange Controls and Economic Development', pp. 442-5, below.

Attempts at corrective measures usually take the form of subsidies to compensate for the inadequate remuneration afforded by the utility rates. But subsidies do not restore the psychological incentives to private investment in those sectors. An alternative remedy is increased government investment to fill the gap left by the stagnation or withdrawal of private domestic and foreign investment. Ignoring the fact that the operating efficiency of the government enterprise may be lower, the mere displacement of private by government investment does not strike at the root of the difficulty.

First, the maintenance of utility rates which are low relative to other prices and costs acts as a subsidy to consumption. If, on the one hand, it contributes to lower production costs, it releases, on the other hand, purchasing power for expenditure on other goods and services. Thus, it rarely has an anti-inflationary or stabilizing effect and to the extent that, by increasing demand and discouraging the expansion of supply, it results in overloading of facilities and accelerated obsolescence, the overall productivity of the economy is lowered, with attendant inflationary effects.

Second, to the extent that prices for government-controlled public services are maintained inflexible while money incomes rise, it can be said that the marginal rate of taxation yielded by the basic sectors tends to be lower than the average rate of taxation, although the opposite is desirable on development grounds. The basic services become incapable of generating sufficient savings to provide for the expansion of facilities or even, at times, to maintain the physical plant.[1]

Third, to the extent that the government finances operation or new investment for low-tariff public utilities by running government deficits, the net effect will be unquestionably inflationary.

Inflation is thus likely to be detrimental to the expansion of overhead capital by shifting the incentives to invest in the direction of the price-flexible sectors. If rates for the basic services are maintained rigid, bottlenecks become almost unavoidable through the combined effect of subsidized demand and disincentive to supply.

---

[1] See W. Arthur Lewis, *The Theory of Economic Growth* (London, 1955), p. 402. The theory of indirect benefits, that is to say, the theory that rates for public services should be maintained low to subsidize the growth of industry and agriculture has no validity except in the case of unused social overhead capacity. In fact, three different rate-making criteria can be conceived, each adapted to a special demand-supply situation for overhead capital. Full-cost pricing, including normal expansion costs, is the criterion applicable to situations of balanced supply and demand. Development pricing, which involves establishment of differential rates designed to ration demand and accelerate expansion of supply, is the criterion applicable to bottleneck situations. Subsidy pricing becomes fully applicable only in the case of excess capacity.

3. *Inflation and Distortions in Industrial Growth*

Inflation may also cause imbalance in the composition of industrial investment to the detriment of the heavy or capital goods industries, when the opposite is desirable on developmental grounds. As noted by Kaldor, 'to accelerate the rate of growth of the economy, the prime technological requirement is to devote to the capital goods industries (iron-steel, cement, engineering, fuel, power) a higher proportion of their current output than would be required for a balanced expansion of all sectors'. This will, of course, be unnecessary if the export sector has an ample horizon of growth. In that case the capital goods required for development can be obtained more economically through foreign trade. In practice, however, the growth of primary exports is often limited by the sluggish price elasticity of foreign demand and cannot be expanded indefinitely without risk of worsening the terms of trade. In this case, internal production of basic materials and capital goods may give the developing country a greater degree of flexibility and a better chance for continuous growth, independent of the vagaries of trade and external payments.

Provided, therefore, that reasonable economic preconditions for industrialization exist, in terms of internal markets and resources, the acceleration of the tempo of development presupposes that an adequate share of resources be devoted to capital goods production. In fact, while a *stable* rate of growth requires merely a balance between the development of consumer and capital goods industries, the acceleration of the tempo of development may require a disproportionate growth of the heavy industries.[1] To the extent that inflation creates artificial disincentives to the expansion of the heavy industry sector, it will thus exert a decelerating influence on economic development.[2]

The unfavourable influence of inflation on the propensity to invest in heavy industry is traceable to a number of direct and indirect reasons. First, the long gestation period involved increases the risk in an environment of unstable prices and rising costs. In

[1] For a stimulating discussion of the growth potential of the investment goods sector as compared to the consumption goods sector, see the report of Nicholas Kaldor's lecture at the Fundação Getulio Vargas in *Revista Brasileira de Economia*, March 1957.

[2] It should be noted, however, that inflation may exert two conflicting effects on heavy industry. On the one hand, it may create conditions for the full utilization of existing capacity. This is a short-run favourable effect. But, paradoxically, it is usually incapable of creating strong-enough incentives for the expansion of capacity due to the reasons discussed above. The short- and long-run effects are thus contradictory. This typifies the easiness with which bottleneck situations are created during the inflationary process. Inflation promotes the full utilization of existing capacity, but creates conditions unfavourable for expansion of capacity.

fact, the longer the planning horizon, the greater the budgetary and financial difficulties due to instability of costs and the risk of changes in overall supply and demand conditions.

Second, because of their pervasive effects on the entire cost structure of the economy, the prices of the products of heavy industry are likely to be less flexible than the prices of the products of light industry. Even when the prices of basic products are not formally subject to control, the difficulty of making rapid price adjustments and the length of delivery periods for basic products tend to render investment in such industries relatively less profitable during inflationary upsurges than speculative activities or quick-yield investments in the consumer goods fields.

But inflation may also have an indirect effect tending to lower the profitability of basic industry relatively to that of other industrial activities. If, as is usually the case, inflation results in balance of payments deficits and rationing of foreign exchange, the brunt of import restrictions is likely to fall on secondary products and luxury goods, while basic industrial products are usually the object of a more favourable exchange or tariff treatment. The prices of basic products tend, therefore, to rise relatively less than the prices of secondary products and luxury goods. This in itself would be desirable were it not for the fact that the relative increase in the profitability of less essential industries tends to bring about a shift of factors and investment away from the basic industry sector. This effect can be offset by excise taxes and other internal fiscal controls aimed at restricting luxury industries and curtailing non-essential consumption so as to redress the profitability ratio in favour of heavy industry.[1] But, in view of the relative inflexibility of the fiscal apparatus, this effect can be brought into operation only after a lag. In the meantime, the relative decrease in the profitability of heavy industry in the face of inflationary costs acts as a disincentive to its growth.

Inflation has two other unfavourable effects on the development of basic industries. If the prices of their products tend to rise less than the general level of prices, depreciation allowances become increasingly more inadequate. This is, of course, a natural consequence of inflation, but it tends to hit those industries which are capital-intensive and which suffer a loss in relative profitability. To the extent that obsolescence of equipment ensues, there is a lowering of productivity in the heavy industry sector, which acts as a negative

---

[1] On the distortions in the pattern of investment deriving from import restrictions, see R. Nurkse, *Problems of Capital Formation in Underdeveloped Countries* (Oxford, 1953), ch. v.

multiplier for the entire economy. Another possible effect is the substitution of government for private investment in the heavy industry sector. The tendency in this direction will be greater the larger the profitability gap between heavy and light industry becomes during the course of inflation.

Aside from the problem of the relative efficiency of government versus private enterprise, which is extraneous to our discussion, to the extent that government operation results in greater rigidity of the prices of heavy products (because governments frequently attempt to combat inflation through sectoral price controls rather than through a general curbing of monetary demand), it tends to act as a subsidy to consumption, leading to supply bottlenecks and the rationing of basic products. If overall monetary demand is not adequately curbed, the difference in profitability in favour of light industry will be increased because low prices for the products of heavy industry act as a disguised subsidy to the consumption sector. From the development view-point this is an unhappy situation, for the marginal rate of saving generated in the heavy industry sector tends to fall below the average rate, thus decreasing the saving potential that could increase the rate of capital accumulation.

IV. INFLATION AND EXTERNAL IMBALANCE

This discussion can best be approached from the view-point of the influence of inflation on the capacity to import. It can be readily seen that, for under-developed economies, the capacity to import plays a crucial rôle in economic growth. While, in industrialized countries capable of producing a wide range of capital goods, growth depends largely on the relationship between saving and investment opportunities, in under-developed countries the conversion of saving into investment requires the importation of a wide range of capital goods. Again, because of the relatively less flexible economic structure of under-developed countries, any upsurge of growth will run into short-run supply inelasticities, which can only be alleviated by an increase in imports. In certain stages of growth when the economy has become more diversified and emphasis has been shifted from export production to the growth of import-replacing secondary industries or to the development of services, the rate of growth of import demand usually exceeds the rate of increase of income. Thus, it is usually found that an inadequate capacity to import is a frequent bottleneck in the process of growth.[1]

External imbalance may at times be due to causes other than inflation or internal imbalance. If, for instance, a country grows at a faster rate than its trading partners, an external disequilibrium may occur, irrespective of inflation. Similarly, shifts in the structures of world demand may render a country, unless it has great resource flexibility, unable to meet its import requirements even in the absence of imbalance between aggregate effective demand and productive capacity.

But inflation will almost inevitably produce an external imbalance or aggravate an existing one. This conclusion becomes obvious if the components of the capacity to import — the quantum of exports, the inflow of foreign capital, and the terms of trade — are analysed.

The effects of inflation on the quantum of exports are likely to be negative. By definition, an inflationary situation is one in which aggregate effective demand exceeds productive capacity. This has a double effect. On the one hand, it increases the import demand, and, on the other, it decreases the export supply. If the pattern of production moves in the direction of greater self-sufficiency, the excess demand may concentrate on home goods. Both imports and exports may then decline, but the rate of decrease of exports will exceed that of imports.[2]

The impact of inflation on import or export demand will depend fundamentally on the exchange rate policy of the developing country suffering from inflation. Barring internal deflation as an unacceptable remedy, and barring also the utilization of reserves which can only be a temporary expedient, the major alternatives that remain are fixed exchange rates, single or multiple, usually in combination with exchange controls, or fluctuating rates.[3]

---

[1] Barring the cases where the impulse to economic growth originates from the export sector, or from an inflow of foreign capital, pressure on the balance of payments can be regarded as an almost inevitable accompaniment of phases of rapid growth for a number of reasons. First, the increase in investment and the change in its composition will usually stimulate the demand for imported capital goods. Second, increased imports of raw materials and semi-manufactures will be needed. For example, if the food supply is inelastic, part of the increase in income will spill over in the form of food imports : see M. Kalecki, 'El Problema del financiamento del desarrollo económico', *El Trimestre Económico*, October, December 1954.

[2] For a discussion of this, see United Nations, *World Economic Survey*, 1956 ; see also E. M. Bernstein, 'Strategic Factors in Balance of Payments Adjustment', a paper presented at the Conference on International Economics, April 14, 1956.

[3] In Brazil, since the exchange reform of October 1953, a system of fluctuating (auction) rates for imports has been combined with multiple fixed rates for exports. For a thorough discussion of the Brazilian experience see Alexandre Kafka, 'Brazilian Exchange Auction System', *The Review of Economics and Statistics*, August 1956.

The most common policy in Latin America has been multiple rates in combination with exchange controls. The rationale of exchange controls and multiple rates has varied from country to country but, as noted by Jorge Marshall, a number of general objectives seem to underlie the use of exchange controls by countries suffering from inflation and balance of payments difficulties.[1] These include correction of balance of payments deficits, protection of domestic economic activities, shifting of import expenditures from non-essential to essential goods, regulation of foreign investment, revenue production, and regional or currency discrimination.

In practice, exchange controls have had the effect of maintaining overvalued export rates for the traditional exports (combined at times with subsidy rates for new exports) for various assumed or implicit objectives. Thus, a major aim of the Brazilian exchange overvaluation was to assure better terms of trade. Because of coffee shortages during the post-war period, this policy was, indeed, successful in influencing the terms of trade favourably. Another motive for overvaluation is the desire to shift resources and factors from traditional export production to import-replacing industries on the assumption that the relative price inelasticity of foreign demand places a serious limitation on export possibilities, and renders imperative a diversification of production in favour of import-replacing industries. In this case the overvalued export rates represent disguised export taxes which are used to subsidize essential cost of living import items or, more often, imports of equipment and raw materials for industrial development.

The usual consequence of multiple overvalued export rates, such as were adopted by Argentina, Brazil, Chile, and other countries in the post-war period, has been a progressive decline of the quantum of exports, leading to a retardation of growth in the export sector and a shrinkage of the capacity to import. Thus, during the post-war period there has been a substantial decline in the export quantum of Argentina and Brazil, and stagnation in Chile.

The effect on the inflow of capital can also be said to be negative. In periods of inflation, fixed rates, single or multiple, inevitably generate the impression that devaluation will eventually become unavoidable. Not only is the inflow of capital discouraged, but flights of capital recur periodically. Multiple rates manipulated by administrative action involve also the risk of arbitrary decisions. In practice, however, multiple exchange rates have often been associated

[1] See Jorge Marshall, 'Exchange Controls and Economic Development', pp. 431-4 below.

with a free rate for financial transactions and remittances, intended to facilitate an unrestricted flow of capital.

Thus, the effect of inflation on the two components of the capacity to import — the quantum of exports and the inflow of foreign capital — may be regarded as negative. However, the situation is much less clear in regard to the terms of trade. Here the relationship is only indirect. Because exchange reserves are limited, inflation cannot long continue without forcing exchange devaluation. But the effect of a devaluation on the terms of trade is anything but unequivocal. The traditional view that devaluation was inevitably reflected in worsening terms of trade has been questioned by Joan Robinson, Professor Haberler, and R. Hinshaw.[1] Professor Haberler has shown that, theoretically at least, devaluation may result in an improvement of the terms of trade of the devaluing country if the product of the demand elasticities for imports and exports of the devaluing country is greater than the product of the elasticities of the supply of imports and exports.

In Latin America the preference for partial devaluation — that is, for multiple exchange rate systems which leave some exports at a grossly overvalued rate — has been founded in part on the desire to avoid a deterioration in the terms of trade for major exports. In the case of Brazilian coffee this policy appears to have been successful. Between 1947 and 1955 the improvement in Brazil's terms of trade amounted to 68 per cent. However, this favourable result can also be explained in terms of the supply shortage that prevailed throughout the post-war period. Chile and Argentina also appear to have used overvalued export rates both for terms of trade reasons and to subsidize industrial diversification.

In all these countries, the association of inflation with overvalued export rates stunted the growth of the export quantum and led to an inadequate growth of the capacity to import, despite the fact that both Brazil and Chile benefited from a very substantial improvement in the terms of trade. In Argentina the reduction of export volumes was aggravated by a parallel deterioration of the terms of trade and the capacity to import was sharply reduced.

Of the various exchange techniques available for correcting a balance of payments disequilibrium provoked by inflation, none appears less likely to distort the pattern of growth and to avoid an

---

[1] See Joan Robinson, 'Beggar-My-Neighbour Remedies for Unemployment', *Essays in the Theory of Employment* (Oxford, 1947) ; G. Haberler, 'Currency Depreciation and the Terms of Trade', in *Wirtschaftliche Entwicklung und soziale Ordnung* (Vienna, 1952), reprinted in *Revista Brasileira de Economia*, March 1952 ; R. Hinshaw, 'Currency Appreciation as an Anti-inflationary Device', *Quarterly Journal of Economics* ; Kurt Rothschild, 'The Effects of Devaluation on the Terms of Trade', *International Economic Papers*, No. 5.

artificial shrinkage of the export sector than the system of freely fluctuating exchange rates. Yet flexible rates have been tolerated rather than accepted in the market for financial transactions, and have seldom been used in the regular market for exports and imports.[1] This is all the more strange as, on theoretical grounds, a better case can be made for flexible exchange rates than for any of the alternative mechanisms, such as direct controls, multiple rates, or the use of exchange reserves. Moreover, on practical grounds, flexible rates eliminate the need for administrative intervention and minimize its disruptive effects. In fact, flexible rates seem the only device capable of maintaining an incentive to export in the situation, all too common in under-developed countries, of internal inflation bound up with a balance of payments disequilibrium.[2]

Automatic adjustment of exchange rates to increases in internal costs avoids the penalization of the export sector which often occurs with fixed single or multiple rates, when the export rate is readjusted with a lag by arbitrary administrative decision. On the other hand, the flow of exports may also be interrupted under a system of flexible rates if exporters decide to hoard stocks in the expectation of further downward movements of the rate. But unless the rate of external depreciation exceeds the rate of increase of internal prices, this result is unlikely to occur and can be prevented through appropriate credit policies designed to discourage commodity hoarding.

Some of the arguments advanced against the use of flexible exchange rates are clearly based on wrong assumptions concerning the efficacy of alternative methods. Flexible exchange rates, for instance, need not be inherently more unstable than rigid exchange rates. On the contrary, the difference seems to be that, while fluctuating rates show small continuous oscillations, rigid rates produce tensions that explode periodically in violent rate readjustments. Nor in inflationary situations do flexible rates increase the uncertainty. If internal prices are inherently unstable, a rigid rate that comes to be generally regarded as unrealistic generates even more uncertainty than day-to-day rate variations, which can be hedged against through a futures market. Two other important advantages deserve mention. First, fluctuating rates serve as an alarm bell, announcing immediately any aggravation of inflationary pressure and creating a psychological

---

[1] I have drawn heavily throughout this discussion on Milton Friedman's essay, 'The Case for Flexible Exchange Rates', in *Essays in Positive Economics* (Chicago, 1953).

[2] See A. Kafka, *op. cit.* p. 318 : '. . . under inflationary conditions, discontinuous revisions of the export rate are clearly inferior to automatic flexibilities. Administered adjustments are dramatic events which almost invariably disrupt the flow of exports.'

pressure in favour of anti-inflation measures. Fixed rates, on the other hand, tend to conceal the acuteness of internal inflation. Second, fluctuating rates do not tend to conceal real costs and thus to lead to misallocation of resources as multiple rates frequently do.

V. Summary and Conclusions

Today's under-developed countries seem peculiarly vulnerable to inflation, in comparison, first, with the countries that underwent their development process during the nineteenth century, second, with the younger countries of recent settlement. For the first case, a possible explanation can be found in the derived nature of the process of development of most of today's backward countries, which finds its motivation on the demand side rather than in the entrepreneurs' drive to produce. The asymmetrical impact of the demonstration effect, which fosters the importation, by today's under-developed countries, of the habits of consumption of richer economies without a corresponding importation of production techniques, explains in part their smaller saving potential out of a given income by comparison with countries of earlier development.

With respect to the second case, it was suggested that the countries of recent settlement owed their greater resistance to inflation to having a relatively elastic food sector, based on the adoption of crops and agricultural techniques developed in the temperate zones of Europe, and capable of yielding a food export surplus. The countries specializing in mineral production or in exportation of agricultural raw materials, by contrast, are characterized by a relatively inelastic and low-productivity food-producing sector. Thus, in the one case, increases in income and demand originating from higher investment levels tend to impinge upon export surpluses and the balance of payments without affecting immediately domestic food prices, while in the other case the full immediate impact is exerted on domestic prices. The important capital-saving features of large-scale immigration of trained manpower were also stressed as a factor making possible a higher rate of development with a lower inflationary pressure.

The degree of structural vulnerability to inflation is not a measure, however, of the development potential. This depends on a host of other factors, such as the composition of natural resources, entrepreneurial supply, and so forth. Nor should the fact that the inflationary bias of many of the currently under-developed countries is partly explained by institutional and structural factors, be used to condone lax monetary policies or lead to an under-estimation of the importance of an adequate monetary management to ensure compatibility between development and stability.

Consideration was then given to the subject of inflation and balanced growth. The three questions raised at the outset were whether and under what conditions inflation can be regarded as a stimulant to growth. The controversy on the matter was briefly reviewed. The conclusion reached was that moderate inflation, particularly if interspersed with periods of stable and falling prices, may exert a stimulating influence. The difficulty is to extract the savings potential of mild occasional inflation without slipping into the spiral of progressive inflation. The notion of balanced growth, if interpreted as the absence of any disproportionality, was found to be inconsistent with the actual development experience of the capitalist system, which has been characterized by surges and relapses and by the disproportionate expansion of the 'leading growth sectors', which have shifted from time to time, and provoked corrective readjustments in the supplementary and derived growth sectors. A distinction was suggested between *self-corrective disproportionalities*, inherent in the growth process, and *induced disequilibria*, the avoidance of which can be made a policy objective.

The rôle of inflation in begetting two types of *induced* disequilibria — sectoral imbalances and external payments imbalance — was discussed. Inflation was found often to generate an imbalance to the detriment of agricultural growth by releasing pressure for the control of food prices, with resulting disincentive to the expansion of agriculture for home consumption. Moreover, export agriculture is often stunted by the rigidity of export rates, which tend to become overvalued for protracted periods as inflation runs its course. Inflation is also likely to discourage investment in price-rigid economic overhead services, such as power, transport, and communications, by shifting the incentive to invest in the direction of price-flexible and quick-yielding sectors. A wrong disproportionality in industrial development is also nurtured, since the investment goods industries, which require a long maturation period, suffer a loss in relative profitability as compared to light industry. These *induced disequilibria* brought about by inflation tend to slow down or stifle the rate of growth.

External payments imbalance may arise independently from inflation. But inflation will inevitably generate or aggravate balance of payments difficulties. It impinges unfavourably on the two main components of the capacity to import, the quantum of imports and the net inflow of foreign capital. Its effects on the terms of trade are more difficult to trace for they are exerted indirectly through the currency devaluation that sooner or later results from inflation. Although it is usually held, on the basis of limited empirical evidence, that the terms of trade move against the devaluing country, the opposite result is theoretically possible.

Of the various possible mechanisms for coping with an external payments imbalance induced by inflation, the most attractive on theoretical grounds, the flexible exchange rate system, appears to be the least employed by under-developed countries. Fixed rates periodically readjusted, or multiple rates in association with exchange restrictions are widely used. More often than not, overvalued export rates which act as an export tariff have been adopted either to ensure better terms of trade or to transfer resources to import-replacing or home goods industries.

The ultimate effect of inflation, via its repercussions on the exchange system, has often been a distorted investment pattern and an artificial impediment which prevents the under-developed economy from realizing the full growth potentialities of the export sector.

COMMENTS ON DR. CAMPOS' PAPER

BY

FLAVIAN LEVINE
University of Chile

I. The Problem of Living with Inflation

I FIND myself in complete agreement with Dr. Campos' conclusions on the evils of inflation. The basic problem Latin American economists have to cope with is one of learning to live with inflation. A high rate of population growth, increasing urbanization, the need to promote basic changes in the economic structure, insufficient saving coupled with inadequate financial institutions to channel the available saving into productive investment, the working of the demonstration effect, the great influence of foreign trade on economic growth, and the persistent relative decrease in international capital movements : all these factors combine to create an economic environment with a bias towards inflation.

The pressing challenge to Latin American economists is how to develop institutional mechanisms that can counteract the growing inflationary pressures. We must learn to absorb these pressures that appear to be inherent in the dynamics of development without affecting the incentives that are needed to bring about a rapid increase in real *per capita* income. This conclusion is, I think, very much the same as Haberler's statement that the 'under-developed countries would be better advised to learn to live with a certain degree of cyclical instability in their terms of trade and balance of payments'.

Instability, disequilibrium, distortions, and waste all seem to be unavoidable concomitant effects of the dynamics of growth. The most we can do is to improve the mechanisms of social control to avoid the excesses inherent and necessary to any process of rapid structural change. It may well be that too much order, too much desire for equilibrium, an excessive emphasis on balance may prove detrimental to progress.

II. THE INADEQUACY OF MONETARY AND FISCAL MEASURES

It seems that although Dr. Campos considers the task of monetary and fiscal officials of under-developed countries to be a hard one, he still relies mainly on such traditional weapons as a means of achieving relative stability. I am not sure that I agree with him.

Let us recall the elementary notion, so often forgotten by governments, that a rise in the price level may be the easiest way to get rid of an inflationary pressure if we are sure that we can depend on the labour unions not to start a movement of wage increases that will lead to a cumulative inflationary process.

Let us assume that the initial inflationary pressure originates in a cyclical fall of the terms of trade. If no exchange reserves are available, we must either depend on direct import restrictions or, accepting a rise in the price level, we must adopt a flexible rate of exchange. If the labour unions cannot be convinced by moral suasion not to start a follow-the-leader search for wage adjustments to compensate for the increase in the cost of living, the monetary authorities will have a very scanty chance of success in their efforts to control inflation. They can only succeed by drastic credit restriction which creates sufficient unemployment to curb the pressure for wage increases. Such drastic credit restriction, coupled with the extreme inflexibility of under-developed economies, will not only stifle growth but will also result in a decrease of the gross national product. Unfortunately, this has been the result of recent experience in Chile.

Moreover, since fluctuations in the terms of trade or in the capacity to import are frequent in Latin America, a permanent restrictive credit policy will be necessary unless sufficient exchange reserves can be built up or unless there is a very responsible labour movement. It is not surprising, therefore, to find in Latin America instances of slow growth either with or without inflation as well as instances of strong growth with inflation but not of strong growth without inflation.

To learn to live with fluctuations in the terms of trade, countries in the process of growth must learn to depend on exchange reserves, the International Monetary Fund and International Bank must learn how to become more useful, and a great amount of political effort and judgment must be directed towards the education of labour in the basic principles of economics.

In addition, if we are to have an adequate rate of development, action against inflation must also be strengthened. Monetary and fiscal measures are not sufficient alone. They must be supplemented by an overall economic policy that can deal with the real factors that give rise to the disequilibria that express themselves in rising price levels. The expansion of the food supply, the relief of housing shortages, the promotion of balanced growth, and development of wage policies must all be given high priority.

III. Growth and Productivity in the Agricultural Sector

Dr. Campos rightly insists that a relatively inelastic food supply is one of the basic causes of inflationary pressure and that, once inflation is under way, agricultural production will be adversely affected.

There seems to be wide agreement not only that the food supply is important for stable growth but also that the development of the agricultural sector is necessary for balanced growth. In his paper, 'International Trade and Development Policy',[1] Professor Nurkse states that the 'concept of balanced growth, based on the diversity and hence complementarity of consumers' wants, is not an argument for industrialization as such. On the contrary, it stresses the futility of trying to set up manufacturing industries without a complementary advance on the farm front.' Kaldor has also recently insisted that the extent of industrialization is conditioned or limited by the growth in productivity in agriculture and that balanced growth requires that food supplies *per capita* increase in proportion to the growth in industrial production.

It seems to me that an increase in the rate of balanced growth requires more than a mere increase in food supplies *per capita* proportional to the increase in industrialization. If, as is the case in some Latin American countries, the average income per gainfully employed person in the agricultural sector is very low compared with the average income per gainfully employed person in other sectors of the economy, any process of growth that does not alter this relationship in favour of the agricultural sector will tend to be rather slow and to render the economic system susceptible to rather intensive inflationary pressure. That is to say, the concept of balanced growth requires that the average income per gainfully employed person in the agricultural sector should grow at a faster rate than the average income for the economy as a whole.

Now, of course, inflation tends to cause a deterioration in the relative position of the agricultural sector. Price controls are eventually imposed on foodstuffs and there is an increase in the inefficiency that is so often a characteristic of industry in under-developed countries.

[1] See below, p. 234.

IV. GROWTH AND THE CAPACITY TO IMPORT

Again, I find myself in complete agreement with Dr. Campos on the negative effect of inflation on the capacity to import. But I do want to comment on the capacity to import in relation to growth. It is frequently true that, quite independently of fluctuations in the terms of trade, the capacity to import of countries that are in the process of development shows a long trend tendency to decline as a proportion of the gross national product. Only too often this trend is explained solely with reference to the inelasticity of the foreign demand for the country's products. The fact that industrialization to supply the domestic market may itself slow down the expansion of exports is usually not sufficiently stressed. If industries which supply the local market expand faster than the gross national product, the relative share of exports in the national income must logically decline. This effect is greater if, as is very often the case, industries which supply the domestic market are characterized by inefficient production or if protection allows an excessive rate of profit in these industries.

DISCUSSION OF DR. CAMPOS' PAPER

MOST of those who participated in the discussion of Dr. Campos' paper expressed themselves in agreement with his general anti-inflationary attitude. There was less agreement among the speakers as to what should be done to stop inflation.

I. CAUSES OF INFLATION

Professor Haberler accepted as a fact that inflationary pressures today were greater than they had been during the nineteenth century. This, however, was not a full explanation, he said, of the actual occurrences of so much inflation. More important than differences in the degree of inflationary pressures were ideological differences between attitudes then and now which reduced resistance to inflation. *Dr. Marshall* believed he saw a tendency among economists, reflected also in Dr. Campos' paper, to overrate the importance of supply factors, such as shortages and inelasticities, as causes of inflation. But demand factors, among them the effect on aggregate demand of the wage policies pursued by the labour unions, and central banking policy, did not seem to get the attention they deserved. *Professor Wallich* supported him, arguing that supply factors were important mainly for changes in relative prices, but that the level of money prices was predominantly influenced by the volume of money and the demand that it engendered. Only if it were made a rule of policy that no sector of the price level should ever be allowed to fall would sectoral price increases due to inelasticities necessarily lead to general inflation.

Dr. Adler observed that the effects of monetary expansion depended basically upon supply conditions. Because of the limited supply elasticities, he said, or, more generally, because of the limited responsiveness of factors of production to economic incentives, monetary expansion in under-developed countries, even with substantial disguised unemployment, resulted in inflationary price increases rather than increases in output. Where factors were responsive to incentives and shifted easily from one use to another the outcome was more satisfactory than where they were sticky. This also applied, he said, to the question whether or not economic overhead should be built ahead of needs. Stickiness of factors strengthened the case for balanced growth. Responsiveness strengthened the case for creative imbalance and advance overhead.

Professor Brahmananda argued that the rôle of the demonstration effect as a cause of inflation had not been tested. He wondered whether savings had really declined anywhere because of this effect, or whether they would be higher if the advanced countries ceased to exert the effect. On the other hand he pointed to the positive rôle of incentive goods. *Dr. Campos* suggested that though these questions could not be answered it seemed quite possible that the demonstration effect had reduced the marginal rate of savings to the level of the average, whereas it ought to be much higher.

II. Repressed Inflation

Professor Haberler thought that much of the harm done by inflation was due to its partial repression and to the distortions that resulted from partial repression. As examples he mentioned price control in agriculture, control of public utility rates, the maintenance of unrealistic exchange rates. *Dr. Kafka* agreed with Professor Haberler that one-sided repression was the special evil of Latin American inflation. The tendency toward one-sided repression, in contrast to open inflations or complete repression, he attributed to the long duration of Latin American inflations. In the end, however, repression would not prevent inflation from turning into wage inflation. Yet, although wage inflation was adverse to development, it was perhaps less damaging in Latin America than elsewhere, because prices tended to move upwards very quickly whenever a wage push occurred. *Professor Nurkse* regarded inflation as a special case of unbalanced growth. Such growth had no clear welfare meaning — if the wrong things were produced, real income was not increased. He restated his interpretation of horizontally balanced growth as an obvious principle and not as a special or arbitrary goal. In practice, of course, there would be always some degree of imbalance. The case of vertical imbalance, as manifested by the creation of advance overhead, he regarded as different.

III. Inflation and Agriculture

Dr. Schultz pointed to the interesting fact that mild inflation during the early years of the twentieth century had been very beneficial to agriculture.

Since the First World War, however, agriculture in Latin America had suffered during a period of inflation. The effects of partial repression were clearly evident in this pattern. Nevertheless, he wondered what might have happened to the production and price of coffee if new plantings had not been discouraged in Brazil by a very unfavourable exchange rate.

IV. INFLATION AND THE BALANCE OF PAYMENTS

Professor Haberler blamed inflation for most of the balance of payments troubles experienced by Latin America. Given proper monetary policies, he had faith that the elasticities of international supply and demand would be high enough to make balance of payments difficulties disappear. *Dr. Marshall* pointed out that in some countries the government's intervention in the balance of payments by means of multiple rates served fiscal purposes rather than those of economic control and allocation. Chile's treatment of copper exchange was a case in point, and much of Argentine's exchange policy could be so explained. *Professor Levine* argued that the balance of payments troubles of countries suffering from inflation were not exclusively due to inflation. They also reflected, in many cases, the growing absorption of resources into the industrial sector. *Dr. Campos* added that, in the long run, industrialization would change the structure of comparative advantages and would give rise to 'acquired comparative advantages'.

V. ACTION TO STOP INFLATION

Despite the almost universal agreement that inflation was bad for development, there appeared to be, with few exceptions, little inclination to take vigorous action against it. *Professor Levine* thought that the traditional weapons of monetary policy were not effective, if inflationary pressure came from wages. If large-scale exchange reserves were available their use for additional imports would help to keep down domestic prices. The International Monetary Fund and the International Bank must come to understand the importance of exchange reserves as anti-inflationary weapons and 'learn to be more useful'.

Professor Haberler thought that it would be a mistake to accept inflation as inevitable. Admittedly inflation was not the worst of all possible evils — uneconomically high wages leading to large-scale unemployment were worse. But that did not mean that inflationary conditions did not very definitely call for correction. *Dr. Marshall* thought that some governments were now reacting to inflation by establishing free exchange markets and exchange rates. In practice, however, governments were still hesitant to allow exchange rates to be truly flexible, as they ought to be as long as inflation persisted.

Professor Wallich argued that as Latin American economies became more complicated, and distortions potentially more serious, the need for stability became more urgent. The growing importance of monetary assets such as savings deposits and bonds pointed in the same direction. The potential benefits of inflation diminished as continued inflation came to be more completely expected. Only when inflation was expected to come to a halt was it likely to promote investment. Though in practice we might have to resign ourselves to live with inflation, this was no reason whatever for not trying to keep it to a minimum. *Dr. Campos*, in summing up, said that whether one should resign oneself to living with inflation depended on whether one regarded inflation as a force for growth or as a hindrance to growth. This meant — did one expect profit inflation or cost inflation ? Monetary and fiscal policies were effective tools. Sometimes, however, their use was painful. Policy decisions would have to be made in the light of these facts.

Chapter 5

THE RÔLE OF CAPITAL IN ECONOMIC DEVELOPMENT [1]

BY

MAURICE BYÉ

University of Paris

I. INTRODUCTION

IN this paper I propose to discuss principles only.

(a) *The Distinction between Development and Other Similar Concepts, in particular, Growth*

The growth of a quantity is its increase. Growth of national *per capita* income is increase of national *per capita* income. The growth of an economy is generally characterized by growth of net national income *per capita*.[2]

Any economic system, for example a national economy, may experience growth either while its structure remains unaltered or while its structure changes. The development of an economy is its growth in conditions of changing structure. It is the transition from a structure with relatively low *per capita* productivity to a structure with relatively higher *per capita* productivity. An economy is fully developed when its structure is such that *per capita* productivity is as high as it can be with given national and world resources and given technical knowledge. In the contrary case we speak of an under-developed economy.

Thus, a poor economy does not necessarily mean an under-developed one. Nor is every economy under-developed which lags behind in growth. It is true that the problems of development cannot entirely be dissociated from problems of growth, because

[1] Translated from the French by Elizabeth Henderson.
[2] On this point see four papers by François Perroux : *La Généralisation de la 'general theory'* (Istanbul, 1950) ; 'Matériaux pour une analyse de la croissance économique', *Cahiers de l'I.S.E.A.*, Series D, No. 8, 1955 ; 'Trois Outils d'analyse pour l'étude du sous-développement', *Cahiers de l'I.S.E.A.*, Series F, No. 1, 1955 ; 'Les Mesures des progrès économiques et l'idée d'économie progressive', Paris, *Cahiers de l'I.S.E.A.*, Series I, No. 1, 1956.

growth always implies some structural change. But developed countries are capable of strong growth with little structural change, while under-developed countries are capable of even modest growth only by means of considerable structural change.

This distinction, which is much the same as Perroux's, enables us to advance two propositions. First, the problems of the development of under-developed economies are very different from those of the growth of developed ones ; and second, low *per capita* income is a very inadequate standard of classification. Not only are the development problems of the Middle East profoundly different from those of Latin America, but even within Latin America the differences between the various countries' economic and social structures are such that we cannot really speak of under-development in all cases, notwithstanding the fact that all these countries are definitely backward in growth.

(b) *The Differing Rôles of Capital in Economic Development and in Economic Growth*

First of all, what are we to understand by capital ? Any definition of capital is arbitrary and must depend upon the purpose at hand. If we mean by development the transition to a more productive structure, we must define capital as everything which increases the productivity of society. Besides investment goods in the proper sense of the term, capital must therefore include also durable consumer goods, such as housing, as well as services apt to promote technical advance, such as education. However much I regret having to disagree with an authority such as Kuznets, I cannot include military investment in my definition of capital, because its relation to social productivity is too uncertain.[1]

Second, are we to consider gross or net figures ? It seems to me that since development is very often a matter of replacing existing equipment by better equipment, depreciation cannot be regarded as neutral. Depreciation policy is one of the aspects of the behaviour of firms and governments. For our purposes gross figures seem much more indicative than net ones.

(c) *What is Structure ?*

For our purpose it will suffice to distinguish two concepts. In the perspective of the market, a structure is a set of proportions and

---

[1] On the concept of capital see Simon Kuznets, 'Population, Income and Capital', in L. H. Dupriez, ed., *Economic Progress* (Louvain, 1955) ; see also Kuznets, 'International Differences in Capital Formation and Financing', National Bureau of Economic Research, *Capital Formation and Economic Growth* (Princeton, 1955).

relations capable of being represented, at least in part, by input-output tables. But, important as these tables are, they are not enough for an analysis of development. The inequality of decision centres, their 'integrating capacity', the effectiveness of their plans and periods of anticipation cannot be measured in quantitative flows. We shall have to say, then, that a structure is a system of constraints between specific decision centres.

To this specific concept of structure there corresponds a specific concept of capital, such as that which Lachmann has developed.[1] Capital is the use of non-specific services for the creation of specific producer goods. Capital is heterogeneous by nature.

Now if we have to apply a heterogeneous concept of capital to a heterogeneous concept of development, any *a priori* definition of the rôle of capital in economic development becomes impossible and the problem cannot be solved purely in terms of aggregate quantities. The structural changes characterizing development can be properly analysed only by considering the effects of each use of capital by each decision centre, or type of decision centre.

In this context I shall discuss in Section II the shortcomings of growth analysis in aggregate terms ; in Section III, the specific use of capital in various sectors and inter-sectoral relations ; and in Section IV, the conditions of the effect of capital on structural changes.

II. THE SHORTCOMINGS OF AGGREGATE ANALYSIS

The growth models with which we are familiar from the work of Harrod, Domar, and Hicks establish relations between the saving coefficient (domestic and imported saving/income) and the capital coefficient (capital/output).[2] These models are useful enough for a short-period determination of the internal and external conditions of equilibrium growth, but they say nothing about changes in the coefficients. Yet structural change, that is, development, implies changes in these coefficients. No distinctions can be made in this respect between so-called structural coefficients such as the average propensity to import, technical coefficients such as the capital-output ratio, and behavioural coefficients such as the average propensity to save. All the coefficients are affected by structural changes.

[1] On the heterogeneity of capital see L. M. Lachmann, *Capital and Its Structure* (London, 1956), p. 11 ; A. J. Youngson, 'The Disaggregation of Investment in the Study of Economic Growth', *Economic Journal*, June 1956.

[2] For a critical review of these models see François Perroux, 'The Quest for Stability : The Real Factors', in Douglas Hague, ed., *Stability and Progress in the World Economy* (London, 1958).

Let us consider the capital coefficient. It might seem logical to argue that the capital-output ratio is initially low, capital being applied first where its productivity is highest, and that the ratio assumes higher values as development proceeds. This, it is often pointed out, agrees both with the marginal principle and, by satisfying the law of factor proportions, with the theory of international specialization. Nevertheless, it is in actual fact a very doubtful proposition.

We possess only a few series going back for any length of time and they give no very clear indications about long-term movements of the capital-output ratio in either direction.[1] In a United Nations study we find that the capital-output ratio has remained relatively constant in the United States, the effects of technical improvements having been offset by other effects. In Europe, the capital-output ratio seems to move in one direction or the other according to the choice of periods.[2]

From such few reliable figures as are available from countries in the early stages of development, it seems that the capital-output ratio depends upon the nature of the production which is the first to develop, which in turn depends upon everything but the law of factor proportions. We need only look at the difference of the capital-output ratio in Venezuela, Colombia, and Brazil, according as initial development is in agriculture, mining, or manufacturing.

The average propensity to save depends upon the country's social structure and the size of its firms. It is not at all clear that the savings ratio increases with development. Personal saving in a subsistence economy is, as Yamey has shown, larger than used to be thought and it may occasionally shrink with development, either because of the disappearance of tertiary producers or local artisans, or as a result of the demonstration effect. Thus, in the United States the average propensity to save fell from 16·2 in the period 1889–98 to 10·2 in the period 1919–28.[3]

The applicability of growth models in terms of aggregate quantities to development problems is further limited by the interdependence of changes in the saving and capital coefficients. It is a fact

[1] See the figures furnished by S. Kuznets, *Economic Progress, op. cit.*, p. 46.

[2] 'In the United States the product-capital ratio, notwithstanding continual fluctuations over short periods, tends to remain constant, owing to factors of another order. This would appear to indicate that those effects of an improvement in technique which tend to increase the product-capital ratio have been offset by others having the opposite results': United Nations, *Analyses and Projections of Economic Development I, An Introduction to the Technique of Programming*, p. 7.

[3] W. Fellner, 'The Capital-Output Ratio in Dynamic Economics', in *Money, Trade and Economic Growth*, in Honour of J. H. Williams (New York, 1951), table on p. 131, calculated from Kuznets' figures.

that saving by firms is at least in part determined by the firms' own capital needs for re-equipment or market expansion.

For all these reasons we must disallow any long-term forecasts based on coefficients which are stable only in the short term. We cannot discuss structural change with the help of tools devised for the study of growth in conditions of unchanging structures. We need to consider not society as a whole, but the action of the decision centres or groups of decision centres making up that society.

III. DEVELOPMENT AND SPECIFIC CAPITAL

If the existence of non-communicating sectors is an essential feature of under-developed economies, we have to define these sectors. Input-output tables tend to define sectors in terms of frontiers between real flows. For our purposes it is more appropriate to consider the frontiers between sources of finance. One sector's saving finances that, and only that, sector's investment. We may speak of closed investment sectors, or sectoral investment autonomy.

Where such closed investment sectors exist, the economy as a whole is not integrated. We speak of an integrated economy when the plans of all its decision centres are subject to the same determinants and constraints. This, in Perroux's terminology, makes the plans compatible. From the point of view of decision centres an economy is non-integrated when the plans of each sector (group of decision centres) are determined by expectations regarding independent variables.

This can happen when each sector's saving is tailored to its own investment needs. In these circumstances the marginal productivity of capital applied to various uses can never be expected to become equal. Indeed, it is immediately obvious that the divergences in the average efficiency of capital are so great that they certainly imply differences in marginal efficiency as well. For instance, in 1954, North American capital invested in Latin America yielded 17 per cent. in the oil industry and only 6 per cent. in manufacturing industry.[1] The non-integration of closed investment sectors is, in our view, a characteristic structural feature of under-developed economies. This concept is wider than Boecke's or Myrdal's concept

[1] Calculated from Tables 3 and 10, Samuel Pizer and Frederick Cutler, 'Growth of Foreign Investments in the United States', *Survey of Current Business*, August 1956.

of dualism characterized by the failure of real flows to pass from a subsistence sector to a monetary sector.[1]

Unless sectoral investment autonomy is reduced, a less productive structure cannot be transformed into a more productive one. If the saving of a sector with low marginal efficiency of capital cannot move to a sector with higher efficiency, it will in some way find its way into consumption, speculation, or investment abroad. Growth will be checked. Thus there can be development only if an economy characterized by non-communicating investment sectors can be transformed into an integrated economy.

Three sectors may become the leading sectors of growth and development : export agriculture, export industry, and domestic industry.

(a) *Export Agriculture*

Neo-classical tradition, the United Nations studies of tropical Africa and, one would think, common sense, all concur in looking to export agriculture for the development of very backward countries. At any rate, development hinged on export agriculture has two important advantages from the point of view here under discussion. First, it attracts foreign capital towards the public services necessary for export agriculture such as railways or ports. Second, it determines the progressive formation of domestic capital. The capital coefficient in agriculture is very variable, ranging from near zero in under-developed and overpopulated countries to a value somewhere in between that for heavy industry and that for many light industries in the United States.[2] Consequently, the 'colonization' of subsistence agriculture by export agriculture is generally possible by means of investment in transport and education, and, above all, by means of some system of stabilizing agricultural incomes, the latter being rather difficult to achieve.

Most under-developed countries, and particularly those where more land is available, thus stand to gain from the impulse of export agriculture and should in any case expand it to the point where its marginal productivity equals that of other branches of production. Development founded on export agriculture, however, has the

[1] See, particularly, United Nations, *Enlargement of the Exchange Economy in Tropical Africa* ; United Nations, *The Scope and Structure of Monetary Economies in Tropical Africa* ; G. Myrdal, *Development and Under-Development*, National Bank of Egypt, Fiftieth Anniversary Commemoration Lectures (Cairo, 1956).

[2] In the United States the capital-output ratio is 1·4 in agriculture, lying between that of heavy industry (petroleum : 4·3) and those of many light industries (sugar refining : 0·3) ; see W. Leontief, *Studies in the Structure of the American Economy* (New York, 1953).

drawback that that sector's saving is highly specific. Not only is agricultural saving in search of productive use generally placed in agriculture itself, but indeed in the same branch of agricultural production whence it came in the first place. It follows that countries, such as Brazil, where cycles of production succeed each other, have known successive phases of investment and disinvestment in sugar, cotton, and coffee, without any considerable amount of these specific sectors' saving having found a new home elsewhere in the same country.[1]

Furthermore, if agricultural saving looks for non-agricultural uses, it is often either invested abroad or spent on durable consumer goods, such as residential buildings. Although, therefore, the capital-output ratio in export agriculture may seem low and hence initially desirable, the capital-output ratio in sectors of induced activity, such as residential building, may be much higher and altogether undesirable. For example, in Egypt, where the capital-output ratio is generally 2 : 1, it is 8 : 1 in residential building financed mainly by the profits of cotton exporters.[2]

(b) *Export Industry*

In a poor country an industry working for foreign demand is often an extractive industry with a high capital-output ratio. Its position is that of a branch of a foreign firm. The large inter-regional unit of which that industry is part appears as an autonomous centre of saving and investment acting throughout the world according to its own plan.[3] For example, copper mining in Chile and in Canada, or oil drilling in Saudi Arabia and in the United States, employ the same techniques and have the same capital-output ratios regardless of country. The saving originating in such an industry may be transferred from the under-developed to the developed country just as much as in the opposite direction, but will only in exceptional cases move spontaneously to other sectors, agriculture or industry, of the same country.

The law of factor proportions is thereby violated only in appearance. What happens is that the law of factor proportions operates within the sphere of action of the decision centre, and the territories which an international firm controls may be situated in several different countries.

[1] João F. Normano, *Brazil, A Study of Economic Types* (Chapel Hill, 1935 ; R. Courtin, *Le Problème de la civilisation économique au Brésil* (Paris, 1941) ; J. Lambert, *Le Brésil* (Paris, 1953) ; A. Barrère, 'À teoria do crescimento et do desenvolvimento econômico', *Revista Brasileira de Economia*, June 1953.
[2] G. Myrdal, *op. cit.*
[3] M. Byé, 'L'Autofinancement de la grande unité interterritoriale et les dimensions temporelles de son plan', *Revue d'Économie Politique*, May-June 1957.

(c) *Domestic Industry*

There are some apparent contradictions with respect to the rôle of capital in industries working for home demand, even within Latin America or within one country of Latin America. On the one hand, the requirements of balanced growth in a country lacking capital make it seem logical that the first to develop should be either industries with low capital intensity or else those techniques in any particular industry which have low capital intensity — and in theory this applies to nearly all industries.[1] In this manner the scarce capital would be used to best effect.

It does in fact appear that before and during the last war the textile industry was the typical new industry in countries lacking capital and that, in Latin America, it was often launched with second-hand equipment. But this apparently logical rule has naturally never applied to the investment of public funds, and only infrequently to branch establishments of foreign firms (tariff factories), these subsidiaries generally tending to employ the same techniques wherever they happen to be.

The advantages of long-term planning by firms are such that an industry financed by local capital and faced with the prospect of rapidly becoming obsolete and being squeezed out of the market, ultimately has the choice only between starting out with modern equipment or not starting at all. Thus the effects of capital scarcity on the modernness of equipment vary widely according to branches, countries, and periods. In this respect the conditions of anticipation count much more than the law of factor proportions in its static aspect. The average capacity of blast furnaces in India is 800 tons, in Great Britain 666 tons. The average capacity of a cement mill is 400,000 tons a year in Chile, and 258,000 tons in the United States. The Peruvian textile industry has installed automatic looms requiring 65 per cent. less labour than non-automatic ones, and 35 per cent. of all looms are automatic. The capital coefficient of cotton spinning is lower in Mexico than in the United States.[2] Thus the apparently logical connection between disguised under-employment and technique adopted seems in fact rather doubtful.

It also happens that in one and the same branch there are at the same time firms with low and with high capital-output ratios, as a result of heterogeneity in the origin of the capital, the time of

---

[1] R. Nurkse, *Problems of Capital Formation in Underdeveloped Countries* (Oxford, 1953).
[2] V. V. Bhatt, 'Capital Intensity of Industries', *Bulletin of the Oxford University Institute of Statistics*, May 1956 ; see also Netherlands Economic Institute, *The Economics of Mill vs. Handloom-Weaving in India* (Rotterdam, September 1956), mimeographed.

establishment, the wealth or temperament of the entrepreneur. Disparities of this kind are not unusual, particularly in the Latin American textile industry. It would seem at first sight that in a competitive market competition, within one and the same branch of industry, between firms with a low capital-output ratio and firms with a high one, the latter should squeeze out the former. But in economies with little domestic saving the acquisition of modern equipment represents a heavy financial charge which firms cannot meet unless they maintain an oligopolistic structure and high prices. Thereby they may for quite some time save the plants working with obsolete equipment. Thus the fact that a branch of industry has to rely on its own saving may be at least partly responsible for the low productivity of that branch.

III. CAPITAL AND STRUCTURAL CHANGE

If we want to consider the problems of development and of growth together and to concentrate on the former, we have to ask ourselves how structural changes are induced by growth, which is mainly capital formation, and how in turn structural changes induce growth.[1]

In passing from growth to development, we have to consider not only the incompatibility of plans and the checks to which it may lead, but also disequilibria in the social structure. It has been shown that social asymmetries and their economic consequences, far from straightening themselves out in the long run, tend to become aggravated by cumulative processes. Whenever, therefore, the disintegrating forces which we have tried to describe come into play, no spontaneous development process can at first sight be expected.

The essential factors here are the differences in the geographical or sociological position of peoples commonly described as equally developed or equally under-developed by the standard of an average level of income. These differences explain why it is impossible to establish any rule either about the historical trend of capital-output ratios in growth or retrogression, or about the choice between more and less capitalistic investment. The answer always depends on circumstances.

If a country's economic sectors are on the road to imperfect integration or even disintegration, only the intervention of a large decision and planning centre can establish the necessary growth relations.

[1] 'A closer analysis will show that it is only by studying the transformation with which economic growth is combined that we can find the key to the problem of determining the level of investment', Ingvar Svennilson, *Growth and Stagnation in the European Economy* (Geneva, 1954), p. 7.

(a) *The Consequences of Non-communicating Sources of Finance*

Sectors which are closed off against each other so far as sources of finance are concerned may be related indirectly through labour, demand, or the monetary system. This inter-relation may lead : first, to integration under the lead of one sector, with 'progressive' results, that is to say, results favouring growth and development in the national economy ; second, to integration with 'retrogressive' results ; or, third, to an 'explosive' pattern implying a check on growth.

Progressive Patterns. Optimum conditions of progress were achieved in the nineteenth century in certain thinly populated areas occupied by European immigrants. I have in mind the United States and Canada. The immigration of people was accompanied by an influx of capital and technical knowledge. A complex society was created, of which only a moderate proportion worked directly on the land. Cultivation of high marginal productivity was made possible by the abundance of land. A sufficient level of development was reached by transmitted growth.

Retrogressive Patterns. Several types of retrogressive patterns are known. If they have not in fact all led to actual retrogression, the danger was avoided only by constructive policies. The risk of retrogression is especially inherent in the following situations :

(i) If mobile labour moves into speculative employments, abandoning lines of production or regions where it would have been more useful in the long run. For instance, the economic history of Brazil is a succession of periods of monoculture, each entailing the abandonment or under-employment of previous investment for the benefit of new production which itself was doomed to failure.

(ii) If agricultural labour is drawn into industrial employment without raising the productivity of agriculture. This may be done for the purpose of increasing the output of an industry protected by oligopoly or tariffs, and is by no means an hypothetical case, as Eugenio Gudin has pointed out.[1]

(iii) If the balance of payments effect of one export product (oil) tends to raise the rate of exchange so much that export by other sectors ceases to be viable. For instance, in some countries where mineral exports earn the bulk of foreign exchange, certain traditional exports can be maintained only by some form of subsidy.[2] In such

---

[1] Eugenio Gudin, 'O case das nações subdesenvolvidas', *Revista Brasileira de Economia*, September 1952, and 'Orientação e programação do desenvolvimento econômico', *ibid.*, September 1956, especially p. 29.

[2] It seems that by leading to 'too high' a rate of exchange, the development of oil production and export caused a contraction in the traditional cocoa and coffee exports.

circumstances the decline of the domestic sector can be compensated for by the progress of the sector financed by foreign capital only if a fiscal policy which taxes the latter sector and makes appropriate use of the revenue is adopted.

Explosive Patterns. Certain explosive patterns in agriculture and export industry tend to obstruct the whole economy. If, for example, the growth of export agriculture is limited by foreign demand or by deficient domestic demand, the decreasing inducement to invest ceases to match the sector's own savings ratio. The same generally happens in export industries working with foreign capital. In either case the excess saving is used in accordance with the originating sector's own interests which do not necessarily coincide with the national interest. Investment with high capital-output ratios springs up; for instance, residential building.[1]

Moreover, capital tends to leave the under-developed countries for more active economies which are world development poles. This centripetal movement is contrary to optimum distribution of capital throughout the world, but it corresponds to the actual existence of active poles enjoying external economies and capable of innovation.

Even in periods of complete political calm saving has sometimes flowed from dependent African territories to France. And United States statistics show that while in 1955 United States assets grew by $589 million in Latin America and by $661 million in Asia and Africa, there is also an opposite movement of foreign assets to the United States, Latin America accounting for $263 million and Asia and Africa for $448 million.[2]

(a) *Inflationary Pressure*

Inter-sectoral pressures capable of arresting growth find expression in inflationary situations and in a tendency towards permanent external deficit, as Raul Prebisch has pointed out.

Inflationary situations are common to economies possessing non-integrated sectors, that is, both to under-developed economies and to certain mature ones afflicted by partial inertia. If inflationary pressure leads to open inflation it will arrest growth at a lower level than could have been attained without open inflation and import restrictions. This has been seen in certain Latin American countries as well as in France.

---

[1] Gunnar Myrdal, *op. cit.*
[2] Samuel Pizer and Frederick Cutler, *op. cit.* Table 2.

(b) *The Aims of Development*

The aims of controlled growth cannot be the same in various phases of development, even if one could be sure about the succession of these phases. We must in the first place distinguish between economies whose essential problem is to build a sizeable subsistence sector into the market, and others where it is mainly a matter of co-ordinating different sectors of the market type.

From the purely economic point of view investment with a very low capital-output ratio would be the most effective for giving impulsion to the subsistence sector. An example is the diffusion of simple agricultural tools in French Tropical Africa, which serves a number of purposes at the same time. It helps to transform local production into export production, raises the productivity of production for home consumption, promotes the technical training of agricultural labourers, and gives them an incentive to save a little.[1]

On the other hand, if the creation of new inflationary pressure is to be avoided, a considerable part of the available funds will have to be devoted to developing the transport system, to improving the commercial sector, which must cease to be monopolistic, and also to stabilizing prices by accumulation of stocks. Such stabilization is indispensable for the containment of inflationary pressures, but it is difficult to protect against abuses by vested interests which would perpetuate obsolete structures.

Finally, organic development, especially of agriculture, in a poor country in which marginal demand is mainly for foodstuffs, cannot neglect certain facts. First, in certain areas rural overpopulation blocks the slightest agricultural progress. There must be some industrialization before there can be any agricultural progress. Second, certain systems of feudal structure, where the main source of income is land rent, cannot in practice be altered. One must try to transform the social structure by the creation of urban settlements. Third, for all its arbitrariness, the myth of industrialization has such compelling force that it cannot be ignored by any policy designed to transform mental attitudes.

In economies which are already largely market economies, government action aimed at integration takes the form of development plans such as are a common feature of our times. These plans are

[1] United Nations, *Enlargement of the Exchange Economy in Tropical Africa* ; United Nations, *The Scope and Structure of Monetary Economies in Tropical Africa* ; United Nations, *Processes and Problems of Industrialization of Under-Developed Countries*, 1955 ; A. Lawrence, 'Les Investissements dans les territoires d'outre-mer', *Journal Officiel de La République Française, Avis et Rapports du Conseil Économique*, March 7, 1956.

made up of specific development schemes, such as have been so well described in the valuable reports of the Economic Commission for Latin America on economic development in that area. However, such programmes can be executed only on certain conditions.[1] First, in large countries such as Brazil, programmes must be on a regional and local industrial basis. This has been attempted for the State of Minas Gerais in Brazil.[2] Second, the chosen development objective must fit in with the national specialization which the principle of comparative advantage is expected to impose upon the country in the near future. Third, the investment of public or foreign capital must not lose sight of the aim of sectoral integration and must not in effect discourage saving, but must collect it and channel it into a national capital market.

(c) *The Means*

It is impossible to over-emphasize the importance of education and training for escaping from the kind of stranglehold from which non-integrated economies suffer. Saving, too, may be a necessary condition of any break with the traditions of a society based on land rent.

Fiscal policy must not remain neutral. Its task is to integrate each sector's saving capacity into the national economy. It may depend on fiscal policy whether a certain structure ends up in complete deadlock or becomes a source of development. We have only to think of the very different uses made of the tax revenue from the great extractive industries operated by foreign capital in various countries. If a development policy taking a sufficiently long view

[1] Celso Furtado, 'Capital Formation and Economic Development', *International Economic Papers*, No. 4 (translated from *Revista Brasileira de Economia*, September 1952, by J. Cairncross) ; Celso Furtado, *A economia brasileira* (Rio de Janeiro, 1954) ; R. Nurkse, 'Notas sobre o trabalho do Sr. Furtado', *Revista Brasileira de Economia*, March 1953 ; M. Fleming, 'External Economies and the Doctrine of Balanced Growth', *Economic Journal*, June 1955 ; H. G. Aubrey, 'Investment Decisions in Underdeveloped Countries', National Bureau of Economic Research, *Capital Formation and Economic Growth* (Princeton, 1955) ; M. J. Levy, 'Some Social Obstacles to Capital Formation in Underdeveloped Areas', *ibid.* ; J. Mouly, 'Note sur les proportions de facteurs et l'intensité capitalistique des investissements dans les pays sous-développés', in *Cahiers de L'I.S.E.A.*, Series F., No. 3 ; United Nations, *Analyses and Projections of Economic Development, II, The Economic Development of Brazil*, 1956 ; J. P. de Almeida Magalhães, *A teoria moderna do crescimento e o problema do desenvolvimento*, Rio de Janeiro, 1954 ; A. Barrère, *op. cit.*

[2] G. F. Loeb, 'Numeros indices do desenvolvimento fisico da produção industrial do Brasil', *Revista Brasileira de Economia*, March 1953 ; J. Boudeville, 'Contribution à l'étude des pôles de croissance brésiliens — Une industrie motrice. La sidérurgie du Minas Gerais', *Cahiers de L'I.S.E.A.*, Series F., No. 10.

acts on the principle of 'sowing the oil', this may lead to diversification and development of the economy.[1]

Any policy making a choice of objectives must be selective in its means. If a certain source of saving is to be encouraged and certain uses of it discouraged, the best tax system is one with very unequal rates, combining a tax on high-productivity incomes with a tax on expenditure. It is essential, however, to remember that in such cases efficiency of enforcement is at least as important as the nominal figure of the tax rate.[2]

While integration demands the creation of a homogeneous money and capital market under the leadership of a central bank in the true sense of the word, this requirement must be reconciled with the need for a very unequal supply of credit to various sectors in certain phases of development.

Finally, multiple exchange rates, while implying much arbitrariness and a host of controls, seem to be well suited to a policy of choice and transformation of structures, provided that these long-run objectives are not violated. Indeed the practice may be applied both in young countries and in mature ones which, like France, are in need of a fundamental transformation of their foreign trade structure.[3]

But nothing must ever obscure the point that while domestic capital formation is always indispensable for development, it is equally necessary to have the help of foreign capital, which, throughout history, has brought economic development with it. No doubt the most desirable form of development requires conditions which are not those proper to a market economy. No doubt also the great financial centres in the richest countries have little resemblance to that ideal capital market sustained by innumerable small savings, which may have existed in the nineteenth century. But all this only accentuates the need for organized international capital movements.

Neither the increase of savings in the developed countries nor the execution of development plans in the so-called under-developed areas can be treated in isolation. We must hope that a new spirit will be born within nations and between nations, which will reconcile the principle of national sovereignty and the desire of democratic countries to choose their own development aims with the need for interdependence of saving and investment and long-term specialization.

[1] M. Byé, *op. cit.* p. 307.
[2] United Nations, *The Economic Development of Latin America and its Principal Problems*, 1954.
[3] Eugenio Gudin, 'Multiple Exchange Rates: The Brazilian Experience', *Economia Internazionale*, August 1956.

IV. CONCLUSIONS

It was not the purpose of this paper to raise innumerable problems, let alone to discuss them. The suggestions it contains may be imprudent — they were made with one sole end in view. I wished to show that under-development is not simply a matter of backwardness in quantitative terms, but that this backwardness is connected with certain structural features, more particularly with insufficient integration of the various sectors of the economy. In these circumstances the theory of development, as distinct from the theory of growth, cannot be based on one single model for all economies and all the stages of their transformation. Nor can such a model be established in terms of aggregate quantities.

We are led to the idea of a morphology classifying various types of under-development. We should, above all, abandon discussion in terms of averages, we should take account of economic and sociological discontinuities, and we should study sectoral coefficients and their movements.

My subject was: 'What is the rôle of capital in development?' To my regret, I must give a somewhat vague answer. Neither the amount of capital to be used, nor the forms of its use, nor the optimum origin of saving can be the same in various types of economy seeking development. This may seem negative. I believe it to be true, and therefore useful.

COMMENTS ON PROFESSOR BYÉ'S PAPER

BY

J. H. ADLER and K. S. KRISHNASWAMY

I. INTRODUCTION

THROUGHOUT Professor Byé's paper the reader is made aware of the difficulty of arriving at satisfactory generalizations, not only when he speaks about the rôle of capital but also when he deals with other aspects of the development process. There is, of course, virtue in any attempt to get away from the generalized models of the pure theorist and to take account of the social, institutional, and cultural differences between economies. This is particularly important if we want to move from analytical reasoning to the more difficult but, in practice, more important plane of policy advising and policy making. But, like any other virtue, it can be overdone. The economist who is circumspect, who takes account of more than the two or three variables which make up the moving parts of a model, who lifts the veil of the *ceteris paribus* stipulations and breaks down such convenient aggregates as consumption and capital formation, deserves our approval and applause. But the economist who substitutes such concepts as socio-cultural differences and dynamic group equilibrium for supply and demand, the size of the market, income flows and income distribution, is bound to get lost in the maze of ill-defined sociological notions, and does not come to grips with the problems of economic growth.

The lack of easily discernible central tendencies, and of conformity to a pattern, has led some students of the processes and problems of economic development to treat each economy as *sui generis* to which the general propositions of theory do not apply. This kind of approach represents, we suggest, an abdication of systematic enquiry, an essential ingredient of economic analysis. The intellectual dissatisfaction with this method of approach has led to attempts to analyse the process of economic growth, and to develop a theory of economic development on the basis of historical data. In practice, this means that the long time series for a handful of advanced countries are worked over and over and the firm parameters that emerge — the capital-output ratios, the savings ratios, the monetary and balance of payments patterns — are accepted as if their validity were timeless and economic development in the middle of the twentieth century could proceed, and succeed, only if the same pattern of behaviour and the same set of institutions that characterized the economies of the United States and of Western Europe in the last fifty years before the First World War were adopted.

This is not to deny the important contribution that an analysis of the historical process of economic growth and development can make to an understanding of the problems of economic development today. But we are rather uneasy about the indiscriminate application of the old rules to the new problems, an application which fails to take account of the changes which have occurred in the last hundred years in national and international political institutions, in the rôle of governments, in the concept of a desirable income distribution, and in the pattern of international trade and capital movements. And we wonder whether it would not be a most rewarding extension of historical enquiry to scrutinize the development process of the last ten or fifteen years in the countries of Latin America, Asia, and Africa to determine what the relation between capital and the growth of output has been, how and where saving has been generated, and what investment patterns have produced the best results in terms of income growth and income distribution. It may well be that the results of such an enquiry would permit us to modify the lessons of the nineteenth century and to apply them less indiscriminately and more fruitfully to an understanding of today's development process, and to the formulation of economic policies which economists are, rightly or wrongly, expected to devise.

II. The Supply of Capital and the Supply of Other Factors

Given the diversity of development aims and the structural changes required to attain them, what can we say, in general terms, about the rôle of capital formation in the development process? We may start from two limiting positions. At the Santa Margherita meeting of the International Economic Association, Professor Cairncross expressed, and elaborated, the view that in the light of the experience of the Victorian era, capital formation was a concomitant phenomenon of the process of economic growth and not a causal impelling factor. The driving forces of growth were technological innovations on the supply side and steadily widening markets on the demand side, which resulted in large business profits, which in turn financed capital formation. Professor Cairncross concluded, or, at any rate, came close to the conclusion, that the level of aggregate capital formation was not the key variable, perhaps not even one of the key variables determining the rate of economic growth, but that changes in productive efficiency, the compounded result of technological change, the growth of markets, and entrepreneurial ingenuity and daring, were responsible for the economic advancement of the period.

On the opposite extreme of the spectrum of views is the proposition that the rate of economic growth and development is uniquely determined by the level of new investment. It is not surprising that this view is expressed, with a frequency that makes it monotonous, at international political conferences and meetings, in the debates of the United Nations and the Organization of American States, and in the various documents prepared for such conferences and debates. But it is surprising that in technical discussions and writings, in analytical models as well as in policy papers, the relationship between capital formation and economic development is stressed to the exclusion of all other causal factors and relations.

We submit that two issues must be distinguished — and kept apart. One is the problem of capital formation, to which we shall return later ; the other is the meaning of the capital-output ratio. Professor Rosenstein-Rodan has pointed out that the marginal productivity of capital is a partial derivative, the supply of all factors other than capital remaining constant, while the marginal capital-output ratio is a full derivative, the supply of all factors other than capital being variable. In other words, the increase in total output associated with an addition to the stock of capital is determined not only by the amount of additional capital but also by additions of some other units — labour, land, technical skill, management. Only if it is assumed that the supply of these other factors is infinitely elastic, is the increase in output determined solely by the amount of additional capital. If we do not make this assumption — which gives us an analytical description of a limiting case — we become immediately concerned with the elasticity of supply of other factors or, more generally, with the responsiveness of other factors to economic incentives.

In recent years, a great deal of attention has been given to the supply of entrepreneurship as the strategic factor which, aside from capital, determines the rate of growth and development. Without in any way denying the importance of entrepreneurship, we suggest that the emphasis on this single factor has led to a neglect of the analysis of the supply conditions of other factors. How does the subsistence farmer, whom we usually do not include in the entrepreneurial class, respond to higher prices of commodities which he *could* produce for the market ? How does entrepreneurship enter into the picture if a large proportion of total saving accumulates in the hands of the government ? Or conversely, what is the rôle of entrepreneurship if the most important factor limiting the development of a region is the lack of transportation facilities and the government does not have enough funds (capital) to build highways ? Can entrepreneurship make up for lack of technical knowledge and productive skills ?

These questions suggest that for an understanding of the process of development it is insufficient to concentrate on an analysis of entrepreneurship. It is essential to broaden the analysis into a more general enquiry into economic incentives and the response of various factors to them. It is equally necessary to determine — perhaps in general terms and perhaps case by case — under what institutional arrangements and under what economic and social conditions the supply of capital and entrepreneurship and technical skill can best be matched. There are numerous examples of economies where capital is held idle — for example, in the form of foreign balances — by a group of capitalists while entrepreneurial talent and technical skill go begging. There are cases in which capital and entrepreneurship are available but technical skills are lacking, or are so expensive as to make production unprofitable. Finally, there are instances in which both entrepreneurship and technical skills are available but capital is lacking.

Thus, the conceptual link between the marginal productivity of capital and the capital-output ratio is the fact that the magnitude of both depends on the supply of all other factors of production ; the greater the supply, the higher the marginal productivity and the lower the capital-output ratio.

Limitations on the supply of factors other than capital explain, at least in part, a phenomenon which is characteristic of under-developed economies. On the one hand, we find that the return on capital in established enterprises is remarkably high — rates of return of 30 or even 50 per cent. are frequently mentioned as typical of some economies. On the other hand, we find that the expected return on new ventures is low, or even negative. This apparent paradox can be explained only by the difference in the supply conditions of factors other than capital. Old enterprises have solved their supply problem. Knowledgeable management knows the conditions in the input and the output markets, it has been able to acquire the necessary labour skills, and it has found the right technology which permits that combination of inputs which corresponds to the price relations among inputs. All or most of these conditions are absent when it comes to the setting up of new enterprises. Management lacks experience and knowledge of the market, skilled labour is expensive or simply not available and therefore has to be trained, and the technology appropriate for the size of the market and for the supply conditions of the non-capital inputs is untried or has not even been invented. In technical terms, we could say that we are faced with a steeply down-sloping marginal productivity curve of capital, or a pronounced discontinuity. But the technical terms do not give an indication of the fact that this sharp drop in the productivity curve is due to the limitations on the supply of factors other than capital.

How does the argument so far developed affect the magnitudes of the marginal capital-output ratio ? When we turn from the concept of marginal productivity to the capital-output ratio, we have to drop the assumption that the supply of all other factors is given and have to think in terms of a flow. As long as the rate of capital formation remains constant and the distribution of capital among its various uses remains the same, and there is a steady automatic growth in the supply of all other factors, we should expect the capital-output ratio to remain unchanged, or, if external economies make themselves felt, to decline gradually. If, however, the supply of capital expands suddenly — for instance, as an indirect result of a drastic improvement in the terms of trade, or because of a sudden increase in government revenues such as oil revenues — while the rate of supply of all other factors remains constant, the capital-output ratio is likely to increase because the efficiency of utilizing additional capital is bound to decline. Some capital is poorly used, or goes to waste, or remains idle, accumulating in the form of bank deposits or foreign balances.

If, on the other hand, the supply of factors other than capital increases more rapidly than the stock of capital, we should expect an improvement in the efficiency of the utilization of capital, and a decrease in the capital-output ratio. With management improving, labour becoming more efficient, and technical skills increasing, capital 'goes further'. Since the existing stock of capital is committed to particular uses, and is combined with other factors in rather inflexible proportions, an improvement in the supply conditions of the non-capital factors will be reflected primarily in the marginal capital-output ratio, the relation of new, additional capital to additional output. But there may be some improvement in the use of existing capital as well. As in the case of a sudden spurt in the supply of capital, an at least temporary oversupply of non-capital factors may occur. Entrepreneurship may be frustrated, and labour skills may go to waste.

The relationship between new capital and additional output is a complex relationship since it depends not only on the composition of investment, which may change over time and cause an increase or decrease in the capital-output ratio, but also on the supply of all non-capital factors. Given a certain rate of capital formation and, we may add, a certain state of technology, there is an appropriate, or optimum, flow in the supply of all non-capital factors of production which corresponds to it.

III. IMPORTANCE OF CAPITAL FORMATION IN DETERMINING THE RATE OF GROWTH OF TOTAL OUTPUT IN UNDER-DEVELOPED COUNTRIES

The preceding observations modify, but do not destroy, the emphasis which much of the literature has put on the rôle of the rate of capital formation as determining the rate of growth of total output. For it may still be argued that conditions in most under-developed countries today are such that the supply of non-capital factors is adequate to take care of a considerable increase in the rate of capital formation ; or that an increase in the rate of capital formation is more difficult to bring about than an increase in the supply of the non-capital factors and therefore deserves most attention ; or — and this seems to us to be the most pertinent argument — that we are dealing in reality with conditions of joint supply of capital and non-capital factors. Professor Cairncross has emphasized the fact that in the nineteenth century entrepreneurship provided its own capital by ploughing entrepreneurial income back into the economy. But just as entrepreneurship creates its own capital, the availability of additional capital permits the exploitation of economies of scale in larger productive units and the use of technological improvements. It also creates new markets for technical skills and managerial talent, and provides new opportunities for skilled and unskilled labour. An increase in the supply of one factor of production sets in motion a complex rearrangement of the flow of all other factors and brings about an increase in their supply.

This increase in the supply of non-capital factors is not automatic in the sense that economic policy can be concerned only with the rate of capital formation and that the supply of non-capital factors will take care of itself. But it is automatic in the sense in which the term is used in economic theory. An increase in the supply of capital brings into play new incentives and new market forces changing the demand for non-capital factors of production. It depends on the speed and intensity of the response on the supply side whether the flow of non-capital factors can be left alone, or whether some form of intervention is called for. It is impossible to generalize on this point. The conditions as to the responsiveness of the non-capital factors to economic incentives (that is, higher rewards or more demand at the existing level of rewards) differ from economy to economy, and, within each economy, from factor to factor. Where the response is spotty and sluggish, as, for instance, in societies in which the attractiveness of leisure is greater than the attractiveness of higher income, or where mobility is impeded by social and cultural institutions, intervention — in the form of measures to eliminate those impediments and to reinforce incentives — is called for. But whatever the specific shortage — of particular skills, of technical knowledge, of institutions to bring capital and entrepreneurial talent together — its elimination will in most instances result in an increase of output only if it is accompanied by an increased availability of capital.

The emphasis on capital requirement and capital formation and, as a supplement, on the inflow of foreign capital, is particularly justified in those under-developed countries where productive techniques have not kept pace with the advances in technology elsewhere. In order to absorb, with appropriate adaptations, the technological advances of the last fifty or eighty years — which according to the studies of the National Bureau of Economic Research account for the major part of the annual increase in productivity of $1\frac{1}{2}$ per cent. — substantial amounts of capital are required, not only to increase the total capital stock (or capital per worker) but also to replace that part of capital stock, including economic overhead capital, that has become obsolete.

IV. Capital Formation and the Pattern of Income Distribution

Let us turn now to a brief consideration of the supply of capital, that is, the process of capital formation. It will be agreed that an increase in the aggregate savings-income ratio is a necessary, though not a sufficient, condition for economic growth in under-developed countries. If we hold with Professor Byé that the essence of economic development is structural change of a type that tends to be progressive, a major manifestation of this will have to be an increase in the supply of capital, or in saving as a proportion of national income. Thus the argument for structural change itself derives, at least in part, from the fact that the prevalent economic and social structure in under-developed countries is such as to perpetuate a relative shortage of capital. Further, for the policy-maker at any rate, some guide is necessary to judge whether the changes that are occurring in the structure are conducive to growth or not. From this point of view, capital growth is something which, despite its complicated character, is less difficult to handle than, say, spread of technology or change in social attitudes.

The changes which occur in an under-developed country in the process of raising its savings ratio from, say, 5 to 12 per cent. of national income are, or ought to be, a vital part of the argument of those who stress capital growth as the prime mover in the situation. This becomes apparent when one looks at the so-called paradox referred to by Professor Lewis : 'because the rich save more than the poor, it used to be expected that every country must save more as income per head rises. It was found, however, that in the wealthier countries, real income per head doubled in fifty to seventy years without any increase in the savings-ratio.' Professor Lewis's explanation of this is that 'the rate of savings is determined not by whether countries are rich or poor, but by the ratio of profits to national income, and both these ratios cease to increase once a certain stage of development has been reached'.[1]

We may or may not agree with all that Professor Lewis has said in this context. But it serves to bring out the fact that an increase in savings-ratio in under-developed countries is important because the process of achieving it necessarily involves a change in the structure of income and economic relationships. That is why it constitutes a major target in the programmes of under-developed countries. Advanced countries are able to maintain a high savings-ratio because, presumably, the economic and sociological changes necessary for it have already occurred there. As observed earlier, it is futile to try to determine which came first in the developed countries, greater additions to the stock of capital or all the other things that help the better utilization of productive equipment. The two had to go hand in hand, and either of these by itself would not have led to economic development. But greater availability of capital was an indispensable element in the process.

Raising the relative share of what Professor Lewis calls capitalists' profits — or incomes out of which more is saved for productive invest-ment — is not an easy thing for under-developed countries to do. This is a question not of making prices rise faster than costs, but of making the productivity of factors increase more rapidly than costs. It is this differ-ence that gives rise to a surplus out of which capital is accumulated, particularly when it accrues to sectors of the community with a high propensity to save and invest. It involves, among other things, restraint in transferring an increasing part of the national income to those whose standards of consumption are low and need to be raised rapidly. Politi-cally and socially, this is a hard policy to implement, since it clashes with modern conceptions of equity and social justice. But all under-developed countries have to try to resolve this conflict between greater saving and more equal distribution of income in some way.

There is considerable need for a clearer appreciation of the relation between capital growth and income distribution in under-developed countries and of all the structural changes that an adjustment in the latter implies. With so many of the people in under-developed countries having incomes barely sufficient for subsistence, all or most of the saving will have to be done by a small group of high-income earners, business firms, and the government. Clearly, the smaller the relative share in national income of this small group of savers, the larger must be the difference between average individual income in that group and the average income in the subsistence sector for a given level of the aggregate savings-income ratio in the economy. If the relative share of the savers in the national income remains unchanged, any increase in the savings-income ratio can only come about through a widening of the difference between average individual incomes in the two sectors.

[1] W. Arthur Lewis, *Theory of Economic Growth* (London, 1954), pp. 238-239.

Two corollaries follow from this. If for political and humanitarian reasons a widening of individual income differences cannot be countenanced, stepping up the savings-income ratio becomes a function of reducing the relative share of the so-called subsistence sector in national income. This must inevitably be a comparatively slow process. Further, since the process cannot go so far as to reduce the absolute income of the subsistence sector — except in the unlikely event of a fall in the number of income-earners in that sector — there is clearly a limit set to the increase in the savings-income ratio, given the initial pattern of relative shares. And the faster the growth of population in the subsistence sector, the lower this limit is likely to be.

Second, it adds point to the importance of public saving in underdeveloped countries. Fiscal policy directed towards reducing inequalities in individual incomes cannot contribute to additional savings and capital formation unless it also contributes *inter alia* to a shift in the relative share of the savers in national income. One of the ways in which this double condition is sought to be met is through the government's appropriating an increasing proportion of the additional income generated in the economy for purposes of public investment. If there is to be a net gain from such a policy, the greater portion of the additional income diverted to government must come from the potential consumers rather than the potential savers outside government. How this can be done and in what measure are questions that have to be judged against the circumstances of each country. But the basic problem of having to alter the pattern of income remains, and it is not rendered any easier by the effect different patterns of income-distribution could have on the supply of factors of production that are co-operant with capital.

FURTHER COMMENTS ON
PROFESSOR BYÉ'S PAPER

BY

JOSEPH A. KERSHAW[1]

I. STRUCTURAL CHANGE

PROFESSOR BYÉ states that the process of development is a change in economic structure rather than a mere growth in income, total or *per capita*. Professor Byé defines a structure as a 'system of relations and constraints between centres of decision'. This phrase conveys little or nothing to me. But perhaps what is meant by structure is the usual notion of relative emphasis on different economic sectors. I think it can

[1] I should like to thank my colleague, Mr. Norman Kaplan, for valuable help in the preparation of this comment.

be established that economic growth invariably brings with it a shift of the labour force out of agriculture into non-agriculture, and an increasing relative importance of tertiary industries. These are certainly structural economic changes and they seem of more interest and significance than changes in income, with which of course they are usually associated.

In this connection it is interesting to point to the experience of the Soviet Union. Here is an economy which, since the Plan period began in 1928, has experienced development on a tremendous scale. Since that time, to be sure, there has been an increase in income *per capita*, though probably rather little in consumption. The striking feature of this economic development, however, is that there were great and continuous structural shifts so that the economy is now scarcely recognizable as having evolved from what it was in 1928. Incidentally, I would argue that, notwithstanding the tremendous industrial growth, the Soviet Union is still under-developed, as evidenced by the fact that about half the labour force is still in agriculture.

There is one other lesson that the Soviet experience can teach students of economic development. Professor Byé tells us that 'while domestic capital formation is always indispensable for development, it is equally necessary to have the help of foreign capital — which, throughout history, has brought economic development with it'. I believe that Soviet experience refutes this statement. While there was some capital imported in the early and middle thirties, this was minimal, and can hardly be regarded as having been critical. The Russians have demonstrated that if a government is willing and able to interfere sufficiently with consumers' time preferences, the necessary volume of saving and investment can be generated internally. The current efforts of China to emulate this experience, and the political importance of the race between India and China, lend special significance to this observation.

II. The Savings-Income Ratio and the Capital-Output Ratio

I would like to turn now to the question of what analytical or predictive use can be made of aggregates, specifically the savings-income and the capital-output ratios. In good part I share Professor Byé's scepticism of their utility, although I should have been less hard on the savings ratio and even harder on the capital-output ratio.

Professor Byé is agnostic on the utility of these ratios on the grounds that development brings substantial structural changes, a fact which is surely beyond dispute. He feels that as economic structure changes, the meaning of these aggregate ratios becomes at best ambiguous, at worst quite misleading. Furthermore, they shift substantially over time, largely as a result of these structural changes, and hence one cannot be quite sure how they will behave during the process of development.

With respect to the savings-income ratio, most of this is true enough. Even so, I feel that the analyst must pay attention to the ratio. In particular, he must consider ways of influencing it. Once there is any monetary sector at all in an economy, the process of growth requires a certain minimum, and approximately specifiable, share of non-consumption. I think this is true regardless of the stage of development or of the structure of an economy. It is quite true that the ratio will change in the process, but I think that these changes may well be predictable. Furthermore, and most important, we know the direction in which we want the ratio to move as an aid to development, and governments can induce it to move in that direction, as indeed Professor Byé points out. Such a minor effort as the establishment of a rural savings system seems to me a constructive step in most under-developed economies, because it induces the aggregate savings ratio to rise. The Indians are stressing this in their second Five-Year Plan.

Professor Byé is troubled by the fact that many savings decisions are not independent of investment decisions. A farmer decides to refrain from consumption in order to build a barn or invest in an irrigation ditch ; he would not make the savings decision except for the specific investment decision. I agree that this diminishes the analytical utility of the ratio, but, as Professor Byé says, many modern investment-saving decisions are also of this sort. I think one can believe that highly developed capital markets are much to be desired without being driven to the conclusion that their absence renders the savings-income ratio analytically valueless.

Finally, let me say a few things about capital-output ratios. I gather that Professor Byé dislikes and distrusts them in large part because they are so variable. My own distrust goes a good deal deeper than this. I feel that they may even detract from, rather than add to, our understanding of the development process. There is nothing inherently wrong with expressing two economic variables in the form of a ratio. If the variables are carefully enough defined, a capital-output ratio can tell us that so much investment will bring so much output. Such an impeccable arithmetic statement can sometimes be useful.

However, people who make use of capital-output ratios seem inevitably to introduce a normative aspect which seems unwarranted. They talk about favourable and unfavourable capital-output ratios, and they frequently recommend choice among projects in accordance with their capital-output ratios. Professor Byé's paper illustrates some of the confusion which results from this. In it there are passages which suggest approval of high ratios (pp. 115, 118) and others which suggest approval of low ratios (pp. 116, 120). My own conviction is that, although some ratios are high and others low, they are not favourable or unfavourable, good or bad.

In this connection I want to make two general points. The first has to do with the use of capital-output ratios as an aid to investment decisions. It seems to me that one runs a danger of paying insufficient attention to the time dimension. It is not enough to know that a given investment will generate so much output in this or the following year. The important point is how long the stream of outputs will continue to flow from this investment. It is quite possible that two investment projects have identical capital-output ratios, but that one is much more durable than the other. If we try to define the capital-output ratio to take this into account, we move towards a rate of return concept. Perhaps this is a way in which the capital-output ratio can be usefully rehabilitated.

Capital-output ratios also ignore other variables. In particular, the impact on population growth of various types of investment may be quite critical. Professor Leibenstein seems to make a lot of sense when he writes about the interaction between economic and population growth. I hope he will have something to say on this during the conference.

My second general point concerns capital-output ratios for broad aggregates, including the economy as a whole. Here I am troubled by the fact that, at least where governments take an active rôle in the planning process, the capital-output ratios turn out to be in good part the result of planning policy decisions, and hence are not technologically determined. Although the data are hard to come by, I think that both average and marginal capital-output ratios in the Soviet Union for industry as a whole have been consistently lower than in the United States, or in most other Western economies. Does this mean that the Russians are more efficient in their investment ? Not at all. Soviet planners long ago made a decision to favour certain areas, such as heavy industry, and to slight others, such as housing and other social overhead. In the former sector capital-output ratios are relatively low, in the latter they are high. In the United States we pay more attention to consumer preferences, and housing is a very important investment sector. The only conclusion one can draw, therefore, from the fact that the capital-output ratios are different in the two countries is that they have elected different policies. This means that where governments take an active part in directing the development process, and they do everywhere these days, it is idle to hope to find numerical values for the capital-output ratio which will be characteristic of stated stages of economic development.

III. INTER-SECTORAL RELATIONSHIPS

Perhaps I may conclude with an observation on the inter-sectoral problem posed by Professor Byé. If I understand him correctly, he tells us that we cannot profitably use aggregate models of the Harrod-Domar type, that sectoral analysis is dangerous because the inter-sectoral questions are likely to be overlooked, and that the real problem is to integrate and control the sectors so that none becomes a brake on the others. One can agree with the diagnosis while lamenting the lack of a helpful prescription.

It is true that various sectors of the economy play different rôles in economic development. Heavy industry provides capital goods for future growth. Light industry provides consumer goods for the population. Agriculture provides labour for industry and consumer goods, some indirectly via light industry. Transport provides services to industry. Housing provides consumer services and permits the urbanization necessary for industrialization. These inter-relationships are complex and imperfectly understood. We are indebted to Professor Byé for reminding us that our planning and predictive models should take these things into account. Unfortunately, it is not yet clear how such models should be constructed, and, without them, predicting may be as hazardous as with the over-simplified aggregative Harrod-Domar models.

DISCUSSION OF PROFESSOR BYÉ'S PAPER

PROFESSOR BYÉ's paper produced a variety of reactions, which found expression in the succeeding discussion. Opinions differed widely as regards the relation between investment and economic growth. Among the possibilities discussed, the following three were particularly characteristic : (1) the rate of growth may be in large measure independent of the rate of investment ; (2) growth and investment may move together, but the chain of causation may run from growth to investment, rather than the other way about ; and (3) the classical case in which saving and investment are causes and growth the effect. In addition, the discussion threw interesting sidelights upon the capital-output ratio and the saving-income ratio.

I. GROWTH WITHOUT CORRESPONDING INVESTMENT

Professor Schultz took the position that, in the United States, a large and perhaps dominant proportion of the growth that had occurred since 1870 could not be attributed to traditional investments. He based his view upon studies by Abramovitz and Kendrick, as well as on an unpublished paper by Robert Solow. These studies suggested that 50 per cent. of her capital growth could not be explained by additions to the traditional capital stock alone. Analogous results, he said, had been obtained from a study of Mexican agricultural development. Further evidence of the subordinate rôle of this capital came from the experience of American agriculture during the 1930s, when a rapid expansion in output had gone hand in hand with a reduction in the amount of capital employed.

Various explanations were volunteered. Technological improvements ranked high among these, although *Professor Schultz* warned that the investigators whom he had quoted stopped short of assigning full responsibility to technology. *Dr. Adler* pointed out that technological improvements affected growth in proportion to *gross* investment, while additions to the capital stock represented only *net* investment. Investment in human resources was cited by *Professors Schultz* and *Brahmananda* and *Dr. Adler*. *Dr. Adler* qualified the 'investment in human resources' thesis, however, by arguing that the utilization of such improvements was nevertheless inseparable from the application of additional capital. *Professor Hirschman* mentioned the 'Leontief paradox' which asserts the seemingly illogical fact that the United States, a capital-rich country, exports principally labour intensive commodities, as possible evidence that the United States had made large though non-statistical investments in the quality of the labour force. The proponents of this point of view — not including Dr. Adler — joined in the comment that 'we are taking capital much too seriously'.

II. INVESTMENT AS THE CAUSAL FACTOR

Dr. Adler, after saying that investment was not uniquely related to growth, nevertheless went on to argue that it deserved special attention because it represented the most manageable focus for policy. The public authorities could do something about capital formation while they could do little about entrepreneurship and similar growth factors. He warned, however, that aggressive policy measures to lift capital formation might unfavourably affect the distribution of income. *Professors Kershaw* and *Wallich*, in their analysis of the Russian and German advances, left room for the interpretation that, despite all qualifications, investment had played a strong initiating rôle. *Professor Wallich* added that it would be unfortunate if the present debate were interpreted to mean that 'investment did not matter'.

III. THE RÔLE OF CAPITAL AT DIFFERENT STAGES OF DEVELOPMENT

No specific view-points emerged with regard to possible differences in capital requirements at different stages of development. *Professor Kershaw* observed that Russia had enjoyed a low capital-output ratio but did not argue that this necessarily reflected a condition typical of under-developed economies. Russia's low capital-output ratio, he said, was the result of decisions taken by the Russian planners that were not necessarily inherent in the process of development. *Dr. Adler* felt that in under-developed economies a relatively large amount of capital might be required in order to make use of available advanced techniques. Much of the existing equipment, including parts of the economic overhead capital, was obsolete, he said. *Professor Boudeville* thought that there were differences between capital-output ratios not only among the various sectors of an economy, but also within each sector, and that such differences made generalizations impracticable. *Professor Ellis* observed that the stage of development might make some difference with regard to the relation between investment and growth, and that in capital-poor countries the relation might be close, while in capital-rich countries the causal contribution of capital to growth might be rather low.

IV. Saving-Income Ratio and Capital-Output Ratio

A variety of doubts were expressed regarding two familiar tools of analysis : the saving-income ratio and the capital-output ratio. Particularly the latter received adverse comment, in line with the doubts expressed regarding the closeness of the relation between investment and growth. Nevertheless, the capital-output ratio found some defenders. *Dr. Adler* argued that while it was no tool of forecasting, it constituted a 'handy concept'. It could also be made to serve in analysing the operation of other factors affecting growth, whose impact would change the ratio. He was concerned that changes in the ratio were frequently interpreted as reflecting merely shifts in the composition of investment, when changes in the supply of co-operating factors were a more fundamental explanation.

Professor Kershaw voiced sympathy with the views of the sceptics. Nevertheless, he said, such were the sort of tools economists had to work with, and we would just have to keep trying. The saving-income ratio he regarded as more solidly founded than the capital-output ratio. Professor Byé, whose paper had been interpreted by some as rejecting both ratios altogether, corrected this impression by saying that he did not think them analytically useless and that observed changes in them required investigation of the underlying causes, which would probably lead to interesting results.

Chapter 6

THE SERVICING OF FOREIGN CAPITAL INFLOWS BY UNDER-DEVELOPED COUNTRIES

BY

GERALD M. ALTER

International Bank for Reconstruction and Development [1]

I. INTRODUCTION

AN under-developed country wishing to secure foreign capital to accelerate its economic development faces various tests by potential investors. These tests — whether they relate to the likelihood of war, revolution, civil strife, expropriation without compensation, the availability of suitable investment projects, or the future balance of payments position of the country — stem from the fact that the ordinary investor expects to receive a return on the funds committed to a country. The entity receiving such funds, if it is a private enterprise or a public corporation operating along business lines, is willing to pay the required return when the use of such funds in a specific project is expected to yield the required surplus over cost directly. If the receiving entity is the government, a specific project may or may not be expected to yield the required surplus over cost directly. The government requires, however, that the overall yield to the whole economy from employing the funds should in some sense justify payment of the return required by the investor.

The fact that both parties to the use of regular investment funds must find it mutually and directly rewarding is well recognized, both in the domestic and in the international sphere. In the international sphere, however, investors recognize special risks which are associated in their minds with the transferrability of the return they require. These risks induce investors to appraise the future balance of payments position of the country to which they commit their funds. The individual enterprise in the capital-importing country wishing to secure funds from abroad may be able fully to demonstrate

[1] The paper does not necessarily reflect the views of the International Bank for Reconstruction and Development with which the author is associated.

that the employment of funds will yield the necessary surplus, at least at present exchange rates, and such a surplus may indeed be earned. Yet, the future balance of payments of the country may be such that interest, dividend, or principal payments due the investor cannot be transferred, or can only be transferred, if denominated in local currency, at a greatly depreciated exchange rate. Similarly, a government borrowing abroad may be able to give adequate assurance that the country's real income will be sufficiently increased by the employment of additional investment resources to justify a payment to the foreign lender. Yet serious obstacles to the transfer of service payments on such loans may be encountered when such payments are to be made.

The economic conditions which must be fulfilled if foreign debt service payments (interest, dividends, or principal) are to be met can be stated in terms of the familiar equation on total resource availabilities and uses. If an economy is to make service payments in any year equal to X, the output produced plus capital inflow, including any net use of foreign exchange reserves, must exceed domestic consumption and investment by X. This proposition may also be put in terms of the saving and investment equation. Domestic saving plus foreign capital inflow must exceed domestic investment by the volume of service payments.

In addition to these equations relating to total resource availabilities and uses, there is the equation relating to foreign exchange availabilities and uses. Total foreign exchange receipts, including gross capital inflow and net use of foreign exchange reserves, must exceed imports of goods and services by the volume of service payments. It is obvious that the payment of debt service requires the fulfilment of all three conditions : other claims on total resources, other claims on savings, and other claims on foreign exchange resources must be less than availabilities by the amount of debt service.

These elementary equations can also be reformulated in terms of increments and decrements. If, for example, there is a decline in national income, no change in capital inflow, and no decline in required debt service payments, domestic consumption and investment must decline by the amount of the decline in national income. Further illustrations are unnecessary. They only serve to emphasize the point that the fulfilment of debt service obligations is dependent on the economy's capacity to adjust the claims on total resources, saving, and foreign exchange in any given year and over time so as to release the amount required for debt service.

In appraising the capacity of a country to service foreign capital inflows, the first problem, therefore, is to determine the conditions under which these competing claims are likely to be resolved in favour of debt service. If such conditions do not exist, even a small amount of debt service is not safe. At the opposite extreme, if conditions in a country are such that the resolution of these competing claims in favour of external debt service can be taken for granted, the capacity of such a country to service foreign capital inflow is dependent only upon its ability to employ additional capital effectively. In this case an upper limit is imposed on external servicing obligations by a case-by-case examination of the projects and programmes proposed or considered for foreign financing. In between these two extremes there is a third alternative : the conditions under which these claims will be resolved in favour of debt service may involve a complex relationship between the amount of debt service payments which are owed and the overall economic performance of the country. In this case some appraisal must be made of the country's future economic performance, taking into account varying levels of capital inflow and associated debt service payments.

With respect to the first alternative, it is clear that there is nothing in the economic mechanism as such which makes it impossible to adjust the claims on total resources, on saving, and on foreign exchange, so that debt service payments can be met. This is true either under the assumptions of the gold standard and the classical adjustment mechanism, or under the modern panoply of fiscal and monetary policy with or without direct controls. But such a formal solution has only limited significance. The environment of policy objectives in which the economic system must operate and the economic performance which is in fact achieved necessarily condition the process through which competing claims on resources are adjusted.

Under the gold standard and the classical adjustment mechanism it can be taken for granted that so long as the system is adhered to and the government sticks to the rules of the game, competing claims on resources will, under all conditions, be adjusted in favour of debt service. Very few countries today are willing to accept the implications of the classical adjustment mechanism as a primary principle of economic management. Its unconditional acceptance is often believed to be in conflict with many of the primary objectives of modern governments, including the objective of relatively full employment, accelerated economic development, more equitable income distribution, and so forth.

Let us, therefore, consider the conditions under which competing claims are likely to be resolved in favour of debt service and whether in the modern day such conditions can ever be taken for granted.

Discussion of the major situations giving rise to balance of payments difficulties in which the priority of debt service is likely to be challenged and of the problems which may be encountered in adjusting competing claims may conveniently be divided into two parts. The risk of a world depression and the problems posed by short-term variations in the real value of exports will be considered first. Most of the subsequent discussion will deal with the risks that arise in the longer-term context of economic growth and with the relationship between debt service capacity and overall economic performance in the long term.

II. IMPORTANCE OF SHORT-TERM DISTURBANCES

The balance of payments problems which led to a suspension of service payments in the past were frequently associated with world-wide depressions. While some countries continued to service external debts even in the depression of the thirties, many countries did not. Since the thirties governments have become more intent on maintaining high levels of economic activity, consumption, and investment, and if a depression of similar magnitude and duration should occur in the future the balance of payments problems initiated in the first instance by a decline in exports are likely to be compounded by an even more active domestic compensatory policy. Debt service is unlikely to be given a high priority in such circumstances unless the capital resources available to debtor countries are increased substantially by governmental and inter-governmental action. This might provide an incentive to maintain debt service. Of course, to the extent that debt service consists of dividends paid out of current earnings, debt service claims are likely to decline, particularly when a foreign-owned enterprise is producing primarily for the export market.

Thus, the risk of a major world depression, if such an occurrence is deemed highly probable, severely limits the international flow of private capital, particularly fixed-interest capital. At the time that the International Bank for Reconstruction and Development was established it is clear that such a contingency was taken into account. The Bank, in effect, considers that it was authorized to bear the risk of suspension of debt service payments in a world depression and the Bank has stated that it assumes this risk.[1] The risk of a major

[1] *The International Bank for Reconstruction and Development, 1946–1953* (Baltimore, 1954), p. 42.

world depression does not appear, at the present time, to be very great. The pressure to continue to maintain high levels of economic activity in the major economic centres and the history of the post-war period give some assurance even to the private investor abroad that future downturns in economic activity may be limited in depth and duration.

Let us then dismiss the risk of a major world depression, at least in so far as it affects the capacity of under-developed countries to service loans from such agencies as the International Bank. There are shorter-term risks which cannot be so easily dismissed, particularly in Latin America, where all countries export only a few primary commodities and where in many countries exports constitute a large percentage of the national product. These risks include temporary reductions in real export receipts resulting from minor recessions abroad, harvest failures at home, and sharp drops in export prices resulting from the return to more normal supply and demand situations, often accentuated in its impact on export receipts by accumulation of stocks in exporting countries.

A country which experiences great variability in its real export receipts — and this is characteristic of most of the Latin American countries — has a special problem in adjusting claims on total resources, saving, and foreign exchange. The performance of the country in meeting this problem is significant in judging its capacity to service foreign debt in two senses. First, a country which succeeds in maintaining some degree of stability (preferably along a rising trend) in domestic consumption and investment is likely to enjoy a sounder and more rapid growth over the longer term than a country which alternates between periods of rapidly increasing consumption and investment and periods of enforced curtailment of consumption and investment. Second, a country which is forced to curtail domestic consumption and investment rapidly is likely to experience difficulty in reconciling all of the competing claims on resources, including the claims of foreign creditors.

In the face of a considerable fluctuation in real export earnings, some degree of stability in consumption and domestic investment can be achieved by building up foreign exchange reserves and repaying external debts in periods when real export receipts are above the longer-term trend and by reducing reserves and incurring external debts in periods when real foreign exchange receipts are below the long-term trend. The policies that are required to pursue this course and the practical difficulties that may be encountered are well known.[1] The adoption of such compensatory policies is, nevertheless, advisable in countries eager to accelerate development and particularly so in countries wishing to attract foreign capital for this purpose.

Of course, if a country is willing to permit a reduction in export receipts to exert its full deflationary effect on domestic income and if foreign suppliers of capital expect such a policy to encounter no opposition in the future, creditors need not fear that a temporary reduction in foreign exchange receipts will jeopardize debt service claims. Only to the extent that extreme variability in domestic consumption and investment leads to an environment unfavourable to long-term development will such a non-compensatory policy be interpreted as an unfavourable course.

There is, moreover, a third method of dealing with fluctuations in real export earnings. This is the practice, if not policy, of stretching available resources to the limit, and beyond. This practice involves, in the extreme case, an expansionary fiscal and monetary policy in periods of abnormally high and rising export receipts, accompanied by the drawing down of international reserves and, in some cases, by the indiscriminate incurring of short- and medium-term external debts. Expansionary fiscal and monetary policies are continued when export receipts decline, but every effort is made to limit the decline in consumption and investment by rationing foreign exchange resources. Such a practice, experience has shown, strains to the utmost the policy-making and administrative capacities of even the best-equipped government. Consumption, investment, and all direct claims on export receipts are ultimately reduced, but in an inflationary environment in which all claimants to a share of the income produced fear that their share is in constant jeopardy. It is no wonder that the suppliers of foreign capital share this fear. Fortunately, there is evidence that this extreme policy of straining resources to the breaking point in economies where export receipts are subject to considerable fluctuation is being rejected by one country after another.

It must, however, be conceded that the policy of straining resources to the limit, if not beyond, is particularly attractive to, and it is widely practised by, countries enjoying a fast rate of growth and by countries aspiring to a fast rate of growth. This policy will now be considered as a part of the problem of the rôle of foreign capital in accelerating economic development, and of the conditions which

[1] See Bruno Brovedani, 'Latin American Medium Term Import Stabilization Policies and the Adequacy of Reserves', International Monetary Fund, *Staff Papers*, February 1955, vol. iv, No. 2.

determine the capacity of under-developed countries to service capital inflow in the long term.

III. DEBT SERVICE AND LONG-RUN GROWTH

The analysis so far has been restricted to the short-term balance of payments difficulties that may jeopardize external debt service claims, particularly in economies where exports are high relative to the gross national product and where the real value of export receipts is subject to substantial variation from year to year. The performance of an economy which is subject to volatile changes in adjusting competing claims on total resources, saving, and foreign exchange resources in the short term is important in judging its capacity to reconcile such claims over the long term. This is, however, only one part of the picture. While debt service claims do not vary with year to year changes in resources there is at least a presumption that the increased debt service claims arising out of capital inflows used for productive investment can be met over the long term from the increased income which the investment produces. Why should one be concerned over the long term with the competing claims on total resources, savings, and foreign exchange resources ?

The economist, educated in the tradition of classical economics, may be disposed to argue that the problem arises simply from the unwillingness of countries to follow the classical blueprint. On the other hand, he recognizes that the automatic adjustment process envisaged by the classical system may involve unemployment and shifts in income distribution which governments are today loathe to tolerate. It may also require reductions in the volume of investment which development-minded governments accept with great reluctance. The automatic adjustment process also presupposes an economy in which capital is invested in a manner which will promote external and internal equilibrium. While the classical blueprint was able to handle with ease the principles which private investment will and should follow to secure this result, it never developed operational guides for government investment or for the policies which government must adopt in the economic sphere if private investment does not respond properly to the guide-posts of changing relative prices. When we add to all this the short-term instabilities which the classical mechanism imposes on countries exporting a few primary products, it is no wonder that the classical adjustment mechanism is regarded with distrust. Thus, the classical adjustment mechanism frequently conflicts with some primary objectives of government policy and the blueprint for action which it provides is inadequate in several respects. At the same time, the experience of the last ten years, particularly in Latin America, indicates that a country which violates completely the doctrines of financial responsibility and the guide-posts of a functioning price system does so at its own peril, simultaneously increasing the risks faced by foreign creditors!

Thus deprived of the fully automatic adjustments of the classical economic system, how can we appraise the capacity of a country to reconcile the competing claims on total resources, saving, and foreign exchange resources ? What conditions must be fulfilled in order to develop a margin for debt service, and under what conditions can this margin be substantial ?

A minimum condition for developing even a small sustainable margin for debt service over the long term would appear to be some increase in *per capita* income. Even for countries where neither the populace nor the political leaders have experienced the revolution of aspirations which characterizes so many under-developed countries today, it may be assumed that the revolution is highly contagious. In countries where the revolution has not occurred and where it is not expected to occur for some time, the claims of foreign debt service may be met even in the absence of a rise in *per capita* income if the yield on the foreign capital invested is sufficient to permit complete repayment of debt in a relatively short period or to permit a very high rate of return on an equity investment. Additional assurance is provided if the foreign capital finances a project which itself produces not only the necessary surplus in local currency but also in foreign exchange. In such a case one need not even rely on the classical adjustment mechanism.

In countries where the revolution of aspirations has occurred — and I suspect this is true in varying degrees of virtually all Latin American, most South-east Asian, and some Middle Eastern countries — some increase in *per capita* income over the long term appears to be a necessary condition. Unless *per capita* income rises it will become increasingly difficult to reconcile the claims of some economic groups to a larger share of the national income and the aspirations of the populace for higher consumption levels. Debt service payments, particularly if they increase relative to national income, saving, or exports, are likely to be jeopardized. It seems clear that where the basic conditions for economic development and for a rise in *per capita* income are absent — even if investment is stepped up — either the rising aspirations will be frustrated or grants must be made available by other countries. The risks facing a supplier of foreign capital expecting a return are too great.

This case, however, need not detain us, for it seems quite evident that despite the high rate of population growth now prevailing in Latin America some growth in national *per capita* income will continue in virtually all countries in the area so long as the economic growth in the outside world continues. In seventeen countries in Latin America for which some data on growth are available for the post-war period it appears that six have enjoyed a rate of growth of *per capita* income of over 3 per cent., five of between 2 and 3 per cent., one between 1 and 2 per cent., and only five below 1 per cent. Even if some part of the growth of income which Latin America has enjoyed is directly and indirectly attributable to the effects of a favourable turn in the terms of trade, which may not last, growth in *per capita* income is likely to continue. In so far as Latin America is concerned, therefore, one is justified in being relatively optimistic. One can assume that in most countries economic growth will continue at a rate in excess of population growth. This conclusion is strengthened if the current trend towards modification of policies which have hampered the growth of the external sector continues.

What then imposes an upper limit on the amount of external service payment obligations which can be incurred over the long term ? To what extent can these limitations be determined by a case by case examination of the projects and programmes proposed for foreign financing and to what extent *must* they be determined by analysis of future economic prospects along aggregative lines ?

Starting with the assumption that a given rate of growth of *per capita* output is required to satisfy the aspirations of the populace for rising living standards and to resolve the competing claims on available resources, it is possible to set forth the conditions which must be fulfilled in order that both debt service claims and the income growth target be met. Assuming that the income growth target is in excess of what the country can achieve on the basis of domestic savings and that in order to achieve the target foreign capital inflows are necessary for a period, a model was constructed which yields these conditions.

The mathematical model provides a method for considering primarily the availability of, and claims on, total resources and saving in the context of economic growth. The availability of foreign exchange and the claims on foreign exchange do not enter explicitly, although we shall consider this aspect too in the discussion that follows.

The following variables were incorporated into the mathematical model :

p—projected rate of growth of population, assumed to be constant.

r'—target rate of growth of *per capita* real income, or output.

r—target rate of growth of aggregate real income or output.

K—projected incremental capital-output ratio, assuming a one-year lag between investment and income.

$S_o{}^a$—initial average savings ratio.

i—projected rate of return on foreign capital, for interest and dividends.

n—year after start of process in which foreign debt must be completely repaid, or alternatively reach a maximum, or alternatively year in which rate of growth of debt rises no faster than rate of growth of national income.

s'—required marginal savings ratio, with required growth of *per capita* savings in the numerator and target growth of *per capita* income in the denominator.

Formulae have been derived [1] employing these variables which permit us to appraise the conditions under which a country can develop a margin for debt service, and to determine how much the margin for debt service and the corresponding volume of capital inflow is influenced by the values which are assigned to the variables.

Certain characteristics of the definitions, assumptions, and structural relations incorporated in the model should be noted.

The following variables — the projected rate of growth of population, the target rate of growth of *per capita* and aggregate income, the incremental capital-output ratio, and the rate of return on foreign capital — are treated in the model as constants *over time*. This was done solely in the interests of mathematical simplicity. It is quite evident that they might well be expected to vary substantially over time. The values assigned to these variables may thus be looked upon as weighted averages of values which in fact vary over time.

The incremental capital-output ratio is an admittedly broad concept since it carries within it *all* of the factors affecting growth of output, not only investment. Included, for example, are the effects of the growth of the labour force (even though population growth as such is introduced as a separate variable for other purposes), the abundance or scarcity of national resources, technological progress, the availability of labour and managerial skills, and even changes in the terms of trade ! Our only excuse for using such a concept is that we have been unable as yet to develop any simple yet more appropriate mathematical concept in which the influence of investment is clearly separable from the influence of the other factors.

[1] See Appendices I and II.

The marginal savings ratio is treated in the formula as the derived variable or the dependent variable, that is, the variable whose value is derived after assigning values to the other variables. We could as well project the marginal savings ratio and treat *one* of the other variables, such as the incremental capital-output ratio, as derived or dependent. An important characteristic of the marginal savings ratio is that it is defined in *per capita* terms, as noted above. It can be argued that the growth of savings, to the extent that it is determined primarily by corporate savings, is more likely to be related to the growth of aggregate income than to the growth of *per capita* income. If this is the case, the concept employed here is awkward. On the other hand, the *per capita* concept is useful because it takes better account of the possibilities for saving by individual households and governments.

Let us now consider some of the implications to be derived in applying the formula which yields the marginal savings ratio required to meet debt service claims and investment requirements associated with different rates of income growth. It is perhaps obvious that all other things being equal the target rate of increase of *per capita* income, compared with the rate that can be achieved in the absence of foreign capital inflow, may be put at a higher level and a larger volume of foreign capital inflow is permitted when :

(1) the marginal savings ratio is higher ; [1]
(2) the incremental capital-output ratio is lower ;
(3) the rate of population increase is lower ;
(4) the required rate of return on foreign capital inflow is lower ;
(5) the degree of independence of foreign capital that must be achieved within a given time period is lower ;
(6) the time period in which a given degree of independence must be achieved is longer.

Some word of explanation may be required on the last two points and on the inter-relationships which may in fact exist among these variables. The independence criterion was introduced into the formula to reconcile two propositions on capital inflow. First, foreign capital inflows must be available on a net basis for some period of time if they are substantially to accelerate development. Second, it is impossible to assume that new capital inflows will be available to any one under-developed country in unlimited amounts for an indefinite period. Both of these propositions are incorporated

---

[1] This is not universally the case. When the initial savings ratio is less than Kp, which is equivalent to the rate of investment required to maintain *per capita* income, a higher rate of growth of income may actually permit some reduction in the marginal savings ratio.

into the model by judging the capacity of a country to service a series of additions to its external indebtedness extending over a number of years and by posing the requirement that the country must, within a prescribed period, achieve a complete or partial independence of foreign capital inflow. The proviso that a country must be capable of achieving complete independence of capital inflow within a defined period of time is, in a sense, analogous to the repayment requirement on a specific loan. While individual loans may have to be repaid, equity investment and the total of loans may not. Therefore, formulae have also been derived to show what is required to achieve a situation where *net* capital inflow is no longer required or where the rate of increase of net capital inflow is progressively reduced. It is particularly interesting to note that all three criteria — complete repayment of external debt, achievement of independence of further net capital inflow, and progressive reduction of the rate of net capital inflow — require exactly the same performance, except for the time period. To put it more exactly, a country which is capable of repaying debt completely in twenty-five years will have reached a maximum volume of external indebtedness somewhat earlier and will have reduced the rate of net capital inflow even earlier. In other words, one can state a more liberal repayment requirement either in terms of complete independence to be achieved over a long time period or a lesser degree of independence to be achieved over a shorter time period.

An additional note on the possible inter-relations among the variables is in order. In countries with abundant natural resources relative to the present size of population, a high rate of growth of population and consequently of the labour force may contribute to a low capital-output ratio. But with a high rate of population growth the growth of income must also be high in order to increase *per capita* income, and it may be necessary to undertake investments which tend to raise the capital-output ratio in order to maintain this high rate of growth of income. Moreover, the terms on which external capital is available may become less favourable if a greater volume of foreign capital, associated with a higher rate of growth of income, is to be attracted. Most important, the feasibility of achieving a required marginal savings ratio is likely to be positively associated with the rate of growth of *per capita* income.

Given the political pressures contributing to a rise in the government's current expenditures, and the economic pressures leading to a demand for increased real wages and increased levels of personal consumption ; and assuming that the capital-output ratio and the projected rate of return on foreign capital do not increase with higher rate of growth of income — it can be shown with this model that the likelihood of being able to service a larger volume of foreign capital is greater than the likelihood of servicing a smaller volume of capital inflow. This follows from the fact that very small increases in the required marginal savings ratio are associated with very large changes in *per capita* income, particularly in countries where population is increasing at a rapid rate. This is illustrated in the model where the required marginal savings ratio has been calculated for a country in which population is growing at a rate of $2\frac{1}{4}$ per cent. per year, the initial average savings ratio is $8\frac{1}{2}$ per cent., and the incremental capital-output ratio is 3·5 : 1 and is invariant with respect to the rate of growth of income.[1]

MARGINAL SAVINGS RATIO REQUIRED TO SERVICE CAPITAL INFLOW
ON CERTAIN ASSUMPTIONS

Target Rate of Growth of *per capita* Income	Required Marginal Savings Ratio	Capital Inflow as ratio of	
		Initial National Income	Aggregate Net Investment
$\frac{1}{2}\%$	0·23	0·23	0·07
1%	0·28	0·61	0·14
2%	0·31	1·42	0·22

Under these assumptions capital inflows over six times as large can be serviced with an increase in the marginal savings ratio from 0·23 to 0·31. Moreover, with the incremental capital-output ratio invariant with respect to the growth of income, the rate of growth of *per capita* consumption goes up from less than $\frac{1}{2}$ per cent. to $1\frac{1}{2}$ per cent.,[2] with a higher rate of growth of income and larger capital inflows. Clearly in this case it should be much easier for the country to reconcile the conflicting claims on resources, including both the claims represented by debt service payments, and investment required to maintain a continued rate of growth, with larger capital inflows than with smaller capital inflows. This case illustrates the highly favourable savings effect which a big push makes possible.

Now let us consider the risks which have been removed by our assumptions. If we assume that with a rate of growth of *per capita*

---

[1] Also, we assume that the required return on foreign capital is $4\frac{1}{2}$ per cent. and that external debt will reach a maximum in twenty-five years.

[2] Since a constant *per capita* savings ratio over time is assumed, the rate of increase in *per capita* consumption at the beginning is equal to $\dfrac{r'\,(l-s')}{l-S_o{}^a}$. The rate of growth of *per capita* consumption accelerates over time and approaches the rate of growth of *per capita* income.

income of 2 per cent. it will be possible to save 0·31 and no more of the increments, debt service claims of the magnitude associated with a 2 per cent. growth of *per capita* income will be met only if the capital-output ratio does not rise above 3·5. If the incremental capital-output ratio should rise to 4 : 1, more than a third of the increments in *per capita* income must be saved.[1] Also, the model assumes that net foreign capital inflows will be available to the country in question over a twenty-five-year period. If they were actually available for a shorter period and debt had to be completely repaid, for example, in twenty-five years, the required marginal savings ratio would exceed one-half. A still higher marginal savings ratio would be required if population growth was accelerated, or if the required rate of return on capital were increased. Clearly, the risks facing the supplier of capital in this highly artificial model are formidable!

This model demonstrates that it is possible to define — albeit in a highly mechanical way — the upper limits of debt service capacity in an environment where debt service claims are not necessarily given the highest priority. The practical significance of this model is limited by the difficulty of assigning realistic values to the variables, small but lasting changes in which are found to produce substantial differences in the final outcome. Nevertheless, the model illustrates that a creditor secures some assurance that debt service claims will be met if *per capita* income can be expected to increase at a fairly high rate. If, in addition, an environment is created which is favourable to a high marginal savings rate in the private sector and if government tax systems can be adapted to contribute to a high marginal savings rate in the public sector, the stage is set for accelerating economic development through foreign capital inflow. On the other hand, the model also indicates the great risks which the creditor faces wherever the politically, socially, and economically determined targets of income growth are set in an unrealistic fashion and then inflexibly adhered to.

The creditor's expectation of a high rate of growth of income is a favourable factor. If, however, the debtor country rigidly insists on maintaining — in the interests of a higher target rate of growth — a rate of investment which is beyond its capacity to finance, this frequently results in a lower capacity to service foreign debt and may even raise doubts as to whether the country will be willing to service foreign debt in times of strain. Even in this case, if the

---

[1] It should be noted that the incremental capital-output ratio in the post-war period has averaged close to 3 : 1 in Latin America. An increase to 4 : 1 is not likely in the short term but cannot be excluded if we look ahead twenty-five years.

higher rate of investment desired by the debtor country is associated with attainable income targets, why should not foreign capital inflows fill the gap as an alternative to eliminating the gap by reducing investment ? Whether the adjustment is more appropriately accomplished by increasing capital inflow or reducing investment depends on whether the income target associated with the higher rate of investment is feasible..

It is particularly in judging whether a target rate of growth of income is reasonable that it becomes important to consider the growth of foreign exchange availabilities and claims in the context of long-term growth. This model subsumes but does not illuminate these foreign exchange aspects of debt servicing capacity. It is, of course, clear that a country must produce sufficient additional goods for export or sufficient import substitutes, so that as income rises the increase in demand for imported goods (or for goods that used to be imported) plus the service on debt can be met from the available flow of foreign exchange. This directional aspect of economic growth has many dimensions, not just the foreign exchange dimension. Thus, form of investment and the composition of output must be adapted to the structure of demand sector by sector, if any given rate of increase of output is to be maintained over time. The foreign sector, however, can play a crucial rôle because foreign exchange is a highly flexible resource. It can be used to fill any temporary gaps in the adaptation of the domestic supply to changing domestic demand, gaps arising in some cases from improper directional policies. It can also be used to secure any of the goods and services which income growth requires but which the domestic economy can produce, at a given stage of development, only at a high or even prohibitive cost. A tight foreign exchange situation may arise because such a temporary gap has occurred or because of a structural deficiency, that is, the rate of growth of the economy is being pushed so fast that the economy cannot produce all of the particular kinds of goods and services, including exports, which the economy requires at this rate of growth.

The balance of payments deficits which recur periodically in countries seeking to accelerate their development rapidly may thus reflect not only the difficulties encountered in adjusting to year to year variations in the real value of exports ; they may reflect, not only the inability or unwillingness of the country to live within its means over the long term, they may also reflect an inability or unwillingness to produce within its means.

In this last case, the main problem is to determine whether a gap in the adaptation of domestic supply to changing domestic demand is temporary so that the target rate of growth of income can be achieved if foreign capital inflows are increased, or whether the gap reflects deficiencies in national resources, labour skills, and management abilities upon which the projected rate of growth also depends. If the gap is temporary and will be corrected fairly quickly by market forces without government action, there is no reason for concern. If, however, the gap is itself attributable to government policies which, for example, penalize the growth of the export sector, or if the gap reflects the inability of the economy to produce the types of goods and services which are required to sustain the rate of growth, corrective action is required. The country must reconcile itself to a lower rate of growth or, if the gap is attributable to government policy, it must change those policies which influence the direction of resource use. It has no alternative but to reduce the rate of growth if the more fundamental limitation is present.

IV. Conclusion

Let us now return to our original question. To what extent are the limitations on the amount of external debt service obligation which can be assumed over the long term subject to determination by a case by case examination of the various investment projects and programmes proposed for foreign financing and to what extent must these limitations be determined by some kind of aggregate analysis of future economic prospects ?

It seems clear that in countries where the revolution of aspirations has already occurred or where it may be expected to occur the case by case approach is not sufficient. Some type of aggregative analysis of future economic prospects is essential.

In the case of many Latin American countries, where a rapid rate of growth has been achieved in recent years, it may, however, be possible to move towards greater reliance on case by case examination of projects and programmes. The dynamic character of these economies is being demonstrated and case by case examination of investment projects and programmes should itself reveal to some extent potentialities for future economic growth. However, unless many of the countries in this area show a better capacity to adjust to short-term variations in available resources by the use of appropriate monetary and fiscal policy, foreign investors will tend to discount heavily the potentialities uncovered by investigations of investment projects and programmes. Perhaps part of the difficulty of adjusting to short-term variations will be removed as tax structures are improved and governments become able to discharge their modern-day responsibilities without inflationary excesses. Moreover, in some countries there is already a growing appreciation of the damage produced by inflation, and the example of growth with stability may prove even more attractive than the example of growth with inflation. The continued expansion of the world economy is already producing a revaluation of government policies on the use of resources, particularly as between exports and the home market. Reliance upon improving terms of trade to increase real export earnings is giving way to a search for ways to increase the volume of exports.

If a greater degree of financial responsibility is firmly established as a conscious policy and if positive measures, including proper exchange rate systems, are taken to encourage the economy to produce the types of goods and services which are required to sustain growth rates, it may be possible to secure some of the advantages of the classical mechanism of foreign investment. Foreign investors may feel less compelled to centre their attention on general uncertainties concerning the debtor country's economy and more able to concentrate on the merits of the projects and programmes proposed for financing.

APPENDIX I[1]

DERIVATION OF DEBT FORMULA (FORMULA A)
DERIVATION OF S_n

Symbols:

Primes (') denote *per capita*. Subscript ($_n$) refers to time-period ; first period denoted by subscript ($_o$).

S_n — aggregate domestic savings.
$S_o{}^a$ — initial average savings ratio.
Y — national income (geographical).
P — population.
p — rate of increase of population, a constant.
r' — target rate of increase of *per capita* income, a constant.
r — target rate of increase of aggregate income, a constant.
s' — *per capita* marginal savings ratio, a constant.

Thus by definition :

1.0
$$Y_n = Y_n{}' P_n.$$
$$S_n = S_n{}' P_n.$$
$$r' = \frac{Y_n{}' - Y'_{n-1}}{Y'_{n-1}},$$

---

[1] The author wishes to acknowledge the assistance of Mr. Charles Goor and Mr. Kenneth Bohr.

$$\text{or}\quad r'Y'_{n-1} = Y_n' - Y'_{n-1}.$$

$$s' = \frac{S_n' - S'_{n-1}}{Y_n' - Y'_{n-1}}.$$

Then, substituting the above in the denominator,

1.1
$$s' = \frac{S_n' - S'_{n-1}}{r'Y'_{n-1}}.$$

From compound interest formula :

$$Y_n' = Y_o'(1+r')^n.$$
$$P_n = P_o(1+p)^n.$$

Then, from 1.1 :

$$s'r'Y'_{n-1} = S_n' - S'_{n-1}.$$
$$S_n' = S'_{n-1} + s'r'Y'_{n-1}.$$

1.2
$$S_n' = S'_{n-1} + s'r'Y_o'(1+r')^{n-1}.$$

For initial period by definition $S_o' = S_o{}^a Y_o'.$

From definition for $S_n(1.0)$ and from 1.2 :

$$S_o = S_o{}^2 Y_o'P_o.$$
$$S_1 = (S_o{}^a Y_o' + s'r'Y_o')P_o(1+p).$$
$$S_2 = [S_o{}^a Y_o' + s'r'Y_o' + s'r'Y_o'(1+r')]P_o(1+p)^2.$$
$$S_3 = [S_o{}^a Y_o' + s'r'Y_o' + s'r'Y_o'(1+r') + s'r'Y_o'(1+r')^2]P_o(1+p)^3.$$

After factoring out $Y_o'P_o$, the general expression S_n becomes,

$$S_n = (Y_o'P_o)(1+p)^n[S_a{}^o + s'r' + s'r'(1+r') + \ldots + s'r'(1+r')^{n-1}].$$

Using formula for summing geometric progression and substituting Y_o for $Y_o'P_o$,

$$= Y_o(1+p)^n\left[S_o{}^a + s'r'\frac{(1+r')^n - 1}{r'}\right].$$

1.3
$$S_n = Y_o(1+p)^n\{S_o{}^a + s'[(1+r')^n - 1]\}.$$

By definition,
$$(1+r')(1+p) = 1+r.$$

1.4 Thus, in 1.3,
$$(1+p)^n[(1+r')^n - 1] = (1+r)^n - (1+p)^n.$$

Substituting 1.4 in 1.3, we obtain :

1.5
$$S_n = Y_o(1+p)^n S_o{}^a - Y_o s'[(1+r)^n - (1+p)^n].$$
$$S_n = Y_o\{(1+p)^n S_o{}^a + s'[(1+r)^n - (1+p)^n]\}.$$

DERIVATION OF I_n

I — Net domestic investment required to secure target rate of increase of income.

K — Incremental capital-output ratio.

By definition :
$$K = \frac{I_n}{Y_{n+1} - Y_n}.$$
$$I_n = K(Y_{n+1} - Y_n).$$

1.6 Since $Y_n = Y_0(1+r)^n$, from 1.6,
$$I_n = KY_0[(1+r)^{n\pm1}(1+r)^n] = KY_0(1+r)^n(1+r-1).$$
1.7 $\quad I_n = Kr Y_0(1+r)^n.$

DERIVATION OF F_n

F — Excess of gross capital inflows over all service payments on foreign debt (interest, dividends, and amortization) required to secure target rate of increase of income. F is thus the gap between domestic investment requirements and domestic savings, equivalent to the required surplus in the balance of payments on capital account, under the geographical concept of national income.

$$F_n = I_n - S_n.$$

Substituting 1.7 and 1.5, we get

$$F_n = Kr Y_0(1+r)^n - Y_0\{(1+p)^n S_0{}^a + s'[(1+r)^n - (1+p)^n]\},$$
$$= Y_0\Big(Kr(1+r)^n - \{(1+p)^n S_0{}^a + s'[(1+r)^n - (1+p)^n]\}\Big).$$
1.8 $\quad F_n = Y_0[(Kr - s')(1+r)^n - (S_0{}^a - s')(1+p)^n].$

DERIVATION OF D_n

D — Foreign debt at the end of each year.
i — Required rate of return on foreign debt, a constant.
X — Interest and dividend payments on foreign debt.

We assume that interest and dividend payments begin in the second year and that interest and dividend payments for any given year are computed from the debt at the end of the preceding year — or $X_n = iD_{n-1}.$

Since debt is the sum of the required surplus in the balance of payments on capital account in the present year, interest and dividend payments on the volume of debt outstanding at the end of the previous year, and the volume of debt at the end of the previous year, we get

$$D_n = F_n + X_n + D_{n-1}$$
$$= F_n + i(D_{n-1}) + D_{n-1}.$$
1.9 $\quad D_n = (1+i)D_{n-1} + F_n.$

It is assumed that no debt is outstanding at the beginning of the first year. Hence, given 1.9 :

$$D_0 = F_0.$$
$$D_1 = F_0(1+i) + F_1.$$
$$D_2 = F_0(1+i)^2 + F_1(1+i) + F_2.$$
$$D_3 = F_0(1+i)^3 - F_1(1+i)^2 + F_2(1+i) + F_3.$$
2.0 $\quad D_n = F_0(1+i)^n + F_1(1+i)^{n-1} + F_2(1+i)^{n-2} + \ldots + F_n.$

From 1.8, $F_n = Y_0[(Kr - s')(1 + r)^n - (S_0{}^a - s')(1 + p)^n]$.

Let : $Kr - s' = A : S_0{}^a - s' = B$.

Therefore, from 2.0, we get

$$D_0 = Y_0[A(1 + r)^0 - B(1 + p)^0].$$
$$D_1 = Y_0\{(1 + i)[A(1 + r)^0 - B(1 + p)^0] + A(1 + r) - B(1 + p)]\}.$$
$$D_2 = Y_0\{(1 + i)^2[A(1 + r)^0 - B(1 + p)^0] + (1 + i)[A(1 + r)$$
$$- B(1 + p)] + A(1 + r)^2 - B(1 + p)^2\}.$$

2.1 $D_n = Y_0\{(1 + i)^n[A(1 + r)^0 - B(1 + p)^0] + (1 + i)^{n-1}[A(1 + r) - B(1 + p)]$
$$+ (1 + i)^{n-2}[A(1 + r)^2 - B(1 + p)^2] + \ldots + A(1 + r)^n - B(1 + p)^n\}.$$

Thus, we have in 2.1 two geometric progressions, the first, with the 'A' term is added, and the second, with the 'B' term is subtracted ; each term in turn has two geometric series which are multiplied.

2.2 $D_n = Y_0 A[(1 + i)^n(1 + r)^0 + (1 + i)^{n-1}(1 + r) + (1 + i)^{n-2}(1 + r)^2 + \ldots$
$$+ (1 + i)^0(1 + r)^1] - Y_0 B[(1 + i)^n(1 + p)^0 + (1 + i)^{n-1}(1 + p)$$
$$+ (1 + i)^{n-2}(1 + p)^2 + \ldots + (1 + i)^0(1 + p)^n].$$

In both progressions the first term is $(1 + i)^n$; in the first progression the common ratio is $\dfrac{1 + r}{1 + i}$ and in the second progression the common ratio is $\dfrac{1 + p}{1 + i}$.

We assume here that r is not equal to i.[1]

Thus, from the formula for summing a geometric progression, when $i \neq r$, 2.2 becomes

2.3 $$D_n = Y_0 \left\{ A(1 + i)^n \left[\frac{\left(\dfrac{1 + r}{1 + i}\right)^{n+1} - 1}{\dfrac{1 + r}{1 + i} - 1} \right] - B(1 + i)^n \left[\frac{\left(\dfrac{1 + p}{1 + i}\right)^{n+1} - 1}{\dfrac{1 + p}{1 + i} - 1} \right] \right\}.$$

Simplifying, we obtain,

$$D_n = Y_0 \left\{ A\left[\frac{(1 + r)^{n+1} - (1 + i)^{n+1}}{r - i} \right] - B\left[\frac{(1 + p)^{n+1} - (1 + i)^{n+1}}{p - i} \right] \right\}.$$

Substituting for A and B,

$$= Y_0 \left\{ (Kr - s')\left[\frac{(1 + r)^{n+1} - (1 + i)^{n+1}}{r - i} \right] - (S_0{}^a - s')\left[\frac{(1 + p)^{n+1} - (1 + i)^{n+1}}{p - i} \right] \right\}.$$

Or, if the first year is denoted by the subscript 1 instead of 0,

2.4   Formula A [2]

---

[1] If $i = r$ the 'A' term becomes $nA(1 + r)^n$.

[2] If $i = r$, we use the above for the A term and get

$$D_n = Y_1 \left\{ n(Kr - s')(1 + r)^{n-1} - (S_0{}^a - s')\left[\frac{(1 + r)^n - (1 + p)^n}{r - p} \right] \right\}.$$

$$D_n = Y_{\scriptscriptstyle\mathrm{I}}\left\{(Kr - s')\left[\frac{(1+r)^n - (1+i)^n}{r-i}\right] - (S_o^a - s')\left[\frac{(1+p)^n - (1+i)^n}{p-i}\right]\right\}.$$

APPENDIX II

DERIVATION OF REQUIRED MARGINAL SAVINGS RATIO

THE required marginal savings ratio is derived by imposing a prescribed constraint upon the volume of debt in a future year and solving Formula A, subject to this constraint, in terms of s'. The following solution is for the common case, where $i \neq r$.

From Appendix I we have Formula A (2.5):

$$D_n = Y_{\scriptscriptstyle\mathrm{I}}\left\{(Kr - s')\left[\frac{(1+r)^n - (1+i)^n}{r-i}\right] - (S_o^a - s')\left[\frac{(1+p)^n - (1+i)^n}{p-i}\right]\right\}$$

(When first year is denoted by subscript $_{\scriptscriptstyle\mathrm{I}}$.)

A. Debt to reach zero in nth year :

Denoting the first year by $_{\scriptscriptstyle\mathrm{I}}$, if debt is to reach zero at the end of n years, D_n must equal zero. Placing $D_n = _o$, we solve for s'.

$$Y_{\scriptscriptstyle\mathrm{I}}\left\{(Kr - s')\left[\frac{(1+r)^n - (1+i)^n}{r-i}\right](S_o^a - s')\left[\frac{(1+p)^n - (1+i)^n}{p-i}\right]\right\} = 0.$$

Simplifying and rearranging terms, we get

Formula I:

$$s' = \frac{S_o^a\left[\dfrac{(1+p)^n - (1+i)^n}{p-i}\right] - Kr\left[\dfrac{(i+r)^n - (1+i)^n}{r-i}\right]}{\dfrac{(1+p)^n - (1+i)^n}{p-i} - \dfrac{(1+r)^n - (1+i)^n}{r-i}}.$$

B. Debt to reach absolute maximum in nth year.

Denoting the first year by $_{\scriptscriptstyle\mathrm{I}}$, for debt to reach a maximum at the end of n years, the increase debt between the year n and $n+1$ must equal zero. Placing $D_n + 1 - D_n = _o$, we solve for s'.

$$Y_{\scriptscriptstyle\mathrm{I}}\left\{\frac{Kr - s'}{r-i}[(1+r)^{n+\mathrm{I}} - (1+i)^{n+\mathrm{I}}] - \frac{S_o^a - s'}{p-i}[(1+p)^{n+\mathrm{I}} - (1+i)^{n+\mathrm{I}}]\right.$$
$$\left. - \left[\frac{Kr - s'}{r-i}[(1+r)^n - (1+i)^n] - \frac{S_o^a - s'}{p-i}[(1+p)^n - (1+i)^n]\right]\right\} = 0.$$

Simplifying and rearranging terms, we get

Formula II:

$$s' = \frac{S_o^a\left\{i\left[\dfrac{(1+p)^n-(1+i)^n}{p-i}\right]+(1+p)^n\right\}-Kr\left\{i\left[\dfrac{(1+r)^n-(1+i)^n}{r-i}\right]+(1+r)^n\right\}}{i\left[\dfrac{(1+p)^n-(1+i)^n}{p-i}\right]+(1+p)^n-\left\{i\left[\dfrac{(1+r)^n-(1+i)^n}{r-i}\right]+(1+r)^n\right\}}$$

C. Ratio of external debt to national income to reach maximum in nth year.

For ratio of debt to national income to reach maximum at the end of n years, the rate of increase of debt between the nth and the $n+1$ year must equal the rate of increase of national income.

Thus $\dfrac{D_{n+1}}{D_n}=1+r$. From Formula A (2.5),

$$\frac{Y_1\left\{(Kr-s')\left[\dfrac{(1+r)^{n+1}-(1+i)^{n+1}}{r-i}\right]-(S_o^a-s')\left[\dfrac{(1+p)^{n+1}-(1+i)^{n+1}}{p-i}\right]\right\}}{Y_1\left\{(Kr-s')\left[\dfrac{(1+r)^n-(1+i)^n}{r-i}\right]-(S_o^a-s')\left[\dfrac{(1+p)^n-(1+i)^n}{p-i}\right]\right\}}=1+r.$$

Simplifying and rearranging terms, we get

Formula III:

$$s'=\frac{S_o^a[(1+p)^n(p-r)+(1+i)^n(r-i)]-Kr[(p-i)(1+i)^n]}{[(1+p)^n(p-r)+(1+i)^n(r-i)]-(p-i)(1+i)^n}.$$

COMMENTS ON DR. ALTER'S PAPER

BY

OTAVIO G. DE BULHÕES
University of Brazil

I. Transfer Risks and the Gold Standard

In my opinion, it is essential to make it clear that, although the gold standard guarantees the transfer of the returns on foreign capital invested in under-developed countries, it by no means ensures the profitability of foreign investment. I cannot, therefore, understand why the author lays so much stress on the gold standard as a means of guaranteeing the foreign capital invested in a given country. At the end of the nineteenth and the beginning of the twentieth century, a series of loans were floated in London, Paris, and New York, under which borrowers bound themselves inflexibly. This inflexibility had no connection whatsoever with the gold standard. The various borrowing governments undertook a solemn, legal obligation to pay their various foreign creditors in the latter's own currencies, whether sterling, francs, or dollars.

II. Case by Case Examination a Sufficient Guide to Investment

The history of finance also reveals that a good many such loans were not guided by any productive criterion. Their purpose was either to cover the increase of consumption, to balance budgetary deficits resulting from current expenditure, or, alternatively, to support the price of export products as in the case of the coffee valorization loans contracted by Brazil. When the World Bank was founded at Bretton Woods, an attempt was made to prevent borrowing for unproductive purposes by linking investments directly and exclusively to economic activities. Hence the policy of associating each loan with a specific project.

From the investor's point of view, individual analysis of each projected enterprise with a view to determining its profitability is in itself an adequate guarantee because interest and amortization represent a small fraction of the aggregate return which the enterprise will produce. Even when the projected enterprise for which a loan is needed calls for substantial financing, as is the case with external economies, the same criterion is relevant since the social marginal income will exceed the amount of debt service.

III. Transfer Risks and Monetary Policy

It may be argued that while such a guarantee may be adequate for domestic investors, it is insufficient for foreign creditors because, in addition to the usual risks, foreign creditors run the risk that there will be a depreciation in the foreign exchange rate of the borrowing country. Balance of payments disequilibria stem rather more frequently from monetary policy than from any other cause. Nowadays one frequently observes a propensity to import which is excessive compared with the amount of foreign exchange provided by the export of goods. One often sees, also, a substantial outflow of foreign exchange to meet expenses incurred by tourists abroad and an equally substantial outflow of saving to be invested in foreign countries. Such situations reflect the lack of a proper monetary policy and by no means imply that foreign borrowing has been excessive in relation to the growth of marginal income. Balance of payments difficulties have not arisen from past foreign investment, nor is there any reason to believe that in the near future the inflow of capital from abroad is likely to reach a level that will make its service excessive in relation to national income.

The author does not make a direct analysis of transfer risks. In other words, he considers that this is a matter of secondary importance, provided that there is a continuous increase of national *per capita* income, and provided further that an adequate ratio between foreign debt service and the increase in national *per capita* income is maintained. Now to attain such a ratio or proportion it is not essential to examine saving as a whole. Case by case examination of specific projects provides the most desirable formula. The only overall study needed is that of the monetary and financial situation of the borrowing country. This is fundamentally a short period analysis which falls within the sphere of the International Monetary Fund. It is not a problem of long term financial agencies, such as the International Bank.

IV. PRODUCTIVITY THE RELEVANT GUIDE FOR INVESTMENT

The rate of growth of national income is obviously incapable of extrapolation over the long run, particularly when the initial phase is characterized by marked inflation. During such a phase, numerous investments may be made, each of which increases national income without strengthening the all-important foundations for the country's progress. Statistics may reveal an increase in real income without a corresponding increase in capital formation. On the contrary, past investments may be being wasted.

During a prolonged inflationary process, one observes not only a decline of net investment but even disinvestment in railways, ports, canals, and many other public utilities, particularly in those fields where profits can only be reaped in the distant future such as, for example, the building of laboratories, the execution of research programmes, and education. Concomitantly, one notes a substantial upward trend of investment in buildings, houses, factories for production of consumer goods, and the provision of urban services, such as hotels, insurance companies, and innumerable other activities which increase the national income but which fail, for the most part, to stimulate any improvement in productivity. There can be no question that it is the raising of productivity that enables the rate of growth of the national income to surpass the rate of growth of population. An increase in productivity should be the main guide of the case by case examination of projects seeking foreign loans.

FURTHER COMMENTS ON DR. ALTER'S PAPER

BY

DAVID L. GROVE
Bank of America

To my mind the most interesting part of Alter's paper is the section on debt service in the context of long-run growth. The models developed there can play a most useful rôle in allowing one to isolate and relate correctly the variables relevant to the problem of debt service in a growth context. I think the use of the models could have been more fruitful, however. Specifically, it would be interesting to trace out the probable directions which the variables may be expected to take through time as a function of the development process. The importance of this problem is obvious. From the standpoint of ease of debt service, some values of the variables are more desirable than others. It is important to know, therefore, what values the variables are likely to take over time, and what their interrelations are likely to be under varying policy conditions and at different stages of development. It is important to know also which of the variables, if any, are subject to policy manipulation. These would provide leverage for guiding the development process so that the relatively non-manipulable variables will follow optimum paths. While Alter could not be expected to go into this problem to any great extent, recognition of its importance and some tentative discussion of its dimensions would be desirable.

It is worth pointing out that Alter's models do not include one of the crucial variables in the saving-investment equation, namely replacement investment. Alter states that his model 'provides a method for considering primarily the availability of, and claims on, total resources and savings in the context of economic growth'. Now the gross national product represents the availability of total resources. The claims against it consist of consumption, net domestic investment, replacement investment and the net export balance. Alter takes account of all of these except replacement investment. This lack is, perhaps, not fatal since in under-developed areas the capital stock is small and replacement requirements correspondingly slight relative to the need for net additions to the stock. As development proceeds, however, and the capital stock grows, replacement requirements are of increasing relative importance. In a developed economy like that of the United States, replacement takes over 60 per cent. of total gross investment. If the capital stock is to be maintained, replacement investment has a first priority claim on the resources of an economy. Therefore, it cannot be ignored, particularly in the context of Alter's problem.

The explicit introduction of replacement investment into Alter's model would, of course, change the numerical results yielded by the model, all other things equal. In general this change would tend to raise the saving required to provide for a given amount of debt service. But, perhaps more important, it could also change the ordering of optimum paths of development. This follows from the fact that replacement requirements and required net additions to the capital stock (determined by the marginal capital-output ratio and the rate of income growth) may be moving in opposite directions. Thus a development path which appears most favourable when looking only at net savings may seem less favourable when replacement requirements are taken into account.

I have one final, and minor, criticism. Throughout this paper Alter refers to dividend and interest payments as though they were identical from the standpoint of debt service. Of course they are not, and the differences are sufficiently great to make their separate treatment important.

DISCUSSION OF DR. ALTER'S PAPER

THE discussion of Dr. Alter's paper developed initially around the issue of project analysis *v.* overall analysis. Later it branched out to include questions relating to the transfer problem, the importance of *per capita* income growth as an index of debt service capacity, and the internal consistency of Dr. Alter's model.

PROJECT ANALYSIS

Dr. Bulhões led the attack upon the overall analysis proposed by Dr. Alter with a strong argument in favour of single project analysis. The rate of income growth, he said, had little to do with whether or not a project was credit-worthy. If it was, the only adverse circumstance that could be discovered by overall analysis was the existence of a balance of payments problem. If this existed, however, it was a short-run phenomenon attributable to faulty monetary and fiscal policy. It could be eliminated by a change in policy, much as a sound balance of payments situation existing at the time of the loan could later be destroyed by bad policies. Project analysis therefore was all that could and should be undertaken.

Dr. Alter commented that, in view of the difficulty of any kind of lending to countries with balance of payments problems, Dr. Bulhões' approach tended to create two groups of countries : those with sound balances of payments, which were eligible for loans subject to project examination, and those with weak balances of payments, which were ineligible for any sort of loan. This criterion appeared to be more rigorous with respect to the ineligible countries than any he himself had meant to apply.

Professor Hirschman likewise sought an escape from the simple alternative of overall *v.* project approach. Neither seemed satisfactory to him, yet he doubted the value of old-fashioned credit rules of thumb, such as that debt service should not exceed 10 per cent of external earning. He concluded that a lending agency like the International Bank should try to identify potential 'growing-points' and place its funds there, leaving other matters to 'a wise and salutary neglect'.

Professor Brahmananda, on the other hand, felt that the analysis ought to be expanded to comprise the condition not only of the borrowing country, but also that of the countries with which it maintained close economic relations. Only in that way, he argued, could the economic outlook of the borrowing country really be established.

Some of the comments on this topic seemed sceptical more of Dr. Alter's detailed analystical model than of the principle of overall appraisal as such. Dr. Alter seemed to be in agreement with this more generalized approach.

TRANSFER PROBLEM

Dr. Bulhões had implied that the transfer problem was a matter of good monetary and fiscal policy. Various other speakers, on the other hand, stressed the possibility of a structural transfer problem. It was agreed that conceptually a country living within its means, *i.e.* maintaining a surplus of total resources over domestic uses, and of saving over investment, was bound to generate a corresponding surplus for debt service. But this did not, of course, dispose of the concrete problem. *Dr. Campos* and *Dr. Domingues* referred to the case of Brazil and Argentina, respectively, as demonstrating the existence of transfer problems in countries with strong domestic economies. *Dr. Kafka* reminded the group that this discussion seemed to lead back to the classical debates between Keynes and Ohlin on reparation problems, when Ohlin had forgotten the price effect and Keynes the income effect.

Dr. Alter questioned the propriety of saying that a country was doing well incomewise and savingwise, when its balance of payments position was fundamentally bad. In the short run, such a contrast might exist, and the country in question might appear to be suffering from nothing worse than a balance of payments difficulty within an otherwise healthy economy. In the longer run, this would reveal itself as fallacious. If the balance of payments problem was structural, it would show itself to be also an income problem. For either the lack of foreign exchange would begin to affect adversely the country's general economy, or desperate measures would have to be taken to push exports, deteriorating the terms of trade and otherwise affecting income. In the longer run, therefore, his income criterion included the balance of payments criterion.

IMPORTANCE OF PER CAPITA INCOME GROWTH AS A LOAN CRITERION

Various speakers pointed out that Dr. Alter's entire model hinged upon the concept of a minimum *per capita* income growth as a criterion of credit worthiness, and questions were raised whether the concept could bear this burden. *Professor Brahmananda* asked whether *per capita* income or *per capita* consumption was the more relevant criterion. This distinction might become important in countries where the government was imposing forced saving upon the population. Income growth might be quite satisfactory, but the temper of the people still not favourable to the fulfil ment of loan contracts.

Professor Wallich noted that ideally the criterion ought to be not absolute income growth, but growth in relation to the increase in expectations. During a process of industrialization, expectations sometimes rose faster than income. He also observed that in view of the many circumstances that affected a country's loan performance, it seemed doubtful that *per capita* income growth could account for more than a modest fraction of the total complex of causation. In the past, countries with little or no *per capita* growth had met their obligations because that was the climate of the times, or because they expected new loans.

Dr. Adler suggested that the income growth criterion would in practice have to be replaced by an appraisal that took into account a large variety of factors. Among these he listed : (1) the nature of the project ; (2) the general prospects of the debtor country, including factors like the saving ratio and capital-output ratio which figured prominently in the Alter model ; (3) the fiscal and monetary policies pursued which reflected the 'competing claims on resources' emphasized by Dr. Alter ; (4) the balance of payments outlook, and (5) the past debt record, especially performance during difficult periods.

Dr. Kafka argued that a quantitative approach in such matters was doing it the hard way and probably doomed to failure. As a practical matter, the lender would do well to limit himself to qualitative analysis. Such analysis, however, was implicit in good project analysis, so that there was no need for overall analysis in addition to project analysis.

Professor Schultz stressed the importance of political factors and pointed to the great difficulty of linking them up with an economic analysis.

Dr. Alter, in replying to those points, agreed that many factors other than income growth were important, and might counsel against a loan. But he upheld his criterion on the grounds that without some evidence of prospects for income growth, even a whole range of otherwise favourable factors would not offer a sound basis for lending, and that with a high rate of income growth in prospect the capacity, though not necessarily the willingness, of a country to service external debt was higher.

CONSISTENCY OF THE MODEL

Opinions were divided about the internal consistency of the model. *Professor Hirschman* observed that minor changes in the variables employed by the model produced large variations in indicated loan capacity. In practice, a lender could never hope to reach firm conclusions with respect to even the approximate magnitude of a country's borrowing capacity by use of the model which, therefore, could not be regarded as having operational value.

Professors Schultz and *Ellis* countered that Dr. Alter had stated all the necessary qualifications, and that after all this was a model and not a statement of fact. *Professor Ellis* nevertheless expressed concern over the possibility that a large volume of foreign loans, such as indicated by the model under certain favourable conditions, might prove inflationary. The resulting high rate of investment, moreover, might increase the lender's risk because it increased the danger of misallocation.

Dr. Alter clarified the rôle of the capital-output ratio in the model by saying that a low ratio was 'favourable' only in so far as it applied to the entire economy. With regard to a particular project, or sector, the ratio depended upon many factors and nothing could be said about its being good or bad. Moreover, even for the entire economy a low ratio was desirable only over a long period of time, but not at any particular moment.

Professor Wallich questioned the consistency of the model by pointing to the conclusion which emerges from it that debtors are creditworthy only if they reduce their rate of borrowing over time. This, as Dr. Alter had said, meant that all borrowers sooner or later were moving towards a position of net exporters of capital. The logical implication of this trend seemed to be that today's creditor countries, principally the United States, must eventually reduce their rate of lending and later become net importers of capital. While such a condition might come about as a result of some catastrophe, it could scarcely be envisaged as the logical end of a normal evolution. In fact, the behaviour of a borrowing country's debt level depended not only on its own evolution, but also on that of others, and was subject to the familiar conditions governing demand and supply in the capital markets.

Dr. Alter and *Dr. Adler* rejected this allegation of internal inconsistency of the model on the grounds that while today's debtor countries might eventually become creditors, this did not mean that today's lenders would have to become debtors. There would always be new countries which would begin to borrow.

Chapter 7

FINANCIAL INSTITUTIONS AND ECONOMIC DEVELOPMENT

BY

JAVIER MÁRQUEZ

Centro de Estudios Monetarios Latinoamericanos

I. INTRODUCTION

THIS paper deals mainly with the structure of Latin American financial systems and the appropriateness of these systems for fostering economic development. Financial institutions are appraised with reference to the gathering and employment of funds. The respective rôles of private institutions and of government institutions and government controls are discussed briefly in connection with the employment of funds.

Although this paper refers to Latin American countries in general, specific conditions in Mexico have unavoidably influenced many of the statements made. Hence, the generality of some statements may be queried.

Finally, although financial institutions are assumed to be important for economic development, no judgment is implied regarding the importance of financial institutions relative to other institutions or other aspects of economic policy.

II. SOURCES OF FUNDS OF VARIOUS FINANCIAL INSTITUTIONS

1. *Total Amount of Funds*

In some Latin American countries there are a few financial institutions, mainly foreign banks, which hold substantial excess reserves. These institutions are exceptional. Even in those Latin American countries where such institutions exist, lending by other institutions operating on the basis of rediscounts at the central bank far exceeds any excess reserves. The basic problem of Latin American financial institutions is a shortage of non-inflationary funds. At the prevailing rates of interest they cannot obtain as much as they could use.

With a few exceptions, the proportion of the total supply of funds which finds its way into the hands of Latin American financial institutions is fairly low compared with more developed countries. What determines this proportion and what determines which institutions get the funds ?

Obviously, the proportion of funds which finds its way into the hands of financial institutions is largely a function of the level of incomes. In countries where incomes are low, savings are low because people seldom earn more than is absolutely necessary for day to day expenditure. Second, this proportion depends on willingness to surrender funds to financial institutions ; nowadays this is a problem which is important only in those regions where incomes are lowest. Third, this proportion is influenced by the extent to which cheques are acceptable for current payments. On the whole, however, lack of education and of convenient savings outlets and instruments and fear of a decline in the value of money have probably been more important in determining the direction of investment and the type of institution to which funds are entrusted than in determining the total volume of funds that are entrusted to financial institutions.

2. *Sight Deposits*

Private financial institutions seem to have accomplished all that could be expected in gathering the liquid working balances of individuals and corporations. These institutions may even pay high rates of interest in countries where such a practice is not legally allowed. They compete with one another for depositors — in some countries this competition is cut-throat — by lowering the charges for banking facilities, by multiplying the number of their branches, by advertising and so forth. Thus, although in most countries there is a striking contrast between the success of private institutions and the lack of success of public institutions in gathering sight deposits,[1] there seems to be no reluctance to hold sight deposits.

3. *Savings Deposits*

The efforts of banks to induce people to hold savings deposits have been a function of the banks' freedom of action with respect to savings deposits, the rate of interest which banks have to pay on these deposits, the level of legal reserves required against savings deposits as compared with the level of reserves required against

---

[1] Uruguay and Brazil — especially if the Banco do Brasil is considered to be an official institution — are exceptions to this generalization.

sight deposits, and the total volume of sight deposits. The relative scarcity of sight deposits and the relative freedom of action which banks enjoy with regard to savings deposits have probably been the main inducements leading banks to seek savings accounts.

Their success in attracting savings deposits has been influenced to some extent by the rate of inflation but not as greatly as might have been expected. A steady rise in savings deposits is common, in countries with a fairly high rate of inflation, even in countries which do not have exchange controls, and indicates that small savers are generally trapped by a slow inflation. It is only in countries like Chile or Bolivia which have strong inflation that one finds stagnation or an actual decline in the volume of savings deposits. Here, it must be pointed out that, with a few exceptions, it is usually the commercial banks operating through specialized departments, rather than official institutions, which serve as gatherers of savings deposits.[1]

4. *Mortgage Bonds and* Cédulas

I come now to a discussion of those savings instruments which, in contrast to both sight deposits and savings deposits, are both inflation-elastic and income-elastic. That is to say, the amount of funds which these forms of savings attract varies inversely with inflation and directly with income. This is because these fixed interest securities, being riskless and easy to handle, are attractive to the middle income groups, the more conservative section of the population. This sector of the population, when faced with persistent or recurring inflation, may easily shift from bonds into investments which provide a hedge against inflation such as real estate. Real estate may be a less desirable, more cumbersome form of investment but it may avoid capital losses and may even, when towns grow rapidly, yield substantial capital gains.

In some countries mortgage bonds and *cédulas* issued by mortgage banks have met with success. However, the stream of funds gathered by mortgage banks has, for the reasons given above, been very uneven, abundant at times, very thin at other times. In supported markets, mortgage bonds and *cédulas*, together with bank acceptances, are often used as temporary investments, until something better is found. (It goes without saying that once the market is supported, it is extremely difficult to withdraw support without running the risk of collapse.)

---

[1] In some countries savings deposits are, or have been, a monopoly of official institutions. Their experience has not been different from that of private institutions.

5. *Life Insurance,* Títulos, *and Deposits with Savings and Loan Associations*

Life insurance has grown slowly and steadily, in spite of inflation, while capitalization banks, a fairly new phenomenon in Latin America, had considerable success when they were first started. The record of capitalization banks in gathering funds is attributed to good salesmanship based on the lottery feature of their securities, *títulos,* which appeals to the middle classes. *Títulos* are also used by some medium-sized corporations as a way of accumulating reserves.[1]

In most Latin American countries savings and loan associations are of even more recent provenance than capitalization banks. Savings and loan associations have also been successful for they have exploited the helplessness of the lower middle classes faced with the increasing cost of urban homes brought about by rapid urbanization and sometimes faced also with general inflation. These groups seek to hedge by building a home before they have accumulated the necessary funds.

The success of all these institutions is affected by inflation and by all the other ups and downs, both economic and non-economic, to which the under-developed countries of Latin America are subject. As in the case of mortgage securities, the flow of funds which savings and loan associations have been able to gather — after some initial, fairly spectacular successes — has been slow and uneven. Since this supply of funds comes largely from the middle class, the class which is hardest hit by inflation, it will diminish further even if there is no flight into hedge-investments. If this class wants to maintain its standard of living, its savings will become an increasingly smaller proportion both of its own and of national income as inflation progresses.

6. *Financieras*

The *financiera* is a typically Mexican institution which other Latin American countries are interested in developing. A *financiera* is a sort of investment bank which receives savings and time deposits and trust funds to support its own lending and investment. It may also underwrite issues. These institutions grew rapidly when they were first started, mainly because of official support and some success with their sales of bonds, but their sources of longer term

---

[1] In Mexico, the official *Patronato del Ahorro Nacional* began by issuing savings bonds. Later, these savings bonds acquired all the characteristics of *títulos.* As a result of this competition, the growth of capitalization banks has been fairly slow in Mexico.

funds have dried up with inflation. The high income groups which might be interested in purchasing their bonds are not satisfied, any more than the middle income groups which purchase mortgage bonds, with 8 or 9 per cent. interest, particularly if official support and the liquidity of the bonds are not guaranteed. Moreover, this is a group which thrives on inflation, which speculates when there is fear of devaluation and so forth. It is also the group whose income falls sharply when national income declines. The further progress of *financieras* at this time depends on the profits of their past investments, their short term borrowing, and their trust funds — which, in fact, resemble time deposits more than real trust funds. Their success may also depend on the outcome of a new development, the establishment of investment companies.

7. *Investment Companies*

The development of investment companies is one more instance of the efforts being made by Mexican financial institutions to attract the long term funds which are not forthcoming at fixed rates of interest in periods of inflation or of expectation of inflation. By selling shares in investment companies some *financieras* hope to attract the funds which they cannot get by selling bonds. However, this is a very recent development and it is too soon to say what the outcome will be.[1] A similar institution has been started by the Mexican development corporation, *Nacional Financiera*, although this institution does not have all the characteristics of an investment company. It appears that private interests in Colombia are also contemplating the establishment of at least one such corporation.

8. *Social Security Contributions*

This paper will not deal with funds collected by any institution for the administration of social security, but will deal only with funds surrendered voluntarily to financial institutions. It seems to me that social security contributions are, in most cases in Latin America, more in the nature of a tax than of voluntary contributions. This, of course, is not to minimize the importance of social security funds as a factor in the capital market.

[1] There are some quasi-investment companies in Brazil. Apparently these, too, have been created by already existing financial institutions. I do not know what resemblance they bear to Mexican investment companies. See Alexandre Kafka, 'Brazil' in B. H. Beckhart, ed., *Banking Systems* (New York, 1954), p. 64, 'Very recently some investment trust banking, as well as quasi-investment trust operations of banks, have begun to appear'.

9. *Commercial Banks the Most Important Gatherers of Funds*

The purpose of this long, yet incomplete, enumeration of the sources of funds of different types of financial institutions has been to show that commercial banks, with or without savings departments, are the only type of financial institution that has been able to secure a fairly steady flow of funds in spite of inflation and the various other upheavals to which Latin American countries are subject. Nevertheless, even the commercial banks are not satisfied with the volume of funds which they are able to attract. Their pressure for central bank, or foreign bank, accommodation is continuous.

10. *Interrelationships between Various Financial Institutions*

The low level and uneven flow of specialized funds, the legal and psychological obstacles to diversified operations by commercial banks, and, to some extent, the widespread control of the rate of interest charged by banks : all these factors have served to bring about close interrelationships between various types of financial institutions wherever there is specialization of financial institutions. This is very apparent in Mexico where there is considerable specialization. *Financieras* have recently begun to establish investment companies. Moreover, some *financieras* are themselves the creations of commercial banks. By establishing *financieras*, commercial banks were able to tap a new source of funds, to charge a higher rate of interest than commercial banks are allowed to charge on certain transactions, mainly instalment sales, and to sponsor specific industries and activities which would not ordinarily be considered eligible for finance by a commercial bank.

Commercial banks have also established mortgage banks through which they have benefited from the rise in real estate values or from real estate speculations. They have established savings and loan associations, general warehouses to hold the commodities on which they have lent, insurance companies to insure these commodities, and so forth.

Development has also proceeded in the opposite direction. While independent *financieras* have sometimes borrowed from commercial banks, some have not been satisfied with this unreliable and at times expensive source of funds and have therefore bought or established their own commercial banks. The result is to create a whole series of separate, specialized institutions among which funds may be shifted back and forth and which profit by each others' operations.[1]

Generalizing on the basis of Mexican experience — admittedly a dangerous exercise — one can say that it does not pay to specialize when, because of inflation, psychological attitudes, low income levels, uneven income distribution, fluctuations in income due to balance of payments difficulties and various other reasons, there is an insufficiency of specialized funds as well as considerable unevenness in the supply of specialized funds. Mexican legislation has probably forced a greater diversification of financial institutions than the market allowed. As a result, the burden of supplying funds for the whole financial system has fallen on the commercial banks while other financial institutions have either gone into commercial banking or have come very close to it on their liability side. I believe that since development is both a continuous process and a process of diversification, the specialization of financial institutions — if it is to be more than a façade — requires a steady flow of funds to all types of financial institutions. Such a steady flow of funds is unlikely in under-developed countries which are subject to all sorts of upheavals both internal and external. If the specialized Mexican financial institutions had not found ways of shifting funds between themselves, and if the regulations of the central bank had not, in great measure, counteracted the spirit, if not the provisions, of the laws aiming at greater specialization, Mexico would have had an even more unbalanced development than she has actually experienced.

Moreover, neither the complexity of a financial system — that is, the extent of diversification, specialization, and interrelationships between the various financial institutions — nor the volume of funds which the financial system is able to gather, is any indication of its contribution to economic development.[2] The contribution of the financial system to economic development depends largely on the employment of the funds which it is able to collect.

[1] When all private sources of funds have been exhausted, two other sources still remain, the budget and the central bank. The budget is a source of finance for government financial institutions, the central bank is a source of finance both for government and for private financial institutions.

Central banks are a source of infinite funds. The size of the flow is a matter of policy. It is becoming fashionable to estimate the maximum increase of the money supply compatible with stability, given a certain rate of development, a certain marginal propensity to import, a certain historical maximum velocity of turnover of deposits, and so forth. A discussion of this point is outside my subject.

It does seem, however, that central banks have become convinced that, as the economy develops, a certain annual increase in the supply of money is desirable. Their efforts are directed to injecting their share of the desired increase at the points which the authorities consider to be critical.

[2] Of all Latin American countries, Uruguay has probably the least complex financial system. It is also probable that there is no other Latin American country in which financial institutions have made a greater contribution to economic development than they have in Uruguay.

However, the employment of the funds collected by the financial system may be influenced by specialization. If agricultural banks are the most successful gatherers of funds — this is not the case in any Latin American country — the contribution of the financial system to economic development will be greater than if financial institutions engaged in financing the importation of luxury automobiles or the building of luxury homes are the most successful collectors of funds.

III. Employment of Funds by Various Financial Institutions

1. *The Origin of a Financial Institution influences the Employment of its Funds*

The origins of Latin American financial institutions influence the direction of their lending and investment and are therefore of interest in appraising their contribution to economic development. In many cases these institutions have been established either as adjuncts to well-developed activities, or in response to pressure from groups that did not previously have access to financial facilities. That is, they have been created to meet the needs of specific activities or specific groups and not as independent institutions. The entrepreneurs who will use the facilities they provide already exist. They do not appear as a result of the establishment of the new financial institutions.

This is not a mere theoretical subtlety. The first banks established in Latin American countries after they achieved independence were usually foreign banks set up to facilitate the foreign trade of other countries, a foreign trade which already existed. These banks were therefore not interested in other economic activities in Latin America. The official agricultural banks that have multiplied in many Latin American countries are a response to pressure from farmers who do not have access to private bank finance. Again, industrial groups or groups of entrepreneurs have frequently established their own banks or have acquired already established banks in order to supply their own needs.

The influence of the origins of Latin American financial institutions on the direction of their operations is particularly obvious in the case of government financial institutions. Mexico, for example, has, in addition to a central bank and a general development corporation, a mortgage bank, two agricultural banks, one for the *ejidos* and one for small farmers, a government bank for foreign trade, largely another agricultural bank, a bank for the army and navy, a bank for small trade, a bank for the motion picture industry, a bank for the sugar industry, a bank for transportation, and a bank for co-operatives.

In countries where financial institutions are specialized, the influence of their origins on their operations is very noticeable. When financial institutions are less specialized, the traces of their origins may be less apparent.[1] But whenever the origin of a financial institution influences the direction of its operations, there is a degree of arbitrariness in its selection of borrowers so that selection is not necessarily determined by the rate of interest and the degree of risk.

2. *The Conservatism of Private Bankers Prejudicial to Certain Sectors of Economic Activity*

The conservatism of private bankers also introduces a degree of arbitrariness into their selection of borrowers. Unless a private banker has connections with a would-be borrower, he is frequently shy of new ventures. Fortunately, many entrepreneurs have diversified interests. In several of the more advanced countries, including Brazil and Mexico, there has emerged an aggressive class of entrepreneurs who are interested in promoting new activities. These entrepreneurs can obtain bank finance on the strength of their personal prestige and wealth without much reference to the purpose of the loan. However, the number of entrepreneurs in this class is always fairly small, and newcomers encounter great difficulties because the established entrepreneurs may absorb all the funds available from financial institutions. No doubt, private bankers in all countries are conservative. Nevertheless, a conservative attitude towards new ventures is more prevalent in under-developed countries where the problem of income inequality is greater.

This difficulty is intensified by the fact that the rate of interest is controlled in many Latin American countries. When this is the case, even well-established activities may have great difficulty in obtaining private bank finance.

It is undeniable that agriculture producing for the home market is an extremely important sector of every under-developed country in Latin America. Yet agriculture producing for the home market has always been a Cinderella as far as private financial institutions are concerned. Apart from the great risks involved in agriculture, particularly tropical agriculture, there is only one consideration

---

[1] Foreign banks are increasingly engaging in the finance of activities other than foreign trade.

which influences a sound banker — individual credit-worthiness as judged by the banker himself. If a small industrialist and a small farmer compete for a limited supply of funds, there is little doubt which the private banker will favour. Indeed, in many countries, private banks prefer to keep funds idle rather than to lend to the small farmers who constitute the majority and the most needy part of Latin American producers.

3. *Use of Bank Finance as a Substitute for Capital Market Finance*

Personal or business connections with banks, ownership of financial institutions by groups of industrialists or by entrepreneurs in general, ownership of financial institutions by specific industries : all these factors have also had a part in bringing about another, related problem. Some corporations make greater use of institution finance than is necessary and absorb funds which could be better used for other purposes. Firms which are strong and profitable enough both to create a market for their securities and also to have good connections with financial institutions — the two usually go together — do not make use of the capital market but obtain their funds from various types of banks. In this way, the present owners of the corporation in question avoid sharing their substantial profits with new shareholders.

When confronted with a request for a loan from a powerful, profitable corporation, financial institutions seldom ask themselves whether the corporation should try the capital market instead. Moreover, when capital markets are thin, as they are in Latin America, businessmen seldom turn to them for any capital which they are able to get from financial institutions. This is natural and legitimate if there is little or no market for their securities. I contend, however, that institutional finance is used by those who have access to the capital market as well as by those who do not.

Inflation has probably accentuated this practice, both by increasing profits and by making bonds unsaleable. Similarly, control of the rate of interest which commercial banks are allowed to charge has strengthened the preference for bank finance since the rate of interest charged by banks will probably be lower than that which would have to be paid for funds on the open market.

4. *Interrelationships between Business and Financial Institutions May Favour Economic Development*

The various interconnections between business and financial institutions may, however, be favourable to economic development in one respect. Groups of entrepreneurs and/or financiers may, by forming one financial institution to hold their several corporations and other resources, not only spread their risks but also facilitate investment in new ventures which would have been too large for any one of them to have attempted individually.[1] The range of possible investment is considerably enlarged and the inducement to plough profits back is accordingly enhanced. Moreover, there is less danger of unbalanced growth of some activities because new ventures are beyond the scope of individual entrepreneurs. This point does not, however, lessen the desirability of tapping the capital market whenever possible.[2]

5. *Criticisms of the Use of Funds by Financial Institutions*

The reluctance of financial institutions to lend to certain economic groups and their preference for lending to others is unfortunate but not directly objectionable. However, Latin American financial institutions are constantly blamed — usually by Latin Americans — for speculative transactions and a total disregard for economic development. There is probably no private financial institution which has escaped such criticism. Mortgage banks are blamed for promoting real estate speculation, investment banks and capitalization banks are blamed for wasting their resources on non-essential activities, and commercial banks are criticized on all scores.

Moreover, financial institutions are sometimes blamed for promoting or supporting directions of effective demand which are not considered favourable to economic development. They are also blamed for not correcting entrepreneurs' erroneous judgments on the best long term opportunities for profitable investment.[3] Subjective valuations are difficult to avoid in this matter.

(a) *Criticisms of the Finance of Foreign Trade and Real Estate.* Financial institutions are most often attacked for their operations in two fields, foreign trade — especially the financing of imports — and real estate. It is difficult to justify the first criticism because the volume and value of imports are controlled. Strangely enough, this

---

[1] A few Mexican *financieras* are good examples of this type of financial institution.

[2] Not infrequently one hears the argument that government financial institutions should sell their corporations as soon as these have proved their worth, but we seldom hear the same argument applied to private institutions. Most people appear more interested in private enterprise than in the distribution of ownership in private enterprise. Both are important.

[3] The criticism that financial institutions, especially commercial banks, impede development because their expansion of credit has inflationary consequences is not dealt with in this paper. It is assumed that the financial institutions provide as large a volume of credit as the monetary authorities will allow and no larger.

criticism is most frequent in those countries where it seems least warranted, that is, in those countries where fewer imports of non-essentials are allowed because of shortages of foreign exchange.

The criticism that financial institutions lend too much for building luxury homes, apartment houses, and office buildings and so con-tribute to speculation has been frequent in Latin America in recent years and it is quite warranted. This is probably the clearest ex-ample of an objectionable activity by Latin American financial institutions. Perhaps all types of these institutions have participated in some way and in some degree in such activities. Some have tried to justify their actions by saying that they are acting in response to a demand which results from an inflation which is not of the banks' making. Some claim that this lending creates employment and promotes productive activity. The fact remains that they are en-couraging luxury investments, investments which usually have a very high capital-output ratio.

The resulting waste of financial and real resources cannot be estimated but in some countries — Brazil is an outstanding example — it may have been substantial. It is true, however, that the main — although not the sole — responsibility for this situation rests with the authorities that permit inflationary situations to develop and do not use the tax system to discourage it.[1]

(b) *Criticisms Relating specifically to Commercial Banks.* Other criticisms of financial institutions are less valid. Three of these criticisms are directed mainly against commercial banks. It is claimed : first, that they promote inflation by financing the specu-lative holding of inventories ; second, that they lend to commerce rather than to productive industry or agriculture ; and, third, that they lend short whereas economic development, which involves the building up of capital equipment, requires medium and long term loans.

It is not denied that the overall instability of Latin American economies, together with inflation, balance of payments difficulties, and other factors, may at times have encouraged bank financed speculative holdings of inventories of those commodities whose production is subject to seasonal variation or whose prices are subject to particularly sharp fluctuations. However, there may be some question about the frequency and volume of these operations. Unless the rate of interest is lower than the anticipated annual increase in prices, it will not pay to use bank credit to finance speculative

---

[1] It is only fair to add that even if financial institutions had tried to avoid using their funds for such transactions, the diversity of activities of Latin American entrepreneurs would have made control extremely difficult, if not impossible.

holdings of inventories. Statistics show that the rate of price increase has been uneven in most Latin American countries, and that in a few Latin American countries the years when prices have actually fallen have been not infrequent. Statistics also show that, in most cases, the average annual price increase is lower than the average rate of interest. Moreover, the cost of storage, insurance, and other expenses, plus some allowance for possible obsolescence and deterioration, must be added to the rate of interest.

In Chile and Bolivia, which have experienced rapid inflation, everything would seem to point to the desirability of holding bank financed speculative inventories. However, the shortages in these countries seem to have been brought about only in small part by the increase in inventories. If continuous inflation produced a concomitant increase in inventories, Chile, Bolivia, and several other Latin American countries would by now resemble nothing so much as enormous warehouses.

In any case, working inventories of certain goods may necessarily be higher in under-developed than in developed countries. There are a number of reasons for this — the structure of retail trade, bad communications, the importance of agriculture, and so forth.[1] None of these can be held to result from the behaviour of financial institutions unless these institutions can be said to be partly responsible for the structure of retail trade and the increase in the number of middlemen generally.

The two other criticisms commonly directed against the commercial banks — that banks lend to commerce rather than to productive industry and agriculture and that banks lend short rather than long — reveal a misunderstanding of the processes of production and distribution and a disregard for the fact that production has no meaning without distribution and vice versa. It also shows confusion between the legal terms in which the financial paper is drawn and the economics of the transactions which are financed.

At first glance, the criticism that banks lend to commerce rather than to production would not seem to deserve mention. It is true that merchants have had and still have easier access to bank finance than do producers. However, unless bank credit is used to build up excess inventories, it should not matter which part or parts of the total process it finances.

---

[1] In many countries, the substitution of domestic production for imports is the most important part of economic development. When this is the case, the same volume of consumption logically requires larger inventories, or working capital. Even assuming that domestic production is no more expensive than imports, it requires inventories of raw materials and wage-goods as well as inventories of the finished product. With imports, only inventories of the finished product are necessary.

However, monetary authorities in Latin America have undertaken strict regulation on this point. Moreover, there is one important argument in favour of granting credit to producers rather than to merchants.[1] By shifting credit from merchants to producers, the bargaining power and, probably, the profits of producers are increased. This may be favourable to economic development because producers are more likely than merchants to invest in further production. Moreover, the regulation which has compelled banks to shift some credit from merchants to producers has taught the banks that this sector, from which they previously shied away, can be a good subject for credit. Thus, the indirect effects of these attempts to foster production as opposed to commerce are both real and favourable to economic development.

The criticism that banks lend short rather than long is valid only if we assume that inventories are greater than normal. If, given the specific circumstances of production and distribution in a given country, inventories at the various stages of production and distribution are normal, any reduction of these inventories will be harmful to the processes of production and distribution and therefore detrimental to development.

I have already hinted at the extent to which financial institutions in Latin America finance the normal working balances of corporations. The rigidity of the portfolios of our financial institutions is a further proof of this situation. Any central banker will vouch for the fact that credit cannot be contracted without endangering production and/or distribution.[2] This is bound to be the case when capital markets are narrow and commercial banks finance, directly or indirectly, a substantial part of domestic production.

I contend, therefore, that funds for working balances are as long term as funds for fixed capital and that it does not matter, from the point of view of economic development, what institution finances the one or the other. The inflationary impact on the economy will

[1] The author has tried to arrive at a working distinction between commerce and production to be used in connection with the granting of bank credit. At times, the distinction is clear, as when banks finance the importation of consumer goods. But in the case of domestically produced goods, the only possible distinction seems to be that made with reference to the applicant for credit. The only defensible definitions seem to be : a merchant is someone who sells products which he does not produce ; a producer is someone who produces and sells the same product.

[2] The smaller the proportion of foreign trade within total income and the smaller the proportion of lending to foreign trade within total lending, the more this is the case.

Recent experience in Chile provides a dramatic example of the effects of a slowing down of the rate of increase in bank credit on the economic system. In Chile, an anti-inflationary policy in regard to bank credit resulted in substantial unemployment in the building industries.

depend on the total volume of financing and will be the same whatever the proportion provided by financial institutions.

Once we grant that commercial banks may legitimately finance working balances, we must also grant that they may legitimately finance fixed capital, which they probably do in many cases. Indeed, it is obvious that the larger the share of a country's total capital (fixed capital plus working capital) provided by financial institutions, the more likely financial institutions are to have to provide fixed capital.[1] Moreover, if we want financial institutions to contribute substantially to economic development and if these institutions are able to gather only small amounts in savings deposits, we will have to accept the fact that a significant part of the sight deposits gathered by these institutions will have to be used to finance long term capital. This is neither worse nor better, more or less inflationary and so forth, than if financial institutions finance only the working capital of producers and merchants.

The banking side of the problem should present no particular problem. First, the use of modern central banking tools can always provide financial institutions with all the liquidity they may require. Second, in a growing economy all the elements in the financial structure may be expected to grow as production grows. And, third, in such an economy the liquidity needs of lenders are not as sensitive to fluctuations in incomes as is the case in a slowly growing economy.[2] Of course, banks may suffer losses if they extend long term finance to a corporation that fails but they may also suffer losses when merchants fail. There is no excuse for bad financing, whether short or long term.

In short, I do not believe that, in a growing economy, there is much justification for or possibility of specialization of financial institutions according to whether their transactions are short, medium, or long term.

6. *Need for Specialized Financial Institutions to Finance Specific Activities*

The specialization of financial institutions according to the activities which they finance — foreign trade, agriculture, industry,

---

[1] This is so because working balances, which consist mainly of inventories, are smaller than annual production and the value of annual production is, as a rule, less than the value of the fixed assets required to produce it.

[2] The argument that with the advance of modern technology, fixed capital has become of increasingly shorter duration and, therefore, it is today more legitimate to finance fixed capital with short or medium term funds, does not seem as applicable to under-developed countries where technology changes less rapidly as it is to, say, the United States.

construction, and so forth — is a different matter. If there is a sufficient volume of business in the different sectors and if the various institutions are able to collect the necessary funds, specialization on this basis may have good results because a specialized institution will have greater knowledge and insight into the problems of the sector of the economy with which it deals.

It does not seem necessary to examine the employment of funds by the various specialized institutions. In Latin America, all specialized financial institutions — with the possible exception of mortgage banks and savings and loan associations — either do the same sort of business or shift funds between them in such a way as to make the distinctions between them purely artificial. There may be legal or psychological obstacles which tend to keep specialized financial institutions within the boundaries of their specified field of operations. This situation is, however, exceptional except in so far as delimitation of their field of operations is in the institutions' own interest.

IV. FINANCIAL INSTITUTIONS AND ECONOMIC DEVELOPMENT

1. *The Need for Selective Credit Controls and for Public Financial Institutions*

If we were content to see investment determined by effective demand and to see entrepreneurs and financial institutions follow the line of least resistance, we would have a slow rate of development. Effective demand is, at the present time, concentrated in the middle and upper income groups. It will be a long time before the incomes of the lower income groups increase sufficiently to call the attention of entrepreneurs to the profitability of producing goods to satisfy their wants. Moreover, the fact that the middle and upper income groups constitute a small part of the total population sets a limit to the profitability of investment in production to fill their wants. This argument is valid whenever there are substantial inequalities of income. However, the smaller and more undeveloped the country, the more valid this argument is, and the larger, absolutely, the middle and upper income groups and the larger and more concentrated the total population, the less valid this argument.

If development of any social value is to be speeded up, considerable investment must go into fields producing goods and services for the large sectors of the population which, in Latin America, have very low incomes. However, private financial institutions will voluntarily undertake investment of this sort only to a limited extent because the short run profitability of such investment is necessarily small. Because this is so and because, also, of the attitudes of private financial institutions discussed in the preceding Section, many Latin American countries have undertaken selective credit controls, including — most important of all — the establishment of public financial institutions.

2. *Controls over Lending by Commercial Banks*

On the one hand, selective controls may take the form of inducements to private institutions to channel their finance in certain directions. On the other, they may be direct and compulsory in nature. Among the first type we find : first, an increase to one year in the length of paper which central banks are willing to accept for rediscount ; second, different rediscount rates for paper representing different types of transactions — both these changes are designed mainly to favour agricultural production ; and, third, an increase in the length of credit which commercial banks may grant so that a certain percentage of their lending may now be in medium term loans. Also, banks' earning assets are now sometimes linked to the banks' capital rather than to deposits, a higher percentage of capital being required against assets representing less desirable transactions. Another new development is the establishment of credit insurance for agriculture and small industries to make these sectors more eligible for finance from private institutions.

Controls may also be compulsory. Thus, in Mexico, the central bank will rediscount only for those private banks whose portfolios are made up of not more than a certain proportion of commercial paper and not less than a certain proportion in paper representing productive activities. In some countries, such as Colombia, the authorities require private banks to hold certain bonds, mainly as reserves against savings deposits. In other countries, such as Mexico, extremely high reserve requirements have been imposed and banks are given the option of keeping these reserves idle or of investing them in specified assets, some of which are provided by the central bank itself. At times banks have been prohibited from granting credit to finance deposits required against imports or from financing more than a certain percentage of import letters of credit.

3. *Controls over other Financial Institutions*

Investment banks, mortgage and capitalization banks, savings and loan associations, insurance companies, and so forth, have also been required, sometimes by law and sometimes by more or less formal agreements or regulation, to invest their capital or reserves in certain ways or to eschew certain transactions. The value of their buildings may not exceed a certain amount. Mortgage bonds must not be used to finance buildings worth more than a certain sum. Investment in foreign assets or corporations is forbidden and so forth.

4. *Effectiveness of Controls*

There is naturally much controversy regarding the effectiveness of these controls. It seems fairly well agreed that their effectiveness is related to the time of their introduction. As the economy expands, compulsory investment probably becomes an increasingly smaller proportion of total investment because financial institutions, corporations, and individuals find ways to circumvent the regulations. Nevertheless, these controls have had a salutary effect, particularly when they were first introduced. In particular, they have helped to teach private financial institutions that certain groups of borrowers who were previously not considered eligible for bank finance are good subjects for credit.

5. *Responsibility for the Structure of Demand that Makes Controls Necessary*

No doubt the structure of demand which has made some of these qualitative controls — as well as quantitative controls — necessary was brought about partly by the authorities themselves through monetary expansion and inflation. To that extent these controls represent an attempt by the authorities to temper the secondary effects of their own actions since they are not able to accomplish this through the use of the tax system. Indeed, in some cases, monetary expansion itself can be partly attributed to the inexpediency of using the tax system soon enough if at all. Thus, an excessive part of the task of adjustment has been thrown upon the credit system.

Not all the blame can be laid on the authorities. The income inequalities which are mainly responsible for the structure of demand which is considered unfavourable to development did not result from inflation but existed before inflation began. Moreover the authorities are not solely responsible for inflation. Inflation has frequently resulted from pressure from the upper income groups or from attempts by the authorities to accomplish what the upper income groups were unwilling to undertake or from attempts by the authorities to obtain in an expedient way funds that the upper income groups were unwilling to supply in the form of taxes. Starting from a situation where there are sharp inequalities of income and where the upper income groups can exert considerable political pressure which allows them to resist successfully the imposition of taxes, the structure of demand in these countries would probably not have been much different from what it is today even if these countries had had no inflation. This is not to deny that inflation has accentuated the problem.

6. *Limitations of Controls of the Private Financial Institutions*

Control of the private financial system is, generally speaking, a negative action. Private financial institutions can be forbidden to do certain things. On the other hand, attempts to induce private financial institutions to take actions which they oppose are likely to have little effect, or may amount to doing through private institutions what could equally well have been accomplished by the authorities directly. Moreover, methods which force private financial institutions to take actions which they oppose — assuming that this is politically possible — imply more regimentation of the financial system than seems either necessary or desirable. If the authorities wish to favour certain activities or groups with access to funds which these activities or groups cannot ordinarily obtain from private financial institutions, the most expedient and clear-cut solution is the creation of official financial institutions which will undertake this financing, even though this may mean reducing considerably the amount of total financing done by private financial institutions.

7. *Official Financial Institutions*

The need for official financial institutions, with various degrees of government interference, to supplement the work of the private financial system has been felt all through Latin America. In several countries the official sector today covers almost the whole field of financing. Official institutions were first set up to finance the domestic market — as opposed to foreign trade, a field financed by foreign banks in the old days — but, at that time, economic development, as we understand it today, was not a primary objective. Agricultural and mortgage banks followed and were followed in their turn by development corporations. The full and, to me, impressive list of Mexican official financial institutions was given above.

It is beyond the scope of this paper to appraise in detail the work done by government financial institutions in Latin America.

A few remarks will suffice. Many of these institutions have been bitterly criticized. They are accused of yielding to political pressure in the direction of their financing and in the selection of their borrowers. They are accused of being used as political instruments by governments and government officials. They are accused of exerting pressure on the central banks in their search for funds, and so forth. But the general contribution which government financial institutions have made to development cannot be denied. They have undertaken projects of great social significance such as low cost housing. They have undertaken public utility projects such as railways, electric plants, and the like. They have undertaken investments which require more funds and yield lower and/or slower returns than private enterprise requires, such as steel mills. They have also undertaken the ordinary financing of agriculture and industry.

Their outlook has been broader than that of private enterprise. Considerations such as the short and long run balance of payments situation have had a great influence on their operations and their work has frequently been co-ordinated with investments made out of budgetary funds. They have taken more risks than private financial institutions and have carried out basic research. Not only is the volume of their loans and investments important, it is also very strategic.

Moreover, there are few examples in Latin America of conflict between private and public financial institutions. First, the two sectors generally finance different activities and different customers. Second, unless the terms offered by government institutions are much more favourable than those offered by private institutions, individuals and corporations prefer to borrow from private institutions. Third, since the public sector has had an expansionary effect on the total volume of money but is a poor gatherer of savings and of sight deposits, the private sector has benefited from their operations. The private sector has also benefited because government institutions have created credit-worthy borrowers or have helped some borrowers to become credit-worthy.

V. Conclusion

This paper has attempted to make a case for unspecialized banks, for banks that offer to the public all sorts of savings opportunities and engage in all sorts of transactions, both short and long term. This recommendation is based on the fact that the flow of specialized funds is uneven whereas development must be a continuous process and on the fact that the processes of production and distribution are economically identical so that the distinction between working capital (short term financing) and fixed capital (long term financing) is meaningless. I do not consider the financing of fixed capital out of short term funds to be dangerous either from an economic or from a banking point of view.

This paper also accepts and recommends the establishment of public financial institutions as a supplement to the private financial system. This recommendation is based on the fact that the investments of the private financial institutions are determined by structure of effective demand which, in Latin America, reflects sharp income inequalities and is not conducive to economic development. The case for public financial institutions is also based on the semi-closed group attitude of private banking and its narrow outlook.

COMMENTS ON DR. MÁRQUEZ' PAPER

BY

JORGE AHUMADA

I. SPECIALIZATION OF FINANCIAL INSTITUTIONS

I AM glad to see that Dr. Márquez does not share the view of many Latin American economists that the financial problem can be solved simply by opening new banks and inventing new types of financial assets. I wholly agree that financial institutions are a function of economic development and that the higher the level of *per capita* income, *ceteris paribus*, the greater the quantitative importance of financial transactions per unit of gross national expenditure. There are several reasons for this but two seem especially important. First, the larger *per capita* income, the larger the value of *per capita* real assets and, consequently, the larger the possibility of transactions on capital account and the greater the opportunity for profitable operations by specialized institutions. Second, the larger average *per capita* income, the more likely it is that some earning units — families or enterprises — will have surpluses for deficits on current account that need to be mobilized.

One should, however, be aware of the danger of falling into the opposite position. The functional relationship between *per capita* income and the need for financial institutions is not necessarily unique. It is not correct to say that at each level of income there is only one efficient set of financial institutions. At each stage of development there are probably several sets of financial institutions which are efficient, and it does not pay to go beyond the limit thus imposed on specialization. Perhaps this is what Dr. Márquez meant in saying that the share of funds going into financial institutions depends partly on the expediency of surrendering funds to financial institutions.

If financial institutions were a unique function of the rate of growth of income and if the rate of savings were another function of the same type, one could accept the statement that savings are institution-inelastic. But financial institutions, as well as savings, are affected by factors other than income. If this is the case, the possibility of institution-elastic savings should not be dismissed so lightly. For example, farmers hoard for transaction and precautionary motives. These hoards are not savings but they will become savings if some financial institution gets hold of them and lends them to someone who wants to invest. Alternatively, hoardings can be counterbalanced by monetary or credit expansion. Is it better to establish institutional financial facilities to reduce hoarding to a minimum or to compensate for hoarding by monetary expansion? The trouble with the second alternative is that it reduces the effectiveness of monetary policy for anti-inflationary purposes.

One can also find institution-elastic savings in the middle income groups. There is no *a priori* reason to believe that it is impossible to expand considerably the market for bonds and shares among the middle and lower income groups. In this field, as in many others, promoters are badly needed. I do not deny Dr. Márquez' statement that Latin American experience in this matter has been disappointing but I contend that in Latin America all sellers, including governments, concentrate their efforts too heavily on the upper income groups.

Should financial institutions specialize? I agree in general with Dr. Márquez' objection to the distinction between short and long term finance. There is no good reason to forbid commercial banks to undertake long-term finance. Whether they would do so if authorized is another matter. There is no doubt that short term finance is more profitable than long term to commercial banks. If the rate of interest were not controlled, it is unlikely that long term borrowers could pay a competitive rate. Nevertheless, it is true that at present long-term borrowers are financing a large amount of fixed capital with short-term loans and are paying a corresponding interest rate. In addition, they are increasing their risk and inconvenience.

If history teaches us anything, it is that the financing of private capital accumulation in the past has been made mainly out of undistributed profits and depreciation reserves. As Domar has shown, given price stability, the usual straight line depreciation leads to the accumulation of reserves which are much greater than the amount actually needed for replacement of worn-out capital. However, in view of the tremendous increase in the minimum size of plant that has taken place in the last fifty years, it is possible that history will not repeat itself in Latin America. Ploughing back is becoming increasingly difficult. But the solution does not lie in greater facilities for long-term borrowing but in greater facilities for equity financing. What we need is investment banks, not authorization to commercial banks to grant long maturity loans. Such authorization will do no harm, but its contribution to the solution of the problem of capital accumulation may be rather small.

The question whether commercial banks should be authorized to act as investment banks is another matter. To me the strongest argument against this is the danger of too great concentration of economic power. On the other hand, excessive caution in this direction may result in a lower rate of economic development.

If the main problem in Latin America is equity finance, then efforts to strengthen the institutional set-up should lie along three main lines. First, the legislation affecting corporations and stock markets should be improved. In Latin America we discriminate against corporations in tax matters, in salary matters and by all kinds of social legislation. On the other hand, there are few facilities for floating new issues and the whole market is surrounded by a liturgy that scares away all potential investors who are not members of the clique. Second, the legislation concerning the operations of insurance companies should be revised. Existing legislation is usually extremely conservative and compels the channelling of this very important and growing source of savings into real estate. Third, it seems a pity that social security legislation is tending more and more away from accumulation of reserves.

I have no objection to Dr. Márquez' recommendation for sectoral specialization. I believe that this development can be expected, *a priori*, to take place as the possibility of profitable operations in any sector increases with income. Indeed, it has already taken place in some sectors. It seems that regional specialization is most likely to be successful at lower stages of economic development, but there is one point that disturbs me. Economic development, being a continuous process of change in the structure of production, implies the need to transfer surplus funds from more mature sectors to less mature sectors. How will this transfer take place if all financial institutions are sectorally specialized? Will financial institutions not tend to over-expand in their own sectors as Dr. Márquez fears individual savers are inclined to do?

To summarize, I agree with Dr. Márquez that financial institutions are a function of economic development but recognize the possibility of a time gap which justifies a conscious effort to improve these institutions. Perhaps the most serious lack in Latin America today is in the field of equity finance. The traditional instruments will probably continue to serve in our countries as they did in the old. In my opinion, the development corporation, a new instrument, is much more important as a promoting agency than as a financial institution.

II. Financial Policy

Dr. Márquez deals with two questions of financial policy. First, he discusses whether the government should channel resources through institutions or should use them directly. He favours the first alternative because institutions are able to form better judgments of investment opportunities. This was also Schumpeter's view. Schumpeter believed that the banking system should be the planning or priority rating agency of a capitalist society but that the mistaken commercial banking theory had perverted the mechanism. It seems surprising to me that Schumpeter took this view. A bank judges investment by the contribution that investment makes to the bank's own profits and not by the contribution it makes to real national income. The investment priority ratings determined by individuals, whether persons or corporations, are much more biased by considerations of income distribution than are the investment priority ratings determined by government agencies.

The second policy question discussed by Dr. Márquez is closely tied to the first. Where should finance preferably go ? Dr. Márquez deals mainly with the question of commerce versus production. Here I disagree to some extent. I believe that one finances investors, not investments. If a certain quantity of resources is lent to an investor, the stated purpose of the loan is of little importance. The borrower will have one indivisible, homogeneous pool of financial resources. But investors do not engage in all kinds of productive activities, they specialize. If loans go mainly to merchants, agricultural producers are not being helped except to the extent that merchants themselves become financiers. If entrance to every line of business were free, as is assumed in the theory of production, it would not matter who got the credits. But in the real world the existence of financial facilities is a very significant help in entering any business. Consequently, a proper distribution of finance may contribute to a balanced structure of production.

To my mind, one of the most difficult problems in the field of financial policy is how to channel financial resources in the directions in which they can do the most good. Financial institutions have, in fact, had a very great influence on the distribution of finance but the priority criteria they employ are mainly based on the collateral offered by borrowers. Naturally, borrowers will not offer their property as collateral unless they are certain that the loan will serve a useful purpose and will yield at least an amount equal to interest and other charges. Beyond this, credit is distributed only on the basis of first come, first served. Is there another, more rational way of distributing credit ?

FURTHER COMMENTS ON DR. MARQUEZ' PAPER

BY

DORIVAL TEIXEIRA VIEIRA
University of São Paulo

I. Specialization of Financial Institutions

Dr. Márquez believes that the charges that commercial banks promote speculation because they finance hedging operations, because they lend more to trade than to production, and because they prefer short to medium or long term loans, are unjust. I do not entirely agree with Dr. Márquez. The fact that speculation results from inflation and difficulties in international trade does not excuse speculation by the commercial banks. Moreover, it remains to be seen whether, in fact, speculation is becoming more sporadic, as Dr. Márquez believes. This does not seem to me to be the case.

It also seems somewhat far-fetched to say that the commercial banks' preference for short term investment and for investment in trade does no harm to production when it is at the same time admitted that the commercial banks are the best gatherers of funds. Since capital is scarce, to the degree that short term finance is given to purely trading and speculative activities, the finance of production is jeopardized. Moreover, distribution itself is disturbed by inventory hoarding and by market manipulations when there are expectations of price increases.

This state of affairs is, in a measure, caused by the banks, although not always directly. In a free enterprise society, banks cannot be denied the right to select their clients and to determine the way in which they invest their funds. However, defence of this principle obliges us to accept the principle of specialization of bank credit, at least to the extent of specialization between commercial banks and investment banks. This, of course, would require the central banks to take steps to guarantee a greater equity in the distribution of funds between these two types of financial institution.

Dr. Márquez does not seem to accept this argument. He says that there is no reason for specialization of this type, although he admits that financial institutions may specialize in financing certain sectors of the economy. This point of view does not seem to me to be very felicitous. Both in agriculture and in industry there is a need for both short term loans to meet day-to-day requirements and for medium and long term loans to finance programmes of development and plant adjustment. Although specialization of banking establishments in the under-developed countries will encounter various difficulties, specialization is necessary because financial institutions in general and commercial banks in particular do not know how to select or do not wish to select their clients in a manner that is rational and conducive to economic development.

II. Inflation in Latin American Countries

It seems to me that Dr. Márquez wavers a little on the effects of inflation. On the one hand, he admits that inflation is a disturbing factor in the investment market. On the other, he considers it one of the factors which are favourable to the increase of deposits.

I think it is necessary to divide the inflationary process in the under-developed countries into two distinct phases. In the first phase, while the rate of increase of prices is lower than the prevailing rate of interest, new financial institutions spring up by attracting deposits. This was especially true during and immediately after the war when artificial price controls prevented the rate of price increase in certain sectors of the economy from exceeding the increase in average salaries in some professional classes. As a result the lower and middle income groups were able to save and there was, in addition, the attraction of a rate of interest which was higher than the rate of inflation. However, the inflation of credit resulting from the investment of these savings in purely financial rather than developmental activities, the financial difficulties of the State, the lack of monetary and credit control, and the disturbance of international trade which forced exports without compensating imports : all these factors contributed to an aggravation of inflation. In Brazil at the present time the rate of inflation exceeds the rate of interest. Hence the market for capital, even short-term capital, experiences greater and greater difficulties. The consequences are a hunger for money, successive issues of paper money in response to pressure from the financial institutions themselves, and investment in speculative activities, to which the financial institutions have finally surrendered. If, as Dr. Márquez points out, commercial banks establish wholesale businesses and industrial groups set up their own banks, are they not seeking to defend themselves from the spiral of inflation which frustrates their economic planning and upsets their normal activities ?

Dr. Márquez does not enquire into the origins of chronic inflation in the under-developed countries. For one thing, scarcity of capital, low productivity of labour, and low real incomes are responsible for a lack of incentive to invest. In endeavouring to compensate for this and to avoid a stalemate, the state has been striving to feed the financial market by increasing the total of working capital. But the smallness of the market on the one hand and the absence of a comprehensive programme of development on the other have caused this increase in the supply of money to result in price inflation. Other causes which are of greater interest to us, considering the nature of the subject under discussion, are : the effect of inflation on the investment market ; the effect of inflation on the distribution of national income and hence on the structure of effective demand ;

and the effect of inflation on the capacity and disposition of private individuals to save and invest and on the direction of their investment. The conclusion that inflation is adverse to the healthy development of the underdeveloped countries seems inescapable.

Dr. Márquez says that the problem of income inequalities in underdeveloped countries antedates inflation. As far as I have been able to ascertain, inflation in most Latin American countries is chronic in character. There are periods of recrudescence followed by periods in which inflation slows down. Although it may be true that inequalities of income were not originally provoked by inflation, it is also true that inflation has accentuated the disequilibria and has brought about transfers of wealth from some holders to others without lessening the degree of concentration of wealth. In the past the landed gentry were the holders of the greater part of the wealth. Nowadays, the wealth of the country has passed from the landed gentry into the hands of newcomers. The newly rich are the subject of countless caricatures in Latin America. A more systematic study of this socio-economic phenomenon, the rise and decline of fortunes, is needed. Perhaps this phenomenon explains the disdain of bankers and entrepreneurs for long run economic soundness.

Inflation has been, in part, the result of pressure exerted by economic groups holding great wealth and anxious to retain it. This is a serious state of affairs when coupled with a loss of tradition and of patriotic sentiment. In part, also, inflation results from the governments' attempts to force the financial institutions to do what they are reluctant to do and, at the same time, to increase tax revenue. I shall deal with the first point when I discuss the problem of state intervention. As to the second point, the demand of governments for higher revenue is not necessarily the cause of inflation. An efficient tax system can rectify inequalities in the distribution of income and allow the government to co-operate actively in a programme of balanced economic development. The cause lies, rather, in bad administration, in the low productivity of the public services, in the lack of a well-orientated programme of comprehensive economic development, and in the use of public revenue for programmes that are themselves inflationary.

Latin American countries are not prepared to wait patiently until private entrepreneurs change their attitude and manage their enterprises in a sound way. In any case, entrepreneurs can scarcely manage their enterprises efficiently when inflation constantly frustrates economic expectations. Perhaps, as the author points out when he deals with reinvestment in profitable enterprises, this is one of the main reasons for the almost chaotic procedure of financial institutions.

III. PUBLIC FINANCIAL INSTITUTIONS

Nor is the state completely to blame. If it is admitted that private financial institutions have accomplished all that can be expected in gathering sight deposits and that these institutions are in no position to operate satisfactorily in the field of long term investment and that therefore they abet unbalanced economic development, state interference is a natural consequence. Indeed, the establishment of public financial institutions is often sought by private enterprise in order that guidance of the national economy along a given road may give rise to satisfactory economic development which will increase production, savings, accumulation, and finance and thus increase the rate of capital formation and direct investment in ways more consonant with national requirements.

IV. MONETARY POLICY

I come now to the question of the government's actions in monetary management. Dr. Márquez admits that in the under-developed countries the state has endeavoured to provide funds for financial institutions in order to foster the expansion of investment. In his opinion a rise in the volume of money in circulation is not prejudicial if the volume of money increases in the same proportion as national income, provided that liquidity preferences remain constant. In practice, the increase of the money supply has been greater than the increase in national income. In other words, there has been inflation — real inflation and not false inflation — and this has changed liquidity preferences.

Control of the interest rate is of especial importance. Dr. Márquez admits that there are social, economic, and even moral motives for controlling the interest rate and that control of the interest rate may contribute to a speeding-up of the financial development of under-developed countries because one of the aims of this control is the favouring of productive enterprises with cheap money. However, he does not believe that this control has proved very satisfactory.

Dr. Márquez believes that intervention by the state in the financial field, including the establishment of public financial institutions, has been beneficial because it has permitted the banking system greater flexibility and because the state is able to undertake investments which are desirable but which private enterprise will not finance. State intervention can also contribute to the re-establishment of equilibrium in the balance of payments of under-developed countries and to the training of industrialists, administrators, and technicians for a more efficient development programme.

Not all the results of state intervention are, however, beneficial. There are some points on which I would criticize the efficiency of the controls which the state has imposed. There is no doubt that there is political interference in the choice of personnel both in the control organs and in the public financial organizations and also in the selection of loans. As a result, public financial institutions have high costs and earn low profits, or even incur losses, on their investments.

Beyond this, state intervention brings up two fundamental problems on the relationship between the state and private enterprise in under-developed countries. First, to what extent can the capital market be left to the free play of interest rates ? Second, to what extent can private enterprise alone carry out an economic development programme and rescue the economy of an under-developed country from the vicious circle of poverty ?

The efficiency of the interest rate usually rests on the assumption of a perfect competitive market. But the financial market is in reality imperfect. The savings of various income groups are inelastic with respect to the interest rate paid on deposits, because the various groups have different standards of living which determine different margins of available net income. Looking at the problem in terms of real product and real income, available net income is relatively constant within each class of savers in the short and medium run. In the under-developed countries, the supply curve may not be perpendicular to the x-axis but may, after a certain point, be parallel with it. We must also distinguish between the supply curves of various groups, keeping in mind the division between groups resulting from differences in the distribution of produced and consumed income. If the market were free and if the demand of the various financial institutions for savings were homogeneous, we should have not only multiple rates of interest on deposits but rates inversely proportional to levels of savings. Groups with low savings power would entrust their savings to financial institutions only if they were given higher interest rates. However, if we admit that savings are concentrated and that the demand for savings of the various financial institutions is not homogeneous, the market is, if not monopolistic, at least oligopolistic. This results in a rigidity in the supply of savings which gives rise to rigidity in the financial institutions' supply of funds for investment.

Regarding the demand for loans, we should distinguish at least three main divisions of the market, commercial loans, industrial loans, and agricultural loans. Each of these divisions has its own demand curve. Each is differently sensitive to variations in the rate of interest. If the capital market were free, there would be multiple interest rates on loans and neither industry nor agriculture would be able to bear the rates of interest that commerce could pay. Therefore, control of interest rates is necessary.

Moreover, we must distinguish between the official rates of interest charged in under-developed countries and the real rates of interest, because financial institutions have various artifices by which they succeed in collecting higher rates of interest than the law allows. Moreover, we must take into consideration non-institutional loans. These two facts together make a mockery of the usury laws.

It follows that a free capital market is not feasible. A free capital market, far from permitting the quickest possible development of under-developed countries, would only aggravate difficulties which already exist. It would not remove the underlying difficulties and it might give rise to new difficulties.

V. Conclusion

The problem of investment in under-developed countries consists partly in striving to increase real non-inflationary savings and in directing these savings into investment that is conducive to economic development. In addition, investment must be in accordance with an overall harmonious plan so as to avoid the hypertrophy of certain sectors of economic activity and the atrophy of other sectors and a consequent imbalance in economic development. If it is true that the financial markets in the under-developed countries are limited by the smallness of demand, it is equally true that this can be remedied by a plan of multiform investments to promote the expansion and consolidation of the domestic market. The efficiency of investment depends not only upon how, but also where, and by whom it is made.

I come now to the last problem. Can private enterprise solve the problems of development not only in the banking sector but in all the other sectors of economic life ? I have already pointed out the short-comings of private financial institutions and of private enterprise in the financial market. From the past history of under-developed countries we also know that private enterprise has been found insufficient in other important sectors. I therefore consider that it is impossible to preclude active collaboration by the state at least in the first stages of a balanced development programme. If such intervention is guided by the overall potentialities of the countries and is planned intelligently, it should be possible to change the financial market completely and to accelerate economic development considerably. To me, the state is not a self-sufficient entity, all-powerful, superior to, and coming before individuals. The state is the manifestation of the behaviour of a group which represents and expresses its power through the state. The quality of the intervention of the state is a function of the values of this group. It is therefore in terms of men that we can speak of good or bad state intervention. In the same way we can speak of the good or bad results of private enterprise.

DISCUSSION OF DR. MARQUEZ' PAPER

THE discussion of Dr. Márquez' paper revealed a wide variety of views. As Dr. Márquez himself pointed out, opinions on the merits of particular financial institutions were apt to be coloured by the experience of particular countries. A rich variety of country experience was reflected among the participants.

I. Speculative Lending

Dr. Márquez had argued in his paper that bank lending for the purpose of carrying speculative inventories, of which Latin American banks had often been accused, was not quantitatively important. The rate of interest usually was so high that the prevailing rate of inflation would not generate very sizeable profits. *Professor Teixeira Vieira* thought that inventory speculation in Brazil had nevertheless been substantial, and quoted cases of banks charging effective rates of up to 3 and 4 per cent. per month for such operations. *Dr. Sol* said that in his experience the situation varied from country to country. At times when certain commodities were moved from one exchange rate category to another, or when new tariffs were imposed, large price movements might occur that would enable a speculator to pay such rates. *Professor Brahmananda* added that speculative financing by banks had been a problem in India, and had been countered through the forward Market Board and selective credit control.

II. Distribution of Credit

Dr. Márquez had stated that specialization of lending institutions by sectors of the economy was desirable. It did not matter a great deal, however, in his opinion, at what stage between the primary producer and the final consumer credit was injected. It would in any case be passed on to the other links of the chain.

Professor Wallich said that this seemed to run counter to the philosophy underlying development of the credit structure in the United States and, to his knowledge, in other Latin American countries. It had usually been found that credit was not readily passed on from one stage to another. Hence it had become necessary to establish special credit facilities for such producer groups as did not have automatic access to credit. He asked whether the failure to channel credit to small farmers, for instance, would not lead to their being charged exploitative rates by the merchants who would then finance them. *Dr. Márquez* replied that in such cases he would favour the establishment of governmental institutions. He saw no reason, however, to be concerned about the point of injection of private bank credit in the economic process.

Professor Hirschman argued that there seemed to be a tendency for Latin American institutions to become overspecialized. Whenever a gap in the credit structure was discovered, some new public institution was likely to be set up, and some new source of funds assigned to it. One of the results often was a complete absence of relation between the source of the funds and their use.

Professor Levine said that Chile had at one time possessed a considerable number of specialized banks. It had found it desirable to integrate them into one large bank with a proportionate number of fairly independent departments.

Professor Teixeira Vieira complained that in Brazil the distribution of credit in the Banco do Brasil was acutely uneven. Less than 10 per cent. went to agriculture, which was, after all, the main activity of the economy. Only half of the Banco do Brasil loans went to commerce and industry out of agriculture in the aggregate. The other half went to government organizations, by no means all for development purposes. The Economic Development Bank had helped, however, to bring credit to industry.

Professor Brahmananda said that India did not have specialized credit institutions, specializing in particular commodities, although their creation had at one time been considered. There existed, however, several specialized agencies to meet sectoral deficiencies.

Dr. Márquez wound up this part of the discussion by rejecting the implication that governmental credit institutions had earned more severe criticism for their policies than private institutions. Both had advantages and disadvantages, and neither kind of institution seemed clearly preferable to the other.

III. Maturity Distribution of Loans

Dr. Márquez had expressed the view that there was no reason why commercial banks should not make medium and long term loans in whatever volume they considered appropriate. The liquidity of short term inventory loans was economically meaningless. Inventories, he said, were after all just as permanent a part of the economy's capital structure as were plant and equipment. If the banks financed the one, they could just as well finance the others. Embarrassment of the banks as a result of a shrinkage in the total volume of deposits was not to be expected nowadays since such shrinkage was unlikely. The Central Bank, moreover, could always help them out if necessary. All he insisted upon was that the loans should be sound.

Professor Wallich argued that, even if total deposits should never decline, individual banks might still experience fluctuations in the volume of their deposits. Consequently, they had to maintain a certain amount of short term assets. He agreed that a substantial volume of medium and long term loans could be taken on, particularly by banks with a good amount of savings deposits. He would like to see this proportion limited, in some form, however, by law.

Dr. Sol suggested that the proper proportion of long term loans should reflect the rock-bottom level of deposits below which, in such bank's experience, the deposits were not likely to fall even in a major cyclical fluctuation. He added, however, that the central bank must stand ready to bail banks out of long term commitments. This implied a willingness on the part of the central bank to face the inflationary repercussions of such expansion on the price level and the balance of payments.

Professor Byé suggested that some amount of long term financing was inevitable. He wondered, however, how in a banking system with substantial long term commitments restrictive credit control could be made effective by the central bank.

Dr. Márquez in his reply, said that the laying down of fixed rules was not practicable. The bank supervisory authorities should have power to intervene, however, if the banks' long term commitments seemed to become excessive in the light of circumstances.

EQUITY FINANCING

Dr. Sol and *Professor Wallich* both favoured some measure of equity investment by banks. *Dr. Sol* pointed to the precedent of Continental banks which often had prefinanced industrial expansion and had later liquidated such credits with common stock issues, and which also held common stocks in their permanent portfolios. This practice did not exist in the United States and Great Britain, where adequate capital markets were available to industrial borrowers. Latin America, however, was more like Continental Europe in this respect. The co-operation of the banks was important for industrial financing. *Professor Wallich* said that he would favour common stock investment by banks particularly if they had a reasonable rate of turnover, so that the banks in effect became underwriters but would not convert themselves into holding companies.

V. SAVINGS INSTITUTIONS

An inconclusive argument developed around the usefulness of private financing institutions as promoters of individual savings. *Dr. Márquez* thought that private financial institutions had done in Latin America as much as could have been expected of them, in their search for deposits, by establishing branches and similar devices. In areas of very low incomes, still untapped by private financial institutions, trying to get more savings would not be a business proposition. In Latin America, savings are more 'income-elastic' than 'institution-elastic'.

Professor Hirschman replied that this was too pessimistic a view. In a developing country, new social groups were constantly reaching a level at which they could begin to save. It was important to acquaint them fully with the possibility of saving, which then would often be utilized at least until these groups had adjusted their living standards. The banks should be alert to such opportunities, combining the collection of savings with the granting of personal credit.

Professor Brahmananda added that in India consumer savings had shown themselves to be 'institution-elastic'.

Dr. Márquez remained unconvinced and suggested that if anything was to be done to capture small savings, the job should be left to official institutions.

Chapter 8

PRIVATE VERSUS PUBLIC FOREIGN INVESTMENT IN UNDER-DEVELOPED AREAS

BY

FELIPE PAZOS
Banco Continental Cubano

I. CLASSIFICATION OF INTERNATIONAL CAPITAL TRANSACTIONS

THIS paper is intended to examine a policy issue that has been widely discussed in the last decade and its title is worded in the simplified terms in which the issue has been commonly debated. Since the terms private and public are not completely clear and precise when referring to investment, we will begin by discussing their meaning.

It is not always easy to classify a capital transaction as private or public because the saving-investment process normally entails three types of participants : savers, financial intermediaries, and end users of the funds. Any one of these three may be either a private party or a public body. When all the participants in a particular saving-investment process are of the same nature, the process can be easily labelled. But when the participants are of different natures, should the transaction be classified according to the nature of the saver, of the intermediary, or of the end user ?

Both in the national and in the international spheres, the flow of private savings to governments and of public funds to private enterprises, either through private or public intermediaries, is very common and assumes many different forms. If we stop to examine the possible combinations, we find examples in real life of all but one of them.

This list is not exhaustive because it does not contemplate cases where there is more than one intermediary, for example, in International Bank loans in which New York banks or investment houses participate, or where saving of both public and private origin is merged, as in the example above or the construction of the Suez Canal, or where the end user is an enterprise owned partly by the government and partly by private interests. But even without taking into consideration these more involved cases, the picture is too complex to permit any clear-cut classification of investments as public or private. If strict logic were to be applied, three separate

TABLE 1

COMBINATIONS OF TYPES OF INTERMEDIARIES

Saver	Intermediary	End User	Example in the International Field
1. Private	Private	Private	Direct * and portfolio investment in private enterprises in foreign countries
2. Private	Private	Public	Loans to foreign governments floated in the market by private financial institutions
3. Private	Public	Private	International Bank loans to private enterprises (directly or through Fomento Corporations) financed with funds obtained in the market ; International Finance Corporation loans
4. Private	Public	Public	International Bank loans to governments financed with funds obtained in the market
5. Public	Private	Private	Export-Import Bank loans to foreign private enterprises through private financial institutions
6. Public	Private	Public	No example known by author
7. Public	Public	Private	Export-Import Bank loans to foreign private enterprises through Fomento Corporations
8. Public	Public	Public	Export-Import Bank loans to governments ; International Bank loans to governments financed with its own capital

* Although in direct investments there are no intermediaries, they obviously belong to the category where all parties are private.

classifications should be made for each transaction, one according to source, one according to intermediary, and one according to end user.

In current language, however, direct and portfolio investment is considered to be private. All other kinds are explicitly or implicitly considered to be public, even if the source and the end user are private and only the intermediary is public. Moreover, in discussion of capital flows to under-developed countries, the private category is in practice restricted to direct investment because of the virtual disappearance of portfolio investment as a form of capital movement to under-developed areas. The types of international investment discussed are, therefore, direct investment on one side and, on the other, international loans of public agencies, whether to governments or to private enterprises, and whether financed with funds obtained from public or private sources.

As already explained, this classification is not strictly logical from the point of view of the public or private character of the parties intervening in the saving-investment process. On the other hand, this classification is highly meaningful from an economic point of view. Direct investment and loans are quite different economic phenomena, which originate in different sources, respond to different stimuli, move through different channels, pursue different objectives, and produce different effects. It is perfectly valid, therefore, to classify and study them separately.

II. DIRECT INVESTMENT

According to the International Monetary Fund, 'a direct investment of a country is the amount invested by its residents in an enterprise or other commercial property abroad effectively controlled by its residents'.[1] A small part of direct investment is made by individuals, through the acquisition of real estate abroad, or of securities of foreign enterprises controlled by their co-nationals. However, by far the larger part of direct investment is made by corporations through the establishment of foreign branches or subsidiaries to exploit the same line of business in which the parent company is engaged or to produce raw materials or semi-manufactured goods for the parent company. In 1950, 90 per cent. of United States direct investment abroad was owned by corporations and only 10 per cent. by individuals.[2] Moreover, as a rule, direct investment is made by large companies. The Census of 1950 showed that 40 per cent. of the total investment at the end of that year was held by 10 corporations and an additional 10 per cent. by another fifteen companies.[3]

Since most direct investment is made by corporations, its source is business savings, that is, the undistributed profits, both of the parent companies and of the subsidiaries themselves. From 1946 to

[1] International Monetary Fund, *Balance of Payments Manual* (Washington, 1948).
[2] *Direct Private Foreign Investment of the United States*, Supplement to *The Survey of Current Business*, 1953, p. 21, and Appendix Tables 10 and 11.
[3] *Ibid.* p. 21.

1951, 45 per cent. of the increase in United States direct investment was financed by reinvestment of the earnings of subsidiaries.[1] A substantial part of the remainder, although registered as an outflow of capital from the United States, was probably reinvestment of branch profits.[2]

Direct investment does not supply all the funds for the enterprises it creates. Part is supplied by investors in the recipient country as equity capital. Yet another very substantial part is supplied by investors and financial institutions of either the investing country or the recipient country as loans. In some countries, foreign investors are legally required to associate with local capital. Even where regulations to this effect do not exist, the practice is widespread and is becoming progressively more common because of its many advantages to both foreign investors and local business men. Participation of domestic interests reduces the financial commitment of the foreign investors and links the enterprise to the local business community.

The 1950 Census estimates non-American participation in United States direct investment enterprises at about 20 per cent.[3] The data on non-American participation mainly reflect partnership between United States and host country interests, but associations of United States interests with British, Canadian, and European capital in investment in third countries are also included. Unfortunately the Census does not break down non-United States ownership of United States controlled foreign enterprises into host country and third countries owners.

A substantial part of the financial needs of direct investment enterprises is supplied by loan capital. It is a general practice of entrepreneurial investors, whether they invest at home or abroad, to borrow as much as possible and to reduce equity capital to the minimum required to offer a sound guarantee to lenders. The share of loan capital in total financing varies greatly from enterprise to

[1] S. Pizer and F. Cutler, 'Foreign Investments and Income', *Survey of Current Business*, November 1954, Tables 2 and 10.

[2] Earnings of subsidiaries, which are separate legal entities incorporated in the host country, are not registered as accruing to United States residents unless actually remitted, but earnings of branches, which are a part of the parent company, are registered as accruing to the parent company in the United States whether they are remitted or not. In balance of payments statistics, unremitted profits of branches are therefore registered twice : once as an inflow of profits and once as an outflow of capital.

[3] *Direct Private Foreign Investment of the United States*, Table 13, 'Total Assets, Owners' Share and Liabilities of Direct Investments, 1950', shows United States investments in equity capital of $9.9 billion and foreign owners' investment of $2.3 billion, or 19 per cent. of the total equity capital. But Table 16, 'United States and Foreign Investments in Foreign Corporations, 1950', shows United States investment of $1.4 billion less, thus elevating the share of non-Americans to 22 per cent. The difference seems to be due to the different definitions used in the two tables.

enterprise, depending on the nature of the assets, the velocity of turnover, and the rate of expansion, and it frequently exceeds equity capital. In the past, direct investors used to borrow in their own countries, where loan funds were abundant and cheap. But since the 1930s this practice has been progressively discontinued. Loans are obtained, whenever possible, in the country where the investment is made, even if interest rates are higher and funds more difficult to raise. This shift is an outcome of the fear of nationalization, exchange controls, and depreciation, which moves entrepreneurs to reduce their commitments to a minimum. In the case of currency depreciation, it is not only a question of fear but of sound business practice, since it is good business to borrow in a depreciating currency. In

TABLE 2

CAPITAL STRUCTURE OF UNITED STATES DIRECT FOREIGN
INVESTMENT IN 1950

(In percentages)

	Equity Capital	Creditor Capital	Total
Owned by or due to residents of the United States	45	8	53
Owned by or due to residents of other countries	10	37	47
Total	55	45	100

Source : *Direct Private Foreign Investments of the United States*, Supplement to *The Survey of Current Business*, 1953, Table 13.

countries with a depreciating currency, interest rates are high, but are generally not high enough to outweigh the decrease in value in real terms of the amounts loaned. In fact, there are times when interest rates in real terms are negative.

In 1950, according to the Census of that year, United States direct investment enterprises had total assets amounting to $22·2 billion, total liabilities, creditor capital, of $10·4 billion, and total net worth, *i.e.* equity capital, of $1·18 billion. Of the total liabilities, $1·9 billion was owed to United States creditors and $8·1 billion to creditors from outside the United States. Of the total net worth, $9·9 billion was owned by United States residents and $2·3 billion by residents of other countries. This means that 53 per cent. of the financing of United States direct investment enterprises was supplied by United States capital and 47 per cent. by non-United States funds, mostly by capital of the recipient countries. The surprising size of non-United States capital is explained by the fact that more than 80 per cent. of loan capital was raised in the recipient countries. Table 2 shows these percentages in tabulated form.

Capital is directly invested in foreign countries in practically all fields of economic activity, from agriculture to services. But there is a marked preference for investment in primary industries and public utilities in under-developed countries and for investment in manufacturing in industrial nations. In 1950, 75 per cent. of United States private capital in Latin America was invested in agriculture, mining, and public utilities, while that in manufacturing was limited to 16 per cent. In Western European dependencies (the Middle East, Africa, and South-east Asia), 88 per cent. of United States investment was in petroleum and mining, manufacturing being only 2 per cent. of the total. On the other hand, in Canada and Western Europe manufacturing receives more than half of United States investment while primary industries take about one-fourth. The distribution of United States direct investment in 1950 by industries and areas is shown in Table 3.

TABLE 3

INDUSTRIAL DISTRIBUTION OF UNITED STATES DIRECT
INVESTMENT IN 1950, BY AREAS

(In percentages)

	Western Europe	Canada	Latin America	Western European Dependencies	Other Countries	Total
Agriculture	—	1	11	2	3	5
Mining and smelting	1	9	13	20	4	10
Petroleum .	25	12	29	68	64	29
Manufacturing	54	53	16	2	16	32
Public utilities	1	8	22	4	4	12
Trade	11	6	5	3	6	6
Finance and Insurance	2	9	2	—	—	4
Miscellaneous	6	2	1	—	2	2
Total	100	100	100	100	100	100

Source : *Direct Private Foreign Investments of the United States*, Appendix, Table 5.

Until the 1930s, railways and public utilities used to be a preferred field which absorbed more than one-fifth of United States direct investment in Latin America and probably more than one-half of United Kingdom direct investment in that area. But these fields have lost their attraction and the amount of private capital being invested in them is very small. The share of transportation, com-

munication, and public utilities in total United States direct investment in all areas diminished from 21 per cent. in 1929 to 18 per cent.
in 1943 and to 12 per cent. in 1950. The increase in the value of
United States direct investment in transportation, communication,
and public utilities between 1943 and 1950 was only 1 per cent. of
the total increase in value of United States direct investment during
that period. The decrease in Latin America has been somewhat
less drastic but also very pronounced. As shown in Table 4, the value

TABLE 4

INDUSTRIAL DISTRIBUTION OF UNITED STATES DIRECT
INVESTMENT IN LATIN AMERICA IN SELECTED YEARS *

(In percentages)

	1914	1929	1943	1944–53
Agriculture	19	24	14	5
Mining and smelting	43	22	14	19
Petroleum	10	21	20	35
Manufacturing	3	6	11	26
Transportation, communication and public utilities	21	22	31	7
Trade	3	3	5	7
Finance, insurance, and miscellaneous	1	2	5	1
Total	100	100	100	100

* Figures for 1914, 1929, and 1943 show value of total investment at a given moment
in these years. Figures for 1944–53 register the flow of investment during that period.

Source : United Nations, *Foreign Capital in Latin America* (New York, 1955),
and Samuel Pizer and Frederick Cutler, 'Foreign Investment and Income',
Survey of Current Business, November 1954.

of United States investment in transportation, communication, and
public utilities in Latin America represented 31 per cent. of the total
United States direct investment in that area in 1943, but only 7 per
cent. of the new direct investment in that area from 1944 to 1953.

The fall of investment in public utilities is the result of the sharp
decline in their yield, which has fallen to less than one-tenth of the
yield in other fields. As shown in Table 5, from 1948 to 1951 the
average ratio of earnings to book value of United States investment
in public utilities was only 1·9 per cent., while that in other fields
averaged 20 per cent. Squeezed between rising costs and government regulated rates, public utilities in Latin America yield less than
United States Government bonds and, hence, are not attractive to
private capital, either foreign or domestic.

Tables 4 and 5 show that, as would be expected, direct investment
is moving into those fields that yield higher profits, the only major

exception being agriculture, which is markedly receding in importance as a field for foreign investment despite its high yields.

Geographically, direct investment flows to countries where known
natural resources offer the best prospects and to countries that have
a large and expanding domestic market. A favourable investment
climate and a non-discriminatory attitude towards foreign investment
is a necessary but not a sufficient condition for capital to move into a

TABLE 5

RATIO OF EARNINGS TO EQUITY, UNITED STATES DIRECT
INVESTMENTS IN LATIN AMERICA, 1948–51 *

(In percentages)

	1948	1949	1950	1951	Average 1948–51
Agriculture	22·2	13·6	17·3	20·6	18·4
Mining and smelting	18·1	9·4	11·6	16·6	13·9
Petroleum	35·1	21·5	18·7	29·0	26·0
Manufacturing	20·2	15·6	15·9	21·8	18·4
Trade	27·3	17·6	13·7	20·2	19·7
Miscellaneous	19·3	20·9	21·6	19·8	20·4
Sub-Total	24·2	15·5	16·4	23·3	20·0
Public Utilities	1·3	1·2	2·5	2·6	1·9
Total	19·2	12·4	13·4	18·8	16·0

* Earnings represent total income accruing to United States investors, including
equity in undistributed profits of foreign subsidiaries and earnings blocked by exchange
restrictions. Earnings are net of Latin American taxes — but before United States
income taxes. Equity represents net worth at book value at beginning of year.

Source : United Nations, *Foreign Capital in Latin America* (New York, 1955),
Table XXI ; and original data from United States Department of Commerce.

country. Countries without well-known natural resources or with
known natural resources that are more difficult to exploit than those
of their neighbours do not attract foreign capital to their extractive
industries even if they offer very favourable treatment to foreign
capital. Small countries and large countries with stagnant economies
do not attract investment for the establishment or expansion of
manufacturing industries. Cuba has huge iron deposits, but United
States capital is exploiting the higher grade deposits of Canada and
Venezuela, and keeping Cuba's in reserve. Manufacturing corporations establish subsidiaries in Brazil and Mexico, which have large
and expanding domestic markets, but not in El Salvador, Costa Rica,
or Ecuador, despite the good treatment received by foreign capital
in these countries.

Table 6 shows that investment is going mainly to countries with well-known rich natural resources, Venezuela, Chile, and Peru, and to those with large and expanding domestic markets, Brazil and Mexico. The influence of government attitudes is probably reflected

TABLE 6

AVERAGE ANNUAL ADDITIONS TO UNITED STATES DIRECT
INVESTMENT IN LATIN AMERICA, 1944–50 AND 1951–53

(In millions of United States dollars)

	1944–50	1951–53
Argentina	3·5	18·7
Bolivia	2·4	1·3
Brazil	58·8	119·7
Chile	30·2	42·0
Colombia	10·9	14·0
Costa Rica	4·2	0·3
Cuba	16·6	14·7
Dominican Republic	5·0	5·0
Ecuador	0·5	1·0
El Salvador	0·5	1·0
Guatemala	2·7	0·3
Haiti	0·2	1·0
Honduras	3·5	6·7
Mexico	18·3	31·7
Nicaragua	0·7	—
Panama	35·4	16·7
Peru	10·5	38·0
Uruguay and Paraguay	6·6	7·0
Venezuela	88·6	105·0
Total	287·7	422·0

Source : *Direct Private Foreign Investment of the United States*, Appendix, Table 12 ; Samuel Pizer and Frederick Cutler, *op. cit.* Table 6.

in the relatively small flow to Argentina, in spite of Argentina's large domestic market and rapid rate of industrial development during the period. Low investment in Guatemala in 1951–53 may also be attributed to an unfavourable investment climate. But Costa Rica, where a favourable environment prevails, received the same low amount of investment in these two years, and Nicaragua, which maintains a most friendly attitude towards United States capital, received practically none during the entire period 1944–53. Panama's high figure does not reflect true capital movements but is largely due to the registration of United States ships and tankers under Panama's flag. Honduras' figure is also nominal, probably for the same reason.

III. INTERNATIONAL LONG TERM LOANS

In the nineteenth century and in the first three decades of the current century, under-developed countries borrowed freely in the capital markets of Europe and the United States. National, provincial, and municipal governments, and private corporations, mainly railways, floated loans in the United Kingdom, France, Belgium, Germany, Holland, Switzerland, and the United States. Before 1914, the flow of loans from Europe to Latin America seems to have been substantially larger than the flow of equity capital. It is estimated that 31 per cent. of the total investment of the United Kingdom in Latin America in 1914 was in bonds of national, provincial, and municipal governments and 46 per cent. was in railway securities.[1] Assuming that 60 per cent. of railway securities were bonds or debentures, 58 per cent. of United Kingdom investment was in the form of loans. French investment in Latin America at the eve of World War I had approximately the same composition.[2]

Before 1914, the bulk of United States capital in Latin America was in the form of direct investment, but in the 1920s the volume of loans increased considerably, amounting to about 42 per cent. of total United States foreign investment from 1919 to 1930.[3]

The Great Depression put an end to international long term credit from private sources. In the middle thirties the United States established the Export-Import Bank to fill part of the vacuum created by the cessation of international private long term loans. In the middle forties, the International Bank for Reconstruction and Development was established with the same purpose. As private capital markets of the United States and Europe continue to be closed to under-developed countries, the only external sources of loan funds for these countries are the two agencies mentioned above, the United States government itself, and the governments of a few other industrial countries which extend loans and grants to their colonies and possessions. In discussing Latin America, however, we may limit ourselves to the operations of the Export-Import Bank and of the International Bank since these are, for all practical purposes, the only sources of international long term credit for this region.

The Export-Import Bank and the International Bank for Reconstruction and Development lend to governments or government agencies and to private enterprises. The International Bank requires that loans to private enterprises be guaranteed by the government,

---

[1] United Nations, *Foreign Capital in Latin America*, 1954, p. 5.
[2] United Nations, *op. cit.* p. 5.
[3] United Nations, *op. cit.*, Appendix, Table V.

while the Export-Import Bank lends to private enterprise both with and without government guarantee. In some cases, governments or government agencies use the proceeds of loans themselves to finance overhead capital projects. In other cases, they re-lend the proceeds

TABLE 7

INTERNATIONAL BANK LOANS TO LATIN AMERICA,
CLASSIFIED BY PURPOSE *

(In millions of United States dollars)

Overhead capital

Public works

Ports and inland waterways	6		
Roads	114		
Irrigation and flood control	20		
Land clearance and improvement	2		
		142	

Public utilities

Electric power	312		
Railroads	127		
Telephone, telegraph, and radio	24		
		463	
			605

Specific capital

Agriculture and forestry

Farm mechanization	22		
Crop processing and storage	2		
Livestock	1		
		25	

Industry

Pulp and paper	20		
Other industries	2		
Development banks	1		
		23	
			48
Total			653

* Total credits authorized since beginnings of operations; includes loans repaid and credits not yet utilized.

Source : International Bank for Reconstruction and Development, *Eleventh Annual Report, 1955–1956* (Washington, 1956).

to business. Direct and indirect loans to business go both to domestic and foreign enterprises.

The records of the Export-Import Bank and of the International Bank show that 57 per cent. of their current loans to Latin American countries have been used to finance specific projects in public utilities and public works, 21 per cent. to finance specific projects in agriculture, mining, and manufacturing, and 22 per cent. to cover general balance of payments deficits. The Export-Import Bank's

TABLE 8

EXPORT-IMPORT BANK LOANS TO LATIN AMERICA
CLASSIFIED BY PURPOSE *

(In millions of United States dollars)

Overhead capital

Public works

Ports and inland waterways	17.7	
Roads	77·4	
Irrigation and flood control	22·5	
Waterworks	14·7	
Airports	2·0	
Hospitals	0·7	
	—	135·0

Public utilities

Electric power	108·8	
Railroads	149·5	
Communications	1·4	
Trucks and buses	2·1	
Shipping	42·5	
Airlines	3·1	
	——	307·4
Balance of payments	401·9	
	—— ——	844·3

Specific capital

Agriculture and forestry

Farm mechanization	17·3	
Processing and storage	2·2	
General development	20·6	
	——	40·1

Manufacturing

Steel	124·1	
Other	107·9	
	——	232·0
Petroleum	8·5	
Mining and smelting	57·7	
Hotels	7·7	
	——	346·0
Total		1,193·2†

* Total disbursement on current loans.
† Total exceeds the sum of partial items because of rounding of figures.

Source : Export-Import Bank of Washington, *Report to the Congress for the Period January-June 1956* (Washington, 1956).

portfolio is much more diversified than that of the International Bank, 71 per cent. of which is concentrated in public utilities and 22 per cent. in public works. Export-Import Bank loans to finance public works and utilities comprise 37 per cent. of its portfolio ; balance of payments loans, 34 per cent. ; and loans to agriculture,

TABLE 9

TOTAL LOANS RECEIVED BY LATIN AMERICA FROM THE EXPORT-IMPORT BANK AND THE INTERNATIONAL BANK *

(In millions of United States dollars)

	Export-Import Bank	International Bank	Total
Argentina	102	—	102
Bolivia	44	—	44
Brazil	672	156	828
Chile	144	23	167
Colombia	83	60	143
Costa Rica	12	—	12
Cuba	72	—	72
Dominican Republic	3	—	3
Ecuador	34	2	36
El Salvador	1	16	17
Guatemala	1	5	6
Haiti	33	—	33
Honduras	1	—	1
Mexico	252	113	365
Nicaragua	5	8	13
Panama	6	2	8
Paraguay	6	3	9
Peru	17	17	34
Uruguay	17	35	52
Venezuela	23	—	23
Various	27	—	27
Total	1556	440	1996

* Cumulative disbursements from beginning of operations of each institution to June 30, 1956.

Source : Export-Import Bank of Washington, *Report to the Congress for the Period January-June 1956* ; International Bank for Reconstruction and Development, *Eleventh Annual Report, 1955–56* (Washington, 1956).

mining, and manufacturing, 29 per cent. Two-thirds of this third group are loans to manufacturing industries, principally steel. Tables 7 and 8 show a more detailed classification of International Bank and Export-Import Bank loans.

Geographical distribution of Export-Import Bank and International Bank loans to Latin America seems to show that loans are going to the countries that are developing fastest, Brazil, Mexico, Chile, and Colombia. The only exception is Venezuela, which is receiving all the dollars she can use through direct investment.

The reason for this correlation between a large inflow of foreign capital and a rapid rate of growth does not seem to be so much that

TABLE 10

GEOGRAPHICAL DISTRIBUTION OF UNITED STATES CAPITAL
FLOWS TO LATIN AMERICA

(In percentages)

	Direct Investment *	Loans †
Argentina	2·1	5·2
Bolivia	0·1	2·2
Brazil	25·1	41·9
Chile	10·1	8·4
Colombia	3·5	7·2
Costa Rica	0·6	0·6
Cuba	4·4	3·6
Dominican Republic	1·4	0·1
Ecuador	0·2	1·8
El Salvador	0·2	0·8
Guatemala	0·4	0·3
Haiti	0·1	1·7
Honduras	1·4	—
Mexico	7·0	18·5
Nicaragua	0·1	0·7
Panama	7·3	0·4
Peru	6·8	1·7
Uruguay and Paraguay	1·9	3·1
Venezuela	27·2	1·1
Total	100·0	100·0

* Additions to direct investment in the period 1944–53.
† Cumulative disbursements of Export-Import Bank and of International Bank as of June 30, 1956.

Source : For direct investment, sources listed in Table 5 ; for loans, International Bank for Reconstruction and Development, *Eleventh Annual Report* and Export-Import Bank, *Report to the Congress for the period January-June 1956*.

loans help the development of countries which receive them, but rather that countries that are developing rapidly have large needs for capital and can present the Bank with many suitable and attractive projects for financing. In the case of private investment also, development attracts capital and capital fosters development. Table 10 shows that public loans and private investment are going to much the same geographical areas.

The volume of international loans to Latin American countries in recent years has been substantially lower than the volume of direct investment. From 1949 to 1952, Latin American countries received $337 million in Export-Import Bank and International Bank loans (net of repayments) and $1144 million in direct investment (counting both capital movements and re-invested earnings). Of the total inflow of capital to Latin America in these years, 23 per cent.

TABLE 11

FLOW OF UNITED STATES LONG TERM CAPITAL
TO LATIN AMERICA, 1950–52

(In millions of United States dollars)

	1950	1951	1952
Direct private investment			
Actual flows (net)	40	166	277
Re-invested earnings	109	249	303
Total	149	415	580
Loans to public agencies			
Export-Import Bank and United States non-military grants	35	85	56
International Bank	39	56	66
Total	74	141	122
Other long term capital	– 27	– 29	– 34
Total	196	527	668

Source : United Nations, *Foreign Capital in Latin America*, Appendix, Table XVII.

was in the form of loans. This percentage is well below that prevailing before 1930. According to estimates quoted above, loans accounted for 58 per cent. of United Kingdom investments in Latin America before 1914 and 42 per cent. of United States investments from 1919 to 1930.

IV. RELATIVE REQUIREMENTS FOR EQUITY CAPITAL AND LOANS

Having examined the characteristics and functions of direct investment and loans, and having seen the relative volumes in which these two types of capital are flowing to Latin America, we may now ask whether these relative volumes have been adequate. Have the relative needs for each been satisfied ? Would the current relationship between foreign direct investment and international loans be appropriate if the total flow of capital were increased ? What are the relative needs of a developing country for foreign direct investment and international loans ?

TABLE 12

CONTRIBUTION OF EQUITY CAPITAL TO THE FINANCING OF
PRIVATE INVESTMENT IN THE UNITED STATES, 1950–53

(In billions of United States dollars)

	1950	1951	1952	1953	1950–53
Increase in equity in non-farm residences and in real property of non-profit institutions	2·76	1·98	2·13	2·15	9·02
Increase in equity in non-farm unincorporated enterprises	– 1·90	2·39	0·36	3·79	4·64
Increase in equity in farm enterprises	– 0·16	0·12	– 0·37	– 1·61	– 2·02
Corporate common stocks	0·82	1·21	1·36	1·33	4·72
Total personal saving invested in equity	1·52	5·70	3·48	5·66	16·36
Undistributed corporate profits	12·93	9·61	8·08	8·92	39·54
Total saving invested in equity	14·45	15·31	11·56	14·58	55·90
Net private investment	28·50	33·52	25·21	22·39	109·62
Ratio of equity to private investment	0·51	0·46	0·46	0·65	0·51

Source : Data from Securities and Exchange Commission and Department of Commerce quoted in A. O. Dahlberg, *National Income Visualized* (New York, 1956), Table 6 ; data on corporate common stock, *Survey of Current Business*.

Since a country's total investment is financed by domestic equity capital, domestic loan capital, foreign equity capital, and foreign loan capital, the problem as to the optimum relationship between the two types of foreign capital has to be examined in two steps. First, it is necessary to ascertain the relative needs of a country for equity capital and loan capital, whatever the geographical origin of the capital. Second, one must study the relative need for each type of capital from each source. Neither question has a precise and invariable answer, but I shall attempt to obtain an idea of the orders of magnitude involved.

I do not know of any estimates of the relative share of equity capital and loans in the financing of investment in the United States, but available data seem to permit an estimate. Such an estimate, based mainly on Securities and Exchange Commission data on personal saving, is shown in Table 12. According to this estimate, from 1950 to 1953 net private investment in the United States amounted to $109·6 billion. During this period, personal saving invested in equity amounted to $16·4 billion and undistributed corporate profits

TABLE 13

UNITED STATES INVESTMENT AND ITS SOURCES OF FINANCE, 1950–53

	Billions of United States dollars	Percentage
Investment		
Net private investment	109·6	74
Public construction	38·7	26
Total	148·3	100
Financing :		
Private equity capital	55·5	37
Government equity capital	26·3	18
Loans	66·5	45
Total	148·3	100

Source : Table 11 ; A. O. Dahlberg, *National Income Visualized*, Table 31 ; International Monetary Fund, *International Financial Statistics*, January, 1955.

amounted to $39·5 billion. Equity capital, therefore, financed $55·9 billion or 51 per cent. of United States net private investment during the period. Loan capital, in its various forms, financed the remaining 49 per cent. Roughly speaking, equity and loans each financed one-half of private investment.

If we bring public investment into the picture, the share of private equity capital in the financing of total investment is reduced. In the four years, 1950–53, public construction in the United States amounted to $38·7 billion. Total net investment, private and public, during the period amounted, therefore, to $148·3 billion. As public debt increased in these years by $12·4 billion, it may be considered that $26·3 billion of public construction was financed from current revenue. On the basis of these figures, it may be said that 37 per cent. of total net investment was financed by private equity capital, 18 per cent. by current government revenue, which we may properly call government equity, and 45 per cent. by loan capital. Table 13 shows these figures in tabulated form.

The 50:50 ratio between equity and loans for private investment found in the United States in the years 1950–53 seems a reasonable formula to use in our estimates. The ratio in direct investment enterprises, shown in Table 1, is very close to it (55-45).

TABLE 14

CAPITAL STRUCTURE OF THE UNITED STATES ECONOMY IN 1939

Industry	Fixed Capital Stock	
	Millions of United States dollars	Percentage of total
Agriculture and fishing	16,683	6·5
Mining	10,859	4·2
Manufacturing	42,412	16·5
Construction	1,435	0·6
Public utilities	48,807	19·0
Trade	10,602	4·1
Residential	70,578	27·5
Miscellaneous services	7,222	2·8
Total Private	208,598	81·2
Government	48,400	18·8
Total	256,998	100·0

Source : Figures for private capital stock from W. Leontief, *Studies in the Structure of the American Economy* (New York, 1953), p. 492 ; figures for 'reproducible physical assets of the Federal, State, and local government', excluding gold and silver, from J. E. Reeve, 'Government Component in the National Wealth', Conference on Research in Income and Wealth, *Studies in Income and Wealth*, XII (Princeton, 1956), p. 467.

Taking a 50:50 ratio between equity and loans for private investment, the overall ratio of equity and loans in total investment will depend on three factors, the volume of public investment, the way in which investment in public utilities is financed, and the proportion of public investment financed with current revenue.

The relation of public investment to total investment varies widely from country to country, depending on the field covered by government economic activity. However, we will base our estimate of public investment requirements on those investments that have necessarily to be made by the government and have traditionally been made by it, such as roads, streets, ports, waterworks, sewage systems, dams, public hospitals, public schools, and administrative buildings. In the United States these reproducible public assets were estimated to account for 19 per cent. of the total fixed capital stock of the country in 1939 (see Table 14). Moreover, in the years 1950–53 public construction absorbed 26 per cent. of total net investment in the United States. Similarly, the Nacional Financiera-International Bank Report estimated that from 1941 to 1950 public investment in Mexico constituted 40 per cent. of total investment,[1] and deducting government investment in other fields from this figure we get 25 per cent. for investment in public works. Finally, the International Bank Report on Colombia recommended investments in the public sector to an amount equivalent to 32 per cent. of total investment.[2] These various figures seem to indicate that in a normal growth process public works absorb from 20 to 30 per cent. of total investment.

When public utilities are profitable they re-invest part of their earnings and, if necessary, issue new stock to cover about 40 per cent. of the capital they need to expand, borrowing the remainder. But when their profits are very low or non-existent, they have to resort to the government to obtain all, or practically all, the capital they need, generally in the form of loans. This naturally raises the proportion of loan capital in overall financing. According to Leontief, investment in public utilities represented 23 per cent. of private fixed capital stock in the United States in 1939 or, according to the estimate in Table 14, 19 per cent. of the total of both public and private investment.[3] In Mexico, investment in public utilities in 1950 seems to have absorbed 22 per cent. of total investment in that year.[4]

As I said before, the ratio of private equity to loan capital is largely affected by the proportion of public investment that is financed from current revenue. If all public investment is financed from revenue, the overall ratio remains equal to the private ratio. But if part or all of public investment, which we have estimated above amounts to 20 to 30 per cent. of total investment in a normal growth economy, is financed by government borrowing, the proportion of loans in total financing rises from 50 per cent. to between

[1] Combined Mexican Working Party, *The Economic Development of Mexico* (Baltimore, 1953).
[2] The International Bank for Reconstruction and Development, *The Basis of a Development Program for Colombia*, Report of a mission headed by Lauchlin Currie (Washington, 1953).
[3] W. Leontief, *Studies in the Structure of the American Economy* (New York, 1953), p. 492.
[4] Combined Mexican Working Party, *op. cit.*

50 and 65 per cent. The proportion of public investment financed from current revenue varies from country to country and from year to year. Hence no constant figure can be used as a basis of estimate. But this difficulty does not hamper our calculations, because our purpose is to find the optimum ratio of equity to loans in the inflow of capital from abroad. This capital, which supplements domestic resources, cannot, by definition, be provided out of the current revenue of the government of the recipient country but has to come as either equity or loan capital.

The average requirement of capital by various economic sectors seems to be roughly as follows : public works, 20 to 30 per cent. of total ; public utilities, 15 to 25 per cent. ; agriculture, mining, manufacturing, trade, and other services, 30 to 40 per cent. ; housing, 20 to 30 per cent. (see Tables 14 and 15). Assuming that public

TABLE 15

CAPITAL REQUIREMENTS BY ECONOMIC SECTORS IN
THE UNITED STATES AND MEXICO
(In percentages)

	United States *	Mexico †
Agriculture and fishing	6·5	7·2
Mining	4·2	3·8
Manufacturing and construction	17·1	21·7
Trade	4·1	—
Miscellaneous services	2·8	—
Sub-total	34·7	32·7
Residential	27·5	20·3
Public utilities	19·0	21·9
Government	18·8	25·1
Total	100·0	100·0

* Fixed capital stock in 1939.
† Gross investment 1941–50. Original figures have been rearranged in the following manner : irrigation, which appears in the original under 'Public Investment in Agriculture', and roads, ports, and airports, which appear under 'Public Investment in Transportation and Communications', have been classified under Government.

Source : For United States, see Table 11. For Mexico, Combined Mexican Working Party, *The Economic Development of Mexico* (Washington, 1953), Table 15.

works are financed entirely by loans, as is the case with supplementary public works financed from abroad, and assuming that the average ratio of equity to loans in other sectors is 50:50, the overall ratio would be 40 per cent. equity to 60 per cent. loans or 35:65, depending on whether the share of public works is 20 or 30 per cent. This estimate is based on the assumption that public utilities are privately financed. If public utilities are entirely financed by loan capital, the proportion of loans would rise to about 70 per cent. Since in most Latin American countries public utilities are, indeed, almost entirely financed by loans, the proper ratio should be this latter, that is, 30 per cent. equity to 70 per cent. loans. This is approximately the reverse of the ratio of equity to loans in the current flow of United States capital to Latin America.

The ratio between the two types of capital inflow does not have to be exactly proportional to the recipient country's requirements because domestic capital may adapt itself and fill the gaps. If, for instance, foreign capital supplies 20 per cent. of total requirements and brings 14 units in equity and 6 in loans, domestic capital may limit its contribution to equity to 16 units and supply 64 units in loans. But it is possible that the adaptation of domestic capital may not be complete. Hence, some sector, for example, public utilities, may be left insufficiently supplied. It is also possible that domestic savers may not be willing to invest in government securities and that, in order to finance public works, the government may have to resort to inflation.

It should also be noted that, given the lower yield of loan capital, the shift from loans to equity increases earnings and vice versa. Assuming an average yield of 20 per cent. for equity and 6 per cent. for loans, in the example above, foreign capital would earn 15·8 per cent. and domestic capital 8·8 per cent.

The fact that the composition of capital inflow does not correspond to the relative needs of the recipient country does not create an insoluble problem, but is not an ideal pattern. When the share of foreign capital in total investment is below 20 per cent., as is currently the case in all Latin American countries except Venezuela, the problems created by this pattern are not overwhelming. But if the flow of capital is going to increase, its composition must change, adapting itself better to the relative needs of the recipient countries for different types of capital.

It might be objected that Venezuela, which has the highest ratio of equity to loans, is not suffering any ill consequences from this high ratio. However, it should be borne in mind, on the one hand, that petroleum investment supplies its own needs for power, transportation, housing, sanitation, and other services, and, on the other, that it pays huge royalties which enable the government to cover the country's requirements for overhead capital liberally. This is not the case with direct investment in other industries in other countries. Petroleum investment in Venezuela is frequently presented as a typical example of foreign direct investment but, in many respects, it is as atypical as the geology of Venezuela.

V. Possibilities of Substitution between Direct Investment and Loans

This paper has tried to show that direct investment and international loans play different rôles and cover needs of different natures in the economic development of a country. Direct investment is an entrepreneurial activity performed by large corporations which have all the facilities — organization, experience, technical and managerial skills, patents, trade marks, and marketing channels — to establish new production units, or to expand existing ones, with a very high probability of success. International loans are purely financial transactions which supply supplemental funds to private enterprises, or to governments for re-lending to private enterprises or for financing public works and public utilities.

Direct investment is not a substitute for loans for the financing of public works. Moreover, although it could finance those capital needs of private enterprises that are customarily financed through loans, this shift would not be welcomed by entrepreneurs, nor would it represent any improvement in financial practice. Direct investment is not, therefore, a substitute for loans.

It could be argued that although direct investment cannot cover loan needs, it raises income and hence saving, and is thus an indirect source of loan capital. But this reasoning does not take into consideration the fact that direct investment itself, and the income generated by the export or import substituting industries created by it, have income-expansionary effects that raise the demand for capital. In most cases, this secondary increase in the demand for capital is probably as large, if not larger, than the increase in saving and does not leave any capital free to cover the *ex-ante* deficiency in loan capital.[1]

[1] Ignoring the temporary income effects of direct investment through the investment multiplier, and taking into consideration only its permanent income effects through the international trade multiplier, income expansion may be calculated by the well-known formula: $\Delta Y = \Delta X \left(\dfrac{l}{s+m-sm} \right)$ where $Y =$ increment in income; $X =$ increment in export or import substituting production brought about by direct investment; $s =$ marginal propensity to save; and $m =$ marginal propensity to import. Saving forthcoming from this additional income will, hence, be: $\Delta S = s\Delta X \left(\dfrac{l}{s+m-sm} \right)$. The increase in capital requirements is given by the formula: $\Delta K = k\Delta X \left(\dfrac{l-(s+m-sm)}{s+m-sm} \right)$ where $K =$ increment in capital requirements and $k =$ capital-income ratio. In order that $\Delta S = \Delta K$, the marginal propensity to save must be: $s = \left(\dfrac{k\,(lm)}{l+k\,(l-m)} \right)$. Giving k a value of 2·5

International loans, on the other hand, may be a substitute for direct investment in some circumstances, owing to government participation in the transaction. The capital needed to expand the capacity of public utilities may be entirely financed by loans if public utilities are government owned or if the government makes or guarantees the loans. The same may be true of enterprises in other fields owned by the government or which the government wants to favour. Governments may use borrowed funds to supply all or part of the equity capital needed to create new industries or may lend them more funds than would be warranted by the amount of equity capital invested in those new industries. In such cases, loan funds are, in part or in whole, a substitute for equity finance.

In contradistinction to direct investment, loans do not bring with them the entrepreneurial activities and skills supplied by direct investment. Because of this fact, the substitution of loan for equity capital may not be successful if there are in the country no technicians and managers able to organize and operate the new industries, unless they are brought from abroad.

VI. POLICY CONSIDERATIONS

To the extent that international loans can be used as substitutes for direct investment, there is reason for discussing which of the two is better for development. According to the estimates worked out in this paper, the relative needs of developing countries for loans and equity investment are in a ratio of 7 : 3. Given the indirect character of the estimates and the margins of error to which the data are subject, it is quite possible that the relative need for loans may be less than 70 per cent. of total capital requirements, perhaps 60 per cent., or even 55 per cent., but, barring gross errors in the estimates, not less than the latter figure. To be conservative, we

and m a value of 0·3, s would be 0·64, which is a completely unattainable figure. With higher values for k and lower values for m, s would be even higher.

If direct investment is not entirely devoted to export or import substituting industries but goes in part to meet the needs of secondary expansion (public utilities, other services, expansion of already established industries producing for the domestic market, etc.), the required value of s decreases very sharply ; for instance, if one-half of direct investment is devoted to secondary expansion, the marginal propensity to save necessary to equate the supply of and the demand for capital would be 0·22, which is still high but not unattainable.

The foregoing analysis is based on the assumption that *ex-ante* domestic saving is fully used in *ex-ante* investment and, hence, not available to cover the additional capital needs created by the secondary income expansion induced by direct investment. Since this does not always happen, the additional capital needs may be covered in whole or in part by *ex-ante* domestic saving. But, when this is the case, direct investment is not satisfying, directly or indirectly, the country's needs for loan capital but is relying on domestic saving to cover those needs.

may take 55 per cent. as the minimum proportion of international capital that should be in the form of loans if the needs of developing countries are to be adequately covered. The remaining 45 per cent. may take the form of loans or of direct investment, depending on the development policy that is followed. In regard to this 45 per cent., much can be said in favour of direct investment and much in favour of international loans.

Direct investment has the great advantage of bringing with it all the elements necessary to create new production units. It brings prefabricated industries, so to speak, ready for use and guaranteed to operate satisfactorily. Direct investment brings with it ready made development in the particular field to which it belongs. Practically no effort is needed from the residents of the recipient country. There is no wait for the training of technicians and managers, nor for tryouts and the gaining of experience. If it comes in adequate volume to the proper fields and is accompanied by the necessary amount of loans to finance overhead capital facilities, direct investment is a short cut to development.

On the liability side, direct investment has disadvantages that are an immediate counterpart of its advantages. Direct investment is the easiest way for a country to acquire new manufacturing industries or to exploit its natural resources, but, as frequently happens with easy solutions, it is costly in the long run. As shown in Table 5, United States direct investment in Latin America in fields other than public utilities is bringing an annual yield of 20 per cent. Since the purely financial cost of this capital is about 5 per cent., Latin America is paying an additional 15 per cent. per annum for entrepreneurial services. These services are fully worth their cost and should be used as long as there are no local entrepreneurs to perform them, but their cost is high enough to justify a strong and sustained effort by Latin American countries to train their own entrepreneurs, managers, and technicians.

As an alternative to direct investment, the Economic Commission for Latin America has proposed that new industries be financed by international loans to governments and that their organization, management, and operation for the first few years be contracted for with foreign firms.[1] In this way, the developing country obtains capital at its purely financial cost, amortizes it in a reasonable period, and receives the benefits of foreign technical and managerial skills. In fact, the system has been tried successfully in some instances, such as the Huachipato steel mill in Chile, and deserves the most

[1] United Nations, *Economic Co-operation in a Latin American Development Policy*, 1954.

careful consideration of economists and policy makers. The system has the further advantage of giving the initiative to create new industries to the developing countries themselves. They do not have to wait until foreign investors find that their domestic markets or natural resources have become as attractive as those of other producing countries.

Many more arguments could be presented on the relative merits of direct investment and loans, but it does not seem useful to prolong a discussion of the best way to cover needs that can be satisfied by either type of capital movement, when in actuality specific loan requirements are being left uncovered. Before weighing the advisability of using loans as a substitute for direct investment, one must consider the necessity of increasing loans to cover unsatisfied, or poorly satisfied, needs that can *only* be covered by loans.

Table 11 shows that in the three-year period 1950–52, Latin America received direct investments, including re-invested earnings, at an annual rate of $381 million and Export-Import and International Bank loans, net of repayment, at an annual rate of $112 million. Of the total inflow, 23 per cent. was therefore in the form of loans.[1] This proportion is considerably below the 55 per cent. which we have found necessary for balanced growth. If this latter percentage had been realized, annual loans during these years would have amounted to $466 million, more than four times their actual rate. With an annual volume of loans of this or similar magnitude, Latin American countries would not be experiencing the bottlenecks in overhead capital facilities which now hamper their development. Nor would they probably face as many financial disorders as they currently do, because these difficulties are, at least in part, a consequence of their efforts to augment public saving in order to finance their increasing overhead capital requirements.

It is the conclusion of this paper that in order to obtain the optimum contribution of foreign capital to the balanced development of Latin America, the share of loans in total foreign investment in Latin America should be considerably raised. Given the current volume of direct investment, the recommended relative increase of loans would also represent a large increase in absolute amounts.

---

[1] 24 per cent. if outflows of 'other long term capital' are deducted from the total.

COMMENTS ON DR. PAZOS' PAPER

BY

LORETO M. DOMINGUEZ
Organization of American States

I. INTRODUCTION

ALTHOUGH I am in sympathy with the policy conclusion contained in the paper, I do not agree with the analysis leading to it nor do I find the statistical formula which it offers valid. One of the difficulties of the policy conclusion drawn from the formula is that it leads to problems of implementation which are not dealt with in the paper and which would be quite difficult to solve. For instance, must we conclude that under-developed countries should impose controls so that foreign capital may flow in the proportions required to preserve the ideal ratio ? Do we prohibit further entrance of foreign equity capital unless the set quota for loans has been fulfilled ?

II. THE STABILITY OF THE RATIO BETWEEN EQUITY AND LOAN CAPITAL

The evidence in support of the contention that more loans are needed is in reality limited. We are shown that in the United States, investment is financed — or at least was financed during 1950–53 — in approximately equal parts by equity and loan capital. If public investment and public utilities, where loan capital is relatively more important, are added, the ratio between equity and loan capital in total United States investments changes to approximately 30 per cent. equity and 70 per cent. loan. At another stage, and this time in connection with Latin America, we are led to accept the ratio of 50 : 50 between equity and loan capital in total private investment as a desirable and reasonable one. Public investment and investment in public utilities, or at least the part of them financed from abroad, are assumed to require loan financing. If it is further assumed that these two sectors absorb 40 per cent. of total investment, it follows that the financing of overall investment in Latin America would require loan capital in the proportion of 70 per cent., with only 30 per cent. in the form of equity. These proportions, which coincide with those found for the United States, are assumed to apply also to foreign invest-ment, but for the sake of conservatism they are later reduced to 55 per cent. loan and 45 per cent. equity. In practice, and for the period 1949–52, of a total flow of United States capital amounting to $1,481 million, Latin American countries are shown to have received only 23 per cent. in the form of loans. Hence the need for additional loans.

In appraising the method we should realize that since foreign investment going to the public sector must take the form of loans, the attainment of the ideal ratio really implies a flow of public loans from abroad at least as large as the flow of direct private investment. The ratio could be maintained with public loans of smaller relative magnitude only if some of the foreign private investment were of the portfolio kind. In fact, once the validity of the ratio is accepted, the need for a greater share of loans in the flow of foreign investment is a foregone conclusion.

Let us investigate the meaning and degree of stability of the loan-equity ratio in the financing of the total private investment of a country. The ratio appears to be a relatively stable one and the 50 : 50 figure determined by Pazos coincides rather well with similar ones computed by Raymond Goldsmith.[1]

According to Goldsmith, for the period 1897–1949 as a whole, 'approximately one-third of total personal saving took the form of equities and two-thirds that of claims. . . . The proportion of saving through claims was substantially higher during the two wars and the Great Depression. As a result personal saving was about equally divided between claims and equities for the normal periods'.[2] This stability is perhaps explainable by institutional factors.

Entrepreneurs and equity investors naturally seek some kind of balance between their desire to maximize profits in case a venture is successful and their desire to minimize capital losses in case of failure. Owners of, and institutions controlling, loan capital, on the other hand, require collateral warranties for their loans, and financial customs and practices determine within broad limits the maximum loan that will normally be advanced against a given collateral. It is possible that owners of financial capital willing to invest in equity and owners of financial capital wishing to avoid direct risks and still earn an income on their capital, may be in approximate balance. But this may be true only in very general terms, for one can easily imagine circumstances, such as an inflationary and speculative atmosphere, under which the ratio might change or be greatly distorted. In fact, Raymond Goldsmith's data indicate that equity investments, which in normal years amounted to a little over 50 per cent. of the total, dropped to as little as 5 per cent. during 1934–39 and 1940–45, increasing extraordinarily between 1930–33.[3]

It seems, then, that we should not place too much faith in the stability of the loan-equity ratio nor feel free to accept it as ideal or in any way linked to the process of growth itself. The most we can say in this respect is that in a monetary economy the net increase in financial capital, whether in the form of claims or equities, will match the net increase in real capital or real investment.

[1] R. W. Goldsmith, *A Study of Savings in the United States* (3 vols.) (Princeton, 1955–56).
[2] *Ibid.* vol. i, p. 157.
[3] *Ibid.* Table S-46, p. 317.

III. THE GENERALITY OF THE RATIO

As to the generality of the ratio, there does not seem to be a sound *a priori* reason to expect that any one ratio, empirically determined for a certain country, say the United States, should be similar to those of other countries with different economic and institutional backgrounds.

To assume that the empirical ratio applying to total investment within a country should also apply to its own foreign investment, or to the investment it receives from abroad, is, in my opinion, unwarranted. Pazos himself points out that the type of capital inflow need not be exactly proportional to the recipient country requirements because domestic capital may adapt itself and fill the gaps. This being the case, we need not be concerned about disruptions in the process of economic growth as a result of the composition or allocation of foreign investment going into a given country or area.

To be sure, balanced growth requires specific allocation of investment as between directly productive and social overhead facilities and also as between the various productive industries, but this is only an overall requirement. Whether foreign or domestic capital, in equity or loan form, is invested in a given industry or social overhead facility is immaterial as far as it concerns the mechanics of growth, provided the investment is a needed one at that stage of the growth process.

It is true, however, that of the total investment needed during any given period, some, such as public works and perhaps some public utilities, must be undertaken by the government. If current government income or domestic loans cannot cover their cost, successful flotation of foreign loans will make the difference between economic growth or lack of it. For this reason, a government in good financial standing, undertaking a sound development plan should be able to obtain abroad loans to finance essential social overhead facilities which cannot be financed otherwise. To the extent that this is not happening the flow of public capital to Latin America should be increased.

But the same applies to the private sector where foreign capital may also be the key to development if domestic capital, technical knowledge, or entrepreneurial talent are insufficient to establish certain productive units required for balanced growth. If all three elements are lacking, the only possible answer is to attract foreign private equity investment. If all of them are available to some extent, a variety of combinations — from outright partnership with foreign investors to simple royalty agreements or even portfolio investment — becomes possible.

In brief, then, we may safely say that the problem confronting countries where saving is insufficient to finance the minimum investment programme which development requires is simply to obtain the balance abroad. Nevertheless, this balance must include enough loans to the public authorities to allow them to finance the social overhead facilities which cannot be financed domestically. It must also include a sufficiently large flow of direct or portfolio investment to make possible the establishment of the directly productive enterprises needed for balanced growth which could not be established otherwise. But the proportion between loans and equity in foreign investment which is needed to implement any given investment programme will vary with the country and with its stage of development. Any fixed rule or percentage must necessarily be arbitrary.

IV. The Cost of Foreign Capital

The above discussion has omitted an important point in the private versus public foreign investment issue in under-developed areas, namely, the problem of the real cost of foreign capital.

Leaving aside matters which concern sociologists and social anthropologists interested in economic development problems, there is no doubt that a sufficiently large volume of investment will develop even a barren desert. But no country has access to unlimited resources and its ability to obtain abroad the supplementary ones needed to assure a given rate of economic growth cannot always be taken for granted. Perhaps this problem can best be approached by stating that the volume of foreign capital that a country can obtain for economic development purposes depends, in the final analysis, on the evolution that it can expect in its balance of payments. This must be so, for unless foreign capital expatriates itself or comes in the form of grants, its servicing will demand that foreign exchange availabilities at the stage where growth can proceed without further assistance from abroad, be large enough at least to cover essential imports and the service payments of the capital up to that time.

The size of the foreign exchange availabilities, other than those resulting from capital movements, that a developing country may expect as it develops cannot be estimated with any degree of certainty. We may, however, analyse the main elements of the problem and arrive at a general answer. To this end we need only think of countries as members of a complex world system linked by trade currents. And just as individual producers within a closed national economy can expand output only at certain rates, determined by the overall rate of growth of the economy and by the price and income elasticities of demand for their respective products, individual producing countries in a world system — given the levels of world income — can produce and offer specific commodities for export only up to certain levels without encountering unit or less than unitary demand elasticities. Beyond this point additional exchange availabilities can only be acquired by entering into new production lines for export — a possibility which will be influenced by the evolution of the country's comparative cost situation, that is, by changes in the supply conditions of all commodities and by changes in the foreign and domestic demand for every item. Whether the resulting volume of exchange availabilities will be sufficient to maintain the desired rate of economic growth must depend on the magnitude of the import needs of the developing country and on the foreign exchange surplus required for servicing the borrowed foreign capital.

Import requirements are related to a country's endowment in natural resources. If domestic resources are great in depth and variety, the need for imports at each level of income will be comparatively small. If they are limited in quantity or undiversified, the need for large imports at each level of income will be comparatively pressing. In the first case the country may be able to buy its essential imports merely by offering certain primary commodities, which it has in abundant supply at comparatively low cost and for which foreign income and price elasticity of demand is high, or a few manufactures in a line with which it can compete advantageously against other manufacturing countries. If, on the other hand, the need for imports is large, success in obtaining them will depend on the country's ability to compete with the rest of the world along a broad front of productive activities.

To a large measure, the volume of capital needed to attain a given rate of economic growth must also be related to a country's supply of natural resources. Other things being equal, a base limited in depth, undiversified, and of poor quality will require comparatively greater investment and probably greater assistance from abroad.

These general considerations indicate a limit in the volume of foreign capital which, subject to the restriction of repayment and servicing, a country can obtain from abroad. This volume may, or may not, be sufficient to assure a given rate of economic growth.

But in either of the two cases, conditions will be improved and growth accelerated, or made possible, if the cost of foreign capital can be reduced. Grants or expatriated capital cost nothing. At present, loan capital is cheaper than equity capital. A reduction in cost from, say, 15 or 16 per cent. to 5 or 6 per cent. would permit a considerable increase in the volume of capital that can be serviced with a given volume of foreign exchange. This may easily make the difference between economic growth or stagnation. The same reduction in cost, in connection with a fixed volume of foreign capital, will have a similar effect through the release of additional domestic resources for investment purposes.

From a practical point of view it is important for under-developed countries to search for ways of reducing the cost of foreign capital. Dr. Pazos suggests foreign loans to governments to be used for re-lending to private entrepreneurs. Other possibilities such as the promotion of partnerships between domestic and foreign equity capital, royalty and patent agreements with foreign firms, and even ways and means of attracting foreign portfolio investment deserve exploration. Enlightened foreign investors could also consider to a greater extent than they now do the possibility of disposing gradually of part of their equity investment in exchange for portfolio securities, perhaps with a warranty given by the government of the recipient country with regard to transferrability and external value of such securities.

It is encouraging, however, to note that the under-developed countries' current preference for loans as against equity investment reflects faith in their development prospects and the anticipation that new enterprises will earn profits considerably in excess of the cost of loan capital. Not too many years ago governments objected to the high cost of foreign loans. At that time the average performance of foreign enterprises, considering failures and losses, was not as satisfactory as it has been in recent years or as it can be expected to be in the future.

DISCUSSION OF DR. PAZOS' PAPER

D R. PAZOS' paper, which was presented in his absence by Dr. Campos, brought out reactions which initially revolved around Dr. Pazos' concept of a desirable ratio between equity and loan investment. From there the discussion went on to the relative cost of equity and loan financing as well as their other merits and demerits, and ended on the subject of new devices and policies for foreign financing.

I. THE RATIO OF EQUITY AND LOAN FINANCING

Dr. Pazos had argued in his paper that the ratio of equities and claims in the American financial structure was approximately 50 : 50 in normal times. From this he derived an optimum ratio for Latin America, under certain assumptions, of 70 per cent. claims and 30 per cent. equity. Under less demanding assumptions this might be reduced to a ratio of 55-45 per cent. To adapt United States capital exports to Latin America to this ratio, a very material increase in the proportion of loans would be required.

Dr. Bulhões took issue with Dr. Pazos' reasoning. If utilities were allowed to charge remunerative rates, he said, they could attract some equity financing which would bring down the ratio. *Dr. Dominguez* rejected any attempt at generalizing some particular ratio. Inflation and speculation were bound to raise the proportion financed by equity investment. *Professor Haberler* agreed with both speakers and termed the ratio problem 'secondary'. *Professor Wallich* added that in practice the structure of financing depended on the preferences of lenders as well as of borrowers, on tax considerations, availability of public savings, interest rates, and a number of other factors. No generalized ratio would be established. *Dr. Dominguez* finally noted, as *Dr. Pazos* had himself pointed out, that small changes in the structure of domestic financing could easily compensate for the high equity ratio of imported capital, since imported capital accounted for only a small fraction of total financing.

II. Relative Cost of Equity and Loan Capital

Dr. Pazos' paper had stated that the average earnings of American equity investment abroad amounted to 20 per cent., which contrasted with rates on loans of 5 or 6 per cent. Various speakers proceeded to whittle down this difference. *Dr. Campos* noted that the 20 per cent. yield on equity capital was due mostly to high returns on oil and mineral investments. It did not apply to manufacturing. The cost of equity money included payment for know-how, while the cost of loans did not. In some fields, such as chemicals and oil, the know-how could not be bought separately at all ; it was tied to the equity money. Equity money did not impose a cost during the construction period, whereas loan money usually did. *Dr. Bulhões* argued that the high return on equity money was due in part to inflation. *Dr. Dominguez*, however, cautioned that one could not just leave the high profits on oil and mining out of the picture in arriving at an average return because these investments constituted a large part of the total.

Dr. Adler calculated that the debt service of loans, including amortization, came to about 10 per cent. annually or more. Since more than half of the 20 per cent. return from equity investments was being ploughed back, the out-of-pocket cost of loan money actually was higher than that of equity investment. He also referred to a calculation by the United States Department of Commerce, showing that United States direct investment abroad had generated exports from the host countries of 4·5 billion dollars annually while the service of this investment amounted to only 2 billions.

Professor Wallich finally speculated that even a 20 per cent. yield might not be unduly expensive, if one was prepared to assume that this type of investment mobilized some local capital and labour that would otherwise have remained idle and thereby added materially to national income.

III. Relative Merits of Equity and Loan Investments

Dr. Campos reminded the meeting of the familiar advantage of transfer flexibility which equity investment offered. He qualified this, however, by pointing to the frequent increase in manufacturing profits during depressions, as a consequence of exchange controls. This might create increasing balance of payment liabilities at inopportune moments. Their transfer, however, could of course be blocked by the same controls. *Dr. Márquez* pointed out that any reference to postponement of transfers took for granted the existence of foreign exchange control, which certainly was not warranted for all countries. *Dr. Alter* observed that in the long run the transfer of profits could not be suspended anyway, and in the short run the problem could be met without exchange controls if a country were prepared to carry larger foreign exchange reserves. *Professor*

Brahmananda said that India had been inconvenienced during the depression by the need to transfer the earnings of British-owned railways. At present, however, he said, there was a strong demand for equity capital in India.

Professor Hirschman observed that where the alternative was between equity participation and management contracts with foreign firms, there was sometimes an advantage in the former because, besides technical and managerial 'know-how', the foreign investors would teach the art of ploughing back profits to their local partners, who often want quick dividends.

Dr. Márquez replied, however, that in Mexico the domestically owned corporations also ploughed back most of their earnings.

Professor Haberler questioned the merits of direct investment if its profits resulted from high protection. In any case he thought that, at a profit level of 20 per cent., 'know-how' might be purchased rather dearly if it was derived from basically inefficient hothouse industries whose profitability depended on exorbitant tariffs or allocation of foreign exchange at fantastically unrealistic exchange rates, as was often the case.

IV. Improved Methods of Financing

Professor Hirschman thought that foreign investors could count on a more favourable reception if they were willing to sell parts of their holdings to local capitalists. *Dr. Kafka* noted that this might be welcome only provided they reinvested the proceeds in the country. *Professor Wallich* drew attention to the potentialities of portfolio investment by individual or institutional American investors in the shares of Latin American corporations. This form of foreign investment avoided the problems of intervention and control. It nevertheless offered transfer flexibility in so far as dividends declined during depressions. Its practicability depended, however, he said, upon the willingness of Latin-American corporations to meet United States standards of corporate disclosure and accounting. *Professor Haberler* observed that what was mainly needed was a change in the policies of the host countries. If they chose to re-establish a favourable climate for foreign capital there was hope that after some time, despite all past experience, foreign investors might once more begin to buy Latin-American bonds.

Chapter 9

INTERNATIONAL TRADE THEORY AND DEVELOPMENT POLICY [1]

BY

RAGNAR NURKSE
Columbia University, New York

I. INTRODUCTION

THE case for international specialization is firmly based on considerations of economic efficiency. The world is not rich enough to be able to despise efficiency. The optimum pattern of specialization is governed by the principle of comparative advantage. This principle remains as valid today as it was in Ricardo's time. And yet there is some question whether it alone can give all the guidance needed by countries whose dominant and deliberate aim is economic development (that is, increasing real income *per capita*).

Trade between countries rests on the realization of mutual gains. Objection may be raised to the uneven division of these gains. Within the range of opportunities for gainful trade, it is true that one country may be able to improve its terms of trade at the expense of another. For a single country, therefore, the logic of the classical position does not necessarily lead to a free trade recommendation, but only to one of some trade as opposed to no trade at all. Moreover, the effects of trade restriction on a country's barter terms are not necessarily offset by retaliation, since different countries have different demand and supply elasticities. It may be that primary producing countries are in a relatively favourable position for playing this kind of game. But even for them the possibilities suggested by the so-called optimum tariff argument are limited and in the long run very unreliable. These possibilities are discussed in Professor

[1] Some parts of a preliminary draft of this paper were presented for discussion at a seminar of the RAND Corporation's Economics Division in Santa Monica, California, in July 1957. In addition Professor W. R. Allen of the University of California at Los Angeles was kind enough to read my manuscript and comment on it in detail. My colleague Professor J. W. Angell gave valuable help in a similar way at a later stage. The criticisms received from these sources, for which I am extremely grateful, have led me to revise or expand a number of points. It goes without saying that no one except myself is responsible for the views advanced or any errors remaining in the paper.

Haberler's paper on 'The Terms of Trade and Economic Development', and need not be dwelt upon further.

Whatever the distribution of the gain from trade, so long as some gain accrues to each party the case for trade remains. In fact, it can be argued that to under-developed countries trade is more important than to advanced countries. There is therefore a *prima facie* presumption in favour of promoting development by means of — or at least side by side with — foreign trade, rather than at the cost of sacrificing the economic efficiency derived from specialization.

The traditional theory of international specialization centres on the comparison of a trading situation with a no-trade situation, and on the demonstration of the superiority of the former over the latter. This is essentially the Ricardian procedure. The mental process which we perform when, starting from a state of isolation with different pre-trade ratios of exchange in each country, we let the barriers be stripped and then study the effects of trade, is still the core of international trade theory. The assumption of a fixed initial stock of factors can be relaxed by allowing factor supplies to change in response to trade itself, without altering the essential character of this demonstration of the gains from international specialization. The demonstration is conclusive. If one asks what help it offers here and now to low-income countries in search of development, the answer is not altogether clear. If these countries were each of them isolated from the rest of the world, they could indeed rise to a higher income level by simply stripping the barriers to trade. But in fact they have long been closely linked to world trade. Their export products do not in general encounter any very severe restrictions in world trade, and their import controls, as will be seen below, are mainly designed either to curb an excessive appetite for foreign wares or to modify the composition of their imports, rather than to force an actual reduction in total volume. There is undoubtedly a good deal of senseless restrictionism that hampers their trade as a whole and hence their economic growth. And yet they may also have reason to wonder what international specialization, an essential base for their existing position, can do for their development.

The present interest in growth economics has so far had little impact on the theory of international trade. In trying to give a specific focus to the discussion of the very broad topic assigned to me, it may be worth considering whether the notion of balanced growth is compatible with the principle of international specialization or whether, on the contrary, it means throwing away the benefits obtainable through trade. In many of the less developed countries today the dominant practical question is whether the available investment funds, limited as they are, should be used to promote activities specialized along lines of comparative advantage internationally or diversified so as to provide markets for each other locally. In Western eyes the pursuit of balanced growth only too often causes a pathetic misdirection of scarce resources. The under-developed countries, on the other hand, feel that they cannot always rely on an expansion of external demand for their primary products, a demand that is typically inelastic with respect to price. Is there any assurance, they ask, that the overspill of prosperity from the advanced countries (through changes in the volume and terms of trade and possibly, in response thereto, through private foreign investment in primary production for export) will induce a satisfactory rate of development — satisfactory in relation, for instance, to population change ?

The clash of prescriptions on the policy plane reflects what looks like a deadlock on the theoretical level also. As everyone has noticed, on·the theoretical plane there exists a gap between the neo-classical allocation economics and the current preoccupation with growth economics. The former operates under the constraint of fixed amounts of resources, directing attention to the price system as a means to efficient allocation and maximum output. In the field of growth economics this particular constraint is removed, but allocation of resources — or more particularly, of resource *increments* — still remains a crucial problem. Indeed, we may distinguish between two principal subdivisions in the field of growth economics : first, resource mobilization, relating to the increase in quantity and improvement in quality of productive factors (capital accumulation, technical training, mass education, and so forth) ; and, second, resource allocation in the process of economic growth. The present paper concerns itself mainly with the allocation aspect of growth economics. Although the mobilization aspect can only be touched upon incidentally, the discussion that follows will not be bound by the static assumption of a constant stock of resources.

II. The Traditional Pattern of Trade and Development

Before we attack the main problem it will be instructive to take a look at past experience and see how economic growth in certain areas was induced through international trade in the nineteenth century. The areas involved in this process of growth through trade were chiefly the so-called regions of recent settlement in the temperate latitudes outside Europe. These areas, in which the United

States may be included, received a large inflow of labour as well as capital from Europe, but a basic inducement that caused them to develop was the tremendous expansion of Western Europe's, and especially Great Britain's, demand for the foodstuffs and raw materials which they were well suited to produce. Growth at the periphery was induced, through trade, by growth in the rising industrial centre.[1]

Alfred Marshall referred to 'the splendid markets which the old world has offered to the products of the new'.[2] He forgot to mention the crucial point that these were growing markets, but this he probably assumed as a matter of course. The penultimate chapter of his *Principles* is entitled 'General Influences of Economic Progress' and begins as follows : 'The field of employment which any place offers for labour and capital depends, firstly, on its natural resources ; secondly, on . . . knowledge and . . . organization ; and thirdly, on . . . markets in which it can sell those things of which it has a superfluity. The importance of this last condition is often under-rated ; but it stands out prominently when we look at the history of new countries.'[3]

It was under the impression of this experience that Marshall made the following pronouncement : 'The causes which determine the economic progress of nations belong to the study of international trade'.[4] In the second half of the twentieth century this may seem to us a curious statement. It can be understood only in the light of certain historical conditions, and it embodies the particular experience of Britain's economic relations with the new countries overseas. Economic growth in these areas was due not to international specialization alone but more particularly to the fact that the character of trade was such that the rapid growth which was taking place in the centre was transmitted to the outlying new countries through a vigorous increase in the demand for primary products.

Trade in the nineteenth century was not simply a device for the optimum allocation of a given stock of resources. It was that too, but it was more than that. It was above all 'an engine of growth'. This profoundly important observation is one which we owe to Sir Dennis Robertson.[5] It helps us to see things in perspective, but in doing so it serves also to limit the significance of classical trade

[1] In the course of the nineteenth century (*i.e.* 1815–1914) Great Britain's population tripled, while judging from such estimates as are now available her real national income may have increased roughly tenfold and the volume of her imports about twentyfold.
[2] Alfred Marshall, *Principles of Economics*, 8th ed. (London, 1920), pp. 668–669.
[3] *Ibid*. p. 668.
[4] *Ibid*. p. 270.
[5] D. H. Robertson, *Essays in Monetary Theory* (London, 1940), p. 214.

theory to its proper sphere. The conventional tendency has been to credit international specialization as such with the spectacular growth of the new countries in the nineteenth century. In the light of Robertson's remark it may perhaps be suggested that classical specialization theory, which in the nature of the case is a static analysis, has derived more prestige from nineteenth-century experience than it has deserved. The dynamic nature of trade as a transmitter of growth was overlooked during an era in which progress was taken for granted, like the air we breathe.

There is no doubt that international trade was peculiarly important in the conditions of the nineteenth century. In real volume it increased tenfold between 1850 and 1913, twice as fast as world production. Imperialism had very little to do with the expansion of trade. As was shown by J. A. Hobson himself,[1] the tropical colonies took a minor share in the growth of British trade. Continental Europe and the new countries outside as well as within the British Empire took the major share. The regions of recent settlement were high-income countries from the start, effective markets as well as efficient producers. Their development was part of the growth of international trade itself.

So much for the new countries. Elsewhere, in the truly backward areas, economic growth induced through international trade in some cases carried with it certain features that were, and still are, regarded as undesirable. It sometimes led to a lopsided pattern of growth in which production of primary products for export was carried on with the aid of substantial investment of foreign capital, while the domestic economy remained far less developed, if not altogether primitive. This picture applies especially to tropical areas. It is the familiar picture of the dual economy resulting from trade and from foreign business investment induced by trade. Areas of outpost investment producing for foreign markets often showed a lack of social as well as economic integration internally. Moreover, their export activities were subject to the familiar hazards of cyclical instability.

Nevertheless, even unsteady growth through foreign trade is surely better than no growth at all. Mr. Bauer has given impressive examples of progress resulting from peasant production for export in some parts of West Africa during the early half of the twentieth century.[2] Elsewhere foreign capital working for export has usually led to an additional demand for local labour, increased wage incomes, expenditures on local materials, new sources of taxation, and, in the

[1] J. A. Hobson, *Imperialism*, 3rd ed. (London, 1938), ch. 2.
[2] P. T. Bauer, *West African Trade* (Cambridge, 1955).

case of mineral concessions, lucrative profit-sharing arrangements. All these benefits have helped to promote expansion in the domestic economy.

The traditional pattern of development through production for expanding export markets is not to be despised and ought not to be discouraged. Indeed, I should like to assume that all opportunities in this direction are fully exploited. The trouble is that in the mid-twentieth century, with a few notable exceptions, conditions for this type of growth do not, by and large, appear to be as promising as they were a hundred years ago.

Since 1913 the quantum of world trade has increased less than world production. To be sure, in the last five or six years we find the volume of trade in the non-communist world increasing at just about the same pace as production. But when we look at it more closely we find that it is chiefly among the advanced industrial countries that international trade has been expanding in the recent past. These countries, including above all the United States, are themselves efficient primary producers, especially of food. Their demand for exotic raw materials like crude rubber, silk, nitrates, jute, vegetable oils, hides, and skins has been, and will probably continue to be, affected by the growth of the chemical industry in the twentieth century. The latest technological casualty among American imports that I have heard of is chicle, which we used to import from Latin America for the manufacture of chewing gum. It appears that the American chemical industry has developed a substitute that is just as good or even better.[1] Professor D. D. Humphrey in his voluminous study, *American Imports*,[2] attaches great importance to the technological factor. He estimates that, in its effect on total United States imports, the displacement of imported raw materials by synthetic products has more than offset the 75 per cent. reduction in the American tariff which has taken place in the last twenty years partly through duty reductions and partly through the effect of price inflation on the burden of specific duties. While tariff changes have mainly affected imports of manufactured goods from other industrial countries, technological displacement has particularly affected United States imports from the less developed countries.

Only for minerals are conditions generally favourable, although

---

[1] It may be that owing to deficiencies in the producing countries the supply of the natural product was inflexible, unreliable in quantity, and uneven in quality. But if this was the main trouble, why did not the American chewing-gum manufacturers set up their own chicle plantations in Guatemala or Mexico? Evidently it was not worth their while, in view of technological advances in the synthetic field.

[2] D. D. Humphrey, *American Imports* (New York, 1955).

even here it should be noted that, first, the demand for metals is affected by the increasing efficiency of scrap collection and recovery in the industrial countries. Second, mineral deposits are gifts of nature, and if a country does not happen to have any, it can do nothing in response to the rise in world demand. Some countries that have deposits fail to exploit them. Nevertheless, the point remains that while Guatemala, for example, can at least try to grow chicle, she cannot try to grow nickel. Third, the export of minerals involves in an obvious sense an element of living on capital.

The growth of synthetic materials is undoubtedly one explanation of the findings which Professor Kindleberger reaches in his book on *The Terms of Trade: A European Case Study*. This study lends some support to the view that the poorer countries' terms of trade have shown a tendency to deteriorate. Kindleberger has calculated industrial Europe's terms of trade separately for various parts of the world, including in particular two groups of countries overseas, the areas of recent settlement, not including the United States, and the poorer countries (the rest of the world in his grouping). Difficulties due to quality changes and transport costs apply to both groups. Both the new countries and the poor countries are exporters of primary products and importers of manufactured goods. From 1913 to 1952, according to these estimates, Europe's terms of trade with the areas of recent settlement showed a 20 per cent. improvement, while in trade with the poorer countries Europe's terms seem to have improved by as much as 55 per cent.[1]

Other recent studies have provided evidence that world demand for the poorer countries' export products has tended to rise much less than in proportion to the production and incomes of the advanced countries.[2] It is therefore not surprising that, according to the report of the Contracting Parties to the General Agreement on Tariffs and Trade, we find the following distribution of international trade in the non-communist world in 1955. The exports of twenty advanced industrial countries (United States, Canada, Japan, and Western Europe) to each other constitute as much as 40 per cent.

[1] C. P. Kindleberger, *The Terms of Trade: A European Case Study* (New York, 1956), p. 234.

[2] For the post-war period this conclusion is documented in United Nations, *World Economic Survey*, 1956, and also in the annual report of the Contracting Parties to the General Agreements on Tariffs and Trade, *International Trade, 1955* (Geneva, 1956).

For a longer period, Professor Cairncross has made a careful statistical study of world exports of manufactured goods since 1900 showing that the manufactured goods which the industrial countries export to each other have constituted a steadily increasing proportion of their total exports of manufactured articles ; A. K. Cairncross, 'World Trade in Manufactures since 1900', *Economia Internazionale*, November 1955.

of total exports. Exports from these twenty countries to all less developed countries outside the communist orbit amount to 25 per cent. of the total. Exports from the less developed to the advanced countries represent another 25 per cent. Only 10 per cent. of the total are exports of the less developed countries to each other, even though the more than hundred countries in this group contain two-thirds of the total population of the non-communist world.[1] Why is it that so little of the coffee, tea, rubber, and tin produced in these countries goes to other countries in the same group ? Obviously the main explanation is the low purchasing power of people in these countries, which in turn is a reflection of their low productivity.

The fact that the economically advanced countries are each others' best customers is now more than ever a central feature of world trade. It is chiefly within this small circle of countries that international trade is now expanding. With the leading exception of petroleum and a few other minerals, it can hardly be said that primary producing countries are enjoying a dynamic expansion in world demand for their exports. The unprecedented boom which the industrial countries have been enjoying in the last two years (1955–56) has had no perceptible effect in improving the terms of trade of primary producing countries.[2]

In view of the tremendous growth of the American economy it is an extraordinary fact that, according to an official index, the real volume of American imports of agricultural products in 1955 was 15 per cent. below the 1929 level. The 1955 quantum of United States imports of crude materials (excluding foodstuffs but including minerals) was only 23 per cent. higher than in 1929, although the United States gross national product had increased by 116 per cent. since 1929.

Professor T. W. Schultz in his paper on 'Economic Prospect of Primary Products' shows that the demand for all raw materials, whether imported or domestically produced, has lagged far behind the increase in output in the United States.[3] What we are considering therefore is merely the international aspect of a fairly general tendency. In a country amply supplied with capital and technical know-how, it seems a perfectly natural tendency for investment in research and development to displace crude materials with synthetic products made from a few basic elements of mostly local origin. These trends

[1] *International Trade, 1955.* The figures given in this report exclude trade within the communist orbit. For the sake of comparability I have adjusted them so as to exclude trade between communist and non-communist countries as well.

[2] This is clear from a special table published in *International Financial Statistics*, April 1957.

[3] See below, p. 311 ff.

are not confined to the United States. They are affecting the trade of other advanced areas as well.[1]

If this is the situation of the mid-twentieth century, the mental habits which economists have inherited from the mid-nineteenth may no longer be altogether adequate. It will be recalled that Professor Hicks's analysis of the long-run dollar problem was based on what he described as 'a change in economic atmosphere between the nineteenth and twentieth centuries'.[2] His analysis in regard to the dollar problem was open to criticism, yet I believe that in emphasizing the varying incidence of productivity changes on international trade he made an important point, a point that had been noted some years earlier by Professor Haberler.[3] While Britain's ratio of imports to national income showed a rising tendency during most of the nineteenth century, the United States import ratio has been practically halved in the last five decades.[4] This has happened in spite of the fact that in short period comparisons the United States typically shows a rather high income elasticity of imports. There seems to have been a long-run downward shift in the United States import function, resulting from changes in economic structure. It is not certain that tariff policy provides the major part of the explanation. It seems very likely that the incidence of technological advance has had a good deal to do with it.

The slight increase which has occurred in the last few years in the United States import ratio has been due to increased imports of finished and semi-finished manufactures. This has meant increased trade with other industrial countries, Canada, Western Europe, Japan. Imports of crude materials, largely from under-developed areas, have not regained their pre-war position in relation to United States gross national product. All this does not mean that the absolute volume of United States imports has failed to expand. It increased by 44 per cent. from 1929 to 1955.[5] But notice two things.

[1] A. K. Cairncross and J. Faaland, 'Long-Term Trends in Europe's Trade', *Economic Journal*, March 1952, pp. 26-27.

[2] J. R. Hicks, 'An Inaugural Lecture', *Oxford Economic Papers*, June 1953, p. 130.

[3] G. Haberler, 'Dollar Shortage ?', in S. E. Harris, ed., *Foreign Economic Policy for the United States* (Cambridge, Massachusetts, 1948), pp. 438-439.

[4] United States exports as a percentage of gross national product fell from 5·7 per cent. in the period 1896–1914 to 2·97 per cent. in 1955. See W. Lederer, 'Major Developments Affecting the United States Balance of International Payments', *Review of Economics and Statistics*, May 1956, p. 184.

[5] The quantum of crude material imports, as already stated, increased by only 23 per cent. The other commodity groups showed the following percentage increases from 1929 to 1955 : crude foodstuffs, 33 per cent. ; manufactured foodstuffs, 55 per cent. ; semi-manufactures, 76 per cent. ; finished manufactures, 52 per cent. Is it not possible, however, that the relatively small rise in imports of crude commodities may be due, not to a low rate of growth of United States demand, but rather to a deficiency on the supply side ? The answer is in Professor Schultz's paper, where the strategic rôle of demand is clearly demonstrated.

This increase is much less than proportional to the growth of United States output. Moreover, it is much less than the rate of growth of British imports in the nineteenth century, which during any comparable period showed a two to threefold increase in volume.[1]

It is useful to keep in mind these elementary facts about American imports because the United States is now the dominant economy not only in world production but also in world trade. Some economists are more inclined to stress the future prospect of expansion in United States imports, but that is a debatable matter. It is never quite safe, and for present purposes really unnecessary, to engage in predictions. The facts for the recent past are sufficient to indicate a change in the economic atmosphere of international trade between the nineteenth and twentieth centuries.

It will be remembered that in Hicks's analysis of the dollar shortage, the balance of payments problem resolves itself into a terms of trade problem. This seems a plausible simplification. Any country in foreign exchange difficulties can normally restore its balance of payments by accepting a worsening in its terms of trade.[2] In Hicks's model external balance is maintained by changes in terms of trade.

But can we not go a step further? There has been a tendency, in Britain and elsewhere, to exaggerate both the actual extent and the economic significance of changes in the terms of trade. We are sometimes apt to think of these changes as if the resources of each country were for ever committed to the existing export industries. This view may be all right for the short run, but in the longer run labour and capital within each country can usually move to other occupations, and do in fact move. If the relationship of export prices to import prices undergoes a marked increase or decline, it is entirely natural that factors of production should tend to move from export industries to import-competing industries or vice versa. This may involve simply changes in the allocation of *increases* in factor supplies rather than movements of existing factors. In any event, the point is that a change in the terms of trade tends to induce shifts in production and in the distribution of resources, which will tend to

---

[1] W. Schlote, *British Overseas Trade from 1700 to the 1930's* (Oxford, 1952), p. 131 ff.

[2] This will tend to occur as a by-product of price adjustment through exchange rate variation or alternatively through the gold standard mechanism. Actually, import restriction for improving the balance of payments may be preferred on terms of trade grounds, but this seems to assume that unused opportunities in the optimum tariff direction do in fact exist. Trade restriction as a means of doctoring the terms of trade is really a separate case, of which mention has already been made.

reverse or counteract the change in the terms of trade.[1] What remains is growth and change in the volume of productive activity induced through international trade. On this view, changes in the terms as well as in the balance of trade are a transient and relatively insignificant element in the mechanism by which processes of economic growth (or decline) may be transmitted from one country to others.

This does not imply that shifts in external demand do not matter. Fortunate indeed is the country with an expanding export market for the commodity in whose production it has a comparative advantage ; for it can then draw increasing supplies in limitless variety from the outside world. The suggestion is merely that, because of the possibility of internal factor shifts in response to varying price relationships, long-term trends in external demand conditions need not be reflected fully, if at all, in changes in the terms of trade.

In considering the international mechanism of development it is necessary at any rate to admit the possibility of variation in the conditions of growth transmission through trade. Just as the limited extent to which the United States economy transmits its own growth rate to primary producing countries is fully understandable in the light of its own abundant natural resources combined with its ample capital supplies and technical know-how, so the nineteenth century experience was conditioned by the fact that the industrial revolution happened to originate on a small island with a limited range of resources, at a time when the chemical industry was yet unborn.

As a result, the rate of growth in the import demand of the dominant economy of the twentieth century seems different from that of the nineteenth. If this is so, it is not certain that the less developed countries can rely on economic growth being induced from the outside through an expansion of world demand for their exports of crude materials.[2] In these circumstances reliance on

[1] By way of illustration, if a devaluation restores external balance but causes for the present a deterioration in the terms of trade, in the longer run factors will respond to this change in price relationships by moving from export industries to import-competing industries. This movement need not affect the balance but will at least tend to repair the terms of trade. Kindleberger's discussion of the comparative ease and difficulty of entry into and exit from various industries is relevant, though not of central importance, in this context.

[2] To ask the less developed countries to increase their export quantities of primary products in the face of a price inelastic and not an upward shifting demand schedule would be to ask, in effect, for an income transfer from poor to rich countries through a change in the terms of trade in favour of the latter. If one of several countries exporting the same primary commodity were to cut its export costs and prices, its export proceeds could indeed increase, but only at the expense of a fall in the other countries' export proceeds. The balance of payments adjustment process alone (whether through exchange rate variations or domestic price changes) would lead the latter to cut their export prices too, and all will be worse off at the end than they were at the start.

induced expansion through international trade may not be able to provide the main solution to the problem of development. It is not surprising, therefore, that countries should be looking for other types of solution. It will be useful to keep these things in mind, because they form the background to the case for balanced growth which is now so greatly in vogue.

III. The Pattern of Home Market Expansion

The circumstances indicated do not by any means apply to all under-developed countries today. Kuwait and Iraq, for example, may have nothing to worry about so long as the petroleum boom continues. But in so far as these circumstances do prevail, it is clear that the poorer countries, even if they are only to keep pace with the richer, to say nothing about catching up with them, must expand production for their own domestic markets or for each others' markets. Now, their domestic markets are limited because of mass poverty due to low productivity. Private investment in any single industry considered by itself is discouraged by the smallness of the existing market.[1]

The solution that presents itself is a balanced pattern of investment in a number of different industries, so that people working more productively, with more capital and improved techniques, become each others' customers. In the absence of a vigorously upward shifting world demand for exports of primary products, a low-income country through a process of diversified growth can seek to bring about upward shifts in domestic demand schedules by means of increased productivity and therefore increased real purchasing power. In this way a pattern of mutually supporting investments in different lines of production can enlarge the size of the market and help to fill the vacuum in the domestic economy of low-income areas. This, I take it, is what lies behind the notion of balanced growth.

Isolated advance is not impossible. A solitary process of investment and increased productivity in one industry alone will have favourable repercussions elsewhere in the economy. There is no denying that through the normal incentives of the price mechanism other industries will be induced to advance also. But this may be a snail's pace of progress. The price mechanism works, but, in the

[1] The limits set by the small size of the local market for manufactured goods are so plainly visible to any individual businessman that we are justified in taking for granted conditions of imperfect competition, and not the pure atomistic competition which even in advanced economies does not exist to any great extent.

conditions prevailing in many backward economies, it may work too slowly. That is one reason for the frequently observed fact that foreign direct investment in extractive export industries has created high-productivity islands and has had little impact on the level of productivity in the domestic economy.

Within the domestic economy itself, advance in one direction — say, in industry A — tends to induce advance in B as well. But if it is only a passive reaction to the stimulus coming from A, the induced advance of B may be slow and uncertain. And B's slowness and passiveness will in turn slow down and discourage the initial advance in A. The application of capital to one industry alone will be subject to sharply diminishing returns. As a way of escape from slowness or stagnation the balanced growth principle envisages autonomous advance along a number of lines more or less simultaneously.

Viewed in this way, balanced growth is a means to accelerated growth. Mr. Nicholas Kaldor in his stimulating lectures in Rio last year [1] treated the problem of achieving balanced growth as conceptually distinct from the problem of speeding up the rate of advance in a backward economy. On this point I cannot quite follow him. In my view balanced growth is, above all, a means of getting out of the rut, a means of stepping up the rate of growth when the external forces of advance through trade expansion and foreign capital are sluggish or inoperative.

In the existing state of affairs in low income areas the introduction of capital-using techniques of production in any single industry may be inhibited by the small size of the market. [2] Hence the weakness of private investment incentives in such areas. As Marshall said : 'The efficiency of specialized machinery . . . is but one condition of its economic use ; the other is that sufficient work should be found to keep it well employed'. [3] The techniques that have been developed in production for mass markets in advanced countries are not well adapted and sometimes not adaptable at all to output on a more limited scale. The relationship between the amount of investment and the size of the market required for efficient

---

[1] See the report of Nicholas Kaldor's lectures at the Fundação Getulio Vargas in *Revista Brasileira de Economia*, March 1957.

[2] As Professor Viner pointed out at the Congress of the International Economic Association in 1956, this need not deter investments that are cost-reducing rather than output-expanding. The former will displace existing high-cost sources of supply and need not be in response to any expansion of demand, current or anticipated. Just like the latter, however, they lead to a higher real income per head, *i.e.* an increase in the size of the market, creating inducements to invest in other lines. (*Stability and Progress in the World Economy*, London, 1958.)

[3] Alfred Marshall, *op. cit.* p. 264.

operation is of considerable importance for the balanced growth theory.

Now the objection is sometimes made, but why bring in machinery ? Why adopt capital-using methods in areas where labour is cheap and plentiful ? Why not rather employ techniques that are labour intensive instead of capital intensive ? The answer is that the pursuit of labour intensive production methods with a view to economizing capital may be perfectly correct as an adaptation to existing circumstances, including the existing factor supplies. But the study of development must concern itself with changing these circumstances, not accepting them as they are. What is wanted is progress, not simply adaptation to present conditions. And progress depends largely on the application of capital, which in turn depends on adequate and growing markets, which in the absence of a strongly rising world demand for the country's exports means a diversified output expansion for domestic use.[1]

Reference has been made to the need for autonomous advance in a number of mutually supporting lines of production. How is this achieved ? Autonomous advance involving capital investment in different branches simultaneously may come about through the infectious influence of business psychology, through the multiplier effects of investment anywhere which can create increased money demand elsewhere, or through deliberate control and planning by public authorities. The widely held view that balanced growth necessarily calls for overall programming strikes me as dubious. Indeed, as a means of creating inducements to invest, balanced growth can be said to be relevant primarily to a private enterprise system. State investment can and often does go ahead without any market incentives. Planning authorities can apply capital, if they have any, wherever they may choose, though if they depart too far from balance as dictated by income elasticities they will end by creating intolerable disproportionalities in the structure of production. It is private investment that is attracted by markets and that needs the inducement of growing markets. It is here that the element of mutual support is so useful and, for rapid growth, indispensable. There is no denying, however, that government policy may play an important part in initiating a process of balanced expansion, or in helping to push sectors insufficiently responsive to price inducements. The agricultural extension service in the United States has long been a classic example of a non-price method of development policy in a predominantly market oriented economy.

---

[1] An increase in capital supply is here taken for granted. A word on the mobilization problem in this respect will be added presently.

It should be noted that the doctrine under consideration is not itself concerned with the question where the capital is to be found for all the balanced investment which it envisages. My discussion of it, in Rio in 1951 and elsewhere later, tried to make it clear that the argument is related primarily to the problem of the *demand* for, or allocation of, capital; it takes an increased *supply* of capital for granted.[1] In reality, of course, capital supplies are hard to come by. The need for state investment stems partly from the fact that capital is scarce and that government efforts are necessary to mobilize all possible domestic sources of saving. Measures to check the expansion of consumer demand may be needed to make resources available for investment, but may at the same time weaken the private inducement to invest. This is a famous dilemma to which Malthus first called attention in his *Principles of Political Economy*. A case for state investment may arise if and when the mobilization of capital supplies discourages private investment activity and so destroys the demand for capital. But this case is entirely separate from the principle of balanced growth as such.

It is easy to see how this principle is related to the classical law of markets. Aside from the savings leakage, which should not be a problem in developing economies, an increased supply of consumables does create its own demand, provided that the supply is properly distributed among different commodities in accordance with consumers' wants. Each industry must advance along an expansion path determined by the income elasticity of demand for its product. Needless to say, the distribution of consumption and output does not remain the same in successive stages of development. The consumption pattern of a man with a thousand dollars a year will differ from that of a man with only a hundred dollars.[2]

The relation between agriculture and manufacturing industry offers the clearest and simplest case of balance needed for economic growth. In a country where the peasantry is incapable of producing a surplus of food above its own subsistence needs there is little or no incentive for industry to establish itself. There is not a sufficient market for manufactured goods. Conversely, agricultural improvements may be inhibited by lack of a market for farm products if the non-farm sector of the economy is backward or undeveloped. Each

[1] *Revista Brasileira de Economia*, December 1951.
[2] Why this emphasis on income elasticity to the neglect of price? There is no denying that price elasticities, too, help to determine the community's pattern of demand. But changes in relative prices have no close or determinate connection with economic growth, whereas income changes are a direct reflection and measure of growth.

of the two sectors must try to move forward together. If one remains passive, the other is slowed down.[1]

It is desirable in this connection to keep a clear distinction between two concepts frequently confused, the marketable surplus and the investible surplus of the farm sector. The former reflects the farm sector's demand for non-agricultural commodities. This is the concept relevant to the balanced growth principle. By contrast, an investible surplus of farm products represents an act of saving in the farm sector. This concept relates to the problem of capital supply. It may be of some importance because in backward economies, in which agriculture occupies the great bulk of the population, capital mobilization may well have to start in the farm sector. Here again the basic distinction is between allocation and mobilization of additional resources in the process of growth.

Within the manufacturing field alone the case for balanced investment implies a horizontal diversification of industrial activities all pushing ahead, though naturally at varying rates. The objection has been made that such diffusion of resources must mean a loss of dynamic momentum in the economy. This is possible. The dispersal of investment over a variety of consumer goods industries can certainly be carried to excess. The balanced-growth principle can be and has been interpreted far too literally. Producing a little of everything is not the key to progress. The argument is concerned with establishing a pattern of mutually supporting investments over a minimum range of industries wide enough to overcome the frustration of isolated advance, precisely in order to create a forward momentum of growth. The factors determining the optimum pattern of diversification have to do with technology, physical conditions, and other circumstances that may vary from country to country. The minimum size of efficient plant in different industries is an important practical consideration. There can be no standard prescription of universal applicability. We are concerned with a point of principle and cannot enter into the concrete forms of its implementation in practice. Just as it is possible for manufacturing industry as a whole to languish if farmers produce too little and are too poor to buy anything from factories, so it is possible for a single line of manufacturing to fail for lack of support from other sectors in industry as well as agriculture, that is, for lack of markets. That the market deficiency may be of some importance as an obstacle to

[1] Adam Smith states this two sector view of balanced growth in his chapter on the Natural Progress of Opulence : 'It is the surplus produce of the country only, or what is over and above the maintenance of the cultivators, that constitutes the subsistence of the town, which can therefore increase only with the increase of this surplus produce', *The Wealth of the Nations*, Book III, chap. i.

private investment is suggested by the remarkable difference between the occupational distribution of United States direct investment in relatively advanced countries, on the one hand, and in underdeveloped countries, on the other.

The case for diversified investment which emerged from these considerations stands in sharp contrast, first of all, to the great concentrations of capital needed for public overhead facilities such as transport and electric power. The notion of balanced growth discussed above is a limited one, confined to the horizontal pattern of supply and demand for consumables.[1] It is not applicable in any simple way to the relationship between the overhead facilities sector and the consumer goods industries sector, which is essentially a vertical relationship, since the basic services like transport and power are significant chiefly as producers' services. Moreover, technical indivisibilities combined possibly with considerations of deliberate development policy may lead to the building of overhead facilities well in advance of the demand for them. In the process of capital expansion a lack of balance in the vertical structure of production may be unavoidable or even desirable.

What is more relevant to our present subject, the diversification argument seems to contrast sharply with the teaching of the doctrine of comparative advantage which is that countries gain by concentration on a limited range of activities. Having surveyed the argument for balanced investment for local markets in low-income areas, we turn to consider the way in which this relates to the case for international specialization. On the face of it, there is a conflict.

IV. SPECIALIZATION THEORY AND TRADE POLICY

Classical trade theory shows that at least up to a point a country can benefit by concentrating its productive effort along lines of international comparative advantage. This is an important and familiar truth which no country seeking development can afford to ignore. But once a country has adopted an optimum pattern and an optimum degree of specialization along these lines (making use, perhaps, of any opportunities it may have for improving its terms of trade through commercial policy), how is it to achieve continued further growth if external demand conditions do not induce it?

---

[1] The notion is sometimes used in a far wider connotation, embracing capital goods industries and public overheads as well as final consumer goods. I confess that I am not able to make sense of it except in terms of income elasticities and complementarities of consumer demands. The arguments for capital-goods production and trade will be referred to in Section IV below.

There is no doubt that the opening up of trade can bring tremendous gains to a primitive economy. But let us imagine that an economy has adjusted itself to foreign trade and that there remains no unused opportunities for gainful specialization in production for export. Is there any guarantee that trade will thereafter induce a rate of growth that can be regarded as satisfactory in the light, for instance, of population increase at home or of the living levels prevailing abroad ? There is no such guarantee, especially if the export products which the comparative advantage principle leads a country to produce face an external demand schedule which is inelastic with respect to price and which shows only a sluggish rate of secular upward shift. Granted all the benefits of international specialization, there remains a possibility of deadlock and comparative stagnation. And this need not surprise anyone. Why indeed should international trade be expected to solve all problems of development ? Unfounded expectations may be due to the influence of a certain historical association.

In the nineteenth century growth was created through international trade not only because countries which were previously isolated decided to specialize. This was an important factor, for example, in the opening up of Japan, and more widely as a result of improvements in transport. But it was not all. Economic development was diffused through trade because the pattern of advance in the industrial centres happened to be such as to cause a rapidly rising demand for imported foodstuffs and raw materials. In so far as this was the operating factor, it should be kept distinct from the act of specialization. The conventional trade theory has enjoyed a very understandable, yet analytically illegitimate, association with nineteenth-century experience, an experience which in some ways was unique.

The theory of international specialization as such is a static analysis. Much of it assumes given levels of productivity and given stocks of resources in each country. The theory can be and has been supplemented (by Ohlin, J. H. Williams, and others) by considering the way in which factor supplies react to the opening up of trade, but even in this form it remains essentially a study in comparative statics.

Static theory does not exclude change, but the type of change it deals with is of the once-for-all variety. The gains from trade which the classical theory contemplates are of this character. Once a certain adjustment has been made, a higher level of real income is attained. (The theory can accommodate without difficulty the optimum tariff modification, which, as Professor Haberler points out in his paper, is similarly static in nature.) This type of trade theory is, of course, not wrong. It is absolutely basic ; it can be extremely useful. It is, however, limited in scope, and the more clearly we recognize its limitation the better it will be for the relevance and realism of international economies.

Dynamics, by contrast, is concerned with effects of continuing changes and with rates of change.[1] The transmission of growth from an expanding industrial centre is an essentially dynamic story, in which a rapidly rising demand for imports of primary products is the decisive feature which in its turn may generate outflows of productive factors to the peripheral areas to meet this demand. My point is that the argument for specialization as such is just as strong as ever, but that the forces making for growth transmission from advanced to less developed countries are not as powerful in the trade field as they were a hundred years ago. In these circumstances there may be a case for output expansion for the home market. If the amount of resources available is increasing at a sufficient rate — through population growth, capital accumulation, and the spread of knowledge — this can be done without giving up the benefits achieved through international specialization. Only on this condition is the case at all clear. Indeed it should not prevent a country from responding to such increases in export demand as may occur.

Suppose that some output expansion for the home market is possible without neglect of any gainful opportunities for export production. Now the process of domestic expansion must of necessity observe a certain balance dictated by income elasticities if the additional supply is to create its own demand, or, more concretely, if the new industries are to find adequate markets for their products. This concept of balanced growth, based on the diversity and hence complementarity of consumers' wants, is not an argument for industrialization as such. On the contrary, it stresses the futility of trying to set up manufacturing industries without a complementary advance on the farm front. Agriculture too is an industry in the framework of this concept. Since in low-income countries a large part of any income increment is likely to be spent on food, agricultural improvement is bound to be a crucial element in any process of balanced growth.

Nor is this an argument for autarky. There is room for home market expansion without reducing the volume of foreign trade. This becomes clear in particular if we remember the existence of transport costs, a factor often neglected in trade theory in the past. If transport costs were zero, then a country's production pattern

[1] See R. F. Harrod, *Towards a Dynamic Economics* (London, 1948), p. 8.

would not depend at all on the pattern of its own consumption. There would be no localization of demand, to use a term which Professor Samuelson has applied in a related context.[1] Actually we find very considerable localization. Countries usually spend most of their income on their own output. The cost of transportation is a basic reason for this. It is largely for this reason that in poor countries, where income is spent mostly on food, the bulk of the labour force works in food production. This is often true even of countries, such as Bolivia, that are net importers of food.

Transport costs alone are an important barrier to complete international specialization. They create in each country a range of domestic goods and services within which the notion of balanced investment is applicable without prejudice to international trade. But transport costs are, after all, an unfortunate necessity. Is it not foolish to impose in addition artificial barriers in order to promote balanced development? The case for and against import restrictions is a well-worn subject, but one which we cannot avoid altogether. In my own opinion the restriction of imports may sometimes help but should never be relied upon. Actually it is apt to be overdone because it is such an easy thing to do.

The argument for balanced growth stresses among other things the relation between investment incentives and the enlargement of domestic markets. For an imported product evidently a market already exists in the country. Hence import restriction will stimulate the domestic production of import substitutes.

Now in the first place this is an essentially unneighbourly thing to do. It hurts our neighbour, and even though he may be comparatively rich and strong, it may weaken his demand for our own export products.[2] Moreover, if nothing else is done, it is not at all certain that it will lead to a cumulative growth of the domestic market. The output of a certain commodity is increased until imports are replaced and at that point the expansion may stop if it is based on nothing broader than import restriction and import substitution.

---

[1] P. A. Samuelson, 'The Transfer Problem and Transport Costs', *Economic Journal*, June 1952.

[2] While this is the general position, it must nevertheless be recognized that there is in reality a marked lack of symmetry in the relations between a dominant economy such as the United States and the low-income countries exporting primary products. On this point some of the considerations adduced in United Nations, *International Co-operation in a Latin American Development Policy* (New York, 1954), pp. 62-64, seem to me entirely realistic. For one thing, the United States can hardly have a balance of payments problem so long as it has over half the world's gold reserves and so long as its own currency is a coveted means of international payment and international liquidity, as sterling was in the nineteenth century.

There is a possibility that import substitution will draw resources away from export production, which may force up prices of export products and so increase the country's real income through better terms of trade. But this is a risky policy. The world may learn to do without those export products. Technology in advanced countries has created countless substitution possibilities which may become economic at any moment. Crude raw materials may therefore face a kinked demand curve. A fall in price will increase the quantity sold very little, while a price rise, by stimulating the development of synthetics, may hurt sales a great deal. Any policy of trying to improve the terms of trade along the lines of the optimum tariff theory is for this reason (among others) very unreliable as a means to development. But the chief point to be stressed here is that increased production for the home market need not impinge on the export sector at all. The purpose of the balanced investment policy should not be to draw labour away from export industries but to raise the productivity of people now working in subsistence agriculture and other activities for domestic consumption.

The drawback of import restriction is that it leads to import-substitute production which, at least initially, is relatively costly and inefficient. The market for an imported commodity, small as it is to start with, becomes even smaller in real volume as the price to the consumer increases. The initial effect on real income is bad and may well lead to a fall in domestic saving. A high level of foreign trade may be very useful as a source of saving (as it was, for instance, for Japan). It is not to be denied that import restrictions can help in a policy of balanced domestic investment, but their adverse effect on real income and hence possibly on savings should be kept in mind. They should therefore be used sparingly. Import restrictions enforced in spite of such unfavourable effects can be justified only on the grounds of greater future benefit. This is the infant industry argument for protection.

Corresponding to our two applications of the balanced growth principle, there are two ways of applying the infant industry case. The first aims at stimulating manufacturing industry as a whole, as distinct from agriculture. In this two-sector view of balanced growth, infant industry protection could take the form of a uniform tariff on imports of all manufactured consumer goods. This is essentially a proposal which Mr. Kaldor made in his Rio lectures last year. The merit of a uniform tariff over a whole range of manufactures is that it preserves the selective principle of comparative advantage in the sphere of manufacturing industry and avoids wasteful attempts at import substitution in all lines. But if the balanced growth argument is also applied *within* the manufacturing field, it might be necessary to have a differential system of protective duties so that each of a group of industries which it is desired to create gets the degree of protection needed for its initial establishment. This would mean raising the price of each commodity to the level of marginal cost at which the home market could be supplied by the domestic industry.

The way in which infant protection is supposed to work has been widely discussed in the literature and cannot here be dwelt upon at length. In even a short survey it is necessary to distinguish the external economies case for protection from the more usual infant industry argument. The former is based on a downward sloping supply curve, the latter on downward *shifts* of a supply curve (which itself may be upward sloping). In the former case, as Professors H. S. Ellis and W. Fellner have shown,[1] we must distinguish between reversible and irreversible external economies. The case of irreversible economies implies some displacement of the curve (that is, a change in conditions of production) and shades into the infant industry case proper. In the infant industry argument the protection needed is in principle *temporary*. The case of reversible external economies is very different in that it calls for *permanent* protection. Professor Meade has recently pointed out, however, that if the cost curve in each country declines rapidly at first and then flattens out horizontally, and if in each country there is a market large enough to permit operation in the horizontal range, the continued existence of the industry need not depend on protection.[2]

The infant argument proper is based on supposedly irreversible changes in conditions of production. Capital, know-how, and public services must be provided, and paid for, separately ; but there are things that can be learned only by actual operation of the industry. It is this on-the-job training of labour and management that the infant subsidy (direct or indirect) is intended to pay for. On this view the unit cost of the product may be a decreasing function, not of the scale of output, but of the volume of output cumulated over time. The fact that, in most countries, protection is apt to be retained long after infancy may be ascribed to vested interests similar to those that oppose tariff reduction in the United States, where by and large the infancy argument has long ceased to be applicable, though even there any new project may exhibit the

[1] H. S. Ellis and W. Fellner, 'External Economies and Diseconomies', *American Economic Review*, September 1943.
[2] J. E. Meade, *The Theory of International Economic Policy*, vol. ii, *Trade and Welfare* (London, 1955), p. 260.

'learning curve' linking unit cost with cumulative output in the way just indicated.[1]

In the circumstances in which the less developed countries find themselves today, the question may be raised why, instead of promoting output of import substitutes, they do not promote manufacturing for export so as to benefit from the expansion of markets in, and trade among, the more advanced countries. This is indeed a possible alternative. In fact it has not yet been practised to any marked extent. Infant protection to export industries can only be given through direct subsidies, the financing of which puts additional strains on fiscal administration. From the standpoint of international trade theory there is not much to choose between protection for home market industries and industrial export promotion through direct subsidies. Both are departures from the free trade position. In practice, for obvious reasons, manufacturing for export is usually a later stage, based on prior development for the home market. Once the infancy phase has been passed in home-market production it may well be possible to develop an export trade in manufactures, even without resort to subsidies. Indian textile exports, though largely due to special factors, can be cited as a recent example.

Manufacturing for home markets in the less developed countries comprises also production in such countries for export to each others' markets. This is particularly important for the smaller countries. According to the ECLA report cited above, 'industrialization is developing in water-tight compartments of national economies, and trade in industrial products between Latin American countries is very rare' (p. 72). The liberalization of import restrictions among under-developed countries, even if it does not offer a basic remedy for under-development, can be an effective measure of infant-industry protection.

In any event it is likely that many of the less developed countries, in their trade with the more advanced centres of industry, will long continue to have an outstanding comparative advantage in primary production for export. It is in their interest at least to maintain, if not to increase, production of primary staples so as to keep up their foreign exchange proceeds from this source at the highest possible level. We are all indebted to Colonel Perón for an excellent demonstration of the loss which a country can suffer by sacrificing its traditional exports and hence its import capacity also. We have in Australia a good example of a high income country, already pre-

[1] A good illustration of this curve appears in a study by H. Asher, *Cost-Quantity Relationships in the Airframe Industry*, The RAND Corporation (Santa Monica, California, 1956). I am indebted to Mr. Charles J. Hitch for calling my attention to this particular study as well as to the general point which it illustrates.

dominantly industrialized at home, yet continuing to rely almost entirely on primary commodities for its foreign earnings, because that is where its comparative advantage lies.

If primary production for export is fully maintained or, as world demand expands, increased in accordance with comparative advantage, import restrictions in under-developed countries do not reduce total imports but only change their *composition*. This has been plausibly argued in the study of the Economic Commission for Latin America cited.[1] Imports of manufactured consumer goods are stopped ; imports of capital goods take their place. Domestic production of manufactured consumables provides substitutes for imports of such products. The attendant losses — which, it is hoped, will be temporary — in consumer welfare have already been stressed. Another point to note is that the additional equipment imported represents increased investment which must be financed by increased saving. It is only with a complementary domestic policy of mobilizing additional saving that the new equipment imports can make a *net* contribution to capital formation. If the necessary saving can somehow be found, the switch in the composition of imports from consumables to capital goods may be regarded as being due to a basic shift in demand conditions reflecting development policy.

Import substitution in the field of manufactured consumables is largely an accomplished fact. About half of the imports which under-developed countries now receive from advanced countries consists of capital equipment. The other half includes some food and essential materials as well as industrial products for consumers' use. If balanced growth is based on import substitution alone, there is little scope for it left. But in principle it need not be based on import substitution. It should mean above all an *enlargement* of the domestic market rather than the mere exclusion of foreign supplies from the small existing market. In short, import substitution is not enough and may, in the long run, or even initially, not prove to be necessary at all.

A word should be said about import substitution in the field of capital goods. To many countries this seems a desirable goal, for reasons that, at any rate in economic terms, are often obscure. The idea that each country has to have its own steel and engineering industries derives no support from the balanced growth principle as interpreted above. Nor is there much to be said for setting them up ahead of demand on the ground that, although they must typically be built in big units, the growth of the national economy will

[1] United Nations, *International Co-operation in a Latin American Development Policy*, p. 60.

eventually lead to their full and profitable utilization. One thing, among others, that distinguishes such industries from public utilities such as transport and power is that machinery and other metal products can be imported and are in fact being imported in ever-increasing volume. The international division of labour is becoming increasingly vertical in the sense of concentrating on capital goods. By contrast, basic services such as inland transport cannot be imported and, if they are to be had at all, the facilities for producing them must be installed on the spot. The absence of such facilities can be an absolute barrier to development while lack of home-produced steel and equipment is not. Priority in investment planning should be given to the former so long as the latter can be got through foreign trade.

At a later stage, when this priority has been met, it may be that, where conditions are suitable, the infant industry case for protection can be applied to capital goods industries too. But here, even more than in the light manufacturing field, it should be remembered that infant creation is far more important than infant protection. Positive measures in the field of capital formation, education, and technical training are needed far more than the easy but negative method of import restriction. If a vigorous pace of development is not attainable through international trade alone, at least we should take care that expansion of the domestic economy does not involve needless extra costs by destroying such gains as are being realized from international specialization.

The upshot of the balanced growth argument in the limited sense in which it has been considered is that, under certain conditions discussed above, output expansion for domestic consumption can go ahead side by side with international specialization. It need not be a substitute for international specialization. It is a substitute rather for the growth transmission mechanism which, for reasons indicated, is not as powerful today as it was in the nineteenth century. However, while the expansion of external demand for primary products is not as strong an engine of growth as it used to be, great harm can result from neglect of existing opportunities of specialization for the world market. Since the available resources, even if growing over time, are at any moment limited, development policy in regard to resource allocation must exercise extreme care to avoid starving the established export sectors or choking off possible new lines of export production.

With this proviso, our two protagonists — specialization for the world market and diversified advance on the home front — are really friends, not enemies. Filling the vacuum in the domestic economy is the best foundation for foreign trade since it means increasing the level of productivity and real purchasing power. That is why the advanced nations are each others' best customers. And that is the best hope for expanding world trade, even though trade as a proportion of total output is likely to decline as the domestic economies of the low-income countries become more fully developed.

V. THE BALANCE OF PAYMENTS PROBLEM

There is, however, a further question that worries some economists. If production is pushed for domestic markets, will that not lead to balance of payments difficulties ? The belief that it will is widely held. We find it expressed, for example, in Professor Lewis's *Theory of Economic Growth* (*e.g.* pp. 282 and 387). Do we have a conflict here between balanced growth and external equilibrium ? If external disequilibrium is an inevitable result of output expansion for home consumption, then this may lead to balance of payments restrictions on imports and so indirectly after all to a destruction of foreign trade.

First, it must be recognized that investment expenditure not covered by concurrent saving (domestic or foreign) is a potent source of disequilibrium in the balance of payments. But this is a separate problem — the problem of living within one's means. If means are inadequate for a certain volume of investment, there may still remain possibilities for remedial action on the side of capital mobilization.

The argument that stresses home market expansion as a cause of external imbalance is concerned, not with the effects of excessive investment outlays, which are obvious, but with the *operation* of investment projects already completed in the domestic economy. It points out that a new industry producing something new for the home market is likely to create an increased demand for imports, because it may need some imported raw materials and because part of the additional incomes created in this industry may be spent on imported goods. If export proceeds remain unchanged, the result will be a foreign trade deficit.

All this is true, but it is not the whole story. If the new industry sells its products on the domestic market, the rest of the economy will have to divert its expenditure away from imported products, provided that expenditure is not increased by inflationary means, through a reduction in saving, through dishoarding, or through credit expansion. If inflation can be avoided, then the products sold by the new industry — given the constraint of limited income in the rest of the economy — will necessarily act as import substitutes indirectly, even if they look totally different from anything imported previously.[1] If there is a balance of payments deficit it is a result of inflation, not of output expansion for the home market. In the absence of inflation the rest of the economy will have to reduce its imports in order to buy the products of the new industry, and this will tend to offset the increase in imports caused by the new industry.

It may seem strange that an expansion of income in this model is not necessarily accompanied by any net increase in imports. The marginal propensity to import would seem to be zero, which looks like a rather unnatural result. But there is nothing strange about it if we remember that in this case there has been a structural change in the economy, the creation of a new industry. The usual concepts of income analysis in international trade, just like those of the Keynesian income analysis in general, assume a given economic structure. Development means changes in economic structure and in this dynamic context the functional relationships between income and imports need not behave in the usual manner.

This does not render income analysis useless in studying balance of payments problems. On the contrary, it is indispensable. That import restrictions can correct an external payments deficit is usually taken for granted. In fact, their efficacy for this purpose is questionable and needs to be closely examined. Classical theorists have always been inclined to maintain that import restrictions alone are not capable of improving the trade balance. It is easy to see that in a state of full employment this view, though subject to qualifications, is basically valid.

Income analysis shows three ways in which import restrictions can help to remove an external deficit. First, if there is unemployment of the Keynesian type, import restrictions will lead to increased production in import-competing industries without having to impinge on the export sectors. The increase in total output and income is likely to generate increased saving also ; the country will once again live within its means. Second, the import controls can directly lead to increased saving if the money income previously spent on imported goods now remains unspent. Even at full employment, external balance can in this case be restored through import controls alone.

If there is full employment, and if expenditure on imports,

---

[1] Whether the goods are direct or indirect import substitutes is, contrary to common belief, immaterial. Physical resemblances are irrelevant. The distinction between competitive and non-competitive imports current in the United States rests on a similar case of misplaced concreteness, though admittedly it is of interest to industries immediately affected.

instead of being saved, is simply diverted into domestic spending, then prices will tend to rise, exports will decline, and the balance of payments deficit will not have been eliminated by the cut in imports. Third, if, in this inflationary position, exports enjoy an inelastic demand abroad, then the value of exports will increase, tending to close the external deficit. This is a rather unlikely possibility. For one thing, any country that is trying to apply the optimum tariff argument will, like an individual monopolist, already be operating on the elastic portion of the demand schedule which it faces abroad, and a further increase in export prices will therefore reduce the value of exports, even though in its lower ranges the external demand schedule has an elasticity of less than one. Quite apart from that argument, we must remember that the external demand schedule cannot conceptually remain inelastic for ever as the price is increased. And even supposing that it does remain inelastic over the relevant range, a favourable outcome for the balance of payments is possible only to the extent that the increment in income from exports is saved.

In all three cases increased saving is seen to be the *sine qua non* of external equilibrium. There is the further possibility that a general price rise resulting from import restrictions, even if it discourages exports, may yet make room for a net improvement in the trade balance by leading to an increased demand for cash and hence, if the money supply is held constant, to a rise in interest rates which will force a reduction in investment. Thus balance of payments policy operates through one or both of the two determinants of capital growth : only by way of an increase in saving or a reduction in investment can a restriction of imports be effective in righting the balance of payments. For short periods import controls may bring relief through unintended inventory reductions or cash balance accumulations ; but such involuntary changes will soon lead to corrective reactions by firms and individuals and hence to renewed pressure on the foreign accounts.

In general, without a change in the relation between national income and expenditure import restrictions cannot produce any improvement in the foreign balance. Exchange-rate adjustment by itself may be equally ineffective unless it is accompanied by such a change as an act of policy or unless, as is conceivable though not at all certain, it induces such a change automatically. All this is clear from the fundamental identity of income analysis, $X - M = Y - E$, where the letters stand for exports, imports, national income and expenditure (on consumption, investment, and government activities). This equation must be interpreted in an *ex-ante* sense if it is to have any explanatory significance. *Ex post* it is true at all times, though it can be true at very different values. The formula acquires pragmatic interest for policy purposes when we impose constraints upon it by postulating that $X - M$ be reduced to zero and, if we are interested in internal balance also, that Y be kept at a level corresponding to full employment without inflation.[1]

If we ask how it is possible for national expenditure to exceed income and so to cause an external deficit, there is no better answer than that given by Professor Robbins : '. . . as David Hume recognized in a moment of unsurpassed intuitive insight, it is the existence in different areas of independent sources of supply of means of payment which is the essential condition for the emergence of disequilibria in balances of payments'.[2] Independent countries have, as a rule, their own centres for the 'manufacture of credit'. The balance between saving and investment is of special significance in the relation between Y and E because investment is a respectable object of at least partial financing through the credit system.

The interrelation between the national income accounts and the foreign exchange accounts is only too often overlooked. Nowhere in the field of international economics is the fallacy of misplaced concreteness so prevalent as in balance of payments policy. Nothing is more common than the attempt to cure a balance of payments problem by cutting out imports — or by pushing production for export — of this or that commodity. For instance, Turkey is at present trying to deal with her foreign exchange crisis by stopping all imports of coffee. The British government has, quite recently again, urged the motor industry to increase the proportion of cars exported. The commodity approach to balance of payments policy seems to flourish everywhere. And balance of payments crises continue.

Another favourite approach, often recommended by economic advisers in under-developed countries, is to try to strengthen the balance of payments by changing the composition of investment (without reducing its total amount) in such a way as to increase investment in either import competing or export industries or in both. This is an unwarranted interference with the principle that capital increments should be applied to those places where, allowing for external economies or diseconomies, they make the greatest contribution to national product. As Professor Ellis has put it, 'invest-

---

[1] These matters are more fully discussed in Sections IV and V of my paper on 'The Relation between Home Investment and External Balance in the Light of British Experience, 1945–55', *Review of Economics and Statistics*, May 1956.

[2] Lionel Robbins, 'A Note on the Formal Content of the Traditional Theory of International Trade', in *Contribuições à análise do desenvolvimento econômico*, Essays in Honor of Eugenio Gudin (Rio de Janeiro, 1957), pp. 269–270.

ment that seems best from the standpoint of the country's domestic economy is also best from the standpoint of its balance of payments with the outside world'.[1] The reason is simple. The higher a country's national income in relation to past peaks at home (the 'ratchet effect') and to current levels observed elsewhere (the 'demonstration effect'), the easier it will generally be for the country to live — and grow — within its income.

A truly effective way of coping with external payments difficulties is not to tamper with the distribution of investment, but to cut down the total amount of investment expenditure. This is easy ; but it is bad for development. There is, however, an alternative, mobilizing additional saving. Even if this cannot easily be done out of current consumption, it can usually be done out of current increases in output, achieved through improvements in methods of production or through the fuller utilization of labour and other resources. I am inclined to the view, therefore, that the balance of payments is not a basic factor limiting a country's development. It is always to some extent within the country's own control. There is another factor which is beyond a country's control, and that is the expansion of world demand for its exports of primary products. If that expansion is relatively sluggish, there is something to be said, under suitable conditions, for promoting economic growth through output expansion for the home market. It seems to me that this has in fact been the case in the last quarter-century or so.

On the main point of this concluding section enough has been said to suggest that it is not home market development as such that makes foreign exchange crises inevitable. It is the excess spending associated with inflation that creates balance of payments disequilibria. In practice, no doubt, home market development and inflation may often be closely associated, but that is no reason for failing to sort out their effects in the analysis of the problem. And inflation is generally due, in its turn, to the difficulty which the poorer countries have in living within their means, when there is so much investment to be done and when there are so many temptations to spend on consumer goods as well. Here indeed is the central difficulty of financing economic development. It lies outside the scope of the present topic — and I am only too glad to leave it alone.

---

[1] N. S. Buchanan and H. S. Ellis, *Approaches to Economic Development* (New York, 1955), p. 391.

COMMENTS ON PROFESSOR NURKSE'S PAPER

BY

HARVEY LEIBENSTEIN
University of California

PROFESSOR NURKSE has made the task of the commentator a rather difficult one. It is easy to comment on and quarrel with an extreme position. But Professor Nurkse presents his position — and it appears to be a rather mild deviation from the orthodox view — in a reasonable and most conciliatory manner. Furthermore, as one reads along, additional qualifications are introduced one at a time. At various junctures I thought I had a point to make only to find, upon turning the page, that the possible difficulty has been recognized, and that what appeared as an initially strong position has been qualified and watered down accordingly. Indeed, when all the qualifications are made, the position that emerges seemed to me to be considerably different from the bold thesis I was led to expect by a rapid perusal of the first section.

On page 235 of his paper Professor Nurkse points out that he intends to consider 'whether the idea of balanced growth is compatible with the principle of international specialization . . . [and] whether the available investment funds, limited as they are, should be used to promote activities specialized along lines of comparative advantage internationally or diversified so as to provide markets for each other locally. In Western eyes the pursuit of balanced growth only too often causes a pathetic misdirection of scarce resources.' One might be led to expect, on the basis of these and other remarks, and on the basis of some of Professor Nurkse's other writings, a defence of balanced growth even in the case where balanced growth proves to be incompatible with comparative advantages. But that is not exactly what we get.

The question that Professor Nurkse really considers is whether international trade can be the generating force for economic development, *i.e. per capita* income growth. Can it stimulate a degree of economic expansion greater than the rate of population growth, and great enough for some of the national aspirations that may be involved ? And especially can this be achieved through the expansion of primary industries in backward economies ? Whereas this may have been the case in the nineteenth century, Nurkse argues that this is unlikely to be the case in the twentieth century. The reasons, we are told, are in part technological, and in part economic. In many cases synthetics have replaced and are replacing raw materials previously exported by under-developed economies. In other cases the possibilities for expansion are limited because the price elasticity of demand for raw materials is less than unity. Furthermore, recent trends, as determined by various empirical studies, suggest that the secular expansion of the demand for exports is unlikely to be large enough to stimulate adequate growth. Hence, Professor Nurkse argues, since international trade cannot do the job, the demand necessary to stimulate adequate expansion must be created locally, and this can be achieved most expeditiously through balanced growth. But, according to Professor Nurkse, balanced growth and comparative advantage are not incompatible. The under-developed economies should retain their comparative advantage and export markets in primary goods, while at the same time expanding the local market. Thus, the old (comparative advantage) and the new doctrine (balanced growth), when seen in this conciliatory light, are really friends rather than enemies.

But if Professor Nurkse has not shattered our faith in the doctrine of comparative advantage, he has cast doubts on notions some of us might have harboured about the factual nature of international specialization. Part 2 of the paper argues that we should not expect international specialization to remain what it was. With respect to primary products the world is becoming somewhat more self-sufficient than it used to be. Also, since economic development implies changes in factor proportions, it also implies changes in the commodities in which a country will have a comparative advantage. Therefore, Professor Nurkse implies, it seems to me, that we should not necessarily expect today's exporters of primary products to continue to be the primary product exporters of tomorrow.

We may readily agree with Professor Nurkse that the twentieth-century expansion of the less developed economies will differ from its nineteenth-century counterpart. We may perhaps also agree that we cannot rely on the expansion of the international demand for primary products to generate economic development. Yet it may be that these notions somewhat understate the possible rôle of international trade in economic development because the problem is approached from the viewpoint of a single country. Under a free market, as economies expand, comparative advantage will change, and trade patterns will change accordingly. Why not attempt to apply the concept of balanced growth to a group of countries rather than a single country, and attempt to achieve a balanced expansion of trade as the economies of these countries expand ?

In stressing the changing pattern of international specialization, the tendency of many raw materials to be displaced by synthetics, and the worsening terms of trade for raw material and primary product producers, Professor Nurkse indirectly emphasizes the danger involved in extreme specialization. In a world of uncertainty extreme specialization should bear a high discount rate for risk. To overcome the risk element some degree of diversification may be a virtue even if such diversification implies a resource allocation that is not strictly in accordance with comparative advantage. The risks involved are probably in part due to the different, and usually unforeseeable, growth rates of different economies. Such considerations do weaken somewhat the case for a strict reliance on comparative advantage.

Professor Nurkse recognizes that international investment in primary industries, especially extractive industries such as oil, may be exceedingly profitable. Through the expansion of one industry others will normally be induced to expand. But, he argues, 'The price mechanism works, but it may work too slowly. That is one reason for the frequently observed fact that foreign direct investments in extractive export industries have created high productivity islands and have had little impact on the level of productivity in the domestic economy.' Is it really the price mechanism that is entirely to blame ? This is a point worth considering. It seems to me that there are three roads to income growth. One is through greater efficiency in the allocation of resources (and this includes the employment of resources previously unemployed). A second is through increases in the quality of the labour force — *i.e.* increases in skill, knowledge, energy level, etc. And a third is through increases in the non-human resources *per capita* — roughly put, through a rate of capital accumulation that is greater than the rate of population growth. The comparative advantage doctrine stresses allocation efficiency with given resources. Now the difficulty with foreign investment in extractive export industries as a growth generator may not be due to the fact that the price mechanism works too slowly, but to the fact that population growth may have been considerable in many of these countries. As a result, the average quality of the labour force has not increased but may have been diluted through population growth among the unskilled. In addition, the increase in resources per head that might otherwise have come about may also have been diluted as a result of population growth. Furthermore, in some of these instances conditions that even roughly approximate free markets may not have existed. I mention these possibilities simply to suggest that perhaps the price mechanism is not the only culprit.

Let us now return to the central problem that Professor Nurkse has set himself — the compatibility of comparative advantage and balanced growth. Are the two quite as compatible as the paper implies ?

It is not clear to me whether balanced growth is necessarily presumed to be consistent with allocation according to profit maximization. I suppose that this is not the case. If it were, then there would be no need to worry about balanced growth at all. We would simply advocate allocation in accordance with profit maximization and the balance problem would take care of itself. But if balanced growth allocation is not consistent with profit maximization allocation, then it seems to me that there is the possibility that balanced growth may be incompatible with the comparative advantage allocation of resources. In a free market economy profit maximization will result in an allocation that is in accordance with comparative advantage. But if the balanced growth allocation is not consistent with the profit maximization allocation, then it also will be inconsistent with the comparative advantage allocation.

Professor Nurkse urges countries not to sacrifice their traditional exports while developing their local market through balanced growth. He points to the unfortunate situation created by Perón in Argentina as a case in point. But pushing balanced growth (where it is incompatible with profit maximization) will alter factor prices. It may conceivably so affect the factor prices in the traditional export industries that they cease to be profitable. Thus there exists the possibility (although I do not know whether or not it is a likely one) that traditional exports may be sacrificed because of the attempt to develop in accordance with balanced growth. Of course, appropriate subsidies might enable the country to retain its traditional exports, but such procedures might gradually drag the country into a system of controls and possible rigidities that Professor Nurkse might not like to see come about.

On the whole I have found this paper exceedingly stimulating, provocative, and yet somewhat unsettling. I feel that this is in part because it touched on, and much of the discussion and answers to the questions raised really depend upon, an underlying theoretical problem that economists have far from solved. That is to say, while we have a highly refined analysis of the price mechanism as a resource allocator, we know relatively little how the price mechanism operates as a generator of economic growth under conditions of imperfect foresight and uncertainty.

FURTHER COMMENTS ON PROFESSOR NURKSE'S PAPER

BY

EUGENIO GUDIN
University of Brazil

I. INTRODUCTION

IN the first part of his paper Professor Nurkse draws a most interesting comparison of the relative importance of international trade for under-developed countries in the nineteenth and in the twentieth centuries, and concludes that 'It is not certain that the less developed countries can rely on economic growth being induced from the outside through an expansion of world demand for their exports of primary commodities'.

I think this conclusion is in accordance with facts. International trade has undergone a structural change. The pattern of international trade and finance of the nineteenth century, under the leadership of Great Britain and the London financial market, was quite different from that prevailing today. The only comment I would venture as far as Latin America is concerned is that these countries have not always taken advantage of the valuable export possibilities open to them.

II. BALANCED GROWTH OR THE BIG PUSH

In the second part of the paper Professor Nurkse refers to the concept of 'balanced growth' as 'a pattern of mutually supporting investments in different lines of production to enlarge the size of the market and help to fill the vacuum in the domestic economy of low income areas', and adds that 'In the existing state of affairs in low income areas the introduction of capital-using techniques of production in any single industry may be inhibited by the small size of the market'. Professor Nurkse also says that 'his argument is primarily concerned with demand for or allocation of capital. It takes an increased supply of capital for granted.'

I am not certain that I am interpreting Professor Nurkse's paper rightly in stating that his concept of balanced growth is nearer — in fact very much nearer — the big push model than to a growth model isolated as much as possible from horizontal or vertical disequilibria such as was suggested by Nicholas Kaldor in his recent lectures in Rio de Janeiro.

I do not lean towards the big push concept. As Professor Nurkse himself says, isolated advance is not impossible and investment and increased productivity in one industry will have favourable repercussions elsewhere in the economy. However, I do not agree with Professor Nurkse's objection that this progress may be at a snail's pace. It seems to me that Professor Nurkse is considering only two extreme models: one, where investment and an increase in productivity take place in one industry only ; the other, the big push, where investment takes place in a large number of industries at the same time. I do not see why a number of intermediate models cannot be adopted. Instead of investment in one industry, we might have advances in two or three industries at the same time as frequently happens in this country.

My objections to the big push are threefold. First, it is somewhat unreal because it presupposes not only an ample supply of capital but also of other scarce factors in under-developed countries, since otherwise they would not be under-developed. An attempt at a big push would probably amount to starting more projects than the country's resources can cope with, with the result of lengthening the period of investment unnecessarily and uneconomically.

Second, I agree with Professor Viner's statement that, 'The argument of an inadequate market for the product of a single new or expanded industry will have no, or less, weight if the investment under considera-tion : (*a*) is cost-reducing instead of output-expanding ; (*b*) is import-substituting ; (*c*) is for production for export ; or (*d*) is some combination of these.'[1] In most Latin-American countries the field of import substitu-tion alone gives ample scope for development and, in my opinion, it has been overdone to the detriment of export possibilities.

I do not think that, in Brazil at least, development has been hampered by the deficiency of the market. External economies can and should be provided *pari passu* with development. The disequilibria which are known to exist in this and other Latin-American countries due to lack of trans-

[1] Jacob Viner, 'Stability and Progress : The Poorer Countries' Problem', in Douglas Hague, ed., *Stability and Progress in the World Economy* (London, 1958), p. 58.

portation, power, and other external economies, including education, are the result of highly defective governmental policies.

Third, the big push model cannot easily avoid a bias towards government action. It is barely conceivable as a joint and simultaneous procedure by a group of entrepreneurs. And in countries with a precarious level of political education, such as these, government intervention in the private economic sector has proved very harmful indeed.

On the other hand, I do not think that the spirit of enterprise and private initiative is lacking in these countries. What is lacking is know-how ; and what is excessive is industrial protection. These two factors together are largely responsible for the comparatively slow pace of development. The excellent report of the Economic Commission for Latin America on the textile industry in five Latin-American countries gives a typical picture in that respect. Less protection, more challenge, and more know-how would double or treble production in many factories.

The same applies to agriculture. Again quoting Mr. Kaldor in Rio, he said then that he regarded the failure to bring about the conditions for a progressive agriculture as *the most important single factor* which inhibited the economic growth of the relatively under-developed areas of the world during the last hundred years.[1]

All these examples, and others I might quote, show how development can be considerably speeded up in these countries without an organized big push. As far as the size of markets is concerned, there is in these countries a very large and unsatisfied demand for human capacity and ability which can only be satisfied by education or import, or both.

These are the reasons why I cannot adhere to the big push model for the economic development of Latin America. The fact that normal and practical solutions are certainly not intellectually attractive to economists does not alter the fact that statesmen responsible for the conduct of the country's economy have no alternative but to adopt them.

I would just like to add a word of praise for the final paragraph of Professor Nurkse's paper where he so clearly and so usefully explains to us that if there is a balance of payment deficit it is a result of inflation, not of output expansion for the home market ; that saving is the *sine qua non* of external equilibrium ; and that the balance of payments is not a basic factor limiting a country's development. This, I think, is most valuable advice to Latin-American economists.

DISCUSSION OF PROFESSOR NURKSE'S PAPER

MOST of the prolonged and very complimentary discussion that followed *Professor Nurkse's* introductory presentation dealt with the subject of

[1] See the report of Nicholas Kaldor's lectures at the Fundação Getulio Vargas, *Revista Brasileira de Economia*, March 1957.

balanced growth. Other subjects incidental to this major theme were the need for domestically orientated investment, the advisability of import substitution through domestic investment, and the relationship between investment and the balance of payments.

I. Domestically Orientated Investment

The main thesis of Professor Nurkse's paper, *Dr. Kafka* said, was that international specialization did not offer the under-developed countries a prospect of rapid development and that the non-export sector must become the leader in economic growth. *Professor Haberler* was not convinced that the prospects of growth through specialization were as dim as *Professor Nurkse* had painted them. Foreign trade was still the mainstay of the economies of most under-developed countries. Technology worked not only to reduce export possibilities but also to increase them. In addition, under-developed countries often helped to hold down their own exports by virtue of their own protectionist policies. He did not fully accept the ECLA argument that when under-developed countries reduced some particular import they were merely changing the composition of imports without reducing the total. Whenever resources were diverted from exports to home production, exports were cut and hence also imports. Nevertheless, he agreed that Professor Nurkse's belief in a low income elasticity of demand for primary products exported by under-developed countries was not without foundation.

Professor Schultz argued that under-developed countries need not look to primary products only as a means of earning foreign exchange. Japan and Puerto Rico were both exporting manufactures, Mexico was exporting services. Under-developed countries that sought to develop by means of high protection might be cutting themselves off from the discovery of big markets for manufactured exports in the developed countries. *Professor Gudin* associated himself with the idea that under-developed countries should push their exports in the field of manufactures.

The observations of these speakers appeared to be in the nature of qualifications rather than positive rebuttals of *Professor Nurkse*'s general thesis that development had to be sought in production for the home market rather than for the foreign market.

II. Balanced Growth

Professor Leibenstein posed the fundamental question : was Balanced Growth compatible with profit maximization ? If it was, there was no need to talk much about it, since it followed naturally. If it was not, then it presumably was incompatible also with comparative advantage. Professor Nurkse's desire to reconcile specialization and Balanced Growth would then appear to be impossible.

Dr. Kafka asked for a precise definition of 'balance' and enquired whether the principle of Balanced Growth applied to the domestic economy only or to the entire economy including the export sector. In the latter case, comparative advantage would be the true guide to resource allocation. He wondered further whether 'Balanced Growth' was really a new concept or problem. The economies of the nineteenth century presumably had had similar problems and they seemed to have solved them without too much difficulty. 'Balanced Growth', it seemed to him, might become a problem in very small economies, but such economies scarcely existed today. Since local production could always displace and substitute for imports, the domestic sector could enjoy growth without 'balance' up to the point of complete import elimination. Finally, if the price mechanism was at all effective it could make up for considerable 'imbalance' in the pattern of growth. *Professor Nurkse* agreed that the price mechanism could contribute to balance. But some things, he said, the price mechanism could not do, and in those cases he would not object to the government doing them. He did not mean to argue that balanced growth necessarily meant a 'big push'. He was in sympathy with that principle in so far as it meant that under-developed countries had to make a great effort. But balanced growth could also proceed at a snail's pace.

Dr. Alter enquired whether balanced growth had any specific meaning for foreign trade policy or whether it was neutral with respect to tariffs, exchange controls, and the like. *Professor Nurkse* replied that balanced growth did mean something specific with respect to specific problems such as the balance between agriculture and industry.

Professor Wallich expressed uncertainty whether balanced growth was to be regarded merely as an aspect of Say's law, in which case it seemed to be without policy implications, or as a normative concept. There seemed to him to be three areas in which a policy of balanced growth could be pursued : (1) the balance between agriculture and industry, (2) the balance between economic overhead and direct application of resources, and (3) balance within the general manufacturing sector. The first seemed highly desirable, the second Professor Nurkse had rejected in a previous discussion in favour of advance overhead construction. The third seemed to him virtually impossible to implement. To establish productive facilities to meet a wide range of consumer needs would greatly exceed a country's resources and capacity to absorb capital. In practice, growth proceeded without balance, but, thanks to import substitution, largely also without creating an imbalance of supplies. *Professor Brahmananda* agreed with *Professor Haberler* that the foreign trade sector entered into the pattern of growth and thus undermined the concept of balanced growth. But he welcomed the idea in so far as it meant avoidance of bottlenecks and maintenance of balance among the major sectors of the economy.

Professor Levine said that he found it difficult to establish a standard by which to measure the degree of balance obtained. How was the concept to be made operational in this sense ? *Professor Boudeville* suggested that at the theoretical level a model approach could be employed — a growth model that did not explode or oscillate might be said to possess balanced growth. *Professor Hirschman* said that the idea of balanced growth might also be applied to the process of recovery from a depression. There in fact the proper proportions were already fixed in advance. Yet, one hardly ever spoke of a cyclical upswing in this way. Was it because the concept of balanced growth was basically unrealistic ? He himself was strongly impressed with the difficulty of organizing a balanced growth process.

Professor Leibenstein said that differences in the gestation period of investment might interfere with balanced growth. He also asked whether balanced growth really had not to be considered as a 'push' — big or little — which would trigger off the process and allow the free market to take over subsequently. *Professor Levine* wondered how the need to establish social conditions that permitted the price mechanism to work fitted in with the concept of Balanced Growth.

Professor Nurkse reminded his commentators that his paper had specifically assumed the availability of adequate resources. He was not concerned with the origin of these resources. Consequently, his ideas could not be criticized on the grounds that Balanced Growth required a shift of resources from exports to the domestic sector, and thus created the very stagnation of exports that balanced growth was intended to make up for. The economy of Bolivia was an illustration of what he meant — balanced growth there was possible without reducing resources in tin mining. He also cautioned against regarding his paper as a policy recommendation. It was more in the nature of an analysis of what had already happened.

III. Import Substitution

Professor Nurkse was sceptical of deliberate import substitution as a principle of investment on the grounds that it was a misallocation of resources. He also regarded it as a static concept — once a given import had been substituted, there was no further development. Various speakers disagreed with this view. *Dr. Kafka* thought that import substitution could carry the economy forward dynamically. Under static conditions, import substitution was limited to the infant industry case. Under dynamic conditions its scope was much wider. In under-developed countries, resource growth was continually tending to change the terms of trade so as to make new import substitutions potentially profitable. *Dr. Marquez* said that Professor Nurkse himself had argued for intensified investments for the home market. Very often this was impossible without in fact substituting imports. Moreover, import substitution often produced shifts from low productivity to high productivity sectors. This meant a gain in income in addition to the saving in foreign exchange.

Professor Gudin gave his support to those who favoured import substitution.

Dr. Mayobre argued for import substitution as a means of saving foreign exchange as well as promoting immediate growth. In so far as growth occurred at all, demand for imports increased. Given the assumption that export possibilities were limited, some import substitution became essential. *Professor Hirschman* wound up this part of the discussion by saying that Professor Nurkse seemed to have created a problem for himself, since he seemed to see no great prospects for expanding exports, and he disliked aggressive import substitution. Where was expansion to occur ? Import substitution was the best way to encourage entrepreneurs, because it offered them a ready market and a minimum of risk.

IV. Balance of Payments

Professor Gudin welcomed Professor Nurkse's demonstration of the crucial rôle of savings in maintaining balance of payments equilibrium in a developing country. If saving was adequate, higher investment should not necessarily cause balance of payments disequilibrium nor represent a limiting factor in development. By virtue of adequate saving and added inflow of foreign capital, a country could accelerate its investment and still maintain balance of payments equilibrium, provided there was no inflation. He further stressed that disequilibrium in the balance of payments of under-developed countries depended much more than upon developmental investment on (1) the terms of trade, (2) inflation, (3) capacity to attract foreign capital, and (4) ability to push exports such as oil, minerals, or agricultural products. These four factors were more important than the disequilibria that might result from the increment of investments provided corresponding savings were available.

Professor Haberler likewise found himself in accord with Professor Nurkse's exposition on this point. He was not quite comfortable, however, with the *ex-post* simplicity of the algebraic demonstration. One really had to be very optimistic regarding the elasticity of foreign demand for a country's exports in order to assume that any increase in resources available for exports, set free by additional saving, could readily be translated into actual export sales. If exports had to be pushed hard, the terms of trade would worsen and the calculation would no longer work out.

Professor Byé seemed to lean to the view that additional savings would permit growth without balance of payments disequilibrium. *Dr. Furtado* challenged this optimism, however. Any shift from consumption to investment, even if covered by voluntary savings, meant an increase in imports because the import component of investment was higher than that of consumption. He saw no ready increase in exports and hence defended the policy of import restriction and programming. *Professor Nurkse* considered this to imply a 'commodity approach' to the balance of payments. So long as the additional investments were covered by savings, he saw no balance of payments problem, assuming the necessary increase in exports to proceed without difficulty.

Professor Wallich argued that Professor Nurkse's equations should not be taken quite so literally. In practice any displacement of resources towards exports would probably generate some growth that would make additional resources available, which would ease the balance of payment situation.

Chapter 10

TERMS OF TRADE AND ECONOMIC DEVELOPMENT

BY

PROFESSOR GOTTFRIED HABERLER
Harvard University

I. Introduction

THE present essay tries to elucidate various connections between the terms of trade and economic development. It utilizes existing statistical and other factual material, but it does not present any new empirical facts nor does it contain new computations. The paper is, to a large extent, critical and polemical. That is to say, it tries to disprove certain widely held notions, historical generalizations, as well as policy conclusions which have been derived from such generalizations. No originality is claimed for these critical analyses, but no apologies are offered either. It is hoped that a systematic stocktaking of existing facts and arguments may clear the air and lead to useful results. In the first section, I discuss some general propositions of international trade theory concerning the terms of trade in their relation to economic welfare. In the succeeding sections, some applications of these propositions to the problems of economic development are made.

II. The Terms of Trade and Economic Welfare: a Theoretical Discussion

Under-developed countries are rightly much concerned with their international trade position, because for all of them international trade is vitally important as a source of supply of the technological know-how, skill, capital, machinery, implements, etc., which are essential for their economic development. Many of them, for example, all Latin-American countries, are very closely knit into the world economy in the sense that an exceptionally large percentage of their output is exported and an equally large part of their total expenditures on capital as well as consumption goods is made on imports. In view of these circumstances, it is altogether natural that much attention is paid to the terms of trade as one of the factors affecting the supply of badly needed imports.

Later on I shall have occasion to distinguish different types of terms of trade, but throughout the paper, when not otherwise stated, I shall always refer to the ordinary commodity terms of trade, that is to say, to the ratio of the export and import price indices, $\frac{Px}{Pm}$.

Any improvement in the terms of trade, that is to say, any rise in export prices relatively to import prices is generally regarded as a factor favourably affecting economic welfare as measured by real national income per head. (Unless otherwise stated, I shall in this paper disregard possible divergences between economic welfare and real national income.) This proposition as well as many others of this paper applies to developed countries as well as to under-developed ones, except that for many of the latter group, owing to the importance of trade, the terms of trade are a matter of greater quantitative concern than for most members of the first group.

The statement that a deterioration in the terms of trade can usually be regarded as an unfavourable factor does, of course, not mean that if the terms of trade of a country have deteriorated over a certain period the country in question is worse off at the later date. It does not even mean that the chain of events which brought about the deterioration in the terms of trade has unfavourably affected economic welfare. If, for example, productivity in transport or in the production of export goods has gone up by, say, 10 per cent., so that the same factor input yields a 10 per cent. larger output (or the same output can be produced by a 10 per cent. smaller factor input), and if the prices of exports in terms of imports have fallen by less than 10 per cent., the country is still better off than before. The substitution of the single factoral terms of trade for the commodity terms of trade is designed to take care of such a situation. In the case envisaged we would have to say that the single factoral terms of trade have improved, that is to say, the average price of factors exported (embodied in the exported commodities) in terms of imported commodities has gone up despite the fact that the commodity terms of trade have deteriorated. Hence, in this case, the single factoral terms of trade are a better index for changes in economic welfare than the commodity terms of trade.

It is true that factoral terms of trade is a concept much more difficult to define and to measure statistically than the commodity terms of trade, because the problems involved in defining factors of production and an index of factor prices are much more complicated than the index number problem in the commodity field. (This is so at least as soon as we get away from the oversimplified notion that labour is the only factor of production.) In fact, as far as I know, only very few and purely exploratory attempts at statistical measurements of factoral terms of trade, single or double, have been made so far. But that in no way reduces the importance of forming a judgment on whether a given deterioration in the commodity terms of trade reflects only an increase in the productivity of the export industries, or goes beyond such an increase, or is due to altogether different causes.

But even if a given deterioration of the commodity terms of trade is fully or more than fully accounted for by an increase in the productivity of the export industries (that is to say, if the single factoral terms of trade have not worsened), it is still true that the country would be better off if the foreign demand for its exports had been infinitely elastic so that the commodity terms of trade had remained unchanged. In this case, the more elastic the foreign demand and hence the better the terms of trade, the better for the country. Similarly, the less elastic the foreign demand, hence the worse the terms of trade, the worse for the country. But if we use this language, we must not forget that the implied comparison is not between the present situation and a previous one (before the increase in productivity has occurred), but between the present situation and a hypothetical one (one in which the elasticity of foreign demand is assumed to be different from what it actually is).

An improvement in a country's terms of trade which results from a change abroad (a shift, for any reason, of the foreign reciprocal demand and supply curve) is always favourable for a country, unless it leads to widespread unemployment in the country's export industries, as was the case in the United Kingdom in the 1930s. But given the level of employment (or unemployment), an improvement in the commodity terms of trade resulting from an intensification of foreign demand is always favourable. Similarly, a deterioration is always unfavourable.

On the other hand, a change in the terms of trade resulting from a shift in the country's own offer curve cannot be unambiguously said to be good or bad according to the direction of the change, even if full employment is maintained continuously.[1] It is generally recognized that a country or group of countries, if it is large enough

---

[1] I must apologize for having slipped on this point in my *Survey of International Trade Theory*, International Finance Section, Princeton University (Princeton, N.J., 1955), p. 30.

to influence prices in the markets in which it sells or from which it buys (in the world market, or in sheltered regional or bilateral markets), can improve its terms of trade by restricting the volume of trade (assuming, of course, that the improvement is not cancelled by retaliatory measures by foreign countries). But it is equally well known that, from a certain point on, further improvement in welfare resulting from further rise in export prices in terms of import prices is offset by a fall in the volume of trade. Just as the optimum price of a monopolist, the price which maximizes monopoly profits, is not the highest price which the monopolist would be able to charge, the optimum terms of trade which maximize welfare is not the highest price of exports in terms of imports which a country could possibly obtain. The optimum tariff theory has tried to define the optimum tariff and optimum terms of trade. The location of the optimum point depends on the elasticities of foreign demand and supplies. The larger these elasticities, that is to say, the larger the percentage reaction of foreign demand and supply to a given percentage change of the prices charged, the sooner this point is reached, and the lower is the optimum tariff.

Suffice it to say at this point that once the optimum has been reached, a further improvement in the terms of trade, brought about by a further contraction of the volume of trade, will reduce economic welfare instead of increasing it. We may also express this by saying that the terms of trade should be optimized, but there is no sense in trying to maximize them.

It has been suggested that for this reason a better indicator than the commodity terms of trade can be found for the welfare change associated with a given trade change. Specifically, volume changes of trade have to be brought into the picture in addition to price changes. This is done by multiplying the index of the commodity terms of trade $\left(\dfrac{Px}{Pm}\right)$ by an index of the volume of exports Qx. The resulting index has been called the income terms of trade or an index of the export gains from trade or of the total gains from trade.

While it is correct that in order to evaluate a welfare change it is necessary to consider volume changes in addition to price changes, it can be easily shown that the income terms of trade $\left(\dfrac{Qx\,Px}{Pm}\right)$ is not a satisfactory indicator of the direction (let alone the magnitude) of the welfare change associated with a trade change. Suppose $\dfrac{Px}{Pm}$ has risen by 10 per cent. and Qx fallen by 10 per cent. — other things, viz., total output, employment, and the balance of payments remaining unchanged. In that case, the country is better off because it exports less and receives the same volume of imports, but the income terms of trade have remained unchanged. Similarly if $\frac{Px}{Pm}$ is down by 10 per cent. and Qx is up by 10 per cent., the country is worse off, but the income terms of trade are unchanged. In both cases the commodity terms of trade correctly indicate the direction of the change in welfare.

This does not mean, however, that an index of the income terms of trade is of no use at all. For example, the Economic Commission for Latin America in their *Economic Survey of Latin America*, 1949, uses the same measure as an index of Latin America's capacity to import. That seems to me a much more appropriate description and application than to regard it as a measure of the gain from trade or an indicator of welfare change.[1]

The upshot of these discussions is that the relations between the terms of trade and economic welfare are intricate. Therefore, great care must be exercised in the interpretation of given changes in the terms of trade and in the formulation of policy objectives with respect to the terms of trade. The mere knowledge that the terms of trade for a country or group of countries have changed in a certain way over a certain period of time is of precious little importance unless it is combined with other types of information. Did the change originate primarily at home or abroad? In other words, has the foreign or the domestic offer curve shifted? If it was the domestic offer curve which has changed, what was the main reason for that shift? Has the supply of export goods become more plentiful — for example, because of technological improvements — or has the demand for imports changed and for what reason?[2] What changes in the volume of exports and imports have been associated with the given change in the terms of trade?

Some of these questions are not at all easy to answer, especially when long run comparisons are involved. Comparisons between distant years are, of course, also marred by the fact that changes in the statistical measures of the terms of trade themselves (quite apart from the difficulty of ascertaining and interpreting attending circumstances and causes) become increasingly dubious to the point of being completely meaningless for the reason that the composition of

[1] The authors of that report are, of course, fully aware of the fact that the capacity to import also depends on funds made available through capital imports, the necessity of repaying loans and interest payments.

[2] Why the foreign offer curve has changed need not concern us except for the reason that this knowledge may give a clue about its likely future behaviour.

trade changes fairly rapidly over time as a consequence of the appearance of new commodities, of quality changes of old ones, and of shifts of others between the categories of traded or non-traded, or even between the categories of export and import, commodities.

Looking through the trade statistics of any country, or at the shop windows in any city, one is struck by the large number of commodities which did not exist at all ten, twenty, forty years ago, or which have changed their quality profoundly. Examples are : machinery of all description, household appliances, vehicles, aeroplanes, chemicals, pharmaceuticals, and synthetic fibres. At great effort and expense it should be possible to make allowance for some of these changes by introducing new commodities, as they appear, in a chain index number. Existing terms of trade indices are grossly deficient and it stands to reason that neglect of new commodities and of quality changes affects primarily the export indices of the developed industrial countries.

In the light of these general theoretical considerations, I shall now discuss some specific issues relating to under-developed countries.

III. Alleged Secular Tendencies in the Terms of Trade and their Consequences

I will first discuss the well-known theory that the terms of trade have a secular tendency to deteriorate for the exporters of primary goods and to improve for the exporters of manufactured products. We may divide the argument into five phases : first, the alleged fact that the said deterioration did in fact occur from the 1870s to the eve of the Second World War ; [1] second, the proposed explanation of this alleged tendency ; third, the extrapolation based on this alleged tendency ; fourth, the welfare interpretation — what does the alleged tendency imply for the economic welfare of the underdeveloped countries and the contribution thereto made by international trade ? fifth, policy recommendations derived from the foregoing.

Several writers have questioned whether as a matter of historical fact the terms of trade have deteriorated for primary producers or for under-developed countries over the period from the 1870s to the 1940s. It is indeed on the face of it highly improbable that such a broad generalization should hold — that the terms of trade for all, or for the majority, of under-developed countries should have the same trend. Where do we draw the line between developed and

---

[1] The statistical basis is to be found in United Nations, *Relative Prices of Exports and Imports of Underdeveloped Countries* (New York, 1949).

under-developed countries ? It should be borne in mind that while all under-developed countries are, on balance, exporters of primary products, there are developed countries, such as Australia and Denmark, that also are net exporters of primary products.

However we draw the line, it is clear that the economic structure, or at any rate the composition of exports, of different under-developed countries is very dissimilar. Considering for the moment Latin American countries only, it would be a very strange coincidence indeed if, in the long run, the commodity terms of trade, let alone the factoral terms of trade, moved parallel for coffee countries, mining countries, petroleum exporters, and exporters of wheat, wool, and fats. The same holds of the other side of the fence. The dissimilarity of the trade structure of developed countries is hardly less pronounced than that of under-developed countries.

It is well known that the hypothesis under consideration is based entirely on the annual index of the United Kingdom's commodity terms of trade. This is much too narrow a statistical base for the generalization that historically the terms of trade for under-developed countries have deteriorated by 40 per cent. or so from the 1870s to the late 1930s.

There are at least three basic objections. First, this index does not allow for quality changes and makes very insufficient allowance for new products. This introduces a bias because, as has been repeatedly pointed out, industrial products have tremendously improved in quality, and literally every year a host of new products are introduced, while the quality and range of most primary products have remained very much unchanged. Copper remains copper, cotton remains cotton, and wheat remains wheat, while an automobile, a rubber tyre, a radio, an antibiotic, either did not exist at all or was an entirely different, less durable, and infinitely less serviceable commodity in earlier periods.

Second, as is also well known, the terms of trade index leaves out services. In the above-mentioned index of the British terms of trade, import prices are taken c.i.f. at British ports of entry and export prices f.o.b. at British ports of exit. In case of a change in transportation cost, this makes it impossible even in a two country model to regard the terms of trade of one partner as an accurate index of the terms of trade of the other. As has often been pointed out, it is possible that, in a period of falling transportation costs, the terms of trade improve for both countries. That this has often happened has been shown by C. M. Wright in a remarkable article.[1]

[1] C. M. Wright, 'Convertibility and Triangular Trade as Safeguards against Depression', *Economic Journal*, September 1955, pp. 425-426.

Wright cites many cases where in depressions prices of primary products fell sharply in the United Kingdom but rose in the distant ports of shipment. For example, from 1900 to 1904, wool prices fell in London 8 per cent., while prices in Argentine gold pesos rose 12 per cent.[1]

Professor Ellsworth, using more aggregative methods, reaches the conclusion that for the period from 1876 to 1905 a 'large proportion, and perhaps all, of the decline in the British prices of primary products can be attributed to the great decline in inward freight rates. Since the price of British manufactured exports fell in this period by 15 per cent., the terms of trade of primary countries, [if] f.o.b. prices [were] used for their exports as well as for their imports, may well have moved in their favor.'[2] Professor Kindleberger in his monumental study on the terms of trade of Europe has constructed a rough index of 'Current-Account Terms of Trade' (including services) which seems to confirm Ellsworth's findings.[3]

Third, the British terms of trade cannot without verification be taken as representative of the terms of trade of other industrial countries. Professor Kindleberger has computed indices for other European countries and has concluded that they do not support the generalization which is based on the United Kingdom terms of trade alone. In fact, he fails to detect 'much uniformity in the terms of trade between manufactures and primary products'.

We can say, then, that the proponents of the secular deterioration of the terms of trade for primary products have not been able to prove that such a change has actually taken place. It is true, however, that Professor Kindleberger thinks that he found some support for a somewhat different proposition. He states that the question of the terms of trade between developed and under-developed countries should not be identified with that between manufactures and primary products because developed countries also export primary products and relatively under-developed countries often export manufactures.

He believes that in intra-European trade the terms of trade have, on the whole, been favourable for the relatively highly developed (progressive is perhaps a better term) countries and unfavourable for France and Italy whom he regards as relatively less developed. 'Moreover, if the terms of trade of Industrial Europe with other

---

[1] Many other examples are cited in Wright, *op. cit.* p. 726.

[2] Paul T. Ellsworth, 'The Terms of Trade between Primary Producing and Industrial Countries', *Interamerican Economic Affairs*, vol. x, Summer 1956, pp. 55-56.

[3] C. P. Kindleberger, *The Terms of Trade, a European Case Study* (New York, 1956), ch. 11, 'Primary Products and Manufactures'.

areas are computed, and inverted, to get an impression of the terms of trade of the rest of the world with Industrial Europe, it . . . will be found that the under-developed world has fared' less well than, for example, the United States.

Special attention should be drawn to the fact that Professor Kindleberger's unit value index of machinery is computed by dividing values of machinery by their physical weight. Hence, if machines become more efficient but lighter in weight (a very common form of progress), even if the price per machine remains unchanged, the unit value will indicate a rise in price, while the efficiency price has fallen. Machinery, of course, plays a very important, in fact an increasingly important, rôle in the export of the industrial countries to under-developed areas.[1]

The support which these findings provide for the thesis under consideration is, however, very weak. For the underlying indices suffer from all the defects mentioned above. They do not allow for quality changes and allow insufficiently for new commodities, and the inversion of the European terms of trade is of questionable validity for the reasons given earlier. We may conclude that it has not been established that the terms of trade have deteriorated for under-developed countries over the stated period.

I now come to the second phase of the argument, the proposed explanations for the alleged tendency. Two main reasons are given : first, monopolistic manipulations in the industrial countries, and, second, the operation of Engel's Law.

On the first point, it is said that in the industrial countries the fruits of technological progress are not passed on to the consumer in the form of lower prices, but are retained by the producers in the form of higher wages.

It is true that for most periods and countries, monetary policy and wage policies have been such that economic progress has taken the form of rising money wages and stable or rising prices rather than the form of stable money incomes and falling prices. Many economists in the developed countries have felt (and a few still do feel) that from the point of view of cyclical stability and social justice stable wages and falling prices would be a better system than the one we have. But there is no evidence that it has hurt the producers of primary products (except perhaps if it really produced serious instability, which few economists would accept today). The victims are not the farmers and other primary producers who know very well how to protect their interests, but fixed-income receivers in the

---

[1] It is only fair to add that Professor Kindleberger is aware of the weakness of his machinery index ; but he is unable to do anything about it.

developed countries. In other words, the explanation under review confuses movements in the absolute price level with shifts in the relative prices of manufactures and primary products.

In the early nineteenth century, especially before the rise of economic liberalism and free trade, many attempts were made at preventing the export of machinery and technological know how in order to slow down the spread of industry and protect the monopoly of the old countries. However, these attempts were never very successful and even after the demise of the free trade era they were not revived except in isolated cases. There is much more competition between manufacturers and producers of capital goods now than there used to be one hundred years ago, because there are now many countries that supply capital goods, machinery, industrial know how, while there only was one, England, a hundred years ago.

On the second point, it is said that Engel's Law operates in such a way as to reduce secularly world demand for primary products. Engel's Law states that the percentage of expenditure on food is a decreasing function of income.

Now Engel's Law is well established as a description of household behaviour in homogeneous populations, but it is a long way from there to an explanation of an alleged trend in the ratio of world expenditures on primary products to expenditures on manufactures over extended periods.

Engel's Law applies to food but not to raw materials. Moreover, relative prices depend not only on demand but also on supply conditions which are likely to change profoundly over long periods. The importance of this last fact is dramatically revealed by the reflection that the hypothesis of the secular deterioration of the terms of trade for primary products, due to the operation of Engel's Law, is the exact opposite of another hypothesis which has been and still is very popular among an influential group of economists. I am thinking of the theory going back to Torrens, Ricardo, and Malthus to the effect that, owing to the law of diminishing returns in primary production, prices of primary products are bound to rise relatively to prices of manufactures. This pessimistic theory — pessimistic from the point of view of the industrial countries — has held a strange fascination for English economists from Ricardo and Malthus, via Marshall and Keynes (in his controversy with Beveridge in the *Economic Journal*, 1912) to Professor Austin Robinson.[1] This theory was also popular in Germany around the turn of the century among a group of economists who looked with apprehension at the

[1] E. A. G. Robinson, 'The Changing Structure of the British Economy', *Economic Journal*, September 1954.

rapid industrialization and urbanization which was then in progress in Germany. There were, of course, also other considerations in their minds such as the alleged military and social disadvantages of industrialization and urbanization, but the expected unfavourable tendency of the terms of trade for industrial products was one reason why economists such as Richard Pohle,[1] Adolf Wagner,[2] and others asked for increased protection of German agriculture against imports from overseas.

Needless to say, the dire predictions of that school have proved just as unfounded as the *ex post* interpretation of the opposite school of thought which we have been considering. Both schools are wrong, because there has been no clear-cut trend one way or the other, but rather irregular, or at best, cyclical fluctuations.[3]

The reason why those predictions went wrong and why it is impossible to forecast future movements of the terms of trade — this brings us to the third phase of the argument, extrapolation — is the complexity and unpredictability of long-run technological and population changes. Methods of production and transportation, world production and world trade, world population and standards of living have undergone tremendous changes since 1870 and are still changing before our eyes. Nobody could foresee these changes then or gauge their impact on various countries or on the terms of trade, and nobody can perform such a miracle now. Surely Engel's Law and the Law of Diminishing Returns alone or in combination are totally inadequate to predict or interpret, or even to throw much light on, such structural upheavals.

In addition to references to Engel's Law one finds frequently direct appeal to the fact that the import coefficients of the industrial countries, particularly of the United States, have declined. By import coefficient is meant the ratio of national income or GNP to imports, the average propensity to consume or simply the percentage of national income spent on imports.

The fact seems to be fairly well established for recent decades.[4] German economists (especially Werner Sombart) generalized the meagre evidence they had and then elevated the generalization to the dignity of a historical law — the law of the falling importance of international trade.[5]

[1] Richard Pohle, *Deutschland am Scheidewege* (Jena, 1902).

[2] Adolf Wagner, *Agrar und Industriestaat* (Jena, 1902).

[3] Colin Clark has put forward the theory that there are long-run swings in the terms of trade and has freely extrapolated them into the future.

[4] It cannot have been true for earlier periods. The British import-income ratio rose steadily throughout the nineteenth century but seems to have declined somewhat since the 1880s. See Robinson, *op. cit.* p. 458.

[5] See, for example, Sombart, 'Das Gesetz der fallenden Export Quota', in *Die Deutsche Volkswirtschaft im 19. Jahrhundert*, 3rd ed. (Berlin, 1913), p. 371.

To the extent that the fall in import-income ratio is due to protectionist policies in the industrial countries or to any other factor
which shifts the industrial countries' offer curve inward, it tends to
make the terms of trade for the under-developed countries less
favourable. To the extent that it is due to protectionist policies in
the under-developed countries themselves, or any other factor which
tends to shift the under-developed countries' offer curve inward, it
tends to improve the terms of trade for the under-developed countries.
It would not be easy to answer the question which one of these
various forces have been most powerful and I do not know of any
attempt to answer it. In fact, I do not even know of any attempt at a
clear formulation of the issues involved. So long as that is not done, the
mere reference to the simple fact of the falling import-income ratio
does not contribute anything to the solution of the problem on hand.

I now come to the fourth phase of the argument, the welfare
implications of the alleged secular deterioration of the terms of
trade for under-developed countries. As we have seen in section I,
a deterioration of the commodity terms of trade even if it is not
wholly spurious (due to neglect of changes in transportation cost, of
quality changes, and of new products) does not imply a decrease in
economic welfare. When the United Kingdom's terms of trade
improved in the last quarter of the nineteenth century as a consequence of the opening up of new sources of supply of agricultural
products from the United States, Canada, and Argentina — that did
not mean that this was an unfavourable change for the producers in
those then under-developed areas, although they would have been
still better off if the British market could have absorbed the additional
supplies at unchanged prices. We can express this by saying that
the single factoral terms of trade of those areas improved although
their commodity terms of trade deteriorated.[1] The improvement in
the British and other European terms of trade hurt British and
European competitors of cheap imports, that is, British and
European agriculture, but not the under-developed countries whence
the cheap imports came.[2]

[1] In many cases not even the commodity terms of trade deteriorated, for when
we convert the British terms of trade into their partner's terms of trade, and make
proper allowance for changes in freight rates, it may turn out that the latter
improved too.
[2] Professor Kindleberger, it will be remembered, thinks he found some support
for the thesis that the commodity terms of trade of under-developed countries
have behaved unfavourably. He remarks that this would be even more true of the
double factoral terms of trade. His reason is that productivity in the developed
(progressive) countries rises faster than in the under-developed (less progressive)
countries. Hence a representative bale of the developed countries' exports contains, as time goes on, less and less labour (or factors of production in general) than
a representative bale of the under-developed countries' exports. [*Cont. on p. 287*

I now come to the fifth phase of the argument — the policy conclusions drawn from the alleged secular tendency of the terms of trade to deteriorate for the under-developed countries. Tacitly or explicitly it is usually concluded that those countries should protect themselves from, and anticipate, the threatening deterioration in their terms of trade by protectionist measures. It is interesting that the opposite school in the industrial countries often draws the same protectionist conclusion from their contrasting forecast of the future development of the terms of trade. This is, of course, not true of the old classical writers, but it is true of the German group of economists mentioned above, and this line of argument can also be found in Professor Robinson's paper.

We have, then, the intriguing situation that two schools recommend reduction in the trade between developed and under-developed countries starting from contradictory forecasts, but on the basis of a common theoretical proposition, namely, that it is better to anticipate an expected unfavourable development of the terms of trade than to wait until the deterioration actually occurs and induces a shift in production.

A few comments on this theoretical proposition seem to be in order. First, it would seem to be clear that what matters is an *expected* deterioration. The mere historical proposition that the terms of trade have deteriorated in a certain way does not prove anything, unless it can be proved that the economy for one reason or the other has failed to adapt itself fully to the changed conditions. If the latter is claimed, then it has to be shown in which way or for what reasons the adaptation has failed to occur. According to the answer given to that question the argument then becomes a species of one of the familiar *genera* : the infant industry argument for protection ; the unemployment (including disguised unemployment) argument ; or the lower productivity in agriculture than in industry argument.

Second, since future events are involved, the policy recommendations suffer from all the uncertainties to which forecasts are subject.

This may be so, but it should be remembered that what matters for the economic welfare of a country is the single factoral terms of trade, and not the double factoral terms of trade. (If a country receives more or better goods per unit of its exported labour, it is better off irrespective of whether these goods contain more or less foreign labour than before.) And the single factoral terms of trade are not a symmetrical concept in the sense that an improvement in the single factoral terms of trade of one partner implies a deterioration of the single factoral terms of trade for the other partner. They may improve for both trade partners at the same time. Concretely, in the 1880s the United States, Canada, and Argentina received more in terms of import goods per unit of labour contained in the wheat or meat which they exported, while at the same time the United Kingdom received more in terms of goods for a British labour unit contained in the machinery and railway equipment which they sent abroad.

Nobody really knows what changes in the terms of trade the future will bring. It is presumptuous and very incautious, in view of the poor record of economic forecasts, for economists to base policy recommendations on such uncertain foundations.

Third, even if we were sure that certain future changes are inevitable, as long as we are uncertain about the date, it surely would be better not to cross the bridge before it is reached. And if, as is likely, the change comes gradually, if it comes at all, the adaptation too can be gradual and can be left to the forces of the market.

Summing up, we may conclude that this case for protection rests on exceedingly weak foundations. It is therefore not surprising that members of both schools frequently try to strengthen their case with extraneous considerations. Thus the argument for protection based on the alleged historical tendency of the terms of trade to deteriorate for one or the other group of countries is frequently linked with the well-known static terms of trade argument for protection (optimum tariff theory). The latter is entirely independent of the former. The optimum tariff case depends on the elasticities of international demand and supply *at any moment of time* and in no way on the alleged historical development of the terms of trade over time.

In the German discussion mentioned above (of which one finds echoes in Professor Robinson's article), much is made of the argument that the inevitable industrialization of the now under-developed countries will rob the industrial countries both of the supply of raw materials and foodstuffs and of markets for their manufactures. And while it is comparatively easy to industrialize and to draw people from the country into the cities, the reverse process is infinitely more difficult. Even if the terms of trade become unfavourable for agriculture it will be difficult or impossible to get people from the factories in the cities back to the farms on the land.

Leaving aside considerations of military strategy and preparedness for war, the above reasoning overlooks two important and related facts. First, even if the whole world becomes industrialized in the sense that a larger and larger percentage of the working force is engaged in secondary and tertiary production, many countries will retain a comparative advantage in agriculture and hence remain exporters of agricultural products. The United States, Australia, Denmark, and Holland are conspicuous examples.

Secondly, advances in technology affecting agriculture have been so rapid that the surpluses of agricultural products available for export in the industrial countries with comparative advantage in agriculture have remained large. In other words, the terms of trade

288

have not turned permanently or catastrophically against industry. And the same technological advance — we may call it the industrial revolution of agriculture — makes it possible for industrial countries to step up agricultural output even at fairly short notice (*vide*, war experience), although, of course, at higher relative prices than those at which they can import those materials. It may be impossible to reverse the process of urbanization, but it is possible to industrialize agriculture. The greatly increased application on the farms of machinery, fertilizer, scientific know how, and other products of industry means that a larger and larger percentage of food and other agricultural products is virtually produced in cities, or at any rate in factories.

IV. Cyclical Instability of the Terms of Trade of Under-developed Countries

While there is no uniformity or common pattern in the long run movement of the terms of trade of under-developed or primary producing countries, the chances of finding such a pattern in the cyclical fluctuations of their terms of trade would seem to be better. But in this area too the degree of uniformity over time and space is by no means as great as is often assumed. A really comprehensive study is still lacking, although the cyclical and other short run instability of prices of primary products has received a great deal of attention.

It is a well-known feature of the business cycle that prices of agricultural products and primary commodities in general fluctuate more widely than prices of manufactured products and finished goods in general. From that it would seem to follow that the terms of trade of countries whose exports consists largely of primary products and whose imports consist largely of manufactures will tend to deteriorate during business cycle downswings and improve during business cycle upswings. One would expect to find the opposite pattern in the terms of trade of industrial export countries. Thus, while the industrial countries get some relief from their depression pains through an improvement in their terms of trade, the under-developed countries (and other net exporters of primary products) find their depression woes intensified by adverse changes in the terms of trade.

As far as industrial Europe, and especially the United Kingdom, is concerned, these expectations were subjected to some statistical testing by Professor Kindleberger. For the inter-war period he found much support in the facts, although even in this period there are a number of exceptions. For the period before 1914 he found, as others found before him, that the cyclical pattern of the British terms of trade was different. They improved as a rule in booms and deteriorated in depressions. The same was true in some instances of the terms of trade of France and Germany. The reason for the cyclical behaviour of the British terms of trade before 1914 was that coal, iron, and steel prices fell sharply in depressions. After 1914, these items no longer loomed so large in British exports and so the cyclical pattern changed.

But even in the short run of the business cycle, we must not assume, without proof, that the British terms of trade are always indicative of the direction of change, much less of the amplitude of movements in the terms of trade of exporters of primary products. It is true that quality changes and the appearance of new commodities can hardly make much difference in the short span of a cycle. (I am not discussing now the long Kondratieff waves.) But the cyclical pattern of other industrial countries is not always the same as the British. And cyclical changes in ocean freight rates have been often very pronounced. C. M. Wright, in an article already cited,[1] has shown that, especially before 1914, in almost all depressions, due to drastic falls in freight rates (especially in the direction towards the industrial centres), lower prices c.i.f. in Britain meant higher prices f.o.b. at distant ports of shipping.

The Wright effect was perhaps not so regular, pronounced, and pervasive as its discoverer thinks. He believes that it worked in every depression prior to 1931 when the pattern changed because of the disruption of triangular trade and convertibility. Professor Kindleberger did not find it always confirmed by his more comprehensive data. But there can be no doubt that on many occasions the impact of depressions in the industrial centres on the overseas primary producers has been greatly lessened by the cyclical play of transportation costs. This is confirmed also by Professor Kindleberger's finding that the inclusion of services in the terms of trade index (the substitution of what he calls the current account index for the merchandise index of the terms of trade) dampens the cyclical amplitude, even if it does not reverse the cyclical pattern of the terms of trade of the industrial countries.

The converse of Wright's theory, that the cyclical play of transportation costs reduces the improvements in the terms of trade of primary producers during business cycle upswings, has not been explored in detail so far as I know. But it stands to reason that, if

---

[1] 'Convertibility and Triangular Trade', *Economic Journal*, September 1955.

the impact of depressions is reduced, the relative improvement of prosperity is also lessened.

The purpose of these remarks is not to deny that there are cyclical fluctuations in the terms of trade of primary producers or to suggest that they are always negligible. It is rather that we should not exaggerate the magnitude of the problem and the degree of regularity of the cyclical pattern over time and space. Especially we should not allow the consequences of a unique catastrophe such as that of the Great Depression in the 1930s to dominate our thinking.

By and large the terms of trade of under-developed countries usually do deteriorate in depressions. With the same export volume and the same interest and capital balance (in real terms), the fall in the terms of trade obviously reduces the import capacity or foreign buying power of those countries. The cyclical fluctuations in the terms of trade add to the instability of export proceeds. It seems, however, that fluctuations in the physical volume of exports usually contribute more to the instability of export proceeds than do price changes. In other words, the percentage increases in cyclical upswings and decreases in downswings of export volumes of primary products are greater than those of prices (unit values).[1] In the post-World War II period of 1948–52 this pattern changed. In this period fluctuations in the value of the foreign trade of under-developed countries were primarily due to price changes and only to a much lesser extent to quantity changes.[2]

If the cyclical fluctuations in the terms of trade disappeared or became milder, volume changes remaining what they are, it would be better for the under-developed countries. Similarly, if the cyclical patterns were reversed, terms of trade improving during downswings when quantities decline and deteriorating during upswings when quantities rise, it would be nice, provided this cyclical pattern was of the right amplitude, and not so violent as to create again instability in the export proceeds.

But there is not much use in wishful thinking. Let us rather

---

[1] That at least is the conclusion of the United Nations' report, *Instability of Export Markets of Underdeveloped Countries* (New York, 1952), p. 3 and *passim*.

This report states that it makes very little difference whether export prices (unit values) of primary products are taken in United States dollars (United States import unit values which are computed on an f.o.b. basis at the point of exit from under-developed countries exclusive of subsequent transport charges) or in real terms (that is to say, deflated by a price index of U.K. manufactured exports). This is rather strange, because it means that the import prices of under-developed countries remain virtually unchanged during the cycle. The fact that the deflator does not make allowance for changes in transportation cost may provide part of the solution.

[2] United Nations, *Repercussions of Changes in Terms of Trade on the Economies of Countries in Process of Development*, U.N. E/2459, June 1953 (Mimeographed).

think in terms of concrete measures and policies, keeping well in mind that such measures and policies will never operate on the terms of trade alone, but also on other relevant magnitudes such as trade volumes.

I suppose it will be generally accepted that the task of eliminating or drastically mitigating world-wide cyclical swings falls squarely on the industrial centres, predominantly on the United States. Without engaging in undue wishful thinking, we may perhaps assume that very violent depressions, anything approaching the Great Depression of the 1930s, will in future be prevented by fiscal and monetary measures. This will automatically eliminate radical shifts in the terms of trade of the under-developed countries and at the same time stabilize export volumes.

The price which the industrial countries seem to have to pay for that comparative stability in output and employment is a slowly but steadily rising price level — creeping inflation in other words. I am not here going to speculate on how long the developed countries will be willing to accept that condition, what can be done about it, or what the final consequences will be. As far as the under-developed countries are concerned, it seems to me that mild inflation in the industrial centres serves them well so long as full employment and import demand are maintained. Since most under-developed countries, especially those in Latin America, have a strong propensity to inflate, their balance of payments position is somewhat eased if inflation, though in milder form, is going on in the industrial countries too. In addition, the burden of their external debt is lightened by steadily rising prices.

The driving force in the process of creeping inflation is the relentless pressure of monopolistic trade unions for higher wages which, in view of the generally accepted full employment postulate, necessitates continuous monetary expansion. The policy of driving up wages parallel with, and in excess of, the gradual rise in productivity, far from hurting the interests of the importers of industrial products (as the theories previously criticized assert), turns out to be in their interest.

It would be wishful thinking to assume that even mild depressions can be avoided. Depressions of the order of magnitude of the recessions which the American economy experienced in 1946–49 and 1953–54, and probably somewhat more severe slumps than those two will again occur. Also, inflationary booms like the one started by the Korean war together with their aftermaths cannot be excluded. Such occurrences will inevitably have their effects on the price ratios between primary products and manufactured commodities.

If it is impossible to eliminate this type of fluctuation at the source, can they be offset or counteracted by special measures? The special measures which at once come to mind are international commodity agreements and buffer stock schemes. When the fluctuations under consideration can be assumed to be produced primarily by inventory fluctuations, international commodity agreements and buffer stock arrangements can best be regarded as attempts by the authorities in charge of these schemes to offset those inventory fluctuations by means of counter-cyclical accumulation and depletion of government-held stocks.

Innumerable schemes of this sort have been proposed. Few, if any, cases of successful counter-cyclical buffer stock schemes are on record. I cannot hope to give a thorough discussion of the issues involved, much less to make any novel contributions to this much studied and reviewed area, but will confine myself to asserting somewhat dogmatically that national and international experience does not justify optimism that anything decisive can be done along these lines. *Ex post* it looks simple to institute counter-cyclical accumulation and decumulation of commodity stocks. But *ex ante* the difficulties of diagnosing and anticipating cyclical changes are formidable. The dissensions and conflicts of interests are enormous and the pressure by special interests to influence the action of the buffer stock authorities must be terrific. If the difficulties into which the American policy of parity price regulation of agricultural products has run offers any guidance, the obstacles to the satisfactory operation of a similar scheme on an international level must be well-nigh insurmountable.

Rather than try to promote administratively and politically if not economically unworkable commodity price stabilization and buffer schemes, the under-developed countries would be better advised to learn to live with a certain degree of cyclical instability in their terms of trade and balance of payments. It has been claimed that this instability makes for inflation in good years as well as in bad years [1] — in good years because the high export proceeds are all spent, in bad years because the deficit is offset by domestic credit expansion, the government taking up some of the non-exportable surpluses.

This surely is not an inescapable consequence, but the result of faulty financial policies.[2] There is no reason why the central bank

[1] See, for example, United Nations, *Instability in Export Markets of Under-developed Countries* (New York, 1952), p. 1.

[2] This is also the opinion of W. A. Lewis. See his celebrated volume *The Theory of Economic Growth* (London, 1955), p. 291. Similarly, Norman S. Buchanan and Howard S. Ellis, *Approaches to Economic Development* (New York, 1955), pp. 383-385.

should not accumulate foreign exchange in good years, sterilizing at least partly the proceeds, and then maintain imports for development and other purposes by dipping into the accumulated reserves. There are, in addition, the International Monetary Fund and other international or foreign national agencies from which credit may be obtained in depressions. Furthermore, if a country maintains a sound financial position it may be able to get private credits. This is what I mean by learning to live with a certain amount of cyclical instability in terms of trade and export proceeds.

Changes in the terms of trade and export prices are, of course, not the only factors making for instability in export proceeds and the capacity to import, and, as we have seen, often not the most important factor. Export quantities of under-developed countries have been frequently affected unfavourably in depressions by increased protectionism in the developed countries. Under-developed countries surely have a right to protest against such unneighbourly policies on the part of the developed countries. They should raise their voices in GATT and the United Nations in protest, but would be in a much better position to do so effectively if they themselves did not engage, as many of them unfortunately do, in hyperprotectionist policies, and did not claim a special right to such policies based on their being under-developed or in the process of development. Who is not developing nowadays, one might ask ? Saner, more liberal commercial policies would greatly contribute to minimizing cyclical instability of the terms of trade and its consequences.

Another aggravating factor which in many depressions has increased the pressure on the balance of payments of under-developed countries (and of debtor and capital importing countries in general) has been the interruption or even reversal, through credit withdrawals and capital flight, of the capital stream. This is highly disturbing and tends to affect unfavourably the terms of trade of the countries concerned.

This aggravation too is not an entirely inescapable, god-sent concomitant of every depression, but is at least partially preventable or curable. Prevention is usually better than cure. Sounder financial management, less inflation, larger international monetary reserves would go some way to counteract the incentive to withdraw capital and the reluctance to invest new capital, at least in mild depressions. I would argue that up to a certain point such a policy would not really cost anything because the loss involved by the holding of a larger liquid reserve (in the form of gold or short term dollar balances) would be offset by the elimination of the high social cost of continued inflation. Moreover, it surely would be worth some expense to make the financial structure capable of withstanding the high winds of financial crises even if we could not possibly make it fully resistant to the hurricane of a really severe depression. To attempt the latter would be tantamount to living permanently in a storm cellar.

V. SUMMARY AND CONCLUSIONS

International trade is vitally important for all under-developed countries — at least for all those that have a strong urge to push their economic development as quickly as possible. Hence the terms of trade as one of the factors determining the gains from trade in general and the capacity to import in particular are matters of legitimate concern.

It seems to me, however, that the concern with the terms of trade has been greatly overdone. Sinister secular tendencies which simply do not exist have been conjured up. Past developments have been given an unwarranted pessimistic interpretation. Reasons have been advanced for the alleged trend which are either fallacious or are entirely inadequate to explain what they are supposed to explain.

The same criticism applies to the opposite theory, popular among certain economists in developed countries, notably Britain, which states that because of the operation of the law of diminishing returns, the terms of trade must inexorably become unfavourable for the industrial countries.

Nobody can be quite sure about what the future will bring. If synthetic coffee were invented, it would be a catastrophe for the coffee exporters. If all under-developed countries could, in a few years, raise themselves to the level of the developed countries, the latter standing still in the meantime, the developed industrial countries would indeed find themselves in a very precarious position.

But these things are not likely to happen, and at any rate economists are not in the possession of any law which would enable them to predict a price trend for or against primary producers, or for or against under-developed countries, however we define that ambiguous term.

With regard to short-run, especially cyclical, variability, there would seem to exist some possibility of broad generalization. Prices of primary products fluctuate more violently over the course of the business cycle than prices of finished goods. Hence the terms of trade of under-developed countries tend to deteriorate in depressions and to improve in prosperity periods. One would expect the opposite cyclical pattern in the terms of trade of industrial countries.

But the degree of regularity and the magnitude of these cyclical fluctuations have been greatly exaggerated. Theorizing in this field has been unduly dominated by the experience of the catastrophic slump of the 1930s and other recent war-induced changes which are, after all, unique occurrences which we may hope will not continuously repeat themselves.

The amplitude of cyclical fluctuations of different primary products is very different (agricultural products versus minerals, petroleum versus mining products, foods versus fibres, etc.). Many developed countries have sizable exports of primary products, some being net exporters of primary products. Some under-developed countries have begun to export finished goods. For these reasons, the uniformity in the cyclical pattern of the terms of trade as between different developed and under-developed countries is limited with respect to amplitude and subject to exceptions with respect to direction.

Furthermore, the comparative stability or rigidity of finished goods prices is by no means an unmixed blessing for the industrial countries. The other side of the medal is great fluctuations in output and employment.

The excessive stress on terms of trade has deflected attention from more strategic points. It has led to preoccupation with symptoms or with factors which cannot be controlled or eliminated, or which can be controlled only at a heavy price in terms of lost opportunities for profitable trade, bureaucratic regimentation of the economy, and great administrative expense. Instead of learning to live with a certain amount of instability, making the economy flexible, and evolving methods to offset some of the consequences of the fluctuations in international demand and export proceeds, administratively and politically, if not economically, hopelessly unworkable schemes of price stabilization are being proposed and discussed.

The prevention of severe world-wide slumps is, of course, a task which falls squarely on the shoulders of the leading industrial countries, primarily on the shoulders of the dominant economy, the United States. In view of the fact that the prevention of severe depressions is also in the interest of the developed countries and that we undoubtedly know much better now how to control them, it seems to me not unreasonable that severe depressions will in fact be prevented in the future.

The milder ups and downs in business which are likely to persist, and the fluctuations in the terms of trade which they engender, should not be a major handicap and it should be possible for the under-developed countries, acting on their own and in co-operation with the developed industrial countries and international agencies, greatly to soften their impact. What is needed for that purpose is a strengthening of the financial structure of the under-developed countries and a counter-cyclical manipulation of gold and dollar reserves — less inflation, larger reserves, accumulation of reserves, and partial sterilization of export proceeds in boom times. This would enable these countries to maintain their imports in depression years by dipping into the accumulated reserves and would counteract the tendency to capital flight and withdrawal of foreign credits in depression years.

In the commercial policy field, attempts should be made to prevent protectionist reactions which in the past have so often intensified the contraction of trade in depressions. Co-operation in the existing international organizations, especially in the International Monetary Fund and GATT, will further the attainment of those objectives.

———

COMMENTS ON PROFESSOR HABERLER'S PAPER

BY

HELIO SCHLITTLER-SILVA
Brazil

I. Factoral, Commodity, and Income Terms of Trade

Professor Haberler is right in giving preference to factoral over commodity terms of trade when the effects of shifts in the terms of trade on economic welfare in under-developed countries are under consideration. Nevertheless, as Dr. H. W. Singer points out, we cannot say that the factoral terms of trade really supply a better measure of the distribution of the benefits from international trade.[1] Let us assume that the foreign demand for the exports of a country has unit elasticity so that the deterioration in the terms of trade is as great as the increase in productivity. In this case, the factoral terms of trade remain unchanged and the country is no worse off than before. The volume of trade of the exporting country is increased and this country's absolute gains from trade remain unchanged. But we cannot say that the distribution of the gains from trade remains unchanged. The share of the exporting country in the total gains from trade is diminished, and the share of other countries is increased. In this

---

[1] H. W. Singer, 'Terms of Trade — Barter versus Factoral — and Gains from Trade', in *Contribuições à análise do desenvolvimento econômico* (Rio de Janeiro, 1957), p. 306 ff.

case, the benefits of increased productivity in the exporting country are totally transferred to other countries.

In my opinion, it is only if we assume that a country faces an elastic demand for its exports that we can say that a deterioration in the commodity terms of trade does not mean that the country is worse off. If foreign demand is inelastic, the exporting country will be worse off after a deterioration in the terms of trade. In this case, the unfavourable shift in the commodity terms of trade will be greater than the increase in productivity so that the same input of productive factors engaged in producing for exports will command less imports in return. The factoral terms of trade will have deteriorated. As Professor Boulding points out, 'in a progressive society industries whose commodities suffer from an inelastic demand always tend to be relatively unprofitable, and technical progress in these industries if anything accentuates this unprofitability . . . The case of agriculture is an important example of this tendency . . . there is a persistent tendency for agriculture, and therefore for agricultural countries, to be worse off than industry and industrial countries.'[1]

With a given level of employment, an improvement in a country's commodity terms of trade which results from a change abroad is always favourable. Similarly, a deterioration which results from a change abroad is always unfavourable. On the other hand, the effect of a change in the terms of trade resulting from a shift in a country's own supply curve cannot be judged by the direction of change alone, even if full employment is continuously maintained. It is well known that, depending on the elasticities of foreign demand and supply, from a certain point onwards, further improvement in welfare resulting from a further rise in export prices in terms of import prices is offset by a fall in the volume of trade. For this reason a better indicator than the commodity terms of trade must be found for the welfare change associated with a given change in trade. Changes in the volume of trade have to be brought into the picture. This is done by the income terms of trade.

I entirely agree with Professor Haberler that the income terms of trade are a better indicator than the commodity terms of trade of the welfare changes brought about by trade changes. In Brazil and other Latin-American countries this concept has been increasingly used as an important instrument for analysis of foreign trade changes and their repercussions on economic development.

II. Statistical Evidence for Long-term Changes in the Terms of Trade

According to Professor Haberler it is highly improbable that the terms of trade for all, or the majority, of under-developed countries should have deteriorated over the period from 1870 to the 1940s. First, the economic structure and the composition of exports of the various under-developed

[1] Kenneth Boulding, *Economic Analysis* (New York, 1941), p. 778 ff.

countries is very dissimilar. It is unlikely that, in the long run, the terms of trade should move parallel for all under-developed countries. Second, the contention that the terms of trade of under-developed countries have been unfavourable over this period is based entirely on the annual index of the commodity terms of trade of the United Kingdom. This index does not allow for quality changes at all and very insufficiently for new products and does not take account of transport costs. Furthermore, this index cannot be taken as representative of the terms of trade of other industrial countries.

As Professor Haberler points out, the statistical data do not allow a precise evaluation of the long-run changes in the terms of trade. But are the inadequacies of the statistical data serious enough to lead us to doubt the tendency which they indicate ? I think we need a more thorough study of this problem.

Because of the differences in the composition of exports of the various under-developed countries, changes in their terms of trade will vary. But this does not mean that these changes may not all be in the same direction. Calculations made by the Department of Economic and Social Studies of the Pan American Union indicate, for example, that the terms of trade of Latin America and of the United States show the same downwards trend, both for minerals and for tropical products, over the period from 1870 to 1940.[1] It is true that the United Kingdom's commodity terms of trade are not representative of other industrial countries. Nevertheless, the Pan American Union shows that the alleged trend is not changed if we substitute the United States figures for United Kingdom figures.

I am not convinced by Professor Haberler's argument on this point.

III. Explanations of the Alleged Long-term Deterioration in the Terms of Trade of Under-developed Countries

Professor Haberler questions the two main explanations of the alleged long-run deterioration in the terms of trade of under-developed countries.

I agree with Professor Haberler that monopolistic elements are not effectively responsible for changes in the terms of trade against the under-developed countries. As Professor Kindleberger [2] indicates, the reason for the changes should be sought in the elasticities of demand and supply. If demand and supply in international trade are elastic, national price-wage policy can have no effect on the terms of trade. Only if foreign demand and supply are inelastic can differences in price-wage policies bring about a change in the terms of trade. It is, however, questionable whether monopoly elements are responsible for the changes.

[1] *Têrmos do trocas da América Latina: sua evolução e perspectivas*, IV Sessão Extraordinária do Conselho Interamericano Econômico e Social (Rio de Janeiro, 1954), p. 20 ff.
[2] C. P. Kindleberger, *The Terms of Trade: a European Case Study* (New York, 1956), p. 247.

As to the second explanation, it is true that Engel's Law applies only to food, and cannot explain the deterioration in the terms of trade of raw materials. But we must not forget that technical progress, the use of waste products, the substitution of synthetic for natural materials, and a host of other factors have brought about a long-term reduction in the proportion of raw materials to total production. In the United States, for example, the Paley Report states that, allowing for changes in the general price level, a dollar's worth of raw materials in 1900 supported $4.20 worth of finished goods and services but that in 1950 a dollar's worth of raw materials supported $7.80 worth of finished goods and services.[1] From 1900 to 1950 the total *per capita* consumption of raw materials rose by only 25 per cent. whereas real income increased by 150 per cent. and manufacturing output by almost 250 per cent.[2]

I think that both on the side of demand and of supply we can find some evidence in support of the alleged secular deterioration in the terms of trade of the under-developed countries in the period from 1870 to 1940. In the first half of the nineteenth century the rate of growth of population and industrial production was high in Europe, chiefly in England, so that demand for raw materials and foodstuffs increased at a rapid rate. Primary production, however, did not keep pace and the terms of trade seem to have moved steadily against the industrial countries. This was the age when Malthusian fears appeared and the law of diminishing returns was considered to be the most important of all economic principles.[3] However, since the 1880s we have seen a slowing down in the rate of growth of demand and an acceleration in the rate of growth of supply of primary products, especially of agricultural products. The main forces responsible for this development are : on the supply side, the opening up of new countries, improvements in transport, and an increasing productivity resulting from technical progress ; and, on the demand side, the decline in population growth in Europe and America and a slackening of growth of industrial production in the United Kingdom and the United States. In so far as the demand for primary products depends on the growth of industrial production in the industrial countries, it should increase at a declining rate.[4]

Even where population and industrial production have maintained their rates of growth, there are reasons to believe that the rate of growth of demand for primary products will decline : first, low income — elasticity for food as income increases (Engel's Law), and economies in the use of raw materials resulting from technical progress. T. W. Schultz points out that for agricultural production, 'these forces are secular, making themselves felt in the long pull, not only in the American economy but in other countries as well. They may be hidden temporarily by war

[1] United States, President's Materials Policy Commission, *Resources for Freedom* (Washington, 1952).
[2] Kindleberger, *op. cit.* p. 208 ff.
[3] W. A. Lewis, *Economic Survey, 1919–1939* (London, 1949), p. 181 ff.
[4] *Ibid.* p. 208 ff.

or by trade fluctuations. But they are forces that already had their head prior to World War I ; they moved on persistently during the interwar years ; and they have not been checked by what has happened during World War II'.[1]

IV. CONCLUSION

As a result of this disequilibrium, the terms of trade of the under-developed countries have deteriorated since the 1880s and the low levels they reached in the interwar period would appear to have been no more than a natural continuation of the process. The reasons why the under-developed countries could not avoid this eventuality can be found in the difficulties of adjusting their economies to the new conditions of world markets. Before they began industrialization they were not in a position to absorb the excess supply of labour developing in primary production, so that the supply of primary products went on increasing at a high rate despite the long run decline in the rate of growth of world demand.

The deterioration of the commodity terms of trade, even if it is not wholly spurious due to neglect of changes in transport costs, of quality changes and of new products, does not, however, necessarily imply a decrease in the economic welfare of under-developed countries. As we have seen above, this depends on the elasticity of foreign demand. If foreign demand is inelastic, as it is in the case of the exports of Latin-American countries, it is possible that a worsening of the terms of trade will bring a concomitant decrease in the economic welfare of the exporting country.

FURTHER COMMENTS ON PROFESSOR HABERLER'S PAPER

BY

HOWARD S. ELLIS

I. INTRODUCTION

PROFESSOR HABERLER has rendered a very useful service to the evolution of the theory of economic development in pointing to the many pitfalls besetting the generalization that primary producers come off badly in the international exchange of commodities because of the terms of trade. Barter terms can turn adversely even with an improvement in single factoral terms. And even the single factoral terms, while superior to other measures of the gain from a welfare angle, have to be supplemented by other information before final conclusions can be reached as to welfare. Historically, as Professor Haberler has so cogently argued, it is not at all clear that primary producers have fared badly on the score

[1] T. W. Schultz, *Agriculture in an Unstable Economy* (New York, 1945), p. 44.

of the terms of trade ; and still less, that they have failed to gain from international trade. Finally, the probable future behaviour of the terms of trade in any and all senses of the phrase is so unpredictable as to form a completely unreliable basis for policy. The upshot of all these considerations, on any sober and objective basis, is clearly that many other lines of activity and policy are vastly more important for raising *per capita* incomes than operations directed towards influencing the terms of trade. Professor Haberler's lucid analysis makes this conclusion difficult — if not impossible — to avoid.

Sceptics of this position, with which I myself strongly agree, may not, however, be altogether convinced on two points — one pertaining to the secular, and the other to the cyclical behaviour of the terms of trade.

II. Monopoly Practices and the Gains from Trade

With regard to the first, Professor Haberler does not devote much attention to the fact that the industrial exports of the more developed countries may be more widely characterized by administered (that is, monopoly or monopolistic) prices than the exports of primary producers. There are, of course, conspicuous exceptions, at least episodically, such as Bolivian tin, Brazilian coffee, South African diamonds, and the like. But the number of these cases seems to be limited and their duration often less than perpetual. In the case of outright monopoly limitation of supply, an adverse turn of the barter or commodity terms of trade would not be offset in welfare terms by other considerations. This fact, of course, would not be negated but only diminished in importance, if — as Professor Haberler believes — industrial exports have in the course of time become rather more than less competitive. On the other hand, primary producers may, despite the prevalence of administered prices for industrial imports, nevertheless derive substantial gains over the alternative of domestic production.

Professor Haberler's analysis of monopolistic manipulations in the industrial countries takes the form of a contrast between rising money wages and stable prices on the one hand and falling prices and stable money wages on the other. The first alternative is linked in his thinking with monopoly manipulations in industrial countries, and the victims are said to be 'not the farmers and other primary producers who know very well how to protect their interests, but fixed income receivers in the developed countries'. While I agree that fixed income receivers in the developed countries do suffer from monopolistic wage or production policies, this seems in no wise to preclude that foreign purchasers of industrial exports should not also suffer. This possible — and I think real — lessening of the gain from international trade does not rest upon a confusion of 'movements in the absolute price level with shifts in relative prices of manufactures and primary products'. Latin-American countries could avoid any real burden from the high *money* wages of the United

States so far as this is a merely general *monetary* phenomenon ; they could let the dollar depreciate, or they could 'keep up' by an equal degree of domestic inflation. But these devices would avail nothing against an unfavourable turn in their *real* terms of trade to the degree that they sell competitively priced raw materials and buy monopolistically priced manufactured goods.

This fact need not render trade unprofitable nor justify protectionist measures. But it does represent a reduction of gains, and it is a phenomenon which might legitimately be the object of policy by an international authority to regulate trade practices.

III. Measures for dealing with Cyclical Instability in the Terms of Trade

As for cyclical instability in the terms of trade, I quite agree with Professor Haberler that the chief remedy must be domestic stabilization policies in the industrial nations themselves. I agree furthermore that a fairly satisfactory degree of stability has prevailed in the past decade, and that the future does not look very unfavourable in this respect. Small fluctuations are probably a part of anything approaching a freely operating price system, and are worth the cost.

Still, I should be somewhat reluctant to end the chapter merely with the observation that 'under-developed countries would be better advised to learn to live with a certain degree of cyclical instability in their terms of trade'. Protectionist and multiple exchange motives, unwarranted faith in infant industry development, and in vested private and government interests provide, in my view, no sufficient justifications for autarkical trade policies. But in some degree they proceed from fluctuations in the price or quantity of demand for primary products. Granted that these fluctuations may recently have been less violent, it is still true that the 'burnt child fears the fire'. If a working mechanism of international commodity price stabilization existed, it would withdraw one of the chief grounds for autarkical trade policies. I share Professor Haberler's belief that past experiences with commodity stabilization schemes have not been successful. But I do not altogether share his conviction that they never can be made to work.

This is a domain upon which — in view of Professor Wallich's scholarly paper on 'Stabilization of the Proceeds from Raw Materials' — it would be foolhardy for me to venture. Professor Wallich does not take a completely sceptical position concerning national commodity stabilization schemes ; and he sets forth the theoretical conditions of demand and supply favourable to international efforts at stabilization, and the strength and weaknesses of various techniques. Analysis of this sort is useful, and a firm theoretical and practical case against commodity stabilization cannot yet be drawn.

DISCUSSION OF PROFESSOR HABERLER'S PAPER

PROFESSOR HABERLER'S paper was discussed intensively. Among the chief subjects were (1) the long-run trends in terms of trade, (2) the distribution of gains from technological progress, (3) the division of gains from trade, and (4) the impact of the cycle on the terms of trade.

I. THE LONG-RUN TREND OF TERMS OF TRADE

Professor Haberler had questioned the familiar assertion that the long-run terms of trade of under-developed countries had deteriorated over the period from 1870 to the 1940s. On this he was challenged by Professor Schlittler-Silva and Dr. Campos.

Professor Schlittler-Silva said that the statistical data, although inadequate factually and conceptually, nevertheless showed a trend sufficiently pronounced to support the general thesis. *Dr. Campos* likewise thought that the data did support the thesis. For further evidence he pointed to the adverse terms of trade for agricultural products in inter-regional trade, for instance within the United States. Here changes in transport costs made little difference, which Professor Haberler had mentioned as a factor that tended to confuse the picture. The United States example seemed to show a clear tendency of agricultural prices to decline against industrial products. *Professor Wallich*, however, suggested that in the United States productivity in agriculture had run ahead of industrial productivity. A relative decline in agricultural prices was therefore appropriate.

Dr. Campos further supported the thesis of the declining terms of trade by pointing to a practice of foreign companies exporting raw materials from under-developed countries. They tended, he said, to establish their profits in the home part of their operations, instead of in the under-developed countries. He added, however, that this tendency probably was of less significance today than in former years. Under-developed countries had learned to absorb part of the export proceeds by means of taxes. High taxes in the home countries of foreign corporations, moreover, often made it inadvisable to establish the bulk of profits abroad.

Professor Brahmananda said that while India's terms of trade during the first half of the nineteenth century might seem to support the thesis of the declining terms of trade, he questioned the basis of such reasoning. The growth of Indian poverty was mostly due to the steady drain of wealth from India in the form of unrequited exports. The trends in the terms of trade were a reflection of this fundamental cause. Nevertheless, he said, there was downward pressure on prices in under-developed countries because the high elasticity of the supply of labour prevented wages from rising as productivity increased.

Dr. Alter thought that Professor Haberler had tended to underrate the merits of the case for industrialization in connection with the terms of trade discussion. The case for industrialization, for one thing, rested upon a number of other considerations in addition to the terms of trade thesis. Rejection of the terms of trade thesis, therefore, did not invalidate the case for industrialization. Moreover, he did not think that a government should wait for actual deterioration to occur, before it acted to push internal development. Some degree of foresight was possible and should be applied.

Professor Haberler did not think that his case was substantially affected by these points. He also argued that, in so far as his opponents' case rested upon Professor Kindleberger's studies, it should be noted that Professor Kindleberger presented his own findings to some extent, as 'mere impressions' derived from the data.

Professor Hirschman noted that as under-developed countries industrialize, they tended to take up themselves the production of articles whose technology had been rather fully worked out. Thus, their imports were continuously shifted towards lines in which the productivity of the exporting country was advancing most rapidly. This evidently tended to improve the importing countries' terms of trade.

II. DISTRIBUTION OF GAINS FROM TECHNOLOGY

Professor Ellis referred to the theorem proposed some time ago by Dr. Prebisch, that the developed countries failed in some measure to pass on to under-developed countries the gains from their improving technology, because they took these gains in the form of rising wages at constant prices, instead of allowing prices to fall while wages rose. Professor Haberler, he observed, had rejected this view in his paper. He thought, however, that the theorem might have some validity to the extent that these wage and price movements might be concentrated in the export sectors of the developed countries. *Professor Haberler* replied that he had implicitly taken for granted that wage increases, even if they started in the export sector, would spread very rapidly through the rest of the economy. This was indeed the experience in the United States. *Professor Gudin* felt, however, that Prebisch's argument had merits. Taking the case of the United States for instance : higher wages would benefit the under-developed countries which are exporters to the United States, to the extent of the elasticity of the demand for these exports, but not those which are only importers of United States articles (*e.g.* Argentina). No doubt in the long run, if all dollar prices were lowered and foreign demand elastic, exchange rates would have to be readjusted. But let us not forget that the long run is composed of a succession of short runs, not favourable to the under-developed countries so far as the distribution of gains is concerned.

Professor Hirschman thought that the Prebisch argument could be valid in the special case indicated by Professor Arthur Lewis, of an almost infinite elasticity of the labour supply. In that case, productivity gains in the under-developed countries would tend to be siphoned off into the developed countries. *Professor Haberler* expressed his doubts regarding the realism of the unlimited labour supply doctrine. *Professor Hirschman* then reminded the audience that exactly the opposite of the Prebisch thesis had been widely argued in connection with the 'dollar shortage' episode. There it had been said that the more rapid growth of productivity in the United States caused prices in the United States to rise less or fall more than elsewhere. It seemed peculiar that the same alleged facts seemed to be made to support exactly contrary theories.

Dr. Adler argued that the failure of United States prices to fall, about which Dr. Prebisch implicitly complained, might actually be of benefit to the under-developed countries. It enabled them to avoid the increase in imports that very likely would result from a drop in United States exports and thus avoided balance of payments difficulties. *Professor Gudin* replied that balance of payments difficulties would not arise without inflation ; the point was one of terms of trade and not of balance of payments. *Professor Wallich* supported Professor Ellis' statement that the terms of trade depended on real prices rather than money prices and that changes in money prices or exchange rates did not ultimately affect them. Otherwise, he said, the Latin-American countries could increase their share in the gains from technology by simply inflating their price level or depreciating their exchange rates. But if the price movement resulting from gains in productivity led to a change in the structure of relative prices, or if the path to a new equilibrium involved the major changes in the structure of production in either group of countries, the terms of trade might of course be affected in one direction or another.

Professor Schlittler-Silva believed that an increase of productivity could actually make an under-developed exporting country worse off than before. If the terms of trade deteriorated in proportion to the gain in productivity, and if the demand for the country's exports was of an elasticity of less than unity, he said this must happen. *Professor Haberler* disagreed, saying that elasticity of demand would have to be absolutely zero before the exporting country could be made worse off under these circumstances. *Professor Hirschman* argued that an elasticity of less than unity could be shown to be sufficient to make the exporting country positively worse off, if the case were analysed in dynamic terms, by means of a cobweb model. *Dr. Kafka* replied, however, that in order to reach a static equilibrium, zero elasticity was nevertheless necessary to make the country worse off. *Professor Leibenstein* believed that Professor Schlittler-Silva's case could be substantiated, if an infinitely elastic supply curve was assumed — the Arthur Lewis case of unlimited supply of labour.

III. Division of Gains from Trade

Professor Gudin raised the question whether the double factoral terms of trade should not be employed in order to appraise the division of the gains from international trade. *Professor Haberler* argued that this would lead to very uncertain calculations, since it was difficult to compare quantities of labour. Moreover, it seemed less significant to him to discover who had gained more, so long as both sides had gained. The important thing was to establish the size of these gains, and for that purpose the single factoral terms of trade were appropriate.

IV. Cyclical Terms of Trade

Professor Ellis agreed with Professor Haberler in his analysis of the long-run trend of terms of trade, but thought that cyclical changes might be more important than Professor Haberler supposed. The exports of developed countries clearly contained a substantial element of monopolistic and administered pricing. This was bound to have an effect on the cyclical behaviour of the terms of trade. He shared Professor Haberler's view that the practical solution of this problem was the maintenance of stability by the developed countries. *Professor Gudin* questioned Professor Haberler's statement that during the cycle under-developed countries suffered more from a decline in the volume than in the price of exports. This did not, he said, reflect the experience of Brazil, which was one of relatively moderate volume changes and violent declines in price during successive depressions. *Professor Haberler* replied that for under-developed countries as a whole, the data provided by the United Nations seemed to confirm that quantity fluctuations were more important than price fluctuations. He was hesitant to use the depression of the early thirties as an example because it seemed a unique case.

Chapter 11

ECONOMIC PROSPECTS OF PRIMARY PRODUCTS

BY

THEODORE W. SCHULTZ[1]

The University of Chicago

I. INTRODUCTION

ECONOMISTS have long been at odds with one another on what the future holds for primary products. Disagreements run deep and the stakes are important as may be seen from the recommendations for economic development. One school of thought is firmly of the belief that the prospects for primary products are bleak and that the production of these products is likely to be poor business. This group sees the market ahead as unfavourable not only because the prices of these products usually fluctuate widely but also because, in their view, the demand for these products is of slow and uneven growth and their supply prices tend to fall relative to the prices of intermediate and finished goods. Moreover, the expansion of production of primary products is not conducive to economic development. It is, therefore, deemed to be unwise for a country to stake its economic future on this class of products. There are other economists, one can hardly call them a school, who believe that primary products are in a strong and strategic position because of widespread industrialization and because of the upsurge in population growth now under way. Industrialization requires vast additional quantities of raw materials and much more food is needed to feed the growing population and to provide improved diets as incomes rise. Accordingly, it is held that the rapid tempo of

[1] Fellow at the Center for Advanced Study in the Behavioral Sciences during 1956–57, where this paper was prepared. I am especially indebted to Marto Ballesteros for his criticism, for organizing the data appearing in the appendix, and for checking calculations used in the text.

In developing this paper I decided to concentrate on the United States because of the availability of data and of relevant studies, and on Latin America because of the setting in which we meet and the importance of primary products to these countries. The conclusions that emerge, however, appear to be applicable to other parts of the world as well.

economic development in prospect throughout the world will place natural resources once again in the position of limitational factors.

The division on this issue also seems to depend upon where we are, for in general those of us who are closest to countries or sectors that produce primary products foresee for them a bleak future, whereas those who are identified with countries that use them do not share this view. It could be that we are thus divided because we lack the virtue of being independent of our environments. However, an explanation based upon such a country or sector orientation would seem to be a weak reed.

How, then, are we to explain this marked difference in views about the economic prospects of primary products? This paper is an attempt to answer this question. It may be helpful to anticipate the steps we shall take in arriving at an answer. I begin by defining what I mean by primary products and by economic prospects. I then determine, as best I can, the demand and supply characteristics of these products based on the developments of recent decades. Next, I take up the more important implications of these characteristics when they are projected two decades or so. I then return to the question to show that the marked difference in views referred to above is based on a vast confusion in what is meant by economic prospects.

II. A WORD ON CONCEPTS

The term primary products has come to mean those commodities or materials which are entering the economy for the first time and which have undergone little or no processing.[1] We shall use the term to mean raw materials; namely, farm products, both food and non-food, fishery and wild life and forest products, minerals, both metallic and non-metallic, construction materials, and mineral fuels including coal, crude petroleum, natural gas, and natural gasoline. This is the concept of raw materials used in preparing the President's Materials Policy Commission Report of 1952.[2]

The other term, economic prospects, presents real difficulties. It is also the main source of the confusion that plagues us. To get at this confusion it will be necessary to consider three kinds of economic prospects: first, prospects for raw material prices relative to the

[1] Other than that required to obtain them in their original form and to prepare them for marketing.

[2] United States, President's Materials Policy Commission, *Resources for Freedom* (Washington, 1952), 5 volumes. This report is often referred to as the Paley Report. It should be noted that this report includes hydro-energy as a raw material.

prices of all commodities at wholesale ; [1] second, prospects of a country's benefiting from economic development as a producer of raw materials ; and, third, the prospects of a country which is dependent on the availability of raw materials from abroad. The first of these three problems falls naturally within the field of economics. The other two are less amenable to economic analysis. They, however, are the main sources of the disagreements which I mentioned at the beginning. It will be necessary to leave other matters aside although some of them are closely related to these particular prospects. [2]

III. Demand and Supply Characteristics of Primary Products

One cannot use these characteristics as a basis for classifying products. Instead, I have taken raw materials to represent primary products. My task now is to consider some of the economic attributes of these materials that are relevant to our purpose. I take the long view throughout. Thus, I am concerned with normal production, consumption, and price developments over two decades or so. I would like to abstract from the more obvious effects of short-term swings in trade and of war, but this may be wishful thinking. In my appeal to data, I am in the main bound to the United States and to the President's Materials Policy Commission Report of 1952.

1. *Consumption of Raw Materials in the United States*

A few key data on raw materials developments since about 1900 may be helpful in taking our bearings. The declining economic importance of raw materials relative to total input and output in

[1] If we were to classify all products entering wholesale markets as has been done in preparing the new Economic Sector Indexes of wholesale prices in the United States, we would have three classes : crude materials for further processing (12·5 per cent. of all commodities) ; intermediate materials, supplies, and components (42·7 per cent. of all commodities) ; and finished goods or goods to users, including some raw foods and fuels (44·8 per cent. of all commodities). See United States, Department of Labor, Bureau of Labor Statistics, *Economic Sector Indexes, January 1947–July 1955* (Washington, 1955).

As I proceed I shall be considering the movement or change in raw material prices at wholesale relative to the price of all commodities at wholesale. I shall not, however, find it possible to examine the demand and supply forces and thus to determine the drift of real commodity prices, other than those of raw materials in prospect. It will be convenient to look upon the price index representing all finished goods plus all intermediate supplies and components as unaffected by any real changes in their demand and supply, that is, to look upon any rise or fall in this index as an indication of a change in the value of money.

[2] I shall not consider short-run movements in raw materials prices. Nor do I wish to enter into the arguments about the terms of trade.

the United States economy is clear. The rate of increase of raw materials consumption has been much less than the rate of increase of gross national product and of real income and only a little larger than the growth of population. Thus, *per capita* consumption of raw materials rose only 17 per cent. from 1904–13 to 1944–50 although real income *per capita* more than doubled. Measured in 1935–39 prices, total consumption of raw materials in the United States rose from $9·9 billion to $18·6 billion during this period. It fell, however, from 22·6 to 12·5 per cent. of gross national product.[1] Agricultural materials have bulked large throughout, representing 68·7 per cent. of total raw material consumption in 1904–13 and 65·6 per cent. in 1944–50. In the same period agricultural materials declined from 15·5 to 8·2 per cent. of gross national product. Indeed, none of the major classes of raw materials increased as rapidly as gross national product although minerals and fuels came closest to keeping pace. By contrast, forest products not only fell in value but also dropped most sharply relative to gross national product.

2. *Explanation of the Relatively Low Rate of Increase in Raw Materials Consumption*

I shall compress the explanation of the relatively low rate of increase in raw materials consumption into two interacting variables. The rate of increase may have been retarded by a rising supply price, as a consequence of which the United States has been economizing on its use of these materials. Price increases may even have encouraged the discovery and use of important substitutes. On the other hand, the slow rate of increase may have its origin on the demand side. Raw materials, as parts of finished goods entering into consumption, may have low income elasticities. It is the latter that emerges as the principal explanation.

Let me first examine the drift in relative prices since 1929, a year for which the available price data are better than for earlier years. Both 1929 and 1955 were prosperous years with high employment. Between these two years the wholesale prices of two major groups of raw materials, farm products, and fuels (including power

[1] Measured in 1935–39 prices, production of raw materials in the United States in 1904–13 was a little larger than consumption, production amounting to $10·5 billion and consumption to $9·9 billion. The difference of $100 million represents net exports.

In 1944–50 production amounted to $18·5 billion and consumption to $18·6 billion. The difference of $100 million represents net imports. See Appendix, Table 4.

Figures for *per capita* consumption are from *Resources for Freedom*, vol. ii, Table IV.

and lighting materials), which together represent about 84 per cent. of all raw materials,[1] declined about 15 per cent. relative to the prices of all commodities at wholesale. (The cost-of-living index was also down about this much relative to all commodities at wholesale.) The price of metals, however, rose 14 per cent. and the price of lumber and wood products more than doubled.[2] Lumber and wood products were handicapped by a rising relative supply price and the use of these materials was reduced. As I have already observed, consumption of these materials fell more than that of any other class of raw materials relative to the gross national product.[3]

For the most part the drift in raw material prices before 1929 was similar to that from 1929 to 1955. Both 1902 and 1913 were also peak years in economic activity. Between these two years the wholesale prices of chemicals and allied products and of metals and metal products fell substantially relative to all commodities at wholesale. Prices of farm products were down a little relatively. On the other hand, the prices of hides and leather products and of building materials rose a little relatively. As is apparent from Table 6, changes in relative prices from 1913 to 1926 are very similar to those for the period between 1902 and 1913.[4] The cost-of-living index appears to have risen as much as all commodities at wholesale from 1902 to 1913. This index, however, rose more than the wholesale price index from 1913 to 1926.

The slow increase in consumption of primary products in the United States would appear to be explained mainly by the income elasticity of demand. Put in its simplest terms, the demand schedule has shifted to the right at a rate which has exceeded only a little the growth of population. A more than doubling of *per capita* real income has added only about one-sixth to the demand for primary products, indicating a very low income elasticity. I shall have more to say later about our knowledge of the demand situation. On the supply side, I infer that enough additional output has been forthcoming to satisfy the increases in demand at approximately the same, or even at a somewhat lower, relative prices, except in the case of forest products. The fact that virtually all the additional output has come so cheaply raises issues which we shall consider below.

---

[1] As of 1944–50, based on 1935–39 prices.

[2] See Appendix, Table 5.

[3] There has been much substitution among raw materials. For example, mineral products are sometimes used to replace forest products, various minerals are substitutes for various other minerals. In the case of fuels, petroleum, natural gas, and natural gasoline have replaced wood fuels and have also greatly retarded increases in the consumption of coal, as is shown in Table 4 in the Appendix to this paper.

[4] See Appendix, Table 6.

TABLE 1

Consumption of Raw Materials in the United States, 1904–13 and 1944–50

	1904–13 Value*	1904–13 Percentage of Gross National Product	1944–50 Value*	1944–50 Percentage of Gross National Product	Percentage Increase or Decrease Relative to Gross National Product 1904–13 = 100 Value*	Percentage Increase or Decrease Relative to Gross National Product 1904–13 = 100
Total raw materials except gold	9·9	22·6	18·6	12·5	+88	−45
Agricultural materials	6·8	15·5	12·2	8·2	+79	−47
Raw materials other than agricultural and gold †	3·1	7·1	6·4	4·3	+106	−39
Forest products	1·3	3·0	1·1	·7	−15	−77
Minerals (other than fuels and gold)	·5	1·1	1·5	1·0	+200	−9
Mineral fuels	1·2	2·7	3·5	2·4	+192	−11
Agricultural materials						
Food	5·53	12·60	9·90	6·64	+79	−47
Non-food	1·26	2·87	2·29	1·54	+82	−46
Forest products						
Sawlogs	·58	1·32	·48	·32	−17	−76
Pulpwood	·03	·07	·20	·13	+567	+86
Other	·70	1·59	·42	·28	−40	−82
Minerals						
Iron and ferro-alloys	·14	·32	·34	·23	+143	−28
Other metals except gold	·15	·34	·47	·32	+213	−6
Construction materials	·15	·34	·42	·28	+180	−18
Other non-metals	·06	·14	·28	·19	+367	+36
Mineral fuels						
Coal	·99	2·26	1·16	·78	+17	−65
Crude petroleum	·16	·36	2·02	1·36	+1163	+278
Natural gas	·02	·05	·24	·16	+1100	+220
Natural gasoline	·01‡	·02‡	·12	·08	+1100	+300
Fuel wood	·56	1·28	·25	·17	−55	−87

* All values are in terms of 1935–39 prices and in billions of dollars.
† Included in these two figures is fishery and wildlife products. This item is not listed in the sub-totals below. It was $135 million in 1903–14 and $282 million in 1944–1950.
‡ No figures for 1904–13. These are for 1914–23.

3. Consumption of Raw Materials in Latin America

Agricultural materials represent an even larger part of all raw materials produced in Latin America than in the United States. In 1950 agriculture contributed somewhat more than six times as much as mining to the gross product of Latin America.[1]

It is exceedingly difficult to estimate the consumption of these materials. However, it appears that about four-fifths of all agricultural materials produced in Latin America are foodstuffs.[2] Moreover, the production of food rose about 42 per cent. from 1935–39 to 1953–54, while net exports of agricultural food products declined by approximately one-half. Accordingly, the amount of food available for consumption rose 63 per cent. Meanwhile, population was up 45 per cent. Therefore, the *per capita* consumption of food increased about one-eighth. Estimates based on daily *per capita* caloric intake of food point to a slightly larger increase, rising from about 2,270 calories pre-war to 2,625 calories in 1953–54.[3]

At this stage of its industrialization, the rates of increase in the consumption of minerals in Latin America are, for the most part,

[1] The Economic Commission for Latin America has estimated the gross product at \$38·2 billion for 1950, of which \$9·9 billion came from agriculture and \$1·6 billion from mining ; United Nations, *Economic Survey of Latin America*, 1953, Table IX.

[2] In Latin America as a whole about 80 per cent. of all agricultural production is foodstuffs. The four areas or zones show the following percentages for foodstuffs :

	Mexico and Central America	Caribbean Area	Tropical Zone	Temperate Zone
1934–38	63	87	54	83
1953–54	64	88	66	86

Total production, net exports, and the amount of foodstuffs available for consumption in 1935–39 and in 1953 were as follows :

	Production of Foodstuffs	Net Export of Foodstuffs	Amount available for Consumption
	(In 1950 prices and in billions of dollars)		
1935–39	5800	1090	4710
1953	8230	570	7660

Source : United Nations, *The Selective Expansion of Agricultural Production in Latin America* (New York, 1957).

[3] If one takes the food consumption *per capita* as having risen 15 per cent. and assumes the income elasticity of the demand for food to have been 0·7, it follows that real income may have risen a bit over 20 per cent. *per capita*. To the extent that food prices rose relative to other relevant prices, the observed consumption of food was less than it would have been had food been available at the same relative prices as formerly. One would, accordingly, underestimate the rise in income to this extent.

large, but the amounts, except of petroleum, are still exceedingly small. From 1929 to 1950, during which period the population rose from about 103 to 155 million, or 50 per cent., the consumption of iron ore increased sixteen times, yet it was less than 2 per cent. of that used in the United States. Copper consumption rose eleven times, and that of lead, sulphur, and petroleum products from three to four times. Consumption of zinc, tin, and pyrites, however, increased somewhat less than did population.[1]

4. *Useful Knowledge about Demand*

In demand analysis we seek to determine the price elasticity and the income elasticity of the demand for particular products.[2] Both concepts are based on received theory. Both have proved useful in organizing data and in deriving dependable estimates. Among the best estimates are those of the demand for food [3] where time series and cross-section data reinforce one another. We know that in rich countries both these elasticities for food are far over on the low side. We also are confident that they are stable and that a decade from now they will have about the same values as they have at present.[4] Confidence in this knowledge about demand is based, one would suppose, on the fact that it works, strengthened by the way demand analysis is grounded in theory and by the observed stability of consumer tests.[5]

In explaining long-term shifts in a demand schedule where the relative price continues about the same,[6] we may leave its price elasticity aside and concentrate on the income elasticity and the growth in population. In the United States the income elasticity of farm products entering into food is as low as 0·25 or less. It is, of course, not so low in Latin America. Although good statistical

[1] From 1937 to 1955 the consumption of energy doubled. With 1937 = 100, the 1955 consumption of petroleum and derivatives was 425, coal only 106, and vegetable fuels 106. Hydro-electricity rose to 396. (Based on Table 74 of United Nations, *Economic Survey of Latin America 1955*. See, also, Appendix, Table 7.)
We cannot discuss the drift in the relative prices of these raw materials in Latin America because of a lack of meaningful price data.
[2] For a particular population under particular temporal circumstances.
[3] In the main for consumers of food at retail.
[4] There are minor qualifications. As a population becomes somewhat richer, these elasticities become a little more inelastic still. Also, should a change occur in the personal distribution of income, the elasticities will be altered somewhat. However, both the direction and magnitude of the effect of such a change may be estimated.
[5] I have compared the state of our knowledge of demand and supply elsewhere; T. W. Schultz, 'Reflections on Agricultural Production, Output and Supply', *Journal of Farm Economics*, August 1956.
[6] One would want to take periods that begin and end when the economy was fully employed or was at a peak in business activity.

estimates are not at hand, there are reasons for believing that the following income elasticities of the demand for food may characterize Latin America :

TABLE 2

INCOME ELASTICITIES OF DEMAND FOR FOOD IN LATIN AMERICA

Countries *	Population in 1950		Approximate Income Elasticities of Food
	Millions	Percentage of Total	
I. *The very poor:* Bolivia, Ecuador, Paraguay, Guatemala, Honduras, Nicaragua, El Salvador, Dominica Republic, and Haiti	20	13	1·0
II. *Not nearly so poor:* Brazil, Colombia, Costa Rica, Mexico, Panama, and Peru	99	64	0·7
III. *Comparatively well - to - do:* Argentina, Chile, Cuba, Uruguay, and Venezuela	36	23	0·5
Latin America	155	100	0·7

* The bases for this income classification of the respective countries and certain qualifications in using it are set forth in T. W. Schultz, *The Economic Test in Latin America*, Cornell University, New York State School of Industrial and Labor Relations, Bulletin No. 35 (Ithaca, 1956).

5. *Knowledge about Supply*

To get at the mainsprings of supply we seek to determine the production functions of the firms that produce the particular products. The production function is, also, a venerable concept, based on received theory of long standing. It has not been a useful concept, however, in organizing data and gaining from them dependable insights about supply. The difficulty runs deep. For a function to be useful it must either be fairly stable, or we must be able to predict how it will change. The stability of the demand functions, as noted above, is dependent upon what happens to tastes, while the stability of the supply function rests upon technology.[1] Fortunately for demand analysis, tastes remain fairly stable. Technology, on the

[1] It will be convenient to define technology to encompass all knowledge that is useful in production.

other hand, does not. Therefore, as I have pointed out elsewhere,[1] unless we can predict the changes in technology, estimates of production functions are comparatively useless in a logical positivistic sense.[2]

How, then, are we to explain long-term shifts in supply schedules when nearly all major classes of primary products are forthcoming at about the same relative supply price ? Not by an appeal to production functions. Nor will an analysis of conventional inputs provide an explanation, because increases in inputs account for only a small part of the increases in output in a developing economy.[3] In the United States only about one-fifth (17 per cent. according to the data below) of the increase in farm output, from 1910–14 to 1945–49, has come from additional inputs of the conventional types. Similar developments affecting farm production have been under way in Latin America as may be seen from studies of agricultural inputs and outputs in the Argentine, Mexico, and Brazil.

TABLE 3

INCREASES IN AGRICULTURAL INPUTS AND OUTPUTS
AND THEIR RELATIONSHIP

	Total Input	Total Output	Per Annum Input	Per Annum Output	Increased Output Accounted for by Additional Inputs per Annum
	Percentages				
United States 1910–14 to 1945–49	8	59	0·23	1·34	17
Argentina 1912–14 to 1945–49	12	53	0·62	1·65	38
Mexico 1925–29 to 1945–49	27	60	1·19	2·36	50
Brazil 1925–29 to 1945–49	28	56	1·24	2·25	55

Source : Based on studies made by Marto Ballesteros of Argentina and by Clarence A. Moore of Mexico and Brazil, and on information on the United States in T. W. Schultz, 'Reflections on Agricultural Production, Output and Supply'.

[1] T. W. Schultz, 'Reflections on Agricultural Production, Output and Supply'.
[2] Also, in the case of the household we have a concept which is additive when it comes to taking into account increases or decreases in the consuming population. The concept of the firm lacks this important property when it comes to measuring changes in the producing population, namely, increases or decreases in total inputs or in producing capacity.
[3] It is important to note, in addition, that the part accounted for by the additional inputs is by no means stable over time. See studies reviewed in T. W. Schultz, 'Reflections on Agricultural Production, Output and Supply'. See also John W. Kendrick, *Productivity Trends: Capital and Labor*, National Bureau of Economic Research, Occasional Paper, No. 53, 1956.

The input and output patterns of mining in the United States are similar to those of agriculture. If anything, even less of the increase in output can be explained by additional inputs of capital and labour.

For the United States economy as a whole the study of Abramovitz, covering the period from 1869–78 to 1944–53, shows that net national product rose at a rate of 3·5 per cent. *per annum* while total input of capital and labour rose 1·72 per cent. *per annum*, or at a rate about one-half the rate of increase of output.[1] By combining the estimates of Goldsmith of net national product and of wealth with the estimates of Abramovitz for labour in the period 1897–1903 to 1944–49, it can be shown that output rose at a rate of 3·32 per cent. *per annum* and input at a rate of 1·06 per cent. or about one-third the rate of output.[2] Kendrick breaks this period into two parts and reports a rate *per annum* for factor productivity (a net figure based on output minus input increases) of 1·1 per cent. for 1899–1919 and 2·2 per cent. for 1919–53.[3]

III. Implications for the Three Sets of Economic Prospects

1. *Prospects in Terms of Relative Prices*

Will the upsurge in population, plus the operation of Engel's Law as incomes rise, plus all manner of industrialization, succeed in driving raw material prices up the grade of diminishing returns as more capital and labour are applied against natural resources ? Or will the accumulation of capital, plus additions to our stock of useful knowledge and its dissemination, be able to provide for the growth of demand and even succeed in driving the prices of these products down the grade of decreasing cost ? If we restrict our economic horizon to two decades, it would seem plausible that the first question should be answered in the negative. The second question, also, should, in the main, be answered in the negative although a small decline in the relative prices of these products may be in prospect.

There are a number of considerations which support these conclusions. First, the demand for farm products, which represent about two-thirds of all raw materials consumed in the United States, is likely to increase only about 40 per cent. during the next two

---

[1] M. Abramovitz, *Resources and Output Trends in the United States since 1870*, National Bureau of Economic Research, Occasional Paper No. 52, 1956.

[2] R. W. Goldsmith, *A Study of Savings in the United States* (Princeton, 1956), vol. iii.

[3] Kendrick, *op. cit.* Table 3.

decades.[1] Because of the very low income elasticity of farm products, both food and non-food, well over three-fourths of this increase will come from the growth in population now in prospect.

Second, supply developments are likely to keep fully abreast of this increase in the demand for farm products. With the new knowledge already available or becoming available, an increase in farm output of 40 per cent. will be easily achieved with 8 to 10 per cent. more inputs. The combination of inputs will change considerably. The amount of labour will continue to decline and no appreciable change will be made to the amount of land devoted to farming.[2]

Third, the demand for minerals and for mineral fuels in the United States is likely to increase at somewhat more than twice the rate indicated for farm products. Increases in output in prospect do not point to higher relative prices for these two major classes of raw materials.[3]

Fourth, the demand for forest products consumed in the United States may increase about one-fifth during this period. It should not be difficult, meanwhile, to increase the output of forest products by this amount and even somewhat more than this amount during the next two decades. The prices of these products are now at a level which makes it profitable to undertake more productive methods and to draw some land that was formerly idle and also some unimproved farm land into the growing of trees.

Fifth, the demand for farm foods in Latin America will probably increase about 85 per cent. during the next two decades if one assumes that the population will increase by one-half, as it did from 1930 to 1950, and if one also assumes that *per capita* income will rise about 2 per cent. *per annum* and that the income elasticity of farm foods declines to about 0·5 as a consequence.

Sixth, the production of farm products in Latin America in general is likely to increase enough to satisfy this very much enlarged demand, provided public economic policies do not discriminate against agriculture, as they have in many of these countries in recent years, and provided programmes are developed which will make available to farmers knowledge relevant to agricultural production.

[1] T. W. Schultz, 'Agriculture and the Application of Knowledge', in *A Look to the Future,* a report of a conference held at the W. K. Kellogg Foundation, Battle Creek, Michigan, June 1956.

[2] See J. D. Black and J. T. Bonnen, *A Balanced United States Agriculture in 1965,* Special Report No. 65, National Planning Association (Washington, 1956).

[3] Based on *Resources for Freedom,* vol. i. This report indicates a 90 per cent. increase for all minerals and a 97 per cent. increase for all mineral fuels from 1950 to 1975. It should be noted that its estimate of population in 1975 would appear to be somewhat too low in view of the increases that have already occurred since 1950.

An increase in inputs of between 35 and 50 per cent. is likely to be sufficient to achieve the required increase in farm output with the knowledge which is now at hand and which can be made available to farmers throughout Latin America. The developments in agriculture in Mexico during recent years strongly support this view of the production possibilities in prospect.

Seventh, it does not appear that these prospects for raw materials would be altered substantially if one were to take into account not only the United States and Latin America, but also the rest of the free world. Western Europe and those less-developed non-communist countries, not considered here, represent a similar combination to the United States and Latin America.

2. *What Contributions can the Expansion of Production of Raw Materials make to the Economic Development of Countries that produce them?*

Why try to press beyond the price prospects which we have just considered? To achieve and to transform increases in production and output into higher *per capita* real income raises additional problems. Even if the prices of these products were not to decline, the production of primary products might be poor business for poor countries which wish to achieve economic development.

That the production of particular primary products can pay, and in the past has paid, handsome national dividends is easily demonstrated. Oil has greatly increased the income of Venezuela, both for consumption and for capital formation. Mexico has done exceedingly well from its cotton. Coffee and cocoa have also been good income producers for a number of countries. Nor are the raw material producing sectors within major countries always among the laggards. The farm people of Iowa, for example, have achieved a high standard of living at farming. So have the farmers of Denmark and many of the raw material producers of the State of São Paulo, Brazil. In view of these successes and many others, why is the production of raw materials looked upon so adversely by some economists, especially when a country is heavily dependent upon them? Raw materials are, as a rule, subject to conditions that limit substantially the contributions which they can make to the economic development of particular countries. However, I shall go to some pains to show that the limitations which characterize the production of raw materials have not been diagnosed correctly and that as a consequence wrong treatments have been and are being widely recommended and applied.

A rough sketch of the underlying issues will have to suffice.

First, the price risks are relatively large because most primary products are subject to wide and rapid price fluctuations. However, I leave these risks aside because they fall into the domain of Professor Wallich's paper.

Second, it is widely held that poor countries which produce mainly primary products are burdened with a large labour surplus. Many workers are presumed to have a zero marginal productivity, especially in agriculture which always bulks very large in these countries. The inference that is drawn is that agriculture in these countries is very inefficient in the use of resources, especially in the use of labour. Primary products are, therefore, deemed to be poor business.

An analysis of this supposition raises several questions. Are there really many agricultural workers with zero marginal productivity ? I know of no evidence which supports this view. Nor would it be plausible where workers are free to move about, and are not tied to their present jobs by legal, cultural, or other restraints.[1] Is the marginal productivity of workers in agriculture, as a rule, appreciably less than that of comparable workers in other sectors ? The answer is affirmative for countries that have achieved substantial and rapid economic development which has increased real income *per capita* and real wages. For countries that have achieved little or no economic development, and have been stationary for a long while, the answer appears to be negative. This is not to imply that the marginal value productivity of many workers in a poor country with a stationary economy is not exceedingly low. Poverty in such countries is widespread and not restricted to agriculture.

Is it impossible to increase factor productivity in agriculture and in other sectors that produce primary products ? Clearly, the answer is negative.[2] I conclude from these all too brief remarks that it has been a mistake to sell the expansion of production of primary products short in the belief that these sectors are always burdened with surplus labour, that they are necessarily inefficient in the use of a country's resources, and that they are in this respect poor business.

Third, one of the important keys to economic development is the accumulation of capital. It is held by some economists that agricultural producers save and invest less of their income than do

---

[1] See T. W. Schultz, *The Economic Test in Latin America*.

[2] An analysis of these possibilities which firmly supports the answer I have given appears in United Nations, *Measures for the Economic Development of Under-Developed Countries* (New York, 1951) and in A. T. Mosher, *Technical Co-operation in Latin-American Agriculture* (Chicago, 1957).

producers in other sectors. Is this plausible? All that can be said here is that I am not convinced that this is necessarily the case.

Fourth, the underlying limitations are of a different order than those described above. They arise out of the rôle of knowledge in production and the adjustments in production that are required as economic development proceeds. Much, and even most, of the increases in output cannot be explained by additional inputs of the conventional types. Additions to the stock of useful knowledge and its application are an important part of the explanation.[1] It is hard to get this knowledge to farmers who are, as a rule, poorly educated, widely scattered, often isolated, and operating small farms.[2]

Also, agriculture is not a good training school for jobs in other sectors. In this respect it ranks far below industry. Mining and the exploitation of oil also are not particularly effective in transmitting new knowledge to other sectors or in training many workers in skills which serve them well when they enter upon other kinds of work. The techniques of production in mining and oil tend to be specific and do not lend themselves to useful application in other sectors.

The limitation imposed by adjustments of production is more complex. In highly developed countries agriculture and coal mining usually become depressed industries. One way of explaining why they become sick is to say that they are not able to adjust the input mix in production fast enough to stay at or near equilibrium. When the amount of new knowledge becoming available is large and when real wages are rising rapidly, agriculture is especially hard put to make the necessary adjustments in production at a rate that will keep returns to its labour on a par with returns to comparable labour in other occupations.[3]

In a large diversified economy like that of the United States, there are many attractive job opportunities for the labour wanting to leave agriculture or coal mining, although the worker must change his occupation and as a rule also move to a new community. What

---

[1] This other factor may be represented by investment in people which adds to their productivity when we treat them in analysis as agents of production ; T. W. Schultz, 'The Role of Government in Promoting Economic Growth', in L. D. White, ed., *The State of the Social Sciences* (Chicago, 1956). See also T. W. Schultz, *The Economic Test in Latin America*.

[2] However, as one poor country after another is demonstrating, it can be accomplished by organizing a far-flung agricultural extension service. See A. T. Mosher, *Technical Co-operation in Latin-American Agriculture*.

[3] Although the labour force in United States agriculture has declined rapidly since 1940, from about 11 millions to 8 millions, it is still far too large by equilibrium standards. The notion that the difficulty arises out of having too much land committed to farming and the so-called Soil Bank approach rest on a mistaken diagnosis. The maladjustment is basically to be found in the unsatisfactory allocation of the labour force and not of land. See T. W. Schultz, 'An Alternative Diagnosis of the Farm Problem', *Journal of Farm Economics*, December 1956.

happens in countries which do not have a diversified economy? Many poor countries are not only small and undiversified but they also seem to possess resources which are mainly suited to the production of primary products. What are the consequences if such countries achieve important technical advances by using new knowledge in agricultural production? I do not hold that this kind of development in agriculture will give rise to unemployment. There will continue to be work for them in agriculture and the marginal value productivity of farm workers will not become zero. Nor do I hold that such advances in agricultural production will not increase the total real income of a small poor country.[1] There comes, however, a stage in economic development when a ceiling on *per capita* income is reached which will be lower than would be the case if there were job opportunities elsewhere which would reduce the number of workers committed to farming. Had Iowa, for example, been a closed economy with no emigration of workers, the real income *per capita* of that state would probably not be as high as it is at present. In diversified countries like Brazil and Mexico some farm workers can and do migrate to the growing industrial centres. But what will happen when Ecuador, Paraguay, and Bolivia reach this stage in their agriculture? Are farm workers from these countries to migrate to neighbouring countries and there join the ranks of industrial workers? What will happen in Haiti, where the underlying circumstances make this problem even more acute? In the context of these particular questions, the limitations of agriculture can be very real indeed.

3. *Prospects of the Availability of Raw Materials to Countries dependent upon importing them*

I can do no more than raise this issue and acknowledge that it is a matter of vital concern to some countries. All too recent wartime experiences have made it clear that the availability of primary products can become a matter of national survival. The growing dependence of Western Europe and Great Britain on oil and the very unsettled political conditions in the Middle East have dramatically underscored the importance of the availability of a dependable supply of oil. Programmes for stock piling some strategic raw materials also serve to remind us how much may be at stake. The problem arises basically out of political uncertainty and, as such, there is not much that can be contributed by economic analysis.

---

[1] As output is increased, either home consumption can be increased and/or more can be exported without lowering the prices because, by assumption, such a country produces only a very small fraction of the relevant world supply.

V. CONCLUSION

The demand for raw materials is increasing rather slowly in the more highly developed countries, much less rapidly than gross national product or real income and only a little more rapidly than population. The rise in real income *per capita* gives rise to only a little additional demand for raw materials. The relevant income elasticity of demand is low. For farm foods in the United States it is 0·25 or less. In countries that are relatively poor, however, the demand for raw materials is increasing at a much faster rate than in the richer countries as gross national product and real incomes rise. The income elasticity of their demand is not nearly as low. Thus, in Latin America, it may be about 0·7 for farm foods. Moreover, the rate of population growth in Latin America is also much larger. These two facts point to fairly large increases in the demand for primary products in these countries over the next two decades or so.

There will probably be no difficulty in the supply of raw materials. Enough additional output to match the increase in demand is in prospect. In general, looking on ahead say two decades, diminishing returns are not now on the horizon, although more capital and perhaps also more labour will be applied against natural resources. Much of the additional output will come from the application of new knowledge in production. In terms of prices, then, raw materials are likely to continue to hold about the same position as they do now relative to other prices at wholesale. The rise in prices of forest products seems to have spent itself. The price indices of farm products, minerals, and even of fuels may well recede somewhat but probably will not fall enough to change substantially the price picture now before us. We cannot, therefore, give any comfort either to those who wish to see the prices of primary products rise or to those who see them headed down.

Even if the relative prices of raw materials move sidewise and not down, it does not follow that the economic prospects of the countries and of the sectors that produce these materials are necessarily bright. As a means of achieving economic development the production of primary products is beset by important limitations. If all increases in output had to be won by more inputs of the conventional kind, the limitations which we have identified and stressed would be less relevant. The production possibilities would in that case be of a wholly different order. It also would be very much harder than it is now to achieve marked increases in real income, and diminishing returns against land would be present everywhere. But we are spared such a dismal prospect because new knowledge is giving us additional output far in excess of the rise in conventional inputs of capital and labour. It is, however, most difficult to make new knowledge of agriculture available and to get it accepted, especially in poor countries. Moreover, agriculture represents much the larger part of the production of all primary products. Then, too, agriculture is not the best training school for developing in workers the skills they need for other occupations. Mining and the exploitation of oil also rate low because they usually are isolated islands in the economy. Other industries in the main rate better on this score.

Another limitation comes into play as primary producers apply the growing stock of knowledge relevant to their kind of production. The shape of the production possibilities changes in such a way that it becomes necessary to alter the input mix. In advanced Western countries this has meant that fewer and fewer workers have been required to work the land (and other natural resources) which it is economic to draw into production. In such countries the emergence of a diversified economy has made it possible for many workers to leave agriculture, and this emigration has altered the combination of factors favourably to the human effort committed to farming. We observe, however, that even under these favourable circumstances, agriculture has not managed to change its input mix fast enough to stay in equilibrium. Agriculture, like coal mining, has become a depressed sector as a consequence. Poor countries which do not enjoy a diversified economy and where the resources are primarily agricultural are much less favourably situated in adjusting their factor combinations in this respect.

Even so, poor countries can, as a rule, increase their net national product substantially by developing their agriculture, mining, and oil resources. It is a mistake to neglect or to hamper the expansion of output of primary products as has been done in many a less-developed country in the belief that these sectors are necessarily inefficient in the use of labour resources and, therefore, represent poor business for such countries.

Finally, from the point of view of many a country that is substantially dependent upon imported raw materials, the political uncertainty that beclouds the availability of these products is indeed a serious matter.

APPENDIX

TABLE 4

PRODUCTION AND CONSUMPTION OF RAW MATERIALS, AND GROSS
NATIONAL PRODUCT IN THE UNITED STATES, 1904–13 — 1944–50

I. *Production*

	Total Raw Materials		Total Raw Materials except Gold and Agricultural Foods	
	Value	Percentage of Gross National Product	Value	Percentage of Gross National Product
1904–13	10·5	23·9	4·8	10·9
1914–23	11·7	20·6	5·3	9·3
1924–33	13·0	17·6	5·7	7·7
1934–43	14·4	14·7	6·3	6·4
1944–50	18·5	12·4	8·2	5·5

TABLE 4 (*continued*)

PRODUCTION AND CONSUMPTION OF RAW MATERIALS, AND GROSS
NATIONAL PRODUCT IN THE UNITED STATES, 1904–13 — 1944–50

II. *Consumption*

	Total Raw Materials except Gold		Total Raw Materials except Gold and Agricultural Foods		Total Agricultural Materials	
	Value	Percentage of Gross National Product	Value	Percentage of Gross National Product	Value	Percentage of Gross National Product
1904–13	9·9	22·6	4·4	10·0	6·8	15·5
1914–23	11·3	19·9	5·1	9·0	7·6	13·4
1924–33	13·0	17·6	5·6	7·6	8·9	12·0
1934–43	14·7	15·0	6·6	6·7	9·9	10·1
1944–50	18·6	12·5	8·7	5·8	12·2	8·2

II. *Consumption* (continued)

	Fishery and Wildlife Products		Total Forest Products		Total Minerals except Gold		Total Energy, all Types	
	Value	Percentage of Gross National Product	Value	Percentage of Gross National Product	Value	Percentage of Gross National Product	Value	Percentage of Gross National Product
1904–13	·1	·3	1·3	3·0	1·7	3·9	1·7	3·9
1914–23	·2	·3	1·2	2·1	2·4	4·2	2·3	4·0
1924–33	·2	·3	1·0	1·4	2·9	3·9	2·7	3·6
1934–43	·2	·2	1·0	1·0	3·6	3·7	3·0	3·1
1944–50	·3	·2	1·1	0·7	5·0	3·4	4·1	2·8

	Agricultural Materials				Forest Products					
	Foods		Non-foods		Sawlogs		Pulpwood		Other Forest Products	
	Value	Percentage of Gross National Product	Value	Percentage of Gross National Product	Value	Percentage of Gross National Product	Value	Percentage of Gross National Product	Value	Percentage of Gross National Product
1904–13	5·53	12·60	1·26	2·87	·58	1·32	·03	·07	·70	1·59
1914–23	6·18	10·88	1·43	2·52	·48	0·85	·06	·11	·64	1·13
1924–33	7·33	9·91	1·52	2·05	·41	0·55	·09	·12	·54	0·73
1934–43	8·17	8·35	1·77	1·81	·39	0·40	·13	·13	·44	0·45
1944–50	9·90	6·64	2·29	1·54	·48	0·32	·20	·13	·42	0·28

TABLE 4 (*continued*)

PRODUCTION AND CONSUMPTION OF RAW MATERIALS, AND GROSS NATIONAL PRODUCT IN THE UNITED STATES, 1904–13 — 1944–50

II. *Consumption* (continued)

	MINERALS							
	Iron and Ferro-alloys		Other Metals except Gold		Construction Materials		Other Non-metals	
	Value	Percentage of Gross National Product	Value	Percentage of Gross National Product	Value	Percentage of Gross National Product	Value	Percentage of Gross National Product
1904–13	·14	·32	·15	·34	·15	·34	·06	·14
1914–23	·18	·32	·22	·39	·17	·30	·09	·16
1924–33	·17	·23	·25	·34	·26	·35	·11	·15
1934–43	·23	·23	·44	·45	·30	·31	·16	·16
1944–50	·34	·23	·47	·32	·42	·28	·28	·19

II. *Consumption* (continued)

	Total		Coal		Fluid Fuels					
					Crude Petroleum		Natural Gas		Natural Gasoline	
	Value	Percentage of Gross National Product	Value	Percentage of Gross National Product	Value	Percentage of Gross National Product	Value	Percentage of Gross National Product	Value	Percentage of Gross National Product
1904–13	1·17	2·67	0·99	2·26	0·16	0·36	·02	·05		
1914–23	1·70	2·99	1·20	2·11	0·44	0·77	·04	·07	·01	·02
1924–33	2·11	2·85	1·09	1·47	0·87	1·18	·08	·11	·07	·09
1934–43	2·48	2·53	1·01	1·03	1·26	1·29	·13	·13	·08	·08
1944–50	3·54	2·38	1·16	0·78	2·02	1·36	·24	·16	·12	·08

TABLE 4 (*continued*)

PRODUCTION AND CONSUMPTION OF RAW MATERIALS, AND GROSS
NATIONAL PRODUCT IN THE UNITED STATES, 1904–13 — 1944–50

II. *Consumption* (continued)

	Fuel Wood		Hydro-energy	
	Value	Percentage of Gross National Product	Value	Percentage of Gross National Product
1904–13	·56	1·28	·02	·05
1914–23	·50	·88	·06	·11
1924–33	·45	·61	·11	·15
1934–43	·35	·36	·16	·16
1944–50	·25	·17	·27	·18

Sources : Data on production and consumption of raw materials are taken from *Resources for Freedom*, vol. ii, Tables I and II, pp. 176-182. All values are in terms of 1935-39 prices and in billions of dollars.

Gross National Product figures are taken from Rex F. Daly, 'Some Considerations in Appraising the Long-run Prospects for Agriculture', in *Long-Range Economic Forecasting*, Studies in Income and Wealth, vol. xvi, pp. 180-181. Daly's figures are :

	Gross National Product in 1935–39 Dollars (Billions)
1904–13	43·9
1914–23	56·8
1924–33	74·0
1934–43	97·9
1944–51	149·0

TABLE 5

CHANGE IN WHOLESALE PRICES IN THE UNITED STATES
BETWEEN 1929 AND 1955

	Wholesale Price Index (1947–49 = 100)		Increase from 1929 to 1955	Change in Price Relative to all Commodities
	1929	1955		
All commodities	61·9	110·7	179	100
Farm products	58·6	89·7	153	85
Processed food	58·5	101·7	174	97
All commodities other than farm products and food	65·5	117·0	179	100
Rubber and products	83·5	143·8	172	96
Lumber and wood products	31·9	123·6	387	216
Hides, skins, and leather products	59·3	93·8	158	88
Fuel, power, and lighting materials	70·2	107·8	154	86
Metals and metal products	67·0	136·6	204	114
Furniture and other household durables	69·3	115·9	167	93
Non-metallic minerals (structural)	72·6	124·2	171	96
Tobacco manufactures and bottled beverages	86·6	121·6	140	78
Chemicals and allied products	64·0*	106·6	167	93
Cost of living, all items	73·3	114·5	156	87

* Not available for 1929. For 1933 it was 51·2. This figure was increased by 25 per cent.

Source : Indices for 1929 and 1955 from the *Economic Report of the President,* January 1956, Tables D-36 and D-38, pp. 204-205, 208.

TABLE 6

CHANGE IN WHOLESALE PRICE OF INDIVIDUAL ITEMS RELATIVE
TO THE CHANGE IN PRICE OF ALL COMMODITIES IN
THE UNITED STATES, SELECTED PERIODS

	1913–1902	1926–1913	1950–1926	1950–1902
All commodities	100	100	100	100
Farm products	103	98	106	107
Foods	101	109	103	114
Hides and leather products	113	103	119	138
Textile products	98	122	92	109
Fuel and lighting	100	114	83	94
Metals and metal products	84	77	108	70
Building materials	105	123	128	166
Chemicals and allied products	78	87	76	52
Home-furnishing goods	96	124	95	114
Miscellaneous	89	75	75	50
Cost of living, all items	100	125	84	105

Source : Indices of wholesale prices and cost of living from *Historical Statistics of the United States, 1789–1945* and *Continuation to 1952 of Historical Statistics of the United States.*

TABLE 7

APPARENT CONSUMPTION OF SELECTED MINERALS IN SOUTH AMERICA, 1929, 1950, AND 1954, AND IN THE UNITED STATES, 1950, AND CONSUMPTION OF ENERGY IN LATIN AMERICA, 1937 AND 1955

		South America				U.S.
	Unit (1000's)	1929	1950	Percentage Increase from 1929 to 1950	1954 *	1950
Iron ore	Metric tons	73·0	1,190·0	1,630	1,712·0	105,400
Manganese ore	M. T.	23·3	7·8	33	—	1,860
Tin metal	Long tons	3·1	4·0	131	4·7	115
Copper	M. T.	3·8	43·4	1,151	85·7	1,075
Lead	M. T.	21·5	57·8	269	67·3	911
Zinc	M. T.	15·8	19·0	120	49·7	894
Petroleum (crude)	Thousand Barrels	111·8	475·6	426	—	2,115
Petroleum (products)	Thousand Barrels	62·9	199·0	317	—	2,278
Potash	M. T.	6·7	0·8	12	—	1,289
Pyrites	M. T.	2·6†	3·6	141	—	1,158
Sulphur	M. T.	40·4	117·0	290	—	3,773

* All Latin America. † 1938.

	1937	1955	Percentage Increase from 1937 to 1955
Total energy *	43·5	90·0	208
Petroleum and derivatives	11·6	49·3	425
Mineral coal	6·2	6·6	106
Hydro-electricity	2·4	9·5	396
Vegetable fuels	23·3	24·6	106

* Millions of tons, petroleum equivalent of 10,700 Cal/Kg.

Sources : Data on mineral consumption in 1929 and 1950 from *Resources for Freedom*, vol. ii, pp. 186-204.

Data on mineral consumption in 1954 and on energy consumption from United Nations, *Economic Survey of Latin America, 1955*, chapters v and vi.

Economic Development for Latin America

COMMENTS ON PROFESSOR SCHULTZ'S PAPER

BY

JOSÉ A. GUERRA
Cuban Sugar Stabilization Institute

I. ON CONCEPTS

FROM a practical point of view there is no definition of primary products more useful and meaningful than the one given in this paper which equates primary products to raw materials. This concept ignores differences in the stage of production at which these products enter either domestic or international trade and may, therefore, not be considered rigorous because it does not provide for uniformity of the type of product which is considered to be primary. However, differences in the stage of processing are not important for the problems that both economists and policymakers have in mind when discussing the future of primary products.

As regards the concept of economic prospects, I also agree both with the method and the conclusions reached in this paper on the future of demand for primary products. Strictly speaking, while the comparison developed in the paper between the growth of demand for primary products and the growth of gross national product is adequate as a measure of the income elasticity of demand, conceptually this relation is not in itself sufficient to arrive at valid conclusions regarding the demand for particular products. Comparisons should also be made between the rate of growth of total demand, due to population increase as well as to income increase, for a particular product and the rate of growth of population of the main producing countries. In practice, however, we may ignore this second relationship because the rate of growth of the countries producing primary products is generally greater than the rate of population growth in consuming countries. It is, therefore, the income elasticity of demand that emerges as the really significant factor.

II. DEMAND PROSPECTS FOR PRIMARY PRODUCTS

In evaluating the economic prospects of primary products, an analysis of price or, more generally, income risks — since prices may be maintained by reducing supplies — involved in the production of primary products should have had a place in Professor Schultz's paper.

It may be considered that such a discussion falls more properly within the scope of Professor Wallich's paper. However, Professor Wallich's paper may take the existence of these risks as given. Nor should these risks be dismissed on the ground that they are seldom invoked as a reason for abandoning the production of primary products.

In the first place, such risks are invoked more often than is suspected.

332

As the production of primary products is usually associated with a considerable degree of international specialization, and the total income of many primary product producing countries depends largely on the income derived from such production, many primary producing countries are very conscious of the dependence of their economies on the production of products which are subject to severe and sudden price and volume fluctuations. In Cuba, for instance, the instability of the income from sugar is perhaps the most important argument advanced, not for abandoning its production, but for diversifying the economy so as to reduce the importance of sugar production and to achieve a greater stability of total income.

But irrespective of whether these risks are or are not invoked, the fact that these risks either exist or are thought to exist plays a most important part in the decisions of entrepreneurs and governments regarding the production of these products, and also in decisions regarding the development of other lines of production. In the case of Cuba, the instability of sugar income has been a strong deterrent to investment in other fields of production. Either consciously or unconsciously, potential investors in other lines of production are afraid that a severe and sudden drop in the income derived from sugar production may severely reduce internal demand for many agricultural and manufactured products, the production of which would be warranted if demand were assured of stability.

These countries therefore find themselves in a vicious circle. Their economies are weak and unstable because of their dependence on a primary product subject to wide and sudden fluctuations, and this instability deters the only investments that can reduce the instability of the economy.

III. SUPPLY PROSPECTS FOR PRIMARY PRODUCTS

Concerning Professor Schultz's analysis of the supply aspects, I also agree with the idea that, in general, the increase in the supply of primary products necessary to satisfy future demand can probably be achieved without particular difficulty and with the idea that the additional conventional input units will constitute only a fraction of the increase of production obtained. This being the case, no sustained upward trend in prices should be expected. I also share the view that, generally speaking, the demand for primary products will prove to have a steady rate of growth and that, therefore, prices in general will not show any marked downward trend. Thus I am in the happy position of not needing, either way, the comfort that Professor Schultz is in no position to offer.

IV. PROSPECTS FOR PRIMARY PRODUCING COUNTRIES

In this paper an important distinction is drawn between countries in a very under-developed condition and countries which are already achieving substantial economic development that increases real income *per capita.* I certainly agree that, for the first category of countries, the development of agricultural production offers opportunities for expansion and for the increase of their real income. One has only to reflect on the very low nutritional levels in those countries to realize how much agricultural production can expand and living standards can be raised.

On the other hand, for the second group of countries, whether agricultural production will further contribute to raising real income is, in my opinion, closely dependent on the possibilities of proper adjustment of the input mix, and also on export possibilities.

Limiting my comments for the present to the supply aspect of the question, I consider that, for this second group of countries, the really significant limitations on the supply side are : first, the limited value of the production of primary products as a training school for work in other sectors ; second, and much more important, the difficulties related to adjustments of production. This last limitation is a very real and important one and, in my opinion, a most valid reason, if not for abandoning the production of primary products, at least for undertaking serious efforts to develop other lines of production that can offer employment to the capital and labour not required for the production of primary products.

Here, again, the situation in Cuba confirms the point made in Professor Schultz's paper in a general way. Although I have not made any precise calculations of the magnitudes involved, the sugar industry in Cuba could make tremendous changes in its input mix that would greatly increase the productivity of labour and release a considerable number of workers to other undertakings. But as the country is not as yet developing at a rate sufficient to create more jobs in other lines of economic activity than can be filled by the natural annual addition to our labour force, the sugar industry is in practice prevented from carrying out such adjustments as it otherwise could make. Indeed, the rate of development may not even be sufficiently great to provide employment for the entire annual addition to the labour force.

Professor Schultz has not dealt with the difficulties due to the seasonal character of agricultural production. In the case of countries specializing in agricultural production, the wastage involved in maintaining a productive complex geared to an intensive use of capital and labour only during a very short period in the year, is a negative factor that should be taken into account and that could justify efforts to diversify the economy.

On the demand side, once a certain level of income has been reached there must be export markets for agricultural products if agricultural production is to make any real contribution to increased real income. The examples, mentioned in the paper — Denmark, New Zealand, Mexico, and Venezuela — all point to a large production for export. The same is true of Iowa if we drop the none too significant distinction between international and interregional trade. Could Iowa have attained anything approaching its present level of income if output had been sold only to its own population instead of being sold to the rest of the United States ?

V. Need for a Particularized Treatment of Primary Products

Almost all my comments on Professor Schultz's paper so far arise from the fact that significant differences sometimes exist between different individual primary product producing countries. My emphasis on these differences should not, in any way, be construed as a criticism of the general analysis and conclusions stated in the paper, as I fully and sincerely recognize that no other approach than a general one was possible. My aim here is only to emphasize the importance of a more particularized treatment of the products which are the subject-matter of the paper if we are eventually to reach conclusions upon which policy decisions of individual countries can be based.

Very often the production of primary products is associated with a high degree of international specialization. Therefore the discussion of the problems of primary products is usually within the framework of their rôle in international trade, and deals with demand and price trends *vis-à-vis* manufactured goods, the terms of trade resulting from such trends, and the international measures designed to smooth out price fluctuations and to improve or protect the terms of trade of primary products producing countries. Indeed, the discussion of the problem is so closely linked with international trade that one can almost say that the independent treatment of the problem of primary products arises in this context.

One very important factor that affects the position and prospects of the different primary products is the elasticity of domestically produced supply in consuming countries. If consuming countries can easily increase the production of a particular primary product, increases in demand may not have any effect on the prospects of the countries specialized in the production of that product. On the other hand, if the consuming countries cannot appreciably increase production of a particular primary product, then increases in demand have an entirely different effect on the prospects of the countries specialized in its production.

Thus, once we abandon the general analysis and come down to the analysis of particular products, the general evaluation of the trend of demand can be usefully supplemented by an evaluation of the trend of demand for particular primary products and of the supply possibilities in consuming and producing countries considered separately. The considerable increase in the consumption of sugar in the last twenty years has not led to a corresponding increase in the international trade in sugar or in the production of the countries specialized in its production. This is because, in a great many cases, the increase in consumption has been satisfied by parallel increases in the domestic production of the countries where the increases in demand have taken place. On the other hand, it is clear that the increase of demand for coffee in North America and in Europe has been fully reflected in an increase of demand for imports from the coffee producing countries. Therefore, in dealing with individual products, the assessment of the trend of demand and supply, in general, may not be enough to reach conclusions about the effect of demand increases on the production possibilities of countries specializing in such production.

In the field of agricultural production with which we are more familiar, there are some substantial differences between individual products with regard to the long trend of their demand and price in the international market.

The indices of the volume, price, and value of international trade constructed by the Food and Agriculture Organization, which cover the period from 1913 to 1955 and which are based on averages for 1920–38, show marked differences for different products.

Taking the index for the real value of international trade (value of international trade adjusted by a general price index), because it reflects the combined results of volume and price fluctuations, we find that real values of many individual products — corn, linseed and linseed oil, butter, and cotton — show a marked and uninterrupted downward trend. Other products — wheat, rice, hard grains, sugar, and jute — show a marked stability over this long period. And still other products — bananas, coffee, tea, cocoa, paper, wool, natural rubber, and forest products — show important gains over the period.

These differences reflect, in the first place, differences in demand in the international market. With respect to those products that show a downward trend and those that show a stable trend in the real value of their international trade, the trend reflects the influence of either volume or price developments, or both, according to individual products. Let us consider some of the products which fall into the first group. In the case of corn, the reduction in value reflects a tremendous reduction in the volume, more than enough to compensate a slight increase in price. Linseed and linseed oil have experienced appreciable reductions both in volume and in price. Cotton has experienced a reduction in volume, while its price has been steady. In the case of products included in the second group, both wheat and sugar show a moderate increase in volume and a moderate reduction in price. Hard grains and jute show both rather stable volume and price. On the other hand, all products included in the third group, that is, all products whose real value in international trade has increased, show an increase both in volume and price. This last group, no doubt, has a greater income elasticity than the two others.

What has been said shows that, although the differences are not too large, different long-term trends exist in demand for the products when they are considered individually.

But from the point of view of international trade, contrasts in the elasticity of supply in consuming versus producing countries are perhaps more important than differing trends of demand. The significance of these differences has been recognized by the Food and Agriculture Organization, which has constructed a table of the annual average real value of international trade in primary products, classifying these products according to the greater or lesser facility with which they can be produced in the industrialized consuming countries or can be replaced by synthetic substitutes. This table, based on a value index which takes the average of 1920–38 as 100, shows very clearly a stable or slight downward trend in the real value in international trade of products that can be easily produced in all the industrialized consuming centres, such as cereals, sugar, meat and dairy products, and linseed and linseed oil. The same is true of products that can be easily produced in some, but not all, consuming countries and can be easily replaced by synthetic alternative products. On the other hand, products that can be easily produced in some, but not all, consuming centres but cannot be replaced by substitutes, show an upward trend. Lastly, products that cannot be produced in consuming centres show an upward trend also, whether they can be replaced by synthetic substitutes or not. For this last group, the trend over the period from 1913 to 1955 rises more sharply than for any other group and comes very close to or exceeds the trend of manufactured goods. (Table 1, constructed by the Food and Agriculture Organization, shows these differing trends.)

The differences in the elasticity of supply for different products in different countries is especially important because, admittedly — and this is corroborated in Professor Schultz's paper — higher rates of increase in demand for primary products are to be expected in countries of low *per capita* income as they develop their economies and increase their real income. To the extent that economic development increases the production of primary products whose production is today highly specialized internationally, the international demand for primary products will not grow and may even be reduced. Since international specialization in the production of primary products is often associated with serious difficulties in the alternative use of resources and consequently with a low or even perverse elasticity of supply, this development may have important consequences for the trend of prices of primary products in international markets.

VI. Conclusion

In practice, there is no point in restricting increases in production in the countries that have specialized in the production of primary products for export. The production of primary products has, in many cases, important contributions to make to the increase in income of under-developed countries, as we believe Professor Schultz's paper clearly demonstrates. But differences in the productivity of different products in different countries should be taken into account in drawing up region-ally integrated programmes of economic development that would be beneficial to all countries concerned.

The foregoing comments may be open to the criticism that, by empha-sizing the international trade aspects of primary products, we are in fact

TABLE 8

ANNUAL AVERAGE OF THE REAL VALUE OF THE INTERNATIONAL TRADE OF CERTAIN AGRICULTURAL PRODUCTS, GROUPED IN ACCORDANCE WITH THE FACILITY WITH WHICH THEY CAN BE PRODUCED OR REPLACED WITH SUBSTITUTES IN THE MAIN INDUSTRIAL REGIONS *

(1920-38 = 100)

Period	All Agricultural Products	Agricultural Products easily Produced in Industrialized Countries †	Agricultural Products easily Produced in some, but not all, Main Industrialized Countries		Agricultural Products easily Produced in Main Industrialized Countries		Manufactured Goods
			(a) With Natural or Synthetic Substitutes ‡	(b) With no Substitutes §	(a) With Natural or Synthetic Substitutes ‖	(b) With no Substitutes ¶	
1913	92	94	—	84	85	85	93
1920	83	92	100	71	62	56	98
1921–22	81	90	89	74	59	62	82
1923–26	106	103	125	92	114	100	96
1927–30	117	116	117	114	117	124	115
1931–34	93	95	82	100	82	109	94
1935–38	98	94	83	114	117	97	105
1947–49	92	94	65	92	103	115	115
1950–51	119	92	101	111	209	175	147
1952–53	115	99	82	102	163	189	174
1954–55	117	92	81	118	158	225	196

* That is, North America, Western Europe, and Japan. † Cereals, sugar, dairy products, linseed, apples.
‡ Cotton, oil loaf. § Edible oilseeds, oranges, grapes, raisins, tobacco, wine.
‖ Natural rubber, wool, jute. ¶ Coffee, cocoa, tea, bananas, pepper.

Source: Food and Agriculture Organization, The State of Food and Agriculture, 1955 (Rome, 1956).

adding a new element to the concept stated in Professor Schultz's paper. I believe that by giving proper recognition to the fact that there does exist a wide and significant international specialization of production of primary products for export, I am not raising a new conceptual problem. The problems arising from this fact are a proper and most important aspect of the discussion of primary products.

From this point of view, the individualized approach may be important for assessing the contributions that primary products can make to the economic development of countries specializing in their production.

DISCUSSION OF PROFESSOR SCHULTZ'S PAPER

I. FUTURE MARKETS FOR PRIMARY PRODUCTS

Professor Schultz introduced his paper with a few general remarks. His analysis, he said, dealt partly with the demand side of primary products, and partly with the supply side. On the demand side, his approach was traditional. It was based upon present knowledge of income elasticities of demand, which rested on statistical estimates and was well founded. Demand elasticity studies had reached a high degree of proficiency ; the demand for primary products at various levels of income could be estimated with considerable accuracy. These studies of demand elasticities made it possible to estimate future shifts of demand for primary products in the United States. The data showed that the demand for primary products was advancing at a far slower pace than the growth of national income.

On the supply side, he said, his paper broke with traditional analysis. It gave little importance to scale of production and emphasized heavily the rôle of substitution. He had noted that many producers nowadays shifted to new inputs as soon as they encountered a cost squeeze in their old line. This had the same effect as substitution on the side of demand : it served to keep relative prices of all products in line with each other. The implication was, he said, that in the field of primary products we were producing what amounted to 'just one single commodity'.

In the subsequent discussion, Professor Schultz's analysis was subjected to some searching enquiry and its implications for development policies of under-developed countries were noted.

Demand for Primary Products

Dr. Campos suggested that the low income elasticity of demand for primary products which Professor Schultz had established for the United States might not apply in less-developed countries. In the United States, the service sector was expanding, in which products were little used, while the manufacturing sector, a heavy user, was contracting relatively. In under-developed countries, the manufacturing sector was expanding rapidly. *Professor Schultz* was willing to accept this although he objected to the 'service sector' concept. He mentioned that in his paper he had pointed to the very rapid increase in the use of certain metals in Latin-American countries. This, however, was a drop in the bucket that did not affect the world demand situation.

II. Diminishing Returns versus Advancing Technology

Professor Schultz's view that the effect of diminishing returns was likely to be offset by advancing technology, was likewise questioned. Some doubts were expressed also about his view that substitution among primary products would prevent relative prices of individual products from getting out of line. *Professor Brahmananda* said that the assumption of constant returns certainly did not fit the case of India. Indian development thinking was influenced considerably by the assumption of a tendency towards diminishing returns. *Professor Gudin* said that the improvement of agricultural techniques was not a simple matter for Brazil, because most of them had to be worked out locally. Agricultural techniques did not meet Brazilian soil and climatic conditions whereas the importation of industrial techniques was a relatively simple affair. He also called attention to the high-risk element inherent in crops of perennials with a long gestation period such as coffee, oranges, cocoa, etc.

Professor Schultz hesitated to accept the contentions of Professors Brahmananda and Gudin. He argued that there were great possibilities for improving agricultural techniques even at the level of the smallest farmer. Means had been found to bring such farmers in contact with advanced techniques, although these training methods were rather costly. Capital today could be made to substitute for land in many forms; this might help to solve the Indian problem.

III. The Short Run and the Long Run

Various speakers agreed that the relatively constant long-run supply price foreseen by Professor Schultz did not preclude short-run fluctuations. They accepted, however, Professor Schultz's contention that this problem could be dealt with by means of commodity stabilization schemes. The thesis of long-run stability was not affected by short-run fluctuations.

IV. Disguised Unemployment

Somewhat aside from his general subject *Professor Schultz* had observed that in his opinion there was no such thing as disguised unemployment. He was immediately challenged by *Professor Brahmananda* and others. *Professor Schultz* stood his ground with the following explanation : a case of real zero productivity does not exist, since the 'disguised un-employed' in fact do produce something. Disguised unemployment, therefore, could at most mean the existence of very low productivity side by side with high productivity. Where this productivity gap was a result of social factors, such as the presence of poor relations in Indian house-holds, the problem was not economic but social. In those cases, however, where the unproductive labourer was free to move to more productive employment, such a move was part of economic development. The productivity gap was thus revealed as one of the inevitable costs of pro-gress. To call it disguised unemployment was to misunderstand its real significance.

V. IMPLICATIONS FOR UNDER-DEVELOPED COUNTRIES

Dr. Campos, *Dr. Dominguez*, and also *Dr. Guerra*, whose paper was distributed to the group, all found that Professor Schultz's forecast of stability was cold comfort to the under-developed countries. For the industrialized countries it might be pleasant to know that they would not have to pay rising prices for most of the primary products that they were accustomed to import. Most under-developed countries, however, export only one or a few products. There was nothing to assure them that their particular products might not decline in price or that they might not become victims of adverse demand substitution if diminishing returns drove up the price.

Dr. Dominguez noted that the case of product substitution usually did not apply to under-developed countries. Their resources often were very specific, their habits ingrained. *Professor Wallich* observed that it would be a mistake to interpret Professor Schultz's findings as an argument against continued rapid industrialization. The stable price trend predicted did weaken the case of those who argued for industrialization on the grounds that the terms of trade for primary products were in a long-term downward trend. But the fact remained that the elasticity of demand for primary products was frighteningly low. Some countries would, of course, continue to enjoy a comparative advantage in primary products. But all primary producers would have to consider very seriously how far they wanted to depend on a line of production of which the share was shrinking so rapidly.

Professor Schultz would not deny these implications. Some reserva-tions seemed important to him, however. The widespread need for industrialization did not preclude that some countries were clearly marked out to be successful primary producers. The lure of industry should not blind policy-makers to the fact that quite disproportionate productivity gains could be made in many branches of primary production. The primary producing sectors of most countries still could make important contributions by raising their productivity, as American agriculture had done.

Chapter 12

STABILIZATION OF PROCEEDS FROM RAW MATERIAL EXPORTS [1]

BY

HENRY C. WALLICH
Yale University

IN going over the literature on the subject of the stabilization of the proceeds from raw material exports, I find myself following numerous distinguished predecessors. But though the area is well travelled, it still permits occasional discoveries, thanks to the continued shifting of the economic scene. Each age views commodity stabilization in the light of its own special problems. The problems of the 1950s differ, in many important respects, from those of preceding decades. Some merit may attach, therefore, to a periodic survey even when the surveyor must realize that he is not an explorer.

I. THE SETTING OF THE RAW MATERIALS PROBLEM [2]

Casting a glance backwards, we can discern at least three different stages through which the stabilization problem has moved. The first covers the happy days before the Great Depression, the next the Depression itself, and the third — leaving out the war — is the brave new world of post-World War II. Each period features problems, analyses, and proposals all its own.

Economists — be it said to their credit — have not vacillated in this field nearly as much as they have in others. Through boom and depression, through shortage and surplus, their theoretical writings for the most part emphasize the importance of the market mechanism, and of optimum allocation of resources. Commodity

[1] I am indebted for helpful comments to Hans W. Singer and Albert O. Hirschman.

[2] For a broad survey of the nature of the commodity problem, see League of Nations, *Report of the Committee for the Study of the Problem of Raw Materials* (Geneva, 1937) ; League of Nations, *Raw Material Problems and Policies* (Princeton, 1946) ; United Nations, *Instability in Export Markets of Under-Developed Countries*, 1952 ; United Nations, *Review of International Commodity Problems*, annually, 1948–54.

stabilization must not lead to uneconomic production. In other words, there must be no restriction of output, and stabilization measures must not interfere with the long-run price trend, whatever that may turn out to be.

Practical proposals and their rare implementation, however, have not always followed economists' precepts. During the 1920s the commodity stabilization problem seems to have been conceived mainly in terms of special maladjustments affecting isolated commodities. The problem of general surpluses began to be seen rather gradually. The techniques of stabilization were crude, leaning towards price-pegging rather than towards the fixing of a range. The purposes, as in the case of the most prominent stabilization scheme, the Stevenson Rubber Plan, often were one-sided and unashamedly exploitative. In that scheme the producers were out for what they would get, consumer interests were not consulted, and economic sense played no rôle. The Stevenson Plan is perhaps not representative of all the efforts of the period and certainly not of most of the suggestions made by economists. But it does capture some of the dominant features.

During the following depression, concern was not with maximization of profits on a few commodities, but with the elimination of surpluses over a broad range of products, and with the lifting of prices back to more normal levels. Somewhat more flexible technical arrangements were envisaged, as, for instance, under the London Sugar Agreement. Consumer participation came to be accepted.

Since World War II we have faced a new set of conditions. Because prices have been unstable rather than disastrously low, most concrete proposals have not ostensibly aimed at higher prices, but at the smoothing out of fluctuations. A large number of schemes have been proposed, but only a few agreements have actually come into being — those for wheat, sugar, tea, and tin. These have been distinguished by their flexibility. Consumer interests have been given a voice. On the whole, one may say that the new agreements look much more like an economist's conception of a good commodity agreement. Perhaps this is because the world economy, in some respects, has behaved more nearly as economists believe world economies should behave. In any case, any mild glow we may permit ourselves to feel is partly chilled when we remember how few and how relatively modest are the agreements that have actually materialized.

To make headway with our problem it will be helpful to look a little more closely at the contemporary setting of commodity problems.

The really new element today comes not from the commodities

themselves but from the countries producing them. Many of the producer countries have become dissatisfied with their rôle. Part of the great drive for development stems from their disappointments in the past and their scepticism about the future. They pin their hopes on industrialization and diversification, rather than on further raw materials specialization. These new development programmes require a steady flow of foreign exchange receipts to finance the necessary equipment imports. Instability turns programming, at best a guessing game, into a rank speculation.

In addition, the world has become highly terms of trade conscious. This concept, long familiar to economists, has moved out of the ivory tower into government offices and the press. This terms of trade consciousness has injected a certain new bitterness and sense of injury into commodity fluctuations. Feelings are intensified when the contracting parties are governments instead of private traders. It is whole nations instead of individuals who seem to be getting the better of one another.

Moreover, we live in a world where balances of payments are precarious. Flexibility of prices, wages, and other factors has diminished ; inflation undermines equilibrium, and adjustment has become increasingly more difficult. I do not want to be too pessimistic, because recent experience has shown that these disequilibria often yield to energetic monetary and fiscal policy. But it does seem that the instability of raw materials creates greater balance of payments problems today than in the past. This, incidentally, is true not only for the exporting countries but also for the importers. It makes the problem of commodity instability more important to both sides.

Finally, in this progressive world of ours the international capital market continues to languish. Hence it remains difficult to remedy by international loans the harm that temporary fluctuations in the terms of trade can do to an economy. This is a further reason for the increased concern with which commodity price movements are viewed nowadays.

II. Is Price Stabilization the Answer to the Instability of Export Proceeds ?

Instability of export proceeds is the joint result of fluctuations in prices and quantities. Prices can be stabilized, but the more obvious remedy for quantity fluctuations is some form of countercyclical lending or reserve accumulation. It seems hardly worth while, therefore, to spend much time on price stabilization, unless prices can be shown to represent the major part of the problem.

The impression that countercyclical lending holds out more promise than price stabilization will indeed obtrude itself with increasing force in the course of this paper. This impression will be derived, however, from premises other than the relative importance of price and quantity changes. A good argument can be made that price fluctuation is the principal villain and deserves primary attention.

This view of the relative rôle of prices and quantities is not uncontested. The United Nations Secretariat, in what constitutes the most recent full-dress review of the problem,[1] points to the possibility of a different conclusion. In the course of this comprehensive and scholarly study, it is pointed out that, on the surface at least, the price element is by far the smaller of the two. Its elimination, in fact, would dispose of only 17 per cent. of total fluctuations in proceeds. Elimination of quantity fluctuations, with price fluctuations remaining unchanged, would remove 39 per cent. of instability of proceeds. The United Nations study demonstrates, however, that such a negative view of the importance of price would have to be supported by an implicit assumption that is not altogether plausible. In the first place, it would have to be assumed that the present wide divergency between commodity trade and commodity absorption would continue despite price stabilization. This divergence is accounted for, of course, by inventory movements motivated in good part by price fluctuations. If prices were stabilized, the gap between trade and absorption would probably shrink, if not disappear. If past fluctuations in the export proceeds of a few major commodities are analysed on the basis of quantities absorbed, not quantities traded, price fluctuations are shown to have accounted for well over 50 per cent. of total instability.

Moreover, the belief in the primary importance of price fluctuations can be supported by still another argument. It is conceptually difficult to assume that quantity fluctuations are independent of price fluctuations, *i.e.* that after stabilization quantities would fluctuate just as they did before. Most practical forms of price stabilization imply some control of quantities. If, for instance, we are thinking of stabilizing a price movement resulting from a crop variation, we must in fact stabilize quantities in order to stabilize prices. This could be done, say, by an export quota plan, backed, as it ordinarily would be, by national buffer stocks. Price stabilization here leads directly to proceeds stabilization.

[1] United Nations, *Instability in Export Markets of Under-developed Countries* (New York, 1952), p. 57.

If the price change comes from a change in demand, on the other hand, price stabilization, though it will not fully stabilize proceeds, unless an international buffer pool takes up the slack, will limit the drop in proceeds to one proportionate to the drop in demand. Without price stabilization the cut in proceeds would be much larger, given the usual inelastic demand curve.

In summary, there is good reason to think that price stabilization would remove a substantial part of the instability of proceeds.

III. The Economic Rôle of Price Fluctuations [1]

To prove that price fluctuations are important does not imply that they are necessarily bad. Discussions of stabilization occasionally, and no doubt inadvertently, convey the impression that price fluctuations are bad *per se*. Of course they are not; they are the essential mechanism for the allocation of resources. Price movements are the signal to increase or reduce production of a commodity. The question is whether the signal is reliable, and how strong it has to be to produce a given effect.

Doubts as to the reliability of price signals arise when we remember the short-run speculative as well as the cyclical nature of many price movements. Presumably we do not want to see sugar mills dismantled, coffee trees uprooted or neglected, or copper mines abandoned in response to a price drop that fails to reflect the long-run trend of demand.

Doubts as to the effectiveness of a given signal originate precisely from the opposite and more realistic concern. Because price movements in the short run are often misleading, producers may be hesitant to react too quickly or too intensively, although the signal

---

[1] For some important analytical discussions, see J. W. F. Rowe, *Markets and Men: A Study of Artificial Control Schemes in Some Primary Industries* (Cambridge, 1936) ; B. Graham, *Storage and Stability* (New York, 1937) ; J. M. Keynes, 'The Policy of Government Storage of Food-stuffs and Raw Materials', *Economic Journal*, September 1938 ; L. St. C. Grondona, *National Reserves for Safety and Stabilization* (London, 1939) ; F. A. Hayek, 'A Commodity Reserve Currency', *Economic Journal*, June-September 1943 ; J. M. Keynes, 'The Objectives of International Price Stability', *ibid.* ; B. Graham, *World Commodities and World Currency* (New York, 1944) ; A. H. Hansen, 'World Institutions for Stability and Expansion', *Foreign Affairs*, January 1944 ; E. S. Mason, *Controlling World Trade* (New York, 1946) ; J. S. Davis, *International Commodity Agreements: Hope, Illusion or Menace?* (New York, 1947) ; M. K. Bennett, *International Commodity Stockpiling as an Economic Stabilizer* (Stanford, 1949) ; P. T. Bauer and F. W. Paish, 'The Reduction of Fluctuations in the Incomes of Primary Producers', *Economic Journal*, December 1952 ; with comments on the above in the same journal, June 1953, September 1953, and December 1954 ; D. G. Johnson, 'Stabilization of International Prices' in *Policies to Combat Depression*, Universities-National Bureau Committee for Economic Research (New York, 1954).

may later prove correct. For some products, this fact may mean extreme price movements for prolonged periods. A lesser signal might suffice, if the producers were given time to react to it. On the side of contraction, inelasticity of supply usually is even more pronounced. Hence the familiar spectacle of surpluses overhanging the market and depressing prices for many years. And, finally, there is the possibility of a cobweb situation — high prices cause over-production, which depresses prices and production, which leads to high prices and renewed over-production, which in turn leads . . . and so *ad infinitum*.

It is generally agreed that the signals given in raw material markets are frequently so misleading or extreme that it seems entirely legitimate to counteract them, even in a free market system. What is not compatible with a free market is a modification of the long-run trend of prices — the true signal that prices are designed to give.

The merits of stabilization, however, have been questioned from still another point of view. It has been argued that the fluctuations experienced by raw material producing countries may be beneficial rather than harmful to their economic development. The reason suggested is that more capital may be formed when incomes are high only periodically, with large profits going to export producers, than when they are more stable and more evenly distributed.[1]

How strong is this argument? There is considerable doubt about the implied analysis of the savings process itself. It may be that the establishment of a higher living standard, based on a temporarily high income, would cut into saving when income falls again and so lead to lower total saving over the cycle. But there are still other reasons for questioning the boom and depression pattern as a promoter of economic development in raw materials producing countries. One is that during the boom, when savings from export profits are at their peak, the country's resources are already fully employed, in the sense in which this can be said of under-developed countries. There are no idle resources then to be mobilized so as to employ the boom-time saving. As a corollary, the savings themselves are in effect invested in the foreign exchange reserves generated by the export surplus. The liquid resources which the exporters hold are just their counterpart, which can be used without inflationary consequences only by liquidating the foreign exchange holdings.

A second reason for questioning the boom and depression pattern is the fascination that it seems to exert on business men in the

[1] Sir Sydney Caine, 'Instability of Primary Product Prices — a Protest and a Proposal', *Economic Journal*, September 1954.

countries so afflicted. The big killings under such conditions are always to be made in the country's principal commodities, be they sugar, coffee, wool, or cotton. Other profit possibilities seem to pale into insignificance. This engenders a kind of raw material mentality that leans towards speculation rather than towards some more stable but less dramatic activity. It is not an attitude helpful to the development of new industry.

The same is to be said of the general sense of instability that permeates an economy dominated by raw material fluctuations. It moulds the economic climate, infuses uncertainty into all plans, and narrows the investment horizon. Economic development is the victim.

Attempts have been made to salvage the instability doctrine on the grounds that depressions themselves have often been a cause of development. Whereas moderate prosperity allows everybody to carry on in his accustomed way, sudden adversity becomes the mother of initiative. This, however, is a picture appropriate to the 1930s. Today, few countries have need of adversity to stimulate their developmental imagination. Stability — at a high level — seems to be what is most needed.

In the end, the success of the development drive will itself do much to overcome the problem of instability. Through diversification of raw materials output, the impact of fluctuations, whether mitigated by stabilization schemes or not, will be lessened. Through the reduction of raw material exports to a small fraction of the national income, the weight of their instability will be reduced. But many years may go by before this solution is attained. Meanwhile we have to continue to search for a solution to the commodity problems of the present and of the immediate future.

IV. Some Characteristics of Commodities and Commodity Fluctuations [1]

We have established so far that price fluctuations do play a major rôle in the instability of export proceeds. Also, we have

---

[1] For a discussion of the problems of specific commodities, see V. D. Wickizer, *The World Coffee Economy* (Stanford, 1943) ; K. E. Knorr, *World Rubber and Its Regulation* (Stanford, 1945) ; P. T. Bauer, *The Rubber Industry* (Cambridge, Massachusetts, 1948) ; J. W. F. Rowe, *Studies in the Artificial Control of Raw Material Supplies*, No. 1, *Sugar* (London, 1931) ; B. C. Swerling, 'The International Sugar Agreement of 1953', *American Economic Review*, December 1954 ; B. C. Swerling, *International Control of Sugar, 1918–41* (Stanford, 1949) ; V. D. Wickizer, *Tea Under International Regulation* (Stanford, 1944) ; W. Y. Elliot and others, *International Control in the Non-Ferrous Metals* (New York, 1937) ; K. E. Knorr, *Tin Under Control* (Stanford, 1945) ; Food Research Institute, Stanford University, *Wheat Studies*.

noted that these price fluctuations are often larger than necessary to perform their allocative function. The next step must be to take a closer look at individual commodities and the factors determining their fluctuations.

To 'know' a commodity is a lifetime job. Two years spent in dealing with hides, sugar, and wool have quite convinced me that in facing a true expert it is the part of wisdom to plead ignorance. It is subject to this qualification that I venture the following remarks.

Every commodity — and its frequently numerous grades and sub-types — faces demand and supply conditions different from those of any other commodity. It may be helpful to describe these conditions in terms of their elasticities and variability. By elasticity, I mean price elasticity in the usual sense. By variability, I mean factors that may cause shifts in the supply curves and demand curves.

As far as the elasticity of demand is concerned, one of the few safe generalizations is that the elasticity for almost all major commodities is on the low side. The instances, if any, where it reaches unity must be very few. For particular grades and sub-types of a commodity, the case is of course different because of high substitutability. Occasionally, the development of new substitutes may inject long-run elasticity into the demand for a major commodity.

There are a variety of reasons for the low price elasticity of primary products. Many such commodities are foodstuffs which commonly have a low price elasticity. In the case of many others, elasticity is low because the demand for these products is derived demand, *i.e.* their share in the final product is small. This is exemplified, for instance, by the share of copper in the price of a house. Finally, for a great many raw materials the original price paid to the grower is only a small part of what the consumer pays for the final product, after mark-ups for processing, transportation, and distribution. Such commodities can become genuinely surplus, in the sense that even a price of zero would not clear the market, because a price of zero to the producer may mean only a modest reduction in the price to the consumer.

It is harder to generalize about the elasticity of supply. The short-run inelasticity of the supply of most raw materials is familiar. This condition, imposed by the period that it takes to bring new capacity into production, may extend to five years or more, as in the case of coffee trees. Often an increase in capacity is not reversible or is only very slowly reversible. Elasticity in the face of a price drop becomes very small. Moreover, excess capacity or stocks can distort the normal elasticity substantially in the short run.

When we turn from elasticity to variability — shifts in demand

and supply curves — an asymmetry becomes apparent that may have been important in shaping our thinking on commodity agreements.

Fluctuations in supply have a compensatory element : a decline in the quantity supplied causes an increase in price, and vice versa. On the other hand, fluctuations in demand are cumulative with regard to proceeds : a reduction in the quantity demanded causes a drop in price. Of course these propositions are valid only for the world market as a whole. They do not apply to a single country unless it is a dominant supplier. Yet it seems that, in principle, demand fluctuations are a source of more serious, because cumulative, instability than supply fluctuations. This seems to lend support to the emphasis often given to demand fluctuations.

Whether in practice demand fluctuations do deserve such primary attention depends upon their relative frequency and violence as compared with supply fluctuations. This varies of course from one commodity to another.

A brief survey of the main products is interesting in this regard. First, there are those enjoying fairly stable demand conditions but subject to unstable supply conditions. This is typical of foodstuffs, such as sugar, coffee, and wheat, which are subject to varying crop yields. Stability on the demand side diminishes, however, if the product is subject to large-scale inventory speculation and particularly if it suffers from domestic competition in the importing countries, as is the case with sugar or wheat.

Next, there are commodities facing unstable demand and stable or at least adjustable supply conditions. This is typical of most industrial raw materials that are not produced as periodic crops, such as metals and minerals, and, within limits, rubber.

Third, there are commodities that are vulnerable to instability on both the supply and demand side. This is typical of industrial raw materials produced as periodic crops, such as cotton or jute. This group seems to get the worst of two worlds. But that does not necessarily mean that their price fluctuations are more extreme. Supply and demand changes may conceivably compensate each other, and much depends in any case on their strength.

V. Reaction of Price Trend to Stabilization

One important characteristic remains to be discussed ; the reaction of the supply and demand of different commodities to price stabilization. In general, there is reason to assume that the removal of extreme fluctuations will encourage output and consumption.

Instability and uncertainty are, after all, costs. The United Nations experts seem to incline toward this view.[1] But can we really be sure ?

We may assume that the kind of stabilization envisaged tries to keep the current price on or close to its long-term trend. An alteration of the trend is not regarded as desirable by most contemporary writers. The expectation that output will increase, with such stabilization, seems to be appropriate for all those commodities whose producers have a realistic appreciation of this trend or who tend to underestimate it. These producers will feel benefited when certainty increases while returns remain what they would have been, on average, without stabilization.

But what of commodities produced under over-optimistic expectations ? These would be commodities for which capacity expanded only in times of peak prices. This may be a matter of the temperament of the producers but more likely it is a function of the gestation period for new capacity. When it takes several years to raise capacity, prices may remain high for long periods without suffering pressure from new supplies. This may persuade even hardened sceptics that a new era has come, and that prices are on a new plateau. Output of such commodities will increase more slowly, if at all, once the price peaks that call forth spurts of expansion are lopped off.

It is hazardous to assign particular commodities to this last category for which output reacts negatively to stabilization. Conceivably, this category represents only an *ideal* type. But it is quite possible that products of absorbing interest to Latin America, such as coffee, perhaps sugar, quite likely cocoa, fall into this group. These commodities have gestation periods ranging up to seven years, their supply does not shrink even in response to very prolonged periods of low prices, and, historically, their supply has tended to expand after a period of high prices.

What are the economic consequences of stabilization for commodities belonging to the positively and to the negatively reacting categories ?

First, it is clear that for either type stabilization around a trend will make that trend different from what it would be in the absence of stabilization. Stabilization of the positively reacting commodities will make their supply greater and hence their average price lower than would otherwise have been the case.

For the negatively reacting commodities the opposite will be

[1] United Nations, *Commodity Trade and Economic Development* (New York, 1954), p. 13.

true. Their supply will be smaller, and their price higher than if stabilization had not occurred.

This suggests that stabilization of short-run fluctuations without changing the long-run trend is a concept of questionable meaning. If stabilization affects the trend, one cannot aim at leaving the trend unchanged ; one can only stabilize around the modified trend as it emerges from stabilization. It also means that stabilization, even theoretically, is more difficult than appears at first sight — and that is difficult enough. Good judgment as to the probable future price range of the unstabilized commodity is not sufficient. The stabilizers must also make a successful estimate of the impact of stabilization on the trend. If they base their efforts on the wrong trend, these efforts will collapse.

To see this more clearly, consider, for instance, a buffer pool that tries to iron out fluctuations without becoming unbalanced, *i.e.* without becoming overloaded and without losing all its stocks. If it is stabilizing a positively reacting commodity and gears its operation to some past average or base price or range without considering the effect of stabilization, it is likely to find itself in trouble. It will stabilize too high a price and will have to absorb too much of the commodity. The scheme will come to an end when the pool is loaded up with stocks and has exhausted its financial reserves. If the commodity is a negatively reacting one, stabilization on the basis of past fluctuations will result in a price too low to maintain an adequate supply. After a while, the pool will find itself holding all cash and no stocks and facing a world shortage of the commodity. To stabilize successfully, the price goals of the pool must be set low for positively reacting commodities and high for negatively reacting.

Some qualification of these suggestions may be necessary in the light of a possible reaction of demand. It is difficult to think of demand as being negatively affected by stabilization. But it could be favourably affected. Stable prices may attract users who otherwise might stay away. It is not very likely, however, that this effect should prove very powerful except in special cases where potential substitution is involved. The chances are that the demand-increasing effect of stabilization is smaller than the impact on supply.

Once all these effects on supply and demand are visualized, other implications become clear. Countries whose commodities are predominantly of the positively reacting type do not stand to gain from stabilization in terms of exports proceeds. On the contrary, their receipts are likely to suffer, assuming the usual inelastic demand. One might argue that such countries get what they are paying for.

They enjoy greater stability, and they pay an insurance premium against fluctuations.

Countries whose exports consist of negatively reacting commodities will have a more favourable experience. Their export proceeds will benefit from stabilization. Here one might argue that the gain signifies no more than the rectification of an old injustice. Previously such countries had been selling their commodities below their true supply price because supplies had been expanded on the basis of over-optimistic expectations that the actual price trend later failed to justify. Some of Latin America's leading commodities and the countries exporting them might become the beneficiaries of this feature of stabilization.

VI. TECHNIQUES [1]

The time has come to say something about stabilization techniques. The basic tools are familiar. It seems preferable to regard them simply as tools, and not as separate systems, because in practice two or more of them are apt to be used jointly. In this they may be said to resemble the policy tools of a central bank.

Buffer pools, quotas, and purchase contracts appear to be the basic generic types of stabilization tools. Their subvariants are endless — domestic and international, private and governmental versions of buffer pools ; quotas on production, exports, imports, or consumption ; purchase contracts for long or short periods, conditional or unconditional, for small or large parts of total output, with prices fixed or flexible, and so forth.

While there is nothing basically new in this field which seems to call for attention at this time, recent experience has thrown some light upon the respective merits and demerits of the various tools.

1. *Buffer Pools*

From a purely abstract point of view, buffer pools are probably the ideal stabilization device. They resemble the open market

[1] B. C. Swerling, 'Buffer Stocks and International Commodity Problems', *Economic Journal*, December 1953 ; W. W. Riefler, 'A Proposal for an International Buffer-Stock Agency', *Journal of Political Economy*, December 1946 ; R. S. Porter, 'Buffer Stocks and Economic Stability', *Oxford Economic Papers*, January 1950 ; Food and Agriculture Organization of the United Nations, *A Reconsideration of the Economics of the International Wheat Agreement* (Rome, 1952) ; H. Tyszynski 'Economics of the Wheat Agreement', *Economica*, February 1949 ; H. G. Johnson, 'De-Stabilizing Effect of International Commodity Agreements on the Prices of Primary Products', *Economic Journal*, September 1950.

operations of a central bank in that they do not interfere with the working of the market. They merely change the balance of supply and demand. In the abstract, a buffer pool could be operated without danger of running out of money or out of stocks — if men of good judgment, who could adjust their price policy flexibly in the light of events and who were independent of politics, could be found to administer it.

This ideal situation, however, conspicuously fails to prevail. In practice, therefore, buffer pools are probably the least promising of all devices. One important difficulty is the question 'Where is the money coming from ?' The producer countries are those most interested in stabilization but usually also those least able to afford it. The consumer countries often have the resources but lack an immediate vital interest. In fact they must fear that they would be putting prices up against themselves. The United States and Canada, being producers as well as consumers, do not fit into this pattern, but so far this has not necessitated any change in the conclusion that buffer pools are hard to finance.

Next, there is the difficulty of agreeing on policy — on the price range, volume of operations, and the like. Agreement might impose itself during the down phase under the imperative need to make stabilizing purchases. During the upswing, producers would scarcely welcome efforts to hold down prices. Buying is easy, selling is hard.

Then, in the absence of production and export quotas to protect the buffer pool, there is always the prospect that some countries might use it to create easy foreign exchange for themselves. Export subsidies and special exchange rates might provide the means to that end. Finally, the present division of the world into different currency areas would hamper the functioning of buffer pools.

2. Quotas

In the case of quotas of all kinds, the situation is the reverse. Quotas are bad theoretically because they imply misallocation of resources. They protect inefficient producers, freeze markets, and probably keep supply below the optimum. Quotas have the advantage, however, of being manageable. They avoid accumulation of stocks, require no financing, and do not call for continuous operating decisions. Some past base year, however arbitrary, can usually be made to serve as a standard to facilitate delicate decisions. In practice, quotas would probably have to be combined with buffer pools, in order to provide the necessary short-run flexibility of supply.

3. *Purchase Contracts*

Last, there is the long-term contract typified by the International Wheat Agreement. Such an agreement has the advantage of preserving the free market as an allocator of resources and an indicator of trends, provided not all supplies are covered by it. The technical problems of a purchase contract are quite manageable, although difficulties grow as the agreement is drawn tighter to make it more effective. The purchase contract has the grave disadvantage, however, of creating a two-price system. It requires domestic controls of some sort and buffer stocks to implement it, and it is quite apt to put the participating governments into the commodities business. In an extreme case, it may become nothing but a payment by the government of one country to that of another, without ever touching the producer or consumer. I shall argue below that this may be the best way of compensating for commodity fluctuations. There is no reason, however, to conduct such an operation under the guise and with all the paraphernalia of an elaborate commodity stabilization agreement.

Different commodities are likely to react differently to each of these devices and to various combinations of devices. Solutions are complicated by the existence of different commodity grades with corresponding price differentials, by seasonalities, by the currency problems both of producer and consumer countries, by differences of production costs and marketing power among producer countries and the ensuing difference in their respective willingness to participate in restrictive schemes, and a host of other factors. We have too little experience to be able to generalize with any confidence. This brief enumeration of problems seems appropriate, however. It should leave no doubt as to immense practical difficulties to be overcome. If any further evidence were needed it is supplied by the paucity of agreements that have come into existence and by the rather indifferent success of a good part of this small number.

VII. ALTERNATIVES FOR ACTION [1]

The discussion so far has been in good part an account of difficulties, problems, and obstacles. Does any of it point towards some

---

[1] For details of various international commodity agreements, see International Labour Office, *Intergovernmental Commodity Control Agreements* (Montreal, 1943) ; United Nations, *Review of International Commodity Problems, 1950–1955*, (1956); Food and Agriculture Organization of the United Nations, *A Reconsideration of the Economics of the International Wheat Agreement* (Rome, 1952).

particular form of action ? What are the prospects that such action may materialize ?

Action is possible on two planes — the national and the international. It is generally thought that, to be effective, action in the commodity field must be international. This is the explanation often given for the experience of countries that have tried to go it alone, like Brazil, or that have banded together in insufficiently comprehensive groups, like the sugar producers under the Chadbourne Plan. This explanation, however, is only partly correct. It applies where the goal is to improve the long-term trend of prices. It does not apply where the desire is only to eliminate the effects of short-run fluctuations. The benefits inherent in the elimination of short-run fluctuations, which underlie the United Nations' experts' recommendations, can be achieved by purely national action. An international agreement is not absolutely necessary.

The national stabilization that I am referring to has nothing to do with price support schemes of the familiar kind. In fact, it does not attempt to influence the price of commodities. All that a country has to do if it wants to neutralize the effect of price fluctuations is to adopt the technique of the West African Marketing Boards, or some refinement of it.[1]

By means of a flexible tax and subsidy, a country could insulate domestic producers against world market fluctuations. It would sell its commodities for whatever they would bring, paying or taxing its producers in accordance with the difference between the stabilized and the world market price. It would accumulate exchange reserves in good times and draw them down in bad times. The stabilized prices would have to be adjusted from time to time, of course, to keep them in line with evolving trends in the world market. A country following this policy would not stabilize the world price, but its domestic economy and its imports would behave as if the price had been stabilized.

The national approach has certain obvious difficulties, otherwise we should see it in action more frequently. It is lacking in the discipline that international action might provide. It runs into the fact that politically it is not easy to tax away producers' gains from rising prices, nor to sterilize the domestic and foreign exchange resources accruing from this tax. Furthermore, national action would allow different countries to make different assumptions as to future price trends. This might lead to a breakdown of some of the national plans, and also to changes in relative market shares. Shifts

[1] P. T. Bauer and F. W. Paish, 'The Reduction of Fluctuations in the Incomes of Primary Producers', *Economic Journal*, December 1952

in market shares might result also if some producer countries stabilized in this form while others did not, because of the impact of domestic stabilization upon supply.

These are potent objections to the national approach, and I am not suggesting seriously that it is to be widely recommended. The reason why I have emphasized it is rather because the widespread lack of interest in it points to an important conclusion. I shall set it forth briefly.

The national approach, despite its weaknesses, is, after all, a possibility, and one which could be seized by any country without waiting for international agreements which are known to be unlikely. Many countries are practising a rudimentary form of it when they support domestic farm prices, or when they try to conduct a counter-cyclical policy in their foreign exchange reserves. With few exceptions, however, these practices are very far from constituting a clearly conceived and firmly adhered-to system.

The conclusion to which this failure to embrace the national approach points is clear : producer countries are not willing, on the whole, to make major efforts or sacrifices for the sake of the kind of stability that the national approach can provide. This kind of stabilization, as I pointed out earlier, is one that does not seek to modify the terms of trade — it is *pure* stabilization. Pure stabilization evidently is not a goal to inspire great effort and enthusiasm. What underlies the widespread urge to do something for commodities must, therefore, be a desire, not for stable prices, but for higher prices.

This interpretation poses a dilemma for contemporary expert opinion. As I mentioned earlier, the present climate of non-partisan opinion, for which there is a good deal to be said, inclines to the belief that commodity agreements should not be allowed to alter long-run price trends. The unwillingness of policy-makers to make more effective use of the national approach seems to indicate that they do not fully share the views of the technicians.

In this final section of my paper, which deals with action, we must face these political realities. All technical difficulties aside, commodity agreements aiming at pure stabilization are not likely to be adopted because they do not offer enough to the producer countries. Commodity agreements promising better terms of trade may be worth the sacrifices, in terms of political discipline, that are required. The question is whether the consumer countries are prepared to co-operate.

At first sight it would not appear in their interest to do so, and that has been the predominant attitude up till now. However, the consumer countries, and particularly the United States, recognize that the economic development of other countries is in their own interest. Favourable terms of trade are an important resource for development. The consumer countries cannot, therefore, take it for granted that a commodity agreement that worsens their own terms of trade must necessarily be hostile to their long-range interests.

In addition, the consumer countries are interested in establishing reliable sources of supply of raw materials. This is a second reason why, prejudices apart, they should not necessarily look with disfavour upon commodity schemes that do not redound to their immediate price advantage.

An action programme in the field of raw materials stabilization should therefore take account of these two thoughts : first, to be successful, an agreement should hold out to the producer countries some prospect of better terms of trade, and second, the agreement should justify this feature by stressing the developmental aspect for the producer countries and the raw materials supply aspect for the consumer countries. To these principles I would add the proviso that our concept of what constitutes a commodity agreement should not be drawn too narrowly. Countercyclical lending geared in some way to fluctuations in raw materials proceeds would, by this test, fall under the general heading of commodity agreements.

A stabilization agreement between a group of producer and a group of consumer countries that shifts the terms of trade against the consumer countries is, in effect, a transfer of income from one group to the other. The real income of the consumers is reduced, that of the producers is increased. In the abstract, the governments of the consumer countries might as well impose a tax and pay the proceeds to the governments of the producer countries. The effect upon their respective real national incomes would be identical, except for tax friction and the like. But once we begin to think in terms of transfers of income, we are bound to notice that to effect the transfer by paying higher prices for commodities is not a very efficient way.

In the first place, to transfer or redistribute income internationally through higher commodity prices means to give most of the benefits to a particular producer group in the exporting countries. Whether the benefit goes only to the wealthy owner or trickles down to his labour is not the main issue here. In either case, the larger part of the population, which is only indirectly connected with the export industry, benefits only indirectly.

In the second place, the higher prices will tend to intensify the raw material character of the exporting economies. An outright shift of resources to the raw material sector may be impeded by the quantitative restrictions that will probably be required to implement the scheme. But the implications for economic development in general would perhaps not be wholesome.

In the third place, the income transfer reaches the recipient countries in the form of income, not of investible capital. Probably only a small fraction of the additional income will be saved and invested. The bulk will go into consumption. If the same amount were transferred as an investment grant, or even as a loan, it would do much more for economic development.

Finally, an income transfer via high raw material prices depends for its size not only on the price but also on the volume of exports. Quantity fluctuations make up an important part of total fluctuations in export proceeds. An income transfer by loan or grant could be tailored so as to compensate for proceeds fluctuations resulting from both price and quantity fluctuations.

Contrary considerations may no doubt present themselves. The raw material countries may specifically want to increase the income of their export industries, if these have been suffering. Usually these industries are the backbone of the economy, and often it is difficult to shift resources away from them as a part of a countercyclical policy. Alternatively, the raw material countries may siphon off the benefits through taxes or multiple exchange rates. The consumer countries on their side may want to strengthen their sources of supply and may therefore prefer the price stabilization technique to a generalized income transfer.

In the case of the United States, it is even conceivable that commodity agreements may some day be favoured as a means of giving foreign aid if political objections to overt aid continue to build up. Admittedly, the prospect seems remote, in view of the well-known attitude of the American Government toward commodity agreements.

The conclusions that I would derive from this discussion are as follows. The prospect for pure stabilization agreements is poor, because they do not offer enough. Stabilization agreements that aim at changing the terms of trade are not in principle undesirable, because they can be made a vehicle of developmental financing. They are merely inefficient because ordinarily developmental financing can be carried out more effectively by overt income transfers than in the concealed form of better terms of trade. I would suggest, however, that the concept of a commodity agreement be broadened so as to include countercyclical loans and grants designed to compensate for raw materials fluctuations. If that be conceded, a good case can be made for commodity agreements.

I should like to sketch briefly a possible technique for implementing this broader concept of a commodity agreement. It represents a combination of countercyclical lending and price stabilization.

Under this plan, the United States, and perhaps other consumer countries, at times of declining commodity prices, would make loans to producer countries. These loans would be secured by a certain amount of the commodity in question. The loans, which I envisage as of medium term and perhaps flexible maturity, would tide the borrowing countries over financially. They could be tied into the investment programmes of the recipients. The withdrawal from the market of the commodity supply serving as collateral would strengthen prices. It would provide the same benefits that a buffer stock would.

The lending countries would obtain an option to purchase the collateral at a given price or scale of prices above the market price. They could exercise these options prior to the maturity of the loan and would presumably do so when the market price had risen sufficiently. In this way, the lending countries would be protected against a subsequent extreme upsurge of prices.

The proposal would naturally have its difficulties. Like other forms of purchase contracts, it might put the participating governments into the commodities business. It might arouse irritation in the producer countries when the lenders exercised their options. This action would deprive the borrowers of the benefits of rising prices and quite likely would bring the price rise itself to a halt. That, however, is an inevitable feature of all stabilization schemes, if they are not to become permanent stockpiling projects.

I do not put forward this proposal as a major innovation nor as a scheme widely applicable to a variety of situations. Given the appropriate circumstances, the proposal might constitute a feasible compromise between the conflicting needs and interests of the various parties. It is very far from being a general plan. The argument of this paper has shown, I believe, that a general plan is, in the nature of things, not feasible. The problems of commodities, countries, and markets involved are too complex.

I do not mean to imply by this that we must permanently live with commodity instability on its present scale. We shall, I hope, succeed in living through the problem to its eventual diminution, if not disappearance. Commodity agreements, broadly conceived, will have an important contribution to make. But other factors, too, are at work to that end. The most important is the remarkable stability and growth maintained by the industrial countries. Had anyone foretold us of this at the end of the war when we were planning the future, we would have regarded the commodity problem as largely solved thereby.

A second factor is the improvement in information and knowledge. We are still very far from a desirable level in either. But it seems that certain extreme fluctuations, resulting from ignorance of changes in productive capacity, crop conditions, and the like, are less probable today than they were in the past.

Finally, there is the economic development of the producer countries, in the form of diversification as well as industrialization. Both were frequently initiated as antidotes to instability of export proceeds from raw materials. They appear to be making headway towards this goal. We may never eliminate instability, but in the long run economic development should succeed in reducing its importance.

COMMENTS ON PROFESSOR WALLICH'S PAPER

BY

JORGE MARSHALL
International Monetary Fund

I T is very difficult to review a paper as interesting and stimulating as the one Professor Wallich has presented on the subject of 'Stabilization of Proceeds from Raw Material Exports'. I find myself very close to the position he has taken on almost every point and I think the ground has been well covered and each issue has been given appropriate importance.

The crucial problem in any stabilization scheme which aims at keeping 'the current price on or close to its long-term trend', is to agree on the level of that trend. This problem is not solved by the proposal put forward by Professor Wallich which he calls a combination of countercyclical lending and price stabilization. Raw material consuming countries will make loans to producing countries 'at times of declining commodity prices'. In order that the scheme should be a success it is necessary to agree on the level below which prices have to decline before starting the offsetting lending.

I also have serious doubts that Professor Wallich's proposal may only be a buffer stock scheme in a slightly disguised form. Some details are missing. Will the loans be made for the full value of the raw materials offered as collateral ? Under those circumstances prices will not go below the minimum at which producing countries can start borrowing. If amounts that can be borrowed are fixed not at the full value of the raw materials offered as collateral but at a fractional percentage of the full value of the stocks, there is also an implicit minimum price depending on the price at which borrowing may start and the percentage that producing countries can obtain on given raw material stocks. The prices of the commodities will not fall below the borrowing point, unless the demand for these commodities is elastic enough to increase total proceeds over total sales plus borrowings.

During the years since the Second World War we have witnessed a long period of high and stable economic activity which has tended to minimize the effects of raw material price fluctuations. Most of the changes during this period have been of a structural or irregular character, affecting the supply conditions of commodities rather than the demand. Within large areas, such as Latin America, they have been of a compensatory nature. The preservation of conditions of prosperity in the industrial centres and certain forms of countercyclical lending, designed to maintain or to minimize the decline in export earnings, together constitute a good substitute programme for stabilization of the proceeds of individual commodities, and avoid some of the difficulties presented by alternative schemes.

I do not find any specific discussion in Professor Wallich's paper of the different effects of raw material price fluctuations on producing countries as a whole as opposed to the effect on the export industries affected. These differences and the question of to whom the benefits of stabilization will accrue should be an important consideration in any scheme.

There are some other minor points which could also be mentioned in reviewing this paper. First, the reasoning as to whether raw material price fluctuations may be beneficial rather than harmful to the economic development of the countries producing those raw materials seems to me inconclusive. Second, it is asserted that the demand elasticity for basic raw materials is low. I agree if the reference is to the total demand for the commodities. But I have serious doubts that the demand elasticity for any given country is low, as I have pointed out in my paper on 'Exchange Controls and Development'.[1]

DISCUSSION OF PROFESSOR WALLICH'S PAPER

THE discussion of Professor Wallich's paper dealt principally with the pros and cons of commodity stabilization.

I. PROS AND CONS OF COMMODITY STABILIZATION

Dr. Marshall drew attention to the tendency of our present prosperity to reduce commodity price fluctuations. He thought that countries selling

---

[1] See below, p. 440.

raw materials possessing good market prospects, such as Chile, might not want any further stabilization measures. They might only reduce the prospect of eventually selling at higher prices. *Professor Schultz* agreed that prosperity had greatly aided price stability but thought that the favourable experience we had enjoyed should not lead us to underplay the need for stabilization measures. *Professor Teixeira Vieira*, on the basis of a theoretical analysis, came to the conclusion that commodity stabilization was desirable, but it would probably lead to the fixing of low prices. This, he said, would be the likely consequence of the superior bargaining power of the consumer countries.

Professor Ellis thought that there was a strong case for stabilization. He did not agree with the implication of Professor Wallich's paper that producer countries were little interested in stabilization unless it brought them an improvement in their terms of trade. The whole world, he said, was deeply stability conscious. For raw material countries, particularly those with a single export product, price stabilization was an essential condition of income stabilization. He thought that most primary producing countries would be happy to stabilize if they could, even if there was no 'bribe' in the form of improved terms of trade.

Dr. Mayobre saw a strong need for stabilization, provided the United States did not take advantage of its position as a monopolistic buyer to keep prices low. Stabilization would have to be international, however. The experience of Brazil showed what could happen to a country that tried to carry the burden of stabilization all by itself.

Professor Gudin said that one might perhaps admit certain advantages in unstable prices. When prices were high, they provided resources for development. When they were low, they had the virtue of a 'challenge' in the sense of Dr. Kafka's paper. But he, too, would prefer stabilization if it were technically feasible.

Professors Schultz and *Ellis* and *Dr. Adler* mentioned an additional benefit of stabilization, the prospect that it was likely to reduce real costs. *Professor Schultz* thought that in some lines of agriculture the input of resources would be reduced as much as 20 per cent. per unit of output, if the farmer could count on stable prices. Of course there was a public cost involved in stabilization. But this public cost would in most instances probably be smaller than the private benefits. He ventured the guess that the United States could in the long run purchase its coffee more cheaply if it were prepared to assume the burden of stabilizing coffee prices. *Professor Byé* likewise regarded stabilization as important, but warned that a country acting by itself and accumulating commodity stocks would not be able to hold out long.

Professor Wallich said that if in his paper he had taken a rather negative view of commodity stabilization, it was not because of any lack of conviction that the economies of under-developed countries needed greater stability. He felt, however, that commodity stabilization would only do part of the job. It could not deal with the effects of quantity variations.

Moreover, he was not at all hopeful that it was a practical proposition, because of great technical difficulties and the attitude of the consumer countries. Nevertheless, he felt that the growth of under-developed countries was very much in the interest of the developed countries. For this reason, he had sought an approach to the stability problem, via developmental lending, that was broader than the commodity approach.

II. TECHNIQUES OF STABILIZATION

Dr. Kafka questioned Professor Wallich's view that a developed country would invest more if a given volume of resources were transferred to it from the United States in the form of a loan instead of in the form of higher prices for its exports. The gains from higher prices could be captured by means of a tax and channelled into development. Moreover, in the case of a loan the receiving country might reshuffle its own resources and simply displace potential local saving and investment with foreign money.

Dr. Adler thought that Professor Wallich had been unnecessarily pessimistic regarding the possibility of national action, not in the fashion of Brazil supporting coffee but in the sense of the African marketing boards. This technique had been quite successful in practice and he did not see why it could not be more widely adopted. A country that stabilized prices to its own producers and managed its foreign exchange reserves on a countercyclical basis, could expect to get some help also from the International Monetary Fund. All this together might be sufficient to solve its problem. He also argued that the national approach as practised by Brazil held some promise provided a sufficiently moderate support price was chosen.

Professor Haberler thought that the existing international credit machinery, together with the maintenance of a high level of activity in the developed countries was as much as was needed from the side of the consumer countries. He questioned the merits of Professor Wallich's suggestion for stabilization loans collateralized with the commodity in question. *Professor Gudin* added that this particular technique had been successfully adopted by Brazil at the beginning of the depression when a Brazilian loan secured by coffee was floated by Schroeders.

III. PRICE ELASTICITIES

Professor Haberler questioned Professor Wallich's assumption that the elasticity of demand for primary products was always low. As far as long-run tendencies were concerned, this was by no means always the case. Many stabilization schemes had come to grief by underestimating the elasticities of supply and demand. *Professor Hirschman* joined him and pointed to the effect of synthetic substitutes upon the elasticity of demand for the natural product. The presence of such alternative supplies at a relatively fixed price increased the elasticity of demand for the natural product. Though the invention of the substitute might initially be a misfortune for the raw material countries, the greater stability resulting from higher elasticity of demand was a gain.

IV. Positively and Negatively Reacting Commodities

Professor Haberler argued that this distinction was an unnecessary refinement. In practice, we could never know what the price trend would have been under other conditions. We had no means of classifying commodities by this criterion. *Professor Ellis* shared this view and added that concerns of this sort should not be allowed to create the impression that stabilization was technically more complex than it seemed. *Professor Schultz* also appeared to take the position that stabilization could be relied upon to increase supplies and that Professor Wallich's 'negatively reacting' commodities did not exist.

Chapter 13

INVESTMENT PRIORITIES

BY

JORGE AHUMADA [1]

Economic Commission for Latin America

I. THE THEORY OF ALLOCATION AND INVESTMENT PRIORITIES

THE problem of investment priorities is a special case of the general problem of choice. It involves three types of questions : what is being selected, what is the selective norm, and who is making the selection ?

In the case of investment decisions the first question is clearly answered by proper definition of the term 'investment'. To invest means to freeze a complex of resources of a given composition into a definite use for a period of time. Hence, investment requires decisions with respect to uses, such as food versus housing ; decisions on the nature of the complex of resources to be employed in each use, such as low versus high capital intensity ; and choice of the time period during which resources are to be frozen into a given use. This last choice is largely another aspect of the second, so that it can be said that basically there are only two general investment priority problems.

The normative aspect of the problem of investment choice has to be solved for each type of decision-making unit, because different types of unit pursue different economic objectives. The consumer is pursuing his personal welfare, the investor is after profits, while the government is, or should be, looking after social welfare. If these groups act rationally, each tries to maximize its own objective with the resources at its disposal. The consumer must allocate his resources so as not to have too much food and too little housing and both these requirements must be fulfilled at the lowest possible cost. The problem of the producer, on the other hand, is quite different. He wants profits. Whether he makes them by producing potatoes

[1] The author is an expert of the Technical Assistance Administration of the United Nations, but the paper reflects only his personal views. He is grateful for the useful comments received by staff members of the Economic Commission for Latin America, but for all mistakes he takes entire responsibility.

366

or nylon hosiery should make no difference. The selection of uses becomes identified with the choice of a given technique to make profits. In his case there is no dual problem of choice.

As is well known, orthodox economic theory has provided an answer to the problem of efficient resource allocation, an answer which is inclusive in the sense that it solves the problem of all three decision-making groups mentioned above, but which is valid only given certain restrictive assumptions. Abba Lerner [1] has elaborated a very concise, elegant, and improved version of the orthodox solution. Given the distribution of income and conditions of free consumer choice, the optimum division of a factor among different uses is achieved when in every use the value of its marginal product is equal to the price of the factor. As the price of a factor is assumed to be uniform everywhere, the optimum division is achieved when the value of the marginal product of the factor is the same in every use. The equalization of the price and the value of the marginal product of each factor in each use produces the optimum division of each factor, and also brings about the best combination of factors in every use, because in each use it makes the marginal products of the different factors proportional to their prices. Thus, given the equality of factor prices, the *relative* marginal products of the different factors in different uses are equal. This is the condition for achieving the optimum combination of factors in each use.

According to this theory, if there is perfect competition and all firms maximize their profits, both the optimum division of factors among different uses and the optimum combination of factors in every use will be achieved, because firms, behaving in the way prescribed, will shift factors around until the value of the marginal product of each factor is equal in every direction. If the value of the marginal product of one factor in any use happens to be larger than its price, there will be positive profits higher than normal in that use and there will be a net overall gain by bringing in factors from other uses.

In brief, given the amount of productive resources, the optimum division and allocation of these resources is achieved when the total money value of production obtained from them is a maximum. Under conditions of perfect competition the maximum money value of production is obtained if all producers behave so as to maximize their profits. Consequently, if investment projects are selected according to the profits they are able to provide, both society and individuals will be maximizing their welfare.

The practical corollary of this type of reasoning has been the

[1] A. P. Lerner, *The Economics of Control* (New York, 1944).

widespread utilization by government agencies of the benefit-cost ratio as an investment priority criterion. The ratio includes in its numerator the total value of production expected from the project during its whole useful life and in its denominator the sum of all fixed and operating costs.[1] All variables are of course properly discounted.

The benefit-cost ratio as described above differs from the criterion that a private investor will use. He will include fixed and circulating capital in the denominator instead of the total value of inputs and he will put only profits, that is, benefits minus costs, in the numerator. However, both ratios aim at maximizing profits per unit of resources and it is very likely that if several projects were graded according to both ratios their relative positions would be the same in both scales.

But the benefit-cost ratio is not applied in the way just described because it is widely recognized that the profit maximization criterion is a valid norm for resource distribution only given the restrictive assumptions that support its theoretical justification. Among these assumptions, the one stating that the market price of a good or service represents its social opportunity cost — what society has to do without in order to produce it — has been the target of most criticism. Unless market prices and social opportunity costs are equal, the fact that a unit of a given resource or combination of resources produces a higher money value in use *a* than in use *b* should not be taken as evidence that it is advantageous to dedicate resources to *a* instead of *b*.

It is argued that market prices and social opportunity costs differ mainly because of market imperfections and the interdependency of economic activities. Market imperfections arise from indivisibilities, monopolies, and the fact that governments, which should participate in the market only as arbiters, in reality take part in the fight. The interdependency of economic activities means that when a decision is taken to produce *a*, the production of other goods is affected favourably or unfavourably. These effects may or may not be reflected in the market prices of the inputs and outputs of *a*. If they are not, they are called external economies or diseconomies.

A United States Federal Inter-Agency Committee has recommended the utilization of an investment criterion to evaluate river basin development projects in which corrections for the two types of imperfections of the profit concept are introduced.[2]

[1] To be wholly consistent with the underlying theory, costs should include an item representing normal profits.

[2] United States, Federal Inter-Agency River Basin Committee, *Proposed Practices for Economic Analysis of River Basin Projects* (Washington, 1950).

The main elements of the criteria could be symbolically represented as follows :

$$\frac{V_p + U_s + \Sigma V_a}{C_p},$$

where

V_p = Total market value of the products expected from the project, taxes and subsidies eliminated ;

U_s = Increment of profit to the direct users of the goods and services of the project ; if these are final goods or services U_s will be zero ;

V_a = Value added in all the processes which the products expected from the project will go through until they reach the stage of final goods ;

C_p = Total project costs, including operating costs, but excluding taxes and subsidies.

Professor Chenery [1] has also made a recommendation for an investment criterion which uses profit maximization as the behavioural norm.[2] Its main elements are as follows :

$$\frac{V_p + C_p}{K} + \frac{E + rB}{K},$$

where

V_p = Total market value of the products expected from the project, taxes and subsidies eliminated ;

C_p = Operating and fixed costs ;

E = External economies arising from the operation of the project ;

rB = Net balance of payments effects of the project, r being the degree of over- or under-valuation of the currency ;

K = Investment requirements of the project.

The modifications proposed by the Inter-Agency Committee and by Chenery are probably sufficient to correct the shortcomings of the profit maximization norm mentioned above. The main reservations are : first, the fact that the impact of monopolistic practices on the structure of relative prices is almost impossible to correct for ; and, second, that the elimination of taxes and subsidies, although arithmetically possible, will not leave *pure* prices as the residual. Relative prices do not necessarily change to the extent of the taxes and subsidies involved, and hence there is no way of saying *a priori* whether adjustment for taxes and subsidies will give a price structure

[1] H. B. Chenery, 'The Application of Investment Criteria', *Quarterly Journal of Economics*, February 1953.

[2] For a review of several criteria, see United Nations, *Manual of Investment Projects*.

which is closer to the one that would exist without those taxes and subsidies.

It appears then that we can be satisfied with the proposals of the Inter-Agency Committee and of Professor Chenery. However, although their remedies may be quite suited to cure the disease mentioned, the patient — the orthodox theory of allocation — seems also to be suffering from something quite different, much worse and perhaps incurable.

Those who defend the profit maximization criterion seem to forget that the social opportunity cost of a good or service is represented by its price only if the different marginal products of each factor have the same value in every use, and this is true only if the price of each factor including profits is the same everywhere and if the economy is in equilibrium.

If the price of each factor is not the same everywhere, the optimum distribution of factors among alternative uses will not be achieved even if each firm or project-maker behaves so as to equate the value of the marginal product to the price of the factor. On the other hand, if the price of each factor is the same to every producer, but the economy is not in equilibrium, the social opportunity cost of any product will not necessarily correspond to its price, because this correspondence depends on the equivalence of the marginal product of each factor in every direction and this happens only in equilibrium.

Everybody agrees that factor prices are characteristically heterogeneous, although nobody is very clear as to precisely what they are agreeing upon. What, for instance, is the spatial magnitude within which it is proper to postulate the equality of factor prices ? In other words, what are the dimensions of a market ? One could also raise a less sophisticated question, such as, what is a factor ? How many labour factors are there that should have different prices reflecting different qualities ? On the basis of spatial and quality considerations, one might say that factor price differentials are actually not so great as to invalidate the orthodox analysis and argue that what are considered price differentials are actually *bona fide* distance and quality inputs.

In order to live in peace with the modified version of the profit maximization criterion, one could also find arguments in favour of the thesis that monopoly interferences are not really damaging. But I fail to see how one can make a logical structure built on the assumption of equilibrium consistent with reality, unless it is assumed that, if the behavioural norm is respected by everybody, an economy will tend towards equilibrium whenever it is not in that state. Unfortunately, this is not so. If an economy is not in a state of equilibrium, profit maximization will not bring it about. In this connection I would like to quote Professor Koopmans, who says : 'If an inefficient state of resource allocation prevails initially, it is not claimed that adherence by all concerned to the rules stated would lead the mechanism to an efficient point or even close to such a point, in a stated time interval. To establish such a claim would require a dynamic analysis resting on a more precise dynamic specification of the rules in question (*e.g.* how much to expand a profitable activity, etc.). It is claimed only that adherence to the rules will perpetuate an efficient state once it has somehow come about.' [1]

A state of equilibrium may somehow come about after a long time has elapsed during which resources are constant, but the problem of investment priorities arises from the need of directing a continuous flow of *new* resources to the best conceivable uses, including the production of other resources. This problem cannot be solved with the assistance of a behavioural model built upon the assumption of the constancy of resources. Unfortunately, there is no way of manipulating the profit criterion so as to neutralize the shortcomings derived from the static nature of its underlying justification. It is really a pity to have to recognize that after two hundred years of evolution, economics — although it is the science of scarce factors that have alternative uses — still does not have a theory of allocation.

II. Towards a Pragmatic Solution

If the relative profitability of alternative employments is not a satisfactory criterion, what, then, is a reasonable guide to investment decisions which will lead to a maximization of social welfare ? A fruitful discussion of this problem must be preceded by the recognition of two fundamental points. One is the fact that there is no escape from value judgments, and the other is that all investment decisions are interdependent.

The following discussion is based on the value judgment that in the end the distribution of resources among alternative uses should be determined by freely expressed consumer preferences. Given this general frame of reference, the problem of resource allocation is tantamount to finding the most accurate reflection of the position of different potential factor uses in the consumer's scale of preferences. I put the question in terms of a reasonable rather than of a precise criterion because I strongly believe that from a social point of view the allocation of resources among alternative

[1] T. C. Koopmans, 'Efficient Allocation of Resources', *Econometrica*, October 1951, p. 463.

uses can only be done in a really proper way with the help of a dynamic inter-industry relation matrix that takes into account not only inter-industry flows but also relations among different stocks and between stocks and flows. At present we do not have such a matrix, but this does not impede the visualization of the problems which arise in the distribution of investment resources, given the premises of free consumer choice and the interdependence of economic activities.

If it is assumed that net national *per capita* income is the closest available index of social welfare in a given country, the rate of growth of *per capita* income is the variable to be maximized.[1] Given the rate of growth of income, the demand for different goods and services will grow at different rates which will depend upon the coefficients of income elasticity of demand for different types of goods and services, upon input-output coefficients, and upon the rate of population growth. The resulting structure of demand at the higher level of income can then be checked against the existing structure of installed capacity. The sectoral differences together with the sectoral capital coefficients will indicate the investment requirements by activities, sectors, or uses. A further check designed to find out the investment requirements of the capital goods industries may result in a second revision of total investment until by this process of successive approximations a final investment figure is achieved.[2]

The trouble with this scheme is that even if Domar is correct when he asserts that the rate of growth of income depends on the investment coefficient and on the capital coefficient, it is also true that the relation is reversible. Both coefficients vary with the rate of growth of income. This is especially true of the capital coefficient, since it is so much affected by the distribution of investment. Furthermore, the investment coefficient is subject to the influence of economic policy. We cannot know how much can be invested unless we know the rate of growth of income, and we cannot know the rate of growth of income unless we know the productivity of investment, which depends upon its composition. This is the reason why the solution to the investment priority problem must be a simultaneous solution within the context of a dynamic input-output model.

[1] One could argue that consumption is a better index of material welfare, but in a capitalistic world economic security is an important good the consumption of which is closely related to personal wealth.

[2] For a detailed exposition of a method along these lines, see United Nations, *Analyses and Projections of Economic Development*, vol. i, *An Introduction to the Technique of Programming*, 1955.

The simultaneity of the solution provides no answer to the question of what share of resources should be dedicated to the accumulation of capital and how much should be devoted to consumption. Freedom of consumer choice provides only a partial answer.[1] This freedom must be exercised within the context of a given economic policy. To what extent can policy push investment upward to achieve the maximization of the increase in *per capita* income ? It seems to me that the only consistent answer is that policy can push investment only up to a point that is consistent with monetary and balance of payment stability at a full employment level.

The simultaneity of the solution makes it necessary on the other hand to consider public and private investment together. The government should not only select its own investment projects according to some system of priorities, but it should also determine its policy with regard to private investment in co-ordination with its own investment programme. As the whip and the carrot have to be used in a way conducive to the coincidence of public and private interests, it is clear that the government must use one set of priority criteria that will permit it to determine the most probable distribution of private investment and another set of criteria to determine the most desirable distribution from a social point of view. The comparison between these two sets will provide the answer as to how much carrot and whip will be required and where.

In view of the practical impossibility of a simultaneous solution, any substitute procedure that pretends to be satisfactory should lead to similar results : the maximization of the rate of growth of *per capita* income compatible with stability. This means that if the government has a given amount of investment resources, it should select that basket of projects which makes the greatest contribution to national income. In other words, the value added by the selected set of projects should be a maximum.

If the ratio of value added to input is used as a priority criterion, investment resources will be distributed among alternative uses in the same way as if the allocation is made on the basis of the elasticity of demand and input-output coefficients. The higher the elasticity of demand for a given good or service, the higher the increase in monetary expenditure on that good or service as income increases and the

---

[1] Actually this is an insufficient condition because no matter how free, consumer choice is exercised within certain constraints and it is essential to be very clear as to what these constraints are. For an elaboration of this point, see Ragnar Frisch, 'From National Accounts to Macro-Economic Decision Models', International Association for Research in Income and Wealth, *Income and Wealth*, Series IV (London, 1955).

higher the value added in its production. The more accurately this increase is anticipated, the less the price increase of the good concerned and the more real the increment in expenditure.

Now, an optimum distribution of resources is secured only when the ratio of value added to input is equal at the margin in every direction. Consequently, if there are several projects showing different value-added input ratios, to give priority only to those with the higher ratios means that the high ratios will tend to come down while the low ratios will tend to go up, thereby tending towards equalization.

Let us specify in more exact terms the elements that participate in the proposed investment criteria.[1] In the first place we have to define the term 'project.' For operating reasons, projects are normally defined in a way that is suitable to handling by engineers and other technicians. But for purposes of evaluation a project must include a description and evaluation of all the operations necessary to produce final goods or services, whether for consumption or investment. If the production of intermediate goods, such as water for irrigation or transportation facilities, is under consideration, their contribution to economic growth is bound to be underestimated if the project is defined from an engineering view-point. This inappropriate definition of a project has led to many discussions of the pros and cons of, for instance, establishing a steel mill in an under-developed country. Those in opposition to the mill may judge the project from the point of view of the engineer while those who defend it may resort to the idea of the multiplier. This multiplier rests upon the recognition that engineering and economic projects are two different things.

If a project is defined in the usual way, the numerator will contain the value added (V_p) in the project, that is, the payments to all the primary factors, including profits. As is well known, this figure differs from the value of production by the amount of purchases from other enterprises, taxes, and depreciation. Defining a project from an economic point of view, the numerator should also include the value-added in the activities supplying the inputs of the project and the value-added in all the further processes that the project must go through until it reaches the stage of final goods. These two types of benefits derived from the project can be termed those behind and those beyond the project respectively, using these two adverbs in relation to the final stage of transformation. Actually, if taxes and depreciations are deducted, this process of aggregation

[1] See Jorge Ahumada, 'Preparación y evaluación de proyector de desarrollo económico', *El Trimestre Económico*, July-September 1955.

gives the direct value of production of the project valued at factor costs plus the value added beyond the project.

The denominator includes all the inputs, fixed and operating, to be used in the project during its useful life. As profits are considered a payment for the services of a factor of production, they are also included in the denominator. As the indirect value-added by the project also has a cost, the corresponding figure should also appear in the denominator. The cost of obtaining the value-added behind the project is automatically taken into account in the direct costs of the project and is included under the heading of raw materials, or rather purchases from other enterprises. However, those costs connected with the value-added beyond the project are not, but should be, taken account of.

Up to this point and in the absence of taxes and subsidies, the only difference between the numerator and the denominator consists of depreciation, which is included in the denominator and not in the numerator. As the evaluation of the project is made for its whole useful life, the denominator is actually the sum of the payments to the factors of production during the whole life of the project plus the fixed capital employed directly in it and that used to produce the behind and beyond input flows. But there is a further difference which is connected with the price of the items entering the denominator.

If one rejects the idea that market prices reflect opportunity costs, it will be necessary to use actual opportunity costs for inputs and market prices for output. The valuation of indirect benefits and costs must follow the same principles. A symbolic representation of the suggested priority criterion could be as follows :

$$\frac{V_p + V_i}{(C_p + C_i)r},$$

where V_p and V_i are value-added directly and indirectly, C_p and C_i are direct and indirect actual costs, and r is the relation between market prices and opportunity costs.

The numerical value of r will vary not only with the type of project but also with its location. An agricultural project may obtain its manpower from other agricultural activities where wage rates are the same as those to be paid in the project. Consequently, the market price of the labour used by the project will be equal to its opportunity cost. A project for a manufacturing plant, however, may use labour withdrawn from agriculture where labour income is much smaller than the income that labour will earn in the project.

We know very little with respect to the pool that serves as a labour reservoir for different economic activities, but it is very likely that there is a kind of economic ladder, workers moving up from agriculture to services and construction and from there to higher forms of manufacture and services. If this is the case, the opportunity cost of the labour employed in a project involving a high form of manufacture will not be represented by the income earned by the transferred labour in its immediately previous employment, but by labour income at the lowest step of the ladder. In the absence of concrete information, a pragmatic solution to the problem of opportunity cost pricing could be the use of the average labour income per employed person as shown by national income statistics. The same could be done in the case of the income of all other factors.[1]

In the case of foreign currency it would be necessary to make an estimate of the actual overvaluation or undervaluation of the exchange rate and also an estimate of the expected exchange rate averaged over the life of the project. The larger the expected disequilibrium of the balance of payments and the foreign currency content of benefits and costs, the larger both the numerator and the denominator. This would automatically give higher priorities to foreign currency earning and saving projects whenever foreign exchange is relatively scarce.

The problem of selecting techniques is also solved by means of the value-added input ratio. At first sight it may appear that the application of this ratio would lead to the selection of the most inefficient techniques, since the larger the inputs of manpower and capital required to produce a given quantity of a certain good, the higher the value-added in comparison with other techniques that use less of these factors. For instance, it could be argued that the building of a road would make a larger contribution to national income the more inefficient the technique selected for the project. This type of reasoning involves the typical confusion of engineering and economic objectives. A road is not an economic objective. The value derived from that road as represented by its serviceability is the meaningful economic dimension. This dimension is not usually determined by the project maker; it is given by the conditions of the market. The value of production as determined by the market reflects a change of techniques only in the structure of costs. One technique could imply that a larger *proportion* would be paid to labour, while another could signify that the largest share would go to capital owners. Of course the denominator would change considerably with alternative techniques.

[1] See, however, p. 378 below in connection with the opportunity cost of capital goods.

Techniques differ in the qualities of basic factors which they use and in the proportion of their factor mix. Usually the scarcer factors have greater mobility and consequently their market prices and opportunity costs are bound to differ less than those of more abundant factors. The main reason for this is that the higher the degree of scarcity the higher is factor remuneration, so that the cost of mobility is a less important handicap for the mobility of a scarcer factor. If this is true, then the use of the value-added input ratio will automatically give higher priority to those techniques that require less capital per unit of output.

Opportunity cost pricing for evaluating techniques makes it unnecessary to use any of the widely recommended criteria based on the minimization of a single input, such as output per unit of capital, or per unit of foreign exchange or per unit of labour. If any of these resources is relatively scarcer than the others, its opportunity cost will differ less from its market price and its market price will be higher. Consequently the greater the use of that type of resource in any technique the lower will be its priority.

In connection with the application of the value-added input ratio there are two additional points that are worth mentioning. In the first place, a comparison of the basket of projects selected according to the profit maximization criterion with the basket of projects resulting from use of the value-added input ratio would indicate the amount of subsidies and taxes which are justifiable to assure a coincidence between the overall social interest and private individual interests. This has great practical significance, because there has been a great deal of exaggeration in justifying the granting of protection in many of the developing economies.

The second point is related to the application of the profitability norm for judging the advisability of producing at home a good currently imported. The fact that it is cheaper to buy any given good abroad than to produce it internally is not sufficient justification to reject the production of that good. This statement will be quite acceptable to the defenders of the comparative cost doctrine. It is not absolute costs that matter in international trade, because given the assumption of the international immobility of the factors of production, the equality of factor prices cannot be postulated. If the advantages or disadvantages of the substitution of a given good are judged by means of the application of the value-added input ratio, one is actually closer to a comparison of comparative cost than if one uses profitability as the norm. As a matter of fact, opportunity cost pricing is partly a recognition of the spatial inequalities of factor prices derived from factor immobility.

377

Let us now return to the question of the opportunity cost of labour. If we define opportunity cost as the value of production sacrificed in order to transfer a factor from its present use to any specific new use, then the opportunity cost of unemployed labour up to the point of its total absorption is zero, because employing new recruits to the labour force should not be charged against any other type of production. This means that in a country where the population is growing, the opportunity cost of labour is zero up to the absorption of the whole additional labour force even though there is no unemployment in the usual sense of the word.

On the other hand, the opportunity cost of unemployed capital is positive and equal to its maintenance and replacement cost. It sounds odd that these two factors of production should be treated differently, but this is consistent with the treatment given to labour in social accounting and in economics in general. If we are to think of resources as a stock and of income as a flow, then labour should also be considered as a part of the stock with its production, maintenance, and replacement cost. But in this case everything else would also change. The denominator of the priority criterion would no longer contain salaries and wages but the capital value of manpower and also the capital value of natural resources. The numerator would no longer contain the total income payments to the factors, but those payments net of replacement of labour. It is easy to see that the treatment of the problem of priorities on the basis of flow-stock ratios is equivalent to the treatment suggested above, that is, pricing inputs at their opportunity cost. But it has the additional advantage of being less involved, of eliminating discriminatory treatment of the factors of production arising from the confusion of value judgments with scientific thinking, and of being more conceptually consistent with the criteria used by the private investor.

Following the usual procedure, once the projects are prepared and their value-added input ratios calculated, all those with higher ratios are selected for implementation up to the exhaustion of available investment resources. This implies two important tasks : first, to determine the amount of investment resources which will in fact be available ; and, second, to have more projects prepared than are likely to be carried into action.

In connection with the first task, there seems to be no other answer than the one we have already suggested in connection with the simultaneous solution, that is, stipulating a stability condition. It is necessary to project the most likely spontaneous rate of growth, the most likely impact of a change in economic policy, and the saving propensities resulting therefrom. Then a decision will have to be taken as to how much investment is likely to be carried out through private and public channels. Only then will it be possible to start making the selection of projects.

In connection with the question of having more projects than investment resources, one could say that in order to establish priorities one must study projects. As a matter of fact, this task is theoretically fully achieved only when all conceivable alternatives have been scrutinized. This requirement is obviously unattainable, but a considerably more modest goal might also be unattainable because project-making is a very expensive process. It is here that valid generalizations on economic development are most helpful.

I would say that there are two generalizations : the old, the new. The old one says, 'Select for study those projects that will contribute to the elimination of bottlenecks'. Bottlenecks are bound to appear in those sections of the economy where, due to institutional or technological reasons, market forces do not operate satisfactorily. This is the case with regard to transportation facilities and public utility services, because of technical indivisibilities. For institutional reasons, agriculture and skilled services often suffer from bottlenecks too. This is why the old recipe for investment priorities was agriculture, transportation, energy, and training.[1]

The new generalization says : 'Select those projects that will absorb into employment the population that is released from rural areas'. Urbanization is a modern exogenous process that implies the need for introducing changes in the way of supplying goods and in the goods to be supplied. In other words, urbanization implies industrialization, and we have to have it whether we want it or not. There are alternatives — a low rate of industrialization with a lot of social tension or a high rate of growth with tensions of a worse type. According to the new generalization, one should search mainly for non-agricultural projects, a conclusion that has much less normative effectiveness than that of the old generalization.

The new generalization is not so new after all. It bears the mark of the thirties, the fear of depression. The old one belongs to the good world of Marshall. Certainly, if the economy is spontaneously developing at a relatively high rate, bottlenecks are bound to appear, and precisely at those points indicated by the old generalization. But growth is not always spontaneous. That is, priorities are actually a function not only of the level but of the rate of growth as well. The practical corollary of all this is that in establishing investment priorities it is most important to make a good

---

[1] A good combination of new and old can be found in United Nations, *Theoretical and Practical Problems of Economic Growth*, 1951.

diagnosis of the development problem of the country or region for which priorities are to be recommended. Let us consider Brazil. If Brazil has several projects to choose from, how is it going to treat the secondary benefits of the projects when the secondary benefits are to be enjoyed by people in the south ? In other words, if we agree that a project should refer to final goods and exports are final goods, at what point in space do the products of a region become the exports of that region ? How will federal authorities determine their investment priorities if a country is heterogeneous and the population on the whole immobile ? Should they follow the principle that what is already developed should be developed first ? Should they stick to the rule that in selecting alternative locations attention should be paid only to minimization of costs ? The most probable consequence of such a policy in a large heterogeneous country would be the repetition of the pattern of development of the world in the last two centuries : a continuous widening of the gap between high and low *per capita* income areas.

There is no doubt that the process of development involves the spatial concentration of people and income, and consequently different rates of regional development, but which regions are to be developed and how much shall each region be developed ? It is conceivable that in a very heterogeneous country the maximization of overall national *per capita* income is an insufficient or inappropriate criterion.

III. The Case of a Financial Agency

In conclusion, I would like to discuss briefly the investment priority problem from the standpoint of a governmental financial intermediary, such as a bank or a development corporation. The usual criteria are useful only to planning agencies which operate on the basis of a basket of projects, all of which are known to the agency but some of which must be rejected. They are not useful to a financial agency because a financial agency does not become acquainted at one time with all the projects it will deal with within a period. Projects are presented to an agency one or two at a time, and as soon as they are presented an answer must be given as to whether or not they will qualify for a loan. Thus, projects are evaluated by a planning agency against one another, while a financial intermediary must evaluate them against a standard or norm. The norm must be consistent with the aim of the agency and should clearly indicate which kind of projects are to be rejected off-hand.

The aim of a public financial agency should be to mobilize as much *real* resources as possible with the *financial* resources it has at its command. In other words, it should try to maximize the real resources put to work each year per unit of agency resources. The value of real resources which are mobilized by the agency is equal to the total capitalized value of the annual inputs used in the projects financed by the agency, less the capitalized value of the inputs of those projects which would have been carried out even if not financed by the agency.

To be consistent with its aim the agency should reject any project which can obtain finance somewhere else. Accordingly, it should try not to finance the highly profitable projects. But the rejection criterion has to be more precise than that. For a private agency the rejection criterion is simple. No project for which the risk of failure of repayment is larger than a certain arbitrary minimum is eligible. The risk of losing the principal depends on the net worth of the prospective borrower and upon the profitability of the project itself. In the case of a public agency, this criterion is insufficient and it could be inappropriate.

It is insufficient because, if it is applied according to the profit maximization criterion of the private agency it will lead to concentration on short-term loans. These loans permit a larger turnover of agency resources. This norm might be inappropriate because it could lead: first, to a rejection of risky projects which have no other way of obtaining financial resources and which consequently cannot be carried out unless financed by the agency; second, to a refusal of projects which could make an important contribution to gross national product per unit of employed resources but which are not profitable in the private sense; or, third, to the acceptance of projects which are inappropriate from any point of view but which are backed up by good guarantees, such as credits to an already large farm owner for buying more agricultural land.

Of course, the policy of neglecting risks can be over-stressed, leading the agency to the loss of its resources if the government does not contribute additional funds. A zero profit criterion for the lending agency as a whole might prolong its life while relaxing the security requirement. Zero profit does not mean that the agency should charge an interest rate high enough to cover costs on every loan. The agency could charge high rates to highly profitable projects and nothing to non-profitable but socially desirable projects.

The lack of alternative sources of financing, however, is not sufficient condition. The agency should obviously not finance a project only because nobody else wants to finance it. The project should also be socially justifiable, that is, the ratio of value-added per unit of employed resources should exceed a certain minimum. How can the minimum value of the ratio be determined below which no project should be eligible ? A solution could perhaps be found in the use of the coefficient of the value-added per unit of employed resources for the region as a whole in all economic activities, or of the same coefficient for the activity to which the project belongs. If the coefficient for the project has a value equal to the coefficient for the overall economy, then the project would not contribute to the average productivity of employed resources. If average productivity has been secularly growing at, let us say, 2 per cent. per year, a project would tend to reduce that rate of growth unless it shows a coefficient higher than the average. How much would depend on the rate of growth of productivity and on the length of the useful life of the project.

COMMENTS ON DR. AHUMADA'S PAPER

BY

HARVEY LEIBENSTEIN
University of California

I. Mr. Ahumada's Objections to the Profit Maximization Criterion

DR. AHUMADA rejects, in the first part of his paper, what he believes to be the orthodox approach to the question of investment priorities, but the formula that he presents, if I understand it correctly, is much more orthodox than I anticipated. It emphasizes the point that the opportunity cost of a factor may not equal its market price, and that, in determining investment priorities, opportunity costs rather than market prices are significant. This alone does not strike me as a significant deviation from the orthodox position, except in emphasis.

Dr. Ahumada rejects the profit maximization criterion on two grounds that are quite dissimilar. These are : first, that the orthodox solution is correct only if all market prices are in fact equilibrium prices ; and, second, that the solution is based on a static theory that enables us to deduce theorems about the maximization of output for *given* stocks, but it does not tell us how the stocks themselves expand.

Dr. Ahumada is correct in emphasizing that, strictly speaking, actual factor prices are unlikely to be equilibrium prices, and therefore do not reflect opportunity costs. But we do not expect real world conditions to be exactly as the theory orders. The crucial issue is whether the prices are good enough approximations of equilibrium prices. The answer, it seems to me, depends on market structure and factor mobility. Dr.

Ahumada grants these points, if I interpret him correctly, but he seems to go one step further. He argues that even where monopolistic elements are not significant, and where there are no important restrictions on factor mobility, the fact that the existing state is one of price disequilibrium is enough to vitiate the orthodox solution. To make this last point Dr. Ahumada invokes the authority of Professor Koopmans to the effect that the solution of a static system can yield only equilibrium values (*i.e.* an efficient state), but it does not imply any tendency towards equilibrium values (the efficient state in Koopmans' vocabulary) if the initial state is one of disequilibrium.

Strictly speaking it is true that only a dynamic system can tell us whether the disequilibrium state is or is not heading towards equilibrium. But I believe that there is at the very least an implicit dynamics in the neo-classical scheme — one that Hicks and others have tried to make explicit. The general view is that under competitive conditions actual prices do fluctuate around their equilibrium values, that in the fullness of time and in the absence of interferences they would reach their equilibrium values, and that the equilibria under consideration are at least stable in the small. In other words, the belief is that the dynamics of most commodity and factor markets are such that an increase in price decreases excess demand. All of this is not to deny the possibility that there may be actual factor markets where this last is not the case. However, I think that Dr. Ahumada's argument would have been more compelling had he given us some examples of such markets.

In actual cases, of course, non-competitive elements may be significant, and factor mobility may not be all it should be. In such cases Dr. Ahumada's point in emphasizing the importance of the deviation between market prices and opportunity costs is very well taken indeed.

The second ground on which Dr. Ahumada rejects the orthodox position is to my mind the more telling of the two. He argues that 'the problem of investment priorities arises from the need of directing a continuous flow of *new* resources to the best conceivable uses, including the production of other resources. This problem cannot be solved with the assistance of a behavioural model built upon the assumption of the constancy of resources.' Unfortunately, from my view-point, Dr. Ahumada found it optimal or adequate to allocate only a few sentences to this point. I would have very much liked to have seen this theme amplified considerably in connection with the problem of investment priorities. Indeed, I was surprised to find that Dr. Ahumada does not seem to take this aspect of the problem into account in his own priority criterion formula.

In any event, I suspect that it is not quite true that the neo-classical model is necessarily a completely static model that assumes a perpetual constancy of resources. It is a simple matter to turn the static model into a dynamic one in which the growth of the capital stock is determined by the amount of net investment period by period. If we add to this relation, as is commonly done, the assumption that population growth and additions to skills and knowledge are determined exogenously, then we have a model, consistent with the neo-classical model, that is dynamic in character, since one of its relations, the relation between capital and investment, covers more than one time period. Of course, such a dynamic model may not satisfy some of us. There may be many more important relations between flows in one period and stocks in subsequent periods than the fact that the capital stock of one period is the sum of the net investments of all previous periods. My point is simply that the charge of inadequacy against the so-called orthodox model must be based on more than the ground that it is static. We must show that there are some important dynamic relations that cannot readily be incorporated into the model, and/or that they are of such a nature that allocation criteria based on profit maximization do not take these relations into account.

II. DR. AHUMADA'S INVESTMENT ALLOCATION CRITERION

In Section II Dr. Ahumada turns to the very difficult task of developing a pragmatic allocation criterion, and presents some of the arguments supporting his solution. I now turn to some of the questions that came to mind in connection with these supporting arguments. The questions that follow are not intended as criticisms of the paper, but, if I am right in interpreting Dr. Ahumada, they involve aspects of the problem that should be clarified.

First, Dr. Ahumada emphasizes the point that there is no escape from value judgments. He puts forth the value judgment that resource allocation should be determined in accordance with freely expressed consumer preferences, but he also suggests that the rate of growth of *per capita* income is the variable to be maximized. First, is free consumer choice to be applied to the choice between present and future goods? That is to say, is the rate of investment also to be determined on the basis of free consumer choice? If so, is there not a possibility that free consumer choice may be inconsistent with the objective of maximizing the rate of *per capita* income growth? The rate of income growth depends on the rate of investment, and if free consumer choice yields a very low rate of investment, then this may not be consistent with maximizing income growth.

Second, how is the question of knowledge to be treated in connection with free consumer choice? For example, would Dr. Ahumada allocate any funds for consumer education? If one recognizes a need for consumer education does this not imply a lack of faith in free consumer choice?

Third, in his symbolic representation of his priority criterion Dr. Ahumada multiplies the sum of the direct and indirect costs of the project by a factor r that turns market prices into opportunity costs. Dr. Ahumada points out that r will vary with the type of project and its location. But will not r vary for each factor input? Why consider actual direct and indirect costs (C_p and C_i) in the formula ? Why not ignore actual costs and simply put in the denominator the sum of the estimated opportunity costs of the direct and indirect inputs ? Would not such an estimate have to be made, factor by factor, in any event, in order to estimate r ?

Fourth, Dr. Ahumada asserts that urbanization is an exogenous process. Is this true ? Is urbanization really unrelated to economic processes, for example the process of economic development ?

Fifth, Dr. Ahumada seems to support the new generalization that we should 'select those projects that will absorb into employment the population that is released from rural areas.' Why ? Does this follow from the objective of maximizing *per capita* income growth ? I would not think that that is necessarily the case. Is it because the released labour is a free good of which the opportunity cost is zero ? But this would not be a sufficient reason, by itself, for emphasizing labour absorption projects. After all, air is usually a free good but we do not especially seek air absorption projects. Of course, we may desire full or high levels of employment for its own sake. This is indeed a way out, for this proposition is based on a value judgment that most of us would support.

FURTHER COMMENTS ON DR. AHUMADA'S PAPER

BY

GERALD ALTER

International Bank for Reconstruction and Development

I. Dr. Ahumada's Investment Criterion and the Conventional Profit Maximization Formula

Dr. Ahumada's stimulating, if somewhat elusive, discussion of the principles to be followed in the allocation of investment resources starts with a discussion of the limitations of the profit maximization rule as a basis for economic policy designed to maximize the increase in *per capita* income. He accepts consumer preferences as a general frame of reference, cites certain factors that are frequently alleged to produce a discrepancy between market prices and social opportunity costs, and proceeds to argue that the orthodox theory of allocation, even after adjustment for these discrepancies, suffers from a disease that is incurable. The incurable disease is found to be a logical structure built on the assumption of equilibrium. 'If an economy is not in a state of equilibrium, profit maximization will not bring it about.' I believe Dr. Ahumada's argument here rests on weak grounds.

While rules based on the principles of comparative statics do not indicate the process through time by which a result will be achieved, this does not mean that the rules are necessarily inapplicable to a dynamic situation. The fact that 'the problem of investment priorities arises from the need of directing a continuous flow of *new* resources to the best conceivable uses' does not rule out, as Ahumada argues, the 'assistance of a behavioural model built upon the assumption of constancy of resources'. In economics we frequently use models built on the assumption of constancy of resources precisely for the purpose of appraising the effects of changes in the supply of labour, supply of capital, and so forth. After all, an assumption is usually made so that it can be removed.

While Dr. Ahumada's introductory incursion into methodology leads him, needlessly I believe, to a wholesale rejection of conventional economic analysis as a means of grappling with his problem, it is not at all clear that his own solution differs significantly from the profit criterion, once market prices are adjusted to approximate opportunity cost. His exposition requires some clarification on this point.

The conventional rule is that investment resources should be allocated to a particular project when there is a reasonable expectation of a surplus after meeting all costs, and that if this is done — if investors seek to maximize profits — investment resources will be allocated in an optimum manner. In the modified version, gross receipts and costs are to be adjusted for the discrepancy between market prices and opportunity costs and the adjusted surplus used as the guide by a public agency.

Dr. Ahumada's formulation in terms of a value-added input ratio, adjusting the value of inputs to an opportunity cost basis, bears a very close resemblance to the modified version of the profit maximization formula. Defining a project in terms of the resources used to produce goods for final sales, the numerator (value added 'behind and beyond') in the ratio is equivalent to gross receipts adjusted for indirect taxes and subsidies. The denominator, which is to include all the inputs, is equivalent to total costs. Dr. Ahumada does introduce certain modifications by his treatment of profits and depreciation, the rationale of which is not clear to me. For some reason, all profits are apparently treated as an input. One would expect some part of profits to be a real surplus. Investment decisions based on expected benefits and costs cannot count all profits as a cost, even though total profits are treated in national accounting as payments to a factor. Perhaps this is taken care of — rather awkwardly, it would appear — by applying the adjustment factor r, which may adjust profits as well as other factors to an opportunity cost basis. Also, it is not clear why depreciation is not included in the numerator. It seems strange that the numerator, which is a measure of benefits at market prices, should by definition be lower than the denominator, which is a measure of costs. If total depreciation is to be deducted from gross receipts at the point of final sale, it should not be included as a cost in the denominator.

While the treatment of profits and depreciation thus requires some clarification, I shall assume that no substantial difference exists between Dr. Ahumada's treatment and the conventional treatment of these items.

If this can be assumed, the formulation of the investment evaluation criterion suggested by Dr. Ahumada is not substantially different from the modified version of the profit maximization formula, with market prices adjusted to opportunity costs. What is new in this formulation is the suggestion that every project should be appraised in terms of all the productive enterprises which produce the final goods to which the particular project contributes. The numerator includes the value-added in the activities supplying the inputs of the project and the value-added in all the processes that the project must go through until it reaches the stage of final goods. The denominator includes total costs involved in producing the final goods.

II. Market Prices and Opportunity Costs

While this proposal to consolidate the accounts of the project with the accounts of enterprises supplying goods to and enterprises making purchases from the project, up to and including the production of final goods, may make good sense in some cases, its main rationale seems to be that market prices never reflect opportunity costs except at the point of final sale. The first problem is to determine the circumstances under which the prices at which goods are to be sold by a specific project do not properly reflect real economic benefits and the circumstances under which the monetary costs of inputs do not properly reflect real economic costs. Under what circumstances are market prices likely to be a poor indicator of opportunity costs and a poor measure of economic benefits? Under what circumstances and to what extent is the consolidation of enterprise accounts vertically likely to be necessary for proper project analysis?

There is the suggestion that whenever a steel mill is proposed in an under-developed country, consolidation of accounts is required in order properly to appraise the steel-making project as such. I have difficulty in accepting this as a general principle. However, where the contribution of a steel mill to the establishment of other specific projects or to the better utilization of existing capacity is clear and predictable, and where the market risks of establishing the steel mill without simultaneously establishing other projects are great, there is much to be said for considering a whole series of projects as part of a single investment. Under such circumstances consolidation of accounts is called for.

Dr. Ahumada seems to argue that complete consolidation is called for in the case of all intermediate goods. I am afraid that he has been misled by the particular cases — water for irrigation and transportation — which he cites. In the case of irrigation, consolidation of the irrigation project accounts with the accounts of the users of irrigation water is usually necessary because governments are loath to impose charges for irrigation water at a level commensurate with the value of the water to users. In the case of most irrigation projects, however, I question whether it is necessary to consolidate forward beyond the farm to the final consumer.

In the case of road transportation, the apparent need for at least partial consolidation arises from the fact that, except with toll roads, the market test is not applied. In the case of railway transportation, tariffs are usually regulated or set by government action and bear only a loose relationship to the benefit which users derive from the transport facility. The allocation of investment resources to these sectors must be based on different procedures, not because they are intermediate goods or services, but because the gross receipts of the enterprise do not properly reflect benefits for very specific reasons. In practice, the decision to invest in a highway or in a railroad does not ordinarily require — fortunately, it would seem — a forecast of the consolidated accounts of the transport entity and of all the users of transport. Judgments can frequently be based on estimates of the reduction in costs which will be secured by a new or improved transport facility coupled with traffic forecasts and an evaluation of the importance of transport costs for the present or potential economic activity in the area served. While I am personally favourably disposed to introducing as much quantitative analysis into such a procedure as is practicable, I doubt that a forecast of the consolidated accounts of transport and transport users is feasible in most cases and I suggest that consolidation to the point of final sale is in this case unnecessary as well as impracticable.

A judgment must be made as to which prices understate or overstate opportunity costs. Consolidation of accounts along the lines of the vertical integration principle suggested by Dr. Ahumada is a matter of convenience only, except when an investment decision can best be made jointly with respect to a group of separate projects.

Dr. Ahumada cites two cases where prices are unlikely properly to represent opportunity costs — labour costs in manufacturing where labour is withdrawn from agriculture, and foreign exchange.[1] While I am personally willing to accept the thesis that there are countries in which wage rates paid by manufacturing enterprises substantially overstate the marginal productivity of labour in alternative employments, making allowances for costs of labour transfer, I question whether this is an important discrepancy between market prices and opportunity costs in most Latin-American countries. Foreign exchange is another matter and I agree that in many Latin-American countries the costing of foreign exchange inputs and the pricing of products earning foreign exchange on the basis of market prices is likely to be misleading as a basis for investment decisions in view of the wide use of multiple exchange rates and administrative controls on the balance of payments.

With respect to the other factors, capital in particular, Dr. Ahumada seems to imply that the remuneration of capital is likely to reflect opportunity costs and that the adjustment of market prices in the case of such a

---

[1] As Dr. Ahumada notes, the adjustment for the foreign exchange factor modifies the numerator, as well as the denominator, in his formula.

scarce and mobile factor is unnecessary. In fact, the terms on which capital is made available to public enterprises in many countries frequently understates the opportunity cost of capital. In the choice of techniques — hydro versus thermal in the production of power, for example — cost comparisons based on conventional interest rates can be very misleading.

Thus, while I agree with Dr. Ahumada that evaluation of projects in terms of opportunity cost pricing is desirable, I question whether it requires as a general practice the vertical consolidation of the accounts of enterprises. Moreover, consolidation as such does not determine the extent to which market prices and opportunity costs differ, and many difficult judgments must be made in practice.

III. Investment Evaluation by Public Financial Agency

In the concluding section of his paper Dr. Ahumada seeks to differentiate the investment evaluation problem as viewed by a 'planning agency' and as viewed by a financial agency. I find it difficult to accept the distinction he draws. A planning agency is assumed to become acquainted at one time with all the projects it will deal with within a period, while with a financial agency, 'projects are presented to an agency one or two at a time, and as soon as they are presented an answer must be given'. As a consequence 'projects are evaluated by a planning agency against one another, while a financial intermediary must evaluate them against a standard or norm'. I wonder whether this is correct. Unless a planning agency can directly appraise all investment projects considered in the economy, comparison of one with another still involves implicit if not explicit judgments about the benefits to be achieved or sacrificed by placing more or less resources under control.

In practice, both planning agencies and government financial agencies frequently arrive at sub-optimum decisions. Planning agencies neither know so much, nor financing agencies so little, about the projects that can be influenced or financed during a specific period that reliance can be placed on a simple comparison of ratios in the first case and a comparison of a given project with a norm in the second case. Both types of agencies will presumably need to apply some test of minimum social acceptability and both will seek to choose projects exceeding the minimum and are not otherwise likely to go forward with the project.

The most difficult issue facing either a financial agency or a planning agency in this regard is not considered by Dr. Ahumada : the weight that should be attached in investment decisions to the financial losses that may be incurred by selecting those projects which have a high value to the economy but low or negative profitability. If market prices seldom reflect opportunity costs as Dr. Ahumada seems to imply, and if investment decisions are to be made in the government sector solely on the basis of opportunity cost calculations, leaving for the private sector most of the investments which are highly profitable, the direct and indirect burden on the government may be substantial. Under such circumstances the financial transfers which would have to be made via the government budget may create serious problems. As a result of large-scale transfers, resources available for investment might be curtailed, both in the private sector and the public sector.

For this reason considerations of financial profitability cannot be completely ignored even by a public agency interested in the optimum use of investment resources. While I agree that such an agency should evaluate major discrepancies between market prices and opportunity costs, it may be necessary to limit the use of this criterion should the financial burden become excessive.

MORE COMMENTS ON DR. AHUMADA'S PAPER

BY

J. R. BOUDEVILLE
France

FIRST, I have some minor criticisms to make on certain points. Second, I shall try to take Dr. Ahumada's brilliant study further on two essential points, namely, the indispensable need for a regional analysis of polarized growth and the importance of the time perspective in investment plans. Finally, since every criterion of choice is consciously or unconsciously founded upon a decision model, I shall discuss what micro- and macro-economic models may be useful either for government planning or for quasi-public investment by banks.

I. NEGATIVE CRITICISM

Dr. Ahumada criticizes the classical marginal theory on two points : first, in the short period, the classical theory of the market is inapplicable to an under-developed economy because of the imperfections of the internal market and the importance of external economies ; and, second, in the long period, growth cannot be planned with the assistance of an economic model built upon the assumption of the constant resources. I agree on both points but I have two minor observations on their treatment.

Dr. Ahumada has not made it clear enough that the key problem is really whether or not one should promote investments with high capital coefficients in countries where labour is cheap. Second, he has not pointed out sufficiently clearly that the marginal and the neo-Keynesian (Harrod-Domar) models have common limits. In particular, the models of Hicks, Harrod and Domar assume equal time perspectives for all decision units, homogeneous production sectors, and fixed production coefficients. Also, they do not take account of endogenous changes in available resources.

To resolve the problem of investment priorities, we need to show how optimal utilization of given resources at a given time is correlated with the endogenous increase of resources over time (cumulative development). Such an analysis must assume changeable production coefficients and heterogeneous sectors, time perspectives, and locations.

In Section II, Dr. Ahumada tells us : first, that the solution is to be found in a dynamic input-output model ; and, second, that the immediately applicable criterion of choice is a coefficient, total value-added/ total cost.

1. *The Input-Output Model*

To my mind, the input-output model must be understood in a very broad sense, that is, as linear programming (Frisch). Two points must be emphasized. First, sectoral differences in the supply and demand schedules for capital goods create not only bottlenecks but also price movements. There can be no growth without inflationary pressures, which in turn exercise an influence on growth. Second, the use of successive linear models makes it possible to introduce lags which are an important and easily manageable dynamic element. I am therefore inclined to regard apparently static models with rather more indulgence than Dr. Ahumada does and I have grave doubts about the radical procedure of inverting the matrices.

2. *The Coefficient*

The coefficient, total value-added/total cost of input, seems insufficient as an investment criterion and it raises both theoretical and practical difficulties.

On the theoretical side, it neglects the problem of aggregation and the influence of a highly aggregated sector on the results of the calculation. It neglects the problem of sectorally unequal gestation periods. It neglects the fact that within a given period value-added always has two components, final products and net investment goods. Hence, the problem of the choice of investment is also a problem of choice of planning period.

On the practical side, the coefficient r is rather intractable. The ratio, opportunity cost/cost at market price, does not fit the problem of under-employed labour. Also, in under-developed countries technical capital is often overvalued because of its scarcity. (All capital coefficients of Brazil are vitiated by this fact.) In other words, we must take account of monetary external economies. Moreover, the calculation of r should differ by regions. And, finally, the development of exchange rates over time is unpredictable.

In concluding these negative remarks, I wish to stress that geographical distribution is as important as functional distribution and that if one aggregates too much in order to make the analysis simpler, it ends by being wrong. In these circumstances we should not hesitate to use such modern tools of analysis as have been developed by Perroux and Byé in France and by Frisch in Norway.

II. Positive Criticism

In practice the problem of investment priorities comes down to two essential questions. First, should preference be given to investments with low capital coefficients ? Second, should one remove the bottle-necks from existing activities or should one create new industrial systems ? The answer is to be found in two types of modern analysis, regional analysis of polarized growth, and the use of linear decision programmes on the macro- and micro-economic level.

1. *Regional Polarized Analysis and Predominance of External Economies*

Growth is localized. It starts at growth points or poles of varying intensity and spreads through different channels leading to varying end effects for the whole economy (Perroux). In the analysis of growth we distinguish between impulse activities and agglomeration coefficients (external economies). Impulse activities and development poles are not created arbitrarily, but their emergence can be facilitated or precipitated by public investment or subsidies to private investment. Experience shows that the way to develop an area is not to disperse subsidies over the most distressed regions, but to single out likely development poles and to encourage their growth. The growth of France within Europe and the growth of some of the federal states within Brazil are two topical examples.

Taking Brazil as an example, let us describe it synthetically. First, the emergence of internal development poles means the creation of a market economy. With capital diluted in artisan industries having a high labour coefficient and a low capital coefficient, there can be no impulse in the absence of a market economy. The emergence of growth poles also implies the possibility of escaping from external economic fluctuations, the problem with coffee.

Second, the emergence of development poles presupposes the creation of an infra-structure. From this point of view, the choice of technique for road-building must be dictated not by its capital coefficient but by its speed. Thus, the road from Rio de Janeiro to Belo Horizonte will promote very rapid economic development within a five-year period, which is as far as anyone can plan at present.

Such sacrifices of present benefits for the sake of a relatively near future can be brought about only by public intervention. The mechanism of the rate of interest, which translates entrepreneurial expectations, operates in a very imperfect manner in under-developed countries or may even act as an effective brake. When the short-term rate of interest is 3 per cent. per month, no one can take the long view. The government must step in so as to allow a longer range choice. In 1957 public invest-ment in Brazil is to be 72 thousand million cruzeiros and, according to Professor Gudin, this will probably account for some 50 per cent. of total investment. Moreover, public investment is useful in that it replaces sterile real estate speculation and exploits such real estate speculation as cannot be eliminated by making it serve the internal development of the country.[1]

The emergence of development poles also presupposes the creation of dynamic mental attitudes which implies large-scale investment in basic education. In this connection it is important to guard against the danger of dilution under heavy demographic pressure. Schooling and technical training need to be concentrated at strategic growth poles where mental attitudes conditioned by an industrial environment can become the springs of higher poles (Anisto Teixeira).

The exploitation of resources is a function of local polarization co-efficients. Every region has its own coefficients and grows at its own rate. Every impulse industry has its own agglomeration coefficients. Every creation of development poles presupposes and causes associated investments which in turn set off others — the big push.

Planning involves a comparison of the spatial interrelation coefficients, a comparison of the coefficients over time, and modification according to the location, regional dimensions, and extent of the infra-structure. Thus, the results of the Rio de Janeiro–Belo Horizonte road can be assessed on the basis of the results of the Rio de Janeiro–São Paulo road.

It should be noted that any infra-structure means starting the big push from a high level and that, in the beginning at least, it implies the creation of unutilized productive and transport capacity. The concrete problem is this : should one plan the infra-structure with a view to creating new centres with high capital coefficients or should one develop existing development centres with lower capital coefficients? If we want a rational solution, we must use operational growth models.

2. *Operational Growth Models*

In the case we are discussing, we have two double problems : one with respect to aims and the other with respect to means. As regards aims, we have to formulate a short-term objective which is to maximize a given region's production with given capital resources and a long-term objective which is to maximize the resources available at the end of the planning period, in this case, five years. As regards means, we must consider the interdependence of private and public plans as well as the need to render them mutually compatible. For the sake of simplicity, we shall mainly consider the problem of means in discussing overall planning and micro-economic plans.

At the overall planning level, one must try to arrive at the most precise evaluation possible both in regional and in national terms. At the micro-economic level, one must try to foresee how individual entrepreneurs will react and how these reactions fit in with the overall objectives. The policy of the investment finance agency can then be determined accordingly.

(a) *National Planning.* One must co-ordinate the long period and the

[1] Brasilio-Cabo Frio, *Correiro de Manhã*, Brazilian Handbook of Information (Rio de Janeiro, New York, June 30, 1957).

short period and, within the latter, one must co-ordinate price effects and income effects in the broad sense. The combined use of linear programming and polarized analysis enables us to sketch out a solution.

In regard to current activity, we must establish the polarization coefficients which link all the flows. This is a problem of the long period. The linked production vectors are lagged in relation to each other. The coefficients of technical and psychological interdependence proper to each region must also be determined. By taking successive data we can take account of varying production cycles. Finally, the coefficients of regionalization must be established for the different supplies. These will vary over time.

We can then calculate the difference between existing productive capacity and the necessary supplies for each period under consideration. Price increases may result from the varying price elasticities of demand. Wage and cost increases may be induced by the existing lags between the wage level and the cost-of-living vector.

With regard to investment, we must establish the associated investment vectors corresponding on the one hand to the polarization coefficient of current activity and on the other to certain relationships proper to basic investment (residential building).[1] We must also establish the table of capital coefficients so as to be able to calculate induced investment as distinct from associated investment. Successive data make it possible to take account of varying lags. The upper and lower limits deriving from the size of firms furnish additional conditions.

With respect to regionalization, we must establish the boundaries of existing polarized regions according to the criterion of interdependence. By regional comparison within one given period we must look for the location of industries or poles which give rise to most associated activities and which are most effective in calling forth and multiplying other activities throughout the whole economy. Attention must be paid to the danger of spontaneous agglomerations around a single centre stretching out its tentacles, like Paris in France or São Paulo-Santos in Brazil. There are better methods of integrating a national economy.

Three points must be made. First, any growth model can have its own behaviour over time, that is, different lines of evolution depending on the nature of the parameters. In our model there are four types of parameters : the size of the region (limit and coefficient of polarization) ; the technical parameter ; the psychological parameter of the region ; and the region's interconnections with other regions (coefficient of regionalization). Differences in these parameters explain why various economic regions have developed in different ways. Action on these parameters is determinant action which can be expressed in quantitative terms. It must be shown how the proposed investments modify the existing parameters.

---

[1] J. M. Mattial, 'Residential Service Construction', *Review of Economics and Statistics*, November 1956.

Second, the concept of production which is described by the co-efficients of polarization and which is capable of changing the economic size of the region, must be linked to the concept of the big push. This means that apart from national and regional accounting we also need accounting in terms of large functional groups and particularly an analysis of the kind of large international firms which M. Byé has investigated. Thus we pass from the global plan to the micro-economic plan.

(b) *Connection between the Location of Firms, their Investment Policy, and National Planning.* The connection is institutional.

Let us consider the point of view of the firm. The firm must establish a linear programme to determine its own location. This throws into relief the difference between the micro- and the macro-economic model. The theory of games offers a tool for studying the behaviour of customers according to the nature of the market and the industry, the size of the enterprise, and the time horizon. The choice of the planning period is the most significant element in the strategy of large extractive firms such as those in mining or in oil. With given and known deposits, a short plan means large annual production and high prices. The conflict between two types of plan is exemplified by the differences between the Iraq Petroleum Company (long plan) and the Compagnie Française des Pétroles (short plan).

There is a difference of aims between different types of companies. A private company is out to maximize profit over a relatively long period. A government company seeks to maximize production over a relatively short time (foreign exchange earnings). There is also a difference of financial resources between different companies and plans are longer the lower the rate of interest. Foreign companies have the benefit of the capital markets in their country of origin. Finally, there are differences of location. Simultaneous location in more than one place tends to lengthen plans and gives rise to the danger of domination. The foreign company imposes its time horizon on associated and other national companies.

III. CONCLUSION

In conclusion, I agree with Dr. Ahumada on the need to stress economic interdependence. But I want to draw attention more particularly to its regional character and to the connections between public and private plans.

A government agency like the French Commissariat au Plan can take an overall view. Its task is not only to draw up a general development plan but, before all else, to undertake studies of regional growth. These involve : a list of strategic regional growth poles (coefficients of polarization, impulse industry) ; the calculation of the impact of the creation of a transport infra-structure on these coefficients ; and regional input-output tables. By means of these the government can determine investment priorities by which to achieve the aims it has set itself.

The task of subsidizing private enterprise falls to federal and regional investment banks, which must adopt a micro-economic view and co-ordinate it with the macro-economic view of the government planning agency. The investment bank must examine projects from the point of view of private industry (profit maximization). It must co-ordinate the location and the size and duration of investment with the government directives. It must finance and subsidize not only projects which are not viable from the private point of view (little or no profit) but also projects which, while already yielding a profit, are worth speeding up because they have a high polarization coefficient.

Growth and the regulation of growth require the creation of strong points and the mapping out of lines of force. A policy of planned growth must guard against the encroaching monopoly of octopus cities, but should certainly not rest content with just filling the vacuum of depressed areas. The growth of intermediate local poles and of regional economic centres which display vitality, and whose development will pull the region along, must be promoted. A successful development policy needs a list of potential assets rather than a catalogue of what is lacking.

DISCUSSION OF DR. AHUMADA'S PAPER

I. GENERAL

IN Dr. Ahumada's absence, the main points of his paper were summarized briefly by Dr. Alter and Professor Leibenstein. The discussion turned on the following subjects : (1) opportunity cost versus market prices ; (2) the broadening of traditional criteria ; and (3) alternative criteria.

Professor Leibenstein stated that Dr. Ahumada's basic principle was the substitution of opportunity cost for market prices. This seemed to imply a rejection of the profit maximization principle as an investment criterion. Dr. Ahumada's view of the conditions under which a discrepancy between opportunity cost and market prices could arise appeared to be quite broad. It was not limited to monopolistic situations or cases of restricted movement of productive factors. Any situation that was not an equilibrium situation Dr. Ahumada seemed to regard as implying such a discrepancy; since the introduction of new resources necessarily introduced a degree of disequilibrium, the discrepancy tended to become rather general.

Dr. Ahumada's choice of a maximum rate of *per capita* income growth as his basic goal seemed to involve a conflict with free consumer choice. It was possible, of course, that consumers would so allocate their resources as to realize the maximum rate of growth. But there was no necessity and, in fact, little probability that this would happen. What then became of the principle of consumer choice in Dr. Ahumada's scheme ?

Professor Brahmananda seemed in accord with Dr. Ahumada's desire to reformulate the criterion for investment selection but sceptical about his particular proposal. In practice, all criteria encountered the familiar difficulty of quantification and measurement.

Dr. Alter expressed a similar view. Dr. Ahumada proposed to broaden the concept of 'project' by including all inputs and outputs directly or indirectly associated with a particular project, up to the point of final sale. In most cases this was neither necessary nor justifiable. The analytical importance of Dr. Ahumada's proposed criterion, as well as its practical applicability, depended in good part on how pervasive he believed the difference between opportunity cost and market prices to be. Dr. Ahumada appeared to believe that the two coincided but rarely. Dr. Ahumada seemed to derive his analytical scheme from reference to certain examples which, though they fitted the scheme, did not represent very typical cases. Finally, he agreed with Professor Leibenstein that Dr. Ahumada, despite his rejection of the profit maximization principle, had not really got away from it. He had simply substituted opportunity costs for market prices in the same old framework.

Dr. Adler argued in favour of the traditional profit maximization principle but wanted to see it applied broadly. Dr. Ahumada, he said, seemed to argue as if profit maximization meant simply to maximize the return on capital. Actually, profit maximization was, of course, a principle of optimum allocation and return to all resources. The profit margin remained a useful criterion even when discrepancies between market prices and opportunity costs existed. Admittedly, these discrepancies often were considerable and if necessary should be taken into account, but they did not always run in the same direction. In any particular comparison of projects these discrepancies might very well cancel each other out to some extent.

II. Broadening of Traditional Criteria

Profit maximization, *Dr. Adler* continued, had the further advantage, as a criterion, of helping to generate savings. In so far as it differed from other criteria, therefore, it would make an added contribution to growth in the form of extra capital formation.

Professor Wallich questioned the possibility of finding a single investment criterion. Profit maximization in the literal sense was not the sole motivation of the entrepreneur. Its extension to the national level made it even more unsatisfactory as a criterion. In practice, planning decisions involved risk appraisals, political issues, and other non-economic factors that were quite likely to outweigh the purely economic appraisal.

Dr. Alter disagreed by saying that one had to separate these elements of judgment. The economist very often was asked to make an appraisal on purely economic grounds. Naturally his judgment was subject to modification at a political level.

Professor Hirschman said that the traditional criteria of allocation, while important, were quite often confronted with other criteria. The growth inducing effects of a particular project might be considerable even though its direct efficiency might be low.

Dr. Alter observed that if considerations of this sort led the government to take on a lot of initially uneconomic projects, the charge on the budget would become a serious problem.

Professor Byé commented upon the theory of poles of growth as an alternative investment criterion. The creation of centres of growth was a dynamic principle, as opposed to the static principle of resource allocation. An important aspect of it was the creation of external economies. Consideration of the time horizon of different projects was a second major principle. He would like to see these principles applied to Dr. Ahumada's criterion. The concrete questions that had to be answered in the case of such investment were : (1) should projects with low capital intensity get priority ? (2) should priority be given to the elimination of bottlenecks ?

Chapter 14

AGRICULTURAL VERSUS INDUSTRIAL DEVELOPMENT

BY

P. R. BRAHMANANDA

University of Bombay

I. SUMMARY

THE object of this paper is to examine the nature of the factors affecting the relative priority of agricultural investment in a programme of economic development. The analysis deals with over-populated under-developed countries. The demand for and supply of agricultural commodities is examined from the point of view of the pressures created during a programme of increased investment outlay. Section II broadly distinguishes agricultural investment from investment in other fields and poses the crucial problem of the choice of the investment pattern. Section III discusses the various points of view regarding the rôle of agricultural investment. Section IV analyses the way in which interdependence between agriculture and the rest of the economy will be affected during periods of increased investment. Section V examines the conditions determining the supply responses in agriculture to an increased aggregate demand for agricultural products. Section VI makes out a case for accelerated agricultural investment with a view to maximizing the rate of transformation of unproductive labour into productive labour. Section VII examines the effects on the economy of varying rates of agricultural development. Section VIII emphasizes the need for concentrating upon agricultural investment as the initial factor in economic development. Section IX examines the implications of rapid capital formation for the economy in general and for the agricultural sector in particular. Section X points out the reasons why agricultural investment may tend to be secularly neglected. The Appendix to the paper draws attention to certain points of view current in India which influenced the First and the Second Five Year Plans.

399

II. Need for Increased Agricultural Investment

For the purpose of this paper, agriculture is considered to be that particular activity which is directly dependent upon the soil. Agricultural products are those that are land-oriented. Agricultural investment may be of various types. First, some investments introduce a certain degree of regularity into the level of production. Protective irrigation works belong in this category. These works are of little use during periods of normal rainfall. They fill up possible troughs in the course of agricultural production. Second, some investments expand the volume of agricultural production during all types of climatic conditions. Most irrigation works, tanks, wells, and land reclamation projects are to be included in this category. Within this category, we have to distinguish between those investments which raise the productivity of the land now under cultivation and those which bring new land under cultivation. Third, there are investments in industries producing fertilizers and manures. Such investments lead to a rise in the level of productivity, but the extent of their efficacy depends upon the degree of certainty regarding the supply of water. Fourth, there are investments in industries producing tools, machinery, and other equipment needed on farms. Some of these may be directly labour-saving in character while some may bring about a general reduction in costs. Improvements in the quality of livestock and increases in the supply of livestock may also be included in this category. Fifth, some investments, such as the provision of roads, transport and communication facilities, marketing services, and commercial education, seek to create external economies. Lastly, there are investments which seek to improve the level of the technical and general education of the farming classes and which lead to new researches on farming methods and techniques, such as the discovery of new seeds. Investments which improve the quality of the human personnel engaged in agricultural operations are as important as investments in concrete capital stock. Thus, the term agricultural investment is very broad and includes all those activities which have a direct bearing upon production and productivity in agriculture. The manufacture of those materials, tools, and equipment, which are required for large-scale irrigation works and flood control measures, is ancillary to agriculture. These activities seek ultimately to raise agricultural productivity and to augment the stock of land.

There may be considerable disguised unemployment in the agricultural sector in an under-developed economy. This may be because of the accumulation of arrears of investment in relation to the population growth over the long period. In particular, agricultural investment may not have proceeded at the same rate as population growth. Hence, short-period agricultural production may fall short of the supply of agricultural commodities necessary to meet the demand for agricultural products which would arise under full employment. Thus, equilibrium with disguised unemployment is stable. Accumulation of further population pressure will only lead to a widening of the gap between the actual supply of wage-goods and the demand for wage-goods that would arise under conditions of full employment. The main pressure of a raised scale of investment will be upon agricultural commodities and will lead to a rise in the price of food and other products. Furthermore, under conditions of full employment, the demand for precautionary hoarding of food and other products may also widen the wage-goods gap. Technically, the wage-goods gap can be ultimately reduced to a gap between the demand for and supply of food, including the demand for hoarding. Thus the programme of raised investment outlay may tend to be choked either by an increased direct demand for food by the newly employed workers and by the peasants left on the farms, or by an indirect demand for foodstuffs because the demand for non-food commodities or for precious metals is thwarted and diverted into a demand for food and other articles.

If political or other forms of pressures are exerted on the farmers and the workers in the process of raising the investment outlay, the marketable surplus may be reduced in the short period, and in the long period the level of production itself may be curtailed, leading to a magnified impact upon the marketable surplus.

The typical impact in an under-developed economy may, however, be slightly different from that described above. It may be that there is considerable surplus labour on the farms which will become available for alternative employment, provided the techniques of production are altered with a bias in favour of labour-saving methods. Here, some expansion of the production of the capital equipment needed to displace labour is a pre-condition to a raised scale of investment activity. If standards of living are low, such a transfer of labour will have to contend with difficulties similar to those in the case just examined. Whereas labour-saving methods of production may release labour, they may not automatically release the required quantities of food and other agricultural commodities. Thus, even under these conditions, some expansion of agricultural output is necessary for the success of a programme of increased investment. The problem of agricultural surpluses is one of additional investment and not merely one of procurement under conditions of constant or slightly rising production. Even in countries where there is no obvious pressure of disguised unemployment on account of a dis-equilibrium between the rates of growth of population and invest-ment, programmes of increased investment may tend to get bogged down on account of the wage-goods gap.

III. ATTITUDES TO THE PRIORITY OF AGRICULTURAL INVESTMENT

It is possible to adopt three attitudes regarding agricultural invest-ment during rapid economic development. First, it may be decided that agricultural investment should get zero or low priority during the initial stages of development. The idea of the planning authori-ties here will be to obtain the services of the labour power concealed in disguised unemployment with the least amount of economic cost. As large as possible a quantity of the foodstuffs now consumed by the workers now in disguised unemployment will have to be trans-ferred to the industrial sector together with workers. The extreme case here is one where the rise in the marketable surplus of agri-cultural products is proportionate to the volume of labour transferred. Normally, it is difficult to obtain this result. First, the productive workers left on the farm must be prevented from consuming the grains previously consumed by the disguised unemployed. Secondly, the level of production on the farms must not suffer despite the psychological and physical repercussions of the transfer of food supplies.

In actual practice substantial differences exist between the average consumption standards of productive farmers and the consumption standards of those in disguised unemployment. Hence, some rise in real wage rates is necessary in order to attract the disguised un-employed to the new industrial projects. The process of accelerated economic development will be characterized by differences in living standards between the peasants, the newly transferred industrial workers, and those workers currently employed.

This transfer will involve considerable costs. First, there is the additional cost for the transport and storage of the additional grain supply which may be released as a result of the transfer. Then there is the cost of establishing an administrative set-up to carry out the policy. Second, the different additional fiscal, monetary, and other such measures, introduced with a view to preventing the farmers from raising their consumption, will necessitate additional administrative and other costs. Third, the farmers may be prevented from raising their consumption of food grains, but they may have to be permitted some rise in the consumption of industrial commodities. The cost of production of these commodities will be an additional item of cost in the transfer programme. The above transfer programme may be conducted within the market mechanism using price and fiscal instruments, but it may be that the planners will want to stretch the area and intensity of control, with the result that measures of procurement, rationing, grain levies, and so forth may have to be introduced. The administrative burden will be increased. The cost of the additional production of the agricultural and industrial commodities necessary for the success of the intensified programme has to be reckoned as an important item in the transfer programme.

There may also be some structural changes. For example, the number of productive farmers on the land may be reduced through investment in various types of labour-saving machinery. The objective of such a programme will be to release both labour-power and marketable surplus. In some cases, changes in the form of organization such as the introduction of co-operatives, and ultimately collective farms, may take place.

In the model outlined above, the transfer programme is conducted within the orbit of stagnant agricultural production. The next step is to consider the case where agricultural production is allowed to rise slowly. The problems arising in this case will not be qualitatively similar to those so far discussed.

Second, as against the extreme view that agriculture should get zero priority in the investment programme, a programme of raised investment outlay may be initiated which will permit an expansion in agricultural production just sufficient to meet the increased pressure on demand. Here we must assume that the economic mechanism possesses the requisite co-ordinating arrangements and links, so that an increased demand can be met in the long run by increased supplies. Such an approach pins its faith upon either the acceleration principle or upon the profit-investment relationship. In a sense, this approach characterizes the planning in mixed economies where the agricultural sector operates under an atmosphere of relative freedom. Historically, some such implicit assumption has characterized the growth process in some of the developed countries.

The third approach would be to accord top priority in development programmes to agricultural investment and to depend upon rising trends in agricultural output to provide the main lever in the development process, particularly in the programme of transformation of unproductive labour into productive labour.

Until recently, a strong belief prevalent in the under-developed countries was that whatever the political implications of the Soviet planning programme, the pattern of priorities incorporated therein had a fundamental economic significance. In these countries, there-fore, there was a great emphasis upon priority for capital goods industries. Keen observers, however, perceived that the neglect of agriculture involved the Soviet Union in considerable economic strains, which had to be overcome through radical extra-economic measures. Recently, therefore, a change in perspective has taken place. This is partly due to the realization that the Soviet Union itself is conscious that more attention needs to be given to agriculture and partly to the experience of Poland, Hungary, and the other continental countries. The high priority being accorded to agri-culture in China has also strengthened this realization. In other words, the present belief is that the neglect of agriculture may involve the economy in serious strains, which might actually halt the course of development. Emphasis now is upon a balance between the two sectors. Increase in agricultural production is looked upon as the *sine qua non* of the success of a development programme. For example, a shift in emphasis is obvious in the case of India.[1]

IV. Effect of Increased Investment on Prices of Agricultural Commodities

Among the factors which determine the extent to which the agricultural sector depends upon the non-agricultural sector are : first, the farmers' need for money to make cash payments to the labourers ; second, money requirements for the payment of taxes ; third, the extent to which the maintenance of conventional living standards requires the consumption of non-agricultural commodities ; fourth, the extent to which the maintenance of production levels and standards requires supplies of tools, plants, and so forth from the non-agricultural sector ; fifth, the commitments of the farmers in regard to debt redemption and interest payments ; and, sixth, money requirements for emergencies and contingencies, including the need for money to purchase gold and ornaments, as well as for occasional conspicuous social functions. The ratio of sales to farm production is dependent upon the intensity of the pressure exerted through these factors. Under certain conditions, depending upon the urgency of these commitments, the farmers might even reduce their internal

[1] See Appendix.

consumption in order to obtain command over a given amount of monetary receipts.

In most under-developed countries, payments in kind to workers are quite common. These payments usually consist of both the agricultural and industrial commodities, mostly the former. With the spread of the market economy and of social legislation regarding wages, payment in kind is declining in importance, although normally some payment is still made in kind. A prolonged fall in the value of money might, however, bring about an absolute reduction in the current extent of the market as well as a reduction in its rate of growth. In the short period, it is difficult to change the mode of payment. But if inflationary pressures are strong enough in the long period, cash payments may tend to decline in relative importance. This would mean that a part of the marketable surplus flowing to the industrial sector would cease to be available for exchange. On the other hand, other conditions equal, if the purchasing power of money remains constant, and is expected to remain so, there will be an increasing tendency towards extension of money payments and the extent of the agricultural sector's dependence upon the rest of the economy in market terms will tend to rise.

The demand for money, and hence the pressure to sell, will also depend upon the farmers' tax commitments. In the short period a rise in such commitments will tend to have a direct effect upon the ratio of sales to farm production. Sometimes the demand for other commodities may be reduced if tax commitments are heavy.

In the short period, however, the greater the transfer of labour from the farms, the larger the quantity of agricultural output that will be potentially available in exchange for other commodities. In this sense, the proportion of marketable agricultural surplus to total agricultural production will be a function of the volume of non-agricultural employment. Other conditions given, if the transfer of labour goes on increasing, the ratio of surplus available for the market to the potential surplus will go on rising. This is one of the most crucial fundamental propositions in the theory of short-period employment in an under-developed economy beset with population pressure. From Engels' Law, we can say that there are limits on the extent to which the farming sector can absorb an increase in the available surplus through internal consumption. Therefore, as the transfer of labour goes on increasing, and the quantity that is potentially releasable goes on increasing, the capacity of the farming population for additional consumption will go on diminishing, and the proportion actually marketed will go on rising.

Thus, the issue boils down to whether the non-agricultural sector can provide the requisite alternative consumer goods, the capital goods needed on the farms and/or the gold or ornaments, to exchange for the agricultural commodities which will become potentially available as a result of the transfer of labour.

Let us examine the possible reactions on the part of the farmers on the assumption that the increased investment outlay is financed by credit expansion. We shall assume that the initial transfer of labour will not contribute to an immediate additional production of commodity surpluses. The economy has to seek to procure the increments of agricultural surplus which result from the transfer of labour. As a result the farmers' money balances go up.

First, part of the money balances may be utilized for debt redemption and interest payments. This item will constitute a sort of transfer payment. Thus, if the agencies dealing in money and credit are integrated into the general monetary and credit mechanism, the working of the system is not disturbed. If such integration does not exist, it will be difficult to control and direct the increases in money savings to socially desirable channels.

Second, part of the increased money balances may be utilized for purchases of industrial consumption goods. Here, there are two possibilities. If we assume that there is excess capacity in the particular industries to which the additional demand is directed, the level of employment in the industrial sector will rise, though in the short period the prices of industrial commodities may also rise to some extent, depending upon cost conditions. Profits will also tend to rise. The question then is how these profits will tend to be utilized. Other conditions equal, if the required additional agricultural commodity surpluses needed to maintain the increased employment in industrial sectors are not forthcoming, there will tend to be an inflationary pressure. If so, the price level of agricultural products will rise and this may tend to have a depressing influence upon the tempo of the investment programme.

An important conclusion from the foregoing is that a programme for transferring labour will tend to lead to a magnified demand for agricultural commodity surpluses, unless the initial conditions are such that the required expansion in industrial commodities can be brought about without additional employment of labour, and/or programmes of short-period expansion in agricultural production are undertaken simultaneously. The final position will depend upon the quantitative significance of the proportions involved.

In the above, we have assumed that there was surplus capacity in industry. The more realistic assumption may be that, initially, the additional demand of the agricultural sector for industrial consumption goods will be met through depletion of stocks. Gradually, this will lead to higher prices of industrial commodities. A rise in demand for industrial products reflected through a rise in prices of industrial commodities and/or through depletion of stocks will lead to additional demand for credit for expansion of industrial investment. Such expansion will lead to an increased demand for agricultural commodity surpluses. It should be noted here that inflationary pressures will tend to emerge. Hence, a programme of short-period expansion of agricultural production and productivity must be undertaken at the same time that any programme of transfer of labour is undertaken.

Third, suppose the additional money balances result in a rise in internal consumption on the farms. This may occur either directly or because prices of industrial commodities rise and the farmers prefer a higher consumption of their own products to relatively costly industrial goods. The net effect initially will be a reduction in the marketable surplus. Here again an expansion in agricultural production is a necessary concomitant of an investment programme.

Fourth, we may now examine the conditions under which the farmers' reaction will increase the demand for gold, jewellery, and so forth whenever money balances are increased. These demands are obviously for precautionary liquidity purposes. In an open economy this will lead to an increased inflow of gold and will interfere with any programme for the import of the capital goods which are necessary if the investment programme is to be maintained. The net effect will be as if only part of the potentially marketable agricultural surplus resulting from the transfer of labour were available for internal diversion to the investment workers.

Suppose we visualize a closed economy. With given supplies of gold or precious metals, there will be a tendency for a rise in the price of gold. This in turn will lead to an increase in the hoarding of commodities if the purchasing power of money is expected to fall, a valid assumption if the scale of the investment programme is being raised. The net effect will be a reduction in the marginal ratio of the marketed surplus to the potentially available surplus.

In the analysis above, we have taken into consideration a case where a certain potentially marketable surplus emerges as a result of the transfer of labour. This analysis will be valid even if aggregate agricultural production alters or if the conditions determining the farmers' behaviour with given production undergoes a change.

A firm conclusion from all the above is that a programme of increased investment outlay, whatever the direction in which it occurs, tends to raise agricultural commodities, prices, particularly food prices. There is no reason to believe that a rise in food prices will lead to an increase in investment and thus to an ultimate rise in the level of production.

V. Supply Reaction of Agriculture to Increased Demand

Analysis of the supply reaction of agriculture in the face of increased demand may be made either in the perspective of the acceleration principle or of the profit-investment relationship. Many analytical models of the trade cycle assume a steadily growing economy. Autonomous investment which grows at a constant rate lifts the economy out of the slump and raises the level of income via the multiplier process. The rate of increase of income in turn leads to induced investment via the acceleration principle. The actual mechanics of the acceleration principle are a matter that requires greater clarification. Increased demand with a given amount of excess capacity leads to higher utilization of the capital stock. The rate of increase in income leads to an increase in the demand for new capital equipment. Initially this may lead to higher prices of capital goods, but gradually the supply of equipment expands and, in the new equilibrium, capacity has expanded. The actual attainment of a new equilibrium is disturbed because the very process of increased production of capital equipment leads to a further increase in income via the multiplier process and an additional demand for capital equipment and so on. The essential link in the acceleration principle is that between demand and supply. It is only when the economy attains a state of full employment that this relationship is disturbed because of inelasticity in the supply of labour and/or of raw materials, or because of the obstacles in the forms of various bottlenecks and frictions.

The difficulty in applying the acceleration principle in the case of the relation between the demand for and supply of agricultural commodities is that none of the pre-conditions which are required to be satisfied in order that the acceleration principle may function smoothly are fulfilled here. In trade cycle theory the acceleration principle is criticized on the ground that the supply of finance is not elastic, that it assumes only one particular form of expectations, that it abstracts from the practical problems of location, organization, and mobility, that it neglects the significance of the psychological and human factors determining the permissible extent of co-ordination, that it adopts a too mechanistic picture of the investment process, relegating to insignificance the evolutionary aspects thereof, and that it does not emphasize sufficiently the significance of profits in the investment process. The acceleration principle has also been criticized on the grounds of a lack of statistical corroboration. It has also been pointed out that, in a sense, this principle emphasizes only the familiar Marshallian supply and demand relationship within the orbit of different time periods, but that it assumes too much technical rigidity in such a process.

In the case of agricultural investment, particularly in an underdeveloped economy, most of these difficulties operate with greater intensity. Additional agricultural investment may encounter all types of new obstacles. The credit available to the agricultural sector supplies only a small percentage of its needs. The organized money and credit markets contribute little to the needs of the agricultural sector. The terms and conditions under which credit is available are too stringent to enable a quick or an adequate response from the agriculturists. Even the available supply of credit goes largely to the relatively wealthy farmers, and expansion by other groups of agriculturalists is difficult. The farmers have to face the problem of possible low levels of money incomes if production expands too much, so that surplus production may be visualized as a burden rather than a boon. The past experience of bumper harvests may not necessarily be a happy one.

It is also incorrect to assume that the farming classes possess the requisite degree of general commercial knowledge as well as the organizational capacity to take advantage of rising prices and to expand investment. There are a number of difficulties in the way of mobility. The organization on the farms may not easily lend itself to quick reorganization with a view to obtaining the maximum rate and extent of response. Then there are the problems concerning the potential availability of land. Even land that is available may be far beyond the reach of the farmers as individuals or in groups. Another troublesome factor is that high prices might mean high incomes, and high incomes may be more often than not reflected in higher consumption standards, leaving only meagre resources for investment. Thus, the acceleration principle does not provide even a rough guide for the analysis of the farmers' reactions to rising agricultural prices.

These remarks also hold true in respect of the profit-investment relationship. Let us assume that there is near perfect mobility of factors of production between agriculture and the rest of the economy. A programme of increased investment financed by credit expansion is undertaken. The fields directly affected by the outlay belong to the non-agricultural sector. Employment initially must rise. Some transfer of labour or conditions favourable to such a transfer becomes possible. The primary impact of the higher scale of expenditure is upon food and other land-oriented products. The prices of agricultural products will rise. Other conditions being equal, the level of profits or of quasi-rents in agriculture will go up. Hence, investment in agriculture is stimulated. If this investment is to take place, a corresponding supply of co-operative factors must become available at the appropriate time. There will also be a demand for some additional credit expansion. If additional output is not forthcoming and prices start rising, it will become necessary to curtail the rate of investment. Alternatively, it may be that the newly started investment activities may be kept going though some other investments may suffer.

Is it, however, possible to argue that agricultural production will expand in the long run under the stimulus of increased demand, thus reducing profits to a normal level in the long period ?

Several possibilities have to be considered. First, despite increased profits, there may not be an adequate flow of entrepreneurial and managerial talent even in the long run. This may be because of organizational and social immobilities. Second, a rise in the level of income of the agricultural classes may not lead to increased investment. This may be because of an inelasticity of demand for income in terms of effort. The supply curve of agricultural products may be backward-sloping. Third, the new types of agricultural investment needed may be indivisible in character so that the equilibrium will be of a constrained type. It may not be possible for farmers, individually or in groups, to undertake the expansion scheme. External assistance may be necessary, or vast co-ordination arrangements may be needed. The aggregate limits of agricultural expansion are set by the past and current trends in regard to gigantic investments in irrigation, land reclamation, flood control, fertilizer supply, and so forth. There is also the question of inappropriable external economies and of the divergence between private and social returns. Fourth, increased money income in the form of windfall profits may lead to an increased demand for gold and thus offset the effect of increased investment. Thus, in a sense, the normal assumption that a rise in price level will lead to increased investment may not hold true. The time lag required may be longer. The profit mechanism simply may not function here. For all these reasons, agricultural investment may not expand and the forces making for industrial expansion may spend themselves in inflation or may lead to serious balance of payments difficulties.

Hence, under autonomous conditions, either a progamme of

increased investment will tend to be self-defeating, or only a part of the contemplated investment outlay will prove to be possible, if corresponding programmes for increasing agricultural production are not undertaken. If food prices are permitted to rise with no countervailing measures to change the trends in the long period, the effect will be a reduction in the ratio of the surplus.

Hence, it is clear that a part of the investment programme must be devoted to increasing agricultural production and/or productivity. It is not enough to assume that autonomous forces will somehow look after the needs of increased agricultural production. In an international economy, there will be heavy pressure for imports of food grains and other consumption goods, thus obstructing the process of augmented investment.

It is now just a short step to the general picture of a growth process in which the increased agricultural activity and production resulting from an appropriate investment pattern provides the base on which increased investment can be maintained. Here, obviously, the primary emphasis of the investment programme in the earlier stages will be upon improvements in agricultural productivity. The economy's scale of investment is raised under conditions in which the short-period increase in the demand for food can be met through the exploitation of short-period productivity opportunities available on the land. In other words, the base on which agricultural production can expand must itself expand so that a programme of increased investment, whether in industry or in agriculture, is conducted under conditions in which the orbit of agricultural expansion is widening.

VI. The Case for Accelerated Agricultural Investment

First, from the theoretical point of view, under conditions of disguised unemployment, it is necessary that the historical neglect of agriculture relative to industry must be corrected by large-scale countervailing investment in agriculture. The programme of agricultural investment thus tends to make good the accumulated arrears in the growth of agricultural production. This programme has a direct bearing upon the rate of growth of employment. As will be noted, there will be corresponding effects upon the organizational efficiency on the farms. Second, a bias towards agricultural investment frees the economy from the strains and stresses that will be inevitable if the problem of marketable surplus is viewed solely as an organizational problem. In this respect, it permits the growth process to be worked out in an atmosphere of relative freedom. The economy avoids the corrosive implications of the psychological, physical, and political strains imposed by a programme of ruthless transfer of wage-goods.

Third, the programme of agricultural investment maintains intact the atmosphere of relative incentives. The living standard of the farming classes will bear some comparison with that of the industrial classes. The political and other frictions that will be inevitable if disparities in consumption standards have to be enforced will thus be avoided. Fourth, such a programme ensures the economy against possible curtailment of the level of production and productivity by the farmers as a reaction against growing demand. Fifth, the programme builds within itself the requisite markets for the products of the newly developing industries. In the case of some agricultural commodities, supply can create its own demand provided the investment tempo is maintained and the ancillary organizational measures are undertaken. The problem of markets is solved without giving room for disequilibrating upsets.

Thus, there are a number of weighty reasons why agricultural investment should get top priority in programmes of economic development. Any neglect on this score will tend to reduce the rate of growth of the economy and create considerable strains and stresses when the process of development is accelerated. The short-period limits of growth in such an economy will be low.

VII. Desired Rate of Growth of Agricultural Investment

In a closed economy, the rate of growth of agricultural investment together with changes in agricultural productivity determine the maximum growth rate that can be attained in the economy. Given the amount of disguised unemployment, the actual wage level and the extent by which it can be reduced, the current average consumption of those in disguised unemployment and the extent by which this consumption can be reduced, and the average consumption standard of the rentiers and the extent by which this can be reduced, all have a vital bearing upon the determination of potential investment. The marketable surplus of food and similar agricultural necessities determines the employment potential in non-agricultural fields. The net marketable surplus of agricultural as well as of industrial wage-goods will determine the employment potential in the investment sector. In the short period, however, the supply of non-food consumer goods is not so important, for it is possible that peasants and the workers will allow a slight reduction in their consumption of non-food consumer goods. The availability of food, however, affects the physical capacity of workers. When the disguised unemployed are employed in the investment sector, or in the non-farm sector, there is generally considerable extra physical strain involved. This, in turn, creates some additional demand for food. In a sense, the availability of food is a pre-condition for the success of a transfer programme. As seen earlier, it is possible to argue that high rates of investment growth and of transformation of surplus unproductive labour into productive labour can be carried out without any increase in the level of agricultural production and/or of agricultural productivity. In such a programme the net effect will be either a reduction of the average consumption of the disguised unemployed, or a fall in the average level of wages. In some cases, the consumption standard of the rentiers may be affected. Generally, such a programme implies very heavy strains and stresses. From the point of view of long-period development, it is not sufficient that high growth rates are obtained at any particular point of time. The length of time during which such austerity can be sustained is the most critical factor in the whole programme. It is possible here to make errors of judgment which may prove costly in retrospect.

Under what conditions can we assume that the proportion of investible resources devoted to the expansion of agricultural output is out of balance with the requirements of the economy? It is difficult to answer this question exactly. From a long-period point of view, the rate of economic development may be said to be determined, under certain conditions, by the proportion of investible resources devoted to agriculture and the rate of increase or decrease of this investment over time.

Expansion of agricultural output may fail to keep pace with consumption arising from population growth. The proportion of employment in agriculture may, however, remain the same. This situation can lead to any one or more of several consequences. The level of consumption of agricultural products by the farmers may decline. The level of agricultural wages may decline. Indebtedness may increase and there may be a general deterioration in the status and living conditions of agriculturists. Agricultural unemployment may increase or there may be a rise in disguised unemployment. The marketable surplus of agricultural products exchanged against industrial products may decline, either because farmers permit a reduction in the level of their consumption of industrial products, or because the consumption of industrial products by agricultural labour declines due to a fall in their wages or to a rise in unemployment. In this case there is a direct long-period effect upon employment in the industrial sector. The short-period result of such a decline will be a fall in the prices of industrial products, a fall in the level of profits and the emergence of excess capacity, all leading to a gradual reduction in the rate of industrial investment.

Thus, a failure of agricultural production to keep pace with population growth may have serious consequences later on, though it may not affect the volume of employment immediately. Either agricultural investment and/or industrial investment may decline. As a result, the rate of growth of employment in capital formation will decline in the long period.

I conclude that, if the pace of agricultural expansion lags behind the growth of population, it is bound to have an immediate effect upon living conditions on the farms and perhaps upon the level of employment in the industrial sector. From a long-period point of view, the rate of growth of employment will be seriously affected. If these trends persist, the proportion of industrial employment will go on declining and, gradually, the agricultural sector may have to absorb most of the workers previously employed in the industrial sector.

The course of such a process is, however, complicated. In the initial stage, there will be a slackening in the rate of growth. There will then be stagnation followed by retrogression. It will be a very long time before the full effects work themselves out. Thus, if there is disguised unemployment in the initial stage, a fall in the rate of agricultural investment will have serious cumulative repercussions.

So far I have assumed that the fall in the rate of agricultural investment was due to a decline of overall savings. Suppose we assume that the rate of growth of agricultural investment declines because of a forcible shift of resources away from agriculture. Rapid capital formation will be taking place, and a vast programme of industrial expansion will be going on, on the assumption that, at a later stage, it may be possible to provide for agricultural expansion. What will be the repercussions of such a programme ?

Technically, such a programme will call for considerable austerity for a long time. Inflationary pressures will emerge. The programme of capital construction may be disturbed in the process. Alternatively, the programme of capital construction may be completed, but under-utilization may emerge because supplies of agricultural products are insufficient to provide for fuller utilization.

Let us assume that a forcible transfer of resources takes place with a view to producing industrial consumer goods of various sorts. What will be the repercussions of such a programme ? In this case prices will fall, and excess capacity will emerge unless a vast programme of luxury consumption is popularized. This, however, will not remedy the situation inasmuch as unemployment will tend to persist. A shift of resources away from agriculture will tend to reduce the normal level of profits and, hence, slacken the investment process.

VIII. Necessity of Initial Concentration on Agricultural Investment

The mechanism of the process of investment shifts is simple. If any particular field of investment is neglected or if there is a heavy pressure of demand upon any particular product, the price of that product will rise. Abnormal profits will accrue to investors in that field so that there will be a flow of capital and other resources towards this sector until the investment deficiency is remedied. But expansion in agriculture may be neglected for a fairly long period of time. This may lead to an equilibrium with low employment and a low rate of capital formation, neither of which will affect the relative price structure. From a long-period point of view, neglect of agricultural expansion does not tend to be self-correcting. Disparities may go on cumulatively widening without setting in motion any compensating factors that will bring about a realignment of investment allocation.

The important thing is that neglect of agriculture is reflected mostly in reduction of aggregate rates of investment. Hence, the economy has no immediately noticeable countervailing forces.

If agricultural expansion is pressed a little further, what will be the effects? Suppose the proportion of resources for expansion of agricultural production goes up. Will this be reflected in low rates of profit in agriculture? If agricultural output is potentially perfectly elastic and if the capital-output ratio in this field is constant, profits in agriculture need not fall. This is because under conditions of disguised unemployment, surplus production of agricultural products, given organizational reforms, leads to forces which create their own demand. The investment process itself creates the required demand for the agricultural surplus.

It is not correct, however, to assume that surplus agricultural production automatically leads to increased investment. The links are many and tenuous, and various possibilities may be visualized. Different consequences follow on various assumptions regarding the character of the surplus agricultural production, that is, whether it is temporary or continuing. The capacity of the economy to expand investment is also crucial. If the investment process does not expand, surplus agricultural production leads to the collapse of prices, serious losses in agriculture, and creates disincentives to further expansion.

Broadly, two factors must be noted. First, the long-period trends in regard to non-agricultural investment are geared to the rate of growth of agricultural investment. Second, in the absence of investment, at appropriate moments, there will be no incentives to expand agricultural production. The relationship between agriculture and investment is complementary in character.

The cumulative nature of the investment process will depend upon which types of investment are given priority. Surplus manpower and wage-goods can be ploughed back in further production, and hence, the process of reabsorption of the disguised unemployed will be cumulative in character. The entire programme, however, has to be viewed from a long-period perspective of the need to provide a quick solution to the problem of unemployment with the minimum possible social frictions in the process. The various stages have to be clearly marked. In the first stage of such a programme, agricultural investment will proceed at a rate more than proportional to population growth. In the second stage, as living standards rise and consumption demand increases, agricultural investment will rise at the same rate as population growth. Gradually, however, as the process of development catches up, the rate of agricultural investment may have to be slackened *vis-à-vis* the population growth. Thus, in the initial stage, a raised scale of agricultural investment enables successively higher ratios of investment to income and higher rates of growth to employment.

IX. INCREASED AGRICULTURAL PRODUCTIVITY OR INCREASED AGRICULTURAL PRODUCTION WITHOUT AGRICULTURAL REORGANIZATION

The problem of agricultural and agrarian development may be considered either as a problem of reorganization or as a problem of capital formation, within agriculture or without it. In discussions of disguised unemployment, it is usual to argue that extensive agricultural reorganization has to precede any programme for transferring surplus labour to the investment sector. It is contended that an agrarian revolution is a pre-condition of a higher rate of growth of the economy. No doubt this would be the most plausible approach for an economy burdened with surplus population. It is natural to argue that even if there are adequate supplies of wage-goods, the investment programme may be handicapped by the continuance of low levels of organization and old-fashioned methods of production on the farms. Historically, in some countries at least, basic structural reorganizations in farm management and cultivation did occur prior to the revolution in industry. An extreme version of this approach would emphasize the need for reorganization on the farms as the primary and the initial step in a programme of rapid economic development. Technically, the labour force on the farms has to be demarcated into productive and unproductive groups, and the permissible levels of consumption standards have to be determined even at the early stages of a planned programme.

I contend that this insistence on need for reorganization overlooks the short-period and the long-period repercussions of increased investment made possible by improvements in the level of agricultural productivity and/or of increased agricultural investment. If we concentrate upon the long-period equilibrium positions, farm techniques and methods of organization have to adjust themselves to the varied proportions in non-agricultural employment, particularly in the investment sector. Other conditions given, for any given amount of employment in the investment sector or the non-farm sector, there corresponds a combination of methods of organization and production in agriculture. In this picture the ratio of labour and management to land and the sizes of farm units and the techniques of production adopted are all conditioned by the extent of the permanent relief from population pressure that is, or can be, obtained. The methods of organization and cultivation automatically adjust themselves when the surplus labour is siphoned off from the farms. If we exclude the complicating factors in the dynamic course of the economy, we obtain different levels of productivity on the farms depending upon the extent of surplus labour that can be removed from the agricultural sector.

In a sense, the foregoing picture is similar to historical fact. If the rate of population growth outstrips the rate of growth of investment, and the unemployment arising on account of technical change is not reabsorbed, surplus labour gets accumulated on the farms leading in turn to deterioration in organization and cultivation with corresponding effects upon the level of productivity per worker. The reverse process starts operating when the load of surplus labour is gradually taken off the farms. Thus, in substance, there is only one problem, namely, that of procuring the necessary wage-goods complements to enable a rapid rate of transformation of unproductive labour into productive labour. It is not necessary that a revolution in agrarian organization should precede programmes of rapid capital formation.

Thus, the critical point in the whole programme is the initiation of rapid rises in the level of agricultural productivity and concentration upon a high rate of investment to expand the production of agricultural commodities. To take a numerical example, let us assume that in an under-developed economy there are 500 million workers. The total production of wage-goods is 900 million units. The net savings are zero. Technically, only 400 million workers are sufficient to produce the 900 million units of output. Assuming that a clear-cut distinction between productive and unproductive workers can hypothetically be drawn, suppose the wage of the productive worker to be about 2 units. Perhaps, from a potential point of view, the wage per full-time worker may have to be determined on physical and nutritional grounds in order to work out the exact extent of surplus labour as well as of commodities. The available average consumption of the disguised unemployed will be about 1 unit per person. (In the actual world, it is, of course, difficult to distinguish between productive and unproductive workers. The burden of disguised unemployment can be borne in a number of ways. It may be that some workers may actually have higher consumption standards while others may just obtain a bare subsistence. It may be that most workers will obtain a bare subsistence. It may be that the work on the farms may actually be shared or that some persons may remain wholly or partly idle. More often than not, the pressure of disguised unemployment is reflected in small-sized farms and an abundance of under-employed managerial units. Thus, in under-developed countries, the owners of small-sized farms tend to have lower consumption standards even than agricultural labourers.)

In the model just sketched, let us assume an increase in productivity such that the level of agricultural production rises to 1000 million units as against 900, the number of workers on the farms remaining at 400 million. Assuming uniform wage rates, about 100 million workers will now be available for employment in the investment sector. The ratio of savings to income and of investment to income will now be 20 per cent., assuming that the productivity of a worker in the investment sector is the same as that in the agricultural sector.

Alternatively, there may be an expansion in agricultural investment. Let us assume that the productivity per worker continues to be $2\frac{1}{4}$ units per worker on the farms. Additional investment will lead to an increase in the supply of land or in equipment such that the level of production again goes up from 900 million units to 1000

million units. Here the number of workers on the farms will be
$444\frac{4}{9}$ million and the number of investment workers will be $55\frac{5}{9}$
million. The ratio of savings to income and of investment to income
would each be about $11\frac{1}{9}$ per cent. The increase in agricultural
production from 900 million units to 1000 million units in this case
may come about gradually. It may be that the productive farmers
are in a position to reduce their consumption for a certain period in
order that the entire economy may benefit, but the extent of commodity surplus available through such reduction may not be sufficient
to provide full employment. Hence, only a part of the surplus
labour can be siphoned off into the investment sector. However,
increased activity in the investment sector will lead to increased
agricultural production, thus enabling a further transfer, and so on,
until the transfer programme is completed. As and when the
economy reaches a state of full employment and the requisite levels
of agricultural production and surpluses, it will be possible to divert
a substantial proportion of investible resources from expansion of
agricultural production to other fields of investment. The rate of
agricultural investment thereafter may just keep pace with population
growth.

In the case of the under-developed countries, historically, agricultural investment must not have kept pace with population growth.
Further, even if agricultural investment is keeping pace at present,
the economy may have accumulated considerable surplus labour in
the past. What is required in this case, is a deliberate reversal of the
historical process. For a considerable period, therefore, the rate of
agricultural investment must outstrip the rate of population increase,
leading to a rate of increase in agricultural production higher than
the rate of population growth. Such a programme becomes inevitable if the surplus labour on the farms is to be put to productive use.

X. Why Agricultural Investment has often Failed to Keep Pace

The important fact to be noted is that there are no automatic
forces leading to a long-period harmony between population growth
and growth of investment which will preclude disguised unemployment. It is possible that a process of slow industrialization may
start but have no real effect upon the volume and proportion of
surplus labour on the farms. First, there is no automatic mechanism
in the economy to ensure that the rate of overall investment will
always be the maximum possible under the circumstances. Second,

the pattern of investment may be such that maximum possible growth rates through time are not obtained. In a private enterprise economy, profit is the lever which allocates investible resources to the different fields. This mechanism, however, can at best assure the economy of only that increase in the rate of growth of agricultural production that is possible within the limits of organizational possibilities determined by the existing structure of rural organizations. As noted earlier, the prices of agricultural commodities may rise without generating those forces which will lead to an alleviation of shortages of agricultural commodities. It is only within limits and under certain conditions that agricultural investment can be made on the same scale as industrial investment. Most farms are small in size, having already borne for years the brunt of disguised unemployment. The level of education of the farmers may be low. The credit and capital resources available may be inadequate. The required additional supplies of technical or engineering personnel or of managerial capacity may not be available. The pattern of organization may prevent the desired level of co-ordination. The additional investment may require capital resources far beyond the capacity of the farmers as individuals or as groups, and conditions may not be conducive to a free inflow of capital from outside the agricultural sector.

Despite high prices, agricultural investment may not expand for a number of reasons if we depend purely upon free private enterprise and upon the mechanism of automatic adjustments. More often than not, in most old countries, the additional investment required to increase the level of productivity or to bring new land under cultivation requires a type of organization far beyond the possibilities of an individual farmer or group of farmers. Further, the required additional investments may sometimes be so large and of such an indivisible character that only the State or an authority acting under its aegis may be in a position to undertake this investment. Another complicating factor, which is perhaps of considerable importance in the economic history of under-developed countries, is that most investments which lead to an expansion of agricultural output will not yield rates of return which meet current standards, even if we take into account the various possible increases of receipts and revenues obtained as a result of an increase in investment.

XI. CONCLUSION

Agricultural investment which seeks to expand agricultural production with a view to enabling a higher rate of transformation of unproductive into productive workers obviously leads to some increase in the levels of farm income. But the main purpose of this investment is the harnessing of the potential energies of vast masses of idle labour. The resulting improvements in production are seen not merely in agriculture, but even more in the other sectors of the economy. Thus, the rate of development of the non-agricultural sector is initially determined by the rate and pattern of agricultural investment. Hence, it is the general economy which benefits through higher employment, higher rates of growth, and ultimately higher consumption standards. The share of the agricultural sector, now relieved of a large share of the burden of disguised unemployment, in these increases, may be large, though not so large as to reduce the share of the other sectors to unimportance. Hence, conventional calculations of potential increases in revenue to be obtained from irrigation rates, surcharges on land revenue, agricultural income-tax, and so forth will not be a correct measure of the social productivity of these investments. Even in terms of static analysis they cannot yield much in this respect, for it is through an accelerated programme of agricultural investment that the surplus pressure on the land is reduced and the ratio of investment to income substantially raised, thus gradually leading to high rates of growth of income and consumption standards. Agricultural investment operates as the lever which sets the ball of development rolling. It gives the big push which generates cumulative growth. Properly visualized, the great defect of *laissez-faire*, from the point of view of the under-developed economies, was that it neglected those factors which determined the absolute levels of employment and growth rates. Historically, agricultural investment has been usually visualized as a precaution against food shortages, arising as a result of population growth. It has rarely been recognized that agricultural investment is necessary because it sets into motion the development process, involving the speedy transformation of the disguised unemployed into productive workers.

APPENDIX

Agricultural Investment and Planning Experience in India

During the period of India's First Five Year Plan, the dominant emphasis of official policy gradually changed from priority for agriculture to priority for industry. At the time the First Plan was formulated, various forms of capital investment in agriculture obtained the lion's share of attention. This was due to a number of reasons. First, the gravity of the food problem — a result both of the long-period imbalance between population growth and food production and of the short-period repercussions of the partition of the country — arrested the planners' attention. The country had been spending very large amounts of precious foreign exchange upon imports of food grains. Second, it was realized that self-sufficiency in foodstuffs had to be achieved to get rid of the psychological anxiety about impending food shortages. Third, food prices had to be brought down from the then existing high level. Simultaneously, the needs of the cotton and the jute textile industries for agricultural raw materials, of which the supply was disturbed by the partition, had to be made good through increased production at home. Jute and cotton textiles were India's leading foreign exchange earners. The pressures that influenced the planners at the time of the formulation of the First Plan and that caused them to devote a major share of the investible resources to agricultural investment were essentially transitional in character. The large relative emphasis upon agriculture in the First Plan was not the result of a carefully reasoned priority based on an assessment of the various patterns of investment from a long period point of view. The planners did not visualize a direct correlation between agricultural expansion, the level of employment, and capital formation. As the investment outlay of the Plan was more or less within the voluntary savings capacity of the community, the need for additional agricultural production to counteract the inflationary pressure generated by a high level of investment outlay was not visualized. Nor was the expansion of agricultural production determined with a view to raising the level of rural incomes. Therefore, it would be incorrect to conclude that any fundamental vision of the growth process and of the interrelationships between the different factors involved underlay the First Five Year Plan.

As the First Plan progressed, the country was fortunate in having a series of very favourable monsoons. About the third year of the First Plan, the level of agricultural production rose by as much as 20 per cent. over production in the immediate pre-Plan year. It is not unnatural in a country like India, where the bulk of the agricultural production depends upon rainfall, that the level of production should fluctuate very widely from year to year, depending upon the state of the monsoon. The first two years of the First Plan and the years immediately preceding had been marked by adverse climatic conditions. The stocks of farmers had been seriously depleted. The rise in production during the third year in the First Plan was a veritable boon, and as the production level was maintained in the fourth year also, the farmers were in a position to make good the deficiencies in stocks. The country, however, was not in a position to absorb the augmented marketable surplus. Hence, food-prices started falling, and the government had to initiate a number of countervailing measures to stop the fall and to level up depressed rural incomes.

It was in this atmosphere that the Second Five Year Plan was formulated and its broad contours of policy determined. It was felt that the country had turned the corner in regard to the food situation and that it would be enough to provide for additional production just sufficient to meet the requirements of the growing population. Naturally, in the priority scheme adopted for the Second Plan, agricultural expansion obtained relatively less emphasis. As the climate of economic opinion was characterized by considerable optimism, it was held both desirable and necessary to step up the level of outlay during the Second Plan and to concentrate a major portion of investible resources upon heavy industry. But, during the fifth year of the First Plan, the volume of agricultural output was slightly less than in the previous year. It looked as if production had levelled off. Further improvements would depend upon investment. It was not prudent to count upon any favourable windfalls. The experience of the fifth year revealed that even a slight reduction in output would tend to have a magnified impact on the marketable surplus and lead to strong inflationary pressures. The policy of deficit financing which had led to a relatively large expansion of currency during the fourth and the fifth years of the First Plan was gradually causing a rise in the price level.

At the time of the acceptance of the Second Plan, it was realized that the food problem had not been completely solved and that unless the level of agricultural production could be stepped up, inflationary pressures would increase. Then during the first year of the Second Plan, prices started to rise steadily, partly because of a considerable expansion of purchasing power. This was despite the receipt of a two million ton wheat loan from the United States Government. At the end of the first year of the Second Plan it became clear that unless the level of agricultural production could be stepped up significantly beyond the provisional initial targets of the Plan, the success of the Plan would be jeopardized. An expansion of agricultural production seemed necessary to curb the inflationary pressures. Along with the other decisive factors during the period of the First Plan such as the need for relief on the foreign exchange front and the need for self-sufficiency in foodstuffs, the desire to utilize additional food production to overcome inflationary pressures, resulting from a high scale of investment outlay, thus became a decisive factor during the Second Plan.

It is clear from the preceding discussion that the need for additional agricultural production was calculated on the basis of certain assumptions about supplies and requirements. The requirements were usually calculated either in terms of the need to provide for the growing population or in terms of the possible increased demand consequent upon rising incomes. These calculations were partially nullified. Another possible desideratum was the need for additional food production to restrain the level of food prices. However, the fundamental necessity to visualize additional agricultural production in relation to the level of investment was not at all in the forefront of the official discussion. It was only about the end of the first year of the Second Plan that some discussion about the relationship between the marketable surplus and the investment programme was started at the official level. Even then, the marketable surplus was considered as a cushion against rising food prices during a programme of accelerated investment.

COMMENTS ON PROFESSOR BRAHMANANDA'S PAPER

BY

THEODORE W. SCHULTZ
University of Chicago

To get economic development under way in very poor countries, Professor Brahmananda would first increase the production of food. He believes that food is a critical product which acts as a limiting factor on economic growth in such a country. All else in economic development will come to naught unless more food is forthcoming.

First, I want to consider whether the problem that Professor Brahmananda presents is relevant and important. I believe that the problem is of basic importance in the case of some of the very poor countries of South Asia and elsewhere. In these countries there are people who cannot do a day's work because of a low level of energy. Food is in such short supply that there is not enough available to provide them with the necessary minimum energy to work a full day. This kind of shortage, however, does not characterize most of the people of Latin America. There are some exceptions, of course, and if one were to look closely one would probably find many isolated pockets where some people are low on energy because of all too little food. One can see in parts of the Caribbean, for example, in parts of Haiti, a deep poverty characterized by a lack of food that gives rise to the kind of production conditions that Professor Brahmananda has in mind.

I next want to take Professor Brahmananda's problem and cast two parts of it in quite different terms from those he has used. I do this in the hope that it will help us see additional facets of this particular food problem.

Let us look upon food as a producer-good for a moment. The older economists took this view of food frequently. Even during the late nineteenth century, it was Marshall's view that many working people in England were still so short of 'necessaries' that they did not have the energy to do the hard work at which many were then employed. There are, or so it appears to me from observation and the few data I have been able to find, situations in agriculture, if we treat food as a producer-good, where the marginal contribution of a little more food to effective work is far above the average contribution of the going food intake.

To illustrate, suppose 1600 calories are required to maintain a farmer's bodily processes and functions in a state of complete inactivity. Suppose also that 2000 calories will provide a farmer with only enough energy for 3 hours' work. If this farmer's intake of food were to be increased by 400 more calories to a total of 2400 calories, let us suppose he would have enough energy to work 6 hours. In this case, a 20 per cent. increase in food has doubled the effective labour supply.

Leibenstein considers this kind of production possibility in his paper, 'The Theory of Underemployment in Backward Economies'.[1] United States road building administrators have had experience akin to this in improving the effective labour supply on which they were dependent in constructing the Pan-American Highway through parts of Central America. I am told that operators of the major mines in South Africa have also had similar experiences of the effect of supplementary food in increasing the effective work of labour. During the past year I have been able to bring together various data which strongly support the hypothesis that there are circumstances where a little more food will add more than proportionately to the hours that people can and do work. I hope to publish these materials in the not too distant future.

The other economic characteristic which may give some additional insight into the issue at hand, pertains to the backward sloping supply curve of food sold by cultivators under certain circumstances in very poor communities. I first encountered this situation in 1946 when I headed a mission to gauge the famine that was then developing in parts of India. It seemed evident that in some of these areas what had happened was that non-farm people were confronted by famine, not because local crops were below par, but because cultivators were eating more of their crops because they did not have to sell as much as formerly to meet their essential requirements. The price of food being sold had risen relatively, the farmers' real income had gone up, and they were so under-fed and hungry that they simply consumed a larger part of their production. To put the matter more technically, the income elasticity of the demand of the cultivators for their home-produced food was exceedingly high (say, 1·0) and the income effects exceeded the substitution effects that could come into play in the very short run. Accordingly, as non-farm people bid up the prices of one food being sold by the cultivators, even less had to be and was being sold by the cultivators. [2]

In closing, what I have here attempted is not a criticism of the general framework into which Professor Brahmananda has cast his analysis. I have not taken on that task for I fear I may not have fully grasped the analytical apparatus which he has employed. I have instead simply indicated that the problem to which he has addressed himself is both

[1] H. Leibenstein, 'The Theory of Underemployment in Backward Economies', *Journal of Political Economy*, April 1957.
[2] See T. W. Schultz, *The Economic Organization of Agriculture* (New York, 1953).

relevant and important to large populations of the world. I then developed briefly two economic characteristics that one observes in some very poor countries which, I trust, throw some additional light on the very serious problem that exists where many people live under semi-starvation conditions.

DISCUSSION OF
PROFESSOR BRAHMANANDA'S PAPER

I. General

THE lively and prolonged discussion that was provoked by Professor Brahmananda's paper dealt principally with the following topics :

(1) The assignment of priority to industry or agriculture.
(2) Measures to stimulate agricultural development.
(3) The transfer of population from agriculture to other sectors.
(4) Disguised unemployment.

Various speakers expressed the view, which was also reflected in Professor Brahmananda's paper, that agriculture and the rest of the economy were so strongly interdependent that it was better to stress this relationship than to point to any conflict between them. *Dr. Sol* in supporting this point of view, said that the issue of industry *v.* agriculture was fictitious, the need was for balanced growth. Nevertheless there was a problem in finding the optimum combination at each stage.

Professor Schultz took a somewhat different position. The problem of competition between industry and agriculture for the developmental resources seemed real and important to him. *Professor Wallich* supported this view and suggested that the decision was essentially a political problem. If the government could afford to starve agriculture and push industry, the economy as a whole might grow more rapidly. *Professor Brahmananda* rejected this view and maintained that economic development would best be served by giving agriculture a high degree of priority. The Indian First Five Year Plan had done this, and the Second Five Year Plan, after having first gone in the industrial direction, was now being reoriented towards a greater emphasis on agriculture.

II. Measures to Stimulate Agricultural Development

Dr. Sol maintained that Professor Brahmananda had underrated the importance of economic overhead in agriculture. In his opinion, agricultural output responded well to increased demand, once overhead facilities were adequate. This point of view was supported by *Professor Huggins*.

Professor Schultz mentioned two important factors that influenced agriculture's contribution to the development process. One was the frequent tendency of poor farmers, when the price of their products rose, to consume more of their own output and sell less. This could happen so long as the farmer had not reached a fairly advanced stage in which his own products became 'inferior goods' to him, of which he would consume less as he found himself better off. The second was the circumstance that, in many under-developed countries, the level of nutrition was so poor that many farmers could not do a full day's work. A small improvement in their diet under such conditions, often led to a large increase in output. *Professor Wallich* suggested that these two factors might neutralize each other to some extent and that this seemed to strengthen the case for not placing all the emphasis on agriculture. *Dr. Adler* remarked that a backward sloping supply curve for food, such as envisaged by Professor Schultz's first case, would make industrialization itself very difficult. While admitting the existence of this phenomenon in some parts of the agricultural sector, he doubted that even in countries like India it was so widespread as to make aggregate supply curves of foodstuffs backward-sloping.

Professor Brahmananda confirmed Professor Schultz's diagnosis of inadequate nutrition. The average *per capita* income of India, he said, was sufficient for two meals a day. But half of the people of India actually were below this level and had only one meal a day. This was inadequate to keep a man at full working strength. The 'multiplier effect' of one extra meal was great under such conditions. He saw in this an important reason for giving developmental priority to agriculture.

Various other views were discussed regarding the possible effects of an improvement in the prices paid to the farmer. *Professor Hirschman* said that if farm output failed to respond to rising prices it would be an indication to the government that it had to do something to raise output. In this indirect way market signals could be made to work. *Professor Schultz* held that the extent of the response of agriculture to price increases depended on resource endowment. In poorly endowed countries such as Puerto Rico and Haiti, there might be only a small response. In Mexico there would probably be a large one. *Dr. Alter* noted that failure of agricultural output to expand might be attributable not only to low prices, but also to structural distortions introduced by governmental planning in favour of industry.

Dr. Huggins emphasized the rôle of research and extension in raising agricultural productivity. If one followed the example of the more advanced economies, the under-developed territories would devote one per cent. or more of their national incomes to these services. *Professor Byé* added that when an agricultural push of that sort was under way, it was important to induce the farmer to produce for export as well as for the home market. He thought however, that agriculture did not offer much prospect for a cumulative process of growth in answer to such a push. The farmer, in his opinion, did not save much ; likewise he said that the farmer was not a good developmental investor.

III. THE TRANSFER OF POPULATION FROM AGRICULTURE
TO OTHER SECTORS

Professor Brahmananda said that a large-scale transfer of population out of agriculture was essential. In that way the disguised unemployment present in agriculture would be absorbed into useful activity. The food supplies which these people had previously consumed on the farm would have to be shifted to the cities, however ; this process was bound to present difficulties. Agricultural productivity had to improve. In this way the basis would be laid for industrial development and the true complementarity of agricultural and industrial growth would become apparent. *Professor Huggins* wondered whether Professor Brahmananda was not overestimating the need for population transfer. In Japan, he said, there had been no transfer of population out of agriculture, despite an annual increase in productivity of 1–2 per cent. *Professor Wallich* noted that in order to keep the agricultural labour force constant, a transfer equal to the population growth in the agricultural sector would be necessary. *Professor Boudeville* pointed out that in France industrialization was necessary to absorb the population transfer from agriculture to industry needed to increase total production as well as the productivity of the French peasant and also of course to absorb the increase in population.

Professor Brahmananda replied that in India the progressive reduction in the size of the average farm, as population increased, had reached a point where labour could be transferred out of agriculture without cutting output. He insisted that the use of this disguised unemployment was the core of the development process.

IV. DISGUISED UNEMPLOYMENT

Professor Brahmananda's references to disguised unemployment elicited a protest from *Professor Gudin*. He argued that disguised unemployment was a misnomer ; it was in fact a case of low productivity. Even though many people in Brazilian agriculture produced very little, they could not be removed without proportional reduction in output. Nor should unproductive employment resulting from inflation, such as in middle-man activities, banks and other financial intermediaries, be classed as 'disguised unemployment'. The reason why labour that produced less than it consumed was retained on farms had to be sought in family ties and other non-economic motivation. *Professor Haberler* supported the view that disguised unemployment was not a concept that would stand close scrutiny in Latin American countries. He called attention to the fact that Professor Rosenstein-Rodan and Professor Nurkse, both advocates of the idea of disguised unemployment, had said explicitly that they did not think that disguised unemployment was widespread in the sparsely populated countries of Latin America. This was in a glaring contrast to the opinion of ECLA.

Brahmananda — Agricultural v. Industrial Development

Professor Ellis sought a compromise between those who believed in disguised unemployment and those who did not. The concept seemed to evaporate, he said, as soon as one related the apparent disguised unemployment with its possible cause or remedy. For instance, if disguised unemployment could be removed by population transfers, it might be regarded as a case of low productivity owing to the absence of such transfers. If it could be removed by more investment or better technology in agriculture, it was a case of low productivity attributable to the lack of capital or skills. But suppose one took the situation exactly as it was — population could not be transferred, there was no capital available and no means of injecting new skills existed. In that sense the concept of disguised unemployment had meaning. The charge that the employment of such labour was irrational could be answered by pointing to family ties, as Professor Gudin has done, or to laws against lay-offs such as existed in Japan and Italy.

Chapter 15

EXCHANGE CONTROLS AND ECONOMIC DEVELOPMENT

BY

JORGE MARSHALL[1]

International Monetary Fund

I. INTRODUCTION AND DEFINITIONS

THE expressions economic development and economic development policies are used today with a variety of meanings.[2] Here, having in mind the economic structure of most Latin American countries, economic development will be understood to mean the raising of the level of real income *per capita*, mainly through direct and indirect measures aiming at an increase in the rate of capital formation. There are three basic elements in the concept thus interpreted : first, a certain degree of state intervention, in order to promote objectives which would not be attained by the free play of economic forces : second, the direction of intervention more towards the increase of real production than towards its redistribution ; and third, the position of paramount importance assigned to changing the institutional factors, political, administrative, legal, social, educational, or economic, which in a growing and developed economy can be taken as given, but which in an undeveloped economy have to be changed if economic development is to be possible. Recourse to intervention by the state does not necessarily imply regimentation of the economy, the public ownership of enterprises, or even socialism in the conventional meaning of the word. State intervention or direction can be made effective by indirect instruments of policy, which are quite compatible with capitalism or private enterprise. Fiscal, monetary, commercial, exchange, investment, and other policies may be used as instruments for this purpose.

By exchange control is meant here direct government interference

[1] The views expressed in this paper are those of the author and are not necessarily the views of the International Monetary Fund or of its Staff.
[2] See Jacob Viner, *International Trade and Economic Development* (Oxford, 1953) ; see also Celso Furtado, 'Capital Formation and Economic Development' in *International Economic Papers*, No. 4.

with incoming and/or outgoing foreign payments through prohibitions, quotas, or licensing, and/or the existence of an exchange rate system in which a single buying and selling exchange rate are not maintained, with a spread no larger than is necessary to pay for the services of brokers and other exchange dealers. The first type of control will be called quantitative restrictions and the second multiple exchange rates. For the purposes of this discussion I shall not attempt to identify these exchange control measures with any kind of legal exchange standard (national or international), nor shall I try to solve the host of problems which may be presented by this concept, such as the differences between exchange and import restrictions, or the question whether, in any given case, an exchange tax creates a multiple exchange rate situation.

It goes without saying that some forms of exchange control are quite strong and elaborate, while others are simple and of little practical significance.[1] Some countries control foreign exchange receipts and payments only for statistical purposes. Others, Peru, for example, have two exchange markets with only a very small spread between the two market rates, while others, Cuba, for example, maintain a tax on foreign exchange remittances. In this paper, when I speak of exchange controls I mean either quantitative restrictions which significantly reduce import demand and/or multiple exchange rates of a rather elaborate nature. It is rather arbitrary to make this distinction, but it seems more appropriate for the purpose of this discussion to consider countries like Peru, Venezuela, or Cuba as, in effect, not having exchange controls.

The discussion throughout will have in mind the condition of a country where the density of population is low, as is usual in Latin America, and in which the capital stock is rather small compared with the labour supply. Disguised unemployment is usually relatively high, and a substantial percentage of the labour force could be removed without causing a large reduction in the national product. In these circumstances, the manufacturing sector usually contributes less to the national income than agriculture and mining. Exports are generally an important part of the total product, consisting for the most part of one or a few agricultural or mining products.

[1] No attempt has been made to measure precisely the tightness of exchange restrictions. One procedure might be to estimate the degree of overvaluation by comparing the actual exchange rate or rates with a computed purchasing power parity exchange rate which also took into account the effects of changes in custom tariffs. This method has two serious drawbacks : first, purchasing power parity rates are poor indicators of equilibrium rates, not only because of the technical deficiencies of price indices, but also because in the long run many changes occur in demand and cost functions ; and, second, even if a good measure of currency overvaluation could be obtained, the necessary curtailment of the demand for foreign exchange will depend on the elasticity of demand within the relevant range.

Technology is quite advanced in the export industries but much less developed elsewhere, especially in that sector of agriculture which supplies the home market, and where rather primitive methods of exploitation prevail.

As part of the general economic policy of the government, exchange controls may be utilized as instruments to foster economic development in the sense indicated above. Methods of using exchange controls for this purpose and their shortcomings will be briefly described in the next two sections. Section IV will contain a summary discussion of the rôle played by the export industries in economic development, with special reference to Latin American countries. The last section of the paper will survey a group of countries in Latin America, comparing their rates of growth during the post-war years, and attempting to show the relation of their rates of growth to exchange control policies.

II. Exchange Controls as an Instrument for Fostering Economic Development

The uses and abuses of exchange controls for the purpose of economic development have already been discussed in many places and specifically in an International Monetary Fund staff paper.[1] Here we shall summarize what has been said and perhaps elaborate one or two points which deserve further attention.

The ways in which exchange controls may be considered as helping economic development may be classified under six headings. First, exchange controls may be used as a balance of payments corrective. Exchange controls are likely to be used when balance of payments problems result from economic development policies or when a government attempts to improve its foreign exchange reserves position with a view to financing future developmental expenditures abroad.

An economic development programme is bound to produce a rise in domestic prices, even if monetary inflation is not the method selected to finance the programme.[2] Changes produced by the new pattern of income and expenditures may also affect the balance of payments unfavourably.[3] Such balance of payments problems do not have to be solved through exchange controls. If domestic

[1] See Margaret de Vries, *Restrictions and Economic Development in Underdeveloped Areas*, International Monetary Fund, ERD/53/1, March 4, 1953.
[2] See Harold Pilvin, *Inflation and Economic Development*, a paper presented to the Fourth Meeting of Central Bank Technicians, held in Washington and New York, April-May 1954.
[3] See Celso Furtado, *op. cit.* p. 138 ff. and R. Nurkse, *Problems of Capital Formation in Underdeveloped Countries* (Oxford, 1953), p. 104 ff.

stabilization policies are not feasible, equilibrium may be restored in the foreign accounts by devaluation of the exchange rate. The use of exchange control measures as a balance of payments corrective assumes the desirability of maintaining an overvalued exchange rate.

Examples of attempts to strengthen foreign exchange reserves through exchange controls with a view to financing development are less frequent but essentially they do not differ from the case just described.

Second, exchange controls may be used to protect domestic economic activities. Exchange controls may be used to exclude foreign competitors in the interests of domestic industries which the development programme wishes to encourage. Protection may be given through straight prohibitions, quotas, or the maintenance of exchange rates which increase the internal supply prices of foreign goods.

Exchange controls, in the form of favourable export rates, may also be used to stimulate the growth of certain industries by enabling them to compete in foreign markets. Export quotas and prohibitions aimed at reserving a certain amount of supplies for the internal market may also be considered as illustrations in this category.

Third, exchange controls may be used to reshape import expenditures. Favourable licensing conditions or overvalued import exchange rates may be established for imported capital goods and raw materials deemed necessary for economic development. The opposite treatment, or even complete import prohibitions, may be applied to non-essential or luxury goods. This policy is based on the assumption that the composition of total expenditure can thus be influenced, decreasing luxury consumption expenditure and increasing investment expenditure. Furthermore, when an overvalued exchange rate is maintained and import demand has to be curtailed, exchange controls may be used to ensure the use of the scarce supply of foreign exchange in the way most consistent with the economic development plans.

Fourth, exchange controls may be used to encourage domestic and foreign investment. Exchange controls were first established in most countries to prevent capital flights during the 1930s. In so far as they still have that purpose, or in so far as they regulate the rate of remittances of amortization, interest, and profits with a view to having these funds reinvested within the country, they may be thought of as a part of an economic development programme.

Many countries with elaborate exchange control systems have established special treatment for new capital coming into the country, these regulations being intended to promote a larger inflow of foreign investments.

Fifth, exchange controls may be used as revenue-producing instruments. Exchange controls in the form of multiple exchange rates may be a source of fiscal revenue when there is a spread between the buying (or average buying) and the selling (or average selling) exchange rates.

The establishment of preferential exchange rates for government imports and/or payments may also be considered as a method of producing revenue for the government.

Another illustration of this type of exchange control is the widespread use of penalty export rates instead of export taxes, as a means of absorbing the profits of exporters, or as an anti-inflationary instrument. If the revenue produced can be used to finance economic development expenditures, this type of exchange control may be considered to be a means of fostering economic development.

Sixth, exchange controls may be used as instruments for enlarging a protected regional market. Exchange control measures may be used to establish discriminatory regional trade and payments arrangements designed to protect certain industries and to enlarge their markets, thus providing economies of scale for new industries which the economic development programme wants to encourage. This type of policy involves the co-operation of at least two countries. It may take the form of a bilateral or a multilateral clearing settlement, especially when imports from the area covered by the payments system are permitted, while other imports are excluded.

III. Shortcomings of Exchange Controls

For every exchange control measure there is some alternative which would produce equivalent economic effects which may be more desirable for other reasons. For example, in dealing with a balance of payments problem created by internal inflation, the results expected from exchange controls could be obtained by anti-inflationary monetary, fiscal, and wage policies. At the same time some of the shortcomings of exchange control would be avoided, and the problem would receive a more fundamental solution.

The very flexibility which may be regarded as an advantage of exchange controls for one or other of the purposes listed above should in fact be regarded as a disadvantage. The purpose of a policy, the details of which can be readily and quickly changed, will not be understood by the public, and its costs may not be immediately visible. Measures other than exchange controls, particularly taxes and subsidies, are usually less flexible in the sense that they are more difficult to impose, or, when once imposed, to change. This also means that they may be devised so as to give policy a more definite shape, to make its purpose clearer, and to permit an accurate weighing of advantages against costs. For example, if a certain activity is deemed to need a subsidy, it seems more appropriate to give the subsidy through the budget (after parliamentary approval) than by the device of a preferential exchange rate, which easily avoids public scrutiny.

Another general shortcoming of exchange controls in contrast with other measures is that the former throw doubt on the soundness of the currency and the financial policies of the country. This tends to discourage the flow of foreign capital which may be necessary to finance a higher rate of investment.[1] No legal provision guaranteeing remittances of amortization and profits can be more effective in attracting foreign capital than sound financial policies and freedom of exchange. When a country is suffering from inflation, balance of payments difficulties, and strict controls, legal guarantees do not accomplish their objectives. Moreover, if the country has a free market parallel to the official exchange market, strict import restrictions may be circumvented.

When exchange controls take the form of quantitative restrictions, and the country lacks efficient or perhaps even honest administrative machinery — as is the case in many Latin American countries — exchange controls are a major disturbing element for the country's foreign trade and for many productive enterprises linked with or dependent on that trade. Foreign supplies are uncertain, export licences and appropriate exchange rates may not be forthcoming, and it may pay to produce for the domestic market rather than for export. Furthermore, the allocation of quotas is usually made on a historical basis, modified by administrative value judgments about essentiality. When exchange receipts decline, the tendency is to maintain the volume of essential imports, thus increasing their relative importance. If the price mechanism is not working adequately because of an overvalued exchange rate for these essential imports, there is likely to be excessive consumption of these imports. The country may thus be deprived of many import goods — such as spares, raw materials, and machinery — which are rated low by the administrative authorities, but which may be more important for development than some of the so-called essential imports.

[1] The equally important effect of encouraging an outflow of domestic capital, and thus reducing the rate of investment, will be mentioned later.

Moreover, since exchange control authorities are subject to pressure from interested parties, clever entrepreneurs may conclude that it is to their advantage to spend time in obtaining a favourable administrative decision rather than in increasing output, improving the quality, or reducing the cost of their goods.

The difficulties of reaching rational administrative decisions and the inherent temptation to corruption are among the worst features of quantitative exchange controls. They have particularly detrimental effects upon any effort to increase output. These disadvantages can be diminished if a flexible exchange market or a different exchange rate is established. At the same time the unjustified profits which may arise from transactions in import quotas will be diverted to the government.

The effects of exchange controls are sometimes confined to the country applying them. In other cases the advantages which are the purpose of the policy may result in loss or disadvantage to other countries. This is the case when a country attempts to exploit its monopoly power, or depreciates one of its multiple exchange rates in order to get an advantage over foreign competitors. It is therefore always necessary to take into account the possibility of retaliation in one form or another.

The foregoing discussion has shown the disadvantages of exchange controls as compared with other policy measures, which would produce equivalent effects. There are also other shortcomings associated with the use of exchange controls for specific purposes.

The basic problems raised by the use of exchange controls as an instrument for protection need not be discussed here. They are the same as those that arise in any general discussion of tariff policy. It is also clear that exchange controls imposed for other reasons may have unwanted protective effects. If protection for industries which would have no chance of survival without it is condemned as harmful, it makes no difference whether this protection is provided through exchange controls or by other means.

Protective exchange control measures are particularly bad when they completely exclude foreign competition. In many Latin American countries, protection of this kind tends to create highly uneconomic industries and prevents any possibility of future readjustment. The problem is aggravated when the size of the protected market is favourable to a monopolistic structure in the country's industries.

Export quotas or prohibitions intended to protect domestic market supplies usually defeat the objectives of economic development, because their effect is usually to maintain a high level of consumption of certain goods at the expense of exports. But, though the resultant discouragement of exports may intensify balance of payments difficulties, it is scarcely possible for a government to ignore the political and social problems which arise if consumption is cut down.

When exchange controls in the form of multiple currency practices are used with the intention of determining the distribution of national expenditures, as between essential consumption, luxury consumption, and investment, they cannot attain their objective unless domestic measures having a similar objective are applied to domestic production. Even if the penalized imports are not domestically produced, there are other alternatives for luxury expenditure which may entirely defeat the purpose of encouraging productive investment. Another significant factor is that favourable import rates may tend to create quota profits in favour of privileged importers, while the abnormally low prices of favoured imported goods may retard the introduction of industries which would have been economically feasible.

One of the strongest cases for the use of multiple currency practices can be made when they have a revenue purpose [1] in a country which does not have a well-developed or well-organized fiscal system. Even under these circumstances, however, the general shortcomings of multiple currency practices remain valid, and it would be in the best interests of the country concerned to develop an adequate tax system as part of economic development itself as soon as circumstances permit.

The idea of widening the market for certain industries is no doubt commendable, and it may be the only way of eliminating inefficiencies resulting from the small size of certain plants producing for limited markets. But it does not follow that this objective can be best attained through discriminatory regional exchange arrangements. It would probably be more effective to adopt fiscal devices, or to give preferential customs treatment to the industries for which a wider market is desired. This could also provide an opportunity for laying the foundations of a regional custom union.[2] In this way the countries concerned might attain their objectives without foregoing the advantages of a fully convertible system of payments.

In reviewing the reasons for including exchange controls in an economic development programme, the correction of balance of

---

[1] To absorb windfall profits accruing to exporters from booming export markets so that their income will be stabilized over time, or to tax export monopoly profits.

[2] For some economic problems raised by custom unions, see J. E. Meade, *The Theory of International Economic Policy*, vol. ii, *Trade and Welfare* (London, 1955), p. 521 ff. ; and Jacob Viner, *The Customs Union Issue* (New York, 1950), chapter iv.

payments disequilibrium overshadows all the others. Those countries which resort to strict exchange controls are usually those countries with payments difficulties which are the result of strong inflation — whether because of economic development or for other reasons — and an overvalued exchange rate or rates.[1] The exchange control practices of those countries which do not have balance of payments problems and which have imposed exchange controls for other reasons are unlikely to be very significant and they could be readily replaced by other economic policy measures.

Unfortunately, however, exchange controls are an unsatisfactory solution for balance of payments problems. The only sound policy is to attempt economic development within a framework of financial stability. The experience already gained indicates that inflation is not the most desirable means of speeding up the rate of growth of an economy.

The case in favour of resorting to inflation in order to encourage economic development — apart from the expediency of this form of tax collection — rests on the assumption that, in this way, real resources will be transferred to the government or to investors, thus making possible an increased rate of investment. As a result of inflation, it is argued, real wages will drop, thus cutting consumption expenditures. However, it is difficult to conceive that labour — particularly when unions are well organized — will tolerate a large or prolonged reduction in real wages. If increased wages are sought because of the rise in prices, a wage-price spiral will result, with the result that inflation will accomplish little and will cause a great deal of harm to the economy.

The case against inflation is still stronger if considerations of development rather than of income distribution are emphasized.

First, productivity capacity is impaired : by continuous social or labour conflicts ; by the lack of incentives to reduce costs, to improve the quality of goods, or to introduce new techniques ; by the increase of government controls [2] and the difficulties in obtaining machinery, spare parts, and raw materials, and so forth ; and by the deterioration of moral and social values in regard to honest work, speculation, economizing, and frugality, which deprives the economy of the solid foundation necessary to assure its growth.

Second, real savings are reduced, especially if labour unions are successful in gearing money wages to some kind of cost of living readjustment. Also, depreciation allowances are likely to become inadequate, and the consequent swollen corporation profits are taxed

---

[1] The exchange rate or rates may be overvalued without inflation.
[2] Mainly price, credit, and exchange controls.

at a high rate, and offer a strong inducement to both shareholders and employees to press for a more liberal distribution. Also, small savers are discouraged by the impossibility of finding assets which will maintain their purchasing power.

Third, investment is misdirected in the sense that there is a tendency to over-invest in those fields which offer the best hedge against currency depreciation, but which will not necessarily make the most adequate contribution to economic development, such as real estate, excess inventories, or foreign exchange. There is also a tendency to direct economic resources into purely speculative ventures.

Exchange controls can do nothing to cure inflation. On the contrary, import demand suppressed by quantitative controls will express itself in higher domestic expenditure. In some circumstances, some of the damaging consequences of controls discussed earlier may be regarded as debatable. There is, however, no doubt whatever that controls will impair the expansion of a country's exports, thereby making its payments difficulties more acute. Export industries are damaged by the overvaluation of the currency and by the uncertainty and slowness of administrative decisions on exchange rates, quotas, and licences, on which the profitability of foreign trade depends. The basic importance of export trade for development will be discussed in Section IV.

When exchange controls are imposed in response to a balance of payments disequilibrium engendered by inflation, other difficulties are likely to arise which will be damaging to the development programme. Short-term credit to finance foreign trade will be reduced or stopped, and this will make the payments problem more acute. Speculation against the currency will increase payments difficulties. Credit-worthiness and the ability to service foreign commitments will be reduced in such a way that even official foreign investments are not forthcoming. A shortage of exchange will force the country to buy in markets which may not be the best from the standpoint of cost and quality. Finally, the tendency to increase the number of bilateral payments agreements will threaten the disappearance of the advantages of multilateral trade.[1]

IV. DEVELOPMENT INWARDS OR OUTWARDS ? THE RÔLE OF THE EXPORT INDUSTRIES

Should a country engaged in an economic development programme put emphasis mainly on developing its export industries,

---

[1] See J. E. Meade, *op. cit.* vol. ii, p. 499 ff.

or should it attempt to develop industries producing goods to supply the domestic market or to compete with imports ?

Prima facie the strengthening and expansion of those export industries in which the country has a comparative advantage appears to be the most convenient policy, at least as far as the factors of production are more productive in these industries than elsewhere. However, some reasons have been advanced to justify a different approach. It has been said that the elasticity of the foreign demand for exports may be so low in certain cases that an expansion of exports will add little or nothing to total foreign earnings. It has been also said that industrial development, even of high-cost industries (generally for internal consumption), is necessary to keep an increasing population employed. And, finally, it is argued that a diversification of the structure of production will reduce excessive reliance on one or two important export products, and minimize the effects on the internal economy of a slump in foreign markets.

The first and the second of these arguments seem to be interrelated. If the elasticity of foreign demand for exports is very low and the export industries are monopolized, these industries will not expand on their own initiative, and if there is a large number of export producers, there is a case for the exercise of monopoly power by the government with a view to achieving a net gain for the country. However, in estimating how far there is likely to be a real gain, the reduction in foreign trade and the possibilities of retaliation have to be considered. It is in any case very doubtful whether the foreign demand elasticity for most Latin American exports is low.[1]

The third argument implies that a price has to be paid, in the form of smaller real income, to attain greater diversification and stability. The country will have to decide whether it prefers a lower

---

[1] It is difficult to give any conclusive proof of this point. Elasticity of demand will be high for those commodities where the share of Latin American exports in total world consumption is small, or, even if it is not small, if there are close substitutes for the commodities in question. A review of the 21 commodities constituting more than 75 per cent. of Latin American export trade suggests that there is little doubt that demand elasticity is high for Latin American wheat, wool, beef, hides, corn, quebracho, cacao, cotton, nitrates, petroleum, tobacco, tungsten, timber, and rice. Lead and zinc exported by Mexico constitute 13 and 8 per cent. of world consumption, but they are only a small percentage of Mexico's exports. Bolivia contributes 16 per cent. of world tin consumption, Chile 15 per cent. of world copper consumption and Cuba 13 per cent. of world sugar consumption. The elasticity of demand for the exports of these three countries may be smaller than for the commodities mentioned above. In Chile, however, expanding world demand for copper justified an expansion of output.

Its monopolistic organization places the banana industry in a special position. Demand for coffee produced in Brazil may have a low elasticity, because of the large share (40 per cent.) of this country in total world consumption, but for other coffee-exporting countries elasticity of demand must be high.

and more stable income for an extended period of time to a larger income subject to more violent fluctuations.

The importance of export industries to the economic development of Latin America should not be judged only on the criterion of the productivity of the factors of production. One must also bear in mind the fact that, in general, markets in Latin America are small and industry is not well diversified. The production of those capital goods, which are essential for the success of any economic development programme, is either non-existent, or in the early stages of development. Indeed, in most countries the impossibility of developing a sufficiently large market means that it is not worth while even to think about establishing such capital goods industries. Therefore, the maintenance of an adequate and ever-growing supply of imports must be one of the corner-stones of any sound development plan.

It would be interesting to make a complete study of the relation of capital goods imports to total imports in times of high and low export earnings and to observe the movements in the rate of total investment. In Chile, for example, there seems to be a close connection between the rate of investment and the level of current account receipts plus long-term capital inflow.

In Section V a survey has been made of the rate of growth of a group of Latin American countries for some years after the last war. The survey shows that those countries with a more rapid expansion of foreign trade have, in general, also had a higher rate of economic growth. The data on the growth of trade are shown in Table I.

Peru, Venezuela, and Mexico, which experienced the highest rates of growth, are also the countries which had the highest rates of export expansion. The export expansion of Peru and Mexico is the more remarkable because these countries have not experienced as great an improvement in the terms of trade as have Venezuela, Brazil, or Chile.

The position of Venezuela can be attributed to the very special position of petroleum. The volume of exports has expanded, and the terms of trade have also improved. In Chile, on the contrary, the improvement in the terms of trade, due to the strength of the copper market, has not resulted in a big expansion of the quantity exported. The gains which could have resulted from a favourable external position were jeopardized by unsound financial policies, that is, by inflation and exchange controls.

Brazil shows a decline in the rate of growth of exports, if corrected for changes in terms of trade. Assuming that import prices did not change very much during the period, the quantities exported were actually much less in 1955 than in 1947. The importance of changes in the terms of trade can be gauged from the fact that between 1948 and 1954 the movement of the terms of trade in favour of Brazil meant an increase of 6 per cent. in that country's gross national product. Brazil has also had the benefit of a large inflow of official and private capital which has helped to sustain the rate of growth.

In Argentina domestic policies leading to financial instability were superimposed on very unfavourable external conditions. A

TABLE 1

RATE OF GROWTH OF EXPORTS AND OF REAL NATIONAL PRODUCT IN SELECTED LATIN AMERICAN COUNTRIES, 1947–55 *

Countries	Rate of Growth of Exports (percentage)	Rate of Growth of Corrected Exports † (per annum)	Index of Terms of Trade 1955 (1947 = 100)	Rate of Growth of Real *Per Capita* National Product (percentage per annum)
Argentina	− 6·8	− 2·8	74 ‡	0·4
Brazil	2·3	− 4·2	168	1·7 §
Chile	4·8 ‖	1·2	157	− 0·3 ¶
Mexico	6·7 **	5·6 **	108	2·8
Peru	8·0	6·25	110 ††	4·9
Venezuela	13·5	10·5	124	6·1 ‖

* Details in tables in the Appendix.
† Corrected exports are estimated by eliminating from the actual export figures the consequences of changes in export and/or import prices. As changes in import prices were not very great, these percentages approximate closely to changes in the volume of exports.
‡ Other computations suggest a much larger deterioration in Argentina's terms of trade.　§ 1948–54.　‖ 1947–54.　¶ 1947–53.
** If earnings from invisibles are included in exports, the Mexican rates of growth are 7·8 per cent. and 7·2 per cent.
†† Based on estimated figures before 1950.

reduction of the basic export industries resulted in a reduction of actual exports, even after the effects of the terms of trade are taken into account.

V. RATES OF GROWTH IN SOME LATIN AMERICAN COUNTRIES WITH AND WITHOUT EXCHANGE CONTROLS

A survey of a number of Latin American countries suggests, *prima facie*, that the rate of economic growth since the last war has been greatest in countries not using exchange controls.[1] The data

[1] Absence of exchange controls is here interpreted to mean relative freedom from exchange restrictions and a fairly simple exchange rate structure. It does not necessarily mean that the country is complying with the obligations of Article VIII of the Articles of Agreement of the International Monetary Fund.

have to be considered with caution, since for some countries they are not very reliable. Furthermore, allowance has to be made for the special circumstances of each country, which will be discussed later. The survey covers six large Latin American countries : Mexico, Venezuela, Peru, Brazil, Argentina, and Chile.[1] The first three were free from exchange controls throughout the period, while the second three maintained rather strict controls. For each country the *per capita* gross national product [2] has been recorded for the post-war period, after correction for the effects of changes in the terms of trade. The series thus obtained has been reduced to real terms by using the most suitable price index available. The resulting series thus constitutes a kind of index of the real *per capita* growth of the economy.[3]

The percentage rates may have been affected by any special situation existing at the end of the period. However, an examination of each series [4] as a whole does not suggest any such significant abnormality. The effects of the main distorting element, changes in the terms of trade, have been eliminated in computing the rates of growth.

These rates of growth may be compared with the annual rate of 2·2 per cent. by which the real *per capita* national product in the United States increased between 1860 and 1950. The United States annual rate was 4·2 per cent. from 1938 to 1950. During the same period, Canada's real *per capita* national product increased at an annual rate of 4 per cent. These rates are the highest recorded for Western advanced economies.[5]

National income figures are in some cases misleading. As National Income grows, the share contributed by middleman activities, social services, and government employment may increase. This trend is, however, unsatisfactory if it is at the expense of the growth of other elements in National Income. For this reason, it is useful to check the National Income data by reference to changes in the physical production of material goods.[6] For example, the considerable decline in the physical *per capita* production indices in Argentina indicates that National Income figures at least do not exaggerate the stagnation of that country's economy.

In Chile there is no index of agricultural production, but the

---

[1] Colombia and Cuba are the only large Latin American countries excluded. Their inclusion would not have changed the conclusions in any significant way.

[2] For Venezuela National Income is used instead of gross national product.

[3] For details see Appendix, Tables 1, 3, 5, 7, 9, and 11.

[4] See the basic data from which the table has been computed in the Appendix.

[5] See W. Fellner, *Trends and Cycles in Economic Activity* (New York, 1956), p. 68.

[6] See Appendix, Tables 2, 4, 6, 8, 10, and 12.

main crops have not changed for many years, and *per capita* agricultural production may therefore have declined by 10 per cent. from 1947 to 1954. However, declines in agricultural and mining production in Chile have been offset by an expansion of industrial production, which was mostly concentrated in iron, steel, and electricity.

In the other countries, data on physical production are not inconsistent with the gross national product figures. The exceptional rate of growth of the Venezuelan economy has been due to a unique factor. If account were taken of the depletion of its oil resources, the percentage shown in the table on page 449 would be reduced. However, other types of agricultural and industrial production have also expanded considerably in Venezuela, as is shown in Table 11 of the Appendix.

At the other extreme, Argentina has suffered from the weakness of some of her exports and from a drastic deterioration in her terms of trade. But this situation has been aggravated by domestic policies aimed at increasing industrial production at the expense of agriculture and by social objectives which have threatened serious damage to the country's internal and external financial stability. Inflation and strong exchange controls, the results of these policies, have not proved to be suitable instruments for a more rapid rate of economic development.

The experience of Chile has been similar, with the difference that in this country exports, especially copper, have been in a rather strong position. Stagnation has resulted mostly from the harmful effects of inflation and exchange controls.

Brazil has suffered from a considerable degree of financial instability and rather strict exchange controls. However, the very strong position of her exports — no other country included in the group has improved its terms of trade so much — and a large inflow of foreign capital have offset in part the effects of her internal financial policies. But, compared with countries like Mexico or Peru, the rate of growth of the Brazilian economy does not appear at all impressive. Mexico and Peru have not benefited in this period from a drastic improvement in their terms of trade. On the contrary, cotton, which is an important export of both countries, has been a rather weak export product. But their attempts to maintain domestic stability and freedom of exchange and their attitude towards domestic and foreign investment have made possible a considerable expansion of output.

The relatively less favourable external position of Peru and Mexico, as compared with Brazil and Chile, is shown in Table 1.

It is not claimed that domestic stability and lack of exchange controls necessarily mean a faster rate of economic growth. But the survey made in this section provides adequate grounds for concluding : first, that freedom of exchange does not hamper and is quite compatible with very rapid economic growth in Latin America ; and, second, that exchange controls, which are generally a consequence of acute domestic inflation, may be a deterrent to economic development, if they affect, as they generally do, the export sector of the economy and prevent an adequate inflow of foreign investment.

APPENDIX

TABLE 2

ARGENTINA : POPULATION, GROSS NATIONAL PRODUCT, EXPORTS, AND TERMS OF TRADE

Year	Popula-tion Index	Gross National Product * (billions of U.S. dollars)	Exports † (millions of U.S. dollars)	Terms of Trade ‡	Index of *Per Capita* Real Gross National Product §
1947	100·0	8·9	1,530	101	100
1948	100·5	8·3	1,407	118	90
1949	102·0	9·5	934	101	104
1950	107·5	9·5	1,168	100	100
1951	110·0	10·3	1,169	97	106
1952	113·0	10·0	678	73	102
1953	115·0	10·8	1,099	74	109
1954	117·5	10·3	1,029	78	102
1955 ‖	119·5	10·7	928	75	103

* Gross National Product figures given in the source indicated and converted into dollars at exchange rates computed by the Economic Commission for Latin America upon the basis of a normal equilibrium rate of exchange in the early 1930s corrected by price changes in the United States and in Argentina.
† Export figures from the Official Foreign Trade Statistics of Argentina. They have been converted into United States dollars at approximate average buying exchange rates up to 1950. From 1951 on they are official dollar figures.
‡ Other terms of trade computations show a larger deterioration, with an index of 55 to 60 for 1955 based on 1947 = 100.
§ Corrected for changes in terms of trade. This column is computed from previous columns according to the procedure indicated in the text.
‖ Provisional figures and estimates.

Sources : República Argentina, *Producto e ingreso de la República Argentina, 1935–54* (Buenos Aires, 1955), and *Dirección nacional de estadísticas y censos,* Comercio Exterior, October 1956 (Buenos Aires, November 1956).

TABLE 3

ARGENTINA : PHYSICAL TOTAL AND *PER CAPITA* PRODUCTION INDICES
(1947 = 100)

Year	Total Production			*Per Capita* Production		
	Agri-cultural	Pastoral	Industrial	Agri-cultural	Pastoral	Industrial
1947	100	100	100	100	100	100
1948	102	99	101	102	98	101
1949	89	98	98	87	96	96
1950	80	95	101	75	89	94
1951	95	90	106	86	82	96
1952	72	93	95	66	82	84
1953	113	98	93	98	85	81
1954	109	98	101	93	83	86

Source : República Argentina, *Producto e ingreso de la República Argentina,
1935–54* (Buenos Aires, 1955), pp. 144, 145, 146, 147, 148, 149, and 164. The
last three columns have been computed by deflating the first three indices by the
population changes indicated in Table 2.

TABLE 4

CHILE : POPULATION, GROSS NATIONAL PRODUCT,
EXPORTS, AND TERMS OF TRADE

Year	Population Index	Gross National Product * (1947 Purchasing Power Pesos)	Exports (millions of U.S. dollars)	Terms of Trade	Index of *Per Capita* Real Gross National Product *
1947	100	78·2	276	100	100
1948	102	83·5	327	108	105
1949	104	79·5	294	106	98
1950	106	85·0	281	118	102
1951	108	85·0	370	128	100
1952	110	87·0	453	140	101
1953	112	82·0	411	155	98

* Corrected for changes in terms of trade. Computed from the previous columns
according to the procedure indicated in the text.

Source : Gross national product figures are unpublished data of the Economic
Development Corporation of Chile. Population and exports are data from *International Financial Statistics*, various issues. Terms of trade were computed by
Horacio D'Ottone, unpublished paper from the Central Bank of Chile, November
1954.

TABLE 5

CHILE : PHYSICAL TOTAL AND *PER CAPITA* PRODUCTION INDICES
(1947 = 100)

Year	Total Production		*Per Capita* Production	
	Mining	Industrial	Mining	Industrial
1947	100	100	100	100
1948	105	103	103	101
1949	92	107	88	103
1950	91	107	86	101
1951	96	124	89	114
1952	95	135	86	122
1953	86	144	77	128
1954	90	154	79	135

Source : Central Bank of Chile, monthly bulletin. Figures in the last two columns have been corrected by reference to the population index of Table 4.

TABLE 6

BRAZIL : POPULATION, GROSS NATIONAL PRODUCT,
EXPORTS, AND TERMS OF TRADE

Year	Population Index	Gross National Product (billions of U.S. dollars)	Exports (millions of U.S. dollars)	Terms of Trade	Index of *Per Capita* Real Gross National Product *
1948	100·0	10·20	1,181	100	100
1949	102·5	10·70	1,097	119	100
1950	105·0	11·30	1,356	175	100
1951	107·5	11·97	1,771	186	102
1952	110·0	12·68	1,418	181	107
1953	112·5	13·02	1,539	188	107
1954	115·0	14·09	1,562	222	111
1955	117·5	14·40	1,423	168	114

* Corrected for changes in terms of trade. This column is computed from the previous columns according to the procedure indicated in the text.

Source : *Anuario Estatistico de Brasil*, 1955 ; Banco Nacional de Desenvolvimento Econômico, *Exposição sobre o programa de reaparelhamento econômico*, 1954 ; *Revista Brasiliera de Economia*, December 1955, Quadro VII ; *International Financial Statistics*, various issues. The parity rate of the cruzeiro in 1948 is taken as a relatively good measure of the external value of the cruzeiro for converting cruzeiro values into dollars.

TABLE 7

BRAZIL : PHYSICAL TOTAL AND *PER CAPITA* PRODUCTION INDICES
(1948 = 100)

Year	Total Production			*Per Capita* Production		
	Agri-culture	Mining	Industry	Agri-culture	Mining	Industry
1948	100	100	100	100	100	100
1949	105	104	106	102	102	103
1950	110	104	118	104	99	112
1951	110	117	128	102	109	119
1952	115	120	136	104	109	123
1953	115	120	145	102	107	129
1954	123	126	156	107	109	136
1955	129	142	162	109	121	138

Source : *Anuario Estadistico de Brasil*, 1955. The *per capita* figures have been obtained by using the population index of Table 6.

TABLE 8

PERU : POPULATION, GROSS NATIONAL PRODUCT,
PRICES, EXPORTS, AND THE TERMS OF TRADE

Year	Popula-tion Index	Gross National Product (millions of soles)	Price Index	Exports (millions of U.S. dollars)	Terms of Trade	Index of *Per Capita* Real Gross National Product *
1947	100	6,816	100	147	100	100
1948	102	8,264	132	157	—	—
1949	104	12,074	152	157	—	—
1950	106	15,161	170	194	125	119
1951	108	18,708	188	254	147	126
1952	109	20,866	200	242	123	135
1953	111	22,650	218	226	110	138
1954	113	25,080	228	253	118	139
1955†	115	28,000	240	275	110	147

* Corrected for changes in terms of trade. This column is computed from the previous columns according to the procedure indicated in the text.
† Preliminary data.

Source : *International Financial Statistics*, various issues. Banco Central de la Reserva del Perú, *Renta nacional del Perú, 1942–54* (Lima, 1956) and *Boletín*, November 1956. The terms of trade index is relatively accurate from 1950 on.

TABLE 9

PERU : *PER CAPITA* PHYSICAL PRODUCTION
(1947 = 100)

Year	Agriculture	Mining
1947	100	100
1948	119	107
1949	147	109
1950	146	106
1951	141	115
1952	131	120
1953	137	111
1954	132	117

Source : Banco Central de la Reserva del Perú, *Boletín*, November 1956, and *Renta nacional del Perú, 1942–54* (Lima, 1956).

TABLE 10

VENEZUELA : POPULATION, GROSS NATIONAL PRODUCT, PRICES, EXPORTS, AND THE TERMS OF TRADE

Year	Population Index	National Income (millions of bolivares)	Price Index	Exports (millions of U.S. dollars)	Terms of Trade	Index of *Per Capita* Real Gross National Product *
1947	100·0	5,000	100	692	100	100
1948	102·5	—	111	1,114	90	—
1949	105·0	7,352	106	1,078	100	132
1950	107·5	7,109	106	1,240	116	114
1951	110·0	7,195	111	1,450	106	113
1952	112·5	9,158	113	1,550	107	139
1953†	115·0	10,257	110	1,448	112	155
1954†	118·0	11,040	109	1,690	124	154

* Corrected for changes in terms of trade. This column is computed from previous columns according to the procedure indicated in the text.
† Provisional data.

Source : *International Financial Statistics*, various issues, and Central Bank of Venezuela, *Monthly Bulletin*, January–March 1956.

TABLE 11

VENEZUELA : QUANTITATIVE INDEX OF PRODUCTION
IN CERTAIN INDUSTRIES
(1947 = 100)

Year	Crude Petroleum	Iron Ore	Diamonds	Milk	Sugar	Butter
1947	100	100	100	100	100	100
1954	159	4,200	232	560	330	205

Year	Vegetable Fats	Rice	Beer	Soft Drinks	Electricity Output
1947	100	100	100	100	100
1954	400	460	275	340	285

Source : Central Bank of Venezuela, *Monthly Bulletin*, January–March 1956.
As there are no indices of physical production, those commodities whose volume
of production is significant were selected.

TABLE 12

MEXICO : POPULATION, GROSS NATIONAL PRODUCT, PRICES, EXPORTS,
TOTAL CURRENT ACCOUNT CREDITS IN THE BALANCE OF PAYMENTS,
AND THE TERMS OF TRADE

Year	Population Index	Gross National Product (millions of pesos)	Price Index	Exports (millions of U.S. dollars)	Current Account * Credits in Balance of Payments (millions of U.S. dollars)	Terms of Trade	Index of Per Capita Real Gross National Product †
1947	100	29,600	100	482	664	100	100
1948	103	32,300	106	472	700	115	98
1949	105	35,400	112	435	680	100	102
1950	108	43,200	119	521	803	106	103
1951	111	51,900	133	629	981	129	114
1952	113	58,500	153	656	974	131	111
1953	116	56,700	150	589	953	104	109
1954	119	72,300	158	655	1,046	108	128
1955‡	122	83,600	183	810	1,204	108	125

* This column is more significant than visible exports because it contains gross tourist credits and
bracero remittances.
† Corrected for changes in the terms of trade. Computed from previous columns according to
procedure indicated in the text.   ‡ Estimates.
Source : *International Financial Statistics*, various issues, and data obtained in the International
Monetary Fund.

TABLE 13

MEXICO : PHYSICAL TOTAL AND *PER CAPITA* PRODUCTION INDICES
(1947 = 100)

Year	Total Production			*Per Capita* Production *		
	Agri-culture	Mining	Manu-facturing	Agri-culture	Mining	Manu-facturing
1947	100	100	100	100	100	100
1948	112	91	108	108	88	105
1949	117	90	118	111	86	112
1950	135	99	135	125	92	125
1951	153	94	146	138	85	131
1952	159	99	141	141	88	125
1953	159	94	141	137	81	122
1954	189	88	154	159	74	133
1955†	209	101	168	711	83	138

* The *per capita* indices were obtained by using the population index of Table 12.
† Estimates.

Source : *International Financial Statistics*, various issues, and data in the International Monetary Fund.

COMMENTS ON DR. MARSHALL'S PAPER

BY

JAVIER MÁRQUEZ
Centro de Estudios Monetarios Latinoamericanos

I. NEED FOR CONTROLS TO PROMOTE ECONOMIC DEVELOPMENT

WHEN we discuss economic development in Latin America it is not just because we want to know how our growth is progressing or what its mechanism is, but because we want to do something about it. We are not satisfied with the rate and/or the direction of our growth. We want to change something that will not change by itself, or we want to speed up a change which, if left to itself, will take too long. This aim, obviously, implies tampering with market forces. The extent of the interference will depend on the magnitude of the job which we want done and on the degree of our eagerness to see it done. It will also depend on the extent to which we are prepared to sacrifice other objectives, for there is always a sacrifice in tampering with market forces.

The parallel between the effort required to promote economic development and the effort required to win a war seems to me very clear. If it is a minor war there will not be much tampering with market forces, not much sacrifice will be asked of the people, and not many controls will be imposed in orde ' to direct demand and investment. But if it is a major war all sorts of strict controls will be imposed, and much additional revenue will be sought through many new channels. The fact that controls are imposed and that new revenue is raised is sufficient proof that if nature were allowed to take its course, demand and investment would not be sufficient, nor of the proper sort, to win the war. The authorities may dislike controls, but they would dislike still more losing the war. With development it is the same. We must control the economy, because investments are not likely to be made in the desired amount, and in the directions considered most appropriate.

II. Other Economic Controls also have Disadvantages

Jorge Marshall will probably agree with this point of view, for he is not against controls for the purpose of fostering economic development, although he dislikes them in principle as much as I do. He seems especially interested, for example, in using the tax system as a substitute for exchange controls. However, if the tax system is to be used as an instrument of economic development, it will not only raise revenue, but will also influence the direction of investment. I want to emphasize this point. Devices that change the decisions which people would have taken with a given price structure, or devices that change the price structure so that decisions change or do not change in certain directions, may or may not be called controls, but this is just a question of terminology. The purpose and the effect may be just the same. If controls are objectionable, a tax system used to influence the direction of demand for consumption or investment goods should be as objectionable. The same may be said of most tools of monetary or wage policy which Marshall seems to accept. Marshall is not against controls, but just against exchange controls. But why tolerate one and not the other ?

I can understand opposition to the purpose for which a tool is used, but have difficulty in understanding how one can oppose the tool itself, if it really fits the purpose. Yet Marshall's attitude is common. Some people are in favour of tariffs but against multiple import rates. Some people are against tariffs but, if given the alternatives of tariffs or multiple import rates, would object less to the former in spite of the fact that these may put up more obstacles to imports than multiple rates. These positions appear to me to be illogical.

The main difficulty I find with Marshall's paper is that he does not make any concessions in favour of exchange controls. Nor does he present an argument to justify his condemnation of exchange controls. Moreover, although it is difficult to disagree with Marshall's statement that for every exchange control measure there is some alternative which would produce equivalent economic effects, he never examines the disadvantage of these other methods. He states the disadvantages of exchange controls for different purposes and then says that other tools have fewer disadvantages but he offers no proof.

At times I get the impression that he is forgetting the purpose for which exchange controls were imposed, that is, that their purpose may be other than monetary stability. For me it is inconceivable that one policy (especially exchange controls) can be the best, the sound policy, in all actual economic and political circumstances, whatever the historical experience of the country, the psychology of the people, the distribution of income or property, the size of the monetized sector of the economy, the geographical location of the country, and the direction of its trade. It is also inconceivable that any policy, any control, could not be the best, the sound policy, in some circumstances and for some purposes.

If we want to reduce imports of luxury automobiles, is it expedient or advisable to do it through progressive income taxes which will reduce the income of high income groups in such a way that they will not be able to buy imported cars? Do we prohibit banks from granting credit for importing cars? Do we limit the number of cars that can be imported? Do we limit the number of dollars that can be spent on importing cars? Do we raise the tariff on cars? Do we raise the price of the dollars to import cars? If reducing the importation of luxury cars is the problem, any of these alternatives may do the job.

We may have to rule out the income tax device because it may have to be carried too far for the purpose. We may not be able to rely on the tightening of bank credit because of its difficulty of enforcement and mild impact. We may rule out limiting the number of cars to be imported because of the difficulty of allocating imports among the importers, and for the same reason we may rule out rationing the exchange to be spent on such cars. We may also rule out raising the tariff because it may require congressional approval which can be obtained only after a delay during which imports will soar and the purpose of the tariff will be defeated. Moreover, a trade agreement may preclude raising the tariff. In short, a multiple exchange rate may be the only expedient device. Of course, it is possible that the only expedient way may be considered more harmful than the benefits which are expected from the reduction in the importation of luxury cars, so that nothing is done.

If we assume that raising the tariff, establishing an excise tax, or establishing a multiple rate are equally expedient, which do we use? In this case we must weigh the pros and cons of what each of these techniques will do, in addition to curtailing the importation of luxury cars.

Exchange controls have been chosen, together with other policies, in countries as different from one another as England and Nicaragua, Argentina and Ecuador, Belgium and Afghanistan, in all of which there are intelligent people and capable statesmen. Surely there must be some advantage which in specific circumstances makes certain exchange controls preferable to other policies, even if everybody agrees that there are disadvantages to such controls.

Marshall's position also seems to me untenable because he has chosen a dialectic device which is not suited to his topic. 'Exchange controls' is an umbrella expression (the 'tax system' is another) which covers devices which differ widely in purpose and in form. All generalizations with regard to them, when applied to specific conditions, may prove right or wrong depending on which exchange control measure or which tax device is used. Marshall has built the possible disadvantages into inescapable disadvantages. The same arguments he uses against exchange controls could be used against any economic policy, or any control which we might want to substitute for exchange controls.

III. MARSHALL'S ALLEGED SHORTCOMINGS OF EXCHANGE CONTROLS

For example, to consider his first alleged shortcoming of exchange controls, flexibility, I could easily give examples of very flexible tax and subsidy systems. I can also give examples of cases in which the purpose of a tax is far less clear than the purpose of an exchange control device. I just cannot see why a tax measure must always be rigid, clear, and good while an exchange control measure must always be flexible, unclear, and bad. Marshall mentions the disadvantages of flexibility. To the extent that flexibility implies, as he contends, that the purpose of an exchange control policy will not be understood and its costs will not be immediately visible — these requirements would probably do away with more than half the tax systems of the world — I might agree with him. But I do not see why a flexible control cannot be made clear to the public or why its costs cannot be made visible. Marshall says that exchange controls, in contrast with other measures, throw doubt on the soundness of the currency. There is no doubt that exchange controls have this effect, but a tax measure or a measure of monetary policy may do likewise.

Similar comments can be made against most of Marshall's alleged shortcomings of exchange controls. Exchange controls have not always prevented the inflow of foreign capital — in the last page of his paper Marshall himself highlights the rôle of foreign capital in Brazil — while some other policies may prevent it more effectively. The administrative machinery of exchange controls is not necessarily inefficient. It may be, and frequently is, less inefficient than the tax machinery. To produce for the domestic market rather than for export cannot be considered an evil in all cases, and in some cases it may be quite preferable. Politics and graft are no monopoly of exchange controls. In fact, taxation, which Marshall seems to favour, has a more consistently brilliant and notorious history in this respect than the exchange control system of any country.

The charge of flexibility should in my opinion be weighed against the peculiar circumstances of most under-developed countries. The fast development which we want to achieve means constant change. Do we want a rigid policy and rigid instruments in a rapidly changing economy? Moreover, under-developed countries are usually subject to sharp ups and downs. Do we want to use rigid tools to adapt the economy to such fluctuations? Exchange controls may or may not be the answer in specific circumstances, but, if they are not, it is not because of their flexibility. For under-developed countries flexibility may be considered an important asset.

The best case can probably be made for the use of exchange controls as a short run policy instrument. Marshall does not make any distinction between the short and the long run and, accordingly, I assume that he thinks the same about both. On one occasion he says that exchange controls should be replaced by an adequate taxation system — as part of economic development itself — as soon as circumstances permit. But this does not lead him into a discussion of the short and long run. The general tone of his paper suggests that he would even accept that short run movements should be allowed to exercise their full effect, for he argues in favour of rigid devices. I do not accept this position. If he believes the ordinary tools of monetary policy should be used to offset economic fluctuations, my answer is that such tools, when applicable, are only useful to meet mild fluctuations. More direct controls are needed to counteract the sharp fluctuations to which under-developed countries are subject. This does not exclude monetary policy. It just does not assign to it all the burden of short-run adjustments.

Marshall's contention that a developing country needs to export in order to be able to import seems to me to be obvious. His point that exchange controls damage the export capacity of the country, however, is far from proven. Mexico, which he quotes as an example of a country which has expanded its exports without exchange controls, could also have been offered as an example of a country which has experienced a great expansion in exports with multiple export rates and multiple import rates. Each of the Mexican devaluations has been accompanied by the imposition of very high export taxes, and in between devaluations the import tariff has been adjusted almost constantly, and seldom downwards. We may call these practices by whatever names we like, but they are still multiple rates in any meaningful sense. In those cases in which exports have not expanded much, if at all, it would be extremely difficult to prove that it was the fault of exchange controls. I would readily agree that exchange controls are not a good tool for expanding exports, but the expansion of exports is quite compatible with the existence of exchange controls.

The comparison of the rates of development in different Latin American countries with the existence of exchange controls does not seem to me to prove much. It does not prove that slow rates of development were due to the exchange controls, nor does it show how the countries that do not have exchange controls would have fared with them.

IV. PAST DIFFICULTIES WITH EXCHANGE CONTROLS

It seems that exchange controls are not today as fashionable as they used to be. An increasing number of countries are abandoning them or adopting exchange systems that are more akin to a free exchange market than the exchange control systems of ten or fifteen years ago. Why? The reason is probably that exchange controls have been abused, that they have been, in some countries, asked to do a bigger job than they are fit for, and that their administrative structure became too complex. In truth, they became in several countries a sort of panacea for every conceivable situation. They have been expected to provide revenue, to stop imports of all or some goods, to stop capital flights, to protect domestic industries, to diversify exports, and so forth. Monetary and tax policies would also have broken down if asked to do the same.

I believe further that the great harm which exchange controls have done in Latin America is one which Marshall does not mention. By postponing some of the adverse effects of inflation, mainly on the balance of payments, exchange controls may blind the authorities to such adverse effects. They may allow excessive monetary expansion in the hope that some of the harm done may be counteracted by the tightening of exchange controls. To the extent that these situations exist I would certainly condemn the authorities. They should know that the more exchange controls, or the more price controls, wage controls, trade controls, and credit controls they have, the stronger the inflationary pressures to which they will be subject. They should also know that continuous inflation is of no help to economic development even if some of its adverse effects are counteracted by controls, including exchange controls.

V. CONCLUSION

I wish to stress that my criticism of Marshall's paper should not be interpreted as an argument in favour of exchange controls. It does imply, however, acceptance of controls as a possible instrument of economic development. Exchange controls, like monetary policy, tax policy, commercial policy, and wage policy, may indeed be inadequate to meet certain problems of underdeveloped countries. Similarly, they may be too mild, or too strong, in the circumstances of specific countries at specific moments. I see no special virtue in exchange controls or in any economic policy, but neither do I see in exchange controls any special evil. I believe that deliberate development needs many economic tools. The use of one or the other is a matter that cannot be judged in the abstract. It is a matter on which one should not take a doctrinaire position.

FURTHER COMMENTS ON DR. MARSHALL'S PAPER

BY

ALBERT O. HIRSCHMAN
Yale University

I. SITUATIONS IN WHICH THE USE OF EXCHANGE CONTROLS MAY BE JUSTIFIABLE

I AM not sure that the reader of Dr. Marshall's paper becomes aware of the breadth, depth, and resiliency of the forces making for the adoption of exchange control measures in under-developed countries. Let me give just two examples of situations in which the exchange control solution, once known, is rather likely to be tried.

When there are strong fluctuations in the world prices of the country's principal export products, whether upward or downward, such price movements probably should not be allowed to be reflected fully and immediately in the local currency proceeds of exporters. In case of a fall in the world prices of one or several commodities responsible for the bulk of a country's foreign exchange income, a devaluation cannot ordinarily be avoided for long. But in the opposite case, a general revaluation can and should be postponed at least until world prices appear to have reached some new plateau. In the meantime some device implying either a partial revaluation or a partial blocking of foreign exchange proceeds is likely to be adopted.

Dr. Marshall fully recognizes that hesitation to devalue the currency immediately upon the first appearance of pressure on the balance of payments resulting from inflation is the most important cause for the recurrent imposition of controls. But he does so only to state that exchange controls are ineffective in curbing inflation and that the country, instead of dealing with the symptoms of the disease, should go to its roots and stop the inflation. Similarly, it could be argued in our previous case that the principal task is to prevent undue fluctuations in commodity prices. Such 'buck-passing' advice strikes me as a bit unhelpful. If one were to apply it generally, one would soon find oneself entirely unable to act. There is hardly any field of activity in under-developed countries — or indeed in any country — where progress and sense do not depend logically on prior progress and sense being introduced in some other, closely related, field. But a start must be made somewhere. Moreover, the fact that we cannot solve a basic difficulty is not a good reason for not trying to cope as best we can with its practical and, for the time being, unavoidable consequences. Society must deal in as sensible a manner as possible with the usually unpleasant results of its assorted failures, be they war, inflation, or juvenile delinquency. We cannot abstain from formulating

457

a foreign exchange policy for a country suffering from persistent inflation any more than we can refuse to consider problems of penal administration on the ground that it is really crime that ought to be stopped.

In the two cases just mentioned — world price fluctuations and internal inflation — exchange control is primarily a reaction to powerful forces operating on the economy from within or without. Their impact on the foreign exchange situation is often quite sudden and makes it imperative to act. In fact, exchange control was born in this way, as a reflex to the war-and-depression-caused disruptions of international payments. Its administrative flexibility — which becomes intolerable arbitrariness in normal times — is a distinct advantage in such emergency situations. The great danger is that temporary emergency measures, which as such may be perfectly justified, may become permanent controls leading to the well-known distortions and abuses. Societies have a remarkable ability to transform not only means into ends, but also temporary expedients into permanent institutions. Perhaps we should concentrate our attack against exchange controls on this point. We could then formulate two rules.

First, the use of exchange controls should be reserved for crisis situations. They should not be used *à froid*, to initiate action towards longer range economic goals, such as industrialization or export diversification. In this case, Mr. Marshall's argument about the superiority of other available policy devices such as tariffs and tax rebates applies with full force.

Second, when exchange controls are instituted in response to some acute development in the balance of payments, they should contain definite self-liquidating features. In the case of multiple exchange rates, provision might be made for a gradual narrowing of the spread between them over a period not longer than a year or eighteen months. Alternatively and more generally, countries might pass basic legislation providing that exchange controls may not be instituted for a period longer than three months so that they would automatically lapse unless specifically re-authorized. In this way, pressure would be created to replace exchange controls by other suitable devices and the need for their continued existence would be periodically scrutinized. Most important, under the stipulated conditions, adoption of exchange controls would become much less attractive.

II. SOME DIFFICULTIES CONSIDERED

These two rules meet with many difficulties of both a practical and a theoretical order. The practical difficulties consist first in deciding what exactly we mean by the term, crisis situation, that is supposed to justify temporary imposition of exchange controls. In the case of inflationary pressures, is it exclusively a run on the country's foreign exchange reserves ? How would a run be defined ? Some under-developed countries are characterized by somewhat sluggish inflations — price rises of 5 to 15 per cent. per year — and they may therefore experience a steady slow pressure upon their reserves rather than any dramatic decline. Nevertheless, every country has in mind some level of reserves which it considers as minimum or safe. As this level is approached, it will consider itself in crisis regardless of the speed with which the decline proceeds.

The advice that countries ought to substitute tariff protection and export subsidies for exchange controls when they want to promote domestic industries and new exports is easy to give, but is it likely to be followed ? It is, of course, a variation on a familiar theme, namely, the free traders' insistence that tariffs ought to be replaced by overt subsidies to the protected industries. This argument never achieved practical success for the simple reason that governments will not replace a budgetary receipt (customs duties) by an expenditure item (subsidies) just to please the economist. Moreover, domestic producers are unwilling to rely on annual appropriations and open government hand-outs which are attended by psychological indignities rather than on more permanent and more discreet protective measures. Fortunately, neither of these very compelling practical reasons for preferring customs duties to subsidies applies when the alternative is either exchange control measures (quantitative restrictions or discriminatory exchange rates) or tariffs. The latter are in fact likely to be preferred by domestic producers as more reliable instruments of protection. From the point of view of the government's fiscal interests, multiple exchange rates enforced through exchange taxes are equivalent to tariffs, but all other exchange control devices are inferior to them, so that the government's self-interest ought to work here for once in support of the economist's point of view.

The situation is considerably different in the case of export promotion through differential export rates. Here a change-over to export subsidies would mean replacement of an implicit subsidy by an explicit one in so far as the government is concerned. For the producers, it would mean that protection for an indefinite period of time is replaced by protection that is subject to annual appropriation uncertainties. The saving grace is that both preferential export rates and export subsidies are likely to be inadequate incentives for actually developing new exports on any large scale. It has correctly been said that preferential export rates for new export products have much in common with infant industry protection for products intended for the domestic market. But once a country's more obvious export possibilities have been exhausted, the development of a new line of production acceptable in world markets is usually a far more complicated task than the setting up of a domestic industry which is to replace previously imported goods. If that task is not undertaken by foreign capital, the government will often have to support it directly through research, planning, and participation in financing. Such measures, jointly with temporary income tax rebates and import duty exemption for machinery and raw materials, will, in the absence of sharp over-valuation of the country's exchange rate, advantageously replace both preferential export rates and export subsidies — they are really *solutions de paresse*, and ineffective ones at that.

I have one remaining difficulty of a theoretical nature with my own prescription that exchange controls should be considered emergency devices. It can be shown, I think, that the process of economic development will be more rapid when foreign exchange availabilities are fluctuating than when they are stable. Let us see first what happens during the expansionary phase. With foreign exchange availabilities ample and restrictions at a minimum, an under-developed country develops a taste, a need, and a market for a number of hitherto unknown and unappreciated foreign commodities. At the same time, the availability of these commodities is an important factor in unbending backward sloping supply curves of effort and in developing efficient working habits. Then comes the lean period and restrictions are imposed. The absence of previously imported commodities is now felt as a shortage and a deprivation and since entrepreneurs know from the previous phase that the market is there, they will now seriously think of starting domestic production in some of these items. Pending the completion of such projects, the would-be, but now frustrated, purchasers of these foreign imports are not likely to replace them entirely by domestic goods in view of the absence of close substitutes and the general lack of variety of domestic production.[1] In this way, savings will be generated and will in part finance the new ventures. It is indeed unlikely that the supply curves of effort will bend backward right away since working habits, once generated, are likely to persist for some time even if the causes that have given rise to them, have disappeared.

In reality, this is an extended Duesenberry-Modigliani model applied to under-developed countries. All it says is that fluctuations in foreign exchange receipts are not all bad — that they set into motion certain valuable development mechanisms. In other words, if an under-developed country could count on a perfectly stable or a regularly rising foreign exchange income, something might be said for inducing a spending pattern that would result in drawing down exchange during one period and in accumulating it during another. But in the real world our problem has been traditionally how to cope with excessive fluctuations in foreign exchange income, and it seems unlikely that we will ever need exchange controls to simulate, as it were, instability in export receipts. Nevertheless, the foregoing considerations explain to some extent why many under-developed countries do not have nearly as hostile an attitude towards exchange controls as industrial countries. They well remember the considerable forward strides their economies have often made when foreign exchange was short.

---

[1] W. F. Stolper, 'The Volume of Foreign Trade and the Level of Income', *Quarterly Journal of Economics*, February 1947.

III. Two Acceptable Exchange Control Devices

Let us now return to our principal argument. If it is correct that the imposition of exchange controls must be expected under some conditions, then we cannot be satisfied with a blanket condemnation of all exchange controls, but must look for criteria which lead us to prefer some controls to others when their introduction cannot be avoided. The traditional position differentiating between tariffs and quotas was that the former are preferable because they only reduce the play of the price mechanism and of international competition while quantitative restrictions shut these forces out entirely. From this point of view, multiple exchange rates are similar to tariffs. There is in fact no strictly economic criterion which opposes tariffs, taxes, and subsidies to exchange controls when the latter are understood to comprise quantitative restrictions and multiple currency practices (as well as, of course, interferences with the free transfer of foreign exchange in service and capital transactions). The classification nevertheless makes sense because of the considerable differences between these two groups of devices with respect to the possibility of arbitrary and abrupt changes, the scope for corruption, and the propensity to proliferate complications, distortions, evasions, and interferences. Incidentally, it is interesting to note that from this point of view, multiple exchange rates, once much heralded, have proved to be even worse offenders than quantitative restrictions.[1]

I know of only two exchange control devices that do not possess these obnoxious characteristics, or at least seem to possess them in much less degree ; the simple division of imports into a prohibited and an authorized list and the establishment of a wider than usual spread between a unitary buying and a unitary selling rate for foreign exchange.

The establishment of a prohibited list is a simple device which is well suited as a temporary balance of payments defence in a variety of pressure situations. As sudden balance of payments difficulties often result from a conversion of foreign exchange into commodity hoards, the list can comprise many essential items whose inventories will be drawn down in due course. As this happens, the measure also has the advantage of possessing a built-in tendency towards self-liquidation rather than towards self-perpetuation and proliferation. Once the stocks are drawn down, the prohibited list will have to be reconsidered.

Moreover, a prohibited list does not raise as much doubt about the future value of the currency as a multiple exchange rate system. It is true that a subdivision of imports into authorized and prohibited can be viewed as a dual exchange rate system with the value of the local currency standing

---

[1] See Alexandre Kafka, 'The Brazilian Exchange Auction System', *The Review of Economics and Statistics*, August 1956. The recent experience of Colombia, which purposely avoided quantitative restrictions because of bad memories connected with them, also confirms that a multiple exchange rate system has remarkable proliferative and degenerative faculties.

at zero for the prohibited items. But this zero rate is not in evidence as no transactions take place at it.

To let a spread develop between the buying and selling rates of foreign exchange, may be considered another comparatively harmless temporary device in case of sudden balance of payments disturbances.[1] In the case of inflationary pressures, for example, much may be said for making foreign exchange more expensive to importers while leaving exporters' proceeds temporarily unchanged in order not to add more fuel to the fire. As long as the inflation is not stopped, a simple depreciation of the currency is two-edged. With regard to imports, it is effective in absorbing local purchasing power and in reducing the pressure on foreign exchange reserves, but it acts as a super-escalator clause for exporters whose income it increases disproportionately to the general level of costs.[2] Therefore a lag in the downward adjustment of the buying rate may be helpful in slowing the inflation.

The spread between buying and selling rates is essentially a general surtax on all imports and should, of course, be transformed into this instrument if it is to be maintained as a permanent revenue-raising or import-restricting device.

Neither of the two controls deals properly with a sudden rise in the world price of a principal export commodity. If it is desired to prevent the possible inflationary consequences of such a rise and to divert part of the terms of trade gain to capital formation, an appropriate instrument is a partial blocking of exchange proceeds in a special fund which remains the property of the exporters and out of which development loans can be made. Another possibility for dealing with this situation is a flexible export tariff. Finally, the smoothing device proposed by Bauer and Paish is perhaps the most sensible way of dealing with the matter from the standpoint of a single country.[3] All three devices imply the use of fiscal rather than exchange control instruments.

We have now derived the following modification of Mr. Marshall's principles of conduct with respect to the use of exchange controls. First, they ought to be resorted to only in emergency situations when action to protect the balance of payments is imperative. Other devices are more suitable for promoting long-range development goals such as industrial-

[1] See E. M. Bernstein, 'Some Economic Aspects of Multiple Currency Practices', *International Monetary Fund Staff Papers*, vol. i, 1950–51.

[2] This argument applies to countries where resources used in the production of exports cannot readily be shifted and which consume only a very small part of their output of exportable commodities, that is, to countries specialized in exporting raw materials and foodstuffs. In the case of countries which can shift resources out of the production of exports or which export articles of which they are themselves the principal consumers, a failure to devalue the buying rate along with the selling rate in the course of inflation leads to serious balance of payments trouble as exports, or resources devoted to producing exports, are diverted to the home market.

[3] P. T. Bauer and F. W. Paish, 'The Reduction of Fluctuations in the Incomes of Primary Producers', *Economic Journal*, December 1952 ; see also subsequent discussions of the proposal in the 1953 and 1954 volumes of the *Economic Journal*.

ization and export promotion. Second, exchange controls ought to be imposed only as temporary measures. If it is desired to retain their effects, exchange controls should give way to permanent tariff, tax, or exchange rate measures. Third, among exchange control devices, first consideration should be given to the establishment of a prohibited list of imports and/or to the adoption of a simple spread between the buying and selling rates for foreign exchange.

One advantage of elaborating such a set of rules — and I do not pretend that mine is either perfect or complete — is that ministers of finance and central bankers, who for one reason or another have trespassed or are about to trespass on the forbidden territory of exchange controls, are provided with some guidance and approximate notions concerning the degree of their wrongdoing. After all, neither the church nor the law have found it beneath their dignity to establish a hierarchy of sins and crimes, and I fail to see why economics should enjoy a privileged position in this respect.

IV. THE CASE AGAINST EXCHANGE CONTROLS IN TIMES OF EXPANDING WORLD INCOME

The rules here developed certainly are not very liberal in authorizing or condoning resort to exchange controls. This position is not only motivated by the distasteful aspects of the methods by which the controls are usually administered. I would tend to keep it essentially unchanged even if I felt certain that the controls were administered in a scrupulously honest, fair, and efficient manner. My reason is that exchange controls invariably are associated with some over-valuation of the currency : some essential imports come in at lower prices and the exporters of some major export products receive smaller local currency proceeds than would be the case if the exchange rate had to do the job of balancing the country's international accounts without help from the controls.

To pursue such a policy under present world conditions seems to me an anachronism. When world income and trade are shrinking, it is perhaps natural for countries to eye the possibility of improving their position through various beggar-my-neighbour and monopolistic practices even though the attempts in this direction during the thirties by no means met with unqualified success.[1] But in an environment of expanding world income and trade, under-developed countries have most to gain by just keeping in step with the expanding world economy. This they may be hard put to do because of the well-known inflexibilities in their economic structures, and an over-valued exchange rate is an additional hindrance.

What do I mean by keeping in step ? In the first place, that primary producers ought to expand the production of the commodities on which

[1] H. S. Ellis, *Exchange Control in Central Europe* (Cambridge, Massachusetts, 1941), p. 276 ff.

they want the industrial countries to keep on relying. Otherwise, new sources of supply or substitutes may well be developed to satisfy urgent world demands. When times are good, the fact that a country is operating on the inelastic portion of the world demand schedule is not necessarily a good reason for not expanding output. Tomorrow that schedule will have shifted upward and, unless output has been increased, the country may find itself operating on an elastic portion of the demand schedule at high prices that strongly invite competition from newcomers and attempts at substitution. Thus an increase in output would have been profitable both from the point of view of short-run maximization of foreign exchange proceeds and in the longer run interest in maintaining one's position in the world market. This argument applies even if the income elasticity of demand for the country's product is less than unity.

With respect to import substitution, the type of over-valuation usually connected with multiple exchange rate systems is also particularly harmful during good times. Such systems typically discriminate in favour of essential raw material, foodstuff and machinery imports and against non-essential consumer goods. Now, in times of prosperity, when the total foreign exchange income of an under-developed country is fairly satisfactory, the preferential rate at which the essential imports come in may be set at a level that actually discourages domestic production of these items. Moreover, the flow of international investment that increases during this period and that will naturally seek out the most profitable opportunities, will then be tapped primarily for the setting up of miscellaneous light industries, rather than for basic industrial and perhaps even agricultural projects. It seems a bit unfair, after that, to criticize foreign private investments for aggravating in this way the lop-sided character of the economies of under-developed countries! [1]

For these reasons, it seems to me that under-developed countries may wish to err on the side of *under-valuation* of their currencies during times of world prosperity. If they do so, they certainly cannot be accused of exporting unemployment — the traditional argument against this practice. And the risk that their terms of trade may deteriorate seems to me infinitely smaller than the possibility that an inelastic supply may jeopardize their position in international markets and that a preferential rate for essential imports may hold back domestic production of such items.

Naturally this is meant as a very general point, subject to modification in the light of specific country and commodity situations. Nevertheless the experience of Mexico since its devaluation of 1954, widely criticized at the time as excessive, lends, I believe, some substance to my thesis. Dr. Marshall's figures are quite eloquent in this respect.

Why is it, then, that the use of exchange controls is still so widespread in spite of all our arguments against them ? In my opinion, the explana-

[1] See K. P. Dalal, 'American Direct Investments in Under-developed Countries', *Indian Economic Review*, February 1956.

tion lies fundamentally in the desire to manipulate and to make full use of available powers that is characteristic of many policy-makers in under-developed, but developing countries. It is easily understood why these men, anxious to contribute in some positive way to the development of their country, are not particularly impressed by expressions that have strong positive connotations in a different environment, such as equilibrium rate of exchange, freedom from controls, non-interference with the market mechanism, and so forth. Our failure in persuasion may thus in part be inevitable. To some extent it may also be due to poor public relations techniques. Instead of stressing the issue of controls as such, we should perhaps emphasize, as I have just attempted to do, that the important policy choices are between the right and the wrong pressures and between the correct and the perverse incentives. By phrasing our arguments in this way, I feel that we have a better chance to obtain a favourable hearing even from the most *inquieto* of our ministers of finance.

DISCUSSION OF DR. MARSHALL'S PAPER

I. General

In the debate on *Dr. Marshall's* paper on exchange controls, there was a great deal of criticism of most forms of exchange control. Few inherently constructive characteristics were conceded to the device. Nevertheless, no one seemed prepared to argue that exchange controls must be avoided at all costs. The discussion principally touched upon the following subjects : (1) the purposes and effects of exchange controls ; (2) the context of circumstances and alternative policies ; (3) the special case of multiple rates, and (4) trends in control techniques and possibilities of ultimate removal.

II. The Purposes and Effects of Exchange Controls

Dr. Marshall had presented in his paper an impressive list of the uses to which exchange controls had been put. *Dr. Márquez* complained that this list seemed to over-emphasize long-run problems and to neglect the short run. He thought of short-run problems as the principal area for exchange controls. *Professor Hirschman* replied that the long run was a succession of short runs. Exchange controls frequently were introduced to cope with balance of payments pressures. They often produced effects that perpetuated the pressure, and so they tended to perpetuate themselves. *Dr. Marshall* agreed that exchange controls had usually been instituted to cope with an emergency and not to achieve long-term goals. In practice, however, since they were not removed, they had generally been diverted to a variety of long-term purposes.

Dr. Adler agreed that there was a strong temptation for governments to carry exchange control too far, both in time and in intensity. The reason for this he saw in their ease of administration and in the way in which vested interests managed to bring their influence to bear.

In addition to the negative results listed by *Dr. Marshall*, a number of further evils brought about by exchange control were mentioned. *Dr. Márquez* said that perhaps the biggest damage done by foreign exchange control was the way in which it isolated the authorities against the consequences of inflation and thus postponed needed corrections. *Dr. Hirschman* warned of the consequences of over-valued exchange rates for exports. It was conceivable that even the low income elasticity of demand for primary products was due in part to the exchange control manœuvres of the supplying countries. These might drive the importing countries to intensify the search for substitutes. Another adverse effect he saw in the diversion of resources to domestic production of precisely those consumer goods which were kept out of the country by exchange controls because they were non-essential.

Dr. Marshall added that in so far as an over-valued exchange rate reduced export receipts, it engendered a superfluous urgency to substitute imports by domestic production while making it harder to import capital goods for development.

Dr. Márquez made a point in favour of controls by arguing that a development drive was somewhat like a war economy in the sense that it required the shift of scarce factors from their traditional uses and into new ones at a faster pace than the market mechanism would permit if it were to work at a tolerable level. *Dr. Marshall* and *Professor Wallich* protested that this concept would open the door to even stronger measures of consumer repression. Investment could no doubt be increased if a country were prepared to take such action, but this meant a very considerable departure from our existing political principles.

III. The Context of Circumstances and Alternative Policies

Professor Hirschman thought that *Dr. Marshall* had presented too rigid a case against exchange controls. One had to take into account the circumstances. Foreign exchange controls presented something like a meeting ground of conflicting social objectives — growth, freedom, income distribution, and others. *Dr. Adler* also pointed to the varying backgrounds of exchange control measures. They seemed to reflect social pressures which in some cases led to a fairly acceptable balance of forces. In other cases, however, where particular interest groups were politically weak, the results might admittedly lead to severe distortions. *Professor Ellis* agreed that there was always some incompatibility of national stability and international stability and that exchange control might be a means of reconciling them. This was bound to be an uneasy compromise.

By the same token, any decisions that a government took in the exchange control area were also likely to represent an uneasy compromise. One must therefore beware of laying down general rules.

Dr. Márquez went on to argue that exchange control was a tool among others and should not be singled out for special criticism. In recent years it had sometimes failed because it had been asked to do jobs beyond its strength. *Professor Haberler* said that exchange control, like almost any other evil, could be justified by comparing it with some greater evil that was pictured as the only possible alternative, that is to say, applying the modern theory of the 'second best' which might be equally well called the theory of the 'second worst'. He cautioned against comparing an extreme case of one evil with a mild case of an alternative evil. *Professor Wallich* agreed that economists could make a case for using all tools simultaneously up to the point where the disadvantages began to outweigh the benefits. But he observed that political scientists did not always seem to follow this principle. Their teachings often seemed to reflect the desire, not to maximize the effectiveness of government, but to minimize the danger of its misuse. He wondered whether on these principles exchange control should not be used more sparingly than economic analysis might suggest.

Turning to the relative importance of alternative policy tools, *Dr. Márquez* argued that monetary policy was in place where disequilibria were mild. Big pressures call for other controls.

Professor Schultz argued that the virtues of having to stand up to competition should not be overlooked. He cited the case of Puerto Rico, which was unable to adopt exchange control and other protective measures and was competing very successfully with the main body of American industry. The very pressures against which exchange control isolated a country might in the long run prove very healthy.

IV. Multiple Exchange Rates

Multiple rates were singled out by several speakers as one of the more desirable forms of exchange control. *Professor Haberler* said that he would prefer multiple rates to quantitative restrictions. They permitted a better adjustment to market forces and could be used so as to avoid some of the distortions caused by repressed inflation, provided the system was not carried to extremes. *Professor Gudin* discussed the advantages that the shift from quantitative restrictions to multiple rates had brought in Brazil. Under the régime of quantitative restrictions, importers had made unreasonable profits, and there had been corresponding pressure to obtain exchange licences. The multiple rate system had diverted these profits to the government. *Professor Huggins* thought that the multiple rate system nevertheless had certain limitations and wanted to know more about the Brazilian experience. *Professor Gudin* replied that he had found the device of auctioning foreign exchange particularly satisfactory. It was true, of course, that a good system could always be badly administered. Some of the difficulties experienced by Brazil, however, he attributed to the fact that part of Brazil's exchange earnings were inconvertible. This could not be held against the auction system. *Professor Wallich* raised the question whether the existence of any sort of exchange control system did not itself constitute an invitation to other countries to impose bilateral relations upon the controlling country. *Professor Gudin* seemed to doubt this tendency. He added that bilateral trade, although better than no trade, should be got rid of as soon as possible. This was what he had done as Minister of Finance by organizing the so-called Hague Club, establishing convertibility for Brazil's operations with the United Kingdom, Germany, Belgium, Netherlands, and other countries through a clearing.

Dr. Marshall expressed agreement with *Professor Gudin* in his preference for multiple rates over quantitative restrictions. He pointed to the danger, however, that over-detailed subdivision of rates might lead to abuses. The discriminatory benefits and burdens that this system dispensed, moreover, seemed to him of a sort that ideally ought to be decided upon by a legislature.

V. Trends in Control Techniques and Possibilities of Ultimate Removal

Dr. Sol gave a survey of the development of exchange controls in Latin America since the war. The Northern group of countries, he said, had used exchange control very little and predominantly for fiscal purposes. The countries of South America proper had used it heavily. Initially, main reliance had been put on quantitative restrictions. These had worked poorly, however, because they had not been backed up by rationing and allocation as they had been in the British Commonwealth. Beginning with the late forties a trend towards multiple rates and away from quantitative restrictions had become noticeable. A few years later, however, these were seen to have severe distorting effects. As a result, a new tendency was gaining ground towards unified rates that fluctuated freely. Some observers, he concluded, thought that the present move towards unified but fluctuating rates might eventually lead to a single free and stable rate.

Dr. Sol's remarks led to a discussion of possible methods of reducing the adverse effects of exchange control or of perhaps removing the device altogether. *Professor Schultz* expressed his view that governments rarely exerted the self-restraint necessary to keep the adverse repercussions of their policies under effective control. Agricultural price supports in the United States were a case in point. It took a crisis to produce a change in policy. *Professor Wallich* mentioned the European experience in attaining progressive liberalization. Thanks to their close interdependence, these countries had been able to exert enough reciprocal pressure via the Organization for European Economic Co-operation to bring about a high degree of unrestricted trade among themselves. He doubted, however, that the interdependence of Latin American countries was sufficient to achieve such a result.

Professor Hirschman suggested that the adverse repercussions of exchange controls would be minimized if two rules were observed : (1) they should be used only to combat disturbances, not for the promotion of long-term goals, and (2) they should be established for a limited duration, at the end of which they would be removed or replaced by appropriate permanent measures like taxes or tariffs. In the last analysis, countries would probably continue to shift from one expedient to another as they successively experienced the drawbacks of each. But eventually some central ground might be reached where the shifts of policy would no longer be so brusque.

INDEX

Entries in the Index in Black Type under the Names of Participants in the Conference indicate their Papers, the Discussions of their Papers, or Comments by them on the Papers of other Participants. Entries in Italics indicate Contributions by Participants to the Discussions.

Abramovitz, M., 136, 318

Adler, Mrs D., x

Adler, J. H., 8 n., *106*, **124-32**, *136, 137, 138, 166, 167, 232, 306, 363, 364, 397, 427, 466*

Adverse shocks, effect of, 8-14

Africa, French Tropical, 121; West, 238

Agricultural development, and reorganization, 416-19; claims of, as opposed to industrial development, 399-424; difficulties, 410-11; must keep pace with population growth, 414

Agricultural investment, accelerated, 408-12; as an initial factor in economic development, 415-16; and population growth, 416, 417-19; degrees of priority accorded to, 402-404; effects of increased, on prices of agricultural commodities, 404-8; effects of varying rates of, 412-15; in India, 421-4; reasons for neglect of, 419-20; various types of, 400-2

Agriculture, advances in technology affecting, 288-9; adverse effects on, of inflation, 90-2, 105; becomes depressed in highly developed countries, 322; export, as a leading development sector, 115-16; in explosive patterns of growth, 120; in retrogressive patterns of growth, 119; neglect of, 48; reluctance of banks to lend to, 176-7, 180-1

Ahumada, Jorge, **188-91, 366-98**

Allen, W. R., 234 n.

Allocation of resources, theory of, 366-371

Alter, Gerald M., *81*, **139-67**, *164, 165, 166, 167, 232, 271, 304*, **385-90**, *397, 398, 427*

Analysis, case by case, 147, 154-5, 161, 164; on aggregative lines, 112-14, 133-5, 147, 154, 164

Angell, J. W., 234 n.

Argentina: average real income, 3; economic growth, 4, 9, 443, 444, 445, 446; exports, 5, 99, 442; income elasticities of demand for food, 316; increases in agricultural inputs and outputs, 317; inflation, 17, 20, 22, 23, 91; loans received from Export-Import Bank and International Bank, 213, 214; partial devaluation, 99; United States direct investment in, 209, 214

Arndt, H. W., 59 n.

Asher, H., 256 n.

Aubrey, H. G., 122 n.

Australia, a net exporter of primary products, 281, 288

Average real income, alterations in, during inflation, 21-3; as a measure of economic growth, 2-4; distribution pattern of, 15-16, 130-2; stagnation of, 6

Balance of payments, problems of, and debt service, 142; and exchange controls, 432-3, 438-9; and home market expansion, 259-63, 269; —equilibrium, and savings, 263, 273-4

Balanced growth, and the 'big push', 267-9, 271; as a means to accelerated growth, 245-6; compatibility with international specialization, 235-6, 250-9, 266-7, 270; notions of, 88-92, 102, 245-50

Ballesteros, Marto, 308 n., 317

Banks, agricultural, 175; capitalization, 171; central, 174 n., 184, 192; commercial, 173, 178 n., 179-82, 184, 192-193; investment, 171-2, 173, 178, 190; Mexican, 173-4, 175-6, 178 n.; mortgage, 170, 173, 178

Barrère, A., 116 n., 122 n.

Basic foodstuffs, in under-developed countries, price of, 83-5, 91; problems of, 401, 407, 412-13, 421-5, 427

Bator, F. M., 59 n.

Index

Taxes and subsidies, an alternative to exchange control, 435, 452, 454, 459-50

Technique, level of, and economic development, 71-3

Technological advances, gains from, 305-6

Teixeira Vieira, Dorival, **192-7,** *198, 363*

Terms of trade, and economic development, 275-307 ; and economic welfare, 275-80 ; — consciousness, and commodity fluctuations, 344 ; cyclical fluctuations in, 289-95, 296, 303, 307 ; factoral, commodity, and income, 276-9, 297-8, 306-7 ; long-term changes in, 298-9 ; secular deterioration in, for export of primary goods, 280-9, 295, 297-301, 302-3 ; secular tendencies of, 280-9, 295

Thorne, A. P., 50 n.

Torrens, R., 284

Toynbee, A. J., 9 n.

Transfer risks, 139-41, 160, 161-2, 165

Turkey, 262

Tyszynski, H., 353 n.

Unemployment, as a feature of stagnation, 6 ; disguised, 62, 340-1, 400-1, 402, 411, 413, 418, 419, 428-9, 431

United Kingdom : balance of payments policy, 262 ; borrowing from, by under-developed countries, 210 ; economic theory, 284, 295 ; foreign investment, 204 ; terms of trade, 243, 281-2, 286, 290 ; unemployment, 277

United States of America : and depressions, 292, 296 ; average propensity to save, 113 ; borrowing from, by under-developed countries, 210 ; capital-output ratio, 60 n., 135 ; capital requirements, by economic sectors, 219, 220 ; capital structure of economy (in 1939), 218-19 ; declining importance of raw materials, 310-13 ; direct investment abroad, 203-4, 205-209, 210, 214, 215 ; financing of total investment, 217, 226 ; government

intervention in economic planning, 49 ; growth and investment, 136-7 ; imports, 241, 242-3 ; increase in *per capita* national product, 443 ; increases in agricultural inputs and outputs, 317 ; relative shares of equity capital and loans in financing private investment, 216, 217, 226 ; technological advance, 239, 241, 288

Uruguay : financial system, 169 n., 174 n. ; loans received by, from Export-Import Bank and International Bank, 213, 214 ; real exports, 5 ; United States direct investment in, 209, 214

Venezuela : average real income, 3 ; economic growth, 9, 441, 443, 444, 449, 450 ; exchange controls, 431 ; exports, 4, 441, 442 ; foreign capital in, 221-2 ; income elasticities of demand for food, 316 ; inflation, 17, 24 ; loans received by, from Export-Import Bank and International Bank, 213, 214 ; oil production, 320 ; United States direct investment in, 208, 209, 214

Viner, Jacob, 7 n., 246, 268, 430, 437 n.

Vries, Margaret de, 432 n.

Wages, and prices, equilibrium relationship of, 17, 18, 19-20 ; wage inflation, 20

Wagner, Adolf, 285

Wallich, Henry C., ix, x, 6 n., *79, 106, 137, 165, 167, 198, 199, 200, 231, 233, 271, 274, 303, 304, 306, 321, 332, 341,* **342-65,** *363, 397, 426, 427, 428, 466, 467, 468*

White, L. D., 322 n.

Wickizer, V. D., 348 n.

Williams, J. H., 251

Wright, C. M., 281-2, 290

Yamey, B. S., 113

Young, A., 60

Youngson, A. J., 112 n.

THE END

PRINTED BY R. & R. CLARK, LTD., EDINBURGH